Learning Microsoft® Office 2010: Advanced Skills

Katherine Murray

Christy Parrish

Suzanne Weixel

Faithe Wempen

PEARSON

Prentice Hall

Boston • Columbus • Indianapolis • New York • San Francisco • Upper Saddle River
Amsterdam • Cape Town • Dubai • London • Madrid • Milan • Munich • Paris • Montreal • Toronto
Delhi • Mexico City • Sao Paulo • Sydney • Hong Kong • Seoul • Singapore • Taipei • Tokyo

Editor in Chief: Michael Payne
Product Development Manager:
Eileen Bien Calabro
Editorial Assistant: Nicole Sam
Director of Marketing: Kate Valentine
Marketing Manager: Tori Olson Alves
Marketing Coordinator: Susan Osterlitz
Marketing Assistant: Darshika Vyas
Senior Managing Editor: Cynthia Zonneveld
Associate Managing Editor: Camille Trentacoste
Production Project Manager: Mike Lackey
Operations Director: Alexis Heydt
Senior Operations Specialist: Diane Peirano

Text and Cover Designer: Vanessa Moore
AVP/Director of Online Programs, Media: Richard Keaveny
AVP/Director of Product
Development, Media: Lisa Strite
Media Project Manager, Editorial: Alana Coles
Media Project Manager, Production: John Cassar
Editorial and Product Development: Emergent Learning, LLC
Contributing Authors: Kathy Berkemeyer and Hope Campbell
Composition: Emergent Learning, LLC
Printer/Binder: R.R. Donnelly Menasha
Cover Printer: Lehigh-Pheonix Color
Text: 10/12 Helvetica

Credits and acknowledgements borrowed from other sources and reproduced, with permission, in this textbook are as follows: All photos courtesy of Shutterstock.com.

Microsoft® and Windows® are registered trademarks of the Microsoft Corporation in the U.S.A. and other countries. Screen shots and icons reprinted with permission from the Microsoft Corporation. This book is not sponsored or endorsed by or affiliated with the Microsoft Corporation.

Many of the designations by manufacturers and seller to distinguish their products are claimed as trademarks. Where those designations appear in this book, and the publisher was aware of a trademark claim, the designations have been printed in initial caps or all caps.

ISBN 10: 0-13-510841-1
ISBN 13: 978-0-13-510841-3

1 2 3 4 5 6   12 11 10 09 08 07

Table of Contents

Microsoft Access 2010

Chapter 1
Enhancing Queries 384

Chapter 2
Customizing Forms and Reports 422

The following Bonus Chapters are provided in pdf format on the CD that comes with the book. The data files for these Chapters can also be found on the CD.

Introduction

Microsoft Office 2010 is Microsoft's suite of application software. The Standard version includes Word, Excel, Outlook, and PowerPoint. Other editions may also include Access, Publisher, OneNote, and InfoPath. This book covers Word (the word processing tool), Excel (the spreadsheet tool), PowerPoint (the presentation tool), and Access (the database tool). Because Microsoft Office is an integrated suite, the components can all be used separately or together to create professional-looking documents and to manage data.

HOW THE BOOK IS ORGANIZED

Learning Microsoft Office 2010 Advanced Skills is made up of four sections:

- **Word 2010.** With Word you can create letters, memos, Web pages, newsletters, and more.
- **Excel 2010.** Excel, Microsoft's spreadsheet component, is used to organize and calculate data, track financial data, and create charts and graphs.
- **Access 2010.** Access is Microsoft's powerful database tool. Using Access you will learn to store, retrieve, and report on information.
- **PowerPoint 2010.** Create dynamic onscreen presentations with PowerPoint, the presentation graphics tool.

Lessons are comprised of short exercises designed for using Microsoft Office 2010 in real-life business settings. Each lesson is made up of seven key elements:

- **What You Will Learn.** Each lesson starts with an overview of the learning objectives covered in the lesson.
- **Software Skills.** Next, a brief overview of the Microsoft Office tools that you'll be working with in the lesson is provided.

- **Application Skills.** The objectives are then put into context by setting a scenario.
- **Words to Know.** Key terms are included and defined at the start of each lesson, so you can quickly refer back to them. The terms are then highlighted in the text.
- **What You Can Do.** Concise notes for learning the computer concepts.
- **Try It.** Hands-on practice activities provide brief procedures to teach all necessary skills.
- **Create It.** These projects give students a chance to create documents, spreadsheets, database objects, and presentations by entering information. Steps provide all the how-to information needed to complete a project.
- **Apply It.** Each lesson concludes with a project that challenges students to apply what they have learned through steps that tell them what to do, without all the how-to information. In the Apply It projects, students must show they have mastered each skill set.
- Each chapter ends with two assessment projects: **Make It Your Own** and **Master It**, which incorporate all the skills covered throughout the chapter.

WORKING WITH DATA AND SOLUTION FILES

As you work through the projects in this book, you'll be creating, opening, and saving files. You should keep the following instructions in mind:

- For many of the projects you can use the data files provided on the CD-ROM that comes with this book. Other projects will ask you to create new documents and files, and then enter text and data into them, so you can master creating documents from scratch.

- The data files are used so that you can focus on the skills being introduced—not on keyboarding lengthy documents. The files are organized by application in the folders on the CD-ROM.

- When the project steps tell you to open a file name, you can open the data file provided on CD.

- All the projects instruct you to save the files created or to save the project files under a new name that includes your first and last name as part of the file name. This is to make the project file your own, and to avoid overwriting the data file in the storage location.

- Follow your instructor's directions for where to access and save the data files on a network, local computer hard drive, or portable storage device such as a USB drive.

- Many of the projects also provide instructions for including your name in a header or footer. Again, this is to identify the project work as your own for grading and assessment purposes.

- Unless the book instructs otherwise, use the default settings for text size, margin size, and so on when creating a file. If someone has changed the default software settings for the computer you're using, your exercise files may not look the same as those shown in this book. In addition, the appearance of your files may look different if the system is set to a screen resolution other than 1024 x 768.

- Also note that if someone has opened an Office 2010 file in a previous version of Microsoft Office such as Office 2007, the file may open in Compatibility Mode. This means that new features from Office 2010 may not be available for use. If this happens, simply save the file as an Office 2010 document and continue working with it in Office 2010.

WHAT'S ON THE CD

The CD contains the following:

- Data Files for many of the projects.
- Glossary of all the key terms from the book.
- Bonus Chapters, including:
  - Word Chapter 5 – Working with Long Documents
  - Word Chapter 6 – Embedding and Linking Objects and Using Macros

  - Excel Chapter 4 – Importing and Analyzing Database Data
  - Excel Chapter 5 – Collaborating with Others and Preparing a Final Workbook for Distribution
  - Access Chapter 4 – Securing, Integrating, and Maintaining Data
  - PowerPoint Chapter 4 – Publishing a Presentation

TO ACCESS THE FILES INCLUDED ON CD

1. Insert the Learning Microsoft Office 2010 Advanced Skills CD in the CD-ROM drive.
2. Navigate to your CD-ROM drive; right-click and choose Explore from the shortcut menu.
3. Right-click the folder that you wish to copy.

4. Navigate to the location where you wish to place the folder.
5. Right-click and choose Paste from the Shortcut menu.

Learning
Microsoft Office 2010:
Advanced Skills

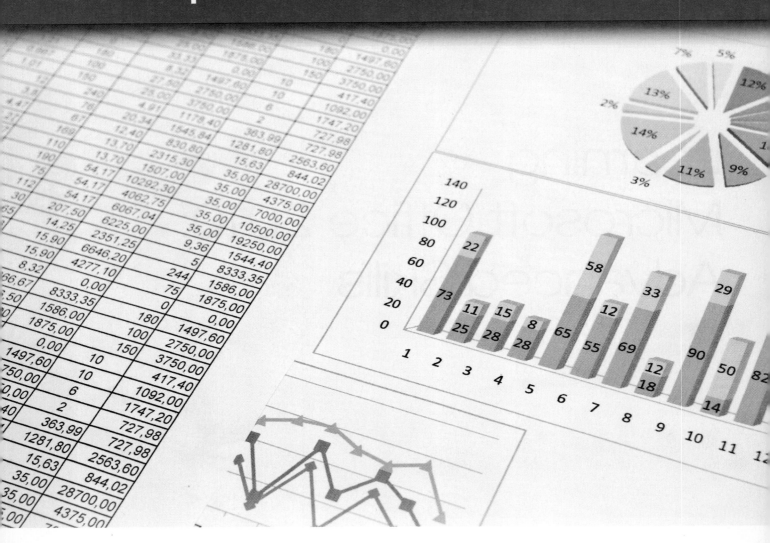

Chapter 1

Using Advanced
Lists and Charts

Lesson 1

Inserting Text Files and Blank Pages

WORDS TO KNOW

Cover page
The first page of a document that usually displays such information as the document title and subtitle, the author's name, and the date.

Electronic portfolio
A collection of digital information and documents that illustrates your abilities and achievements.

Employment portfolio
A collection of documents that illustrates the qualities and abilities of a job candidate.

Reflection
The act of thinking critically about items in a portfolio and communicating the importance of each item to others.

➤ What You Will Learn

Inserting a File in a Document
Inserting a Blank Page or a Cover Page
Setting Up an Employment Portfolio

Software Skills Word has many features that help you save time by reusing existing content. You can insert a file into another file to save time retyping existing text. You can also insert a blank page anywhere in a document, or select a preformatted cover page design from a gallery to insert at the beginning of your document.

Application Skills Liberty Blooms, a flower shop, has asked you to develop a customer handout about selecting rose plants. You have missing content in an existing document, which you can insert on a blank page in the brochure. You will also insert a cover page.

What You Can Do

Inserting a File in a Document

- You can insert one file into another file to incorporate the first file's contents into the second file.
- The entire contents are saved as part of the second file.

- The first file remains unchanged.
- The command for inserting a file is available on the Object menu in the Text group on the Insert tab of the Ribbon.

Try It!   Inserting a File in a Document

1. Start Word and open **WTry01a** from the data files for this lesson.

2. Save the file as **WTry01a_studentfirstname_ studentlastname** in the location where your teacher instructs you to store the files for this lesson.

3. Position the insertion point on the last line of the document.

4. Click the Insert tab.

5. Click the Object drop-down arrow and click Text from File.

6. Navigate to the location where the data files for this lesson are stored.

7. Click **WTry01b**.

8. Click Insert.

9. Save the changes to **WTry01a_ studentfirstname_studentlastname**, and leave it open to use in the next Try It.

Inserting a Blank Page or a Cover Page

- Use commands in the Pages group on the Insert tab of the Ribbon to insert a blank page or **cover page**.
- When you insert a blank page, Word inserts hard page breaks before and after the new page.

- Word includes a gallery of preformatted cover pages that include page layout and design features as well as content controls for standard text, such as the document title and the author's name.
- You replace the sample text by typing new text or by selecting data from the content control's drop-down list.
- You can remove a cover page at any time.

Try It!   Inserting a Blank Page or a Cover Page

1. In the **WTry01a_studentfirstname_ studentlastname** file, position the insertion point at the beginning of the paragraph you inserted in the previous Try It.

2. On the Insert tab, click the Blank Page button.

3. On the Insert tab, click the Cover Page button to display the gallery of cover page styles, and then click the Conservative style.

4. Click the Cover Page button again, and click Remove Current Cover Page.

(continued)

Try It!   **Inserting a Blank Page or a Cover Page** (continued)

5 Click the Cover Page button 📄 to display the gallery of cover page styles, and then click the Alphabet style.

6 On the cover page, click *[Type the document title]* and type Nutrition Class Schedule.

7 Right-click *[Type the document subtitle]* and click Remove Content Control on the shortcut menu.

8 Click *[Pick the date]*, then click the drop-down arrow and click today's date on the calendar.

9 If necessary, replace the default author's name with your own name.

10 Save the changes to WTry01a_ studentfirstname_studentlastname, close it, and exit Word.

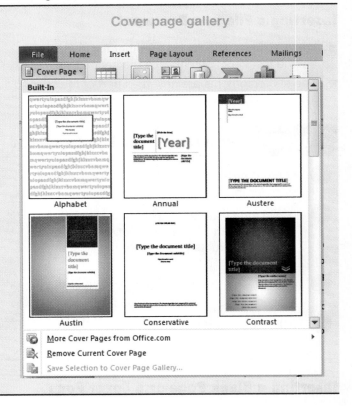

Cover page gallery

Setting Up an Employment Portfolio

- Set up an **employment portfolio** to organize information about yourself that you can use as a reference while looking for a job.

- An employment portfolio may be as simple as a binder in which you store printed documents and a Windows folder in which you store digital documents.

- Printed documents should be placed in the binder in plastic sleeves for protection and to maintain a professional appearance when you bring it to interviews or meetings.

- Documents are usually organized by category or type. For example, store all letters of recommendation together, all certifications together, and examples of achievement together.

- An effective employment portfolio illustrates the progress you make in school and in your career and helps you stay on track to achieve your educational and career goals.

- There are three types of portfolios, but most portfolios are a combination of all three.

  - A *development portfolio* shows the progress of skills over a period of time.
  - An *assessment portfolio* demonstrates competency.
  - A *showcase portfolio* highlights achievements and the quality of work.

- Most employment portfolios include a resume, transcripts, letters of application, lists of references, letters of recommendation, copies of certifications, and examples of achievement.

- An effective portfolio also includes comments or explanations that describe the importance of each item, help define goals, and map a path or plan to achieve those goals. This is often called a **reflection**, or self-reflection, because the owner of the portfolio must think critically about each item and communicate its value to others.

- Throughout your career, you should maintain and update your employment portfolio so that it is always ready if you need it.

- An **electronic portfolio** is a collection of digital information and documents. You learn about electronic portfolios in the PowerPoint section of this book.

Project 1—Create It

Rose Brochure

DIRECTIONS

1. Start Word, if necessary, and save the default blank document as **WProj01a_studentfirstname_ studentlastname** in the location where your teacher instructs you to store the files for this lesson.

2. Apply the **Newsprint** theme and the **Newsprint** style set, then type the following paragraphs using the default Normal style:

   Roses are prized by gardeners around the world. While some roses have a reputation as being difficult to grow or care for, many variations exist that are resistant to disease, offer beautiful blooms and fragrances, and blend easily into different landscapes.

   Other considerations include the size of the garden, the growing conditions, and how much time you want to spend caring for the plants. Drawing a garden plan can help you determine the number of plants you will need and how the colors and shapes of the blooms will relate to the other plants in the garden. Whether you have container pots on a balcony or a large suburban yard, with a little thought and preparation, you can select and grow magnificent roses.

3. Position the insert point at the beginning of the second paragraph.

4. Click **Insert** > **Blank Page**.

5. On the Insert tab, click the **Object** drop-down arrow ⬛ and click **Text from File**.

6. Navigate to the location where the data files for this lesson are stored.

7. Click **WProj01b** and then click **Insert**.

8. Reposition the insertion point at the beginning of the document.

9. On the Insert tab, click **Cover Page**.

10. Scroll down the Cover Page gallery and click the **Newsprint** style.

11. Click **[Type the document title]** and type **Selecting Roses**.

12. Click **[Type the document subtitle]** and type **A Buyer's Guide**.

13. Right-click the **Abstract** content control and click **Remove Content Control** on the shortcut menu.

14. Type your full name in the location where the Abstract content control had been.

15. Click **[Pick the date]**, then click the drop-down arrow and click today's date on the calendar.

16. Reposition the insertion point on the blank line above the Page Break on page 2 of the document.

17. Click **Insert** > **Picture**, navigate to the location where the data files for this lesson are stored, and insert **WProj01c** on the page.

18. Reposition the insertion point on the blank line above the Page Break on page 3 of the document.

19. Click **Insert** > **Picture**, navigate to the location where the data files for this lesson are stored, and insert **WProj01d** on the page.

20. Check and correct the spelling and grammar in the document, and then save the changes.

21. **With your teacher's permission**, print the document. Page 1 should look similar to Figure 1-1, shown on the next page.

22. Close the document, saving all changes, and exit Word.

Figure 1-1

Selecting Roses

A Buyer's Guide

Firstname Lastname

Today's Date

Project 2—Apply It

Rose Brochure

DIRECTIONS

1. Start Word, if necessary, and open **WProj02a** from the data files for this lesson.

2. Save the file as **WProj02a_studentfirstname_ studentlastname** in the location where your teacher instructs you to store the files for this lesson.

3. Remove the current cover page.

4. Change the theme to **Metro** and the style set to **Modern**.

5. Position the insertion point at the end of the last sentence in the second to last paragraph and insert a blank page.

6. On the new blank page, insert the text from the file **WProj02b**.

7. Insert a cover page in the **Sideline** style.

8. In the Company content control, replace the sample text with the text **Liberty Blooms**.

9. Edit the brochure title to **How to Select Roses**.

10. Edit the brochure subtitle to **Your Guide to Buying Quality Blooms**.

11. Replace the sample author name with your own name, and enter today's date.

12. Reposition the insertion point on the blank line above the Page Break on page 3 of the document.

13. Insert the **WProj02c** picture file on the page.

14. Check and correct the spelling and grammar in the document, and then save the changes.

15. **With your teacher's permission**, print the document. Page 1 should look similar to Figure 1-2.

16. Close the document, saving all changes, and exit Word.

Figure 1-2

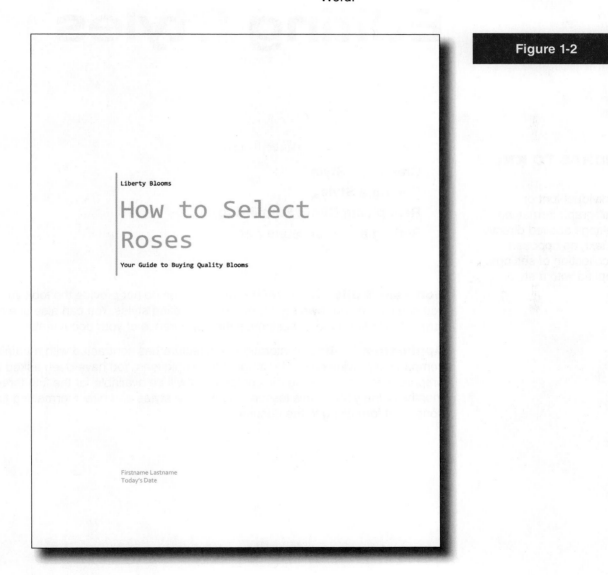

Liberty Blooms

How to Select
Roses

Your Guide to Buying Quality Blooms

Firstname Lastname
Today's Date

Lesson 2

Creating and Editing Styles

WORDS TO KNOW

Direct formatting
Individual font or paragraph formatting settings applied directly to text, as opposed to a collection of settings applied with a style.

➤ What You Will Learn

Creating a Style
Editing a Style
Reapplying Direct Formatting
Setting a Default Style Set

Software Skills   When Word's built-in styles do not provide the look you need, you can create your own styles, or modify existing styles. You can also use direct formatting to fine-tune or customize the appearance of your documents.

Application Skills   Restoration Architecture has contracted with a training company to provide computer training for employees. You have been asked to prepare a document listing the courses that will be available for the first three months of the year. In this lesson, you will use styles and direct formatting to apply consistent formatting to the document.

What You Can Do

Creating a Style

- Recall that you use styles to apply a collection of formatting settings to characters or paragraphs all at once, and that Quick Styles display in the Styles gallery in the Styles group on the Home tab of the Ribbon, and in the Styles task pane.

- You can create a new Quick Style to apply font and/or paragraph formatting to your documents.

- The easiest way to create a style is to format text, select it, and then assign the formatting a style name.

- Style names should be short and descriptive.

- By default, the new style is added to the style sheet for the current document and displays in the Quick Styles gallery.

Try It! Creating a Style

1 Start Word and open **WTry02** from the data files for this lesson.

2 Save the file as **WTry02_studentfirstname_ studentlastname** in the location where your teacher instructs you to store the files for this lesson.

3 Select the first line of text and format it in 24 point Arial, Red, Accent 2, and center it horizontally.

4 On the Home tab, in the Styles group, click the Quick Styles gallery More button [▾].

5 Click Save Selection as a New Quick Style to display the Create New Style from Formatting dialog box.

6 In the Name box, type **Headline** to replace the sample style name.

7 Click OK to create the style and add it to the Quick Styles gallery.

Create New Style from Formatting dialog box

8 Click in the paragraph beginning *Class size is limited*.

9 In the Quick Styles gallery, click the Headline style to apply it.

10 Save the changes to **WTry02_ studentfirstname_studentlastname**, and leave it open to use in the next Try It.

Editing a Style

- You can edit, modify, or delete an existing style.

- Note that you can also remove a style from the Quick Styles gallery, but that does not delete the style.

- When you modify a style that has already been applied to text in the document, the formatting is updated to reflect the changes to the style.

- If you modify a style and give it a new name, it becomes a new style; the original style remains unchanged.

- You can quickly modify a style by changing the formatting and then updating the style in the Quick Styles gallery.

- When you want to modify any or all of the style properties at the same time, you can use the Modify Style dialog box.

Try It!   Editing a Style

1 In the **WTry02_studentfirstname_ studentlastname** file, select the first line of text and apply the Gradient Fill - Gray, Outline - Gray text effect style (middle option on the third row in the Text Effects gallery).

2 On the Home tab, in the Quick Styles gallery, right-click the Headline style and click Update Headline to Match Selection.

3 In the Quick Styles gallery, right-click the Headline style again, and click Modify to open the Modify Style dialog box.

4 Click the Style for following paragraph drop-down arrow and click Normal.

5 Under Formatting, click the Font drop-down arrow and click Times New Roman.

6 Click OK to save the changes to the style.

7 On the Home tab, click the Styles group dialog box launcher [▫] to display the Styles task pane.

8 Click the Headline style drop-down arrow and then click Delete Headline.

9 Click Yes in the confirmation dialog box to delete the style.

   ✓ Note that you can also remove a style from the Quick Styles gallery, but that does not delete the style.

Modify Style dialog box

10 Save the changes to **WTry02_ studentfirstname_studentlastname**, and leave it open to use in the next Try It.

Reapplying Direct Formatting

■ By default, Word does not display information about **direct formatting** in the Styles task pane.

■ You can select to display direct formatting so that you can reapply it to different text without saving it as a style.

■ This feature is similar to the Format Painter, but instead of scrolling through the document to copy the formatting, you can select the direct formatting in the Styles task pane.

Try It!   **Reapplying Direct Formatting**

1 In the Styles task pane in the **WTry02_studentfirstname_studentlastname** file, click Options to open the Style Pane Options dialog box.

2 Click to select the Paragraph level formatting, Font formatting, and Bullet and numbering formatting check boxes.

3 Click OK.

Style Pane Options dialog box

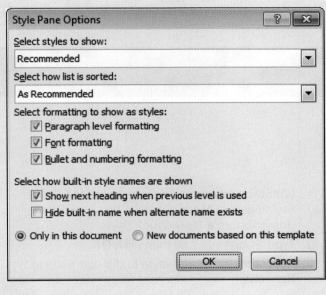

4 Select the first line of text and apply the Heading 1 style.

5 Increase the font size to 24 points and change the font color to standard Red.

6 Select the paragraph beginning *Class size is limited*.

7 In the Styles task pane, click Heading 1 + 24 pt, Red to reapply the direct formatting to the selected text, and then close the Styles task pane.

8 Close **WTry02_studentfirstname_studentlastname**, saving all changes, but leave Word open to use in the next Try It.

View direct formatting in the Styles task pane

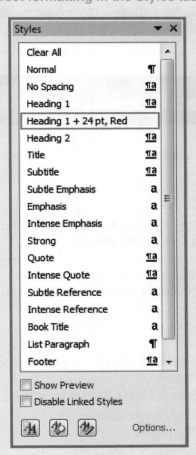

Setting a Default Style Set

- Recall that a style set is a collection of styles that use coordinated font formatting.
- Most templates have a built-in default style set. For example, the default style set for the Normal template is Office 2010.
- You can change the default style set so that all new documents based on the template are created using the new style set.
- You can restore the original style set as the default.
- Take care when changing the Normal template's default style set, as the changes will affect all new, blank documents.

Try It!   **Setting a Default Style Set**

1 In Word, create a new blank document.

2 On the Home tab in the Styles group, click the Change Styles button A.

3 On the menu, point to Style Set.

4 Click Modern.

5 Click the Change Styles button A again, and click Set as Default.

6 Click File > Close > Don't Save to close the file without saving.

7 Create a new blank document. Notice that the styles use the new default style set—Modern.

8 Click Change Styles A > Style Set > Word 2010.

9 Click Change Styles A > Set as Default to restore the original default style set.

10 Exit Word without saving any changes.

Project 3—Create It

Course List

DIRECTIONS

1. Start Word, if necessary, and open **WProj03** from the data files for this lesson.

2. Save the file as **WProj03_studentfirstname_studentlastname** in the location where your teacher instructs you to store the files for this lesson.

3. Double-click in the header and type your full name and today's date.

4. On the Home tab, click **Change Styles** A > **Style Set** > **Formal**.

5. Click **Change Styles** A > **Set as Default**.

6. Click the Styles group dialog box launcher to display the Styles task pane.

7. In the Styles task pane, click **Options**.

8. In the Style Pane Options dialog box, click to select the **Paragraph level formatting**, **Font formatting**, and **Bullet and numbering formatting** check boxes, and then click **OK**.

9. Apply the **Heading 1** style to the company name.

10. Select the company address and change the font size to **10 points** and the font color to **Red, Accent 2, Darker 50%**. Center the paragraph and increase the spacing after to **30 pt**.

11. With the address still selected, click the Quick Styles gallery **More** button and click **Save Selection as a New Quick Style**.

12. Type **Subhead1** and then click **OK**.

13. Apply the **Subhead1** style to the text *Training Schedule*.

14. Select the text *Training Schedule* and change the font size to **12 points** and apply bold.

15. In the Styles task pane, click the **Subhead1** drop-down arrow and click **Update Subhead1 to Match Selection**.

16. Select the text *January*.

17. Change the font to **18 point Times New Roman**.

18. Select the course name *Microsoft Word 1* and then click **Times New Roman, 18 pt** to reapply the direct formatting you applied in step 17.

19. Check and correct the spelling and grammar in the document, and then save the changes.

20. **With your teacher's permission**, print the document. It should look similar to Figure 2-1 on the next page.

21. In the Styles task pane, click the **Subhead1** drop-down arrow, click **Delete Subhead1**, and then click **Yes**.

22. Apply the **Subtitle** style to the company address and the text *Training Schedule*.
23. Close the Styles task pane.
24. On the Home tab, click **Change Styles** 𝖠𝖠 > **Style Set** > **Word 2010**.

25. Click **Change Styles** 𝖠𝖠 > **Set as Default**.
26. Close the document, saving all changes, and exit Word.

Firstname·Lastname¶
Today's·Date¶

RESTORATION·ARCHITECTURE¶

8921·Thunderbird·Road·✦·Phoenix,·Arizona·85022·✦·602.555.6325¶

Training·Schedule¶

January¶

Microsoft·Word·1¶

This·introductory·course·will·cover·the·basics·of·using·Microsoft·Word·2010·to·create·common·business·documents.·By·the·end·of·the·course·you·will·know·how·to·create,·format,·edit,·and·print·text-based·documents·such·as·letters,·memos,·and·reports.¶

Figure 2-1

Project 4—Apply It

Course List

DIRECTIONS

1. Start Word, if necessary, and open **WProj04** from the data files for this lesson.
2. Save the file as **WProj04_studentfirstname_studentlastname** in the location where your teacher instructs you to store the files for this lesson.
3. Double-click in the header and type your full name and today's date.
4. Change the default style set to **Distinctive**.
5. Apply the **Title** style to the company name.

6. Select the text *Training Schedule* and change the formatting to **24 point bold Arial**, centered horizontally.
7. Save the formatting as a new Quick Style named **Subhead1**.
8. Apply the **Subhead1** style to the names of all three months.
9. Modify the **Subhead1** style to be left-aligned with a solid underline.
10. Select the course name *Microsoft Word 1*, change the font size to **14 points**, and center it.

11. Reapply the formatting you applied in step 10 to the names of the other two courses.

12. Format the paragraph describing the Word 1 course in **14 point Arial**, indented 0.5" from both the left and the right, with 0 pt of space before and 6 pt of space after.

13. Create a style named **Course Description** based on the formatting of the course description.

14. Apply the **Course Description** style to the other two course descriptions.

15. Modify the **Course Description** style to change the font size to **12 points**.

16. Check and correct the spelling and grammar in the document, and then save the changes.

17. **With your teacher's permission**, print the document. It should look similar to Figure 2-2.

18. Delete the **Course Description** style.

19. Click the **Subhead1** style in the Styles task pane and click the down arrow. Click **Revert to Subtitle** and then click **Yes** at the prompt to delete the **Subhead1** style.

20. Change the default style set to **Word 2010**.

21. Close the document, saving all changes, and exit Word.

Figure 2-2

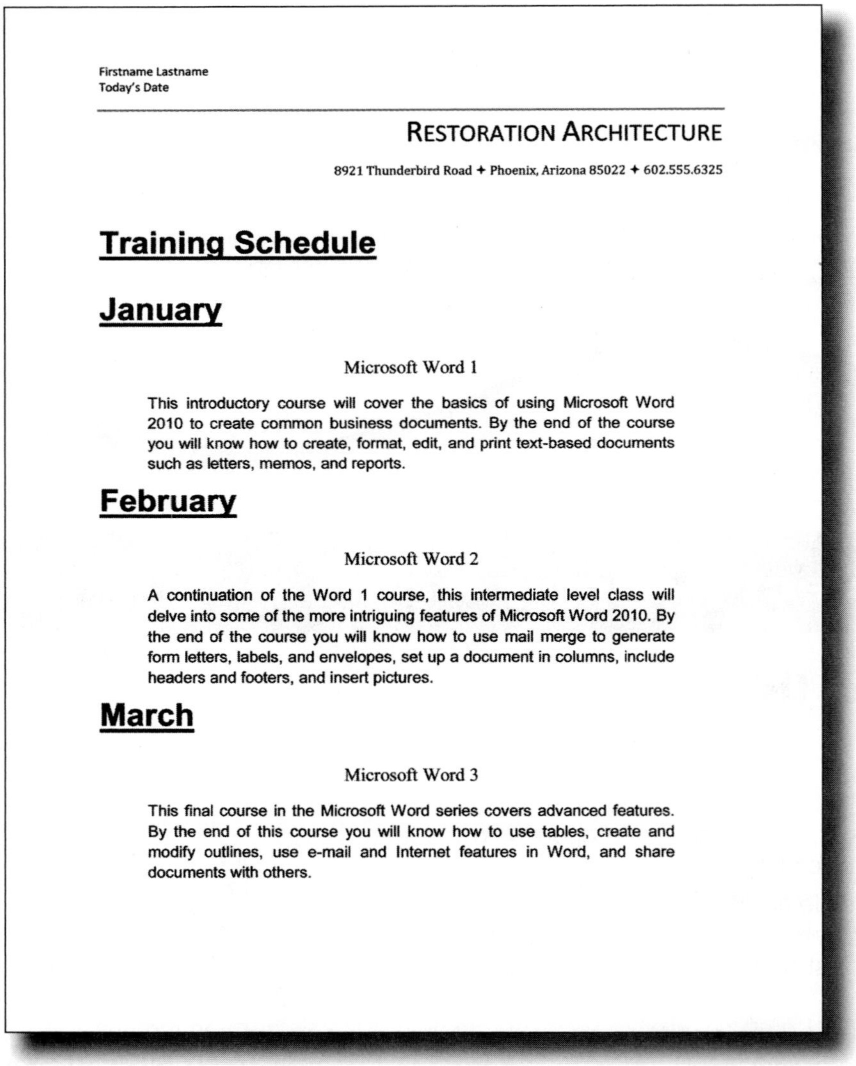

Firstname Lastname
Today's Date

RESTORATION ARCHITECTURE

8921 Thunderbird Road ✚ Phoenix, Arizona 85022 ✚ 602.555.6325

Training Schedule

January

Microsoft Word 1

This introductory course will cover the basics of using Microsoft Word 2010 to create common business documents. By the end of the course you will know how to create, format, edit, and print text-based documents such as letters, memos, and reports.

February

Microsoft Word 2

A continuation of the Word 1 course, this intermediate level class will delve into some of the more intriguing features of Microsoft Word 2010. By the end of the course you will know how to use mail merge to generate form letters, labels, and envelopes, set up a document in columns, include headers and footers, and insert pictures.

March

Microsoft Word 3

This final course in the Microsoft Word series covers advanced features. By the end of this course you will know how to use tables, create and modify outlines, use e-mail and Internet features in Word, and share documents with others.

Lesson 3

Managing Style Formatting

➤ What You Will Learn

Revealing Style Formatting

Tracking Formatting Inconsistencies

Software Skills   Consistent formatting ensures that your documents look professional and are easy to read. Microsoft Office Word 2010 includes tools that help you monitor and track inconsistent formatting. You can use the Style Inspector to reveal details about paragraph and character formatting, and you can track and mark formatting inconsistencies as you work. Once you identify inconsistencies, you can use tools such as styles, themes, and direct formatting to correct them.

Application Skills   You are preparing a document for the Liberty Blooms flower shop that lists programs and events the shop is sponsoring in the coming months. However, the document does not appear to be formatted consistently. In this lesson, you will turn on the check formatting and mark formatting features, and you will reveal style formatting in order to identify and correct formatting inconsistencies.

WORDS TO KNOW

Character style
A collection of formatting settings that can be applied all at once to a single character or multiple characters.

Paragraph style
A collection of formatting settings that can be applied all at once to a single paragraph or multiple paragraphs.

What You Can Do

Revealing Style Formatting

- Use Word's Style Inspector and Reveal Formatting task panes to display specific information about formatting applied to the current text.
- Revealing style formatting can help you identify inconsistent formatting in order to improve the appearance and professional quality of your documents.
- The Style Inspector task pane displays details about the current paragraph and text level formatting, such as the name of the current **paragraph style** and/or **character style**, as well as any direct formatting that has been manually applied.
- You can move the insertion point with the Style Inspector task pane open in order to reveal formatting for different text.

- In the Reveal Formatting task pane, you can view specific details about font formatting, paragraph formatting, and page setup.

- You can also compare the formatting of two selections to display differences between the two.

Try It!   **Revealing Style Formatting**

1 Start Word and open **WTry03** from the data files for this lesson.

2 Save the document as **WTry03_ studentfirstname_studentlastname** in the location where your teacher instructs you to store the files for this lesson.

3 Click on the word *Eat* in the heading *Eat Heart Healthy with Sandra!*

4 On the Home tab, click the Styles group dialog box launcher 🔲 to display the Styles task pane.

5 Click the Style Inspector button 🔄 to display the Style Inspector task pane, and then close the Styles task pane.

Style Inspector task pane

6 In the Style Inspector task pane, click the Reveal Formatting button 🔍 to display the Reveal Formatting task pane.

7 In the Reveal Formatting task pane, click to select the Compare to another selection check box.

8 In the document, click on the word *left* in the sentence *Register now so you won't be left out!* The differences between the formatting of the two selections display in the task pane.

9 Close the Reveal Formatting task pane and then close the Style Inspector task pane.

10 Save the changes to **WTry03_ studentfirstname_studentlastname**, and leave it open to use in the next Try It.

Reveal Formatting task pane

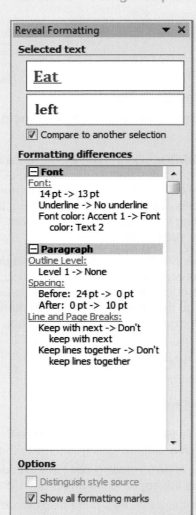

Tracking Formatting Inconsistencies

- You can set Word to check formatting while you work in much the same way that it checks spelling and grammar.
- If Word identifies a formatting inconsistency, it marks it with a wavy blue underline.

- For example, if you change the formatting of an item in a bulleted list without changing the formatting of other items in the list, Word would identify the formatting as inconsistent.
- You can ignore the blue lines and keep typing, or you can use a shortcut menu to correct the formatting error.
- The automatic format checker is off by default; you must turn it on to use it. It remains on in all documents until you turn it off.

Try It!   **Tracking Formatting Inconsistencies**

1 In **WTry03_studentfirstname_ studentlastname**, click File > Options > Advanced.

2 Click to select the Keep track of formatting check box and the Mark formatting inconsistencies check box.

3 Click OK.

4 Reposition the insertion point at the end of the document and press ENTER to start a new line.

5 On the Home tab, click the Bullets button 📋 ▾ and then type the following list, pressing ENTER to start a new line between each item: **Carbs**, **Sugar, Fat, Protein**.

    ✓ *If the default bullet list formatting on your system has been modified, lists may display differently from those in the figures.*

6 Select the item *Sugar* and click the Bold button **B**. Word applies a blue wavy underline to the word, indicating that the formatting is inconsistent.

7 Deselect the word *Sugar*, then right-click it to display a shortcut menu.

8 On the shortcut menu, click Ignore Once.

9 Click File > Options > Advanced, and then click to clear the Keep track of formatting check box. The Mark formatting inconsistencies check box clears automatically.

10 Click OK.

11 Close **WTry03_studentfirstname_ studentlastname**, saving all changes, and exit Word.

Tracking formatting

Make this text consistent with formatting Bulleted, Symbol (symbol), Left: 0.25", Hanging: 0.25"

Ignore Once

Ignore Rule

✂ Cut

📋 Copy

📋 Paste Options:

A Font...

Paragraph...

Bullets |▸

Numbering |▸

Styles   ▸

Hyperlink...

Look Up |▸

Synonyms   ▸

Translate

Additional Actions   ▸

Inconsistent formatting options on shortcut menu

Eat Heart
Are all sugars b
muscle? Should
dietitian, will a
evenings at 7:0

Class size is

Sandra Tsai is
Nutrition from

- Carbs
- Sugar
- Fat
- Protein

Times Ne ▾ 11 ▾ A˄ A˅
B *I* U ⚏ A ▾

Blue wavy underline

Project 5—Create It

Programs List

DIRECTIONS

1. Start Word, if necessary, and save the default blank document as **WProj05_studentfirstname_ studentlastname** in the location where your teacher instructs you to store the files for this lesson.

2. Double-click in the header and type your full name and today's date.

3. Apply the **Aspect** theme and the **Fancy** style set.

4. Click **File** > **Options** > **Advanced**.

5. In the Word Options dialog box, click to select the **Keep track of formatting** check box, and the **Mark formatting inconsistencies** check box, if necessary. (It may be selected automatically when you select Keep track of formatting.)

6. Click **OK**.

7. On the first line of the document, type **Liberty Blooms**, and format it using the **Title** style.

8. Press [ENTER], type **Upcoming Programs**, and format it using the **Subtitle** style.

9. Press [ENTER], click the **Bullets** button [≡▾] to apply bullet list formatting, and type the following list, pressing [ENTER] between each item to start a new line:

    Flower Arranging

    All about Herbs

    Water Gardens

    Edible Plants

    Roses

10. Select the second item in the list and increase the font size to **14 points**. (Word should mark the item as inconsistently formatted.)

11. Click the Styles group dialog box launcher [⌐].

12. In the Styles task pane, click the **Style Inspector** button [🕮].

13. Close the Styles task pane.

14. Click the company name to display its formatting in the Style Inspector task pane.

15. In the Style Inspector task pane, click the **Reveal Formatting** button [🔍].

16. Click the text **Arranging** in the first item in the bullet list.

17. In the Reveal Formatting task pane, click to select the **Compare to another selection** check box.

18. In the document, click the text **Herbs** in the second item in the bullet list. Note the formatting difference.

19. Select the second item in the bulleted list and change the font size to **10 points**.

20. Close the **Reveal Formatting** task pane and the **Style Inspector**.

21. Check and correct the spelling and grammar in the document, and then save the changes.

22. **With your teacher's permission**, print the document. It should look similar to Figure 3-1 on the next page.

23. Click **File** > **Options** > **Advanced**, and then click to clear the **Keep track of formatting** check box. The Mark formatting inconsistencies check box clears automatically.

24. Click **OK**.

25. Close the document, saving all changes, and exit Word.

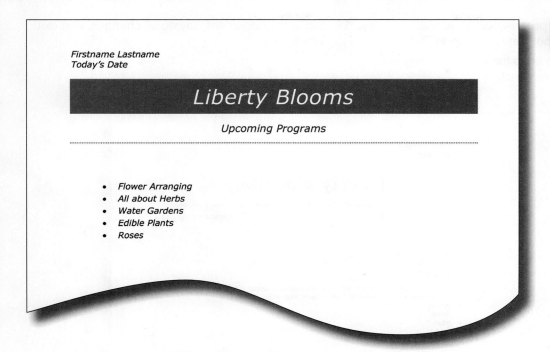

Figure 3-1

Firstname Lastname
Today's Date

Liberty Blooms

Upcoming Programs

- *Flower Arranging*
- *All about Herbs*
- *Water Gardens*
- *Edible Plants*
- *Roses*

Project 6—Apply It

Program List

DIRECTIONS

1. Start Word, if necessary, and open **WProj06** from the data files for this lesson.
2. Save the file as **WProj06_studentfirstname_ studentlastname** in the location where your teacher instructs you to store the files for this lesson.
3. Type your full name and today's date in the header.
4. Set Word to keep track of formatting and to mark formatting inconsistencies.
5. Select the first item that Word marks as having inconsistent formatting—the bulleted item *Irises*.
6. Display the Style Inspector. (If necessary, drag it by its title bar to move it so you can see the selected text.) See if you can identify why Word has it marked as inconsistent.
7. Display the Reveal Formatting task pane. Compare the selected text to another item in the bulleted list.
8. Change the font size of the item *Irises* to **11 points** to match the other items in the list.
9. Clear the **Compare to another selection** check box in the Reveal Formatting task pane, and click in the next word marked as inconsistent— **February**. See if you can identify why Word has it marked.
10. Remove the bold formatting from the text *February* to make it consistent with the other paragraphs formatted with the Heading 2 style.
11. Click in the last paragraph. See if you can identify why Word has it marked as inconsistent.
12. Right-click anywhere in the paragraph to see how Word suggests you fix the inconsistency.
13. Click the option to replace direct formatting with the **No Spacing** style.
14. Increase the spacing before the last paragraph to **12 pt**, and center it horizontally.
15. Close all open task panes, check and correct the spelling and grammar in the document, and then save the changes.

16. **With your teacher's permission**, print the document. It should look similar to Figure 3-2.

17. Turn off the options to keep track of formatting and mark formatting inconsistencies.

18. Close the document, saving all changes, and exit Word.

Figure 3-2

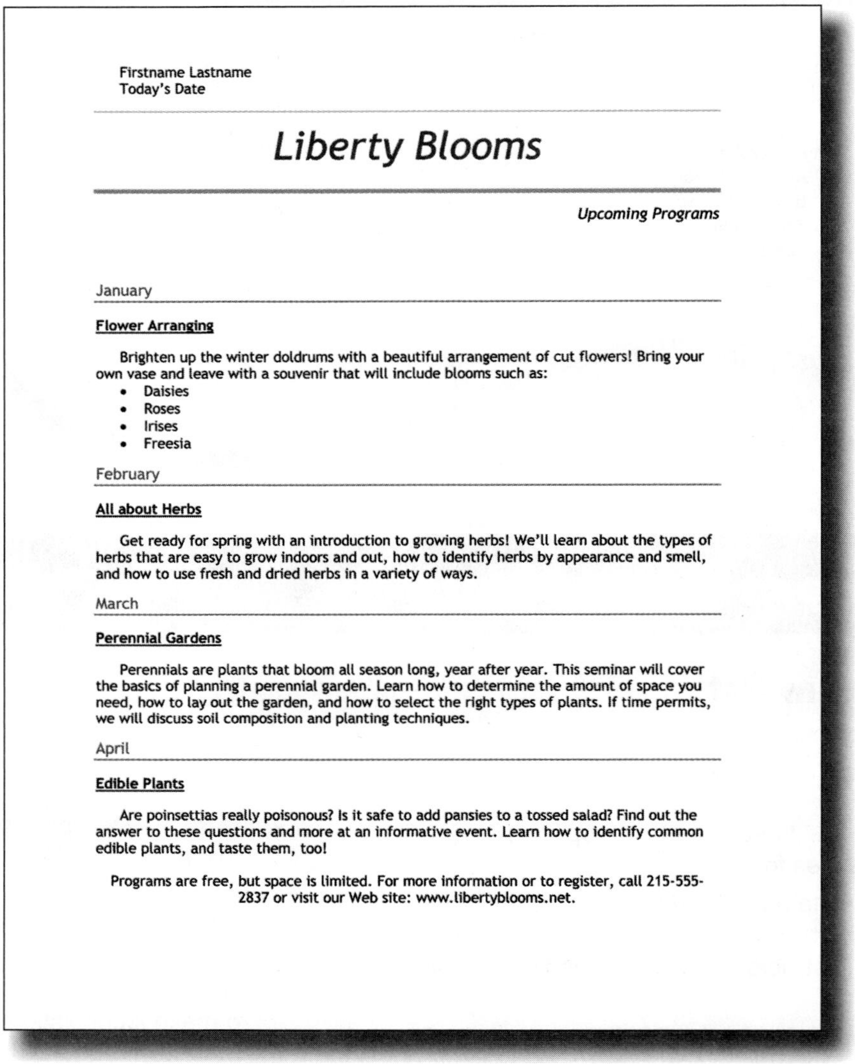

Firstname Lastname
Today's Date

Liberty Blooms

Upcoming Programs

January

Flower Arranging

Brighten up the winter doldrums with a beautiful arrangement of cut flowers! Bring your own vase and leave with a souvenir that will include blooms such as:
- Daisies
- Roses
- Irises
- Freesia

February

All about Herbs

Get ready for spring with an introduction to growing herbs! We'll learn about the types of herbs that are easy to grow indoors and out, how to identify herbs by appearance and smell, and how to use fresh and dried herbs in a variety of ways.

March

Perennial Gardens

Perennials are plants that bloom all season long, year after year. This seminar will cover the basics of planning a perennial garden. Learn how to determine the amount of space you need, how to lay out the garden, and how to select the right types of plants. If time permits, we will discuss soil composition and planting techniques.

April

Edible Plants

Are poinsettias really poisonous? Is it safe to add pansies to a tossed salad? Find out the answer to these questions and more at an informative event. Learn how to identify common edible plants, and taste them, too!

Programs are free, but space is limited. For more information or to register, call 215-555-2837 or visit our Web site: www.libertyblooms.net.

Lesson 4

Creating Multilevel Lists

WORDS TO KNOW

Multilevel list
A list that has a hierarchical structure that indicates the relationship between items in the list.

➤ **What You Will Learn**

Formatting a Multilevel List
Customizing a Multilevel List
Creating and Deleting a Multilevel List Style

Software Skills   Some lists—such as outlines or test questions—require the use of different levels that display different number or bullet formatting. You can easily format multilevel lists using the styles in Word's Multilevel List gallery. If none of the styles in the Multilevel list gallery is what you want, you can define a new multilevel list, or create a new list style.

Application Skills   For Voyager Travel Adventures, you are developing a questionnaire to help potential customers select an appropriate tour. In this lesson, you will use multilevel list formatting to prepare the questionnaire.

What You Can Do

Formatting a Multilevel List

■ Use Word's **multilevel list** styles to format items into a list that has more than one level.

■ Each level in the list has different formatting so you can clearly see the relationship between items.

■ To apply multilevel list formatting, select the list style from the gallery of Multilevel List styles, and then type the list.

■ Decrease the level of an item by pressing TAB or by clicking the Increase Indent button 💠 on the Home tab.

■ Increase the level by pressing [ENTER] twice, by pressing [SHIFT] + [TAB], or by clicking the Decrease Indent [⯇] button.

■ You can change the style of a multilevel list by selecting the list and clicking a different style in the List Library.

<h2>Try It!   Formatting a Multilevel List</h2>

1 Start Word and save the default blank document as **WTry04_studentfirstname_studentlastname** in the location where your teacher instructs you to store the files for this lesson.

2 On the Home tab, in the Paragraph group, click the Multilevel List button [⯇].

3 In the List Library, click the style in the middle of the first row.

4 Type **Microsoft Office 2010** and press [ENTER].

5 Press [TAB], type **Microsoft Word**, and press [ENTER].

6 Click the Increase Indent button [⯈], type **Word processing** and press [ENTER].

7 Press [SHIFT] + [TAB], type **Microsoft Excel**, and press [ENTER].

8 Type **Microsoft PowerPoint** and press [ENTER] three times to end the list.

9 Select all items in the list, click the Multilevel List button [⯇], and click the style on the left end of the second row.

10 Save the changes to **WTry04_studentfirstname_studentlastname** and leave it open to use in the next Try It.

Format a multilevel list

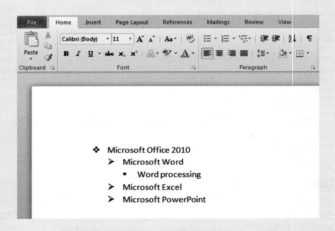

Customizing a Multilevel List

■ You can customize a multilevel list to meet your own needs. For example, you might want to combine bullets and numbers in the same list.

■ When you define a customized multilevel list, Word adds it to the Multilevel List gallery under Lists in Current Documents; the list formatting is only available when the document in which you created it is open

■ Keep in mind that a multilevel list style includes formatting for all levels in the list. You do not have to create a style for each individual level.

Try It!   **Customizing a Multilevel List**

1 In the **WTry04_studentfirstname_studentlastname** file, select all items in the multilevel list.

2 In the Paragraph group, click the Multilevel List button and click Define New Multilevel List to open the Define new Multilevel list dialog box. Level 1 is selected by default.

3 Click the Number style for this level drop-down arrow, scroll to the top of the list, and click 1, 2, 3... This sets the number style for level 1.

4 Click in the Enter formatting for number box, position the insertion point to the right of the number, and type a period.

5 In the Click level to modify list, click 2.

6 Click the Number style for this level drop-down arrow, scroll down, and click the basic round, black bullet.

7 In the Click level to modify list, click 3.

8 Click the Number style for this level drop-down arrow and click a, b, c,...

9 Click in the Enter formatting for number box, position the insertion point to the right of the number, and type a close parenthesis—).

✓ *You can repeat these steps to customize additional levels.*

10 Click OK. Word applies the list style and adds the new style to the Multilevel List gallery.

11 Save the changes to **WTry04_studentfirstname_studentlastname** and leave it open to use in the next Try It.

Define new Multilevel list dialog box

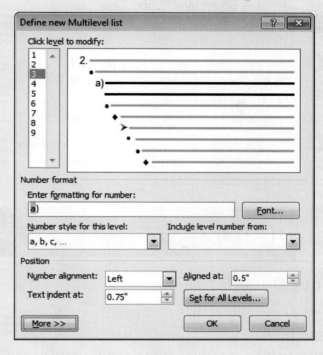

Creating and Deleting a Multilevel List Style

- Use the Define New List Style command to create a multilevel list style that you can use in the current document only, or make available in any document.
- When you make a new list style available in any document, Word adds it to the Multilevel List gallery under List Styles.

- The easiest way to create a new multilevel list style is to define a customized list and then use the Define New List Style dialog box to give it a name.
- You can also change formatting options in the Define New List Style dialog box to create a new style.
- Again, keep in mind that formatting for all levels in the list are part of a single style; you do not create a style for each individual level.
- To delete a multilevel list style, use the Manage Styles dialog box.

Try It!   **Creating and Deleting a Multilevel List Style**

1   In the **WTry04_studentfirstname_ studentlastname** file, select the multilevel list.

2   In the Paragraph group, click the Multilevel List button ⬚ and click Define New List Style to open the Define New List Style dialog box.

3   In the Name box, type **Multilevel List 1** to replace the sample name.

4   Click the Font Color drop-down arrow and click Red.

5   Click the New documents based on this template option button, and then click OK.

    ✓   *To make the new style available only in the current document, select the Only in this document option button.*

6   On the Home tab, click the Styles group dialog box launcher to open the Styles task pane.

7   Click the Manage Styles button ⬚ to open the Manage Styles dialog box.

8   Click the Sort order drop-down arrow and click Alphabetical, then click to select the New documents based on this template option button.

9   In the Select a style to edit list, click Multilevel List 1.

10   Click Delete, click Yes in the Confirmation dialog box, and then click OK to close the Manage Styles dialog box.

11   Close **WTry04_studentfirstname_ studentlastname**, saving all changes, and exit Word.

Project 7—Create It

Tour Questionnaire

DIRECTIONS

1. Start Word, if necessary, and save the default blank document as **WProj07_studentfirstname_ studentlastname** in the location where your teacher instructs you to store the files for this lesson.

2. Double-click in the header and type your full name and today's date.

3. On the first line of the main document, type **Voyager Travel Adventures Questionnaire**, and format it with the **Title** style.

4. Press ENTER and type: **What type of adventure is right for you? How can you decide? At Voyager Travel Adventures, we know that not everyone wants the same travel experience. To help you pick the tour that's right for you, we developed this brief series of questions. Once you complete the form, we'll recommend an adventure we think you'll love.**

5. Press ENTER .

6. On the Home tab, in the Paragraph group, click the **Multilevel List** button ⬚, and then click the style in the middle of the first row.

7. Type **How do you feel about camping?**, and press ENTER .

8. Press TAB and type **I am comfortable in a camper as long as it has electricity and running water.**

9. Press ENTER and type **I am comfortable in a tent as long as there are restroom facilities nearby.**

10. Press ENTER and type **I love wilderness camping.**

11. Press ENTER and type **I will not camp.**

12. Select the items in the multilevel list.

13. In the Paragraph group, click the **Multilevel List** button ⬚ and click **Define New Multilevel List**.

14. Click the **Number style for this level** drop-down arrow, and click **I, II, III,...**

15. Click in the **Enter formatting for number** box, delete the close parenthesis, and type a period.

16. In the Click level to modify list, click **2**.

17. Click the **Number style for this level** drop-down arrow, scroll down, and click **A, B, C,...**

18. Click **OK**.

19. Check and correct the spelling and grammar in the document, and then save the changes.

20. **With your teacher's permission,** print the document. It should look similar to Figure 4-1.

21. Close the document, saving all changes, and exit Word.

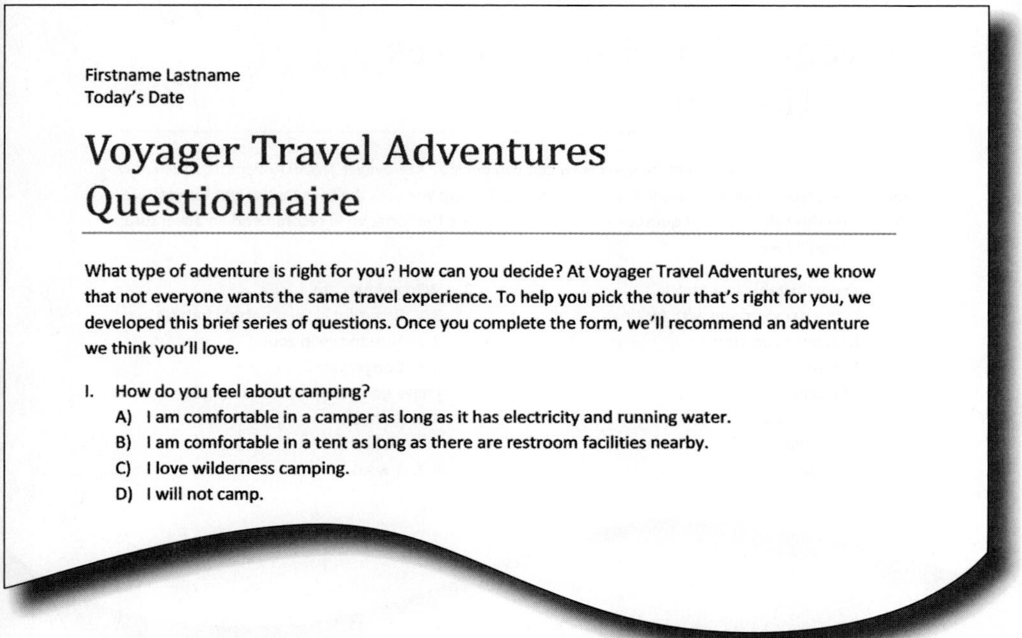

Figure 4-1

Firstname Lastname
Today's Date

Voyager Travel Adventures Questionnaire

What type of adventure is right for you? How can you decide? At Voyager Travel Adventures, we know that not everyone wants the same travel experience. To help you pick the tour that's right for you, we developed this brief series of questions. Once you complete the form, we'll recommend an adventure we think you'll love.

I. How do you feel about camping?
   A) I am comfortable in a camper as long as it has electricity and running water.
   B) I am comfortable in a tent as long as there are restroom facilities nearby.
   C) I love wilderness camping.
   D) I will not camp.

Project 8—Apply It

Tour Questionnaire

DIRECTIONS

1. Start Word, if necessary, and open **WProj08** from the data files for this lesson.

2. Save the file as **WProj08_studentfirstname_ studentlastname** in the location where your teacher instructs you to store the files for this lesson.

3. Type your full name and today's date in the header.

4. Select all of the text beginning with *I am comfortable in a tent* and apply the Multilevel List format that uses 1. for level 1, 1.1 for level 2, and 1.1.1 for level 3.

5. Position the insertion point at the beginning of the text *Wild animals are* and click **Page Layout** > **Breaks** > **Column** to insert a column break.

6. Adjust the levels in the list as shown in Figure 4-2 on the next page.

7. Modify the current multilevel list formatting in the document so level 1 uses an Arabic numeral followed by a close parenthesis and level 2 uses uppercase letters followed by a period.

8. Create a new list style named **Form List 1** based on the current formatting. Change the color of level 1 to purple, and the color of level 2 to red. Make the style available in the current document only.

9. Check and correct the spelling and grammar in the document.

10. **With your teacher's permission**, print the document. It should look similar to Figure 4-3.

11. Close the document, saving all changes, and exit Word.

Figure 4-2

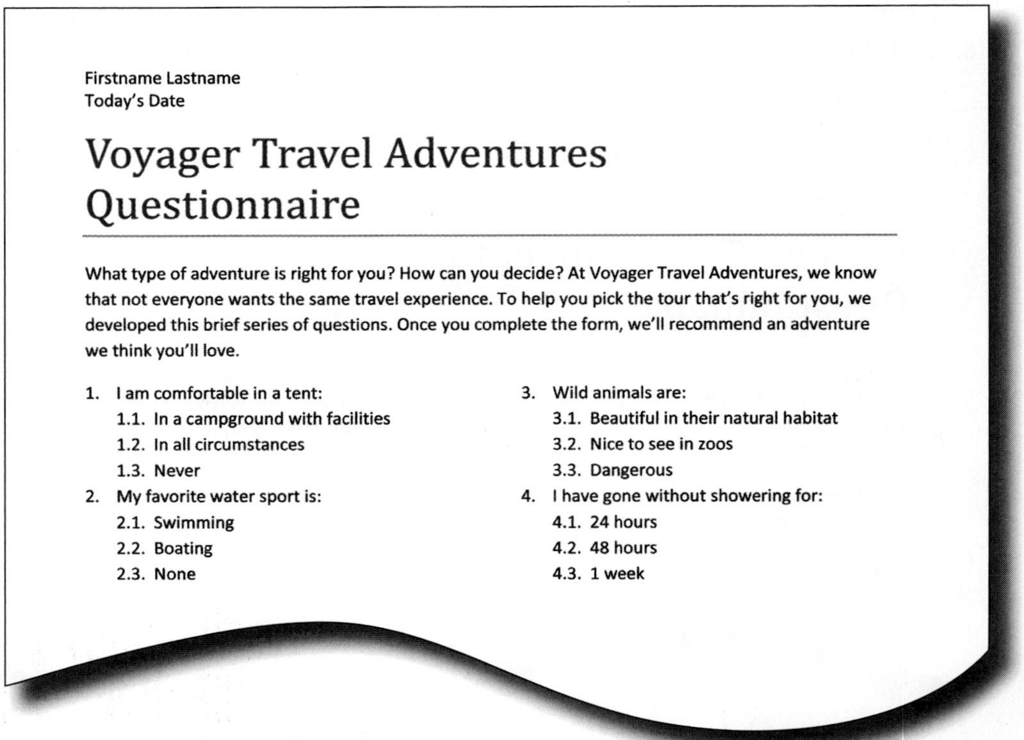

Firstname Lastname
Today's Date

Voyager Travel Adventures Questionnaire

What type of adventure is right for you? How can you decide? At Voyager Travel Adventures, we know that not everyone wants the same travel experience. To help you pick the tour that's right for you, we developed this brief series of questions. Once you complete the form, we'll recommend an adventure we think you'll love.

1. I am comfortable in a tent:
   1.1. In a campground with facilities
   1.2. In all circumstances
   1.3. Never
2. My favorite water sport is:
   2.1. Swimming
   2.2. Boating
   2.3. None

3. Wild animals are:
   3.1. Beautiful in their natural habitat
   3.2. Nice to see in zoos
   3.3. Dangerous
4. I have gone without showering for:
   4.1. 24 hours
   4.2. 48 hours
   4.3. 1 week

Figure 4-3

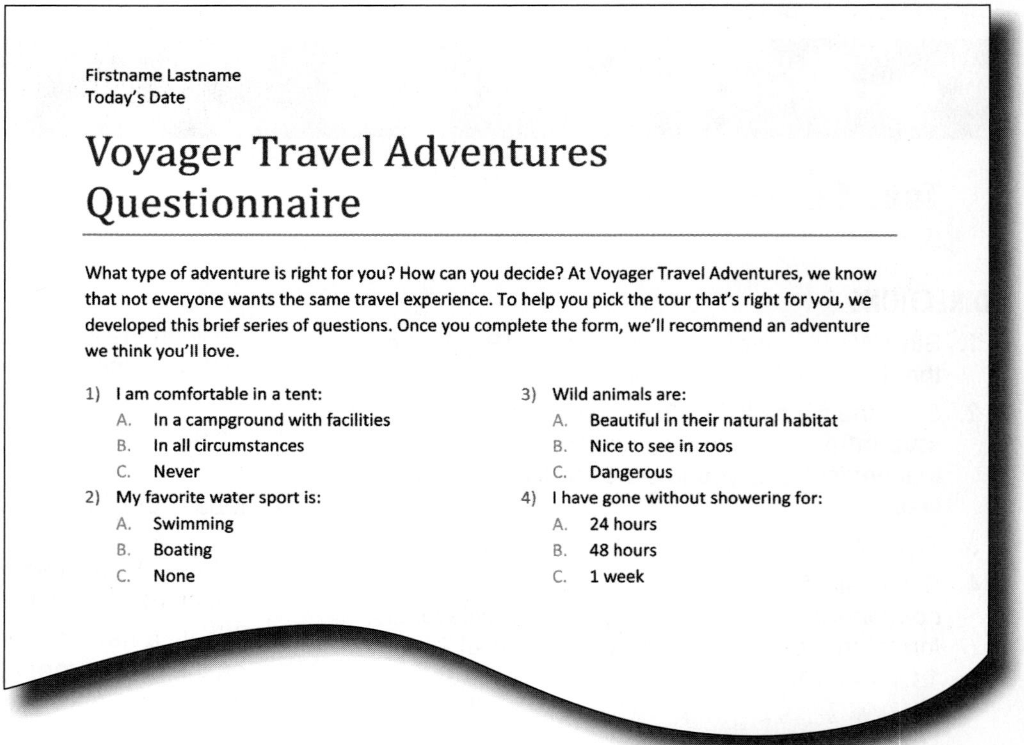

Firstname Lastname
Today's Date

Voyager Travel Adventures Questionnaire

What type of adventure is right for you? How can you decide? At Voyager Travel Adventures, we know that not everyone wants the same travel experience. To help you pick the tour that's right for you, we developed this brief series of questions. Once you complete the form, we'll recommend an adventure we think you'll love.

1) I am comfortable in a tent:
   A. In a campground with facilities
   B. In all circumstances
   C. Never
2) My favorite water sport is:
   A. Swimming
   B. Boating
   C. None

3) Wild animals are:
   A. Beautiful in their natural habitat
   B. Nice to see in zoos
   C. Dangerous
4) I have gone without showering for:
   A. 24 hours
   B. 48 hours
   C. 1 week

Lesson 5

Inserting Charts

WORDS TO KNOW

Chart
A visual representation of information.

Chart object
A chart embedded in a Word document.

Chart title
The name of the chart.

Data axis
The scale used to measure the data in the chart. The Y axis shows the vertical scale, and the X axis shows the horizontal scale.

Data label
Text that identifies the units plotted on the chart, such as months or dollar values.

Data range
A range of cells in which you may enter data.

Data series
A range of values plotted in a chart.

Legend
The key that identifies what each color or symbol in the chart represents.

Plot area
The area of the chart where the data series are displayed.

➤ What You Will Learn

Inserting a Chart
Modifying a Chart
Formatting a Chart

Software Skills   Charts are an effective way to illustrate numeric data and trends. For example, you can use charts to plot sales over time, compare projected income to actual income, or to show a breakdown in revenue sources.

Application Skills   You are investigating the possibility of home delivery service for Fresh Food Fair, a natural food store. In this lesson you will create charts illustrating the results of two customer surveys and include them in a memo to the company owner.

What You Can Do

Inserting a Chart

- Word comes with a Chart tool that lets you use Microsoft Excel charting features to embed a **chart object** in a Word document.
- To create the **chart**, you click the Chart button in the Illustrations group on the Insert tab of the Ribbon to open the Insert Chart dialog box, where you select a chart type and/or subtype.
- Some common chart types include:
  - Column: Compares values across categories in vertical columns.
  - Line: Displays trends over time or categories.
  - Pie: Displays the contributions of each value to a total value. Often used to show percentages of a whole.
  - Bar: Compares values across categories in horizontal bars.
  - Area: Displays trends over time or categories by showing the contribution of each value to the whole.
  - XY (Scatter): Compares pairs of values.

- When you insert a chart, Word creates the chart object in the document, and then displays an Excel worksheet with sample data.

- To create your own chart, you replace the sample data by typing the actual **data series** you want to plot. You may have to increase or decrease the chart **data range**, depending on the amount of data you are entering.

- Charts are linked to the data you enter in the Excel worksheet, so when you edit the worksheet, the chart changes, too.

- You can also create a chart by copying data from a Word table, an Excel worksheet, or an Access table.

Try It!   Inserting a Chart

1 Start Word and open **WTry05** from the data files for this lesson. Save the document as **WTry05_studentfirstname_studentlastname** in the location where your teacher instructs you to store the files for this lesson.

2 Click the Insert tab and then, in the Illustrations group, click the Chart button.

3 In the left pane of the Insert Chart dialog box, click Bar.

Insert Chart dialog box

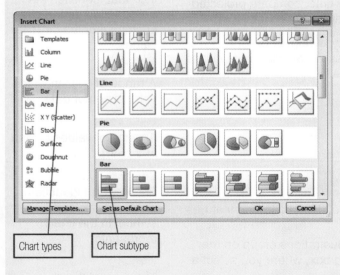

Chart types   Chart subtype

4 Click OK. Word creates a bar chart in the document using sample data and displays an Excel workbook named Chart in Microsoft Word.

5 Replace the sample data with the following, as shown in the graphic on the next page:

	Northeast	Southeast	Midwest
January	32	19	61
February	43	22	45
March	22	35	22
April	52	45	65

✓ To enter data in a worksheet, click the cell and type.

6 Close the Excel program window.

7 In the Word document, scroll down and click in row 2 of the table. Click Table Tools Layout > Select > Select Row, then click Home > Copy.

8 Click the selection frame around the chart object to select the entire chart. On the Chart Tools Design tab, in the Data group, click the Edit Data button to display the worksheet again.

9 Drag the lower right corner of the chart data range down one row, so the data range includes A1:D6.

(continued)

Try It!   **Inserting a Chart** *(continued)*

10 Click in cell A6, then click Home > Paste ⧉.

11 Close the Excel workbook. Save the changes to **WTry05_studentfirstname_studentlastname** and leave it open to use in the next Try It.

Create a chart in Word

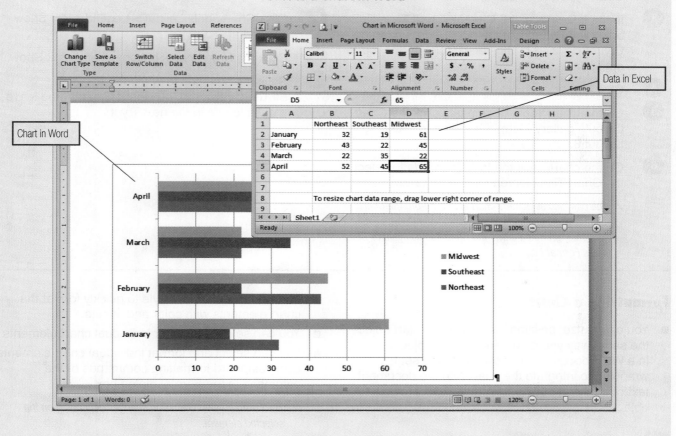

Modifying a Chart

- You can change the chart type by selecting a different type in the Change Chart Type dialog box.

- The Change Chart Type button ▥ and the Chart Layout gallery are on the Chart Tools Design tab on the Ribbon.

- You can apply a chart layout, which controls the way chart elements such as the **chart title**, the **data axis** titles, the data axes, the **legend**, gridlines, the **plot area**, and the **data labels** are positioned in the chart.

- You can position individual chart elements using options on the Chart Tools Layout tab of the Ribbon.

Try It!   Modifying a Chart

1 In the **WTry05_studentfirstname_ studentlastname** file, click the selection frame around the chart to select it, if necessary.

2 On the Chart Tools Design tab, click the Change Chart Type button 📊.

3 In the left pane of the Change Chart Type dialog box, click Column. In the right pane, under Column, click 3-D Clustered Column (the fourth option from the left in the first row).

4 Click OK.

5 On the Chart Tools Design tab, click the Chart Layouts gallery More button ⊡ and click Layout 8.

6 On the chart, click the text *Chart Title* to select the Chart Title element and type **Sales**.

✓ *You can also select any chart element from the Chart Elements drop-down list available in the Current Selection group on either the Chart Tools Layout or Chart Tools Format tab.*

7 Click the text *Axis Title* on the vertical, or Y-axis (left side of the chart), and type **Dollars (in thousands)**.

8 Click the text *Axis Title* on the horizontal, or X-axis (bottom of chart), and type **Month**.

9 Click Chart Tools Layout > Legend 📊 > Show Legend at Right.

10 Click the Data Labels button 📊 and click Show.

11 Save the changes to **WTry05_ studentfirstname_studentlastname** and leave it open to use in the next Try It.

Formatting a Chart

- You can resize, position, and format a chart object the same way you do other graphics objects in a Word document. For example, you set text wrapping to integrate the chart with the document text or apply an outline or shadow effect to the object.

- You can apply a chart style to quickly format the chart elements with color and effects.
- You can select a style for individual chart elements.
- You can select and format individual chart elements using standard formatting commands or the command in the Format dialog box.

✓ *The Format dialog box name changes depending on the selected element.*

Try It!   Formatting a Chart

1 In the **WTry05_studentfirstname_ studentlastname** file, click the selection frame around the chart to select it, if necessary.

2 On the Chart Tools Design tab, click the Chart Styles More button ⊡ and click Style 34 (second to last row, second style from the left).

3 Click the Chart Tools Format tab, then, in the Current Selection group, click the Chart Elements drop-down arrow to display a list of all chart elements.

✓ *The Chart Elements button displays the name of the selected element. In Step 3, it displays Chart Area.*

4 Click Back Wall on the list of chart elements.

(continued)

Try It!   **Formatting a Chart** (continued)

5 Click the Shape Fill drop-down arrow [icon] and click Aqua, Accent 5, Lighter 60%.

6 Click the Chart Elements drop-down arrow and click Series "Midwest".

7 Click the Format Selection button [icon] to display the Format Data Series dialog box.

8 In the left pane, click Fill. In the right pane, click Solid fill, and then click the Color drop-down arrow and click Purple, Accent 4. Click Close to apply the change.

9 Click the selection frame around the chart to select it, then change the value in the Shape Height box [icon] to 4".

10 In the Arrange group, click the Position button [icon] and click Position in Bottom Center with Square Text Wrapping.

11 Close **WTry05_studentfirstname_studentlastname**, saving all changes, and exit Word.

Format a chart in Word

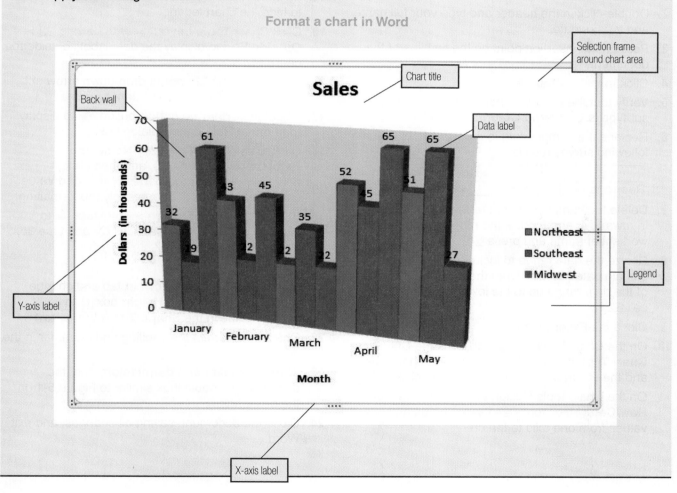

Project 9—Create It

Survey Results Chart

DIRECTIONS

1. Start Word, if necessary, and save the default blank document as **WProj09_studentfirstname_studentlastname** in the location where your teacher instructs you to store the files for this lesson.

2. Double-click in the header and type your full name and today's date.

3. Position the insertion point on the first line of the document.

4. Click **Insert** > **Chart** .

5. Verify that the selected chart type is **Column**, and subtype is **Clustered Column**, then click **OK**.

6. Replace the sample data in the worksheet with the following survey results:

	No	Maybe	Yes	Don't Know
Responses	10	38	49	3

7. Delete the sample data not replaced by new data in rows 3, 4, and 5. Click the row number in the worksheet frame and press DEL .

8. Resize the data range to include only the cells that contain data (A1:E2). Drag the lower-right corner of the data range up to the lower-right corner of cell E2.

9. Close the Excel window.

10. On the Chart Tools Design tab, click the **Change Chart Type** button , select the **Pie** chart type and the **Pie in 3-D** chart subtype, and click **OK**.

11. On the Chart Tools Design tab, click the **Switch Row/Column** button to swap the data series values from one axis to the other.

12. Click the chart title text **Responses** and change the font size to **12 points**.

13. With the chart title still selected, type **Likely to Purchase Home Delivery**.

14. Click **Chart Tools Layout** > **Legend** > **None** to hide the chart legend.

15. Click **Chart Tools Layout** > **Data Labels** > **Outside End** to display the data labels outside the chart.

16. Click the **Chart Elements** drop-down arrow and click **Series "Responses" Data Labels**.

17. Click the **Format Selection** button to display the Format Data Labels dialog box.

18. Click to select the **Category Name** and **Percentage** check boxes, and then click, if necessary, to clear the **Series Name** and **Value** check boxes. Click **Close** to apply the formatting.

19. Click **Chart Tools Design** > **Edit Data** to display the worksheet. Click cell **C2** and type **30**. Click cell **D2** and type **57**.

20. Close the Excel window.

21. Click the **Chart Tools Format** tab and change the value in the **Shape Height** box to **2.5"** and the value in the **Shape Width** box to **4"**.

22. Check and correct the spelling and grammar in the document.

23. **With your teacher's permission**, print the document. It should look similar to Figure 5-1 on the next page.

24. Close the document, saving all changes, and exit Word.

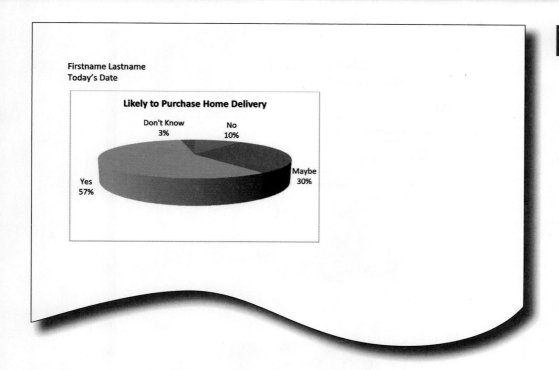

Figure 5-1

Project 10—Apply It

Memo with Survey Results

DIRECTIONS

1. Start Word, if necessary, and open **WProj10a** from the data files for this lesson.

2. Save the file as **WProj10a_studentfirstname_studentlastname** in the location where your teacher instructs you to store the files for this lesson.

3. Replace the sample text *Student's Name* with your own name and *Today's Date* with today's date.

4. Position the insertion point on the last line of the document.

5. Insert a **Clustered Column** chart.

6. Start Excel and open the workbook file **WProj10b** from the data files for this lesson.

7. Copy the data in cells **A4:E8** to the Clipboard, then exit Excel without saving any changes.

   ✓ *To copy the data, click cell A4, press and hold Shift, then click cell E8. Click the Copy button.*

8. Click cell **A1** in the Chart in the Microsoft Word worksheet and paste the data from the Clipboard.

9. Close the workbook.

10. Resize the chart to **2.5"** high by **4"** wide.

11. Apply **Chart Layout 3**. Change the chart title to **Product Preferences by Area**.

12. Apply the **Chart Style 42** to both charts in the memo.

13. Change the font size of the chart titles of both charts to **12 points**.

14. Change the Chart Area color of both charts to a **solid fill Purple, Accent 4, Lighter 60%**.

15. Check and correct the spelling and grammar in the document.

16. **With your teacher's permission**, print the document. It should look similar to Figure 5-2.

17. Close the document, saving all changes, and exit Word.

Figure 5-2

Fresh Food Fair
Route 117, Bolton, MA 01740

MEMO

To: Kimberly and Jack Thomson
From: Firstname Lastname
Date: Today's Date
Subject: Home Delivery Service

Here are two charts showing the results of surveys of our target market. Call me if you have questions.

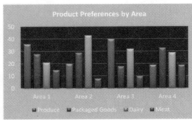

Chapter Assessment and Application

Project 11—Make It Your Own

Employment Portfolio

Use skills you have learned in this chapter to set up an employment portfolio. You can create a digital portfolio by creating a folder on a removable storage device, and you can use a manila or an accordion folder to store printed copies of documents. In this project, set up the folder and create a multilevel list describing the contents of your portfolio.

It is not necessary to have all of the documents now; you can use the multilevel list as a guide for items you plan to include. Create at least one document that uses a chart to illustrate information you think a potential employer might find useful. For example, you might chart improvement in your grades over time, or your performance in athletics. You may also copy or move existing documents into the portfolio, such as a resume, sample cover letters, or a list of recommendations.

DIRECTIONS

1. Use Windows Explorer to create a new folder named **WProj11_portfolio_studentfirstname_ studentlastname** in the location where your teacher instructs you to store the files for this chapter.
2. Start Word and save the default blank document as **WProj11a_studentfirstname_ studentlastname**, in the folder you created in step 1.
3. Apply a theme and a style set.
4. Set up an outline-style multilevel list that includes the items you plan to store in the portfolio. For example, level 1 might be a title, level 2 might be main categories of items, such as job search materials or academic achievements, and level 3 might be specific documents, such as resume, references, or school transcripts.
5. Choose one of the built-in multilevel list styles, or define your own for use in this document only. Use direct formatting to indicate documents you have already created and added to the portfolio compared to documents you plan to create in the future.
6. Insert a cover page for the outline and include your name and the date.
7. Check the spelling and grammar in the document and correct errors as necessary.

8. **With your teacher's permission**, print the document and put the printed document in your portfolio.
9. Close the document, saving all changes.
10. Create a new, blank document in Word and save it as **WProj11b_studentfirstname_ studentlastname**, in the folder you created in step 1.
11. Type your name and the date in the document header.
12. Apply a theme and a style set.
13. Decide what information you want to chart, and type a title on the first line of the document. Create a new style for the title and name it **Portfolio Title**.
14. Type a paragraph describing the information in the chart, and explaining why you are including it in your portfolio. Create a new style for the paragraph text and name it **Portfolio Text**.
15. Insert an appropriate chart type and enter the information. Modify and format the chart to make it easy to read and visually appealing.
16. Check the spelling and grammar in the document and correct errors as necessary.
17. **With your teacher's permission**, print the document and put the printed document in your portfolio.
18. Close the document, saving all changes, and exit Word.

Project 12—Master It

Expansion Proposal

In response to a customer survey, Liberty Blooms flower shop has asked you to draft a proposal for expanding the business. In this project you will create an outline for the proposal, which you will format as a multilevel list. You will insert text from an existing file, and include a chart illustrating the results of the survey and a cover page.

DIRECTIONS

1. Start Word and save the default blank document as **WProj12a_studentfirstname_studentlastname** in the location where your teacher instructs you to store the files for this chapter.

2. Apply the **Angles** theme and the **Manuscript** style set.

3. Type your name and the date in the document header.

4. Set Word to track formatting inconsistencies.

5. Define a new multilevel list using the following formatting for each level:
   - Level 1   None (with no punctuation)
   - Level 2   Uppercase letters followed by a period
   - Level 3   Arabic numbers followed by a period
   - Level 4   Lowercase letters followed by a close parenthesis

6. On the first line of the document, press SHIFT + TAB to make the line level 1, then type **Liberty Blooms Flower Shop Proposal Outline**, and then press ENTER .

7. Press TAB and type **Introduction**.

8. Press TAB and type **Background**.

9. Continue applying indents and typing to create the outline shown in Illustration A on the next page.

10. Select the first line of the text, increase the font size to **18 points** and apply a solid underline. Save the selection as a new Quick Style with the name **Proposal Title**.

11. Insert a new page at the end of the document.

12. Type **Customer Survey Results** and format it with the **Proposal Title** style.

13. Reveal the style formatting and examine it closely. Note that it includes list formatting.

14. Remove the list formatting and update the style to match the selection.

15. Close all open task panes.

16. Position the insertion point on the line below the second page heading, clear all formatting, and insert the text from the **WProj12b** file from the data files for this chapter.

    Using the Normal style, type: **Customers entering the current store location were invited to complete a brief survey. They were asked to rank five statements on a scale of 1 to 10, with 10 being Most Favorable and 1 being Least Favorable. The results have been compiled, and the average ranking of each statement is shown in the chart below.**

17. Apply bold to the text *Most Favorable* and *Least Favorable*.

18. On a line below the inserted paragraph, insert a pie chart using the following data:

	Average Rank
Expand the current store	3.2
Open a new store downtown	9.3
Open a new store at the mall	1.6
Open a new store in the next town	7.8
Don't change a thing	6.6

19. Apply the **Chart Layout 6** and the **Chart Style 42**.

20. Change the chart subtype to **Exploded pie in 3-D**.

21. Format the Chart Area fill to a solid **Blue-Gray, Accent 6, Lighter 40%**.

22. Edit the Chart Title to **Average Customer Rankings**.

23. Center the chart object on the page, horizontally and vertically.

24. Insert the **Exposure** style Cover Page. Remove the business-related content controls and replace the remaining content controls as follows:

   ■ Document title: **Liberty Blooms Expansion Proposal**

   ■ Author: *Your full name*

   ■ Year: *Today's date*

   ■ Abstract: **This proposal examines the pros and cons of expanding the Liberty Blooms flower shop business.**

25. Check the spelling and grammar in the document and correct errors as necessary.

26. **With your instructor's permission**, print the document. Page 2 should look similar to Illustration A, and page 3 should look similar to Illustration B.

27. Set Word to not track formatting.

28. Close the document, saving all changes, and exit Word.

Illustration A

Firstname Lastname
Today's Date

Liberty Blooms Flower Shop Proposal Outline

A. Introduction

B. Background

   1. History of Liberty Blooms

   2. Description of Business

   3. Description of Neighborhood

C. Growth Opportunities

   1. Expansion of Current Location

      a) Pros

      b) Cons

   2. Expansion into New Territory

      a) Pros

      b) Cons

D. Customer Survey

   1. Methodology

   2. Summary of Results

Firstname Lastname
Today's Date

Customer Survey Results

Customers entering the current store location were invited to complete a brief survey. They were asked to rank five statements on a scale of 1 to 10, with 10 being **Most Favorable** and 1 being **Least Favorable**. The results have been compiled, and the average ranking of each statement is shown in the chart below.

Illustration B

Chapter 2

Using Reusable Content and Markup Tools

Lesson 6
Translating Text and Customizing Word Options
Projects 13-14

- Analyzing Effective Communication
- Translating Text
- Customizing the Quick Access Toolbar
- Customizing the Ribbon
- Locating the Default Save Options
- Personalizing Your User Name and Initials
- Customizing the View for Opening E-Mail Attachments

Lesson 7
Using Advanced Find and Replace
Projects 15-16

- Analyzing Conflict
- Collecting Images and Text from Multiple Documents
- Finding and Replacing Formatting
- Using Wildcard Characters in Find and Replace
- Understanding Project Management

Lesson 8
Using Building Blocks
Projects 17-18

- Inserting a Built-In Building Block
- Creating a Custom Building Block
- Using the Building Blocks Organizer

Lesson 9
Inserting Fields from Quick Parts
Projects 19-20

- Inserting a Field from Quick Parts
- Setting Field Display Options
- Analyzing Employment Packages

Lesson 10
Creating Custom Themes
Projects 21-22

- Creating a Custom Theme
- Applying, Restoring, and Deleting a Theme

Lesson 11
Using Comments
Projects 23-24

- Inserting Comments
- Setting Comment Options

Lesson 12
Tracking Changes
Projects 25-26

- Tracking Changes
- Customizing Revision Marks
- Accepting and Rejecting Changes

Lesson 13
Comparing Documents
Projects 27-28

- Viewing Documents Side by Side
- Comparing Documents
- Combining Documents

End-of-Chapter Assessments
Projects 29-30

Lesson 6

Translating Text and Customizing Word Options

WORDS TO KNOW

Active listening
Paying attention to a message, hearing it, and interpreting it correctly.

Communication
The exchange of information between a sender and a receiver.

Nonverbal communication
The exchange of information without using words.

Translate
To change text from one language into another.

User name
A name assigned to someone who uses a computer system or program that identifies the user to the system.

Verbal communication
The exchange of information by speaking or writing.

➤ What You Will Learn

Analyzing Effective Communication
Translating Text
Customizing the Quick Access Toolbar
Customizing the Ribbon
Locating the Default Save Options
Personalizing Your User Name and Initials
Customizing the View for Opening E-Mail Attachments

Software Skills   Effective communication skills are essential for succeeding in any business or career. Microsoft Word 2010 provides tools to help you get your message across, including the ability to translate text to and from English. Customize Word Options, the Ribbon, and the Quick Access Toolbar so you have easy access to the tools and features you use most often.

Application Skills   A Fresh Food Fair store wants to post signs with the company slogan in English, Spanish, and Brazilian Portuguese. In this lesson, you will translate the slogan from English to Spanish and from English to Portuguese to create the signs. You will also practice customizing and personalizing Word 2010 options.

What You Can Do

Analyzing Effective Communication

- In business, it is important to make sure all **communication** is clear and effective, including speeches, e-mail, blogs, and Web posts, as well as more traditional letters, memos, and reports.

- Effective communication is when the receiver interprets the message the way the sender intended.

- Ineffective communication is when the receiver misinterprets the message.

- Talking is usually a very effective form of **verbal communication**. When you write, you lose some of the context, which is the current situation that applies to the communication, which can make the communication less effective.

- **Nonverbal communication** includes visual messages that the receiver can see, such as a smile. It also includes physical messages, such as a pat on the back, and aural, or sound, messages, such as your tone of voice.

- Nonverbal communication also includes the use of visual aids, such as pictures and charts which can help clarify your message and put it in context.

- **Active listening** is a sign of respect. It shows you are willing to communicate and that you care about the speaker and the message. When you listen actively, the other person is more likely to listen when you speak, too.

Translating Text

- Use Microsoft Word 2010 to **translate** document text from one language to another.

- Right-click a word and click Translate on the shortcut menu to display the translation in the Research task pane.

- Use the Translate button in the Language group on the Review tab of the Ribbon to display all translation commands or to set translation options.

  - Use the Translate Selected Text command to display the translation in the Research task pane. You can select the languages you want to translate from and to.

  - Use the Mini Translator to display a pop-up translation. The Mini Translator also includes buttons for opening the Research task pane, copying the text, playing an audio file of the text in its current language, or displaying help.

  - If you have access to an online translation service, you can select the Translate Document command to transmit the entire document to the service.

- By default, Word uses the online dictionary if there is a connection to the Internet.

- Otherwise, only the languages for which you have bilingual dictionaries installed will be available for translation.

- Translation options are not the same as Office Language Preferences. Customize Office Language Preferences on the Language tab of the Word Options dialog box to set the default language of text entry and editing and for displaying Help and ScreenTips.

Try It!   Translating Text

1 Start Word and open **WTry06** from the data files for this lesson.

2 Save the file as **WTry06_studentfirstname_studentlastname** in the location where your teacher instructs you to store the files for this lesson.

3 Select the sentence *My mother went home.* and click Translate on the shortcut menu to display the Research task pane.

4 In the Research task pane, click the To drop-down arrow and click Italian (Italy). The English to Italian translation displays.

(continued)

Try It!	**Translating Text** *(continued)*

Translation in the Research task pane

8 On the Review tab, click the Translate button a⅍ and click Mini Translator. This toggles the feature on; it remains on until you toggle it off.

9 Rest the mouse pointer on the word *mother*. A dim Mini Translator displays.

10 Move the mouse pointer over the Mini Translator to make it display clearly.

✓ *The options may differ depending on whether you are working from an online or an installed dictionary.*

The Mini Translator

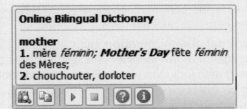

11 Click Review > Translate > Mini Translator to toggle the feature off.

12 Close the Research task pane.

13 Save the changes to **WTry06_ studentfirstname_studentlastname**, and leave it open to use in the next Try It.

5 Click the Review tab, then, in the Language group, click the Translate button a⅍.

6 Click Choose Translation Language to display the Translation Language Options dialog box.

7 Under Choose Mini Translator language, click the Translate to: drop-down arrow and click French (France). Click OK to apply the change.

Customizing the Quick Access Toolbar

■ By default, there are three buttons on the Quick Access Toolbar: Save, Undo, and Repeat. The Repeat button changes to Redo once you use the Undo command.

■ Use the Customize Quick Access Toolbar button ▾ to display a menu of common commands to add or remove from the toolbar, or to choose to display the Quick Access Toolbar below the Ribbon.

■ If the command does not display in the menu, you can locate it on its Ribbon tab, right-click it, and select the command to add it to the Quick Access Toolbar.

■ Alternatively, you can select any command from a list of all available commands using the Quick Access Toolbar tab in the Word Options dialog box.

■ You can also rearrange the order of buttons on the Quick Access Toolbar, and you can reset the Quick Access Toolbar to its default configuration.

Try It! **Customizing the Quick Access Toolbar**

1 In the **WTry06_studentfirstname_studentlastname** document, click the Customize Quick Access Toolbar button ⊡ to drop down a menu of common commands.

✓ *A check mark next to command indicates it is already on the Quick Access Toolbar.*

2 Click Quick Print on the menu. The button for Quick Print is added to the Quick Access Toolbar.

3 Click the Customize Quick Access Toolbar button ⊡ and click Show Below the Ribbon.

4 Click Customize Quick Access Toolbar ⊡ > Show Above the Ribbon.

5 Click the Home tab, right-click the Bold button Ⓑ, and click Add to Quick Access Toolbar.

6 Click Customize Quick Access Toolbar ⊡ > More Commands to display the Quick Access Toolbar tab in the Word Options dialog box.

7 Click the Choose commands from drop-down arrow and click File Tab.

8 In the list of commands, click Close, then click the Add button ⸢ Add >> ⸥.

9 In the list of commands on the Quick Access Toolbar, click Bold and then click the Remove button ⸢ << Remove ⸥.

10 In the list of commands on the Quick Access Toolbar, click Close and then click the Move Up button ⸢▲⸥ twice.

11 Click the Redo button, click the Move Down button ⸢▼⸥, then click OK to close the Word Options dialog box.

Customized Quick Access Toolbar

12 Click Customize Quick Access Toolbar ⊡ > More Commands.

13 Click the Reset button ⸢ Reset ▼ ⸥ and then click Reset only Quick Access Toolbar.

14 Click Yes in the Reset Customizations confirmation dialog box and then click OK.

15 Save the changes to **WTry06_studentfirstname_studentlastname**, and leave it open to use in the next Try It.

Customizing the Ribbon

■ In Word 2010 you can customize the Ribbon by adding commands you use frequently or removing commands you rarely use.

■ You can create new groups on a Ribbon tab, and you can even create a completely new tab with new groups.

■ Commands for customizing the Ribbon are on the Customize Ribbon tab of the Word Options dialog box.

Try It! **Customizing the Ribbon**

1 In the **WTry06_studentfirstname_studentlastname** document, right-click anywhere on the Ribbon and click Customize the Ribbon.

2 On the right side of the dialog box, under Main Tabs, click to clear the check mark to the left of Insert, then click OK to apply the change and close the Word Options dialog box. Notice on the Ribbon that the Insert tab no longer displays.

(continued)

Try It!　　Customizing the Ribbon *(continued)*

3 Right-click anywhere on the Ribbon and click Customize the Ribbon.

4 Under Main tabs, click Home and then click the New Tab button `New Tab`. Word creates a new tab with one new group.

5 Click New Tab (Custom), click the Rename button `Rename...`, and type **Documents**. Click OK.

6 Click New Group (Custom), click the Rename button `Rename...`, and type **Management**. Click OK.

7 Click the Choose commands from drop-down arrow and click File Tab.

8 In the list of commands, click Close, and then click the Add button `Add >>`.

9 In the list of commands, click New, and then click the Add button `Add >>`.

10 In the list of commands, click Save As, and then click the Add button `Add >>`.

11 Click OK, then click the Documents tab on the Ribbon to view the new group of commands.

12 Right-click anywhere on the Ribbon and click Customize the Ribbon.

13 Click the Reset button `Reset ▾` and then click Reset all customizations.

14 Click Yes in the confirmation dialog box and then click OK.

15 Save the changes to **WTry06_ studentfirstname_studentlastname**, and leave it open to use in the next Try It.

Custom tab on the Ribbon

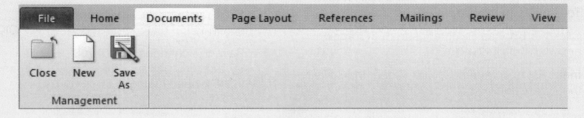

Locating the Default Save Options

- Word 2010 is set to save files using default options.
- By default, Word 2010 saves documents in the Word Document (*.docx) format, in the Documents folder.
- It saves AutoRecover information every 10 minutes.
- You can change the default save options on the Save tab in the Word Options dialog box.

- Additional Save options are available on the Advanced tab in the Word Options dialog box. For example, you can select a default folder for storing specific file types, such as clip art pictures and templates.
- Your system may have been customized to use different save options. For example, files may be saved on a network.

Try It!　　Locating the Default Save Options

1 In the **WTry06_studentfirstname_ studentlastname** document, click File > Options to display the Word Options dialog box.

2 In the left pane, click Save.

3 Examine the Save options.

(continued)

Try It!   **Locating the Default Save Options** *(continued)*

4 In the left pane, click Advanced and scroll down to the bottom of the dialog box.

5 Click the File Locations button to view the storage locations for specific file types.

6 Click Close and then click Cancel to close the Word Options dialog box without making any changes.

7 Save the changes to **WTry06_studentfirstname_studentlastname**, and leave it open to use in the next Try It.

Personalizing Your User Name and Initials

■ When you set up Microsoft Word 2010 on your computer, you enter a **user name** and initials.

■ Word uses this information to identify you as the author of new documents that you create and save, and as the editor of existing documents that you open, modify, and save.

■ In addition, your user name is associated with revisions that you make when you use the Track Changes features, and the initials are associated with comments that you insert.

■ You can change the user name and initials using options in the General group in the Word Options dialog box.

Try It!   **Personalizing Your User Name and Initials**

1 In the **WTry06_studentfirstname_studentlastname** document, click File > Options to display the Word Options dialog box.

2 Under Personalize your copy of Microsoft Office, view the current User name and Initials.

3 Click Cancel to close the Word Options dialog box without making any changes.

4 Save the changes to **WTry06_studentfirstname_studentlastname**, and leave it open to use in the next Try It.

Customizing the View for Opening E-Mail Attachments

■ By default, when you open a document that you receive as an attachment to an e-mail message, it displays in Full Screen Reading view.

■ You can use the Word Options dialog box to disable the feature so that the document opens in Print Layout view.

Try It!   **Customizing the View for Opening E-Mail Attachments**

1 In the **WTry06_studentfirstname_studentlastname** document, click File > Options to display the Word Options dialog box.

2 Under Start up options, click to clear the Open e-mail attachments in Full Screen Reading view check box, if necessary.

3 Click Cancel to close the Word Options dialog box without making any changes.

4 Close **WTry06_studentfirstname_studentlastname**, saving all changes, and exit Word.

Project 13—Create It

Spanish Slogan

DIRECTIONS

1. Start Word, if necessary, and save the default blank document as **WProj13_studentfirstname_studentlastname** in the location where your teacher instructs you to store the files for this lesson.

2. Double-click in the header and type your full name and today's date.

3. Apply the **Origin** theme and the **Modern** style set.

4. Click the **Customize Quick Access Toolbar** button ⏷ and click **Spelling & Grammar** to add the button to the Quick Access Toolbar.

5. Click the **Insert** tab, then right-click the **Clip Art** button 🖼 and click **Add to Quick Access Toolbar**.

6. Click **Page Layout** > **Orientation** > **Landscape**.

7. Click **View** > **Page Width**.

8. On the first line of the document, type **Fresh Food Fair** and format it with the **Title** style. Select the text, then click in the **Font Size** box ⎡50 ▾⎤ and type **50** to increase the font size to **50 points**.

9. Press ⎡ENTER⎤, then type **Organic and Locally Grown for You** and format it with the **Heading 1** style. Increase the font size to **16 points**.

10. Press ⎡ENTER⎤ to start a new line at the end of the document.

11. Select the text *Organic and Locally Grown for You*.

12. Right-click the selection and click **Translate** on the shortcut menu.

13. In the Research task pane, click the **To** drop-down arrow and click **Spanish (International Sort)**.

14. On a blank line at the end of the document, type or copy and paste the translated text: **Orgánico y Localmente Crecido para Usted**.

✓ *To insert the á character, click Insert > Symbol > More Symbols, click the character, click the Insert button, and then click Close.*

15. Format the Spanish text with the **Heading 2** style and increase the font size to **16 points**.

16. Close the Research task pane.

17. On the Quick Access Toolbar, click the **Clip Art** button 🖼. Use the Clip Art task pane to search for a photograph of vegetables, such as the one shown in Figure 6-1, and insert it into the document.

✓ *If you cannot find a suitable clip art picture, insert the file WProj13_picture.jpg from the data files for this lesson.*

18. Close the Clip Art task pane, then select the picture and resize it to 4″ high. The width should adjust automatically.

19. On the Picture Tools Format tab, click the **Position** button 🖼 and click **Position in Top Left with Square Text Wrapping**.

20. On the Quick Access Toolbar, click the **Spelling & Grammar** button ✓. Check and correct the spelling and grammar in the document—ignoring the errors in the Spanish—and then save the changes.

21. **With your teacher's permission,** print the document. It should look similar to Figure 6-1.

22. Click **Customize Quick Access Toolbar** ⏷ > **More Commands**.

23. In the Word Options dialog box, click the **Reset** button ⎡Reset ▾⎤ and then click **Reset only Quick Access Toolbar**.

24. Click **Yes** in the Reset Customizations confirmation dialog box and then click **OK**.

25. Close the document, saving all changes, and exit Word.

Figure 6-1

Project 14—Apply It

Portuguese Slogan

DIRECTIONS

1. Start Word, if necessary, and open **WProj14** from the data files for this lesson.

2. Save the file as **WProj14_studentfirstname_ studentlastname** in the location where your teacher instructs you to store the files for this lesson.

3. Type your full name and today's date in the header and apply the **Hardcover** theme and the **Thatch** style set to the document.

4. Add the **Print Preview and Print** button to the Quick Access Toolbar.

5. Customize the Ribbon to create a new Ribbon tab named **Photos**, with a group named **Formatting**.

6. Add the following buttons for working with pictures to the new group: Picture 🖼, Position 🖼, Wrap Text 🖼, Size Height 🖩, and Size Width 🖼.

7. Change the page orientation to **Landscape** and set the zoom so you can see the entire width of the page onscreen.

8. Format the first line of text in the **Title** style, increase the Font Size to **50 points**, and center it horizontally.

9. Format the second line of text in the **Heading 1** style, increase the Font Size to **22 points**, and center it horizontally.

10. Format the third line of text in the **Heading 2** style, increase the Font Size to **22 points**, and center it horizontally.

11. Insert a new line at the end of the document.

12. Set the Mini Translator to translate to Portuguese (Brazil), and then toggle the Mini Translator feature on.

13. Select the text *Organic and Locally Grown for You*, and rest the mouse pointer over the selection.

14. Move the mouse pointer over the Mini Translator so you can see the translation, then, on the Mini Translator, click the **Copy** button 🖼.

15. Position the insertion point on the last line of the document and click **Home** > **Paste** 🖼.

16. Delete the line with the text *WorldLingo*, and any other blank lines in the document.

17. Format the Portuguese translation with the **Heading 3** style, increase the Font Size to **22 points**, and center it horizontally.

18. Using the Photos tab on the Ribbon, insert the picture **WProj14_picture** from the data files for this lesson. Resize the picture so it is **4˝** high (the width should adjust automatically), and position it in the **Bottom Center with Square Text Wrapping**.

19. Check and correct the spelling and grammar in the document—ignoring the errors in the Spanish and Portuguese—and then save the changes.

20. **With your teacher's permission,** print the document. It should look similar to Figure 6-2.

21. Reset all customizations, and toggle off the Mini Translator.

22. Close the document, saving all changes, and exit Word.

Figure 6-2

Firstname Lastname
Today's Date

Fresh Food Fair

Organic and Locally Grown for You

Orgánico y localmente crecido para usted

ORGÂNICO E CRESCIDO LOCALMENTE PARA VOCÊ

Lesson 7

Using Advanced Find and Replace

➤ **What You Will Learn**

Analyzing Conflict
Collecting Images and Text from Multiple Documents
Finding and Replacing Formatting
Using Wildcard Characters in Find and Replace
Understanding Project Management

Software Skills   Use the Office Clipboard to collect images and text from multiple documents. Use Advanced Find and Replace features to locate and replace existing formatting throughout a document. Use wildcard characters with Find and Replace when you are not sure what text you want to find. Conflict with others can make it difficult to achieve goals. You can manage by being open, honest, and respectful, and by working together to compromise and find solutions.

Application Skills   Two Long Shot, Inc. sales representatives were observed laughing at a disabled golfer while on company business. The legal department has instructed you, a human resources assistant, to assume responsibility for an ongoing project to improve relations within the company and with the community. First, you will draft a letter of apology to the disabled golfer. Second, you will write an internal memo reinforcing the company's position on diversity. To complete these projects, you will use text and images collected from multiple documents and advanced Find and Replace features.

WORDS TO KNOW

Bias
An opinion based on something you think you know, not on the truth.

Conflict
A disagreement between two or more people who have different ideas.

Diversity
People of many cultures, backgrounds, and abilities living and working together.

Prejudice
A negative bias.

Problem
Something that blocks you from achieving a goal.

Project
An activity with a starting date and an ending date designed to produce a product, service, or specific result.

Project management
Using resources such as time, money, and people to plan, organize, and complete a project.

Project manager
The person responsible for overseeing the project.

Wildcard character
A typed character such as an asterisk (*) that represents one or more other characters in a string of text.

What You Can Do

Analyzing Conflict

- **Conflict** with others can interfere with your ability to complete tasks and achieve goals.

- There is a **problem** at the root of all conflict. You may be able to use a problem-solving process to find a solution that will resolve the conflict.

- Managing conflict does not always mean eliminating the conflict completely. It means that you are able to recognize what is causing the conflict, and that you can cope with it in an honest and respectful way.

- Sometimes, **diversity** can cause conflict. Focusing on the common goals you and others share will help you see past the differences.

- Understanding the differences between people makes it easier to communicate. It does not mean you have to always agree with people who are different, or have different opinions. It just means that you are willing to listen to them and show respect.

- You might have a **bias** about people who are different from you, even before you meet them. When a bias is negative, it is called **prejudice**. There is no place for prejudice at work or anywhere else.

- You can work and communicate effectively in a diverse workplace by developing the qualities of tolerance, cooperation, respect, and understanding.

Collecting Images and Text from Multiple Documents

- Use the Microsoft Office Clipboard with the Cut or Copy commands to collect images and text from multiple documents.

- Recall that the Copy command stores a duplicate of the selection on the Clipboard, leaving the original selection unchanged, and that the Cut command deletes the selection from its original location, and stores it on the Clipboard.

- You can then use the Paste command to paste a selection from the Clipboard to the insertion point location in the same file or a different file.

- You can store up to 24 items on the Clipboard task pane at a time.

Try It!   **Collecting Images and Text from Multiple Documents**

1 Start Word, if necessary, and save the default blank document as **WTry07a_studentfirstname_studentlastname** in the location where your teacher instructs you to store the files for this lesson.

2 Click the Clipboard group dialog box launcher to display the Clipboard task pane.

3 In the task pane, click the Clear All button to delete any selections currently on the Clipboard.

4 Open **WTry07b** from the data files for this lesson.

5 Press `CTRL` + `A` to select all of the text in **WTry07b**, click the Copy button to place the selection on the Clipboard, and then close **WTry07b** without saving changes.

6 Open **WTry07c** from the data files for this lesson, select all of the text in the document, click the Copy button, and then close **WTry07c** without saving changes.

(continued)

Try It!   **Collecting Images and Text from Multiple Documents** *(continued)*

7 Open **WTry07d** from the data files for this lesson, right-click the picture, click Copy on the shortcut menu, and then close **WTry07d** without saving changes.

8 Double-click in the header of **WTry07a**, and then click the third selection listed in the Clipboard task pane.

9 Close the header area and click the second selection listed in the Clipboard task pane.

10 Position the insertion point at the beginning of the text *Mission Statement*, and click the first selection listed in the Clipboard task pane.

11 Close the Clipboard task pane, save the changes to **WTry07a_studentfirstname_ studentlastname**, and leave it open to use in the next Try It.

Three selections on the Clipboard

Finding and Replacing Formatting

■ Use options in the Find and Replace dialog box to find and/or replace text formatting.

■ For example, you can find text formatted with the small caps effect and replace the formatting with the all caps effect.

■ Open the Find and Replace dialog box using the Find drop-down list or the Replace button in the Editing group on the Home tab of the Ribbon.

Try It!   Finding and Replacing Formatting

1 In the **WTry07a_studentfirstname_studentlastname** document, click the Home tab, and then, in the Editing group, click the Replace button.

2 In the Find what text box, type **Michigan Avenue Athletic Club**.

3 Click the More button to expand the dialog box.

4 Click the Format button and then click Font.

5 In the Font style list, click Bold, and then click OK.

6 In the Replace with text box, type **Michigan Avenue Athletic Club**.

7 Click Format > Font. Under Effects, click to select Small caps, and then click OK.

8 Click Replace All. When the process is complete, click OK to close the confirmation dialog box.

9 Close the Find and Replace dialog box, save the changes to **WTry07a_studentfirstname_studentlastname**, and leave it open to use in the next Try It.

Find and replace formatting

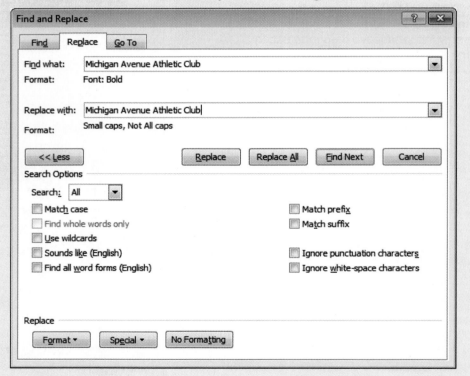

Using Wildcard Characters in Find and Replace

- Use **wildcard characters** with Find and/or Replace when you are not sure exactly what text you want to find.

- For example, you may want to find all occurrences of someone's last name in a document, but you are not sure if it Olden, Oldheimer, or Oldsman. By using wildcard characters, you can find the name, no matter which spelling is used.

- You can use wildcard characters in the Find and Replace dialog box or in the Navigation pane.

- Table 7.1 lists common wildcard characters available for find and replace searches.

Table 7-1	Common Wildcard Characters	
Character	**Description**	**Example**
?	any single character	b?d finds bad, bid, bud, and bed
*	any string of characters	b*d finds all of the above plus bled, blood, and bartered
<	the beginning of a word	<inter finds interesting and interdepartmental but not splintered or disinterred
>	the end of a word	ent> finds sent and represent but not presents or enter

Try It!   Using Wildcard Characters in Find and Replace

1 In the **WTry07a_studentfirstname_ studentlastname** document, click the Find drop-down arrow 🔍 and then click Advanced Find.

2 In the Find and Replace dialog box, click in the Find what text box and then click the No Formatting button, then click in the Replace with text box and click the No Formatting button.

3 Click the More button, if necessary.

4 Click to select the Use wildcards check box.

5 In the Find what text box, type **Peters?n**.

6 Click Find Next.

7 Click the Reading Highlight drop-down arrow and click Highlight All.

  ✓ *Word applies a text highlight color to text matching your criteria.*

8 In the Find and Replace dialog box, click to clear the Use wildcards check box.

9 Click the Less button and then click Close to close the Find and Replace dialog box.

10 Close **WTry07a_studentfirstname_ studentlastname**, saving all changes, and exit Word.

Find and replace using wildcards

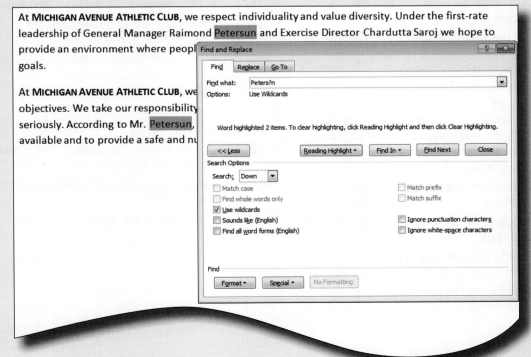

Understanding Project Management

- In order to successfully complete a **project**, it is important to use **project management** skills and techniques.

- Project management includes defining goals, developing a plan to achieve those goals, and then implementing the plan.

- It requires the ability to use available resources including time, money, and people to achieve the goal.

- A well-managed project is completed on schedule and within budget, and achieves the stated goals.

- An effective **project manager** is a strong leader who can guide team members to successfully meet common goals.

Project 15—Create It

Letter of Apology

DIRECTIONS

1. Start Word, if necessary, and save the default blank document as **WProj15a_studentfirstname_studentlastname** in the location where your teacher instructs you to store the files for this lesson.

2. Click the **Clipboard group dialog box launcher** to display the Clipboard task pane.

3. In the task pane, click the **Clear All** button.

4. Open **WProj15b** from the data files for this lesson.

5. Select all the text in the header, click the **Copy** button, and then close **WProj15b** without saving changes.

6. Open **WProj15c** from the data files for this lesson, right-click the logo picture, click **Copy** on the shortcut menu, and then close **WProj15c** without saving changes.

7. In **WProj15a_studentfirstname_studentlastname**, double-click in the header area, and then click the last selection in the Clipboard task pane, to insert the company letterhead.

8. Click **Header & Footer Tools Design > Go to Footer**, then click the first selection in the Clipboard task pane to insert the logo image.

9. Click the image to select it, then click the **Picture Tools Format** tab.

10. Resize the picture to **1.5˝** high by **2˝** wide, and center it horizontally in the footer.

11. Close the header and footer area, and close the Clipboard task pane.

12. Type the letter shown in Figure 7-1, replacing the sample text *Today's Date* with the actual date and *Student's Name* with your own name. Use the No Spacing style and proper page setup and spacing for a full-block business letter.

13. Click **Home > Replace**.

14. In the Find what text box, type **Special O*s**.

15. Click the **More** button to expand the dialog box, and click to select the **Use wildcards** check box.

16. Click in the Replace with text box.

17. Click the **Format** button and then click **Font**.

18. In the Font style list, click **Bold**, and then click **OK**.

19. Click **Replace All**, and then click **OK** in the confirmation dialog box.

20. In the Find and Replace dialog box, click to clear the **Use wildcards** check box.

21. Click in the Replace with text box and click the **No Formatting** button.

22. Click **Close**.

23. Check and correct the spelling and grammar in the document, and then save the changes.

24. **With your teacher's permission,** print the document.

25. Close the document, saving all changes, and exit Word.

Figure 7-1

Long Shot, Inc.

234 Simsbury Drive ⌶ Ithaca, NY 14850 ⌶ 607.555.9191 ⌶ mail@longshot.net

Today's Date

Mr. John Smith
1001 Main Street
Pine Ridge, NY 11111

Dear Mr. Smith,

I am writing on behalf of the entire Long Shot, Inc. organization to express my deepest apologies for the conduct of the two sales representatives last month at the Pine Ridge Golf Club. Please believe me when I say that they do not represent the attitudes of other Long Shot employees.

At Long Shot, Inc. we have a great respect for diversity. We work very hard to insure an open, honest, and respectful environment, and we have a zero tolerance policy for prejudice and discrimination in any form. In accordance with that policy, we have terminated the contracts of the two offending employees.

I want to assure you that we are reviewing our corporate policies, and plan to conduct additional sensitivity training for all employees. We take this responsibility very seriously. In addition, we are making a sizable donation to the Special Olympics, and plan to provide equipment and ongoing support for the Special Olympics golf team. We are also implementing a partnership program between our employees and Special Olympian athletes.

As a token of our goodwill, we are sending you a full set of golf clubs, customized to accommodate your special needs. The package will include other accessories, as well.

Again, we are all deeply sorry for any pain or humiliation you experienced. Feel free to contact me at any time, for any reason.

Sincerely,

Student's Name

Cc: Legal department

Project 16—Apply It

Internal Memo

DIRECTIONS

1. Start Word, if necessary, and open **WProj16a** from the data files for this lesson.

2. Save the file as **WProj16a_studentfirstname_studentlastname** in the location where your teacher instructs you to store the files for this lesson.

3. Replace the sample text *Student's Name* with your own name and *Today's Date* with the actual date.

4. Display the Clipboard task pane, and clear all currently stored selections.

5. Open **WProj16b** from the data files for this lesson and copy the text beginning with *To reinforce...* through the end of the numbered list to the Clipboard.

6. Close **WProj16b** without saving changes.

7. Open **WProj16c** from the data files for this lesson, copy the logo image to the Clipboard, and then close **WProj16c** without saving changes.

8. Insert the text copied from **WProj16b** between the two paragraphs of the memo body (refer to Figure 7-2).

✓ *If necessary, insert a blank line above the pasted text.*

9. Insert the logo image in the document. Position it in the **Bottom Center with Square Text Wrapping** and resize it to **2˝** high by **2.75˝** wide. Close the Clipboard task pane.

10. Use Find and Replace with wildcard characters to apply bold formatting to all occurrences of the text *Special Olympics* and *Special Olympian athletes*.

11. Reset the Find and Replace options to clear the options for using wildcard characters and formatting.

12. Check and correct the spelling and grammar in the document, and then save the changes.

13. **With your teacher's permission,** print the document. It should look similar to Figure 7-2.

14. Close the document, saving all changes, and exit Word.

Figure 7-2

Long Shot, Inc.

234 Simsbury Drive ⌶ Ithaca, NY 14850 ⌶ 607.555.9191 ⌶ mail@longshot.net

MEMORANDUM

To: All Employees
From: Student's Name
Date: Today's Date

By now you are all aware of the unpleasant incident that took place at the Pine Ridge Golf Club last month. You should also all be aware of the fact that the two employees involved in the incident have been let go. There should be no doubt that we have a zero tolerance policy for prejudice and discrimination in any form, and that we will administer that policy if necessary.

To reinforce our policies, we will be conducting sensitivity training classes throughout the coming year. Every employee will be required to participate. There will be no exceptions.

Two positive changes will occur in response to the incident.

1.   Long Shot, Inc. will make a significant financial contribution to the **Special Olympics**, including the donation of equipment and ongoing support to the golf team.
2.   Long Shot, Inc. will implement a partnership program with the **Special Olympics** designed to bring Long Shot employees together with **Special Olympian athletes** as mentors, coaches, and friends.

Information about the training classes and programs with the **Special Olympics** will be posted on the company's Web site. You may also contact the Human Resources Department to learn more.

Thank you.

Lesson 8

Using Building Blocks

WORDS TO KNOW

AutoText
A category of building block displayed in the AutoText gallery.

Building block
A feature of Microsoft Office 2010 that lets you insert reusable pieces of content such as headers, footers, or tables created from saved text and graphics.

➤ What You Will Learn

Inserting a Built-In Building Block
Creating a Custom Building Block
Using the Building Blocks Organizer

Software Skills   Use built-in and custom building blocks to design and save common parts of a document so you can insert them in any document at any time. Use the Building Blocks Organizer to modify, view, insert, or delete a building block.

Application Skills   In this lesson, you will design a header building block for Long Shot, Inc. You will then insert the custom header building block and a built-in footer building block to complete a press release about the company's commitment to the Special Olympics.

What You Can Do

Inserting a Built-In Building Block

- **Building blocks** are a feature of Microsoft Office 2010 designed to make it easy to save content so you can insert it into any document at any time.
- Word 2010 comes with many built-in building blocks which display in galleries available using commands on the Ribbon.
- For example, there are building block galleries for bibliographies, cover pages, headers, footers, equations, page numbers, tables of contents, tables, text boxes, and watermarks.
- Some of the building block galleries are called Quick galleries, because they enable you to quickly insert a formatted object. For example, you use the Quick Tables gallery to insert a table building block.
- Click a building block in a gallery to insert it in a document, then adjust formatting as necessary.

Try It!   Inserting a Built-In Building Block

1 Start Word and open WTry08. Save the file as WTry08_studentfirstname_studentlastname in the location where your teacher instructs you to store the files for this lesson.

2 Position the insertion point on the blank line below the table.

3 Click Insert > Text Box ▣ . A gallery of built-in text box building blocks displays.

4 Click the Alphabet Quote building block.

5 Type **Building Blocks are one way Word 2010 makes it easy to create professional-looking documents.**

6 Save the changes to WTry08_studentfirstname_studentlastname and leave it open to use in the next Try It.

Creating a Custom Building Block

- You can save any selection of text and graphics as a custom building block.

- Use the Create New Building Block dialog box to enter properties for the building block, such as a name and a description.

- The gallery property determines in which gallery the building block will display. For example, if you are creating a header building block, it displays in the Header gallery.

- If the building block does not fit in a particular category, you can select the **AutoText** gallery property. Using the AutoText gallery is covered in Lesson 9.

- You open the Create New Building Block dialog box from the gallery where you want to store the new building block. For example, use the Page Numbers gallery when you want to create a Page Number building block.

- When you exit Word after creating or modifying a building block, the program asks if you want to save the changes to the Building Blocks template.

Try It!   Creating a Custom Building Block

1 In WTry08_studentfirstname_studentlastname, select the table.

2 Click Insert > Table ▦ > Quick Tables to display the gallery of built-in table building blocks.

3 Click Save Selection to Quick Tables Gallery to display the Create New Building Block dialog box.

4 Verify that the Gallery is *Tables*, the Category is *General,* the Save in option is set to *Building Blocks*, and that Options is set to *Insert content in its own paragraph*. If necessary, select these options.

5 In the Name text box, type **Weekly Class Schedule**.

6 In the Description text box, type **High School Class Schedule**, and then click OK.

7 Position the insertion point on a blank line below the table and press ENTER .

8 Click Insert > Table ▦ > Quick Tables, and then scroll down to the bottom of the Quick Tables gallery.

9 Under the heading General, click the Weekly Class Schedule building block to insert it into the document.

✓ *If necessary, position the text box building block in the lower-left corner of the document so it does not split the table.*

(continued)

Try It!   **Creating a Custom Building Block** *(continued)*

10 Save the changes to **WTry08_ studentfirstname_studentlastname** and leave it open to use in the next Try It.

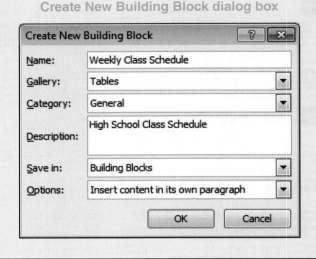

Create New Building Block dialog box

Using the Building Blocks Organizer

- Use the Building Blocks Organizer dialog box to edit, insert, view, or delete a building block.

- Open the Building Blocks Organizer from the Quick Parts drop-down menu on the Insert tab of the Ribbon, or by right-clicking a building block in any gallery and clicking Organize and Delete on the shortcut menu.

- By default, building blocks are listed by gallery. You can change the sort order by clicking a heading at the top of the list.

- Click a building block to view a preview on the right side of the organizer dialog box, or to select it for editing, deletion, or to insert.

- Click the Edit Properties button to open the Modify Building Block dialog box so you change the properties, or display the gallery where the building block is stored, right-click the building block, and click Edit Properties on the shortcut menu.

Try It!   **Using the Building Blocks Organizer**

1 In **WTry08_studentfirstname_ studentlastname**, click Insert > Quick Parts to display the Quick Parts drop-down menu.

2 Click Building Blocks Organizer.

3 In the list of Building Blocks, click the Contrast Cover Page building block. Note that the name and description display below the preview.

4 Click the Name heading to sort the list by building block name.

5 Scroll down the list and click the Weekly Class Schedule Table building block. Note that the category is General—the default for custom building blocks.

6 Click the Edit Properties button to open the Modify Building Block dialog box for the selected building block.

7 Edit the name to **Class Schedule**, then click OK. Click Yes in the confirmation dialog box.

(continued)

Try It!   **Using the Building Blocks Organizer** *(continued)*

8 Scroll down the list and click the Class Schedule Table building block, then click the Delete button.

9 Click Yes in the confirmation dialog box, click the Gallery heading to sort the list by gallery, and then click Close to close the Building Blocks Organizer.

10 Close **WTry08_studentfirstname_ studentlastname**, saving all changes, and exit Word. Click Save in the confirmation dialog box to save the changes to the Building Blocks template.

Building Blocks Organizer

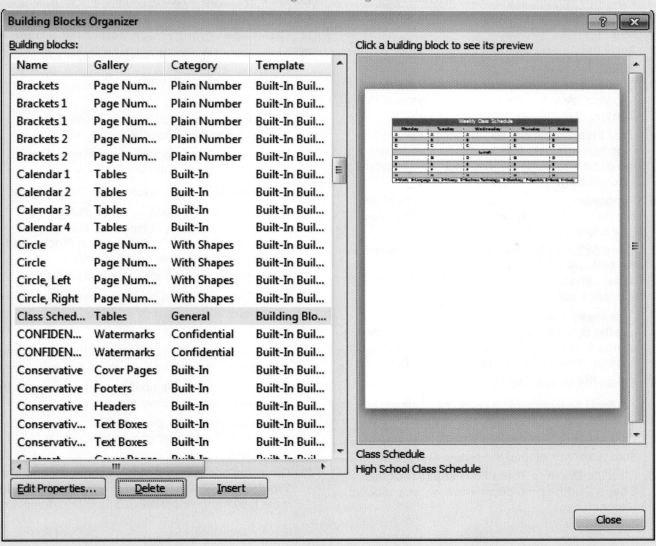

Class Schedule
High School Class Schedule

Project 17—Create It

Header Building Block

DIRECTIONS

1. Start Word, if necessary, and save the default blank document as **WProj17_studentfirstname_ studentlastname** in the location where your teacher instructs you to store the files for this lesson.

2. Apply the **Aspect** theme and the **Distinctive** style set.

3. Double-click in the Header and apply the **No Spacing** style. Set the horizontal alignment to **Center**.

4. Click **Insert** > **Picture** 🖼, then insert **WProj17_ logo** from the data files for this lesson. Resize the picture height to 1˝. The width should adjust automatically.

5. Reposition the insertion point to the right of the picture, increase the font size to **36 points** and type **Long Shot, Inc.**

6. Press SHIFT + ENTER to insert a line break. Change the font size to **10 points** and type **234 Simsbury Drive - Ithaca, NY 14850 - 607.555.9191 - mail@ longshot.net**.

7. Click **Insert** > **Symbol** > **More Symbols**, and use the Symbol dialog box to replace the hyphen characters in the address with the Webdings symbol number 119—a golf flag (refer to Figure 8-1).

8. Select the picture and the text.

   ✓ *Click in the selection bar to the left of the picture to select the first line, then drag down to select the second line.*

9. Click **Insert** > **Text Box** 🄰 > **Draw Text Box** to draw a text box around the picture and the text.

10. Click the **Drawing Tools Format** tab, click the **Shape Outline** drop-down arrow ✏, and click **No Outline**.

11. Click the **Align** button 🄴 and click **Align to Page**.

12. Click the **Align** button 🄴 again, and click **Align Center**.

13. Click the **Align** button 🄴 again, and click **Align Top**.

14. Click **Page Layout** > **Page Borders** ▢ > **Borders**.

15. In the Style list, click the default single line. Click the **Color** drop-down arrow and click Standard **Dark Blue**. Click the **Width** drop-down arrow and click **2 ¼ pt**.

16. In the Preview area, click the **Bottom Border** button ▣ and then click **OK**.

17. With the text box selected, click **Insert** > **Header** > **Save Selection to the Header Gallery**.

   ✓ *You could also save the selection to the Text Box Gallery.*

18. In the Create New Building Block dialog box, verify that the Gallery is Headers, the category is General, Save in is set to Building Blocks, and Options are set to Insert content only.

19. In the Name text box, type **LSI Letterhead**.

20. In the Description text box, type **Company letterhead with logo and address**.

21. Click **OK**.

22. Make the footer active and type your full name and today's date, then close the header and footer area.

23. Check and correct the spelling and grammar in the document, and then save the changes.

24. **With your teacher's permission,** print the document. The header should look similar to Figure 8-1.

25. Close the document, saving all changes, and exit Word. Click Save in the confirmation dialog box to save the changes to the Building Blocks template.

Figure 8-1

234 Simsbury Drive ⚑ Ithaca, NY 14850 ⚑ 607.555.9191 ⚑ mail@longshot.net

Project 18—Apply It

Press Release

DIRECTIONS

1. Start Word, if necessary, and open **WProj18** from the data files for this lesson.

2. Save the file as **WProj18_studentfirstname_ studentlastname** in the location where your teacher instructs you to store the files for this lesson.

3. Apply the **Executive** theme and the **Traditional** style Set.

4. Replace the sample text *Today's Date* with the actual date and *Student's name* with your own name.

5. Insert the **LSI Letterhead** header building block.

6. Click **Insert > Quick Parts** 📋 **> Building Blocks Organizer**.

7. Sort the list by Name.

8. Locate and select the **LSI Letterhead** building block.

9. Edit the Properties to change the name to **Long Shot Header**.

10. Delete the **Long Shot Header** building block.

11. Sort the building block list by Gallery.

12. Close the Building Blocks Organizer Gallery.

13. Insert the built-in **Conservative** footer building block.

14. Check and correct the spelling and grammar in the document, and then save the changes.

15. **With your teacher's permission,** print the document. It should look similar to Figure 8-2.

16. Close the document, saving all changes, and exit Word. Click Save in the confirmation dialog box to save the changes to the Building Blocks template.

Figure 8-2

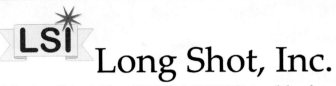

234 Simsbury Drive Ithaca, NY 14850 607.555.9191 mail@longshot.net

FOR IMMEDIATE RELEASE:

Long Shot, Inc. Announces Partnership with Special Olympics

Ithaca, NY – Today's Date – Long Shot, Inc., a manufacturer and distributor of quality golf products, has announced that it is implementing a partnership program with the Special Olympics organization. The partnership will provide ongoing support for many Special Olympian athletes in the area.

According to a company representative, the partnership is designed to encourage Long Shot, Inc. employees to become involved directly with the athletes as mentors, coaches, and friends. It allows for time off from work to participate in Special Olympics activities, and makes grants available to employees interested in participating at a greater level.

In addition, Long Shot, Inc. has also announced a sizable donation to the Special Olympics, as well as a donation of equipment and support for the Special Olympics golf team.

"We are thrilled and excited about this unique partnership," said the company president. "We expect it will continue to bring benefits to both organizations for years to come."

For more information contact:

Firstname Lastname
555.555.5555
contact@longshot.net

Lesson 9

Inserting Fields from Quick Parts

> **What You Will Learn**

Inserting a Field from Quick Parts
Setting Field Display Options
Analyzing Employment Packages

Software Skills   Insert a field into a document as a placeholder for data that might change, such as a date, results of a calculation, or page number. Access the available fields using Word's Quick Parts menu to quickly locate the field, enter field options, and insert the field at the desired location.

Application Skills   As an administrative assistant at Executive Recruitment Resources, Inc., a job search and recruitment agency, you want to show that you are resourceful. In this lesson, you will use fields from Quick Parts to complete a newsletter explaining types of benefits often included in employment packages. You will also save a nameplate for the top of the newsletter as an AutoText building block.

What You Can Do

Inserting a Field from Quick Parts

- Use Word's Quick Parts menu to insert a **field** into a document.
- The available fields are listed alphabetically in the left pane of the Field dialog box.
- Field properties display in the middle pane and options, if any, display in the left pane.
- By default, all fields are listed; you can select a category from the Categories drop-down list to display only the fields in that category.
- Fields display in the document based on field options set in the Word Options dialog box. The default setting is to display the **field value**.

  ✓ *Setting field options is covered in the next section.*

WORDS TO KNOW

Employment package
Compensation offered to employees by an employer, usually including salary, insurance, and other benefits.

Field
A placeholder used to insert information that changes, such as the date, the time, a page number, or the results of a calculation.

Field code
A code that represents the data that Word will display in a document.

Field value
The data displayed in a field.

- If the field value changes, you can update the field to display the current value.
- Most of the fields can also be inserted using other Word features and commands.

- For example, you can insert the date and time using the Date and Time dialog box, which can be opened from the Text group on the Insert tab of the Ribbon.

Try It!   Inserting a Field from Quick Parts

1 Start Word and save the default blank document as **WTry09_studentfirstname_studentlastname** in the location where your teacher instructs you to store the files for this lesson.

2 Click Insert > Quick Parts ⊞ to display the Quick Parts drop-down menu.

3 Click Field.

4 In the left pane of the Field dialog box, click the Categories drop-down arrow and click User Information.

5 In the list of Field names, click UserName.

6 In the Format list, click Uppercase, then click OK. Word inserts the field and displays the name currently entered as the user name, in all uppercase characters.

7 Save the changes to **WTry09_studentfirstname_studentlastname** and leave it open to use in the next Try It.

Field dialog box

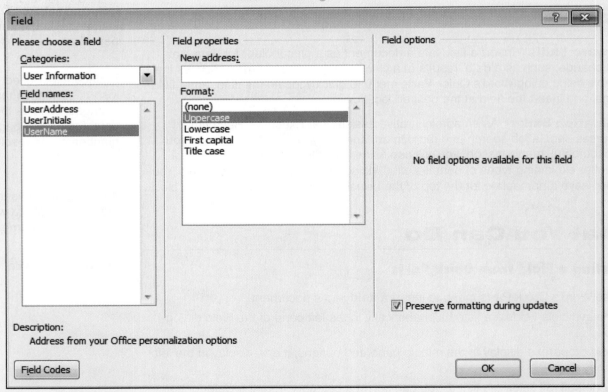

Setting Field Display Options

- In the Advanced tab of the Word Options dialog box, you can select options for how fields display in a document.

- You can select to display **field codes** instead of field values.

- You can select to display shading when a field is selected (the default), always, or never.

Try It!   **Setting Field Display Options**

1. In the **WTry09_studentfirstname_studentlastname** document, click the user name. By default, field shading displays when the field is selected.

2. Move the insertion point off the user name. The field is no longer shaded.

3. Click File > Options > Advanced to display the Advanced tab of the Word Options dialog box.

4. Under Show document content, click to select the Show field codes instead of their values check box.

5. Click the Field shading drop-down arrow and click Always.

6. Click OK to apply the changes and close the dialog box. The field code displays in place of the field value, and shading displays.

7. Click File > Options > Advanced.

8. Under Show document content, click to clear the Show field codes instead of their values check box, then click the Field shading drop-down arrow and click When selected.

9. Click OK to apply the change and close the dialog box.

10. Close **WTry09_studentfirstname_studentlastname**, saving all changes, and exit Word.

Display field codes and shading

{ USERNAME * Upper * MERGEFORMAT }

Analyzing Employment Packages

- When you are offered a job, the company offers an **employment package** that includes benefits as well as salary.

- Most employment packages include some level of health insurance as well as a pension or retirement plan. They usually include vacation time, holidays, and sick/personal days.

- Other benefits that may be offered include:
  - Life insurance
  - Disability insurance
  - Transportation assistance
  - Cafeteria plan
  - Tax-sheltered annuities
  - Fitness assistance
  - Tuition reimbursement
  - Dependent care

- When evaluating an employment package, prospective employees should consider factors such as:
  - The value of the offered benefits.
  - The amount the employee must contribute for benefits and whether the contribution is deducted "pre-tax."
  - Whether the benefits cover family members.
  - Whether benefits are available immediately, or if there is a waiting period.
  - Whether there is flexibility in selecting or changing benefit coverage.

Project 19—Create It

Nameplate

DIRECTIONS

1. Start Word, if necessary, and save the default blank document as **WProj19_studentfirstname_ studentlastname** in the location where your teacher instructs you to store the files for this lesson.

2. Apply the **Black Tie** theme.

3. Apply the **No Spacing** style, and then type the following three lines of text, pressing [ENTER] at the end of each line:

   Executive Recruitment Resources, Inc.

   8921 Thunderbird Road – Phoenix, Arizona – 85022

   Phone: 602-555-6325 – Fax: 602-555-6425 – www.errinc.net

   ✓ *If necessary, right-click the Web site URL and click Remove Hyperlink.*

4. Format the first line of text with the small caps font effect, and increase the font size to **22 points**.

5. Increase the font size of the second line of text to **14 points**.

6. Click **Insert** > **Symbol** > **More Symbols**, and use the Symbol dialog box to replace the hyphen characters in the second and third lines with the Wingdings symbol number 118 (refer to Figure 9-1).

7. Select the three lines of text and click **Page Layout** > **Page Borders** ☐ > **Shading**.

8. Under Patterns, click the **Style** drop-down arrow and click **12.5%**.

9. Click the **Borders** tab, then, in the Style list, click the default single line. Click the **Color** drop-down arrow and, under Theme Colors, click **Blue-Gray, Accent 4, Darker 50%**. Click the Width drop-down arrow and click **3 pt**.

10. In the Preview area, click the **Bottom Border** button ▦ and then click **OK**.

11. Select the three lines of text.

12. Click **Insert** > **Quick Parts** ▤ > **AutoText**, and then click **Save Selection to AutoText Gallery**.

13. In the Name text box, type **ERR Nameplate**.

14. In the Description text box, type **Company name and address**, and then click **OK**.

15. Double-click in the Header and then click **Insert** > **Quick Parts** ▤ > **Field**.

16. If necessary, click the **Categories** drop-down arrow and click **User Information**.

17. In the Field names list, click **UserName**, then, in the Format list, click **First capital**.

18. Click **OK**.

19. Press [ENTER], then click **Insert** > **Quick Parts** ▤ > **Field**, again.

20. Click the **Categories** drop-down arrow and click **Date and Time**.

21. In the Field names list, click **Date**, then, in the Format list, click the third format in the list: **MMMM d, yyyy**.

22. Click **OK**.

23. Click **File** > **Options** > **Advanced**.

24. Under Show document content, click to select the **Show field codes instead of their values** check box.

25. Click the **Field shading** drop-down arrow, click **Always**, and then click **OK**.

26. Close the header and footer, and then check and correct the spelling and grammar in the document.

27. **With your teacher's permission,** print the document. It should look similar to Figure 9-1.

28. Close the document, saving all changes, and exit Word.

{ USERNAME * FirstCap * MERGEFORMAT }
{ DATE \@ "MMMM d, yyyy" * MERGEFORMAT }

Figure 9-1

EXECUTIVE RECRUITMENT RESOURCES, INC.

8921 Thunderbird Road ❖ Phoenix ❖ Arizona ❖ 85022
Phone: 602-555-6325 ❖ Fax: 602-555-6425 ❖ www.errinc.net

Project 20—Apply It

Newsletter

DIRECTIONS

1. Start Word, if necessary, and open **WProj20** from the data files for this lesson.

2. Save the file as **WProj20_studentfirstname_ studentlastname** in the location where your teacher instructs you to store the files for this lesson.

3. Apply the **Technic** theme.

4. Set fields to display values and field shading to display when the field is selected.

5. Position the insertion point at the beginning of the document and insert the **ERR Nameplate** AutoText building block.

6. With the insertion point still at the beginning of the heading *What is an Employment Package?*, insert a continuous section break.

7. Set the spacing before the heading to **10 pt**.

8. Format the second section into two newsletter-style columns, and set the width of the gutter between columns to **0.25˝**.

9. Reposition the insertion point to the beginning of the heading *Evaluating an Employment Package* and insert a column break.

10. Set the spacing before the heading to **20 pt** so it is visually aligned with the heading in the left column.

11. Insert the picture file **WProj20_picture** from the data files for this lesson, and position it in the **Bottom Left with Square Text Wrapping**.

12. Flush left in the footer, type **Prepared by:** and then insert the **UserName** field with uppercase formatting.

13. Centered in the footer, type **Date:** and then insert the **Date** field in the m/d/yy format.

14. Flush right in the footer, type **Time:** and then insert the Time field in the HH:mm format.

15. Delete the **ERR Nameplate** building block.

16. Check and correct the spelling and grammar in the document, and then save the changes.

17. **With your teacher's permission,** print the document. It should look similar to Figure 9-2.

18. Close the document, saving all changes, and exit Word.

Figure 9-2

EXECUTIVE RECRUITMENT RESOURCES, INC.
8921 Thunderbird Road ❖ Phoenix ❖ Arizona ❖ 85022
Phone: 602-555-6325 ❖ Fax: 602-555-6425 ❖ www.errinc.net

What Is an Employment Package?

An employment package—which is sometimes called a benefits package—is all of the compensation that an employer provides for an employee. It includes monetary compensation, such as salary, overtime, and commissions, as well as other benefits, such as insurance coverage.

Benefits and non-monetary compensation have value. Therefore, it is important that everyone who is looking for employment, or who is considering accepting a new position, understands the concept of an employment package. It is also important to know how to evaluate and compare different packages.

An overview of the standard employment package should be discussed during the interview process. A prospective employer should provide a complete, written explanation of the employment package at the time he or she makes a job offer to the prospective employee. It is also advisable for the prospective employee to sit down and discuss the package with a human resources professional or recruitment counselor. The HR professional should be able to answer all questions, and explain the package in detail.

Evaluating an Employment Package

Medical Insurance: Consider the type of plan, what is covered, the amount of the deductibles, co-payments, exclusions, and whether it includes coverage for family members. Also, consider whether there is separate coverage for dental and orthodontic care, as well as for vision and eye care.

Life Insurance: Consider the amount and type of coverage, and whether it is possible to purchase additional coverage.

401(k) plan: A 401(k) is a tax-deferred retirement account. Many companies are replacing pension plans with 401(k) plans. Consider the maximum amount you can contribute, whether the employer matches your contributions, and conditions for transferring the account if you change employers.

Pension plan: Some organizations, particularly government agencies, still offer pension plans for retirement savings. Consider the length of time it takes to become eligible, how the account is managed, and the age at which you can start claiming benefits.

Vacation/holiday/sick/personal days: Consider the number of days for each, when you become eligible, and whether you are paid your full salary for time off. Some companies allow you to carry over unused days from one year to the next.

Other benefits to consider include cafeteria plans which subsidize meals, transportation assistance which subsidizes mileage or public transportation costs incurred while traveling to

Prepared by: SUZANNE   10/8/10   13:51

Lesson 10

Creating Custom Themes

➤ **What You Will Learn**

Creating a Custom Theme
Applying, Restoring, and Deleting a Theme

Software Skills   Word comes with themes you use to apply consistent formatting to your documents. You can create a custom theme to personalize your documents, and save the theme to use again. You can also restore a template theme to its original settings, and delete a custom theme.

Application Skills   The Horticultural Shop Owner's Association is running a two-day conference. As the organization's secretary, you must prepare the **agenda**. In this lesson, you will create a custom theme and use it to format the agenda for the first day. You will then apply it to the agenda for the second day.

What You Can Do

Creating a Custom Theme

- A **theme** includes settings for fonts, colors, and effects.
- You can create and save a custom theme by selecting colors, fonts, and/or effects using the galleries accessed from the Themes group on the Page Layout tab of the Ribbon.
- You can also select theme color and font options from the Change Styles menu accessed from the Styles group on the Home tab of the Ribbon.
- Word comes with built-in sets of theme colors, theme fonts, and theme effects.
- If you do not want to use any of the built-in themes, you can create and save your own.
- Word stores custom themes in the Document Themes folder.
- A saved custom theme displays at the top of the Themes Gallery under the heading Custom so that you can apply it to any document.

WORDS TO KNOW

Agenda
A list or schedule of activities or topics to be accomplished or discussed.

Theme
A set of coordinated colors, fonts, and effects that can be applied to Office 2010 documents.

Try It!   Creating a Custom Theme

1 Start Word and open **WTry10a** from the data files for this lesson.

2 Save the file as **WTry10a_studentfirstname_ studentlastname** in the location where your teacher instructs you to store the files for this lesson.

3 Click Page Layout > Theme Colors ▣ to display a gallery of coordinated theme colors.

4 Click Clarity to apply that set of built-in colors.

5 On the Page Layout tab, click Theme Fonts Ⓐ to display a gallery of coordinated theme fonts, and click Create New Theme Fonts.

6 Click the Heading font drop-down arrow and click Arial.

7 Click the Body font drop-down arrow and click Century.

8 Click in the Name text box and type **Theme Fonts 1**, and then click Save.

9 Click the Theme Effects button ▣ and click Concourse.

10 Click the Themes button Ⓐ and click Save Current Theme.

11 In the File name text box, type **WTry10**, and then click Save.

12 Close **WTry10a_studentfirstname_ studentlastname**, saving all changes. Leave Word open to use in the next Try It.

Custom themes display at the top of the Themes gallery

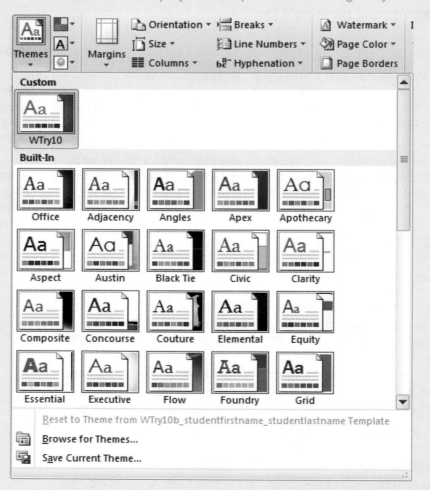

Applying, Restoring, and Deleting a Theme

- Most templates have a built-in, default theme. For example, the default theme for the Normal template is Office.

- You can reset the default template theme, even if you apply a different theme, or a custom theme.

- You can delete a custom theme that you no longer need. Deleting the custom settings does not affect existing documents formatted with those settings.

Try It!   Applying, Restoring, and Deleting a Theme

1. In Word, create a new blank document and save it as **WTry10b_studentfirstname_ studentlastname**, in the location where your teacher instructs you to store the files for this lesson.

2. Click Page Layout > Themes [Aa] to display the Themes gallery.

3. Under Custom, at the top of the gallery, click WTry10 to apply the theme to the template.

4. Type your full name, and format it with the Title style and then save the changes.

5. Click Page Layout > Themes [Aa] > Reset to Theme from Template to restore the default Normal template theme.

6. Click Page Layout > Themes [Aa].

7. Right-click the WTry10 theme, click Delete on the shortcut menu, and then click Yes.

8. Click Page Layout > Theme Fonts [A].

9. Under Custom, right-click Theme Fonts 1, click Delete, and then click Yes.

10. Close **WTry10b_studentfirstname_ studentlastname**, saving all changes, and exit Word.

Project 21—Create It

Day One Agenda

DIRECTIONS

1. Start Word, if necessary, and save the default blank document as **WProj21_studentfirstname_studentlastname** in the location where your teacher instructs you to store the files for this lesson.
2. Apply the **Distinctive** style set.
3. On the first line of the document apply the **Title** style and type **Agenda**.
4. Press ENTER, apply the **Heading 1** style, and type **Horticultural Shop Owner's Association, Day One**.
5. Press ENTER, apply the **No Spacing** style, and then apply the **Strong** style.
6. Type today's date, press ENTER and type **9:00 a.m. to 5:00 p.m.**
7. Click **Home > Clear Formatting**. Click the **Page Layout** tab and set the spacing after to **54 pt**.
8. Insert a table with three rows and four columns. Set the horizontal alignment for columns 1 and 2 to **Left**, and for column 3 to **Right**, and enter the following data (refer to Figure 10-1):

9:00 a.m. – 10:00 a.m.	Introduction Continental Breakfast Welcome Speaker: James Keefe, President	River View Room
10:00 a.m. – Noon	Session 1 Marketing Expanding	Conference Room A Conference Room B
Noon – 1:00 p.m.	Lunch	River View Room
1:00 p.m. – 3:00 p.m.	Session 2 Recordkeeping Legal Issues	Conference Room A Conference Room B
3:00 p.m.– 5:00 p.m.	Demonstrations Wedding Arrangements Valentine's Day Bouquets	Conference Room A Conference Room B

9. Click anywhere in the table, click the **Table Tools Design** tab, and click the **Table Styles More** button ▼.
10. Click the **Medium Grid 2-Accent 2** style, then modify the style by removing the bold formatting from all data in columns 2 and 3.
11. Reposition the insertion point to the line below the table and press ENTER.
12. Type **For more information contact:**, press ENTER and type your full name.
13. Save the changes.
14. Click **Page Layout > Theme Colors** and click **Elemental**.
15. Click **Page Layout > Theme Fonts** and click **Austin**.
16. Click **Page Layout > Theme Effects** and click **Equity**.
17. Click **Page Layout > Themes** > **Save Current Theme**.
18. In the File name text box, type **WProj21**, and then click **Save**.
19. Check and correct the spelling and grammar in the document, and then save the changes.
20. **With your teacher's permission,** print the document. It should look similar to Figure 10-1.
21. Close the document, saving all changes, and exit Word.

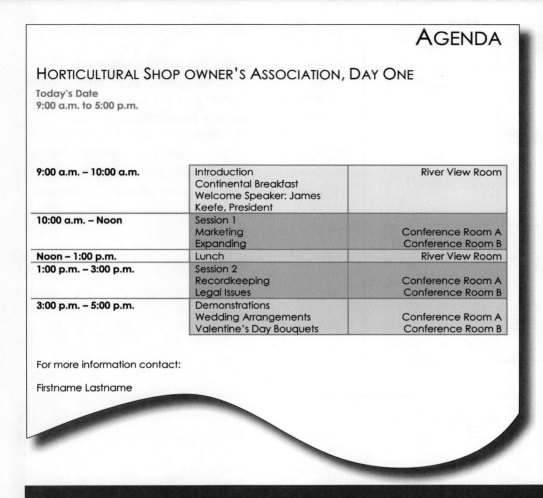

AGENDA

Figure 10-1

HORTICULTURAL SHOP OWNER'S ASSOCIATION, DAY ONE

Today's Date
9:00 a.m. to 5:00 p.m.

9:00 a.m. – 10:00 a.m.	Introduction Continental Breakfast Welcome Speaker: James Keefe, President	River View Room
10:00 a.m. – Noon	Session 1 Marketing Expanding	Conference Room A Conference Room B
Noon – 1:00 p.m.	Lunch	River View Room
1:00 p.m. – 3:00 p.m.	Session 2 Recordkeeping Legal Issues	Conference Room A Conference Room B
3:00 p.m. – 5:00 p.m.	Demonstrations Wedding Arrangements Valentine's Day Bouquets	Conference Room A Conference Room B

For more information contact:

Firstname Lastname

Project 22—Apply It

Day Two Agenda

DIRECTIONS

1. Start Word, if necessary, and open **WProj22** from the data files for this lesson.

2. Save the file as **WProj22_studentfirstname_ studentlastname** in the location where your teacher instructs you to store the files for this lesson.

3. Replace the sample text *Today's Date* with today's date and *Student's Name* with your own name.

4. Format line 1 with the **Title** style.

5. Format line 2 with the **Heading 1** style, and replace the word *One* with the word **Two**.

6. Format lines 3 and 4 with the **No Spacing** style and the **Strong** style, set the spacing after line 4 to **54 pt**, and edit the time from 5:00 p.m. to **4:00 p.m.**

7. Replace the data in the table with the following data:

9:00 a.m. – 10:00 a.m.	State of the Association Continental Breakfast Speaker: Stephanie Moore, Treasurer	River View Room
10:00 a.m. – Noon	Keynote Address Maryellen Rubinsky, Author	Jewel Room
Noon – 1:00 p.m.	Lunch	River View Room
1:00 p.m. – 3:00 p.m.	Workshops Holiday Arrangements Living Wreaths	Conference Room A Conference Room B
3:00 p.m. – 4:00 p.m.	Farewell Reception	River View Room

8. Apply the **Medium Grid 1 - Accent 6** style to the table.
9. Apply the **WProj21** theme to the document.
10. Check and correct the spelling and grammar in the document, and then save the changes.
11. **With your teacher's permission,** print the document. It should look similar to Figure 10-2.
12. Reset the document to the default template theme.
13. Delete the **WProj21** custom theme.
14. Close the document, saving all changes, and exit Word.

Figure 10-2

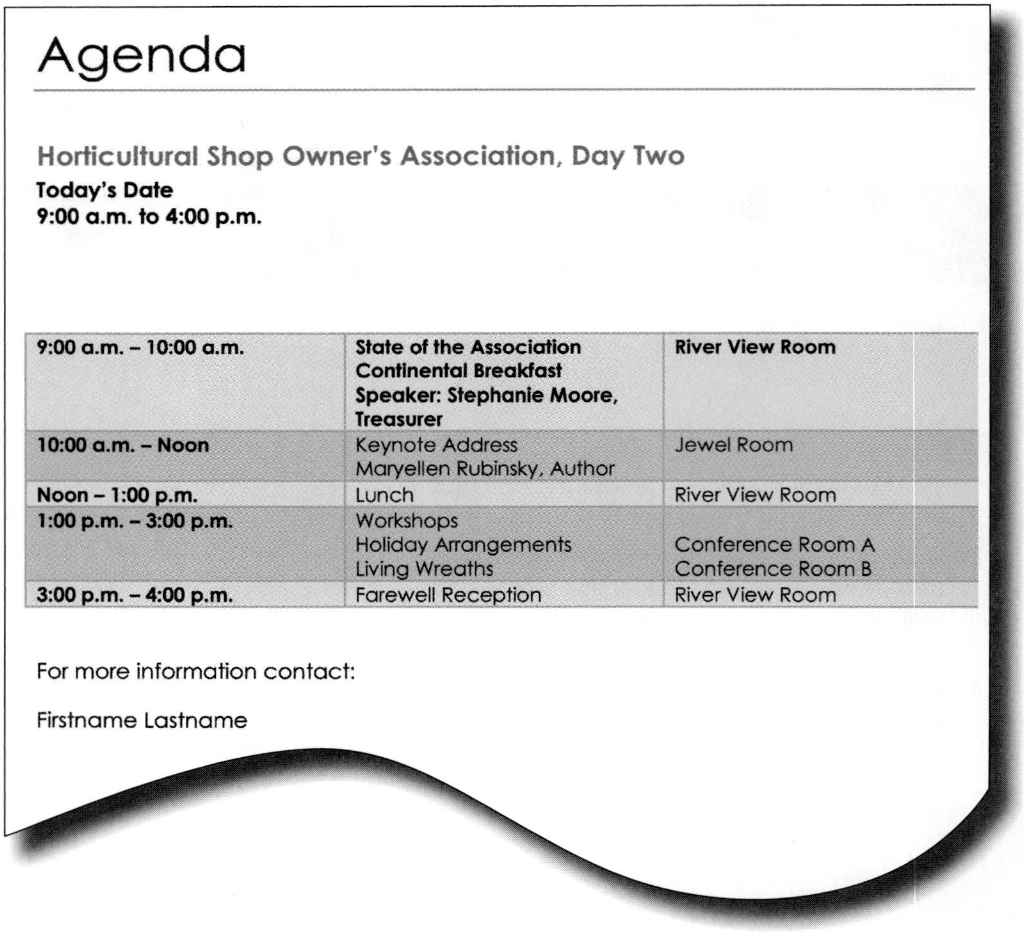

Agenda

Horticultural Shop Owner's Association, Day Two
Today's Date
9:00 a.m. to 4:00 p.m.

9:00 a.m. – 10:00 a.m.	**State of the Association Continental Breakfast Speaker: Stephanie Moore, Treasurer**	**River View Room**	
10:00 a.m. – Noon	Keynote Address Maryellen Rubinsky, Author	Jewel Room	
Noon – 1:00 p.m.	Lunch	River View Room	
1:00 p.m. – 3:00 p.m.	Workshops Holiday Arrangements Living Wreaths	Conference Room A Conference Room B	
3:00 p.m. – 4:00 p.m.	Farewell Reception	River View Room	

For more information contact:

Firstname Lastname

Lesson 11

Using Comments

➤ What You Will Learn

Inserting Comments
Setting Comment Options

Software Skills   Insert comments in a document when you want to include a private note to the author, another reader, or to yourself, in much the same way you might attach a slip of paper to a hard copy printout.

Application Skills   The Director of Training at Restoration Architecture has asked you to prepare a document listing in-house training courses. In this lesson, you will create the document using comments. You will then revise the document based on comments from a reviewer.

What You Can Do

Inserting Comments

- Insert a **comment** to annotate text, communicate with readers, or to attach reminders or questions to a document.
- Comments are part of the revision marking features available with Word.

  ✓ *You learn about other revision marking in Lesson 12.*

- The command for inserting a comment is in the Comments group on the Review tab of the Ribbon.
- When you insert a comment, Word inserts **comment marks** around the word to the left of the current insertion point location, or around selected text.
- By default, in Print Layout view, each comment displays in a **balloon** in the **markup area** on the right side of the document page. The balloon connects to the comment marks by a dotted line.
- In Draft view, comments display in the **Reviewing pane**.
- You can also rest the mouse pointer over the comment marks to display the comment in a ScreenTip.

WORDS TO KNOW

Balloon
An area in which comment text or revisions are displayed.

Comment
A note attached to a document for reference.

Comment mark
Color-coded brackets that mark the location of a comment in a document.

Inline
Within the document text.

Markup area
A 3″ wide strip along the right side of a document where comment and other revision balloons display.

Reviewing pane
A window where revisions and comments can be entered and displayed.

- Comment marks and comment balloons are color coded by reviewer.
- The initials of the reviewer who inserted the comment display with the comment, and each comment by a reviewer is numbered sequentially.

- You can edit the text in a comment at any time.
- You can delete a single comment or you can delete all comments in a document.

Try It!   Inserting Comments

1 Start Word and open **WTry11** from the data files for this lesson.

2 Save the document as **WTry11_ studentfirstname_studentlastname** in the location where your teacher instructs you to store the files for this lesson.

3 Select the text *Michigan Avenue Athletic Club* in the first paragraph.

4 Click the Review tab, and then click the New Comment button to insert the comment balloon.

5 Type **I recommend changing the font color of the club name so it stands out more.**

6 Position the insertion point after the word *Petersun* in the second paragraph and click the New Comment button.

7 Type **Petersun retired. Leave name out until new GM is hired.**

8 Select the text *Mr. Petersun* in the last paragraph, click the New Comment button and type **Omit.**

9 Click to position the insertion point at the end of the text in the first comment balloon, then press SPACE and type **I like the small caps effect!**

✓ *You can also right-click text within the comment marks and click Edit Comment on the shortcut menu.*

10 In the Comments group on the Ribbon, click the Next button to move the insertion point to the next comment.

11 Click the Delete button to delete the comment.

✓ *You can also right-click the balloon and click Delete Comment on the shortcut menu.*

12 Click the Previous button, click the Delete drop-down arrow, and click Delete All Comments in Document.

13 Save the changes to **WTry11_ studentfirstname_studentlastname** and leave it open to use in the next Try It.

Three comments in a document

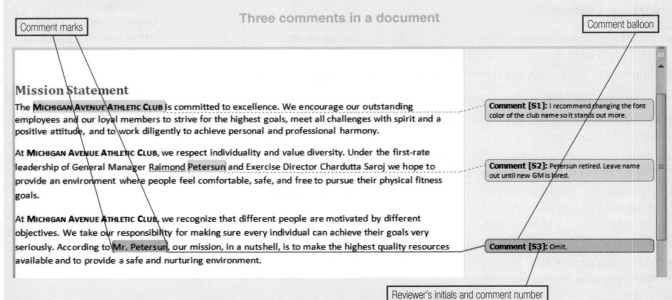

Comment marks

Comment balloon

Mission Statement

The **MICHIGAN AVENUE ATHLETIC CLUB** is committed to excellence. We encourage our outstanding employees and our loyal members to strive for the highest goals, meet all challenges with spirit and a positive attitude, and to work diligently to achieve personal and professional harmony.

At **MICHIGAN AVENUE ATHLETIC CLUB**, we respect individuality and value diversity. Under the first-rate leadership of General Manager Raimond Petersun and Exercise Director Chardutta Saroj we hope to provide an environment where people feel comfortable, safe, and free to pursue their physical fitness goals.

At **MICHIGAN AVENUE ATHLETIC CLUB**, we recognize that different people are motivated by different objectives. We take our responsibility for making sure every individual can achieve their goals very seriously. According to Mr. Petersun, our mission, in a nutshell, is to make the highest quality resources available and to provide a safe and nurturing environment.

Comment [S1]: I recommend changing the font color of the club name so it stands out more.

Comment [S2]: Petersun retired. Leave name out until new GM is hired.

Comment [S3]: Omit.

Reviewer's initials and comment number

Setting Comment Options

- You can choose to show or hide comments.

- You can choose to show revisions **inline**, which means the reviewer's initials and the comment number display to the right of the comment marks in the text, and comments display in the Reviewing pane. There are no balloons.

- You can display the Reviewing pane vertically along the left side of the window or horizontally across the bottom.

- By default, each reviewer's comments display in a different color. You can select one color to use for all comments.

- You can print comments with a document.

Try It!   **Setting Comment Options**

1 In **WTry11_studentfirstname_ studentlastname**, select the name *Raimond Petersun* in the second paragraph, then click Review > New Comment 💬.

2 Type **New GM is Jeanette Silva.**

3 In the Tracking group on the Ribbon, click the Show Markup button 📄, then click Comments to toggle the display of comments off.

4 Click Show Markup 📄 > Comments to toggle the display of comments on.

5 Click Show Markup 📄 > Balloons > Show All Revisions Inline.

6 Click the Reviewing Pane drop-down arrow 📄 and click Reviewing Pane Horizontal.

7 Click the Reviewing Pane drop-down arrow 📄 and click Reviewing Pane Vertical.

8 Click the Track Changes drop-down arrow 📄 and click Change Tracking Options to display the Track Changes Options dialog box.

9 Under Markup, click the Comments drop-down arrow and click Blue. Click OK to apply the change and close the dialog box.

10 Click the Track Changes drop-down arrow 📄 and click Change Tracking Options again.

11 Under Markup, click the Comments drop-down arrow and click By Author. Click OK.

12 Click Show Markup 📄 > Balloons > Show Only Comments and Formatting in Balloons to display comments in balloons instead of inline.

13 Click the Reviewing Pane button 📄 to close the pane.

14 Click File > Print. Click the Print All Pages button and click to select the Print Markup option near the bottom of the menu, if necessary.

✓ *A check mark indicates the option is selected.*

15 **With your teacher's permission,** click the Print button to print the document with the comment.

16 Close the **WTry11_studentfirstname_student lastname** file, saving all changes, and exit Word.

Display comments in the Reviewing pane

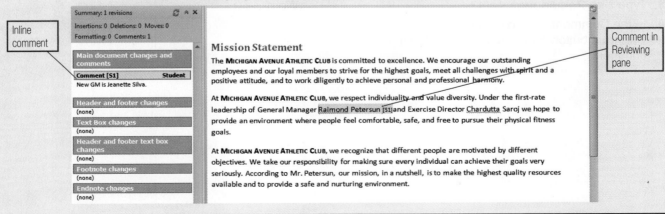

Project 23—Create It

Course Schedule Draft

DIRECTIONS

1. Start Word, if necessary, and save the default blank document as **WProj23_studentfirstname_ studentlastname** in the location where your teacher instructs you to store the files for this lesson.

2. Type your name and today's date in the header, and then type the document shown in Figure 11-1 (without the comments), applying the following styles to match the formatting in the figure:
   - Line 1 – **Title** style
   - Line 2 – **Subtitle** style
   - Line 3 – **Heading 1** style
   - All months – **Heading 2** style
   - All course names – **Heading 3** style
   - All course descriptions – **Normal** style
   - Last line – **Heading 4** style, centered

3. Position the insertion point at the end of the first line and click **Review > New Comment** 🗖.

4. Type **Center?**

5. Position the insertion point after the course name *Microsoft Word 1* and click the **New Comment** 🗖 button.

6. Type **Too much blue.**

7. Position the insertion point after the course name *Microsoft Word 2* and click the **New Comment** 🗖 button.

8. Type **Use Roman numerals?**

9. In the Comments group on the Ribbon, click the **Previous** button 🗖 twice to move to the first comment.

10. Position the insertion point after the word *Center* and type **first three lines**.

11. In the Comments group on the Ribbon, click the **Next** button 🗖.

12. In the Comments group, click the **Delete** button 🗖.

13. In the Tracking group, click the **Show Markup** button 🗎, point to **Balloons**, and click **Show All Revisions Inline**.

14. Click the **Reviewing Pane** drop-down arrow 🗖, and click **Reviewing Pane Horizontal**.

15. In the Reviewing pane, scroll to the second comment and replace the question mark with a period.

16. Click the **Reviewing Pane** button 🗖 to close the Reviewing pane.

17. Check and correct the spelling and grammar in the document, and then save the changes.

18. Click **File > Print** to display the Print tab in Backstage view.

19. Click the **Print All Pages** button and click to select **Print Markup, if necessary**.

20. **With your teacher's permission,** print the document with the comments. It should look similar to Figure 11-1.

21. Click the Review tab, then, in the Comments group, click the **Delete** drop-down arrow 🗖 and click **Delete All Comments in Document**.

22. Close the document, saving all changes, and exit Word.

Figure 11-1

Project 24—Apply It

Course Schedule Revised

DIRECTIONS

1. Start Word, if necessary, and open **WProj24** from the data files for this lesson.

2. Save the file as **WProj24_studentfirstname_studentlastname** in the location where your teacher instructs you to store the files for this lesson.

3. Type your full name and today's date in the header.

4. Set Word to display comments in balloons.

5. Display the Reviewing pane vertically on the left side of the window.

6. Revise the document as instructed by the first comment.

7. Go to the second comment.

8. Insert a new comment and type **I think the current number formatting is best.**

9. Make the correction as instructed by the next comment.

10. Close the Reviewing pane.

11. Change the font color for the course names as recommended by the last comment, and increase the font size to **14 pt.**

12. Insert a comment after the last comment and type **Great suggestion. It looks much better.**

13. Delete the comments by RO that you addressed in step 6 and step 9.

14. Check and correct the spelling and grammar in the document, and then save the changes.

15. **With your teacher's permission,** print the document with the comments. It should look similar to Figure 11-2.

16. Close the document, saving all changes, and exit Word.

Figure 11-2

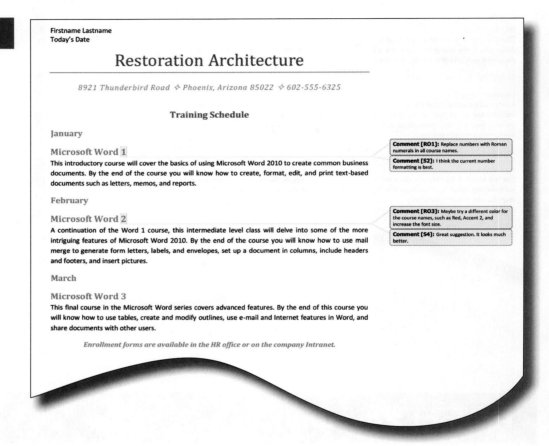

Firstname Lastname
Today's Date

Restoration Architecture

8921 Thunderbird Road ✧ Phoenix, Arizona 85022 ✧ 602-555-6325

Training Schedule

January

Microsoft Word 1

This introductory course will cover the basics of using Microsoft Word 2010 to create common business documents. By the end of the course you will know how to create, format, edit, and print text-based documents such as letters, memos, and reports.

Comment [RO1]: Replace numbers with Roman numerals in all course names.

Comment [S2]: I think the current number formatting is best.

February

Microsoft Word 2

A continuation of the Word 1 course, this intermediate level class will delve into some of the more intriguing features of Microsoft Word 2010. By the end of the course you will know how to use mail merge to generate form letters, labels, and envelopes, set up a document in columns, include headers and footers, and insert pictures.

Comment [RO3]: Maybe try a different color for the course names, such as Red, Accent 2, and increase the font size.

Comment [S4]: Great suggestion. It looks much better.

March

Microsoft Word 3

This final course in the Microsoft Word series covers advanced features. By the end of this course you will know how to use tables, create and modify outlines, use e-mail and Internet features in Word, and share documents with other users.

Enrollment forms are available in the HR office or on the company Intranet.

Lesson 12

Tracking Changes

➤ What You Will Learn

Tracking Changes
Customizing Revision Marks
Accepting and Rejecting Changes

Software Skills   Track changes made to a document to monitor when and how edits are made. Tracking changes lets you consider revisions before incorporating them into a document. If you agree with the change, you can accept it, but if you disagree with the change, you can reject it. You can track changes made by one person, or by many people, which is useful when you are collaborating on a document with others.

Application Skills   The Director of Training at Restoration Architecture has asked you to review a document listing in-house training courses. In this lesson, you will use the Track Changes feature while you review and edit the document. You will then update the document by accepting or rejecting the changes.

WORDS TO KNOW

Ink annotations
Comments, notes, and other marks added to a document using a tablet PC or other type of pen device.

Revision marks
Formatting applied to text in a document to identify where insertions, deletions, and formatting changes have been made.

What You Can Do

Tracking Changes

■ Turn on Word's Track Changes feature to apply **revision marks** to all insertions, deletions, and formatting changes in a document.

✓ *Word 2010 also supports the use of **ink annotations**.*

■ When Track Changes is active, the Track Changes button in the Tracking group on the Review tab of the Ribbon is highlighted.

■ The way that revisions are marked onscreen depends on whether you are using the Reviewing pane or balloons, and on the selected Display for Review option:

✓ *Refer to Word, Lesson 11 for more on the Reviewing pane and balloons.*

- Final: Show Markup (default). This option displays the document with revisions marked. Formatting changes display as they would look in the final document if the changes are accepted.
- Final. This option displays the document as it would look if all of the revisions are accepted.
- Original: Show Markup. This option displays the document with revisions marked. Formatting changes display as they look in the original document without changes.
- Original. This option displays the document as it would look if all revisions are rejected.

- Like comments, revisions are color coded by reviewer.
- By default, Word also inserts a vertical line to the left of any changed line to indicate where revisions occur in the document.
- You can view descriptions of all revisions in the Reviewing pane, or by resting the mouse pointer on the revision to display a ScreenTip.
- The commands for tracking changes are in the Tracking group on the Review tab of the Ribbon.

Try It!   Tracking Changes

1 Start Word and open **WTry12** from the data files for this lesson.

2 Save the file as **WTry12_studentfirstname_studentlastname** in the location where your teacher instructs you to store the files for this lesson.

3 Click the Review tab and then click the Track Changes button 📝 .

   ✓ *The Track Changes feature is a toggle; it remains on until you turn it off.*

4 Double-click the word *outstanding* in the first paragraph and press DEL . Word marks the deleted text in red, with a strikethrough.

5 Position the insertion point after the word *personal* in the first paragraph, and type **, physical,** . Word marks the inserted text in red, with a solid underline.

6 Double-click the word *harmony* at the end of the first paragraph and click Home > Italic. Word inserts a revision balloon in the markup area indicating the formatting change.

Using revision marks to track changes

Vertical line indicating changes

Deleted text

Formatting change

Mission Statement

The **MICHIGAN AVENUE ATHLETIC CLUB** is committed to excellence. We encourage our ~~outstanding~~ employees and our loyal members to strive for the highest goals, meet all challenges with spirit and a positive attitude, and to work diligently to achieve personal, <u>physical,</u> and professional *harmony*.

Formatted: Font: Italic

At **MICHIGAN AVENUE ATHLETIC CLUB**, we respect individuality and value diversity. Under the first-rate leadership of General Manager Raimond Petersun and Exercise Director Chardutta Saroj we hope to provide an environment where people feel comfortable, safe, and free to pursue their physical fitness goals.

At **MICHIGAN AVENUE ATHLETIC CLUB**, we recognize that different people are motivated by different objectives. We take our responsibility for making sure every individual can achieve their goals very seriously. According to Mr. Petersun, our mission, in a nutshell, is to make the highest quality resources available and to provide a safe and nurturing environment.

Inserted text

(continued)

Try It!   **Tracking Changes** *(continued)*

7 Click the Review tab and then click the Display for Review drop-down arrow.

8 Click Final. Word displays the document as it would look if all changes are accepted.

9 Click Display for Review > Original to display the document without changes.

10 Click Display for Review > Final: Show Markup.

11 Click the Reviewing Pane drop-down arrow and click Reviewing Pane Vertical to display the Reviewing pane.

12 Save the changes to **WTry12_ studentfirstname_studentlastname** and leave it open to use in the next Try It.

Tracked changes in the Reviewing pane

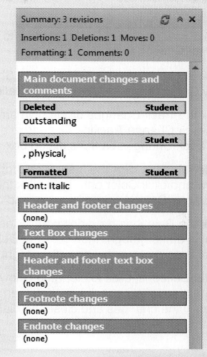

Customizing Revision Marks

- You can customize revision marks using options in the Track Changes Options dialog box.

- For example, you can select the formatting used to indicate changes. You can mark formatting changes with a double-underline, or insertions with color only instead of color and an underline.

- You can select the colors you want to use to mark changes.

- You can customize the location and color of the vertical bar used to mark lines that have been changed.

- You can also customize the way balloons are displayed in a document.

- From the Show Markup drop-down menu you can select which changes you want displayed onscreen. For example, you can display insertions and deletions, but not formatting.

- You can set Word to show only the changes made by one reviewer at a time.

Try It!   **Customizing Revision Marks**

1 In the **WTry12_studentfirstname_ studentlastname** document, click the Review tab if necessary. Click the Show Markup button and click to clear Formatting. Word hides the formatting change revision marks.

2 Click the Show Markup button, click Balloons, and then click Show Revisions in Balloons. Word displays the deletion revision marks in balloons.

✓ *When you display the Original: Show Markup option, insertion revision marks display in balloons.*

(continued)

Try It!   **Customizing Revision Marks** (continued)

3 Click Show Markup 📄 > Balloons > Show All Revisions Inline.

4 Click Show Markup 📄 > Formatting to display formatting revisions again.

5 Click Show Markup 📄 > Balloons > Show Only Comments and Formatting in Balloons.

6 Click the Track Changes drop-down arrow 📝 and click Change Tracking Options to display the Track Changes Options dialog box.

7 Under Markup, click the Insertions drop-down arrow and click Color only, then click the Insertions Color drop-down arrow and click Blue.

8 Click the Deletions drop-down arrow and click Double strikethrough, then click the Deletions Color drop-down arrow and click Bright Green.

9 Under Balloons, click to clear the Show line connecting to text check box, and then click OK to apply the changes and close the dialog box.

10 Click the Track Changes drop-down arrow 📝 and click Change Tracking Options.

11 Under Markup, click the Insertions drop-down arrow and click Underline, then click the Insertions Color drop-down arrow and click By author.

12 Click the Deletions drop-down arrow and click Strikethrough, then click the Deletions Color drop-down arrow and click By author.

13 Under Balloons, click to select the Show line connecting to text check box, and then click OK.

14 Click the Reviewing Pane button 📄.

15 Save the changes to **WTry12_studentfirstname_studentlastname** and leave it open to use in the next Try It.

Customize revision marks

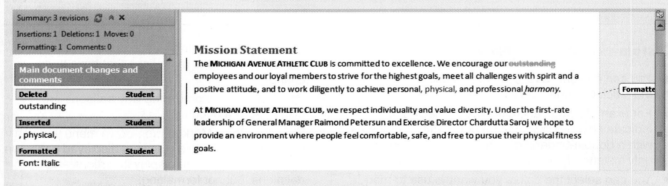

Accepting and Rejecting Changes

- Revision marks remain stored as part of a document until the changes are either accepted or rejected.
- To incorporate edits into a document file, accept the changes.

- To cancel the edits and erase them from the file, reject the changes.
- The commands for accepting and rejecting changes are in the Changes group on the Review tab of the Ribbon.

Try It!   Accepting and Rejecting Changes

1 In the **WTry12_studentfirstname_ studentlastname** document, press `CTRL` + `HOME` to move the insertion point to the beginning of the document.

2 Click the Review tab if necessary, then, in the Changes group, click the Next button ⮞ to move to the next marked change.

3 Click the Next button ⮞ again.

4 Click the Reject drop-down arrow ⮞ and click Reject and Move to Next.

> ✓ You can also right-click the revision marks and click Reject Insertion, or simply click the Reject button ⮞.

5 In the Changes group, click the Previous button ⮜.

6 Click the Accept drop-down arrow ✎ and click Accept Change.

> ✓ You can also right-click the revision marks and click Accept Deletion, or simply click the Accept button ✎.

7 Click the Undo button ↺ on the Quick Access Toolbar, then click the Accept drop-down arrow ✎ and click Accept All Changes in Document.

8 Close **WTry12_studentfirstname_ studentlastname**, saving all changes, and exit Word.

Project 25—Create It

Spring Course Schedule

DIRECTIONS

1. Start Word, if necessary, and open **WProj25** from the data files for this lesson.

2. Save the document as **WProj25_ studentfirstname_studentlastname** in the location where your teacher instructs you to store the files for this lesson.

3. Double-click in the header and type your full name and today's date.

4. Click the **Review** tab, and then, in the Tracking group, click the **Track Changes** button ✎ to turn on the track changes feature.

5. Click the **Track Changes** drop-down arrow ✎ and click **Change Tracking Options** to open the Track Changes Options dialog box.

6. Under Markup, click the **Insertions** drop-down arrow and click **Bold**, then click the **Insertions Color** drop-down arrow and click **Red**.

7. Click the **Deletions Color** drop-down arrow and click **Blue**.

8. Under Balloons, click the **Margin** drop-down arrow and click **Left**.

9. Click **OK** to apply the changes and close the dialog box.

10. In the Tracking group on the Ribbon, click the **Show Markup** button 🗎, click **Balloons**, and click **Show Revisions in Balloons**.

11. In the document, on the address line, select one of the diamond symbols and click **Home** > **Copy** 🗐 to copy it to the Clipboard.

12. Position the insertion point at the end of the address line, press `SPACE`, click **Home** > **Paste** 🗐, press `SPACE` and type **www.rarc.net**.

13. Select the entire address line and decrease the font size to **11 pt**.

14. In the description of the Microsoft Word 1 course, select the text *will cover* and type **covers**.

15. In the same sentence, select *2007* and type **2010**.

16. In the description of the Microsoft Word 2 course, select the text *2007* and type **2010**.

17. At the end of the description of the Microsoft Word 3 course, type the following sentence: **Open only to those who have completed the Word 1 and Word 2 courses.**

18. Select the last line in the document and click the **Italic** button *I* to remove the italic formatting.

19. Click **File** > **Print** to display the Print tab in Backstage view.

20. Click the **Print All Pages** drop-down arrow and click to select **Print Markup**.
21. **With your teacher's permission,** print the document with the markup. It should look similar to Figure 12-1.
22. Press CTRL + HOME to move the insertion point to the beginning of the document.
23. Click the **Review** tab, and then, in the Changes group, click the **Next** button.
24. Click the **Reject** drop-down arrow and click **Reject and Move to Next**.
25. Click the **Reject** button.

26. Click the **Accept** drop-down arrow and click **Accept All Changes in Document**.
27. In the Tracking group, click the **Track Changes** button to turn off the track changes feature.
28. Check and correct the spelling and grammar in the document, and then save the changes.
29. **With your teacher's permission,** print the document.
30. Close the document, saving all changes, and exit Word.

Figure 12-1

Firstname Lastname
Today's Date

Restoration Architecture

Formatted: Font: 11 pt

8921 Thunderbird Road ✧ Phoenix, Arizona 85022 ✧ 602-555-6325 ✧ www.rarc.net

Training Schedule

January

Microsoft Word 1

Deleted: will cover
Deleted: 2007

This introductory course covers the basics of using Microsoft Word 2010 to create common business documents. By the end of the course you will know how to create, format, edit, and print text-based documents such as letters, memos, and reports.

February

Microsoft Word 2

Deleted: 2007

A continuation of the Word 1 course, this intermediate level class will delve into some of the more intriguing features of Microsoft Word 2010. By the end of the course you will know how to use mail merge to generate form letters, labels, and envelopes, set up a document in columns, include headers and footers, and insert pictures.

March

Microsoft Word 3

This final course in the Microsoft Word series covers advanced features. By the end of this course you will know how to use tables, create and modify outlines, use e-mail and Internet features in Word, and share documents with other users. Open only to those who have completed the Word 1 and Word 2 courses.

Formatted: Font: Not Italic

Enrollment forms are available in the HR office or on the company Intranet.

Project 26—Apply It

Summer Course Schedule

DIRECTIONS

1. Start Word, if necessary, and open **WProj26** from the data files for this lesson.

2. Save the file as **WProj26_studentfirstname_ studentlastname** in the location where your teacher instructs you to store the files for this lesson.

3. Type your full name and today's date in the document header.

4. Turn on the track changes features and set tracking options to display insertions underlined in pink and deletions with a strikethrough in bright green. Display balloons in the markup area along the right margin of the page.

5. Show only comments and formatting in balloons, and set the display for review to **Original: Show Markup.**

6. Change the font of the address line to **Times New Roman.**

7. Replace the text *January* with **June**, *February* with **July**, and *March* with **August**.

8. Add the following sentence to the end of the Microsoft Word 2 course description: **If there is enough time, the course will also include basic desktop publishing concepts.**

9. Display the Reviewing pane vertically.

10. **With your teacher's permission,** print the document with the markup. It should look similar to Figure 12-2.

11. Change the display for review to **Final: Show Markup.**

12. Accept the formatting changes in the document.

13. Accept the changes to the names of the months.

14. Reject all remaining changes in the document.

15. Hide the Reviewing pane.

16. Set the insertion and deletion colors to **By author,** and turn off the track changes feature.

17. Check and correct the spelling and grammar in the document, and then save the changes.

18. **With your teacher's permission,** print the document.

19. Close the document, saving all changes, and exit Word.

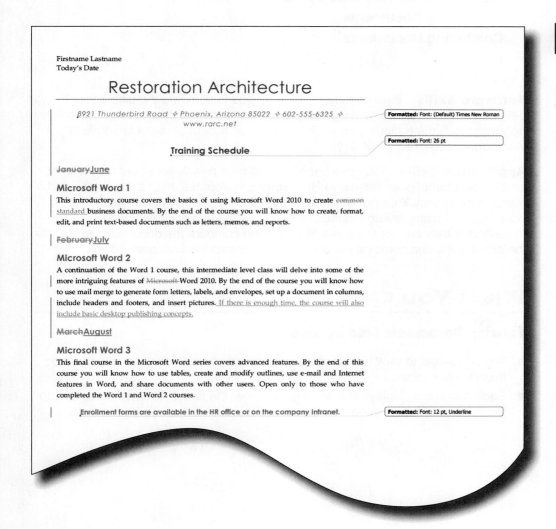

Figure 12-2

Firstname Lastname
Today's Date

Restoration Architecture

8921 Thunderbird Road ✧ Phoenix, Arizona 85022 ✧ 602-555-6325 ✧
www.rarc.net

[Formatted: Font: (Default) Times New Roman]

Training Schedule

[Formatted: Font: 26 pt]

~~January~~June

Microsoft Word 1

This introductory course covers the basics of using Microsoft Word 2010 to create ~~common~~ standard business documents. By the end of the course you will know how to create, format, edit, and print text-based documents such as letters, memos, and reports.

~~February~~July

Microsoft Word 2

A continuation of the Word 1 course, this intermediate level class will delve into some of the more intriguing features of ~~Microsoft~~ Word 2010. By the end of the course you will know how to use mail merge to generate form letters, labels, and envelopes, set up a document in columns, include headers and footers, and insert pictures. If there is enough time, the course will also include basic desktop publishing concepts.

~~March~~August

Microsoft Word 3

This final course in the Microsoft Word series covers advanced features. By the end of this course you will know how to use tables, create and modify outlines, use e-mail and Internet features in Word, and share documents with other users. Open only to those who have completed the Word 1 and Word 2 courses.

Enrollment forms are available in the HR office or on the company intranet.

[Formatted: Font: 12 pt, Underline]

Lesson 13

Comparing Documents

WORDS TO KNOW

Independent scrolling
The ability to scroll a window without affecting the display in other open windows.

Synchronous scrolling
A feature that links the scroll bars in two windows so that when you scroll in one window the other window scrolls as well.

➤ What You Will Learn

Viewing Documents Side by Side
Comparing Documents
Combining Documents

Software Skills   View documents side by side to compare the differences between similar versions. When you compare and combine documents, differences between the two are marked as revisions. You can accept or reject changes to incorporate revisions.

Application Skills   You have been working on a newsletter about the value of employment benefits for Executive Recruitment Resources, Inc., a job search and recruitment agency. Your manager sent you a copy of the newsletter which she edited without using revision marks. You will view the two documents side by side to verify that they are not the same. You will then compare the documents to identify the differences, and combine the documents to create the final newsletter.

What You Can Do

Viewing Documents Side by Side

■ You can select to view two open documents side by side so you can compare them to each other.

■ Each document displays in a separate window; the active document displays on the left side of the desktop and the second document displays on the right.

- If your desktop is not wide enough, or if the monitor resolution is not high enough, Word condenses the Ribbon commands into groups.

- For example, on the Home tab, paragraph formatting commands are condensed to the Paragraph group. Click the group drop-down arrow to display the commands.

- By default, both windows are set to use **synchronous scrolling**, which means that when you scroll in one document, the other document scrolls in the same direction by the same amount.

- You can turn off synchronous scrolling to use **independent scrolling**.

- Changes you make to the view in one window affect the other window as well. For example, if you zoom in on one document, the other document zooms in by the same amount.

- The View Side by Side command is in the Window group on the View tab of the Ribbon.

- You can only view two documents side by side at a time. If more than two documents are open in Word when you select the View Side by Side command, the Compare Side by Side dialog box displays so you can select the second document to view.

Try It! **Viewing Documents Side by Side**

1. Start Word and open **WTry13a** from the data files for this lesson.

2. Save the file as **WTry13a_studentfirstname_ studentlastname** in the location where your teacher instructs you to store the files for this lesson.

3. Open **WTry13b** from the data files for this lesson.

4. Save the file as **WTry13b_studentfirstname_ studentlastname** in the location where your teacher instructs you to store the files for this lesson.

5. Click the View tab.

6. In the Window group, click the View Side by Side button ⊔⊔. Word arranges the document windows side by side, and turns synchronous scrolling on.

7. In the **WTry13a_studentfirstname_ studentlastname** document window, click the scroll down arrow ▼ three times. Notice that the other document scrolls down as well.

8. Press CTRL + END. Both documents scroll down to the end of the document.

9. Click in the **WTry13b_studentfirstname_ studentlastname** window, and then click the Zoom In button ⊕ on the status bar. Notice that the other document zooms in as well.

10. In the **WTry13b_studentfirstname_ studentlastname** window, on the View tab, click the Window group button ⊟, if necessary, and click the Synchronous Scrolling button. This toggles the feature off.

11. Press CTRL + HOME. Only the active document scrolls.

(continued)

Try It!   **Viewing Documents Side by Side** *(continued)*

12 In the **WTry13b_studentfirstname_ studentlastname** window, on the View tab, click the Window group button ▣, if necessary, and click the View Side by Side button ▥. Both windows are restored; the active window displays on top.

13 Close both **WTry13b_studentfirstname_ studentlastname** and **WTry13a_ studentfirstname_studentlastname**, and leave Word open to use in the next Try It.

View documents side by side with synchronous scrolling

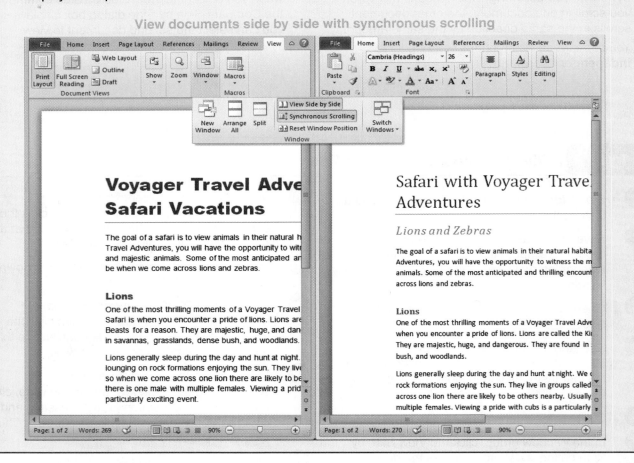

Comparing Documents

- You can compare two documents to mark the differences between them.

- To compare documents, you select the original document and the revised document; Word displays the original document with revision marks showing the differences between the two.

- You can choose to show the original document with tracked changes, the revised document with tracked changes, or both. Word creates a new document named Compare Result1, in which it uses revision marks to indicate the differences between the original and revised documents.

- If you show both, Word displays all three documents onscreen, along with the Reviewing pane.

- By default, the user name of the author of the revised document is used to mark the revisions, but you can use different initials or text if you want.

- Comparing documents is useful if you have more than one version of a document and need to see what changes have been made, or if someone has edited a document without using the track changes features.

■ You can modify the way Word displays differences between the documents. For example, you can choose to display the revision marks in the original document or the revised document instead of in a new document.

■ You can also select the types of differences to compare. For example, you can choose to compare formatting, but not headers and footers.

Try It!   **Comparing Documents**

1 In Word, click the Review tab, click the Compare button 📄, and then click Compare.

2 Click the Original document drop-down arrow and click **WTry13a_studentfirstname_ studentlastname**.

   ✓ *If the document you want is not listed, click the Browse button and navigate Windows Explorer to locate it.*

3 Click the Revised document drop-down arrow and click **WTry13b_studentfirstname_ studentlastname**.

4 Under the Revised document box, click in the Label changes with text box and type your full name.

5 Click the More button to view additional options, and then click OK. Word displays the original document with tracked changes.

6 Click the Compare button 📄, click Show Source Documents, and then click Show Both. Word displays all three documents and the Reviewing pane.

7 Click the Close button in the Original document, and then click the Close button in the Revised document. Only the Compare Result1 document remains open, with the Reviewing pane displayed.

8 Click the Accept drop-down arrow 🖉 and click Accept all Changes in Document.

9 Save the document as **WTry13c_ studentfirstname_studentlastname**, and close it. Leave Word open to use in the next Try It.

Compare differences between two documents

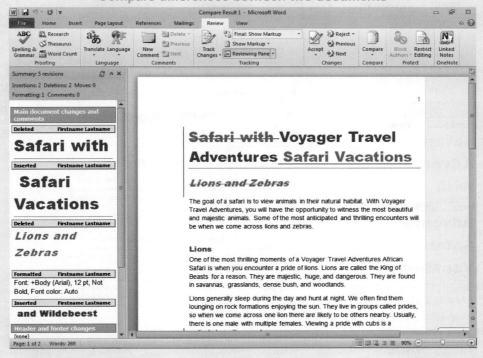

Combining Documents

■ Use the Combine feature to combine revisions made by more than one reviewer into a single document.

■ Word merges the two documents into a final document

■ Word can only store one set of formatting changes in the final document. If necessary, it prompts you to select which formatting changes to keep.

■ By default, Word marks the changes made in the original and revised documents with the user names of each document author. You can change the names if you want.

Try It!   Combining Documents

1 In Word, open **WTry13d** from the data files for this lesson, save it as **WTry13d_ studentfirstname_studentlastname** in the location where your teacher instructs you to store the files for this lesson, and close it.

2 Click the Review tab, click the Compare button , and then click Combine.

3 Click the Original document drop-down arrow and click **WTry13c_studentfirstname_ studentlastname**.

✓ *If the document you want is not listed, click the Browse button and navigate Windows Explorer to locate it.*

4 Your name should display in the Label unmarked changes with text box for the original document. If not, click in the box and type your full name.

5 Click the Revised document drop-down arrow and click **WTry13d_studentfirstname_ studentlastname**.

6 Click in the Label unmarked changes with box for the revised document and type **Reviewer Two**.

7 Click the Less button to hide the options, and then click OK. Word displays the final document with revisions marked.

8 On the Review tab, in the Tracking group, click the Reviewing Pane button . The marked changes indicate whether the change was made by you in the original document or by Reviewer Two in the revised document.

9 Click the Accept drop-down arrow and click Accept All Changes in Document.

10 Save the document as **WTry13e_ studentfirstname_studentlastname**, and close it. Exit Word.

Combine two versions of a document

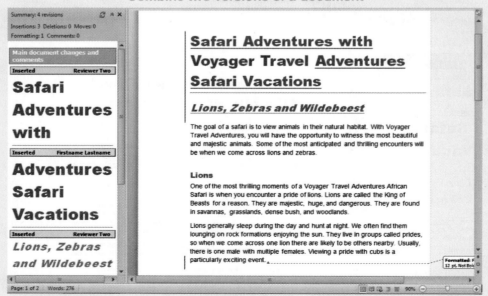

Project 27—Create It

Compare Newsletters

DIRECTIONS

1. Start Word, if necessary, and open **WProj27a** from the data files for this lesson.

2. Save the file as **WProj27a_studentfirstname_ studentlastname** in the location where your teacher instructs you to store the files for this lesson.

3. Double-click in the header and type your full name and today's date. Then, starting on the first line of the document, type the following headings and paragraphs

   Career Planning

   An important aspect of career planning is identifying career opportunities that meet your needs and fit your skills, interests, and abilities. Here at Executive Recruitment Resources, we provide access to many job search resources, which are tools designed to help you find career opportunities. We also provide training and support to help you build your own job search resources.

   Occupational Outlook Handbook

   The U.S. Bureau of Labor Statistics (BLS) is a government agency that tracks information about jobs and workers. BLS publishes the Occupational Outlook Handbook in printed and online editions. The Handbook describes more than 200 occupations, including responsibilities, working conditions, education requirements, salary ranges, and job outlook.

   Networking

   Employers like to hire people who come with a recommendation from someone they know and trust. That's why networking is one of the best ways to find a job. Networking is when you share information about yourself and your career goals with people you know already or new people you meet. One of these contacts might know of a job opening, or be able to introduce you to someone in a field that interests you.

   Networking is more than just chatting with others. It requires you to be focused and organized. It works best if you keep track of all the people you meet and talk to, and if you follow up by e-mail or phone.

4. With the insertion point in the second section of the document, click **Page Layout > Columns** ▦ **> Two** to format the text in two newsletter-style columns.

5. Position the insertion point at the beginning of the heading Networking, and click **Page Layout > Breaks** ⊟ **> Column** to insert a column break.

6. Apply the **Heading 1** style to the three headings (Career Planning, Occupational Outlook Handbook, and Networking).

7. Change the spacing before the Networking heading to **34 pt** so it visually aligns with the Career Planning heading.

8. Check and correct the spelling and grammar in the document, and then save the changes.

9. Open **WProj27b** from the data files for this lesson.

10. Save the file as **WProj27b_studentfirstname_ studentlastname** in the location where your teacher instructs you to store the files for this lesson, and type your full name and today's date in the header.

11. Click **View > View Side by Side** ▭ to arrange the documents side by side with synchronous scrolling.

12. Adjust the view using the zoom and scroll controls so you can see only the left column in both documents.

13. Scroll down and compare the text in the left column of each document.

14. When you identify a difference in the **WProj27b_ studentfirstname_studentlastname** document, highlight it in yellow.

    ✓ *To highlight text, select it, and then click Home > Text Highlight Color* ✎ *.*

15. Scroll to the top of the document and to the right so you can see only the right columns in each document window.

16. Scroll down and compare the text in the right column, and highlight in yellow differences you find in **WProj27b_studentfirstname_ studentlastname**.

17. In **WProj27b_studentfirstname_ studentlastname**, click the **View** tab, click the **Window** group button ⬚ if necessary, and click the **View Side by Side** button ⬚.

18. Close the document, saving all changes, then close and save **WProj27a_studentfirstname_ studentlastname**. Leave Word open.

19. In Word, click the **Review** tab, click the **Compare** button ⬚ and then click **Compare**.

20. Click the **Original document** drop-down arrow and click **WProj27a_studentfirstname_ studentlastname**.

✓ *If the document you want is not listed, click the Browse button and navigate Windows Explorer to locate it.*

21. Click in the **Label changes with** text box and type your full name, if necessary.

22. Click the **Revised document** drop-down arrow and click **WProj27b_studentfirstname_ studentlastname**.

23. Click in the **Label changes with** text box and type your initials, if necessary.

24. Click **OK**.

25. Save the Combine Result document as **WProj27c_studentfirstname_studentlastname**, in the location where your teacher instructs you to store the files for this lesson.

26. **With your teacher's permission,** print the document with markup. It should look similar to Figure 13-1.

27. Close the document, saving all changes, and exit Word.

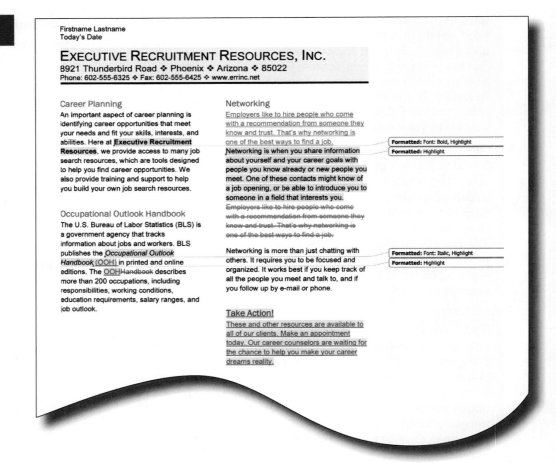

Figure 13-1

Firstname Lastname
Today's Date

EXECUTIVE RECRUITMENT RESOURCES, INC.
8921 Thunderbird Road ❖ Phoenix ❖ Arizona ❖ 85022
Phone: 602-555-6325 ❖ Fax: 602-555-6425 ❖ www.errinc.net

Career Planning

An important aspect of career planning is identifying career opportunities that meet your needs and fit your skills, interests, and abilities. Here at **Executive Recruitment Resources**, we provide access to many job search resources, which are tools designed to help you find career opportunities. We also provide training and support to help you build your own job search resources.

Occupational Outlook Handbook

The U.S. Bureau of Labor Statistics (BLS) is a government agency that tracks information about jobs and workers. BLS publishes the *Occupational Outlook Handbook* (OOH) in printed and online editions. The OOHHandbook describes more than 200 occupations, including responsibilities, working conditions, education requirements, salary ranges, and job outlook.

Networking

Employers like to hire people who come with a recommendation from someone they know and trust. That's why networking is one of the best ways to find a job. Networking is when you share information about yourself and your career goals with people you know already or new people you meet. One of these contacts might know of a job opening, or be able to introduce you to someone in a field that interests you. ~~Employers like to hire people who come with a recommendation from someone they know and trust. That's why networking is one of the best ways to find a job.~~

Networking is more than just chatting with others. It requires you to be focused and organized. It works best if you keep track of all the people you meet and talk to, and if you follow up by e-mail or phone.

Take Action!

These and other resources are available to all of our clients. Make an appointment today. Our career counselors are waiting for the chance to help you make your career dreams reality.

Formatted: Font: Bold, Highlight
Formatted: Highlight

Formatted: Font: Italic, Highlight
Formatted: Highlight

Project 28—Apply It

Combine Newsletters

DIRECTIONS

1. Start Word, if necessary, and open **WProj28a** from the data files for this lesson.

2. Save the file as **WProj28a_studentfirstname_studentlastname** in the location where your teacher instructs you to store the files for this lesson.

3. Type your full name and today's date in the header.

4. Open **WProj28b** from the data files for this lesson.

5. Save the file as **WProj28b_studentfirstname_studentlastname** in the location where your teacher instructs you to store the files for this lesson.

6. Type your full name and today's date in the header.

7. View the documents side by side and use synchronous scrolling to compare the content to identify differences.

8. Remove the side-by-side display, then save and close both documents.

9. Combine the two documents, using the following options:

   Use **WProj28a_studentfirstname_studentlastname** as the original document.

   Use **WProj28b_studentfirstname_studentlastname** as the revised document.

   Label unmarked changes in the original document with your full name, and unmarked changes in the revised document with your initials.

   Choose to show the changes in the revised document.

   ✓ *Click the More button in the Combine Documents dialog box and, under Show changes in, click the Revised document option button.*

10. Save the changes to **WProj28b_studentfirstname_studentlastname.**

11. **With your teacher's permission,** print the document with markup. It should look similar to Figure 13-2.

12. Close the document, saving all changes, and exit Word.

Figure 13-2

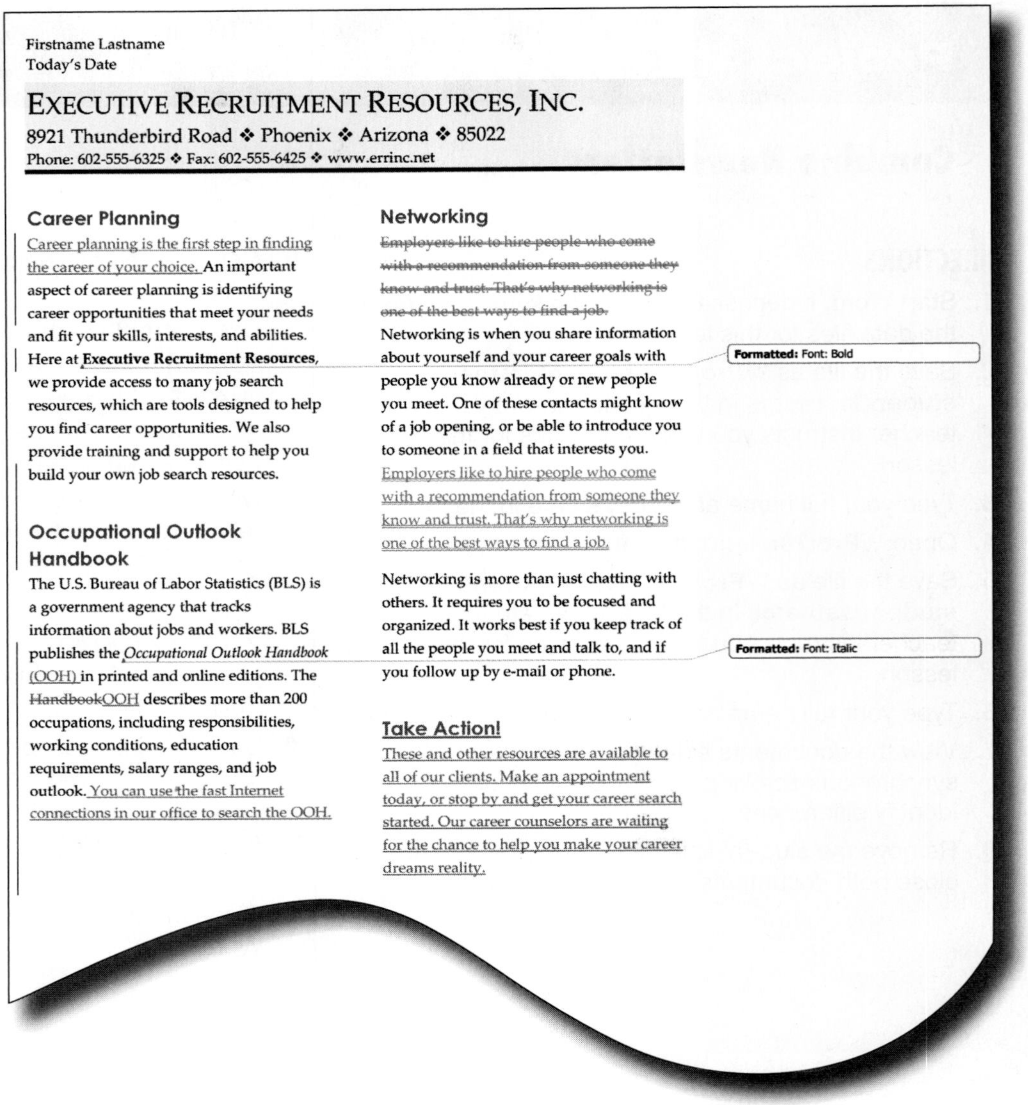

Firstname Lastname
Today's Date

EXECUTIVE RECRUITMENT RESOURCES, INC.

8921 Thunderbird Road ❖ Phoenix ❖ Arizona ❖ 85022
Phone: 602-555-6325 ❖ Fax: 602-555-6425 ❖ www.errinc.net

Career Planning

Career planning is the first step in finding the career of your choice. An important aspect of career planning is identifying career opportunities that meet your needs and fit your skills, interests, and abilities. Here at **Executive Recruitment Resources**, we provide access to many job search resources, which are tools designed to help you find career opportunities. We also provide training and support to help you build your own job search resources.

Occupational Outlook Handbook

The U.S. Bureau of Labor Statistics (BLS) is a government agency that tracks information about jobs and workers. BLS publishes the *Occupational Outlook Handbook (OOH)* in printed and online editions. The HandbookOOH describes more than 200 occupations, including responsibilities, working conditions, education requirements, salary ranges, and job outlook. You can use the fast Internet connections in our office to search the OOH.

Networking

Employers like to hire people who come with a recommendation from someone they know and trust. That's why networking is one of the best ways to find a job.

Networking is when you share information about yourself and your career goals with people you know already or new people you meet. One of these contacts might know of a job opening, or be able to introduce you to someone in a field that interests you. Employers like to hire people who come with a recommendation from someone they know and trust. That's why networking is one of the best ways to find a job.

Networking is more than just chatting with others. It requires you to be focused and organized. It works best if you keep track of all the people you meet and talk to, and if you follow up by e-mail or phone.

Take Action!

These and other resources are available to all of our clients. Make an appointment today, or stop by and get your career search started. Our career counselors are waiting for the chance to help you make your career dreams reality.

Formatted: Font: Bold

Formatted: Font: Italic

Chapter Assessment and Application

Project 29—Make It Your Own

Directory

A directory is a book containing an alphabetical list of names and descriptions of items in a category or group. The items might be people, such as the students in your class, or things, such as companies, countries, sports teams, or books.

Working as a team with other classmates, use skills you have learned in this chapter to create a directory of items in a category approved by your teacher. Each team member will write one page for the directory, and you will collaborate to combine the pages into a professional-quality, multi-page booklet. Enhance the booklet by using a custom theme, and a logo saved as a building block.

DIRECTIONS

1. As a team, work together to select a topic that your teacher approves, and decide who will write each page.

2. Collaborate by designing a custom theme that will give your directory a unique look.

3. Also work together to design a logo you can use on each page, and then save the logo as a building block that you can all access.

4. Design a cover page for your directory using the theme and the building block. Enter all team members' names and the current date on the cover.

5. Individually, start Word and save the default blank document as **WProj29_studentfirstname_ studentlastname** in the location where your teacher instructs you to store the files for this project.

6. Apply the custom theme your team designed, and insert the logo building block somewhere on the page.

7. Insert the user name and date fields from Quick Parts in the footer.

8. Write your directory page. It should have a title, be at least two paragraphs long, and may include a picture or other type of illustration.

9. Use Word's Translation tools to translate your page title into at least one other language.

10. Exchange documents with a teammate and use revision marks and comments to review the document and make suggestions for improvement.

11. When you receive your own document back, accept and reject changes, or compare and combine the documents to create the final.

12. Check the spelling and grammar in the document and correct errors as necessary.

13. **With your teacher's permission,** print the document.

14. Restore all default settings and delete custom themes and building blocks you will no longer need.

15. Close the document, saving all changes.

16. Arrange the printed documents in alphabetical order and staple them together with the cover page to create the booklet.

Project 30—Master It

Information Sheet

You and a co-worker at Fresh Food Fair have been collaborating on a document explaining the benefits of organic farming. In this project, you will start by comparing and combining the two versions of the document. You will then use the skills you have learned in this chapter including translating text, advanced find and replace, building blocks, quick parts, comments, and revision marks to complete the document.

Design a Building Block and a Custom Theme

1. Start Word.
2. In the header of the default blank document, type **Fresh Food Fair** and format it in **48 point Times New Roman**. Select the text and draw a text box around it.
3. Format the text box to have no fill or outline, and resize it to **1˝** high by **5.25˝** wide. Align the text box with the top of the page and with the left margin.
4. To the right of the text box, insert a clip art image of vegetables. If you cannot find a suitable image, insert **WProj30 _picture** from the data files for this project.
5. Size the image to **1˝** high and **2˝** wide, and align it with the top of the page and with the right margin.
6. Select the text box and the image and then save the selection as a building block in the Headers gallery with the name **WProj30 Header** and the description **Header for Fresh Food Fair**.
7. Customize the theme with the **Waveform** theme colors and the **Slipstream** theme fonts.
8. Save the custom theme with the name **WProj30 Theme**.
9. Close the document without saving changes. Leave Word open.

Compare and Combine Documents

1. In Word, open **WProj30a** from the data files for this project. This is the original document.
2. Save the file as **WProj30a_studentfirstname_ studentlastname** in the location where your teacher instructs you to store the files for this chapter.
3. Type your full name and today's date in the footer, then scroll back to the top of the document.
4. Open **WProj30b** from the data files for this project. This is the revised document.
5. Save the file as **WProj30b_studentfirstname_ studentlastname** in the location where your teacher instructs you to store the files for this lesson.
6. Type your full name and today's date in the footer, then scroll back to the top of the document.
7. View the documents side by side and use synchronous scrolling to compare the content to identify differences.
8. When you identify a difference, insert a comment in the revised document describing the difference. For example, insert a comment to identify the different title, and to note that terms beginning with the word *organic* are italicized.
9. When you complete the comparison, remove the side-by-side display, then save and close both documents. Leave Word open.
10. Combine the two documents, using the following options:
    - Use **WProj30a_studentfirstname_ studentlastname** as the original document.
    - Use **WProj30b_studentfirstname_ studentlastname** as the revised document.
    - Label unmarked changes in the original document with your full name, and unmarked changes in the revised document with your initials.
    - Choose to show the changes in the original document.
    - In the next dialog box, choose to keep formatting changes from the revised document.

11. Save the changes to **WProj30a_ studentfirstname_studentlastname**.

12. Save the document as **WProj30c_ studentfirstname_studentlastname** in the location where your teacher instructs you to store the files for this project.

Finalize the Document

1. In the **WProj30c_studentfirstname_ studentlastname** document, delete all comments.

2. Show all revisions inline, and display the Reviewing pane vertically.

3. Accept the title change.

4. Reject the changes to the first heading.

5. Reject the changes to the first sentence, and then accept all the remaining changes in the document.

6. Close the Reviewing pane and set Word to Show Only Comments and Formatting in Balloons.

7. Save the changes to the document.

8. Use Find and Replace to remove all italic formatting in the document.

   ✓ *Hint: Do not enter any text in either the Find what or Replace with boxes. Just select italic as the formatting to find and regular as the formatting to replace with.*

9. Clear all formatting options and then close the Find and Replace dialog box.

10. Insert the **WProj30 Header** building block.

11. Apply the **WProj30 Theme** custom theme.

    ✓ *If necessary, adjust the indent of the subtitle line so it fits on one line, as shown in Illustration A.*

12. Use Word's translation features to translate the last line of text into Spanish, then insert a new line at the end of the document and type the translated text. Format both lines with the **Heading 2** style, centered.

    ✓ *Remove hyperlink formatting, if necessary.*

13. Flush right in the footer, insert the **UserInitials** field with **Uppercase** format and the **Time** field in **HH:mm:ss** format.

14. Check and correct the spelling and grammar in the document, and then save the changes.

15. **With your teacher's permission,** print the document with markup. It should look similar to Illustration A.

16. Delete the **WProj30 Header** building block and the **WProj30 Theme** custom theme.

17. Close the document, saving all changes, and exit Word. Save the building blocks template.

Illustration A

Fresh Food Fair

Organic Farming Information Sheet

What is Organic Farming?

Organic farming is an ecological management system that promotes and enhances biodiversity, biological cycles, and soil biological activity. This system is based on management practices that restore, maintain, and enhance biological harmony. Organic farmers fertilize and build healthy soils by using compost and other biologically-based soil modifications. This produces healthy plants which are better able to resist disease and insects.

Standards of Quality

Organic farmers follow a set of strict standards set by the U.S. Department of Agriculture (USDA). Essentially, the organic standards offer a national definition for the term "organic." The standards also state that all agricultural products labeled "organic" must originate from farms or handling operations certified by a state or private agency accredited by the USDA.

For products to carry the label "Made with Organic Ingredients," at least 70% of their ingredients must be organic. Furthermore, the standards provide information for consumers by requiring manufacturers to state the exact percentage of organic ingredients on the chief display panel of the product.

Benefits and Drawbacks

Because organic farming systems do not use toxic chemical pesticides or fertilizers, organic foods are not exposed to these toxins. Organic foods are also minimally processed to maintain the integrity of the food without artificial ingredients, preservatives, or irradiation, which some people believe makes them taste better.

Generally, organic foods cost more than conventional foods. This is because the prices for organic foods reflect many of the same costs as conventional foods in terms of growing, harvesting, transportation, and storage, but there are added costs as well. Organically-produced foods must meet stricter regulations so the process is often more labor and management intensive, which costs more. Also, organic farms tend to be smaller, which increases costs.

Where to Find Organic Foods

Organic foods can be found at natural food stores, organic farm stands, as well as in the health food and produce departments of most supermarkets. Many restaurant chefs are using organic products because of its growing popularity, as well as its reputation for having superior quality and taste.

Available in Spanish at www.freshfoodfair.org

Disponible en español en www.freshfoodfair.org

Firstname Lastname   FL
Today's Date   17:09:31

Chapter 3

Using Advanced Tables and Graphics

Lesson 14
Customizing Table Styles
Projects 31-32

- Creating a Custom Table Style
- Modifying and Deleting a Table Style
- Adding a Caption to a Table

Lesson 15
Using Advanced Table Features
Projects 33-34

- Inserting Graphics in a Table Cell
- Inserting a Nested Table
- Inserting an Excel Worksheet in a Word Document
- Copying Excel Data to Word and Converting a Table to Text

Lesson 16
Using Advanced Graphics
Projects 35-36

- Using Document Gridlines
- Using Advanced Sizing Features
- Using Advanced Position Features
- Adjusting Objects
- Cropping a Picture

Lesson 17
Linking Text Boxes
Projects 37-38

- Aligning an Object with Another Object
- Linking Text Boxes
- Adding a Caption to a Picture
- Compressing a Picture
- Removing a Picture Background

Lesson 18
Creating WordArt and Watermarks
Projects 39-40

- Creating WordArt
- Creating a Watermark

End-of-Chapter Assessments
Projects 41-42

Lesson 14

Customizing Table Styles

> **What You Will Learn**

Creating a Custom Table Style
Modifying and Deleting a Table Style
Adding a Caption to a Table

WORDS TO KNOW

Caption
A text label that identifies an illustration such as a figure, table, or picture.

Software Skills   Create a table style when none of the built-in table styles are suitable. Add a caption to a table to help readers identify the table you are referring to in the document text.

Application Skills   As the executive assistant to the president of Long Shot, Inc., you are responsible for planning his business trips. In this lesson, you prepare an itinerary for a meeting with a client, in which you include tables that you format by creating a custom table style, and captions.

What You Can Do

Creating a Custom Table Style

- Use the options in the Create New Style from Formatting dialog box to create and save a custom table style.
- As you select formatting, you can specify whether the formatting should apply to the whole table or to parts of the table, such as the header row.
- You can select to make the style available in all new documents based on the current template or only in the current document.
- The style becomes available in the Table Styles gallery so you can use it to format other tables.

Try It! Creating a Custom Table Style

1. Start Word and open **WTry14** from the data files for this lesson.

2. Save the document as **WTry14_studentfirstname_studentlastname** in the location where your teacher instructs you to store the files for this lesson.

3. Click anywhere in the table. On the Table Tools Design tab, click the Table Styles More button and click New Table Style to open the Create New Style from Formatting dialog box.

4. In the Name text box, type **WTry14**.

5. Click the Border Style drop-down arrow and click the triple line style.

6. Click the Borders drop-down arrow and click Outside Borders.

7. Click the Fill Color drop-down arrow and click Blue, Accent 1, Lighter 80%.

8. Verify that the Only in this document option button is selected, and then click OK.

   ✓ Click the Format button to access additional formatting options.

9. Click the Table Styles More button. Under Custom, click the WTry14 table style to apply it to the table in the document.

10. Save the changes to **WTry14_studentfirstname_studentlastname**, and leave it open to use in the next Try It.

Create New Style from Formatting dialog box

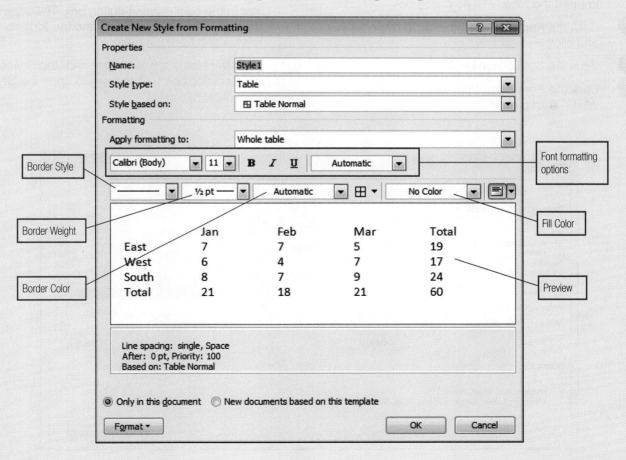

Modifying and Deleting a Table Style

- You can modify a custom table style or a built-in table style.

- All tables formatted with the modified style are updated to show the modified formatting.

- When you delete a custom style, the style is removed from the Table Styles gallery and the formatting is removed from all tables formatted with that style.

- When you delete a modified built-in style, the formatting is removed from tables but the original style remains available in the gallery.

- To delete a table style stored with the current template—not just the current document—you must delete it from the template file using the Style Organizer.

Try It!   Modifying and Deleting a Table Style

1. In the **WTry14_studentfirstname_ studentlastname** file, make sure the insertion point is in the table, and click the Table Tools Design tab.

2. In the Table Styles gallery, right-click the WTry14 custom table style, and click Modify Table Style to open the Modify Style dialog box.

3. Click the Apply formatting to drop-down arrow and click Header row.

4. Click the Bold button B.

5. Click the Font Color drop-down arrow and click White, Background 1.

6. Click the Fill Color drop-down arrow and click Dark Blue, Text 2.

7. Click the New documents based on this template option button, and then click OK.

8. In the Table Styles gallery, right-click the WTry14 custom style, click Delete Table Style, then click Yes in the confirmation dialog box. The style is deleted from the document, and the formatting is removed from the table.

9. Click the Home tab, and then click the Styles group dialog box launcher to open the Styles task pane.

Organizer dialog box

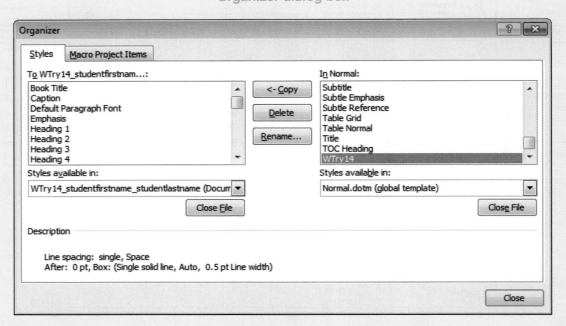

(continued)

Try It!   **Modifying and Deleting a Table Style** *(continued)*

10 Click the Manage Styles button 🗏 to open the Manage Styles dialog box, and then click the Import/Export button to display the Organizer dialog box.

11 On the right side, under In Normal, click the WTry14 style, and then click Delete.

12 Click Yes in the confirmation dialog box, and then click Close.

13 Close the Styles task pane, and then save the changes to **WTry14_studentfirstname_ studentlastname**. Leave the document open to use in the next Try It.

Adding a Caption to a Table

■ Insert a **caption** to label a table so a reader can identify the table referenced in the main text.

■ Each caption includes a text label and a number field.

■ You can customize or edit the label as you would any text.

■ By default, Word uses Arabic numbers and positions the captions below the table. You can customize the number format and select to position the caption above the table.

■ Word automatically updates the numbers for each caption entered; however, if you delete or move a caption, you must manually update the remaining captions.

■ You can insert a caption manually or set Word to automatically insert captions. Once you enable automatic captions, the feature remains on until you turn it off.

Try It!   **Adding a Caption to a Table**

1 In the **WTry14_studentfirstname_ studentlastname** file, position the insertion point in the table.

2 Click the References tab, and then, in the Captions group, click the Insert Caption button 🗏 to open the Caption dialog box.

3 Click the Position drop-down arrow and click Below selected item.

Caption dialog box

4 Click OK to insert the caption.

5 Click the Insert Caption button 🗏 again and click AutoCaption.

6 Click to select the check box to the left of Microsoft Word Table, and then click OK.

7 In the document, move the insertion point to the last line and click Insert > Table. Drag across the grid to insert a table with four columns and three rows. Word automatically inserts the caption *Table 2*.

8 Click References > Insert Caption 🗏 > AutoCaption.

9 Click to clear the check box to the left of Microsoft Word Table, and then click OK.

10 Close **WTry14_studentfirstname_ studentlastname**, saving all changes, and exit Word.

Project 31—Create It

Travel Itinerary

DIRECTIONS

1. Start Word, if necessary, and save the default blank document as **WProj31_studentfirstname_studentlastname** in the location where your teacher instructs you to store the files for this lesson.

2. Apply the **Urban** theme, then double-click in the header and type your full name and today's date.

3. On the first line of the document, type **Long Shot, Inc.** and format it with the **Title** style.

4. Press [ENTER], apply the **No Spacing** style, and type **Itinerary for Mr. Lombardi.**

5. Press [ENTER] and type **Customer Meeting in Chicago, Illinois.**

6. Apply the **Normal** style, press [ENTER] and type the following paragraph:

   You are traveling to Chicago on Tuesday, October 11 to meet with representatives of Golf Equipment, LLC. Refer to Table A for your departure flight information.

7. Press [ENTER] and insert a table with two columns and five rows.

8. Enter the following information in the table:

Departure Flight Information	
Date:	October 11, 2011
Airline/Flight Number:	SouthernWest/191
Scheduled Departure Time:	9:40 a.m. EST
Scheduled Arrival Time:	10:10 a.m. CST

9. Merge the cells in the first row.

10. Click the **Table Tools Design** tab, click the **Table Styles More** button ⩫ and click **New Table Style.**

11. In the Name text box, type **WProj31.**

12. Click the **Borders** drop-down arrow ⊞▾ and click **Outside Borders.**

13. Click the **Borders** drop-down arrow ⊞▾ again, and click **Inside Horizontal Border.**

14. Click the **Fill Color** drop-down arrow [No Color ▾] and click **Blue-Gray, Text 2, Lighter 80%.**

15. Click the **Apply formatting to** drop-down arrow and click **First column.**

16. Click the **Fill Color** drop-down arrow [No Color ▾] and click **Blue-Gray, Text 2, Lighter 60%.**

17. Click the **Apply formatting to** drop-down arrow and click **Header row.**

18. Click the **Bold** button [B].

19. Click the **Alignment** drop-down arrow ▤▾ and click **Align Center.**

20. Click to select the **New documents based on this template** option button, and then click **OK.**

21. In the Table Styles gallery, click the **WProj31** table style to apply it to the departure flight information table.

22. Click the **References** tab and then click the **Insert Caption** button ▤.

23. In the Caption dialog box, click the **Numbering** button.

24. In the Caption Numbering dialog box, click the **Format** drop-down arrow, click **A, B, C, ...,** and then click **OK.**

25. Click the **Label** drop-down arrow and click **Table.**

26. Click the **Position** drop-down arrow and click **Above selected item,** then click **OK.**

27. Check and correct the spelling and grammar in the document, and then save the changes.

28. **With your teacher's permission**, print the document. It should look similar to Figure 14-1 on the next page.

29. Close the document, saving all changes, and exit Word.

Firstname Lastname
Today's Date

Long Shot, Inc.

Itinerary for Mr. Lombardi
Customer Meeting in Chicago, Illinois

You are traveling to Chicago on Tuesday, October 11 to meet with representatives of Golf
Equipment, LLC. Refer to Table A for your departure flight information.

Table A

Departure Flight Information	
Date:	October 11, 2011
Airline/Flight Number:	SouthernWest/191
Scheduled Departure Time:	9:40 a.m. EST
Scheduled Arrival Time:	10:10 a.m. CST

Project 32—Apply It

Expanded Travel Itinerary

DIRECTIONS

1. Start Word, if necessary, and open **WProj32** from the data files for this lesson.
2. Save the file as **WProj32_studentfirstname_ studentlastname** in the location where your teacher instructs you to store the files for this lesson.
3. Double-click in the header and type your full name and today's date.
4. Click in Table A, then click the **Table Tools Design** tab.
5. In the Table Styles gallery, right-click the **WProj31** custom table style and click **Modify Table Style**.
6. Modify the formatting for the whole table to change the single line borders to double lines.
7. Change the formatting for the first column and the header row to make the text bold and White, Background 1, and to change the fill color to Blue-Gray, Text 2.

8. Save the changes for all new documents based on the current template.
9. Turn on the **AutoCaption** feature, set to apply the text label Table followed by uppercase letters (A, B, C, ...) above the table.
10. On the last line of the document, insert a new table with two columns and five rows and enter the following information:

Return Flight Information	
Date:	October 11, 2011
Airline/Flight Number:	SouthernWest/392
Scheduled Departure Time:	5:30 p.m. CST
Scheduled Arrival Time:	8:15 a.m. EST

11. Merge the cells in the first row, and format the table using the **WProj31** custom table style.

12. Position the insertion point on the last line of the document, press [ENTER], insert a table with three columns and five rows, and enter the following:

Meeting Agenda		
Attendees:	Mr. George Lombardi Ms. Kate Sunderland Mr. Philip Katz	President, Long Shot, Inc. President, Golf Equipment, LLC Vice President of Sales, Golf Equipment, LLC
Location:	Golf Equipment, LLC Headquarters	1187 NW 151st Street, Chicago, Illinois
Time:	11:00 a.m. – 4:00 p.m.	Lunch included
Topic:	Joint marketing venture	

13. Merge the cells in the first row and apply the **WProj31** custom table style.

14. Adjust the width of each table to AutoFit the contents (**Table Tools Layout** > **AutoFit** > **AutoFit Contents**).

15. Check and correct the spelling and grammar in the document, and then save the changes.

16. **With your teacher's permission**, print the document. It should look similar to Figure 14-2.

17. Turn off **AutoCaption**.

18. Delete the **WProj31** custom table style from the Normal.dotm template. Do not delete it from the document.

19. Close the document, saving all changes, and exit Word.

Figure 14-2

Firstname Lastname
Today's Date

Long Shot, Inc.

Itinerary for Mr. Lombardi
Customer Meeting in Chicago, Illinois

You are traveling to Chicago on Tuesday, October 11 to meet with representatives of Golf Equipment, LLC. Refer to Table A for your departure flight information. Refer to Table B for your return flight information. Refer to Table C for the meeting agenda.

Table A

Departure Flight Information	
Date:	October 11, 2011
Airline/Flight Number:	SouthernWest/191
Scheduled Departure Time:	9:40 a.m. EST
Scheduled Arrival Time:	10:10 a.m. CST

Table B

Return Flight Information	
Date:	October 11, 2011
Airline/Flight Number:	SouthernWest/392
Scheduled Departure Time:	5:30 p.m. CST
Scheduled Arrival Time:	8:15 p.m. EST

Table C

Meeting Agenda		
Attendees:	Mr. George Lombardi Ms. Kate Sunderland Mr. Philip Katz	President, Long Shot, Inc. President, Golf Equipment, LLC Vice President of Sales, Golf Equipment, LLC
Location:	Golf Equipment, LLC Headquarters	1187 NW 151st Street, Chicago, Illinois
Time:	11:00 a.m. – 4:00 p.m.	Lunch included
Topic:	Joint marketing venture	

Lesson 15

Using Advanced Table Features

➤ What You Will Learn

Inserting Graphics in a Table Cell
Inserting a Nested Table
Inserting an Excel Worksheet in a Word Document
Copying Excel Data to Word and Converting a Table to Text

Software Skills   Insert graphics in a table cell to add visual interest. Use nested tables when you want to create a table within a table. Use Excel features in Word to create a worksheet, or copy and paste Excel data into a Word document as a table. Finally, convert a table to text when you want the content to display in paragraph format rather than in columns and rows.

Application Skills   In this lesson, you will use nested tables, graphics, and Excel worksheet data to create a purchase order for gifts to hand out to attendees at the national meeting of the Horticultural Shop Owner's Association. You will also create an invoice for the items.

What You Can Do

Inserting Graphics in a Table Cell

- You can insert a graphics object into a table cell so it stays positioned relative to other objects and text on the page.
- Use the same commands to insert a graphic into a table cell that you use to insert a graphic in any Word document.
- For example, use the Insert > Picture command to insert a picture, or Insert > Clip Art to insert clip art.
- By default, the cell automatically adjusts in size to fit the dimensions of the graphic.

- You can set the table properties to keep the cell size constant and adjust the size of the graphic to fit.

- If you increase the size of the graphic after inserting it, Word automatically crops the portion that is outside the boundaries of the cell.

Try It!   **Inserting Graphics in a Table Cell**

1 Start Word and save the default blank document as **WTry15a_studentfirstname_ studentlastname** in the location where your teacher instructs you to store the files for this lesson.

2 Insert a table with three columns and three rows, and verify that the insertion point is in the top-left cell.

3 Click Insert > Picture and insert **WTry15_ picture** from the data files for this lesson. Notice that the cell resizes automatically to fit the picture.

4 Click the Undo button ↻ on the Quick Access Toolbar.

5 Click the Table Tools Layout tab and then, in the Table group, click the Properties button 🔧.

6 In the Table Properties dialog box, on the Table tab, click the Options button, then click to clear the Automatically resize to fit contents check box and click OK.

7 In the Table Properties dialog box, click the Row tab.

8 Under Row 1 Size, click to select the Specify height check box, then use the increment arrows to set the row height to 1.5".

9 Click the Row height is drop-down arrow, click Exactly, and then click OK.

10 Click Insert > Picture and insert the **WTry15_ picture** file from the data files for this lesson.

11 With the picture selected, drag the lower-right sizing handle down about 0.5". Notice that Word crops the picture so you only see the portion that still fits within the cell boundaries.

12 Click the Undo button ↻ on the Quick Access Toolbar, then save the changes to **WTry15a_ studentfirstname_studentlastname**, and leave it open to use in the next Try It.

Inserting a Nested Table

- Insert a **nested table** when you need to create a table within a cell of an existing table.

- For example, you might use a table to set up an agenda, and then use a nested table within the agenda to list events occurring in a particular time slot.

- You can use any method of inserting a table to create a nested table, including the Insert > Table command, Draw Table command, or copying and pasting a table from a different location.

- Nested tables make it easy to position and align data relative to other data on a page. They are often used to design Web pages.

- You can format a nested table independently from the primary table. For example, you can apply a style to the primary table, and a different style to the nested table.

Try It!   **Inserting a Nested Table**

1 In the **WTry15a_studentfirstname_ studentlastname** file, position the insertion point in the cell in the lower-right of the table.

2 Click Insert > Table and drag across the grid to insert a table with three columns and four rows. The insertion point displays in the first cell in the nested table.

3 Type **Date**, press TAB, type **Name**, press TAB, and type **Age**.

4 Press TAB. The insertion point moves to the first cell in the second row of the nested table.

5 Select the larger, main table, click the Table Tools Design tab, then, in the Table Styles gallery, click the Medium Grid 1 - Accent 1 table style.

6 Select the nested table, then, in the Table Styles gallery, click the Medium Grid 3 - Accent 2 table style.

7 Save the changes to **WTry15a_ studentfirstname_studentlastname**, and leave it open to use in the next Try It.

Nested table in a table cell

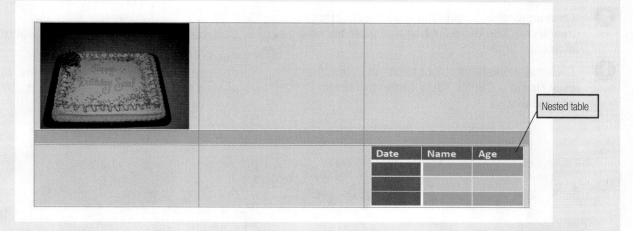

Nested table

Date	Name	Age

Inserting an Excel Worksheet in a Word Document

■ There may be times when you want more advanced spreadsheet functions than a Word table provides.

■ In that case, you can use the Insert > Table > Excel Spreadsheet command to create an Excel worksheet object in your document.

■ Like a chart, the worksheet data is not saved in an Excel file; it is only saved as part of the Word document.

   ✓ *Refer to Word, Lesson 5 for information on creating charts in Word.*

■ When you double-click the worksheet object, the Excel Ribbon becomes available so you can use the Excel tools and commands to enter, edit, and format the data.

   ✓ *For information on working with Excel, refer to the Excel chapters in this book.*

   ✓ *For information on linking and embedding objects saved in a separate file, refer to the lessons in Word, Chapter 6.*

Try It!   Inserting an Excel Worksheet in a Word Document

1 In the **WTry15a_studentfirstname_ studentlastname** file, insert two blank lines below the table and position the insertion point on the last blank line.

2 Click Insert > Table ▦ > Excel Spreadsheet. The worksheet object displays, and the Excel Ribbon becomes available.

3 Type **Balloons**, press [ENTER] , type **Cake**, press [ENTER] , and type **Paper Goods**.

4 Click in cell B1, type **$15.99**, press [ENTER] , type **$19.99**, press [ENTER] , type **$12.99**, and press [ENTER] .

5 On the Home tab, in the Editing group, click the Sum button Σ button and press [ENTER] .

6 Click anywhere outside the worksheet object to deselect it. The Word Ribbon and tools become available, again.

7 Click the worksheet object to select it, and then click Home > Center ≡ to center the object horizontally.

8 Double-click the worksheet object. The Excel tools become available.

9 Double-click the border between column A and column B in the worksheet frame to automatically adjust the width of column A to display all contents.

10 Drag the sizing handle in the lower-right corner up and to the left so only the range A1:B4 displays.

✓ *After resizing the object, you may have to scroll the worksheet to display the correct range.*

11 Select the range A1:B4, in the Styles group click the Cell Styles button ▦, and then click 20% - Accent 1.

12 Click anywhere outside the worksheet object.

13 Save the changes to **WTry15a_ studentfirstname_studentlastname**, and leave it open to use in the next Try It.

Insert an Excel worksheet in a document

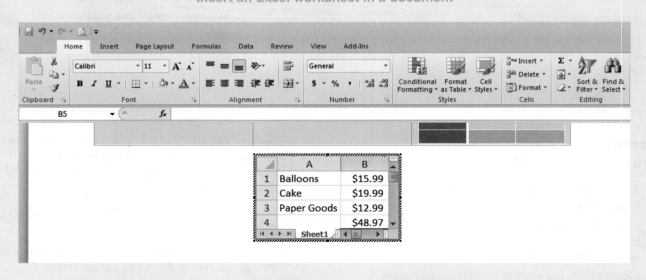

Copying Excel Data to Word and Converting a Table to Text

- If you have existing data in an Excel worksheet, you can copy and paste it as a table into a Word document.

- The pasted table has the same formatting it had in the Excel worksheet, but you can edit and reformat it using Word commands.

- Convert an entire table or selected table rows into regular document text.

- Word inserts the specified **separator character** into the text at the end of each column.

- Word starts a new paragraph at the end of each row.

- If document text is set to wrap around a table, when you convert the table to text Word inserts the text in a text box.

Try It!   Copying Excel Data to Word and Converting a Table to Text

1 In the **WTry15a_studentfirstname_ studentlastname** file, toggle on nonprinting characters, if they are not already displayed, then insert two blank lines below the worksheet object. Position the insertion point on the last blank line and click the Align Text Left button ≣.

2 Start Excel and open **WTry15b** from the data files for this lesson.

3 Select the range A1:C4.

4 On the Home tab in the Clipboard group, click the Copy button 🗐, then exit Excel without saving any changes.

5 In Word, click Home > Paste 📋 to paste the Excel data as a Word table.

6 Select the table you pasted in step 5.

7 Click the Table Tools Layout tab and then, in the Data group, click the Convert to Text button 📑 to open the Convert Table to Text dialog box.

8 Verify that the Tabs option button is selected, and then click OK. Word converts the table to text, separating the columns with tabs.

✓ If the Rating column heading wraps to a new line, drag the second left tab stop a bit to the left on the horizontal ruler.

9 Save the changes to **WTry15a_ studentfirstname_studentlastname**, close it, and exit Word.

Convert a table to text

Restaurant	→	Description	→	Rating¶
Pizza·and·More	→	Family-friendly·casual·dining·at·a·budget-friendly·price.	→	***¶
Main·Street·Café	→	Excellent·service·in·a·neighborhood·setting.	→	****¶
Le·Chat·Noir	→	Pretentious·and·stuffy·bistro·that·does·not·merit·the·high·prices	→	*¶

Tab separators

Project 33—Create It

Purchase Order

DIRECTIONS

1. Start Word, if necessary, and save the default blank document as **WProj33a_studentfirstname_studentlastname** in the location where your teacher instructs you to store the files for this lesson.

2. Insert a table with five columns and seven rows. Rest the mouse pointer over the table and click the **Table Selector** button ⊞ to select the entire table.

3. Click the **Table Tools Design** tab, if necessary, click the **Borders** drop-down arrow ▦, and click **No Border**.

4. If table gridlines are not displayed, click **Table Tools Layout > View Gridlines** ▦.

5. Select the first row and click **Table Tools Layout > Merge Cells** ▦, then position the insertion point in the first cell of the third row and enter the following data in the third and fourth rows, replacing the sample text *Today's Date* with the actual date and *Student's Name* with your own name:

P.O. Date	Ordered By	Shipped Via	F.O.B. Point	Terms
Today's Date	*Student's Name*	Ground	Shipping	Net 30

6. Select the fifth row and click **Table Tools Layout > Merge Cells** ▦.

7. In the third column of the seventh row, type **Authorized by:**, press [TAB], type your name, press [TAB], and type today's date.

8. Position the insertion point in the top-left cell in the table and click **Insert > Table** ▦.

9. Drag across the grid to insert a nested table with three columns and three rows.

10. Rest the mouse pointer over the nested table, and then click its Table Selector button ⊞ to select the entire nested table. Click **Table Tools Design > Borders** ▦ **> No Border**.

11. Select the top row of the nested table and click **Table Tools Layout > Merge Cells** ▦.

12. In the top row of the nested table, type **PURCHASE ORDER** and format the text with the **Heading 1** style.

13. Position the insertion point in the first cell in the second row of the nested table and click **Table Tools Layout > Table Properties** ▨.

14. In the Table Properties dialog box, click the **Row** tab and click to select the **Specify height** check box.

15. Type **2.5** in the Specify height box, and then click the **Row height is** drop-down arrow and click **Exactly**.

16. Click **OK** to apply the changes and close the Table Properties dialog box.

17. With the insertion point still in the first cell in the second row of the nested table, click **Insert > Picture** 🖼 and insert **WProj33_picture** from the data files for this lesson.

18. Select the middle and right cells in the second row of the nested table and click **Table Tools Layout > Merge Cells** ▦.

19. Type the following five lines of text:

    Horticultural Shop Owner's Association

    452 Cathedral Street

    Baltimore, MD 21201

    555.555.5555

    hsoamail@hsoassoc.net

20. Format the first line with the **Heading 1** style, then click **Table Tools Layout > Align Top Right** ▤.

21. In the third row of the nested table, type the following:

| To: Swag Manufacturing | Ship To: HSOA | P.O. Number: 11001 |

22. Position the insertion point in the fifth row of the main table (that you merged in step 6), and click **Insert** > **Table** > **Excel Spreadsheet**.

23. Starting in cell A1, enter the following:

QTY	UNIT	DESCRIPTION	UNIT PRICE	TOTAL
250	Shirt	Blue T with logos	$3.12	=D2*A2
250	Mug	Blue coffee with logos	$3.49	=D3*A3
			SUBTOTAL	=SUM(E2:E3)
			SALES TAX	=E4*.05
			TOTAL	=SUM(E4:E5)

✓ *If Excel marks cell E5 as containing an error, click the error warning button drop-down arrow and click Ignore Error.*

24. Adjust the column widths to display all data, then drag the sizing handle in the lower-right of the worksheet object up and to the left so only the range A1:E6 displays.

25. Select the range **A1:E1** and click **Cell Styles** > **Accent1**.

26. Select the range **A2:E6** and click **Cell Styles** > **20% - Accent1**.

27. Click anywhere outside the worksheet object.

28. Click the worksheet object in the document and click **Home** > **Center**.

29. Insert a second blank line below the main table and position the insertion point on the last blank line.

30. Start Excel and open **WProj33b** from the data files for this lesson.

31. Select the range **A3:A6**, click **Home** > **Copy**, then exit Excel without saving any changes.

32. In Word, click **Home** > **Paste** to paste the Excel data as a Word table.

33. Select the table you pasted in step 32.

34. Click the **Table Tools Layout** tab and then, in the Data group, click the **Convert to Text** button to open the Convert Table to Text dialog box.

35. Verify that the **Paragraph marks** option button is selected, and then click **OK**. Word converts the table to text, separating the rows with paragraph marks.

36. With the converted text still selected, click **Home** > **Numbering**.

37. At the end of the last line, type your name followed by a period.

38. Adjust the width of the two cells where you entered your name in the main table so the text fits on a single line.

39. Check and correct the spelling and grammar in the document, and then save the changes.

40. **With your teacher's permission**, print the document. It should look similar to Figure 15-1 on the next page.

41. Close the document, saving all changes, and exit Word.

Figure 15-1

PURCHASE ORDER

Horticultural Shop Owner's Association
452 Cathedral Street
Baltimore, MD 21201
555.555.5555
hsoamail@hsoassoc.net

To: Swag Manufacturing   Ship To: HSOA   P.O. Number: 11001

P.O. Date	Ordered By	Shipped Via	F.O.B. Point	Terms
Today's Date	Firstname Lastname	Ground	Shipping	Net 30

QTY	UNIT	DESCRIPTION	UNIT PRICE	TOTAL
250	Shirt	Blue T with logos	$3.12	$780.00
250	Mug	Blue coffee with logos	$3.49	$872.50
		SUBTOTAL		$1,652.50
		SALES TAX		$82.63
		TOTAL		$1,735.13

Authorized by: Firstname Lastname   Today's Date

1. Please send two copies of your invoice.
2. Enter this order in accordance with the prices, terms, delivery method, and specifications listed above.
3. Please notify us immediately if you are unable to ship as specified.
4. Send all correspondence to: Firstname Lastname.

Project 34—Apply It

Invoice

DIRECTIONS

1. Start Word, if necessary, and open **WProj34a** from the data files for this lesson.

2. Save the file as **WProj34a_studentfirstname_ studentlastname** in the location where your teacher instructs you to store the files for this lesson.

3. Select the table and apply the **Light Shading - Accent 1** table style.

4. In the top row, insert a nested table with two columns and three rows. Remove all borders from the nested table.

5. Merge the cells in row 1 of the nested table and type **INVOICE**. Format the text with the **Title** style.

6. Set the row height of row 2 of the nested table to exactly **1.75"**.

7. In the left cell of row 2 of the nested table, type the following five lines:

   SWAG Manufacturing Co.

   779 Industrial Avenue

   Marlborough, MA 01752

   555.555.5555

   mail@swagmftg.net

8. Format the company name with the **Heading 1** style.

9. Insert **WProj34_picture** from the data files for this lesson into the right cell of row 2 in the nested table, and align it with the top right of the cell.

10. Type the following in row 3 in the nested table, replacing the sample text *Student's Name* with your own name:

Invoice # HOSA-2C **Invoice Date:** *Today's Date*	**Ship To:** ***Student's Name*** **Horticultural Shop Owner's Association** **452 Cathedral Street** **Baltimore, MD 21201**

11. In the last row of the main table, insert an Excel spreadsheet and enter the following starting in cell A1:

QTY	DESCRIPTION	UNIT PRICE	TOTAL
250	T-shirts with logos	$3.12	=C2*A2
250	Mugs with logos	$3.49	=C3*A3
		SUBTOTAL	=SUM(D2:D3)
		SALES TAX	=D4*.05
		TOTAL	=SUM(D4:D5)

   ✓ *If Excel marks cell D5 as containing an error, click the error warning button drop-down arrow and click Ignore Error.*

12. Adjust the column widths to display all data, then adjust the size of the object to display only the range **A1:D6**.

13. Format the range **A1:D1** with the **Accent 5** cell style and format the range **A2:D6** with the **20% - Accent 5** cell style.

14. Center the worksheet object horizontally in the Word table.

15. Start Excel and open **WProj34b** from the data files for this lesson.

16. Copy and paste the data from cells **A3:A5** to a blank line below the main table (insert a new blank line, if necessary) in **WProj34a_studentfirstname_studentlastname**, then exit Excel without saving any changes.

17. Replace the sample text *Student's Name* in the copied Excel data with your own name, and then convert the copied Excel data to text separated by paragraph marks.

18. Center the last line.

19. Check and correct the spelling and grammar in the document, and then save the changes.

20. **With your teacher's permission**, print the document. It should look similar to Figure 15-2 on the next page.

21. Close the document, saving all changes, and exit Word.

Figure 15-2

INVOICE

SWAG Manufacturing Co.
779 Industrial Avenue
Marlborough, MA 01752
555.555.5555
mail@swagmftg.net

Invoice #: HOSA-2C
Invoice Date: Today's Date

Ship To:
Firstname Lastname
Horticultural Shop Owner's Association
452 Cathedral Street
Baltimore, MD 21201

Salesperson	P.O. Date	Ordered By	Shipped Via	F.O.B. Point	Terms
Jack McGraw	Today's Date	Student's Name	Ground	Shipping	Due on Receipt

Quantity	Description	Unit Price	Total
250	T-shirts with logos	$3.12	$780.00
250	Mugs with logos	$3.49	$872.50
	Subtotal		$1,652.50
	Sales Tax		$82.63
	Total		$1,735.13

Make all checks payable to: SWAG Manufacturing Co.
If you have any questions concerning this invoice, contact Student's Name.
Thank you for your business!

Lesson 16

Using Advanced Graphics

> ## What You Will Learn

Using Document Gridlines
Using Advanced Sizing Features
Using Advanced Position Features
Adjusting Objects
Cropping a Picture

Software Skills   Using Word 2010's advanced graphics options, you can integrate graphics objects with text and white space on the page to create professional-looking documents. You can apply precise settings for sizing and positioning objects, you can change a picture by adjusting or cropping, and you can add a caption to help a reader locate an illustration.

Application Skills   Business owners and managers must continually look for ways to bring in customers, improve products, and develop opportunities. At Liberty Blooms, this means creating newsletters, sponsoring classes, and hosting events. In this lesson, you will create a recipe flyer to hand out to customers interested in growing and using herbs. You will then incorporate the flyer in a newsletter. Both documents will use advanced graphics features.

WORDS TO KNOW

Adjustment handle
A small yellow diamond used to alter the most prominent feature of an AutoShape. The mouse pointer is an arrowhead when resting on an adjustment handle.

Anchor
An element in a document, such as the margin or the page itself, relative to which you can position an object.

Aspect ratio
The relative horizontal and vertical sizes of an object, or the ratio of height to width.

Crop
Trim or hide one or more edges of a picture.

Document gridlines
Nonprinting horizontal and vertical lines that you can display on the page to help you align and position objects.

Outcrop
Use the cropping tool to add a margin around an object.

Scale
Adjust the size of an object based on a percentage of its original size.

Snap to
Align evenly with.

What You Can Do

Using Document Gridlines

- **Document gridlines** display between the margins to help you size and position objects on a page.
- By default the gridlines are spaced 0.13" apart horizontally and vertically. You can change the spacing in the Drawing Grid dialog box.

- You can also select the number of gridlines to display, and whether objects should **snap to** the grid or to other objects.
- You can select to display the gridlines on the View tab on the Ribbon or from the Align drop-down menu in the Arrange group on the Page Layout tab of the Ribbon.

Try It!   **Using Document Gridlines**

1. Start Word and open **WTry16** from the data files for this lesson.

2. Save the file as **WTry16_studentfirstname_ studentlastname** in the location where your teacher instructs you to store the files for this lesson.

3. Click the View tab. In the Show group, click to select the Gridlines check box, and the Ruler check box.

4. Click the Page Layout tab. In the Arrange group, click the Align button ⏢ and click Grid Settings to display the Drawing Grid dialog box.

5. Under Grid settings, set both the Horizontal spacing and Vertical spacing to 0.25".

6. Click to clear the Snap objects to other objects check box, if necessary, and then click OK.

7. In the document, drag the heart shape about 1" to the left. Notice that it snaps to each vertical gridline as you drag.

8. Click Page Layout > Align ⏢ > Grid Settings.

9. Click to select the Snap objects to other objects check box, and then click OK.

10. Save the changes to **WTry16_ studentfirstname_studentlastname** and leave it open to use in the next Try It.

Display document gridlines

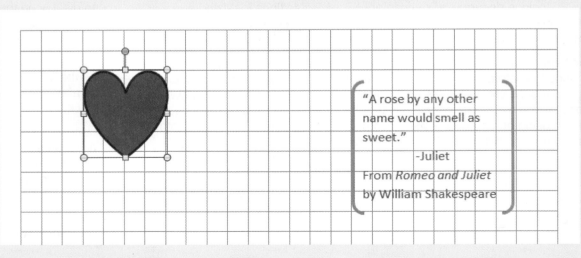

Using Advanced Sizing Features

■ You can easily resize the height and/or width of an object by dragging a sizing handle or entering a precise measurement in the Height or Width boxes in the Size group on the Format tab.

■ Use advanced sizing features to fine tune the size of an object.

■ By default, the **aspect ratio** of most picture objects is locked, so when you adjust one dimension— either height or width—and the other dimension adjusts automatically.

■ You can lock or unlock the aspect ratio for any object.

■ **Scale** an object when you want to adjust its size based on a percentage of its current or original size. For example, scale it by 50% to make it half its original size.

■ Set a relative size for a drawing object when you want to size it relative to the page or margins.

■ Some sizing options are available only for certain types of objects. For example, you cannot set a relative size for a picture, but you can reset a picture to its original size.

Try It!   Using Advanced Sizing Features

1 In the **WTry16_studentfirstname_ studentlastname** file, click to select the heart shape.

2 Click the Drawing Tools Format tab and click the Size group dialog box launcher ▣ to display the Size tab of the Layout dialog box. (You may have to click the Size group button to display the dialog box launcher.)

3 Under Scale, set the Height value to 200%, and then click OK. The shape height doubles, but the width remains the same.

4 Click the Undo button ↺ on the Quick Access Toolbar.

5 Click the Size group dialog box launcher ▣ again.

6 Under Scale, click to select the Lock aspect ratio check box, and then set the Height value to 200%.

7 Click OK to resize the shape.

8 Save the changes to **WTry16_ studentfirstname_studentlastname** and leave it open to use in the next Try It.

Using Advanced Position Features

■ Use Word's advanced position features to position or align an object precisely.

■ You access these features by clicking More Layout Options on the Position drop-down menu on the Picture tools Format tab of the Ribbon.

■ You can position or align the object relative to an **anchor**, such as a column, page, or margin.

■ You can lock the anchor to keep the object from moving when you add or delete text.

■ Object anchors display with other nonprinting characters.

Try It!   Using Advanced Position Features

1 In the **WTry16_studentfirstname_ studentlastname** file, display nonprinting characters if they are not already displayed.

2 Click to select the picture. Notice the object anchor in the upper-left margin.

3 Click the Picture Tools Format tab, then click the Position button ▦ and click More Layout Options to display the Position tab of the Layout dialog box.

(continued)

Try It!   Using Advanced Position Features *(continued)*

4 Under Horizontal, click the Alignment drop-down arrow and click Left, then click the relative to drop-down arrow and click Page.

5 Under Vertical, click the Absolute position option button, and enter 2.5" in the measurement box. Verify that Margin is entered in the below box, and then click OK.

6 Save the changes to **WTry16_ studentfirstname_studentlastname** and leave it open to use in the next Try It.

Position an object precisely

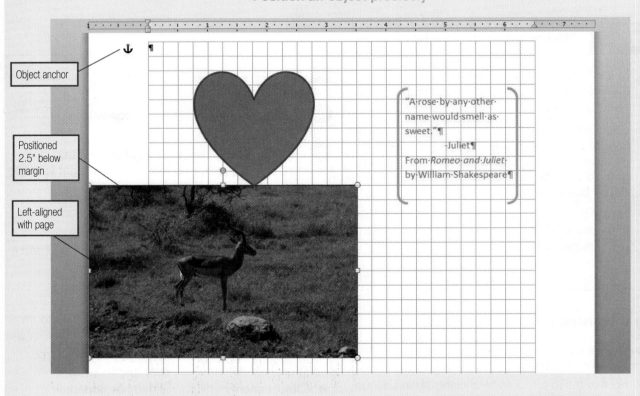

Object anchor

Positioned 2.5" below margin

Left-aligned with page

"A rose by any other name would smell as sweet."¶
        Juliet¶
From Romeo and Juliet by William Shakespeare¶

Adjusting Objects

■ Some—but not all—drawing objects have one or more **adjustment handles** that look like a small yellow diamond.

■ You can drag the adjustment handle to alter the most prominent feature of the shape.

■ For example, you can drag an adjustment handle on a block arrow AutoShape to change the width of the arrow body or the length of the arrowhead.

■ When the mouse pointer touches an adjustment handle, it looks like an arrowhead.

Try It!   Adjusting Objects

1 In the **WTry16_studentfirstname_ studentlastname** file, click to select the text box. Notice the adjustment handle just below the upper-left sizing handle.

2 Drag the adjustment handle down and to the right about 0.5" and then release the mouse button. (You can use the gridlines to estimate the distance.) The text box border adjusts to a rounder, more curved shape.

3 Increase the width of the text box to 2.5" so all the text displays within the box.

4 Save the changes to **WTry16_ studentfirstname_studentlastname** and leave it open to use in the next Try It.

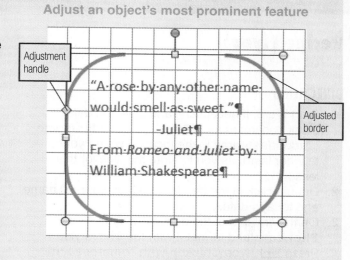

Adjust an object's most prominent feature

Adjustment handle

"A·rose·by·any·other·name· would·smell·as·sweet."¶

—Juliet¶

From·*Romeo·and·Juliet*·by· William·Shakespeare¶

Adjusted border

Cropping a Picture

- **Crop** a picture to remove or trim one or more of the edges.
- You can crop from the left, right, top, and/or bottom.
- Cropping hides the edges, but does not permanently delete them.

✓ *You can permanently delete cropped edges when you compress a picture. You learn about compressing pictures in Word, Lesson 17.*

- You can reset a cropped picture to its original appearance.
- If you want to add a margin around a picture, you can **outcrop** it by dragging a cropping handle out, away from the picture area.

Try It!   Cropping a Picture

1 In the **WTry16_studentfirstname_ studentlastname** file, click the picture to select it.

2 Click the Picture Tools Format tab and then, in the Size group, click the Crop button 📐. Crop handles display around the sides of the picture.

3 Position the mouse pointer over the center crop handle on the left side of the picture, then click and drag to the right about 1" and release the mouse button.

4 Position the mouse pointer over the crop handle in the upper-right corner of the picture, then click and drag down and to the left about 0.5".

5 Click anywhere outside the picture to complete the crop.

6 Click the picture to select it, then click the Crop drop-down arrow to display a menu of cropping options.

7 Point to Crop to Shape to display the Shapes palette. Under Basic Shapes, click the Oval.

8 Click Position 🖼 > More Layout Options.
- Under Horizontal, click the Alignment drop-down arrow and click Left, then click the relative to drop-down arrow and click Margin.
- Under Vertical, click the Absolute position option button, and enter **3"** in the measurement box. Verify that Margin is entered in the below box, and then click OK.

9 Click View > Gridlines to hide the gridlines.

10 Close **WTry16_studentfirstname_ studentlastname**, saving all changes, and exit Word.

Project 35—Create It

Recipe Flyer

DIRECTIONS

1. Start Word, if necessary, and save the default blank document as **WProj35_studentfirstname_ studentlastname** in the location where your teacher instructs you to store the files for this lesson.
2. Double-click in the header and type your full name and today's date.
3. On the first line of the document, type **Recipe Showcase** and format it with the **Title** style.
4. Press [ENTER], type **Chicken with Tomatoes and Herbs**, and format it with the **Heading1** style.
5. Press [ENTER], type **Yield: Four Servings**, and format it with the **Heading 2** style.
6. Press [ENTER], type **Ingredients**, and format it with the **Heading 3** style.
7. Press [ENTER] and type the following eight lines using the **No Spacing** style:
   8 boneless chicken pieces
   1 tablespoon olive oil
   10½ ounces canned diced tomatoes, drained
   ¾ cup chicken stock
   2 teaspoons mixed herbs, chopped
   1½ ounces black olives, chopped
   1 teaspoon sugar
   Fresh basil to garnish
8. Press [ENTER], type **Directions**, and format it with the **Heading 3** style.
9. Press [ENTER], click the **Numbering** button ≣ and type the following list:
   Heat oil in large skillet.
   Add chicken pieces and cook until browned on all sides.
   Add the tomatoes, stock, and mixed herbs and simmer for 30 minutes or until chicken is cooked through.
   Add the olives and sugar and simmer for an additional 5 minutes.
   Garnish with fresh basil and serve with rice or pasta.
10. Click the **View** tab. In the Show group, click to select the **Gridlines** check box.
11. Click the **Page Layout** tab. In the Arrange group, click the **Align** button ≣ and click **Grid Settings** to display the Drawing Grid dialog box.
12. Click to clear the **Snap objects to other objects** check box, and then click **OK**.
13. Click **Insert** > **Shapes** and then under Stars and Banners, click the **5-Point Star**. Click in the upper-right part of the document to insert the shape.
14. Click the **Drawing Tools Format** tab and then, in the Shape Styles gallery, click the **Subtle Effect - Blue, Accent 1** style.
15. Right-click the star and click **Add Text**. Type **From the Liberty Blooms Kitchen!**
16. On the Drawing Tools Format tab, click the **Size** group dialog box launcher 🔳 to display the Size tab of the Layout dialog box. (You may have to click the Size group button to display the dialog box launcher.)
17. Under Scale, click to select the **Lock aspect ratio** check box, and then set the Height value to **250%**.
18. Click **OK** to resize the shape.
19. With the shape still selected, click the **Drawing Tools Format** tab, then click the **Position** button 🖼 and click **More Layout Options** to display the Position tab of the Layout dialog box.
20. Under Horizontal, click to select the **Alignment** option button, then click the **Alignment** drop-down arrow and click **Right**. Click the **relative to** drop-down arrow and click **Margin**.
21. Under Vertical, click the **Absolute position** option button, enter **1"** in the measurement box, click the **below** drop-down arrow, and click **Margin**.
22. Click to select the **Lock anchor** check box, and then click **OK**.
23. With the shape still selected, click and drag the **adjustment handle** up and to the right about 0.25" (use the gridlines to judge the distance), then release the mouse button.
24. Select the text in the shape and increase the font size to **14 points**.
25. Click anywhere outside the shape to deselect it, and save the changes to the document.
26. Position the insertion point at the end of the document, click **Insert** > **Picture** and insert **WProj35_picture** from the data files for this lesson.
27. With the picture selected, click **Picture Tools Format** > **Wrap Text** ⊠ > **Square**.

28. Click **Picture Tools Format > Position** 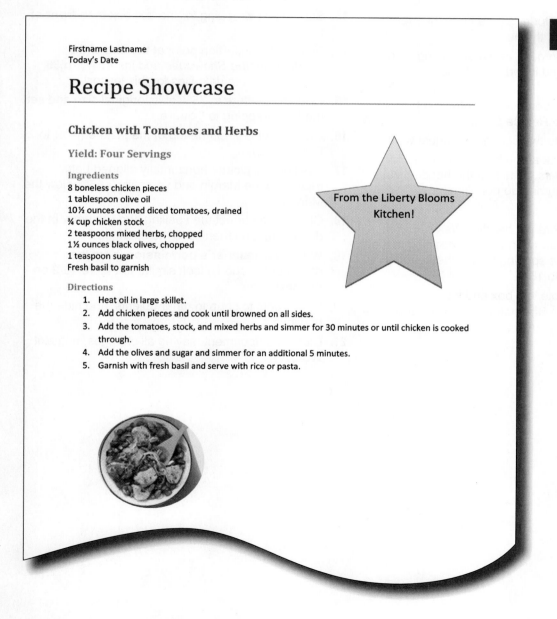 **> More Layout Options**.
29. Under Horizontal, click to select the **Absolute position** option button, set the value to **1.5"**, then click the **to the right of** drop-down arrow and click **Page**.
30. Under Vertical, click to select the **Absolute position** option button, set the value to **5.12"**, click the **below** drop-down arrow and click **Margin**.
31. Click to select the **Lock Anchor** check box and click **OK**.
32. With the picture still selected, on the Picture Tools Format tab, in the Size group, click the **Crop** button.

33. Drag the top **Crop handle** down about 0.5", then click anywhere outside the shape to complete the crop.
34. Click the picture to select it, then click the **Crop** drop-down arrow and point to **Crop to Shape**.
35. On the Shapes palette, under Basic Shapes, click the **Oval**.
36. Click the **View** tab. In the Show group, click to clear the **Gridlines** check box.
37. Check and correct the spelling and grammar in the document, and then save the changes.
38. **With your teacher's permission**, print the document. It should look similar to Figure 16-1.
39. Close the document, saving all changes, and exit Word.

Figure 16-1

Firstname Lastname
Today's Date

Recipe Showcase

Chicken with Tomatoes and Herbs

Yield: Four Servings

Ingredients
8 boneless chicken pieces
1 tablespoon olive oil
10½ ounces canned diced tomatoes, drained
¾ cup chicken stock
2 teaspoons mixed herbs, chopped
1½ ounces black olives, chopped
1 teaspoon sugar
Fresh basil to garnish

From the Liberty Blooms Kitchen!

Directions
1. Heat oil in large skillet.
2. Add chicken pieces and cook until browned on all sides.
3. Add the tomatoes, stock, and mixed herbs and simmer for 30 minutes or until chicken is cooked through.
4. Add the olives and sugar and simmer for an additional 5 minutes.
5. Garnish with fresh basil and serve with rice or pasta.

Project 36—Apply It

Newsletter

DIRECTIONS

1. Start Word, if necessary, and open **WProj36** from the data files for this lesson.

2. Save the file as **WProj36_studentfirstname_studentlastname** in the location where your teacher instructs you to store the files for this lesson.

3. Type your name and today's date in the header and apply the **Clarity** theme.

4. Position the insertion point at the beginning of the line *News in Brief* and insert a continuous section break.

5. Insert another continuous section break at the beginning of the line *Recipe Showcase*.

6. Format section 2 into two columns of equal width.

7. Insert a column break at the beginning of the line *Classes and Seminars*. Note that the headings in the left and right columns do not align.

8. Display gridlines.

9. Set the spacing before the heading *News in Brief* to **14 pt**. It should now align with the heading in the right column. Set the spacing before the heading *Recipe Showcase* to **18 pt**.

10. Insert a Braces Quote text box and type **Introducing Recipe Showcase, a new feature designed to bring your garden into your kitchen.**

11. Select the text and change the font size to **12 points**.

12. Position the text box horizontally at 5.5" to the right of the Margin and vertically -1.25" below the page (type a minus sign or hyphen to enter the negative value), and lock the anchor.

13. Set the text wrapping for the text box to **In front of text**.

14. Position the insertion point at the end of the heading *Recipe Showcase* and insert **WProj36_picture** from the data files for this lesson.

15. Scale the picture to 75% of its original size and set the text wrapping to **Square**.

16. Crop about 0.5" off the top of the picture (refer to Figure 16-2).

17. Position the picture horizontally aligned Left relative to the Margin and vertically 5.45" below the Margin.

18. Check and correct the spelling and grammar in the document, and then save the changes.

19. **With your teacher's permission**, print the document. It should look similar to Figure 16-2 on the next page.

20. Set objects to snap to other objects, and hide the gridlines.

21. Close the document, saving all changes, and exit Word.

Figure 16-2

Firstname Lastname
Today's Date

Liberty Blooms News

Introducing Recipe Showcase, a new feature designed to bring your garden into your kitchen.

"The newsletter than brings your garden to life!"

News in Brief

Plans are progressing on the store expansion. Thanks to everyone who completed a survey.

Spring-planting bulbs are in! Get them in the ground now so you can enjoy a summer of colorful blooms.

We offer a range of natural pest control products. Ask for details.

Classes and Seminars

There is always something going on at 345 Chestnut Street. We try to fill the calendar with interesting and informative activities that the whole family will enjoy.

The following events are scheduled for the coming months. Some events require registration, so please call ahead for more information.

- Edible Gardens   May 13
- Flower Arranging   May 21
- Water Gardens   June 3
- Potpourri Designs   June 11

Recipe Showcase

Chicken with Tomatoes and Herbs   Yield: Four Servings

Ingredients

8 boneless chicken pieces
1 tablespoon olive oil
10½ ounces canned diced tomatoes, drained
¾ cup chicken stock
2 teaspoons mixed herbs, chopped
1½ ounces black olives, chopped
1 teaspoon sugar
Fresh basil to garnish

Directions

1. Heat oil in large skillet.
2. Add chicken pieces and cook until browned on all sides.
3. Add the tomatoes, stock, and mixed herbs and simmer for 30 minutes or until chicken is cooked through.
4. Add the olives and sugar and simmer for an additional 5 minutes.
5. Garnish with fresh basil and serve with rice or pasta.

Lesson 17

Linking Text Boxes

WORDS TO KNOW

Link (text boxes)
Establish a connection between text boxes so that text which does not fit within the borders of the first text box flows into the next, linked text box.

Compress
Reduce in size. A compressed picture has a reduced color format which results in a smaller file size.

➤ What You Will Learn

Aligning an Object with Another Object
Linking Text Boxes
Adding a Caption to a Picture
Compressing a Picture
Removing a Picture Background

Software Skills   Using text boxes makes it possible to position and format text independently from the rest of the document. You can link the text boxes so that the text flows from one to another. Align objects to improve the appearance of the document. Copy objects to save time and to insure consistency between similar objects in a document.

Application Skills   New Media Designs, a Web site design and management company, wants to inspire local students to pursue careers in computer information systems and technology. It is sponsoring a communications contest for students in middle and high school to encourage them to learn more about the available opportunities. In this lesson, you will create two flyers advertising the contest. You will use pictures and text boxes to make the flyers visually appealing and informative.

What You Can Do

Aligning an Object with Another Object

- To create a truly professional-looking document, it is important to have objects properly aligned on the page and with each other.

- When you have multiple objects on a page, you can align them horizontally and vertically relative to each other.

- For example, you can align the tops of text boxes relative to each other.

- Aligning objects with each other can also help you design graphics. For example, if you want to center a star shape over a circle, you can align the centers and middles of the shapes.

- When you select more than one object, Word activates the Align Selected Objects option so you can align the objects with each other.

- Options for aligning objects are on the Align drop-down menu in the Arrange group on the Page Layout tab or the Format tab.

Try It!   **Aligning an Object with Another Object**

1 Start Word and open **WTry17** from the data files for this lesson.

2 Save the file as **WTry17_studentfirstname_studentlastname** in the location where your teacher instructs you to store the files for this lesson.

3 Click the heart shape, then press and hold SHIFT and click the circle shape to select both objects.

4 Click the Drawing Tools Format tab, then in the Arrange group, click the Align button. Notice that the Align Selected Objects option is selected.

5 Click Align Center. The centers of the shapes are aligned vertically.

6 Click the Align button again and click Align Middle. The middles of the shapes are aligned horizontally. The heart shape is now centered over the circle.

7 Click the text box on the left, press and hold SHIFT and click the text box on the right.

8 Click the Drawing Tools Format tab, click the Align button and click Align Top. The tops of the text boxes are aligned.

9 Save the changes to **WTry17_studentfirstname_studentlastname**, and leave it open to use in the next Try It.

Align objects relative to each other

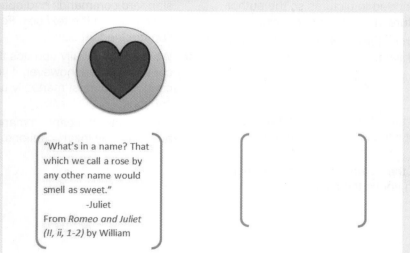

"What's in a name? That
which we call a rose by
any other name would
smell as sweet."
                -Juliet
From *Romeo and Juliet*
(II, ii, 1-2) by William

Linking Text Boxes

- You can **link** text boxes in a document so that text which does not fit within the first text box automatically flows into the next linked text box.

- To link one text box with another, select the first text box, click the Create Link button in the Text group on the Text Box Tools Format tab of the Ribbon, then click the next text box.

- The second text box must not contain text when you establish the link.

- A series of linked text boxes is called a *text box chain*.

- Text flows through the chain in the order in which you link the text boxes, not in the order in which the text boxes appear in the document, or in the order in which the text boxes were created.

- Use the Break Link button to break the link and move all text into the first text box.

Try It! Linking Text Boxes

1. In the **WTry17_studentfirstname_studentlastname** file, click the text box on the left.

2. Resize it to 1.5" high by 1.5" wide.

3. Click the Drawing Tools Format tab, then, in the Text group, click the Create Link button ⮑. The mouse pointer changes to resemble a pitcher with an arrow on it 🝙.

4. Position the mouse pointer over the blank text box on the right—the mouse pointer changes to a pouring pitcher ⬙—and click. The text boxes are linked, and overflow text from the first box displays in the second box.

5. Click in the text box on the left, then click Drawing Tools Format > Break Link 🔗 to break the link and remove the overflow text from the second text box.

6. Click the Undo button ↩ to create the link again.

7. Save the changes to **WTry17_studentfirstname_studentlastname**, and leave it open to use in the next Try It.

Adding a Caption to a Picture

- Captions are often added to pictures so the author can refer to the picture in the main body text.

- As with tables, each picture caption includes a text label and a number field.

  ✓ *For information on adding a caption to a table, refer to Word, Lesson 14.*

- You can customize the label if you want. For example, you might want to change it from *Figure* to *Illustration*.

- You can customize the number format and select to position the caption above the picture.

- When the picture is floating—not in line with text—picture captions are inserted in a text box. Use standard commands and options to format or edit the caption in the text box. For example, you can change the font size.

- Word automatically updates the numbers for each caption entered; however, if you delete or move a caption, you must manually update the remaining captions.

- You can insert a caption manually or set Word to automatically insert captions.

Try It!   Adding a Caption to a Picture

1 In the **WTry17_studentfirstname_studentlastname** file, click the picture to select it.

2 Click the References tab, and then, in the Captions group, click the Insert Caption button 🖹 to open the Caption dialog box.

3 Click the Position drop-down arrow, click Above selected item, and then click OK.

4 Click the Undo button 🔁 on the Quick Access Toolbar to remove the caption.

5 Click the Insert Caption button 🖹 again.

6 In the Caption dialog box, click the New Label button to display the New Label dialog box. Type **Illustration** and click OK.

7 Click the Position drop-down arrow, click Above selected item, and then click OK.

8 Select the caption in the text box and increase the font size to 14 points.

9 Save the changes to **WTry17_studentfirstname_studentlastname**, and leave it open to use in the next Try It.

Add a caption to a picture

Illustration·1¶

Compressing a Picture

- Picture files may be large and therefore take up a lot of disk space or take a long time to transmit electronically.

- You can **compress** a picture to make its file size smaller.

- Compressing reduces the color format of the image, which makes the color take up fewer bits per pixel. In most cases, you do not notice a difference in image quality.

- You can select options to control the final resolution of the compressed picture. For example, if you plan to print the picture, you can select a higher resolution than if you plan to display the picture on-screen or send the picture by e-mail.

- You can also choose to delete cropped areas at the same time that you compress the pictures.

- You can compress the selected picture or all pictures in the document.

- The tool for compressing pictures is in the Adjust group on the Picture Tools Format tab of the Ribbon.

Try It!   Compressing a Picture

1 In the **WTry17_studentfirstname_studentlastname** file, click the picture to select it.

2 Click the Picture Tools Format tab, then, in the Adjust group, click the Compress Pictures button 🗔 to display the Compress Pictures dialog box.

3 Click to select the Print (220 ppi): excellent quality on most printers and screens option button, and then click OK.

4 Save the changes to **WTry17_studentfirstname_studentlastname**, and leave it open to use in the next Try It.

Removing a Picture Background

- You can remove the background from a picture when you want to eliminate details or highlight a focal point.

- The Remove Background tool is in the Adjust group on the Picture Tools Format tab of the Ribbon.

- When you start the removal process, Word displays the Background Removal tab on the Ribbon providing the tools you need to complete the process.

- Word applies a magenta overlay to everything in the background of the picture, and leaves the foreground unchanged. It also displays a selection box.

- By adjusting the size and position of the selection box, you can affect the areas Word identifies as background.

- You can fine tune the removal by marking areas you want to keep and areas you want to remove.

- Because compressing a picture may change its appearance, you should compress pictures and save the file before removing a background.

- Use Undo to reverse the background removal if you are not satisfied with the results.

- Combine background removal with other picture effects, such as cropping and picture styles, to create an interesting graphic.

Try It!   **Removing a Picture Background**

1 In the **WTry17_studentfirstname_studentlastname** file, click the picture to select it.

2 Click the Picture Tools Format tab and then in the Adjust group click the Remove Background button. Word displays the Background Removal tab on the Ribbon, and highlights the picture background in magenta. Note that some foreground areas that you might want to keep— such as the elephant's tusk—are magenta.

3 Drag the top sizing handle down about ¾" to just above the elephant's head. When the selection box is smaller, Word distinguishes the tusk as foreground and removes the magenta. The only area marked for removal that you might want to keep is the tail.

4 On the Background Removal tab, click the Mark Areas to Keep button. The mouse pointer changes to a pencil.

5 Click and drag to draw a line along the part of the tail covered in magenta. (If necessary, you can draw more than one line.) Each line is marked by a circle with a plus sign in it, indicating the area is foreground.

6 On the Background removal tab, click the Mark Areas to Remove button and click on the area inside the curled trunk. The area is marked by a circle with a minus sign in it, indicating the area is background.

7 On the Background Removal tab, click the Keep Changes button ✓. Word removes the magenta areas identifying the background.

8 Save the changes to **WTry17_studentfirstname_studentlastname**, close it, and exit Word.

Marking the background for removal

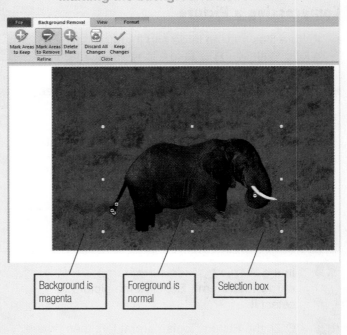

Background is magenta   Foreground is normal   Selection box

Project 37—Create It

Middle Grades Contest Flyer

DIRECTIONS

1. Start Word, if necessary, and save the default blank document as **WProj37_studentfirstname_ studentlastname** in the location where your teacher instructs you to store the files for this lesson.

2. Double-click in the header and type your full name and today's date.

3. Set the font to **Arial** and the font size to **28 points**, and type **New Media Designs**.

4. Press ENTER and type **Proudly Announces**, press ENTER and type **Its First Ever**, press ENTER and type **Communications Contest**.

5. Press ENTER and type **Topic:**. Press ENTER and type **The Future of Computer Technology**.

6. Press ENTER , change the font size to **14 points**, and type **Grand Prize winner will receive a $2,500.00 scholarship and a notebook computer, similar to the one shown in Illustration A. Other prizes include gift certificates, computer accessories, and more. For more information and for an entry form, consult New Media's Web site: www.nmd.com**.

7. Click **Insert** > **Shapes** . Under Stars and Banners, click **Explosion 1**, then click in the upper-right part of the document.

8. With the shape still selected, enter **3"** in the Size group Height box and **2.75"** in the Width box .

9. In the Arrange group, click the **Position** button and click **Position in Top Right with Square Text Wrapping**, then click the **Wrap Text** button and click **Behind Text**.

10. Right-click the shape and click **Add Text**. Change the font size to **16 points** and type **Middle Division: Grades 5 - 8**.

11. Click **Insert** > **Text Box** > **Draw Text Box**, and then click and drag below the line *The Future of Computer Technology* to insert a text box approximately 0.75" high by 1.75" wide.

    ✓ *If nonprinting characters are displayed, the object's anchor should display to the left of the line The Future of Computer Technology.*

12. Click **Drawing Tools Format** > **Wrap Text** > **Top and Bottom**.

13. Click **Drawing Tools Format** > **Position** > **More Layout Options**.

14. Under Horizontal, click the **Alignment** option button, then click the **Alignment** drop-down arrow and click **Left**, and click the **relative to** drop-down arrow and click **Margin**.

15. Under Vertical, click the **Absolute position** option button and enter **0.75"** in the box, then click the **below** drop-down arrow and click **Paragraph**.

16. Click to select the **Lock anchor** check box, and then click **OK**.

17. Select the text box, click **Home** > **Copy** to copy it to the Clipboard, and then, on the Home tab, in the Clipboard group, click **Home** > **Paste** twice to create two copies of the text box. There should be three text boxes in total, overlapping each other.

18. With the top text box selected, click **Drawing Tools Format** > **Position** > and then **More Layout Options**. Under Horizontal, click the **Alignment** option button, then click the **Alignment** drop-down arrow and click **Right**, click the **relative** to drop-down arrow and click **Margin**, then click **OK**.

19. Select the next text box, click **Drawing Tools Format** > **Position** > and then **More Layout Options**. Under Horizontal, click the **Alignment** option button, then click the **Alignment** drop-down arrow and click **Centered**, click the **relative to** drop-down arrow and click **Margin**, then click **OK**.

20. Press and hold [SHIFT] and click to select all three text boxes.

21. On the Drawing Tools Format tab, in the Arrange group, click the **Align** button and click **Align Top**.

22. Click in the text box on the left, apply the **No Spacing** style, set the font size to **14 points**, and set the horizontal alignment to **Center**.

23. Type the following six lines of text, pressing [ENTER] between each line (you will not be able to view all of the text within the text box).

    Category 1

    Writing

    Category 2

    Graphic Design

    Category 3

    Oral Presentation

24. Click the **Drawing Tools Format** tab, then in the Text group, click the **Create Link** button, then click in the middle text box.

25. Click the **Create Link** button again, and click in the right text box.

26. Position the insertion point at the end of the document and press [ENTER] to insert a blank line. (Right-click the Web URL and click **Remove Hyperlink**, if necessary.)

27. Click **Insert** > **Picture** and insert **WProj37_picture** from the data files for this lesson.

28. Resize the picture height to **2"**. The width should adjust automatically.

29. With the picture selected, click the **References** tab and then, in the Captions group, click **Insert Caption** .

30. In the Caption dialog box, click the **New Label** button, type **Illustration**, and then click **OK**.

31. In the Caption dialog box, click the **Numbering** button, click the **Format** drop-down arrow, click **A, B, C, ...** and then click **OK**.

32. In the Caption dialog box, click **OK**.

33. Click the picture to select it, and then click **Picture Tools Format** > **Compress Pictures** > **OK**.

34. In the Adjust group, click the **Remove Background** button .

35. Use the sizing handles to resize the selection box so it is the same size as the picture, then, on the **Background Removal** tab, click the **Mark Areas to Keep** button and click and drag a line along the top of the computer case where the magenta overlay displays. If necessary, mark any other areas of the computer that are overlaid with magenta.

36. On the Background Removal tab, click the **Keep Changes** button .

37. Check and correct the spelling and grammar in the document, and then save the changes.

38. **With your teacher's permission**, print the document. It should look similar to Figure 17-1 on the next page.

39. Close the document, saving all changes, and exit Word.

Figure 17-1

Firstname Lastname
Today's Date

New Media Designs

Proudly Announces

Its First Ever

Communications Contest

Middle
Division:
Grades 5 - 8

Topic:

The Future of Computer Technology

Category 1 Writing	Category 2 Graphic Design	Category 3 Oral Presentation

Grand Prize winner will receive a $2,500.00 scholarship and a notebook computer similar to the one shown in Illustration A. Other prizes include gift certificates, computer accessories, and more. For more information and for an entry form, consult New Media's Web site: www.nmd.com.

Illustration A

Project 38—Apply It

High School Contest Flyer

DIRECTIONS

1. Start Word, if necessary, and open **WProj38** from the data files for this lesson.

2. Save the file as **WProj38_studentfirstname_ studentlastname** in the location where your teacher instructs you to store the files for this lesson.

3. Double-click in the header and type your full name and today's date.

4. Insert an **Explosion 2** shape. Size it to **2"** high by **2.5"** wide and add the text **High School Division!** in **14 point Arial**.

5. Position the object in the top left part of the document relative to the margins, and set the text wrapping to **Behind Text**.

6. Insert an **Explosion 1** shape. Size it to **2.5"** high by **2.5"** wide and add the text **Winners announced June 1!** in **14 point Arial**.

7. Set the text wrapping to **Behind Text**, and align it with the Right margin.

8. Apply the **Subtle Effect - Black, Dark 1** shape style to both shapes.

9. Align the middles of the shapes relative to each other.

10. Position the insertion point in the left text box, set the style to **No Spacing**, set the font size to **14** points, and set the alignment to **Center**.

11. Type the following six lines:

    Category 1

    Video Presentation

    Category 2

    Web Page Design

    Category 3

    Essay Writing

12. Link the left text box to the middle text box, and the middle text box to the right text box.

13. Format the text boxes on the left and right with the **Moderate Effect - Blue, Accent 1** shape style and the text box in the middle with the **Moderate Effect - Red, Accent 2** shape style.

14. Insert a blank line at the end of the document (remove the hyperlink from the URL, if necessary), and insert **WProj38_picture**.

15. Set text wrapping to **Square**, and resize the picture to **1.5"** high by **1.5"** wide. Center the picture horizontally, and position it **0.25"** below the blank line.

16. Add a caption below the picture using the label Figure and Arabic numbers.

17. Compress the picture and then remove its background and other areas as necessary so it looks similar to the picture in Figure 17-2 on the next page.

18. Check and correct the spelling and grammar in the document, and then save the changes.

19. **With your teacher's permission**, print the document.

20. Close the document, saving all changes, and exit Word.

Figure 17-2

Firstname Lastname
Today's Date

High
School
Division!

New Media Designs

Proudly Announces

Its First Ever

Communications Contest

Winners
announced
June 1!

Topic:

The Future of Computer Technology

Category 1
Video Presentation

Category 2
Web Page Design

Category 3
Essay Writing

Grand Prize winner will receive a $4,000.00 scholarship and a notebook computer. Other prizes include a digital camera (see Figure 1), an MP3 player (see Figure 2), a mobile phone, and more. For more information and for an entry form, consult New Media's Web site: www.nmd.com.

Figure 1

Lesson 18

Creating WordArt and Watermarks

WORDS TO KNOW

Watermark
A pale or semitransparent graphics object positioned behind text in a document.

WordArt
A feature of Word used to transform text into a drawing object.

➤ What You Will Learn

Creating WordArt
Creating a Watermark

Software Skills   Use WordArt to transform text into artwork for letterheads, logos, brochures, and other documents. WordArt lets you create special effects using any text that you type. You can stretch characters, rotate them, reverse direction, and even arrange the text in shapes such as circles, waves, or arcs. Place a watermark on a document to make an impression on readers, convey an idea, or provide a consistent theme. For example, a watermark on corporate stationery can create a corporate identity.

Application Skills   Long Shot, Inc. is growing by leaps and bounds. To fill job vacancies, it is hosting an open house and career fair. In this lesson, you will create a notice announcing the event and a handout for attendees. You will use WordArt and a watermark to create the documents.

What You Can Do

Creating WordArt

- **WordArt** is an Office feature similar to text effects that you use to transform text into a drawing object.
- You create WordArt by selecting a style from the WordArt gallery.
- The WordArt text is inserted in a text box which you can size and position anywhere on the page.
- Use the tools in the WordArt Styles group on the Drawing Tools Format tab to customize the WordArt text.
- For example, you can apply text effects to transform the shape of the text, or to add a glow, reflection, or 3-D effect.
- You can also use the standard tools for formatting the text box, such as fill, outline, text wrapping, size, position, and alignment.
- The command for creating WordArt is in the Text group on the Insert tab of the Ribbon.

Try It!   **Creating WordArt**

1 Start Word and save the default blank document as **WTry18_studentfirstname_studentlastname** in the location where your teacher instructs you to store the files for this lesson.

2 Click the Insert tab, then in the Text group click the WordArt button to display the WordArt gallery.

3 Click the first style in the fourth row—Gradient Fill - Blue, Accent 1, Outline - White, Glow - Accent 2. Word creates the WordArt in a text box using sample text.

4 Type **Adventure!** to replace the sample text.

5 Click the Drawing Tools Format tab, then, in the WordArt Styles group click the Text Effects button to display a menu of text effects options.

6 Point to Transform to display a gallery of transform styles. Under Warp, point to the first option in the fourth row—Curve Up—to see how it affects the WordArt.

7 Scroll down to the bottom of the Transform gallery and click the first style in the last row—Slant Up.

8 In the WordArt Style group, click the Text Fill drop-down arrow **A** and click Purple, Accent 4.

9 In the Arrange group, click the Position button and click Position in Top Center with Square Text Wrapping.

10 Save the changes to **WTry18_studentfirstname_studentlastname**, and leave it open to use in the next Try It.

WordArt

Creating a Watermark

- Insert text or graphics objects as a **watermark** to provide a background image for text-based documents.
- Word 2010 comes with a few built-in watermark styles that you can select from the Watermark gallery in the Page Background group on the Page Layout tab.
- You can also create a custom watermark using the options in the Printed Watermark dialog box.
- A watermark may be a graphics object, such as clip art, a text box, WordArt, or a shape.

- You can also create a watermark from text.
- Watermarks are usually inserted into the document header so that they automatically appear on every page, and so that they are not affected by changes made to the document content.
- To remove a watermark, click the Watermark button and click Remove Watermark, or make the header active, select the watermark, and press `DEL` .
- Watermarks are a nice feature to add to a template because every document based on the template will display the same watermark.

Try It!   Creating a Watermark

1 In the **WTry18_studentfirstname_ studentlastname** file, adjust the zoom to display the entire page.

2 Click the Page Layout tab, then, in the Page Background group, click the Watermark button to display the Watermark gallery.

3 Click the CONFIDENTIAL 1 style. Word inserts the watermark on the page.

4 Click the Undo button on the Quick Access Toolbar to remove the watermark.

5 Click the Watermark button again, and click Custom Watermark to display the Printed Watermark dialog box.

6 Click the Picture watermark option button, and then click Select Picture.

7 Navigate to the location where the data files for this lesson are stored and insert **WTry18_ picture**.

8 In the Printed Watermark dialog box, click OK.

9 Click the Undo button on the Quick Access Toolbar to remove the watermark, then click the Watermark button , and click Custom Watermark to display the Printed Watermark dialog box.

10 Click the Text watermark option button, select the text in the Text box, type **Adventure!**, and click OK.

11 Save the changes to **WTry17_ studentfirstname_studentlastname**, close it, and exit Word.

Project 39—Create It

Announcement

DIRECTIONS

1. Start Word, if necessary, and save the default blank document as **WProj39_studentfirstname_ studentlastname** in the location where your teacher instructs you to store the files for this lesson.

2. Double-click in the header and type your full name and today's date.

3. Position the insertion point on the first line of the document, set the font to **72 point Arial**, and type **SOAR**. Center the line horizontally.

4. Press [ENTER], decrease the font size to **20 points**, type **to new heights with**, and press [ENTER].

5. Click the **Insert** tab, and then in the Text group, click the **WordArt** button 🅐.

6. Click the style on the right end of the fifth row— **Fill - Blue, Accent 1, Plastic Bevel, Reflection**.

7. In the WordArt text box, type **Long Shot, Inc.**

8. On the Drawing Tools Format tab, in the WordArt Styles group, click the **Text Effects** button 🅐▾, point to **Transform**, and then, under Warp, click the first style in the sixth row—**Inflate**.

9. With the WordArt text box selected, click the **Wrap Text** button 🔲 and click **Top and Bottom**.

10. Click the **Position** button 🔲, and then click **More Layout Options**.

11. Under Horizontal, click the **Alignment** option button, click the drop-down arrow and click **Centered**. Click the **relative to** drop-down arrow and click **Margin**.

12. Under Vertical, click the **Absolute position** option button and enter **0.6"** in the box, then click the **below** drop-down arrow and click **Paragraph**.

13. Click to select the **Lock Anchor** check box, and then click **OK**.

14. Position the insertion point on the last line of the document, set the spacing before to **132 pt**, and type the following six lines, pressing [ENTER] between each line:

    Please Come to Our

    Open House and Career Fair

    Saturday, April 15th and Sunday, April 16th

    10:00 a.m. – 3:00 p.m.

    234 Simsbury Drive

    Ithaca, NY 14850

15. Click the **Page Layout** tab, and then, in the Page Background group, click the **Watermark** button 🄰.

16. Click **Custom Watermark** to open the Printed Watermark dialog box.

17. Click the **Picture watermark** option button, then click **Select Picture**. Browse to the location where the data files for this lesson are stored, and insert **WProj39_picture**.

18. In the Printed Watermark dialog box, click **OK**.

19. Check and correct the spelling and grammar in the document, and then save the changes.

20. **With your teacher's permission**, print the document. It should look similar to Figure 18-1 on the next page.

21. Close the document, saving all changes, and exit Word.

Figure 18-1

Firstname Lastname
Today's Date

SOAR

to new heights with

LONG SHOT, INC.

Please Come to Our

Open House and Career Fair

Saturday, April 15th and Sunday, April 16th

10:00 a.m. – 3:00 p.m.

234 Simsbury Drive

Ithaca, NY 14850

Project 40—Apply It

Handout

DIRECTIONS

1. Start Word, if necessary, and open **WProj40** from the data files for this lesson.

2. Save the file as **WProj40_studentfirstname_ studentlastname** in the location where your teacher instructs you to store the files for this lesson.

3. Type your full name and today's date in the document header.

4. Insert a WordArt object using the **Fill - Red, Accent 2, Matte Bevel** style.

5. In the WordArt text box, type the text **234 Simsbury Drive**, press [ENTER] and type **Long Shot, Inc.**, press [ENTER] and type **Ithaca, NY**.

6. Resize the WordArt text box to **3.5"** high by **4.5"** wide.

7. Click **Text Effects** > **Transform**, and then, under Follow Path, click the **Button** style.

8. Set the word wrap for the WordArt object to **Top and Bottom**. Position the object horizontally centered on the page and 3" below the page, and lock the anchor.

9. Create a picture watermark using the **WProj40_ picture** file from the data files for this lesson.

10. Check and correct the spelling and grammar in the document, and then save the changes.

11. **With your teacher's permission**, print the document. It should look similar to Figure 18-2 on the next page.

12. Close the document, saving all changes, and exit Word.

Figure 18-2

Firstname Lastname
Today's Date

Welcome

to our Open House and Career Fair

Career Opportunities are available in:

- ✓ Manufacturing
- ✓ Marketing
- ✓ Design

Department managers are stationed in the cafeteria to provide additional information. Please complete a job application to submit along with your resume, letter of introduction, and list of references. We appreciate your interest in working at Long Shot.

Chapter Assessment and Application

Project 41—Make It Your Own

Travel Itinerary

In this project, create an itinerary for yourself and three or four traveling companions. They might be your friends, family, or a club or organization to which you belong. You might start by looking up sample itineraries online, or searching Office.com for itinerary templates to use to create the document.

Include the following information:

■ The names of everyone who will be traveling.

■ The locations, dates, and times of departure and arrival for all legs of the trip.

■ The method of transportation, including schedule and flight, train, or bus numbers. You may choose to include the cost information, as well.

■ Information about accommodations at the destination, such as hotel name, address, and telephone number, and the number of nights.

■ A schedule of activities or sightseeing options.

Create the itinerary using the advanced tables and graphics skills you have learned in this chapter, including table styles, nested tables, advanced graphics sizing and positioning, captions, WordArt, and watermarks.

DIRECTIONS

1. Start Word and save the default blank document or the itinerary template of your choice as **WProj41_ studentfirstname_studentlastname** in the location where your teacher instructs you to store the files for this project.

2. Type your name and today's date in the document header, and apply a theme and style set.

3. Design the itinerary using tables and graphics. For example, you might use a large table to organize the page into columns, then insert a graphic image of your destination in one of the table cells. You might insert a nested table in a cell to enter the names of the travelers and the travel information.

4. Design and save a custom table style to give your tables a unique look.

5. Embellish and enhance the document by including shapes and pictures, and format the objects using advanced graphics features. Use document gridlines to help you make sure objects are aligned evenly on the page, and with each other.

6. When you have completed a first draft, exchange documents with a classmate, make suggestions for improvement, and then exchange back.

7. Make the improvements to your document and then save the changes.

8. Check the spelling and grammar in the document and correct errors as necessary.

9. **With your teacher's permission**, print the document.

10. Restore all default settings and delete custom styles.

11. Close the document, saving all changes, and exit Word.

Project 42—Master It

Invitation

You have been asked to design an invitation to a luncheon honoring the winners of New Media Design's Communications contest. You will use tables, graphics objects, WordArt, and a watermark to create an effective, eye-catching document.

DIRECTIONS

1. Start Word, if necessary, and save the default, blank document as **WProj42_studentfirstname_ studentlastname** in the location where your teacher instructs you to store the files for this project.

2. Insert your name and today's date in the document header, and apply the **Flow** theme.

3. Use the following steps to create the document shown in Illustration A.

4. Insert a WordArt object using the **Fill - Turquoise, Accent 2, Double Outline - Accent 2** style.

5. Type the text **New Media Designs**, and apply the **Chevron Up** transform text effect.

6. Resize the WordArt text box to **1"** high by **5"** wide, set the text wrapping to **Top and Bottom**, and center it horizontally on the page and position it along the top margin.

7. Insert a text box sized to **1"** high by **3"** wide. Position it horizontally aligned with the left margin and vertically 3" below the page.

8. Set the style to **No Spacing** and the font size to **14 points** and type the following seven lines:

   You are invited to celebrate the winners of our first ever Communications Contest!

   Please join us for lunch.

   Friday, October 19

   12:30 p.m.

   New Media Designs

   Highway 73

   Cambridge, WA 53523

9. Draw a second text box of the same size. Position it centered horizontally and vertically 4" below the page.

10. Draw a third text box of the same size. Position it horizontally aligned with the right margin and vertically 5" below the page.

11. Link the left text box to the middle box and the middle box to the right box.

12. Apply the **Subtle Effect - Turquoise, Accent 3** shape style to the left text box, the **Subtle Effect - Blue, Accent 1** shape style to the middle text box, and the **Subtle Effect - Bright Green, Accent 4** shape style to the right text box.

13. Insert a table with four columns and five rows, and drag it down near the bottom of the page (refer to Illustration A). Merge the cells in the top row. Enter the following data in the first two rows:

Communications Contest Winners			
Middle (5–8)	Category 1	Category 2	Category

14. In the second cell of the third row, insert a nested table with two columns and three rows and enter the following data:

1st	Alex Grogan
2nd	Michaela Jackson
3rd	Jaclyn Brown

15. In the third cell of the third row, insert a nested table with two columns and three rows and enter the following data:

1st	Jill Kline
2nd	Sam Lapp
3rd	Dinesh Patel

16. In the fourth cell of the third row, insert a nested table with two columns and three rows and enter the following data:

1st	Matt O'Toole
2nd	Chris White
3rd	Liz Jones

17. In the fourth row, enter the following data:

High School	Category 1	Category 2	Category 3

18. In the second cell of the fifth row, insert a nested table with two columns and three rows and enter the following data:

1st	Keith Feeney
2nd	Brady Kim
3rd	Olivia Tombola

19. In the third cell of the fifth row, insert a nested table with two columns and three rows and enter the following data:

1st	June Tsai
2nd	Leah Gold
3rd	George Wei

20. In the fourth cell of the fifth row, insert a nested table with two columns and three rows and enter the following data:

1st	Jen LeBlanc
2nd	Robbie Maltz
3rd	Jim Shepard

21. Apply the **Light List** table style to the main table. Increase the font size in the first row to **14 points**, and center the text horizontally and vertically.

22. Apply the **Colorful List** table style to all six nested tables.

23. Click outside the table and insert **WProj42_picture1** from the data files for this lesson.

24. Crop about 1.75" from the right side and about 0.5" from the left side.

25. Set the text wrapping to **In Front of Text** and then position the picture 4" to the right of the margin, horizontally, and 1" below the margin, vertically.

26. Insert a caption below the picture that says: **1 Grand Prize Winner, Middle School**.

27. Insert **WProj42_picture2** from the data files for this lesson, and resize it to **2.5"** high.

28. Set the text wrapping to **In Front of Text** and then position it 0.5" to the right of the margin, horizontally, and 4" below the margin, vertically.

29. Insert a caption below the picture that says: **2 Grand Prize Winner, High School**.

30. Compress all of the pictures in the document, and then remove the backgrounds.

31. Create a picture watermark using the file **WProj42_picture3** from the data files for this lesson.

32. Check the spelling and grammar in the document and correct errors as necessary.

33. **With your teacher's permission**, print the document.

34. Restore all default settings and delete custom styles.

35. Close the document, saving all changes, and exit Word.

New Media Designs

You are invited to celebrate the winners of our first ever Communications Contest!

Please join us for lunch.
Friday, October 19
12:30 p.m.

1 Grand Prize Winner, Middle

New Media Designs
Highway 73
Cambridge, WA 53523

2 Grand Prize Winner, High School

Communications Contest Winners								
Middle (5-8)	Category 1			Category 2			Category 3	
	1st	Alex Grogan		1st	Jill Kline		1st	Matt O'Toole
	2nd	Michaela Jackson		2nd	Sam Lapp		2nd	Chris White
	3rd	Jaclyn Brown		3rd	Dinesh Patel		3rd	Liz Jones
High School	Category 1			Category 2			Category 3	
	1st	Keith Feeney		1st	June Tsai		1st	Jen LeBlanc
	2nd	Brady Kim		2nd	Leah Gold		2nd	Robbie Maltz
	3rd	Olivia Tombola		3rd	George Wei		3rd	Jim Shepard

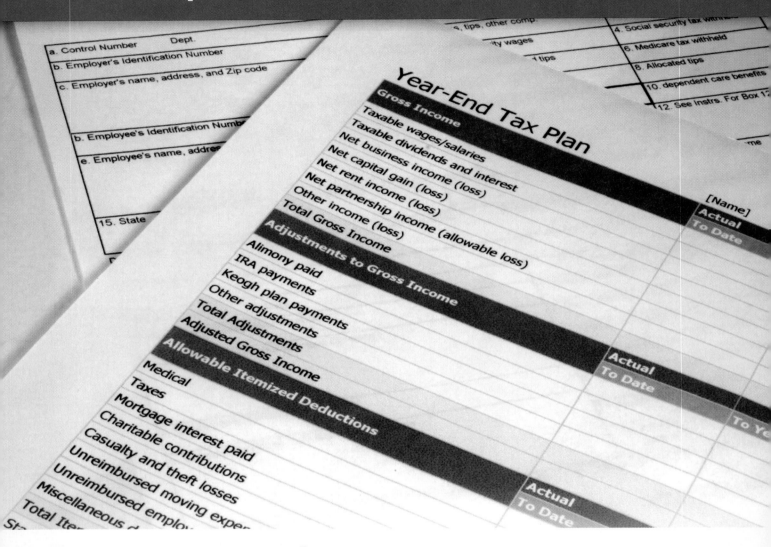

Chapter 4

Protecting Documents and Forms

Lesson 19
Creating Forms
Projects 43–44

- Inserting Content Controls
- Setting Content Control Properties
- Protecting a Form
- Filling Out a Form
- Analyzing Surveys

Lesson 20
Protecting Documents
Projects 45–46

- Restricting Editing and Formatting
- Setting Restriction Exceptions
- Applying Password Protection and Encryption
- Understanding Computer Ethics and Codes of Conduct
- Understanding Computer Security

Lesson 21
Inspecting and Checking Documents
Projects 47–48

- Using the Document Inspector
- Checking Compatibility

Lesson 22
Marking a Document as Final and Using Digital Signatures
Projects 49–50

- Marking a Document as Final
- Understanding Digital Signatures
- Using a Visible Digital Signature
- Using an Invisible Digital Signature
- Verifying Signature Details
- Analyzing Legal Documents

End-of-Chapter Assessments
Projects 51–52

Lesson 19

Creating Forms

WORDS TO KNOW

Content Controls
Tools used to create forms.

Form
A document used to collect and organize information.

➤ What You Will Learn

Inserting Content Controls
Setting Content Control Properties
Protecting a Form
Filling Out a Form
Analyzing Surveys

Software Skills   Use forms to collect information such as names and addresses for product registrations, data for surveys, or products and pricing for invoices or purchase orders. With Word, you can create forms that can be printed and filled out manually. You can also store forms on a computer so they can be filled out on-screen.

Application Skills   As the Manager of in-house training at Long Shot, Inc., you recognize that changes to the business environment affect all departments, including training. You would like to survey employees to learn how to use developing technology to provide the best in-house training to the most people. In this lesson, you will create a form that employees can fill out indicating their attitudes toward different types of teaching methods.

What You Can Do

Inserting Content Controls

- Insert **Content Controls** in a document to create a form for collecting information that can be stored and analyzed.
- For example, a human resources department might use a form to collect and store employee information.
- Use the buttons in the Controls group on the Developer tab of the Ribbon to insert content controls.
- The Developer tab does not display by default; you must set an option to make it available.
- Available content controls include:
  - Rich Text
  - Plain Text

- Picture
- Building Block Gallery
- Combo Box
- Drop-Down List
- Date Picker
- Check Box

■ Instructional text automatically displays in each content control that you insert.

■ For example, if you insert a Text control, it displays *Click here to enter text*. If you enter a Drop-Down List control, it displays *Choose an item*.

■ For best results, create a form as a document template; you can then use the template to create new form documents as you need them.

■ Users can also print the document and fill out the form on paper.

■ When inserting content controls, give some consideration to the form layout. You may want to use a table or tab stops to be sure items are aligned so that it will be easy for users to read and fill out the form.

■ Also, it is important to keep in mind that the insertion point moves from control to control based on the order in which controls are inserted in the document, not based on the order in which the controls are arranged.

■ Versions of Word prior to Word 97 do not support content controls. If you know a form will be used on a system running an older version of the program, you can use Word's Legacy Tools to insert form fields instead of content controls.

Try It!   Inserting Content Controls

1 In Word, open **WTry19** from the data files for this lesson.

2 Save the file as type Word template (*.dotx) with the name **WTry19a_studentfirstname_studentlastname** in the location where your teacher instructs you to store the files for this lesson.

3 Click File > Options 📄 > Customize Ribbon.

4 Under Customize the Ribbon, click to select the Developer check box, and then click OK.

5 In the document template, click to position the insertion point in the table cell in the first row of the right column.

✓ *If table gridlines are not displayed, click to the right of the text Name:, click the Table Tools Layout tab, and click to toggle on the View Gridlines button* 🖽.

6 Click the Developer tab on the Ribbon, then, in the Controls group click the Rich Text Content Control [Aa] button.

7 Position the insertion point in the cell in the second row of the right column, then click the Drop-Down List Content Control button 📇.

8 Move the insertion point down one cell and click the Date Picker Content Control button 📅.

9 Position the insertion point in the second cell in the bottom row and click the Check Box Content Control button ☑.

10 Position the insertion point in the cell on the right end of the bottom row and click the Check Box Control button ☑ again.

11 Save the changes to the document template and leave it open to use in the next Try It.

Content Controls in a form template

Long Shot, Inc.

234 Simsbury Drive ⌶ Ithaca, NY 14850

Telephone: 607-555-9191 ⌶ Fax: 607-555-9292 ⌶ E-mail: mail@longshot.net

Name:	Click here to enter text. → Rich text content control
Department:	Choose an item. → Drop-down list content control
Week of:	Click here to enter a date. → Date picker content control

Full Time	☐	Part Time	☐

Check box content control

Setting Content Control Properties

- By default, Word inserts content controls using basic settings. For example, text controls are set to allow users to enter an unlimited number of text characters.
- You can customize the content control options in the item's Properties dialog box.

- For example, you can set text options to limit users to entering valid dates, or no more than ten characters, and you can assign a style to text entered in a plain text content control.
- You can also change the instructional text that displays in a content control.
- Each type of content control has its own set of properties. For example, you use properties to enter the items for a Drop-Down list content control.

Try It!   Setting Content Control Properties

1. In the **WTry19a_studentfirstname_ studentlastname** file, click on the Rich Text content control to select it.

2. On the Developer tab, in the Controls group, click the Properties button ⬚ to display the Content Control Properties dialog box.

3. In the Title box, type **Name**, and then click OK.

4. Click the Drop-Down List content control to select it, and click the Properties button.

   ✓ Notice that the properties for the Drop-Down List content control are different from the properties for the Rich Text content control.

5. In the Title box, type **Department**.

6. Under Drop-Down List Properties, click the Add button to display the Add Choice dialog box.

7. In the Display Name box, type **Marketing**, and then click OK.

8. Click the Add button again, type **Sales**, and click OK.

9. Click the Add button again, type **Site Support Group**, and click OK.

10. In the Content Control Properties dialog box, click OK.

11. Save the changes to **WTry19a_student firstname_studentlastname** and leave it open to use in the next Try It.

Protecting a Form

- It is a good idea to protect a form template.
- When a form is protected, users can enter information in the content controls, but cannot edit or format any other part of the document.
- The protection is extended to all documents based on the protected template.

- The options for protecting a document are found in the Restrict Formatting and Editing pane, which you can access using the Restrict Editing button on the Review tab of the Ribbon.

  ✓ You learn about other ways of protecting documents in Word, Lesson 20.

- You must stop the protection in order to edit or format the form.

Try It!   Protecting a Form

1. In the **WTry19a_studentfirstname_ studentlastname** file, on the Developer tab in the Protect group, click the Restrict Editing button 🔲 to display the Restrict Formatting and Editing pane.

2. In the task pane under Editing restrictions, click to select the Allow only this type of editing in the document check box.

3. Click the drop-down arrow and click Filling in forms.

4. Click Yes, Start Enforcing Protection, and in the Start Enforcing Protection dialog box, click OK.

5. Try to select the text *Name:* Note that Word only allows you to select content controls.

(continued)

Try It!   **Protecting a Form** *(continued)*

6 In the Restrict Formatting and Editing pane, click Stop Protection. Now, you can edit or format the document.

7 In the Restrict Formatting and Editing pane, click Yes, Start Enforcing Protection, and in the Start Enforcing Protection dialog box, click OK.

8 Close the **WTry19a_studentfirstname_ studentlastname** file, saving all changes. Leave Word open to use in the next Try It.

Filling Out a Form

- To fill out a form manually, simply print it.
- To fill out a form on-screen, create a new document based on the form template.

- If the form is protected, Word automatically selects the first content control so you can begin filling it out.
- If necessary, click to select a different content control.
- You can leave content controls blank.
- Use the following methods to enter data in content controls:

Table 19-1

Rich Text	Type
Plain Text	Type
Drop-down list	Click drop-down arrow and click item to enter
Date picker	Click drop-down arrow and click date to enter
Building block gallery	Click drop-down arrow on control's handle, then click item to enter.
Picture	Double-click icon in control, then use the Insert Picture dialog box to locate and select picture to insert
Check box	Click to select or clear box
Combo box	Click drop-down arrow and click item to enter

Try It!   **Filling Out a Form**

1 Use Windows Explorer to create a new document based on the **WTry19a_student firstname_studentlastname** document template.

  ✓ *Navigate to the location where the template file is stored, and double-click the template name.*

2 Save the file as a Word document with the name **WTry19b_studentfirstname_studentlastname** in the location where your teacher instructs you to store the files for this lesson.

  ✓ *Note that because the template is protected, the document based on the template is protected, as well.*

3 In the *Name* Rich Text Content Control, type your first and last names.

4 Click the *Department* Drop-Down List Content Control. A drop-down arrow becomes available.

5 Click the drop-down arrow and click Sales.

6 Click the *Date Picker* content control, click the drop-down arrow, and click today's date.

7 Click to select the *Part Time* Check Box Content Control.

8 Close the **WTry19b_studentfirstname_ studentlastname** file, saving all changes, and exit Word.

Analyzing Surveys

■ A survey lets you collect information that you can use to analyze trends and changes.

■ Watching and analyzing trends can help managers make informed business decisions.

■ For example, retailers watch for trends in the colors and products customers are buying so they know what items to stock in stores.

■ A well-designed survey makes it easier to identify trends. It usually includes a plan for whom to survey and the questions to ask, as well as a form for entering the answers to the survey questions.

Project 43—Create It

Training Survey

DIRECTIONS

1. Start Word and save the default blank document as a document template with the name **WProj43_studentfirstname_studentlastname** in the location where your teacher instructs you to store the files for this lesson.

2. Double-click in the header and type your full name and today's date.

3. With the insertion point on the first line of the document, press ENTER to insert a blank line.

4. Click **Insert** > **Table** 🔲 and drag across the table grid to insert a table with two columns and six rows.

5. Select the fourth row and click **Table Tools Layout** > **Merge Cells** 🔲.

6. Select the first three rows, and then drag the column divider to the left so the left column is approximately **1.5"** wide and the right column is approximately **5"** wide.

7. Select rows 5 through 6 and then drag the column divider to the right so the left column is approximately **4"** wide and the right column is approximately **2.5"** wide.

8. Select the right cell in row 5 and click **Tables Tools Layout** > **Split Cells** 🔲 > **OK**.

9. Enter the following text in your table:

10. Select the table and increase the font size to **16 points**.

11. If the Developer tab is not displayed on the Ribbon, click **File** > **Options** 🔲 > **Customize the Ribbon**, then, under Customize the Ribbon, click to select the **Developer** check box, and then click **OK**.

12. Click in row 1, column 2, click the **Developer** tab, then, in the Controls group, click the **Rich Text Content Control** button 🔠.

13. Click in row 2, column 2 and click the **Plain Text Content Control** button 🔠.

14. Click in row 3, column 2, and click the **Date Picker Content Control** button 📅.

15. Position the insertion point after the word *Yes* in row 5, column 2, press ENTER, and then click the **Check Box Content Control** button ☑.

16. Position the insertion point after the word *No* in row 5, column 3, press ENTER, and then click the **Check Box Content Control** button ☑.

17. Click in row 6, column 2, and then click the **Drop-Down List Content Control** button 🔲.

18. With the Drop-Down List Content Control selected, click the **Properties** button 🔲.

Name:	
Department:	
Date:	
Were you satisfied with the training class?	Yes	No
If you answered No, please select the option that best explains why not:	

19. Under Drop-Down List Properties, click the **Add** button, type **Too difficult**, and click **OK**.

20. Click the **Add** button again, type **Too easy**, and click **OK**.

21. Click the Add button again, type **Not what I expected**, and click **OK**.

22. In the Content Control Properties dialog box, click **OK**.

23. Check and correct the spelling and grammar in the file, and then save the changes.

24. Click the **Developer** tab, and then click the **Restrict Editing** button.

25. In the Restrict Formatting and Editing pane, under Editing restrictions, click to select the **Allow only this type of editing in the document** check box, then click the drop-down arrow and click **Filling in forms**.

26. Click **Yes, Start Enforcing Protection**, and then click **OK**. Close the task pane.

27. **With your teacher's permission**, print the document. It should look similar to Figure 19-1.

28. Close the file, saving all changes, and exit Word.

Figure 19-1

Firstname Lastname	
Today's Date	

Name:	Click here to enter text.	
Department:	Click here to enter text.	
Date:	Click here to enter a date.	
Were you satisfied with the training class?	Yes ☐	No ☐
If you answered No, please select the option that best explains why not:	Choose an item.	

Project 44—Apply It

Training Survey

1. Start Word and open **WProj44** from the data files for this lesson.

2. Save the file as a document template with the name **WProj44a_studentfirstname_ studentlastname** in the location where your teacher instructs you to store the files for this lesson.

3. Type your name and today's date in the document footer.

4. Display the Developer tab on the Ribbon, if necessary, and display table gridlines, if necessary.

5. In row 1, column 2, insert a **Plain Text Content Control**.

6. In row 2, column 2, insert a **Plain Text Content Control**.

7. In row 3, column 2, insert a **Date Picker Content Control**.

8. In rows 5 and 6, columns 2 and 3, on the line under the text, insert **Check Box Content Controls**.

9. In row 7, column 2, insert a **Drop-Down List Content Control**.

10. Set properties for the Drop-Down List Content Control to add the following items: **Too difficult, Too easy, Not what I expected, Inconvenient time**.

11. In row 8, columns 2, 3, and 4, on the line under the text, insert **Check Box Content Controls**.

12. In row 9, column 2, insert a **Drop-Down List Content Control**.

13. Set properties for the Drop-Down List Content Control to add the following items: **Live instructor, Online classroom, Individual training workstation**.

14. In row 10, column 2, insert a **Rich Text Content Control**.

15. Check and correct the spelling and grammar in the file, and then save the changes.

16. Protect the document so users can only fill in content controls on the form.

17. Close the task pane, and then close the document, saving all changes.

18. Create a new document based on the **WProj44a_studentfirstname_studentlastname** template and save it as a Word document with the name **WProj44b_studentfirstname_studentlastname** in the location where your teacher instructs you to save the files for this lesson.

19. Type your name in the *Name* Plain Text Content Control.

20. Type **Marketing** in the *Department* Plain Text Content Control.

21. Select today's date from the Date Picker Content Control.

22. Select the **Yes** check box for whether or not you have attended in-house training classes.

23. Select the **No** check box for whether or not you were satisfied.

24. For the reason why you were not satisfied, select **Inconvenient time** from the Drop-Down List Content Control.

25. Select the **Maybe** check box for whether or not you are interested in future classes.

26. Select **Individual training workstation** from the training method Drop-Down List Content Control.

27. In the Rich Text Content Control, type **I think there is potential benefit to in-house training but I need a more flexible schedule.**

28. **With your teacher's permission**, print the document. It should look similar to Figure 19-2.

29. Close the file, saving all changes, and exit Word.

Figure 19-2

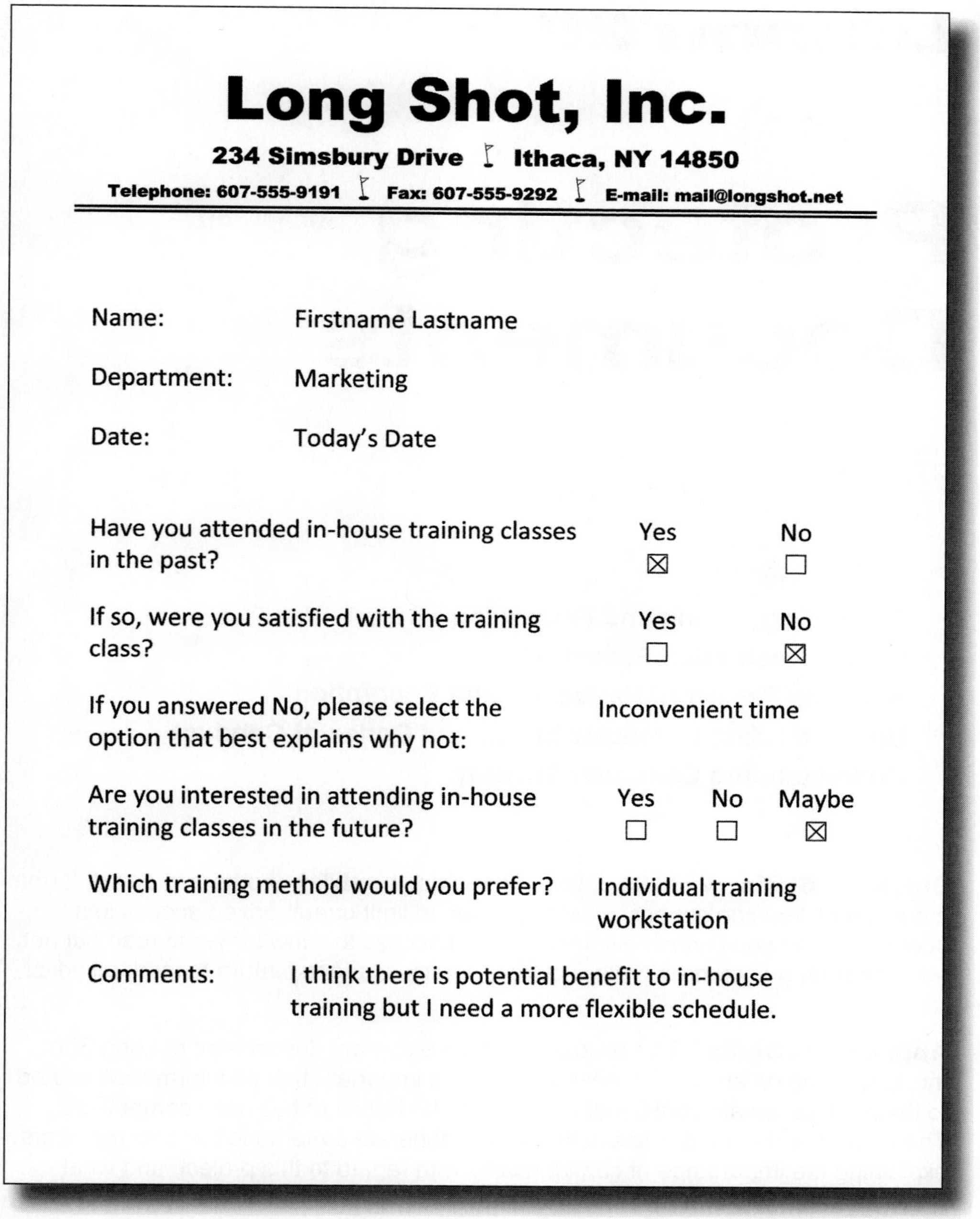

Long Shot, Inc.

234 Simsbury Drive ⌡ Ithaca, NY 14850

Telephone: 607-555-9191 ⌡ Fax: 607-555-9292 ⌡ E-mail: mail@longshot.net

Name: Firstname Lastname

Department: Marketing

Date: Today's Date

	Yes	No
Have you attended in-house training classes in the past?	☒	☐

	Yes	No
If so, were you satisfied with the training class?	☐	☒

If you answered No, please select the option that best explains why not: Inconvenient time

	Yes	No	Maybe
Are you interested in attending in-house training classes in the future?	☐	☐	☒

Which training method would you prefer?   Individual training workstation

Comments: I think there is potential benefit to in-house training but I need a more flexible schedule.

WORDS TO KNOW

Authenticated
Checked and verified as real or legitimate.

Code of conduct
A policy that defines the behavior expected of all employees.

Confidentiality
A legal and ethical principle that prevents the disclosure of secret information to unauthorized parties.

Encryption
Scrambling so as to be indecipherable.

Ethical
Conforming to accepted standards of social or professional behavior.

Firewall
Software or hardware that monitors information as it passes from a network to your computer in order to detect and prohibit the transfer of malicious programs.

Integrity
Adherence to a strict moral or ethical code.

Password
A string of characters used to authenticate the identity of a user, and to limit unauthorized access.

Phishing
A method of tricking computer users into divulging private or confidential information over the Internet.

Unethical
Not conforming to accepted standards of social or professional behavior.

Lesson 20

Protecting Documents

> ## What You Will Learn

Restricting Editing and Formatting
Setting Restriction Exceptions
Applying Password Protection and Encryption
Understanding Computer Ethics and Codes of Conduct
Understanding Computer Security

Software Skills   With Word, you can restrict the ability of others to edit or format a document. You can set password protection to limit unauthorized access to a document, and you can set different levels of access to allow others to read but not edit or format a document, or to require the track changes feature to mark all edits.

Application Skills   The research and development department at Long Shot, Inc. is working on an exciting new product. It is important that all information related to the product remain confidential and out of the hands of business competitors. The department manager has asked you to generate a memo to all team members explaining the importance of confidentiality with regard to this project, and what problems might arise from a breach of confidentiality. In this lesson, you will create the document and then set restrictions so that it cannot be changed.

What You Can Do

Restricting Editing and Formatting

- You can protect a document from unauthorized changes by restricting the ability of others to make edits or apply formatting.

- To restrict formatting changes, you use options in the Formatting Restrictions dialog box to limit the ability of others to modify selected styles and apply direct formatting.

- To restrict editing changes, you may select from four options:
  - Tracked changes. Use this option to force edits to display using revision marks.
  - Comments. Use this option to allow others to enter comments without being able to edit document text.
  - Filling in forms. Use this option to allow changes in content controls only.

    ✓ *Protecting forms is covered in Word, Lesson 19.*

  - No changes (Read only). Use this option when you do not want to allow any changes at all.

- The options for setting restrictions are found in the Restrict Formatting and Editing pane, which you can access using the Restrict Editing button on the Review tab of the Ribbon.

- When you open a protected document, the Restrict Formatting and Editing pane displays information about the changes you may or may not make to the document.

- You can also view information about restriction settings on the Info tab in Backstage view.

- You can remove the protection to enable unlimited editing.

WORDS TO KNOW

Virus
A malicious computer program designed to cause damage to a computer system.

Workgroup
A team, or group of individuals who work together on the same projects, usually connected via a network.

Worm
A self-replicating program designed to cause damage to a computer system.

Try It!   Restricting Editing and Formatting

1. Start Word and open **WTry20** from the data files for this lesson.

2. Save the file as **WTry20_studentfirstname_ studentlastname** in the location where your teacher instructs you to store the files for this lesson.

3. On the Review tab, in the Protect group, click the Restrict Editing 📄 button.

4. In the Restrict Formatting and Editing pane, under Formatting Restrictions, click to select the Limit formatting to a selection of styles check box and then click Settings to display the Formatting Restrictions dialog box.

5. In the Formatting Restrictions dialog box, click Recommended Minimum and click OK.

6. If necessary, in the warning dialog box, click No.

7. In the Restrict Formatting and Editing pane, under Editing restrictions, click to select the Allow only this type of editing in the document check box, then click the drop-down arrow and click Tracked changes.

8. Under Start enforcement click Yes, Start Enforcing Protection, then click OK without entering a password.

9. Click the Home tab on the Ribbon. Note that the Font and Paragraph group commands are not available because of the formatting restrictions.

(continued)

Try It!   Restricting Editing and Formatting *(continued)*

10 Select the heading *Mission Statement* and press `DEL`. The edit is displayed with revision marks because of the editing restrictions.

11 Save the changes to **WTry20_ studentfirstname_studentlastname** and keep it open to use in the next Try It.

A protected document

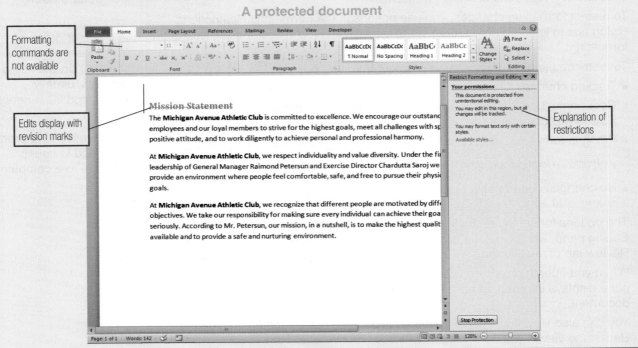

- Note that restrictions apply to documents even when they are copied or saved with a new name.

Setting Restriction Exceptions

- By default, an entire document is protected from changes made by all users.

- If you set formatting, read only, or comments restrictions, you may specify exceptions to allow access to all or parts of the document.

- Parts of the document that may be modified are set off by brackets and shading by default.

- You can use options in the Restrict Formatting and Editing pane to scroll directly to the areas you have permission to change.

Try It!   Setting Restriction Exceptions

1 In the **WTry20_studentfirstname_ studentlastname** document, in the Restrict Formatting and Editing pane, click Stop Protection.

2 Under *Editing Restrictions*, click the drop-down arrow and click No changes (Read only).

3 In the document, right-click the heading *Mission Statement* and click Reject Change.

4 Select the heading, then press and hold `CTRL` and select the second body paragraph.

5 Under *Exceptions (optional),* click to select the Everyone check box, then click Yes, Start Enforcing Protection, and click OK in the Start Enforcing Protection dialog box without entering a password.

(continued)

Try It!   Setting Restriction Exceptions *(continued)*

6 In the first paragraph in the document select the text *Michigan Avenue Athletic Club* and press DEL. Nothing happens, because restrictions are set to allow no changes.

7 In the second paragraph select the text *Michigan Avenue Athletic Club* and press DEL. The text is deleted, because everyone is allowed to edit or format the second paragraph.

8 In the Restrict Formatting and Editing pane, click Find Next Region I Can Edit. The heading is selected.

9 Edit the heading from *Mission Statement* to **Club Mission Statement**.

10 Save the changes to **WTry20_ studentfirstname_studentlastname** and keep it open to use in the next Try It.

Set restriction exceptions

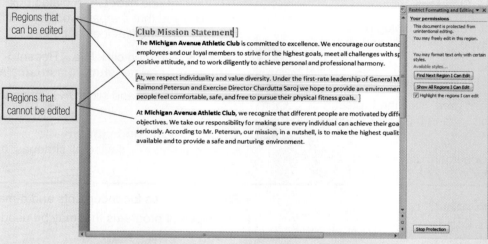

- You can allow access to everyone, or specific individuals or groups who have access.

- To add an individual or group to the exceptions list, you must know the workgroup identification, e-mail address, or Microsoft Windows user account name the he or she uses to log on to the system.

Applying Password Protection and Encryption

- To ensure that users cannot remove or change restriction settings, you can assign a **password** when you start enforcing protection. Only someone who enters the assigned password can unprotect the document or change the restriction settings.

- Note that the password protection applies to documents even when they are copied or saved with a new name.

- You can also assign a password and encrypt a document at the same time using options on the Info tab in Backstage view.

- **Encryption** increases the security of the document, because only **authenticated** owners of the document can remove the protection.

  ✓ *Authenticity is based on the use of a valid digital signature. Digital signatures are covered in Lesson 22.*

- Always create a strong password, which is one that cannot easily be guessed by unauthorized personnel.

- According to Microsoft, a strong password combines upper- and lowercase letters, numbers, and symbols, and is more than 8 characters long.

- Take care when assigning passwords. If you forget the password, you will not be able to access the document.

Try It!   Applying Password Protection and Encryption

1 In the **WTry20_studentfirstname_ studentlastname**, in the Restrict Formatting and Editing pane, click Stop Protection, and then click Yes, Start Enforcing Protection.

2 In the Start Enforcing Protection dialog box, in the Enter new password (optional) box, type **Try?W?20!**.

3 In the Reenter password to confirm box, type **Try?W?20!**, and then click OK.

4 In the pane, click Stop Protection.

5 In the Unprotect Document dialog box, in the Password box, type **Try?W?20!** and click OK.

6 Click the File tab to display Backstage view. The Info tab should display by default.

7 In the Permissions area, click the Protect Document button 🔒 and then click Encrypt with Password.

8 In the Encrypt Document dialog box, in the Password box, type **Try?W?20!** and click OK.

9 In the Reenter password box, type **Try?W?20!** and click OK. Note that under *Permissions* it states that a password is required to open the document.

10 Close the document saving all changes.

11 Click File > Recent and click **WTry20_student firstname_studentlastname** to open it again. A password dialog box displays.

12 In the Enter password to open file box, type **TRY?w20!** and click OK. A dialog box informing you that the password is incorrect displays, and the file does not open.

13 Click OK, and then click File > Recent > **WTry20 _studentfirstname_studentlastname** again.

14 Type **Try?W?20!** and click OK to open the document.

15 Close **WTry20_studentfirstname_ studentlastname**, saving all changes, and exit Word.

Understanding Computer Ethics and Codes of Conduct

- In general, the ethics for computer use should follow the same basic code of ethics for all business and personal conduct.

- In other words, employees and employers should conduct themselves with honesty and **integrity**, according to legal and corporate policies.

- Most companies and organizations establish corporate computer application policies or rules, as well as policies for using the Internet and e-mail.

- These policies address the legal and social aspects of computer use and are designed to protect privacy while respecting personal and corporate values and adhering to federal and local laws.

- Some topics typically covered by corporate computer application policies include:
  - The type of language allowed in documents and messages.
  - Permissions for accessing documents and data.
  - The amount of time allowed for personal Internet and e-mail use.
  - The types of Web sites that may be accessed from corporate computers.

- Storage policies for documents and e-mail.
- The types of programs that may be used on corporate computers.

- Employers expect employees to have integrity and to conduct themselves in a professional and ethical manner.

- Most employers have a written policy called a **code of conduct** that specifies the rights and responsibilities of employees.

- The codes vary depending on the organization. Most list the types of behavior that are considered acceptable, as well as behavior that is considered unacceptable.

- Some typical expectations include:
  - Reporting **unethical** or illegal behavior in others.
  - Respecting the **confidentiality** of clients, co-workers, and employers.
  - Arriving and leaving on time.
  - Wearing professional attire in the workplace.

- Most codes also specify the consequences of failing to meet the standards.

- For a first or minor infraction, the punishment might be a warning letter placed in an employment file.

- For a severe or repeated infraction, the punishment might be dismissal.

Understanding Computer Security

- Maintaining the security of computer systems is a vital part of any business.
- Many situations can put your computer information at risk.
  - Disasters such as a flood or fire might make a hard disk unusable.
  - Accidentally knocking out a power cord might delete unsaved changes to a file.
  - A thief might steal your notebook computer or external hard drive.
  - Malicious software such as a **virus** or **worm** might corrupt your data.
  - A **phishing** Web site might capture private information such as passwords and financial data.
- Some steps you can take to safeguard your data include saving frequently, backing up to a remote location on a regular basis, and storing backup data in a fire- and flood-proof safe.
- You should activate a **firewall** to prevent unauthorized programs from accessing your system via a network.

- You should use a malicious software detector tool, such as Windows Defender, to monitor and protect your system from malware such as worms.
- You should use a virus protection program to prohibit, detect, and remove computer viruses.
- You should also learn about the features and tools that your operating system has for preventing data loss:
  - You can use System Restore to revert to a restore point to undo changes.
  - You can use system recovery tools such as Startup Repair or Memory Diagnostic.
- Computer system security usually includes hardware and software devices as well as managerial procedures that work together to protect the system from unauthorized access, to make sure the data is available when needed, and to maintain the integrity of the data.
- Types of security devices include firewalls, virus detection programs, passwords, and data encryption.
- A breach in security compromises data stored on the system, resulting in lost revenues.
- In addition, there are laws governing computer security, which means businesses may be legally responsible for a breach.

Project 45—Create It

Confidentiality Memo

DIRECTIONS

1. Start Word, if necessary.
2. Create a new blank document and save it as **WProj45_studentfirstname_studentlastname** in the location where your teacher instructs you to store the files for this lesson.
3. Display the rulers and nonprinting characters, if necessary.
4. Set paragraph spacing **Before** to **24** points and paragraph spacing **After** to **36** points.
5. Type **MEMO**, and press ENTER.
6. Apply the **No Spacing** style, and then set a left tab stop at **0.75"** on the horizontal ruler.
7. Type **To:**, press TAB, and type **Team Members**. Press ENTER.

8. Type **From:**, press TAB, and type your own name. Press ENTER.
9. Type **Date:**, press TAB, and type or insert today's date. Press ENTER.
10. Type **Subject:**, press TAB, and type **Confidentiality**. Press ENTER twice.
11. Apply the **Normal** style and type the following paragraphs, as shown in Figure 20-1:

    As you all know, we are working on a new and exciting product which the company expects will completely revolutionize the golf equipment industry. This memo is simply a reminder of the Long Shot, Inc. corporate policy on confidentiality and ethical behavior.

> Confidentiality in business refers to the protection of proprietary and secret information. In some businesses, the information belongs to a client, and it is the responsibility of the business to make sure no one else can access the information. In our case, the information belongs to the corporation, and it is our responsibility to make sure no one outside the company gains access.

12. Check and correct the spelling and grammar in the document, and then save the changes.

13. Click the **Review** tab, then, in the Protect group, click the **Restrict Editing** button.

14. In the Restrict Formatting and Editing pane, under *Formatting Restrictions*, click to select the **Limit formatting to a selection of styles** check box and then click **Settings**.

15. In the Formatting Restrictions dialog box, click **Recommended Minimum** and click **OK**.

16. If necessary, in the warning dialog box, click **No**.

17. In the Restrict Formatting and Editing pane, under *Editing Restrictions*, click to select the **Allow only this type of editing in the document** check box, then click the drop-down arrow and click **Comments**.

18. In the document, select the last paragraph.

19. In the task pane, under *Exceptions (optional)*, click to select the **Everyone** check box.

20. Under *Start Enforcement* click **Yes, Start Enforcing Protection**.

21. In the Start Enforcing Protection dialog box, in the Enter new password (optional) box, type **!45?Project&**.

22. In the Reenter password to confirm box, type **!45?Project&**, and then click **OK**.

23. Select the text *MEMO* and try to apply the Title style.

24. Select the first paragraph and press ⎡DEL⎤.

25. Click **Review > New Comment** and type **What about code of conduct?**

26. Click outside the comment balloon, then in the task pane, click **Find Next Region I Can Edit**, to select the last paragraph. Apply the **No Spacing** style.

27. **With your teacher's permission**, print the document. It should look similar to Figure 20-1.

28. Close the document, saving all changes, and exit Word.

Figure 20-1

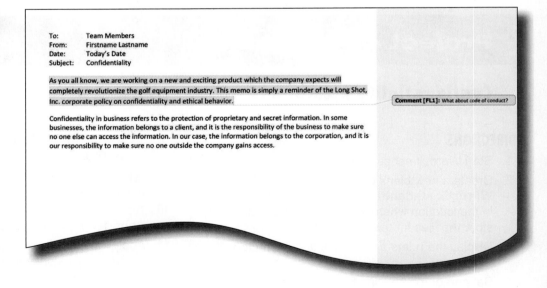

Project 46—Apply It

Confidentiality Memo

DIRECTIONS

1. Start Word, if necessary, and open **WProj46** from the data files for this lesson.

2. Save it as **WProj46studentfirstname_ studentlastname** in the location where your teacher instructs you to store the files for this lesson.

3. Replace the sample text *Student's Name* with your own name, and *Today's Date* with the actual date.

4. Set options so users cannot apply any styles to the document, but do not remove existing styles.

5. Restrict editing to tracked changes, and start enforcement. Do not apply a password.

6. Use the Info tab in Backstage view to encrypt the document with the password **&LSI?46**.

7. Close the document, saving all changes.

8. Open the document, using the correct password.

9. **With your teacher's permission,** print the document.

10. Close the document, saving all changes, and exit Word.

Lesson 21

Inspecting and Checking Documents

WORDS TO KNOW

Compatibility
The ability to work together without conflict.

Hidden text
Text that is formatted with the Hidden font effect.

Invisible Content
Objects that have been formatted as invisible.

> **What You Will Learn**

Using the Document Inspector
Checking Compatibility

Software Skills   Use the Document Inspector to remove personal or confidential information from your Word documents. Check Compatibility to identify features that might not be compatible with earlier versions of Microsoft Office Word.

Application Skills   Long Shot, Inc. has been working on a new mission statement. In this lesson, you will create and edit versions of the document and prepare them for distribution to all department managers for review. Before distribution, you will use the Document Inspector to locate and remove any personal or confidential information that might be part of the document. Also, because you know some managers are using previous versions of Word, you will check the document for compatibility problems.

What You Can Do

Using the Document Inspector

- Run the Document Inspector to identify information you might not want to share with other people working with your document files.
- Once you identify the content, you have the option of keeping it with the file or removing it.
- For example, you might want to delete comments before passing a file on to another reviewer, or remove document properties which might include personal or confidential information.

- After removing document properties, document properties will no longer automatically be saved with the file. You can select to allow the information to be saved on the Info tab in Backstage view.
- When you start the Document Inspector, you can select to check for the following types of information:

- Comments, Revisions, Versions, and Annotations
- Document Properties and Personal Information
- Custom XML Data
- Headers, footers, and watermarks
- Invisible Content
- Hidden Text

Try It!   Using the Document Inspector

1 Start Word and open **WTry21** from the data files for this lesson.

2 Save the file as **WTry21a_studentfirstname_ studentlastname** in the location where your teacher instructs you to store the files for this lesson.

3 Double-click in the Header and type your name and today's date.

4 Select the text *MEMO* and then click Review > New Comment 🗨. Type **Change the font for this heading**.

5 Save the changes to the file, then click the File tab.

6 On the Info tab in Backstage view, in the Prepare for Sharing area, click the Check for Issues button 📄, and then click Inspect Document. By default, all options are selected.

7 In the Document Inspector dialog box, click to clear the Custom XML Data check box, verify that all other options are selected, and then click Inspect.

8 To the right of Comments, Revisions, Versions, and Annotations, click Remove All.

9 To the right of Document Properties and Personal Information, click Remove All.

10 To the right of Headers, Footers, and Watermarks, click Remove All.

11 Click Reinspect, and then click Inspect.

12 Click Close. Note on the Info tab in Backstage view that the author name and other document properties have been removed.

13 On the Info tab in Backstage view, in the Prepare for Sharing area, click Allow this information to be saved in your file.

14 Click the Print tab in Backstage view. Note in the preview area that the comment, watermark and header have been removed.

15 Save the **WTry21a_studentfirstname_ studentlastname** document and leave it open to use in the next Try It.

The Document Inspector dialog box after inspecting

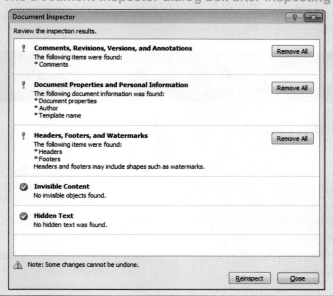

Check Compatibility

- You can check your Word 2010 documents to identify features that might not be supported by earlier versions of Word, such as content controls.

- By default, the compatibility checker feature runs automatically when you use the Save As command to save a document in Word 97-2003 format.

- After checking the document, Word displays a summary list of incompatible features.

- The summary list includes the number of times the feature is used and explains the action Word 2010 will take to resolve the incompatibility issue when the document is saved in an earlier format.

- The changes are made only in the documents saved in Word 2007 or Word 97-2003 format; the original Word 2010 documents remain unchanged.

- You can also start the check from the Check for Issues drop-down menu in the Prepare for Sharing area on the Info tab in Backstage view.

- Use Word Help to view a table listing Word 2010 features that are not available in Word 97-2003 or Word 2007. Start Help, search for 2007 compatibility, and click the link to Compatibility changes between versions.

Try It!   Check Compatibility

1. In the **WTry21a_studentfirstname_ studentlastname** file, click File > Check for Issues 📄.

2. Click Check Compatibility.

3. Click OK.

4. Click File > Save As 🖫.

5. Type the file name **WTry21b_student firstname_studentlastname**, then click the Save as type button, click Word 97-2003 Document, and click Save.

6. In the Microsoft Word Compatibility Checker dialog box, click Continue to save the document in the earlier format.

7. Close the **WTry21b_studentfirstname_student lastname** document saving all changes, and exit Word.

The results of a compatibility check

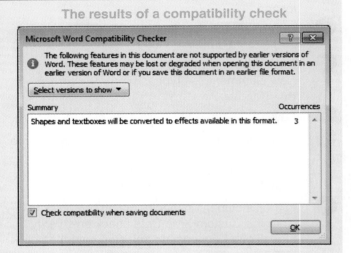

Project 47—Create It

Mission Statement Version 1

DIRECTIONS

1. Start Word and save the default blank document as **WProj47a_studentfirstname_studentlastname** in the location where your teacher instructs you to store the files for this lesson.

2. On the first line of the document type: **Prepared by** and then type your name.

3. Press ENTER, click the **Developer** tab on the Ribbon, and, in the Controls group, click the **Date Picker Content Control** button 🗓.

4. With the Date Picker Content Control selected, click its drop-down arrow and click today's date.

5. Click to the right of the Content Control in the document, press ENTER to start a new line, type **Mission Statement Version 1**, and press ENTER.

6. Type the following two paragraphs:

   Long Shot, Inc. is committed to excellence. In order to meet the needs of our clients, we encourage and support creativity at every level of our organization. Our goal is to maintain the highest standards, pursue the extraordinary, and guarantee customer satisfaction.

   We respect all employees as individuals and believe that fostering a strong community within the workplace strengthens our position in the marketplace. We are confident that our commitment to quality will make us leaders in our industry.

7. Select the word *excellence* in the first sentence, click **Review** > **New Comment** 🗔, and type **Not sure I agree with this!**

8. Click **Page Layout** > **Watermark** 🄰 and, in the Watermark gallery, click the **CONFIDENTIAL 1** style.

9. Check the spelling and grammar in the document, correct errors, and save the changes.

10. Click the **File** tab to display Backstage view. On the Info tab, in the Properties pane, click **Add a title** and type **LSI Mission Statement v.1**.

11. Under Related People, click **Add an author** and type **Communications Assistant**.

12. Save the changes to your document, then, in the Prepare for Sharing area, click the **Check for Issues** button 🗐 and click **Inspect Document**.

13. Verify that all check boxes are selected, and then click **Inspect**.

14. To the right of Comments, Revisions, Versions, and Annotations, click **Remove All**.

15. To the right of Headers, Footers, and Watermarks, click **Remove All**.

16. Click **Reinspect**, and then click **Inspect**.

17. In the Document Inspector dialog box, click **Close**.

18. Click the **Check for Issues** button 🗐 again and click **Check Compatibility**. After reviewing the summary, click **OK**.

19. Click **File** > **Save As** 🖫.

10. Type the file name **WProj47b_studentfirstname_studentlastname**, then click the **Save as type** button, click **Word 97-2003 Document**, and click **Save**.

11. In the Microsoft Word Compatibility Checker dialog box, click **Continue** to save the document in the earlier format.

22. Click on the date. Notice that it has been converted from a Content Control to plain text. It remains a Content Control in the **WProj47a_studentfirstname_studentlastname** file.

23. **With your teacher's permission,** print the document. It should look similar to Figure 21-1.

24. Close **WProj47a_studentfirstname_studentlastname**, saving all changes and exit Word.

Figure 21-1

Prepared by Firstname Lastname

Today's Date

Mission Statement Version 1

Long Shot, Inc. is committed to excellence. In order to meet the needs of our clients, we encourage and support creativity at every level of our organization. Our goal is to maintain the highest standards, pursue the extraordinary, and guarantee customer satisfaction.

We respect all employees as individuals and believe that fostering a strong community within the workplace strengthens our position in the marketplace. We are confident that our commitment to quality will make us leaders in our industry.

Project 48—Apply It

Revised Mission Statement

DIRECTIONS

1. Start Word and open **WProj48** from the data files for this lesson.

2. Save the file as **WProj48a_studentfirstname_ studentlastname** in the location where your teacher instructs you to store the files for this lesson.

3. Replace the sample text Student's Name with your own name.

4. Click the Date Picker Content Control to select it, click the drop-down arrow and click today's date.

5. Save the changes, then run the Document Inspector to identify content you might want to remove before distributing the document.

6. Close the Document Inspector without taking any action.

7. Review the comments in the document.

8. Review the document properties.

9. Note the content of the header and the watermark.

10. Run the Document Inspector again, and remove comments, document properties, and personal information.

11. Save the changes to the document.

12. Check the document for compatibility issues and review the summary.

13. Save the document as a Word 97-2003 Document with the name **WProj48b_studentfirstname_ studentlastname**

14. **With your teacher's permission**, print the document. It should look similar to Figure 21-2.

15. Close **WProj48a_studentfirstname_student lastname**, saving all changes and exit Word.

Figure 21-2

LSI Mission Statement, Final

Prepared by Firstname Lastname

Today's Date

Mission Statement

Customer Satisfaction
Long Shot, Inc. is committed to providing quality service to all of our clients at every level of our organization. Our ultimate goal is to hear our clients say, "Thank you. That is just what we wanted."

Employee Well-Being
Second only to customer satisfaction is the happiness and well-being of our employees. The employees at Long Shot, Inc. are encouraged to set personal and professional goals. We respect all employees as individuals and believe that fostering a strong community within the workplace strengthens our position in the marketplace.

Conclusion
At Long Shot, Inc. we vow to maintain the highest standards, pursue the extraordinary, and guarantee customer satisfaction. We are confident that our commitment to quality will make us leaders in our industry.

Lesson 22

Marking a Document as Final and Using Digital Signatures

> ➤ **What You Will Learn**

   Marking a Document as Final
   Understanding Digital Signatures
   Using a Visible Digital Signature
   Using an Invisible Digital Signature
   Verifying Signature Details
   Analyzing Legal Documents

Software Skills   Use a visible or invisible digital signature to verify the authenticity of a document. Once you add a digital signature, the document is automatically marked as final and cannot be edited. Mark a document as final to indicate to others that they are viewing a completed or final version of a document, and to prevent others from making unauthorized or inadvertent changes to the document. Maintain the integrity and security of your computer system by learning how to protect it from disasters, accidents, and malicious intent.

Application Skills   New employees at Executive Recruitment Resources are asked to sign two documents: a job offer acceptance letter and a non-disclosure agreement. In this lesson you will create versions of each that can be signed using digital signatures.

What You Can Do

Marking a Document as Final

- Mark a document as final to discourage others from editing it.

- A document marked as final opens in Read-only mode, and a Marked as Final icon 📝 displays in the status bar.

- The Ribbon does not display; instead an Information bar displays the message *Marked as Final: An author has marked this document as final to discourage editing.*

- You can click the Edit Anyway button on the Information bar to edit the document.

- The Mark as Final command is available from the Protect Documents drop-down menu on the Info tab in Backstage view.

- To prohibit editing completely, set editing restrictions and password protection, as explained in Word, Lesson 20.

Try It!   **Marking a Document as Final**

1 Open the **WTry22** file from the data files for this lesson.

2 Save the document as **WTry22_student firstname_studentlastname** in the location where your teacher instructs you to store the files for this lesson.

3 Click the File tab to display Backstage view.

4 In the Permissions area, click the Protect Document button 🔐 and then click Mark as Final.

5 Click OK, and then click OK again in the confirmation dialog box. Click the Home tab, and note the changes to the document window.

6 Select the text *Photo* in the title and press `DEL`. A message in the status bar indicates the action is not allowed.

7 Click Edit Anyway on the Information bar, and then press `DEL`.

8 Save the changes to **WTry22_studentfirstname _studentlastnam** and keep it open to use in the next Try It.

A document marked as final

Photo Permission Form

Information bar

By signing below, I am granting permission for my photograph to be published. I understand and agree that I will not be paid or compensated in any way for the use of the image.
I also agree that the image may be published on a Web site, in a book, or in related advertising materials for no compensation.

Click here to enter text.	Click here to enter a date.	
Name	Date	
Click here to enter text.		
Street Address		
Click here to enter text.	Click here to enter text.	Click here to enter text.
City	State	Zip

Marked as Final icon

Understanding Digital Signatures

- You can apply a **visible digital signature** or an **invisible digital signature** to a document.

- A **digital signature** can be used like a written signature to verity the authenticity of information.

- A digital signature indicates the following:
  - The signer is who he or she claims to be.
  - The content has not changed since the digital signature was applied.
  - The signer read and approved the document.

- A digital signature is created using a **digital certificate**, which can be obtained from an authorized vendor or from the internal security administrator responsible for your computer system.

- Windows usually creates a personal digital certificate—called a digital ID—for each user account.

- If you attempt to add a digital signature to a document, but you do not have a digital certificate, Word will display the Get a Digital ID dialog box, from which you can create your own personal digital certificate.

- A personal digital certificate is authorized only on the computer on which it is created.

- Once a digital signature is added, the document is marked as final, and the Signatures icon 🧑 displays in the status bar.

Using a Visible Digital Signature

- A visible digital signature is similar to a standard signature line on a contract or other type of agreement.

- When you add a visible digital signature, Word inserts a **signature line** object into the document.

- You can use the options in the Signature Setup dialog box to add information about the signer, such as a name and a title, as well as instructions for the signer on how to add a digital signature.

- To sign the document, the signer opens the Sign dialog box in which he or she may type a signature or insert a digital image of a signature.

  ✓ If the signer is using a tablet PC, he or she may use the Inking feature to sign the document.

- Once the digital signature is signed, the document is marked as final. If edits are made, the signature becomes invalid, and is removed from the document.

- If there is a signature line in a document that has not been signed, the information bar displays a message that the document needs to be signed.

Try It!   Using a Visible Digital Signature

1. In the **WTry22_studentfirstname_studentlast name** document, position the insertion point in the bottom row of the table.

2. Click the Insert tab, and then, in the Text group, click the Signature Line button 🖊. If a Microsoft Word message dialog box displays prompting you to explore Signature Services, click OK to continue.

3. In the Signature Setup dialog box, in the Suggested signer box, type your name.

4. In the Suggested signer's title box, type **Student**.

5. In the Suggested signer's e-mail address box, type your e-mail address.

6. Click to clear the Show sign date in signature line check box.

Signature Setup dialog box

(continued)

Try It!   **Using a Visible Digital Signature** *(continued)*

7 Click OK. Word inserts the signature line at the insertion point location.

8 Double-click the signature line object. (Again, if Word prompts you to explore Signature Services, click OK to continue.)

  ✓ *If you do not already have a digital ID, Word displays the Get a Digital ID dialog box. Follow your teacher's instructions, or click to select the Create your own digital ID, click OK, fill in your information in the Create a Digital ID dialog box, and click Create.*

9 In the Sign dialog box, in the box to the right of the large X, type your name as you entered it in your digital ID.

  ✓ *If you have an image file of your signature, click Select Image, then locate and insert the image file. Use a scanner to create an image file of your signature.*

10 Click Sign, and then click OK in the confirmation dialog box. Word displays your name on the signature line and marks the document as final.

11 Keep **WTry22_studentfirstname_student lastname** open to use in the next Try It.

Document signed with a visible digital signature

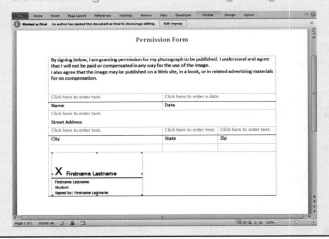

Using an Invisible Digital Signature

■ An invisible digital signature is attached to the document but does not display as an actual signature in the document.

■ You can verify that the document has been signed by viewing the document's digital signature(s) in the Signatures pane.

Try It!   **Using an Invisible Digital Signature**

1 In the **WTry22_studentfirstname_ studentlastname** document, in the Information bar, click Edit Anyway, and then click Yes, and then click OK in the confirmation dialog box.

2 Click the File tab to display Backstage view.

3 In the Permissions area, click the Protect Document button 📄 and click Add a Digital Signature. (Click OK if Word prompts you to explore Signature Services.)

4 In the Sign dialog box, in the Purpose for signing the document dialog box, type **Verify authenticity**, click Sign, and then click OK. Word attaches the invisible signature, and marks the document as final.

5 In Backstage view, in the Signed Document area, click the View Signatures button 🔍. Word displays the Signatures pane listing all signatures attached to the document.

6 Keep the **WTry22_studentfirstname_student lastname** document open to use in the next Try It.

Verifying Signature Details

- An authorized digital signature is listed as having a valid digital certificate.

- If the certificate is not valid, it is listed as Invalid.

- If the status of a certificate cannot be verified, the signature is listed as having certificate issues.

- Some factors that might cause an invalid certificate or certificate issues include:
  - The content of the document has been changed since the signature was applied.
  - The document has been saved with a new name or in a new location.
  - The digital signature has a time limit, which has expired.
  - The certificate associated with the signature is unauthorized.

- You can view information about a signature in the Signature Details dialog box, including information about the certificate. You can also manually change a certificate from invalid to valid in the Signature Details dialog box, by adding it to a list of trusted certificates.

Try It!   Verifying Signature Details

1. In the **WTry22_studentfirstname_student lastname** document, in the Signatures pane, under Valid signatures, rest the mouse pointer on your signature and click the down arrow that displays.

   ✓ *If the Signatures pane is not displayed, click File > View Signatures.*

2. Click Signature Details to display the Signature Details dialog box.

3. Click View to display the Certificate dialog box.

4. Click OK, and then click Close.

5. Close the **WTry22_studentfirstname_ studentlastname** document, and exit Word.

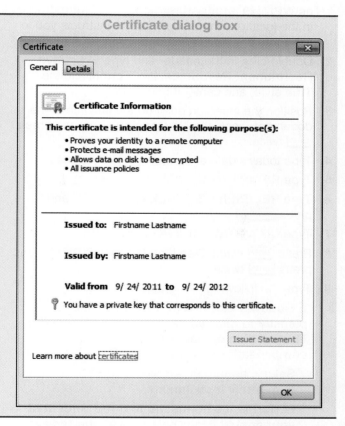

Certificate dialog box

Analyzing Legal Documents

- Legal documents are used to insure the legal rights of people, businesses, groups, or organizations.

- Legal documents may be as simple as a handwritten note that is signed by all concerned parties and witnessed by a third party.

- Alternatively, legal documents may be long, complex, and written using legal terms and language.

- Many legal documents are forms that combine text and blank spaces or form fields where you may enter customized information.

- Other legal documents are reports, case studies, or opinions that include references to legal authorities.

  ✓ *Creating a table of authorities is covered in Word Lesson 28.*

- Some common legal forms include the following:
  - Bill of Sale
  - Last Will and Testament
  - Rental Agreement

- General Release
- Living Will
- Non-disclosure Agreement

- The laws governing legal documents vary from state to state.
- You may be able to find legal document forms on the Internet.

Project 49—Create It

Job Offer Acceptance Letter

DIRECTIONS

1. Start Word and save the default blank document as **WProj49_studentfirstname_studentlastname** in the location where your teacher instructs you to store the files for this lesson.
2. Double-click in the header and type **Executive Recruitment Resources, Inc.** Format it in the **Title** style, and center it horizontally.
3. Position the insertion point on the first line of the document, apply the **No Spacing** style, and press **ENTER** twice.
4. Type today's date and press **ENTER** three times.
5. Type **RECIPIENT'S NAME** and press **ENTER**.
6. Type **RECIPIENT'S STREET ADDRESS** and press **ENTER**.
7. Type **CITY, STATE and POSTAL CODE**.
8. Press **ENTER** twice, then type **Dear RECIPIENT:** and press **ENTER** twice.
9. Type the following paragraphs:

   Executive Recruitment Resources, Inc. is pleased to offer you a position as JOB TITLE. The position comes with the following compensation:

   Salary: annual gross salary of $XXXXX, paid in monthly installments.

   Performance bonus: up to three percent of your annual gross salary, paid quarterly.

   Benefits: standard benefits for salaried, exempt employees, including the following:
   - **401(k) retirement account**
   - **Health, dental, life, and disability insurance**
   - **Educational assistance**
   - **Personal days for vacation, illness, and family care based on length of employment**

   To accept this offer, please sign and date this letter below and return it to me. Please contact me if you have any questions or concerns.

10. Press **ENTER** twice, type **Sincerely**, press **ENTER** four times, type your name, press **ENTER**, type **Human Resources**, and press **ENTER** three times.
11. Type **I**, press the underline key **40** times, and type **, accept the position of JOB TITLE.**
12. Press **ENTER**, press **TAB**, and type **Print Name**.
13. Press **ENTER**, then insert a table with two columns and two rows.
14. Merge the cells in the first row.
15. In the left cell of the second row, type **Type or insert Digital Signature above**.
16. In the right cell of the second row, type **Date:**, then click **Developer > Date Picker Content Control**.
17. Select the table then click the **Table Tools Design** tab, click the **Borders** drop-down arrow, and click **No Border**.
18. Save the changes to the document.
19. Position the insertion point in the top row of the table.
20. Click the **Insert** tab, and then, in the Text group, click the **Signature Line** button. If a Microsoft Word message dialog box displays prompting you to explore Signature Services, click **OK** to continue.
21. In the Signature Setup dialog box, in the Suggested signer box, type **Recipient**.
22. In the Instructions to the signer box, replace the existing text with **Sign here if you accept this offer.**
23. Click to clear the **Show sign date in signature line** check box.
24. Click **OK**. Word inserts the signature line at the insertion point location.
25. Check and correct the spelling and grammar in the document.
26. **With your teachers permission**, print the document. It should look similar to Figure 22-1.
27. Click the **File** tab to display Backstage view.

28. In the Permissions area, click the **Protect Document** button 🔖 and click **Add a Digital Signature**. (Click **OK** if Word prompts you to explore Signature Services.)

29. In the Sign dialog box, in the Purpose for signing the document dialog box, type **Verify authenticity**, click **Sign**, and then click **OK**. Word attaches the invisible signature, and marks the document as final.

30. Close the document, and exit Word.

Figure 22-1

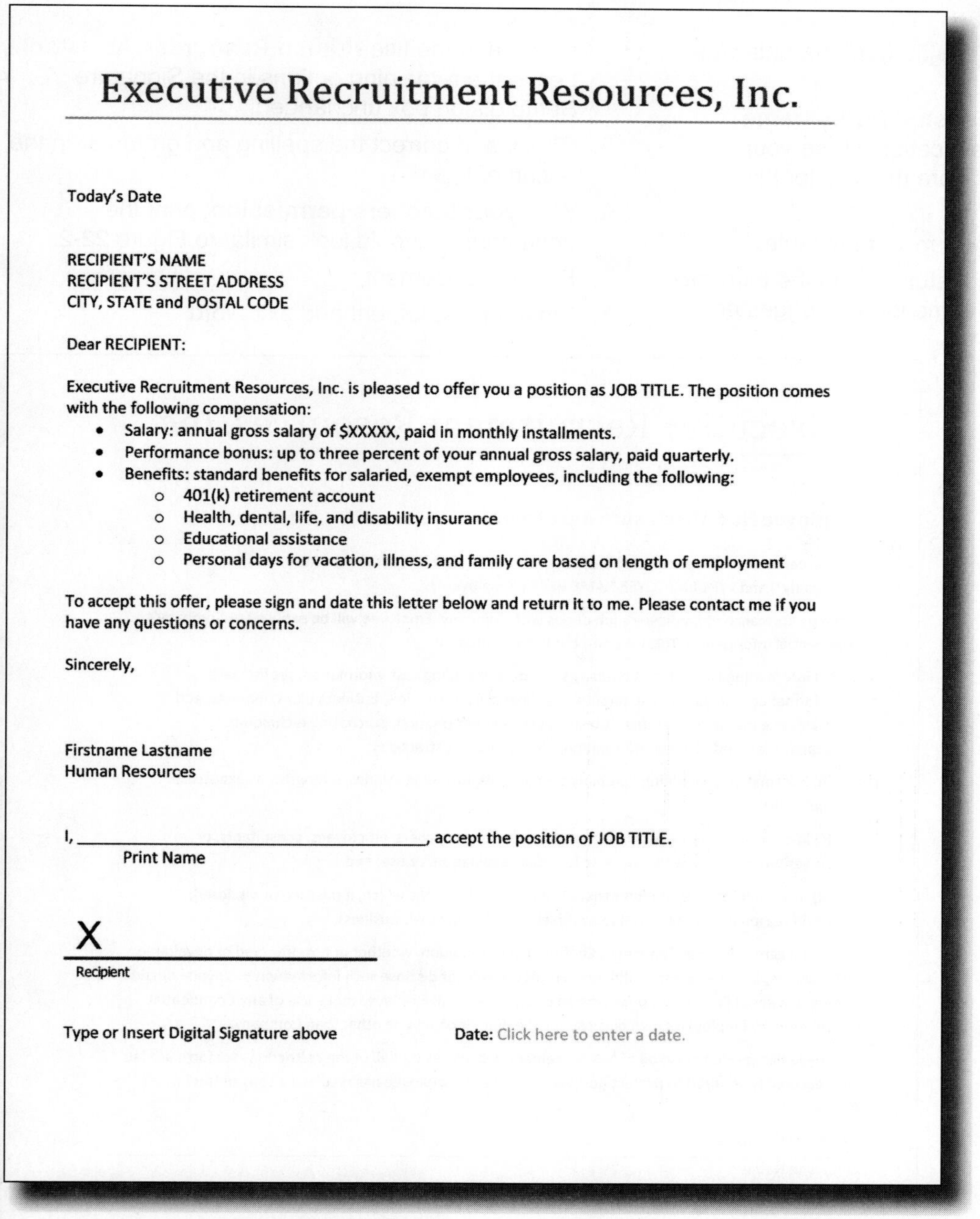

Executive Recruitment Resources, Inc.

Today's Date

RECIPIENT'S NAME
RECIPIENT'S STREET ADDRESS
CITY, STATE and POSTAL CODE

Dear RECIPIENT:

Executive Recruitment Resources, Inc. is pleased to offer you a position as JOB TITLE. The position comes with the following compensation:

- Salary: annual gross salary of $XXXXX, paid in monthly installments.
- Performance bonus: up to three percent of your annual gross salary, paid quarterly.
- Benefits: standard benefits for salaried, exempt employees, including the following:
  - 401(k) retirement account
  - Health, dental, life, and disability insurance
  - Educational assistance
  - Personal days for vacation, illness, and family care based on length of employment

To accept this offer, please sign and date this letter below and return it to me. Please contact me if you have any questions or concerns.

Sincerely,

Firstname Lastname
Human Resources

I, _____, accept the position of JOB TITLE.
     Print Name

X _____
  Recipient

Type or Insert Digital Signature above   **Date:** Click here to enter a date.

Project 50—Apply It

Non-Disclosure Agreement

1. Start Word and open **WProj50** from the data files for this lesson.
2. Save the file as **WProj50_studentfirstname_ studentlastname** in the location where your teacher instructs you to store the files for this lesson.
3. Type your name in the first row of the table.
4. Insert a visible digital signature line in the third row of the table, using your name for the suggested

signer and the title **Human Resources Assistant**. Leave the remaining options in the Signature Setup dialog box unchanged.
5. Check and correct the spelling and grammar in the document.
6. Wit**h your teachers permission**, print the document. It should look similar to Figure 22-2.
7. Sign the document.
8. Close the document and exit Word.

Figure 22-2

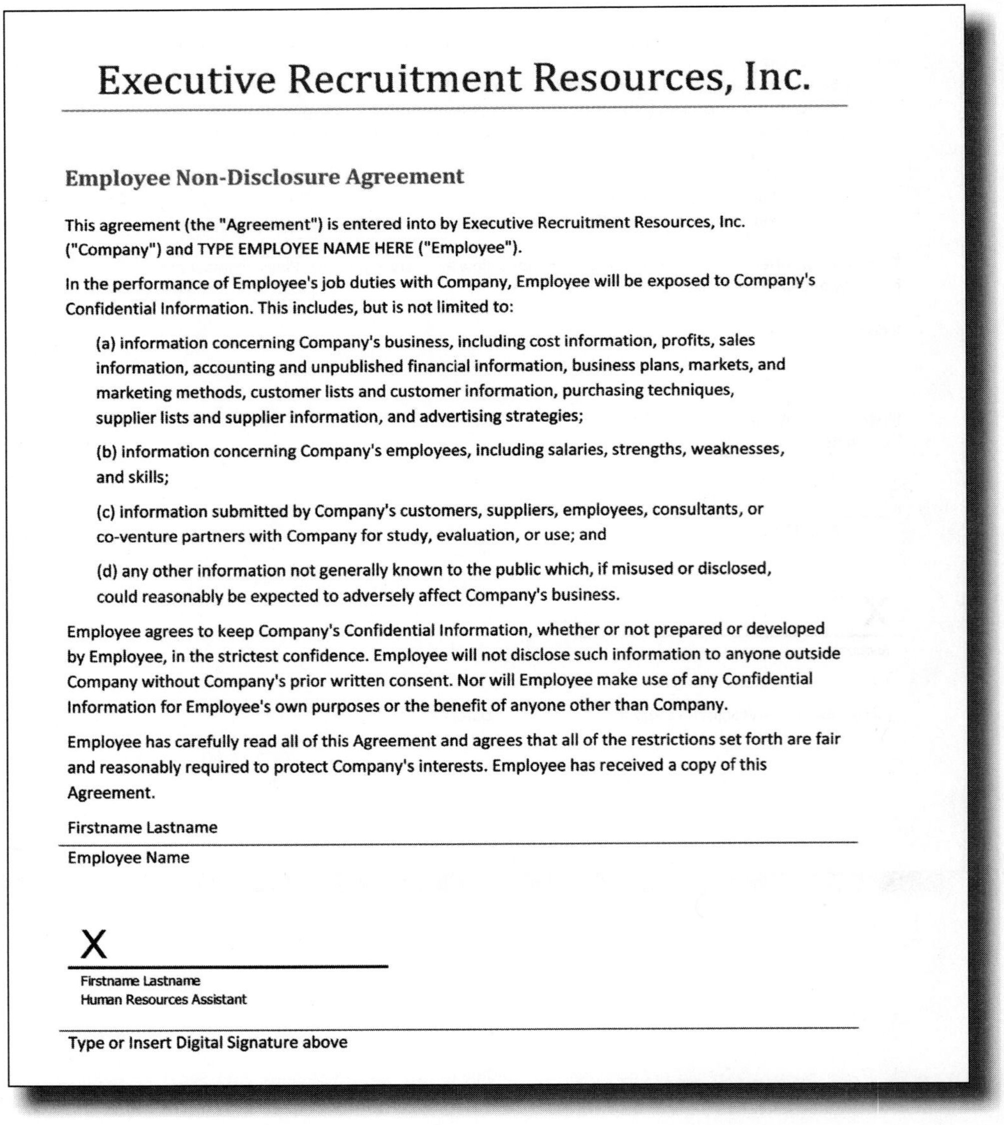

Executive Recruitment Resources, Inc.

Employee Non-Disclosure Agreement

This agreement (the "Agreement") is entered into by Executive Recruitment Resources, Inc. ("Company") and TYPE EMPLOYEE NAME HERE ("Employee").

In the performance of Employee's job duties with Company, Employee will be exposed to Company's Confidential Information. This includes, but is not limited to:

(a) information concerning Company's business, including cost information, profits, sales information, accounting and unpublished financial information, business plans, markets, and marketing methods, customer lists and customer information, purchasing techniques, supplier lists and supplier information, and advertising strategies;

(b) information concerning Company's employees, including salaries, strengths, weaknesses, and skills;

(c) information submitted by Company's customers, suppliers, employees, consultants, or co-venture partners with Company for study, evaluation, or use; and

(d) any other information not generally known to the public which, if misused or disclosed, could reasonably be expected to adversely affect Company's business.

Employee agrees to keep Company's Confidential Information, whether or not prepared or developed by Employee, in the strictest confidence. Employee will not disclose such information to anyone outside Company without Company's prior written consent. Nor will Employee make use of any Confidential Information for Employee's own purposes or the benefit of anyone other than Company.

Employee has carefully read all of this Agreement and agrees that all of the restrictions set forth are fair and reasonably required to protect Company's interests. Employee has received a copy of this Agreement.

Firstname Lastname
_____
Employee Name

X _____
Firstname Lastname
Human Resources Assistant
_____
Type or Insert Digital Signature above

Chapter Assessment and Application

Project 51—Make It Your Own

Survey Form

A survey is an effective method of collecting information that can help you identify business trends and changes. Once you collect the data, you can analyze it so that you can use the information to make business decisions.

Working alone or in teams, use the skills you have learned in Chapter 4 to design and create a form that you can use to survey classmates to collect information about a change or trend. For example, you might survey classmates about changes in cafeteria food purchases, how they spend their money on the weekends, or what color clothes they like to buy.

When you are finished, ask your classmates to fill out the form on screen or in print. You can use the results of the survey to create a chart or table, or to write a newspaper article analyzing the data. Refer to Illustration A to see a sample of a survey form.

DIRECTIONS

1. Pick a topic that you want to use for your survey, and have it approved by your teacher.

2. Plan a form that can be used to collect responses to your survey. Consider the type of content controls you will need, the standard text, and how you want to design the form so that it is easy to fill out.

3. Start Word, if necessary, and create a new document. Save it as a Word template with the name **WProj51_studentfirstname_student lastname**.

4. Insert your name and today's date in the header of the document. If you are working as a team, be sure to include all team members' names.

5. Select to display elements that might help you while you work, such as the rulers, nonprinting characters, and gridlines.

6. Enter all of the standard text you want on your form. You can insert graphics as well, such as a clip art picture, or shapes. Use a table if it helps you line up the information neatly on the page. Alternatively, you might want to use text boxes.

7. Insert the content controls you will need on your form. Remember to enter them in the order in which you want users to fill them out.

8. Restrict editing in the document to tracked changes.

9. Ask a classmate to review the document and offer comments and suggestions.

10. Remove editing restrictions and incorporate the comments and suggestions into the form template.

11. Check the spelling and grammar in the document and correct errors.

12. Restrict editing to filling in forms. Do not require a password.

13. Add your invisible digital signature to the document.

14. **With your teacher's permission**, print the form.

15. Save the template document and close it.

16. Ask your classmates to fill out the form.

17. Collect the results and analyze them. Create a chart, graph, or table illustrating the results, or write an article explaining them.

18. Exit Word.

Illustration A

Firstname Lastname
Today's Date

Computer Usage Survey

Please take the time to complete this survey. The
results are strictly confidential.

Age: Click here to enter text.

Gender: Male   Female
                             ☐   ☐
Date: Click here to enter a date.

How many hours per day do you spend   Choose an item.
using a computer?

On which computer-based activity do you   Choose an item.
spend the most time?

What type of computer do you use? (check all that apply)

   Smartphone   Notebook   Desktop   Tablet
       ☐   ☐   ☐   ☐

Comments: Click here to enter text.

Project 52—Master It

Registration Form

In this project you will create a registration form that New Media Designs
employees can use to offer their services as contest judges. The form will
include a visible digital signature line. You will test the registration form by filling
it out on screen, and you will attach a digital signature to the completed form.

DIRECTIONS

1. Start Word and save the new blank document
   as a Word template with the name **WProj52a_
   studentfirstname_studentlastname** in the
   location where your teacher instructs you to store
   the files for this lesson.

2. Insert your name and today's date in the header.

3. On the first line of the document type **New Media
   Designs**. Press `ENTER` and type **Contest Judge
   Registration Form**.

4. Apply the **Title** style to both lines of text, and
   center them both horizontally.

5. Apply the **Apothecary** theme to the document.

6. Press `ENTER` twice, and then insert a table with two
   columns and 9 rows.

7. Set table properties so all rows are at least **0.5"** high.

8. Split the right cell in row 6 into two cells.

9. Merge the cells in row 8 and merge the cells in row 9.

10. Enter the following text and content controls in the table:

First Name:	Rich Text Content Control	
Last Name:	Rich Text Content Control	
Date:	Date Picker Content Control	
Department:	Drop-Down List Content Control	
Contest for which you would like to be a judge:	Drop-Down List Content Control	
Have you ever been a New Media Designs contest judge before?	Yes Check Box Content Control	No Check Box Content Control
Comments:	Rich Text Content Control	
Rich Text Content Control		
Please insert digital signature above.		

11. Add the following items to the Department Drop-Down List Content Control: Marketing, Human Resources, Accounting, Sales, Other.

12. Add the following items to the Contest for which you would like to be a judge Drop-Down List Content Control: **Elementary, Middle School, High School.**

13. In row 8, click in the Rich Text Content Control and insert a signature line. Do not suggest a signer, signer's title, or signer's e-mail address. Leave the default instructions to the signer, allow comments in the Sign dialog box, and do not show the date in the signature line.

14. Apply single line borders to the bottom of each row in the table, and apply the **Align Center Left** alignment to all cells.

15. Check and correct the spelling and grammar in the document.

16. Restrict editing in the document to filling in forms. Do not use a password.

17. **With your teacher's permission**, print the form. It should look similar to Illustration A.

18. Add your invisible digital signature to the template, and then close it.

19. Use the template file to create a new document. Save the new document as **WProj52b_ studentfirstname_studentlastname** in the location where your teacher instructs you to store the files for this lesson.

20. Fill in the form. Use your own name and today's date. Select the **Accounting** department and the **Middle School** contest. Select the **No** check box. In the Comments: box, type **I am looking forward to being a contest judge.**

21. Digitally sign the document.

22. **With your teacher's permission**, print the form.

23. Close the document saving all changes and exit Word.

Illustration A

Firstname Lastname
Today's Date

New Media Designs
Contest Judge Registration Form

First Name: Click here to enter text.

Last Name: Click here to enter text.

Date: Click here to enter a date.

Department: Choose an item.

Contest for which you would like to
be a judge: Choose an item.

Have you ever been a New Media Designs contest judge before?	Yes ☐	No ☐

Comments: Click here to enter text.

X_____

Please insert digital signature above.

Chapter 1

Managing Large Workbooks and Using Advanced Sorting and Filtering

Lesson 1
Customizing the Excel Interface and Converting Text
Projects 1-2

- Customizing the Quick Access Toolbar
- Customizing the Ribbon
- Customizing Excel Options
- Converting Text to Columns

Lesson 2
Formatting Cells
Projects 3-4

- Using Advanced Formatting of Dates and Times
- Creating Custom Number Formats
- Clearing Formatting from a Cell

Lesson 3
Hiding and Formatting Workbook Elements
Projects 5-6

- Hiding Data Temporarily
- Hiding and Printing Worksheet Gridlines
- Hiding Row and Column Headings
- Using Custom Views

Lesson 4
Customizing Styles and Themes
Projects 7-8

- Customizing a Workbook Theme
- Creating a Custom Table Style

Lesson 5
Using Advanced Sort
Projects 9-10

- Sorting Excel Items
- Understanding the Rules for Advanced Sorting
- Sorting on Multiple Columns
- Removing a Sort

Lesson 6
Using Advanced Filtering
Projects 11-12

- Using AutoFilter to Filter Tables
- Using AutoFilter to Filter by Custom Criteria
- Filtering Items without Creating a Table
- Filtering by Using Advanced Criteria
- Removing an In-Place Advanced Filter
- Extracting Filtered Rows
- Using Sum, Average, and Count in a Filtered Table

Lesson 7
Customizing Data Entry
Projects 13–14

- Entering Labels on Multiple Lines
- Entering Fractions and Mixed Numbers

Lesson 8
Using Find and Replace
Projects 15–16

- Formatting Text with Formulas
- Replacing Text

Lesson 9
Working with Hyperlinks
Projects 17–18

- Using a Hyperlink in Excel
- Creating a Hyperlink in a Cell
- Modifying Hyperlinks
- Modifying Hyperlinked Cell Attributes
- Removing a Hyperlink

Lesson 10
Saving Excel Data in a
Different File Format
Projects 19–20

- Ensuring Backward-Compatibility in a Workbook
- Saving Excel Data in CSV File Format
- Saving a Workbook as a PDF or XPS File

Lesson 11
Working with Subtotals
Projects 21–22

- Using Go To and Go To Special
- Creating Subtotals
- Creating Nested Subtotals
- Hiding or Displaying Details
- Removing a Subtotal
- Manually Outlining and Adding Subtotals

End-of-Chapter Assessments
Projects 23–24

Lesson 1

Customizing the Excel Interface and Converting Text

➤ **What You Will Learn**

Customizing the Quick Access Toolbar
Customizing the Ribbon
Customizing Excel Options
Converting Text to Columns

Software Skills   Like other Office programs, Excel is design to be customized to your needs. You can customize Excel Options, the Ribbon, and the Quick Access Toolbar so you have easy access to the tools and features you use most often.

Application Skills   Your boss at The Little Toy Shoppe wants you to create a newsletter to inform clients of new products and to entice them to return to the store on special sales days. Luckily, Rob the intern has been keeping track of customer names and addresses in a new worksheet. Unfortunately, Rob doesn't know the first thing about creating a workable database. In this lesson you will practice customizing the Excel workspace and then you'll take Rob's list and convert the data in to usable columns.

What You Can Do

Customizing the Quick Access Toolbar

- The Quick Access Toolbar (QAT) appears at the top-left corner of the Excel window. It provides a set of quick shortcuts to the most common functions and features.

- By default it contains three buttons: Save, Undo, and Redo. You can also customize the QAT by adding shortcuts to most other Excel features.

- To add any button to the Quick Access Toolbar, simply right-click it and select Add to Quick Access Toolbar.

- To remove a button from the Quick Access Toolbar, right-click it and choose Remove from Quick Access Toolbar.

- You can also use the Quick Access Toolbar to store shortcuts to Excel features that don't exist on any tab of the Ribbon. Use the Quick Access Toolbar section of the Excel Options dialog box to add additional features to the QAT.

Try It!   Adding Quick Access Toolbar Buttons

1 Start Excel and select the Review tab and then right-click the Spelling & Grammar button ✓.

2 Select Add to Quick Access Toolbar.

3 Click the Customize Quick Access Toolbar button ▼ and select Sort Ascending.

Try It!   Customizing the Quick Access Toolbar

1 In Excel, click File > Options 🔲 > Quick Access Toolbars.

2 Click the Choose commands from the down arrow and select Formulas Tab.

3 In the list of commands, choose the Average formula and click Add.

4 In the list below the Customize Quick Access Toolbar box, select Sort Ascending and click Remove.

5 If you want, you can also check Show Quick Access Toolbar below the Ribbon.

6 Click OK.

7 Leave the Excel Options window open for the next Try It.

Customizing the Quick Access Toolbar

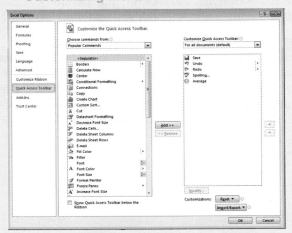

Customizing the Ribbon

- In Excel 2010 you can customize the Ribbon by adding commands that you use frequently or removing those commands that you don't use.

- You can create new groups on a Ribbon tab, and you can even create a completely new tab with new groups.
- Commands for customizing the Ribbon are on the Customize Ribbon tab of the Excel Options dialog box.

Try It! Customizing the Ribbon

1 In the Excel Options window, right-click anywhere on the Ribbon and click Customize the Ribbon.

2 In the Main Tabs list, click to clear the check mark to the left of Page Layout.

3 Click New Tab at the bottom of the dialog box and then select the New Group (Custom) line in the Main Tabs list.

4 Click the Rename button and type **Learning Excel** in the Display name box and click OK.

5 Click the Choose commands from the down arrow, and then click Commands Not in the Ribbon.

6 Click Zoom Out, and then click Add.

7 Click OK to apply the change and close the Excel Options dialog box. Notice that the Page Layout tab no longer appears on the Ribbon and that a New Tab tab displays.

8 Select the New Tab to view the new group of commands.

Modified Ribbon

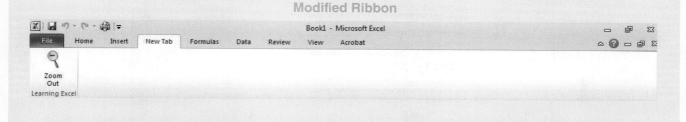

Try It! Restoring the Ribbon

1 In the Excel window, click File > Options 🖹 > Customize Ribbon.

2 Under the Main Tabs list, click Reset.

3 Select Reset all customizations.

4 On the warning message that appears, click Yes. This will reset both the QAT and the Ribbon to the default settings.

5 Click OK.

Customizing Excel Options

- There are over 100 different options and settings that you can use to control the way Excel operates. They are organized to several categories, such as Formulas, Proofing, Save, and Add-Ins.

- You view and set program options in the program's Options dialog box, which is accessed from Backstage view.

Try It!   Customizing Excel Options

1 Open **ETry01** from the data files for this lesson.

2 Save the presentation as **ETry01_ studentfirstname_studentlastname** in the location where your teacher instructs you to store the files for this lesson.

3 Click File > Options 📄 .

4 On the General tab, type your name in the User name text box at the bottom of the dialog box.

5 Click Save in the list on the left side of the dialog box to display the Save options.

6 Click Proofing to display the Proofing options.

7 Click Advanced, and scroll through the options.

8 Under Display options for this workbook, clear Show sheet tabs.

9 Under Display options for this worksheet, click the Gridline color button.

10 Select the last Blue color on the last row.

11 Save the changes to the file, and leave it open to use in the next Try It.

Excel's Advanced Display Options

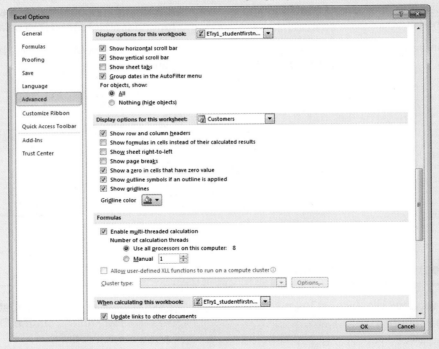

Converting Text to Columns

■ When working with large amounts of text data in Excel, pre-planning is often critical:

- For example, when creating a long list of customers, it's useful to place first names in one column, and last names in another so that you can sort on the single column, Last Names, and arrange the customer list alphabetically by last name.

- It might also be useful to separate out the parts of a customer's address into different columns—one each for street address, city, state, and ZIP Code—so the customer list can be sorted by state or ZIP Code if you like.

■ If such a customer list was not set up properly, you can easily fix it by having Excel split the contents of a cell across several cells.

■ Excel can split the contents of a single cell, a range, or an entire column in one step.

Try It!   Converting Delimited Text to Columns

1 In the **ETry01_studentfirstname_studentlastname** workbook, select the range I6:I57.

2 Click Data > Text to Columns ⊞.

✓ *The Convert Text to Columns Wizard appears.*

3 Click Delimited and then click Next.

4 Under Delimiters, select Comma.

✓ *After selecting the correct delimiter, the fields in the selected cell, range, or column will appear in the Data preview pane, separated by vertical lines.*

5 To skip empty columns, click Treat consecutive delimiters as one and click Next.

6 Click the last column in the Data preview window and click Text under Column data format.

7 Click Finish.

8 Save the changes to the file, and leave it open to use in the next Try It.

Try It!   Converting Fixed Width Text to Columns

1 In the **ETry01_studentfirstname_studentlastname** workbook, select the range F6:F57.

2 Click Data > Text to Columns ⊞.

3 Click Fixed width and click Next.

4 Click the 10 on the ruler in the Data preview window.

5 Drag the line to the end of the first five digits and click Next.

6 Click the second column in the Data preview window, and click Do not import column (skip) under Column data format.

7 Click Finish.

8 Save the changes to the file, and exit Excel.

Project 1—Create It

Splitting Delimited Text

DIRECTIONS

1. Start Excel, if necessary, and open **EProj01** from the data files for this lesson.

2. Save the file as **EProj01_studentfirstname_studentlastname** in the location where your teacher instructs you to store the files for this lesson.

3. Select the column headers for columns C and D, right-click the headers, and select **Insert** from the shortcut menu.

4. Select cells **E2** and **E3** and drag them to cells **C2** and **C3**.

5. Type **First Name** in cell **B5**; type **Last Name** in cell **C5**.

6. Select the range **B6:B57**.

7. Click Data > Text to Columns ⊞.

8. Click **Delimited** and then click **Next**.

9. Under Delimiters, select **Space** and then click **Next**.

10. Click the first column in the Data preview window and click **Text** under Column data format.

11. Repeat for the second column in the Data preview window.

12. Click **Finish** and click **OK** in the warning box. Your worksheet should look similar to Figure 1-1.

13. Click the **Customize Quick Access Toolbar** button ▼, and select **Quick Print**.

14. Repeat to add **Spelling** to the **Quick Access Toolbar**.

15. Close the document, saving all changes, and exit Excel.

Figure 1-1

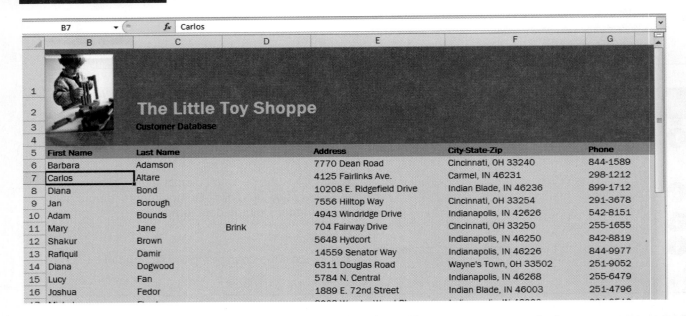

Project 2—Apply It

Splitting Text into Multiple Columns

DIRECTIONS

1. Start Excel, if necessary, and open **EProj02** from the data files for this lesson.

2. Save the file as **EProj02_studentfirstname_ studentlastname** in the location where your teacher instructs you to store the files for this lesson.

3. Two of the names use all three columns; those names have two part first names, which should appear together in column B. You can easily correct this situation, however, and get rid of the third column that you don't need:

   a. Type **Mary Jane** in cell **B11** and **Brink** in cell **C11**.

   b. Type **Chu Gi** in cell **B34** and **Nguyen** in cell **C34**.

   c. Delete column **D**.

4. Insert two columns between columns E and F.

5. Type **City** in cell **E5**, **State** in cell **F5**, and **Zip Code** in cell **G5**.

6. Split the addresses in column E into three columns:

   a. Select the range **E6:E57**.

   b. Display the Convert Text to Columns Wizard.

   c. Select the **Delimited** option, and **Comma** as the delimiter used.

   d. Select **Text** as the format for first column.

7. Split the state and Zip Codes in column F into two columns:

   a. Select the range **F6:F57**.

   b. Display the Convert Text to Columns Wizard.

   c. Select the **Fixed Width** option.

   d. Add a delimiting line at the beginning of the Zip codes in the Data preview window.

   e. Select **Text** as the format for first column, and **General** for the second column.

8. Adjust column widths as needed. (See Figure 1-2.)

9. Add a header with your name.

10. Use the Excel Options dialog box, to turn off sheet tabs in this workbook.

11. **With your teacher's permission**, print page 1 of the worksheet in landscape orientation. It should look similar to Figure 1-2.

12. Close the document, saving all changes, and exit Excel.

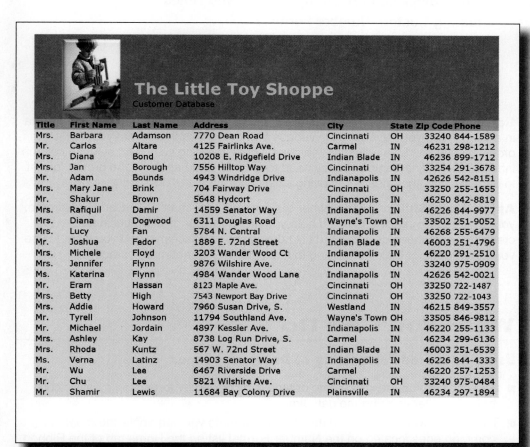

Figure 1-2

The Little Toy Shoppe
Customer Database

Title	First Name	Last Name	Address	City	State	Zip Code	Phone
Mrs.	Barbara	Adamson	7770 Dean Road	Cincinnati	OH	33240	844-1589
Mr.	Carlos	Altare	4125 Fairlinks Ave.	Carmel	IN	46231	298-1212
Mrs.	Diana	Bond	10208 E. Ridgefield Drive	Indian Blade	IN	46236	899-1712
Mrs.	Jan	Borough	7556 Hilltop Way	Cincinnati	OH	33254	291-3678
Mr.	Adam	Bounds	4943 Windridge Drive	Indianapolis	IN	42626	542-8151
Mrs.	Mary Jane	Brink	704 Fairway Drive	Cincinnati	OH	33250	255-1655
Mr.	Shakur	Brown	5648 Hydcort	Indianapolis	IN	46250	842-8819
Mrs.	Rafiquil	Damir	14559 Senator Way	Indianapolis	IN	46226	844-9977
Mrs.	Diana	Dogwood	6311 Douglas Road	Wayne's Town	OH	33502	251-9052
Mrs.	Lucy	Fan	5784 N. Central	Indianapolis	IN	46268	255-6479
Mr.	Joshua	Fedor	1889 E. 72nd Street	Indian Blade	IN	46003	251-4796
Mrs.	Michele	Floyd	3203 Wander Wood Ct	Indianapolis	IN	46220	291-2510
Mrs.	Jennifer	Flynn	9876 Wilshire Ave.	Cincinnati	OH	33240	975-0909
Ms.	Katerina	Flynn	4984 Wander Wood Lane	Indianapolis	IN	42626	542-0021
Mr.	Eram	Hassan	8123 Maple Ave.	Cincinnati	OH	33250	722-1487
Mrs.	Betty	High	7543 Newport Bay Drive	Cincinnati	OH	33250	722-1043
Mrs.	Addie	Howard	7960 Susan Drive, S.	Westland	IN	46215	849-3557
Mr.	Tyrell	Johnson	11794 Southland Ave.	Wayne's Town	OH	33505	846-9812
Mr.	Michael	Jordain	4897 Kessler Ave.	Indianapolis	IN	46220	255-1133
Mrs.	Ashley	Kay	8738 Log Run Drive, S.	Carmel	IN	46234	299-6136
Mrs.	Rhoda	Kuntz	567 W. 72nd Street	Indian Blade	IN	46003	251-6539
Ms.	Verna	Latinz	14903 Senator Way	Indianapolis	IN	46226	844-4333
Mr.	Wu	Lee	6467 Riverside Drive	Carmel	IN	46220	257-1253
Mr.	Chu	Lee	5821 Wilshire Ave.	Cincinnati	OH	33240	975-0484
Mr.	Shamir	Lewis	11684 Bay Colony Drive	Plainsville	IN	46234	297-1894

Lesson 2

Formatting Cells

➤ **What You Will Learn**

Using Advanced Formatting of Dates and Times
Creating Custom Number Formats
Clearing Formatting from a Cell

Software Skills   Sometimes, in order to accommodate the various kinds of data in a worksheet, you have to apply various formatting techniques that you might not ordinarily use, such as adjusting the row heights, merging cells, and slanting column labels. Other refinements you may need to make include applying the proper format to data—even if that means removing existing formats and creating your own.

Application Skills   As the owner of Giancarlo Franchetti's Go-Cart Speedrome, you're interested in using Excel to help you manage your growing business. You've created a worksheet for tracking daily admissions and receipts, and you want to use your knowledge of Excel formatting to make the worksheet more attractive.

What You Can Do

Using Advanced Formatting of Dates and Times

- You can change the way a date or time is displayed by formatting a cell or cells before or after entering the date/time

- There are several standard date and time formats you can apply, the most common ones located on the Number Format list on the Home tab of the Ribbon.

- Other standard date and time formats are applied through the Format Cells dialog box.

- You can also customize the way you want dates displayed, by creating a custom number format.

- After entering a date, you can change its number format as needed. For example, you can change the date 1/14/12 to display as January 14, 2012

Try It! Formatting Date or Time with Standard Format

1 Start Excel and open **ETry02** from the data files for this lesson.

2 Save the file as **ETry02_studentfirstname_studentlastname** in the location where your teacher instructs you to store the files for this lesson.

3 Select the range G6:G20 and select the Home tab.

4 Click the Number Format down arrow `Date` in the Number group and select Short Date.

5 Select the range L6:M20 and click the Number Format down arrow `Custom` in the Number group and select Time.

6 Save the changes to the file, and leave it open to use in the next Try It.

Try It! Formatting Date or Time with a Custom Format

1 In the **ETry02_studentfirstname_studentlastname** workbook, select the Home tab.

2 Select the range G6:G20 and click the Number Format down arrow `Date` in the Number group and select More Number Formats.

OR

Right-click the range G6:G20 and select Format Cells.

3 On the Number tab, click Custom in the Category box and scroll through the available options in the Type box.

4 Select the d-mmm-yy option in the Type box.

5 Click OK.

6 Double-click the column border between column G and column H.

7 Save the changes to the file, and leave it open to use in the next Try It.

Applying a Custom date format

Creating Custom Number Formats

- When a number format doesn't fit your needs, you can create a custom number format:
  - Typically, you use a custom number format to preformat a column or row, prior to data entry. The custom format speeds the data entry process.
  - For example, if you need to type account numbers in the format AB-2342-CO, you can create a format that will insert the dashes for you. And if the account numbers all end in -CO, you can build that into the custom format as well.
- You create a custom number format by typing a series of special codes.
  - ✓ *To speed the process, select an existing format and customize it.*
- You can specify format codes for positive numbers negative numbers, zeros, and text:
  - If you wish to specify all four formats, you must type the codes in the order listed above.
  - If you specify only two formats, you must type a code for positive numbers and zeros first, and a code for negative numbers second.
  - If you specify only one format, all numbers in the row or column will use that format.
  - To separate the formats, use a semicolon, as in the following custom number format: $#,##0.00;[red]($#,##0.00);"ZERO";[blue].
  - This format displays positive numbers as $0,000.00, negative numbers in red and parentheses, a zero as the word ZERO, and text in blue.

- Standard colors you can use by typing the name in brackets include: red, black, blue, white, green, yellow, cyan, and magenta.
- The following table shows examples of codes you can use in creating a format:

#	Digit placeholder
0	Zero placeholder
?	Digit placeholder
@	Text placeholder
.	Decimal point (period)
%	Percent
,	Thousands separator (comma)
$	Dollar sign
-	Negative sign
+	Plus sign
( )	Parentheses
:	Colon
_	Underscore (skips one character width)
[color]	Type the name of one of the eight colors previously mentioned.

- Custom number formats are saved with the worksheet, so if you want to use a custom format on another worksheet, use the Format Painter to copy the format manually.

Examples of formats you can create:

To Type	To Display	To Use this code:
5.56	5.5600	#.0000
5641	$5,641	$#,##0
5641 and -5641	$5,641 and ($5,641) in red	$#,##0;[red]($#,##0)
5641and -5641	$5,641.00 and ($5,641.00) in red	$#,##0.00;[red]($#,##0.00)

Try It! — Creating Custom Number Formats

1 In the ETry02_studentfirstname_studentlastname file, select the range N6:N20.

2 On the Home tab, click the Number group dialog box launcher.

3 In the Category list box, click Custom.

4 Scroll through the Type list and select 000-00-0000.

5 In the Type text box, place the insertion point before the first 0 in the Type text box and type "AB-".

6 Place the insertion point after the last zero and press BACKSPACE five times.

7 Click OK.

8 Click cell N6 and type 35135 and press ENTER to see how the new format is applied.

9 Save the changes to the file, and leave it open to use in the next Try It.

Creating a Custom Number Format

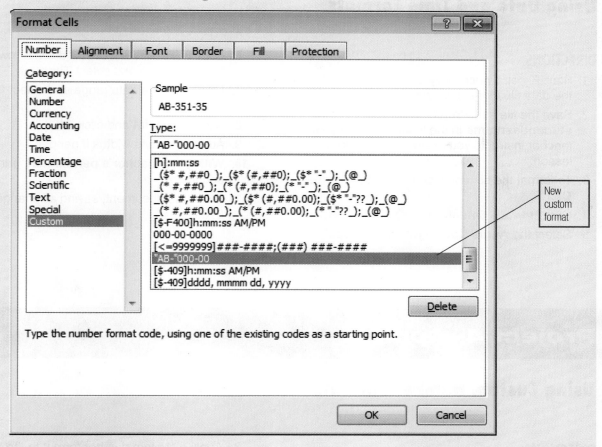

Clearing Formatting from a Cell

- Sometimes, you may want to keep the data in a cell, but remove the formatting you've applied.

- Excel allows you to clear just the format of a cell, without clearing its contents, using the Clear button in the Editing group on the Home tab.

Try It!   **Clearing Formatting from a Cell**

1 In the file **ETry02_studentfirstname_ studentlastname**, select the range E6:E20.

2 Click **Home > Clear** ✐ .

3 Select Clear Formats.

4 Close **ETry02_studentfirstname_ studentlastname**, saving all changes, and exit Excel.

Project 3—Create It

Using Date and Time Formats

DIRECTIONS

1. Start Excel, if necessary, and open **EProj03** from the data files for this lesson.

2. Save the file as **EProj03_studentfirstname_ studentlastname** in the location where your teacher instructs you to store the files for this lesson.

3. To format the column labels, select the range **C8:H8**.

4. Click **Home > Orientation** 📑 .

5. Select the **Angle Counterclockwise** option.

6. Click the **Number Format** down arrow in the Number group and select **Time**.

7. Right-click the data range and select **Format Cells**.

8. Select **1:30 PM** and click **OK**.

9. Adjust columns widths if needed.

10. **With your teacher's permission**, print the document.

11. Close the document, saving all changes, and exit Excel.

Project 4—Apply It

Using Custom Number Formats

DIRECTIONS

1. Start Excel, if necessary, and open **EProj04** from the data files for this lesson.

2. Save the file as **EProj04_studentfirstname_ studentlastname** in the location where your teacher instructs you to store the files for this lesson.

3. Apply a custom number format to the Session Number column.

   a. Select the range, **F9:F20**.

   b. Display the **Format Cells** dialog box, click the **Number** tab, and select **Custom** format.

   c. Replace the contents of the **Type** box with this: **00-00-"Session "0**.

d. Enter the session numbers, without the dashes, and let the format do the work:

F9	10051
F10	10052
F11	10081
F12	10091
F13	10101
F14	10102
F15	10103
F16	10111
F17	10112
F18	10113
F19	10121
F20	10122

4. Remove the formatting in the title area and start over (see Figure 2-1):

 a. Select the range **A1:I7**.

 b. Clear the formats in the selected range.

 c. Apply **Blue-Gray, Text 2, Lighter 50%** fill color to the selection.

 d. Apply bold formatting to the selection.

 e. Change the point size of cell **C3** to **24** point.

 f. Adjust the height of row 3 to **65**.

5. Adjust column widths if needed.

6. Add a worksheet footer that includes your name and the worksheet file name.

7. **With your teacher's permission**, print the document.

8. Close the document, saving all changes, and exit Excel.

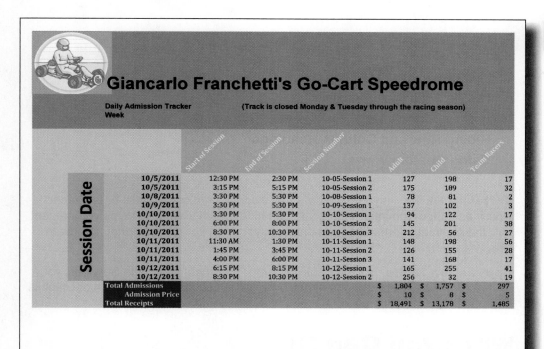

Figure 2-1

Giancarlo Franchetti's Go-Cart Speedrome

Daily Admission Tracker Week　　(Track is closed Monday & Tuesday through the racing season)

Session Date	Start of Session	End of Session	Session Number	Adult	Child	Team Racers
10/5/2011	12:30 PM	2:30 PM	10-05-Session 1	127	198	17
10/5/2011	3:15 PM	5:15 PM	10-05-Session 2	175	189	32
10/8/2011	3:30 PM	5:30 PM	10-08-Session 1	78	81	2
10/9/2011	3:30 PM	5:30 PM	10-09-Session 1	137	102	3
10/10/2011	3:30 PM	5:30 PM	10-10-Session 1	94	122	17
10/10/2011	6:00 PM	8:00 PM	10-10-Session 2	145	201	38
10/10/2011	8:30 PM	10:30 PM	10-10-Session 3	212	56	27
10/11/2011	11:30 AM	1:30 PM	10-11-Session 1	148	198	56
10/11/2011	1:45 PM	3:45 PM	10-11-Session 2	126	155	28
10/11/2011	4:00 PM	6:00 PM	10-11-Session 3	141	168	17
10/12/2011	6:15 PM	8:15 PM	10-12-Session 1	165	255	41
10/12/2011	8:30 PM	10:30 PM	10-12-Session 2	256	32	19
Total Admissions				$ 1,804	$ 1,757	$ 297
Admission Price				$ 10	$ 8	$ 5
Total Receipts				$ 18,491	$ 13,178	$ 1,485

Lesson 3

Hiding and Formatting Workbook Elements

➤ What You Will Learn

Hiding Data Temporarily
Hiding and Printing Worksheet Gridlines
Hiding Row and Column Headings
Using Custom Views

Software Skills   If you have data that's considered confidential or is needed strictly as supporting information, you can hide it from view. This helps you present only the relevant information, and prevents you from accidentally printing private data.

Application Skills   As the bookkeeper for Intellidata Database Services, your job is to produce three versions of one Web traffic statistics report, each of which is distributed to a different office.

What You Can Do

Hiding Data Temporarily

- To prevent data from displaying or printing in a workbook, you can **hide** the data.
- You can hide the contents of individual cells, whole rows or columns, and even whole worksheets.

  ✓ *Hiding data is useful for keeping important supporting or confidential information out of sight, but it won't prevent those who know Excel from exposing that data if they can get access to the workbook. If you need more security, review the protection options in Lesson 20.*

- When a row or column is hidden, the row number or column letter is missing from the worksheet frame. Hiding row 12, for example, leaves the row headings showing 11, 13, 14, and so on.

- Hiding a worksheet makes its tab disappear. If worksheets use a sequential numbering or naming scheme (such as Sheet1, Sheet2, Sheet3), the fact that a worksheet is hidden may be obvious.

- If you hide the contents of a cell, the cell appears to contain nothing, but the cell itself doesn't disappear from the worksheet.

- Even if a cell's contents are hidden, you can still display the contents in the Formula bar by selecting the cell.

- You can also hide all the zeros in a worksheet, displaying blank cells instead.

- If you hide a workbook, its contents aren't displayed even when the workbook is open. This feature is useful for storing macros that you want to have available but not necessarily in view.

- If you copy or move hidden data, it remains hidden.

- Because the data in hidden columns or rows doesn't print, you can use this feature to print noncontiguous columns or rows as if they were contiguous.

- To edit, format, or redisplay the contents of hidden rows, columns, or worksheets, **unhide** the rows, columns, or worksheet.

Try It!   **Hiding and Redisplaying Cell Contents**

1. Start Excel and open **ETry03** from the data files for this lesson.

2. Save the file as **ETry03_studentfirstname_ studentlastname** in the location where your teacher instructs you to store the files for this lesson.

3. Click cell C4 and click the Number group dialog box launcher ▣.

4. In the Category list box, click Custom.

5. In the Type list box, select the contents and type ;;; and click OK.

6. Click the Number Format down arrow in the Number group and select Text.

7. Save changes and leave the file open to use in the next Try It.

Try It!   **Hiding All Zeros for Current Worksheet**

1. In the **ETry03_studentfirstname_ studentlastname** file, click File > Options > Advanced.

2. Deselect the Show a zero in cells that have zero value check box in the Display options for this worksheet and click OK.

3. Save changes and leave the file open to use in the next Try It.

Try It!   Hiding Rows or Columns

1 In the **ETry03_studentfirstname_ studentlastname** file, click the column I heading.

2 On the Home > Format .

3 Click Hide & Unhide > Hide Columns.

4 Right-click the row 6 heading.

5 Select Hide.

OR

Click the border between rows 6 and 7. Drag up until row 6 disappears.

6 Save the file and leave it open to use in the next Try It.

Try It!   Unhiding Rows or Columns

1 In the **ETry03_studentfirstname_ studentlastname** file, select the H and J column headings.

2 Right-click the selection and select Unhide.

OR

Point just to the right of the column H heading.

✓ The pointer becomes ╫ .

3 Point just below the row 5 heading border until the cursor changes to ╪ and then drag down.

✓ Drag down until you reach the bottom of the name Carlos that was in cell 7A. When you release the mouse button the contents of row 7 worksheet contents will shift and the contents of row 6 will appear.

OR

Select the 5 and 7 row headings. Click Home > Format 📋 > Hide & Unhide > Unhide Rows.

4 Right-click the row 6 heading.

5 Select Hide.

OR

Click the border between rows 6 and 7. Drag up until row 6 disappears.

6 Save the file and leave it open to use in the next Try It.

Dragging to unhide a row

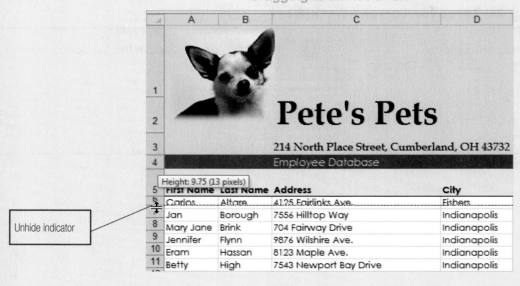

Unhide indicator

Try It!   **Hiding and Unhiding Workbooks**

1 In the **ETry03_studentfirstname_ studentlastname** file, click View > Hide ▢ .

2 Notice the change to the Excel window.

3 Click View > Unhide ▢ .

4 Select the hidden workbook in the Unhide dialog box and click OK.

5 Save the file and leave it open to use in the next Try It.

Try It!   **Hiding and Unhiding Worksheets**

1 In the **ETry03_studentfirstname_ studentlastname** file, select the Customers worksheet.

2 Click Home > Format 🗒 > Hide & Unhide > Hide Sheet.

OR

Right-click the Customers sheet tab and select Hide.

3 Right-click the Employees sheet tab and select Unhide.

OR

Click Home > Format 🗒 > Hide & Unhide > Unhide Sheet.

4 Select the Customers worksheet in the Unhide dialog box and click OK.

5 Save the file and leave it open to use in the next Try It.

Hiding and Printing Worksheet Gridlines

- When presenting Excel data onscreen to a client, you might prefer to present it cleanly, without various on-screen elements such as **gridlines**.

- To turn off gridlines on-screen, you select that option from the View tab or select the View under Gridlines in the Sheet Options group of the Page Layout tab on the Ribbon.

- Regardless of whether you display gridlines on the screen, they don't print unless you select the Print check box under Gridlines in the Sheet Options group of the Page Layout tab on the Ribbon.

Try It!   **Hiding Worksheet Gridlines**

1 In **ETry03_studentfirstname_ studentlastname**, View > Gridlines to deselect it.

2 Save the file and leave it open to use in the next Try It.

Hiding Row and Column Headings

- Even in Full Screen view, the column **headings** that display the letter assigned to each column (such as A, B, and IX) still display.
- The row headings (1, 2, 3, and so on) display as well.

- Although you can easily turn off row and column headings, you want to leave them on until you're finished entering data.
- You can turn off the headings in any view.

Try It!　　**Hiding Row and Column Headings**

1 In the **ETry03_studentfirstname_ studentlastname** file, click click View > Full Screen ▣ and see how the headings appear.

2 Double-click the title bar to go back to Normal view. Maximize the window if necessary.

3 On the View tab, in the Show group, clear the Headings check box.

4 Click View > Full Screen ▣ .

5 Double-click the title bar and maximize the window if necessary.

6 Click View > Headings to redisplay the headings.

7 Save the file and leave it open to use in the next Try It.

Using Custom Views

- You can set up the display of a workbook as you like, then save that setup in a custom view so that you can switch back to it when needed.
  - ✓ For example, you could save one view of the worksheet with all cells displayed, another view with certain rows or columns hidden, and so on.
- Settings in a view include any selected cells, current column widths, how the screen is split or frozen, window arrangements and sizes, filter settings, print setup, and defined print area (if any).

- When creating a view, you can specify whether to save the settings for hidden columns and rows (hidden worksheets are always hidden in the view), and/or the print settings).
- Because custom views can control print settings, you can create the same arrangement of printed data each time you print from that view (for example, printing just the tax deductible expenses from a monthly expense workbook).
- The current view is saved with the workbook.

Try It!　　**Creating a Custom View**

1 In the **ETry03_studentfirstname_ studentlastname** file, you need to create a custom view of the employee database that hides sensitive employee information.

2 Click View > Custom Views ▣ .

3 Click Add and type **Normal** in the Name box and click OK.

4 On the Employees worksheet, click the H column heading, press `CTRL` and click the column headings I, O, and P.

5 Click Home > Format ▣ > Hide & Unhide > Hide Columns.

6 Right-click the Customers sheet tab and click Hide.

7 Click Insert > Header & Footer ▣ > File Name ▣ .

8 Click File > Print > No Scaling and choose Fit Sheet on One Page.

(continued)

Try It!   **Creating a Custom View** *(continued)*

9   Click View > Normal ⊞ .

10   Click cell A8 and click View > Custom Views 🗔 .

11   Click Add and type Schedule in the Name box.

12   Ensure that both options are selected and click OK.

13   Save the file and leave it open to use in the next Try It.

The Workbook Views group

Try It!   **Displaying a Custom View**

1   In the ETry03_studentfirstname_studentlastname file, click View > Custom Views 🗔 .

2   Select Normal in the Custom Views dialog box.

3   Click Show.

4   Click Undo to switch back to the Schedule custom view.

5   Save the file and leave it open to use in the next Try It.

The Custom Views dialog box

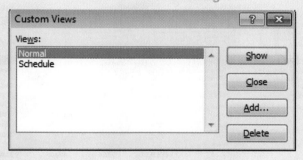

Try It!   **Deleting a Custom View**

1   In the ETry03_studentfirstname_studentlastname file, click View > Custom Views 🗔 .

2   Select Normal in the Custom Views dialog box.

3   Click Delete and click Yes to confirm.

4   Press ESC , close ETry03_studentfirstname_studentlastname, and exit Excel.

Project 5—Create It

Creating a Custom View of a Worksheet

DIRECTIONS

1. Start Excel, if necessary, and open **EProj05** from the data files for this lesson.

2. Save the file as **EProj05_studentfirstname_ studentlastname** in the location where your teacher instructs you to store the files for this lesson.

3. On the **Usage statistics 0704** sheet, click **View > Gridlines** to clear the Gridlines check box for this sheet.

4. Click the row heading for row 8. Press `CTRL` and click the row headings for **9, 12, 13, 16, 17, 20, 21, 24,** and **25.**

5. Click **Home > Format** 📠 **> Hide & Unhide > Hide Rows.**

6. Click **View > Headings.**

7. Click **Page Layout > Orientation** 📄 **> Landscape.**

8. Click **View > Custom Views** 📖 .

9. Click **Add** and type **North** in the Name box.

10. Ensure that both options are selected and click **OK.**

11. **With your teacher's permission**, print page 1 of the worksheet. It should look similar to Figure 3-1.

12. Close the document, saving all changes, and exit Excel.

Figure 3-1

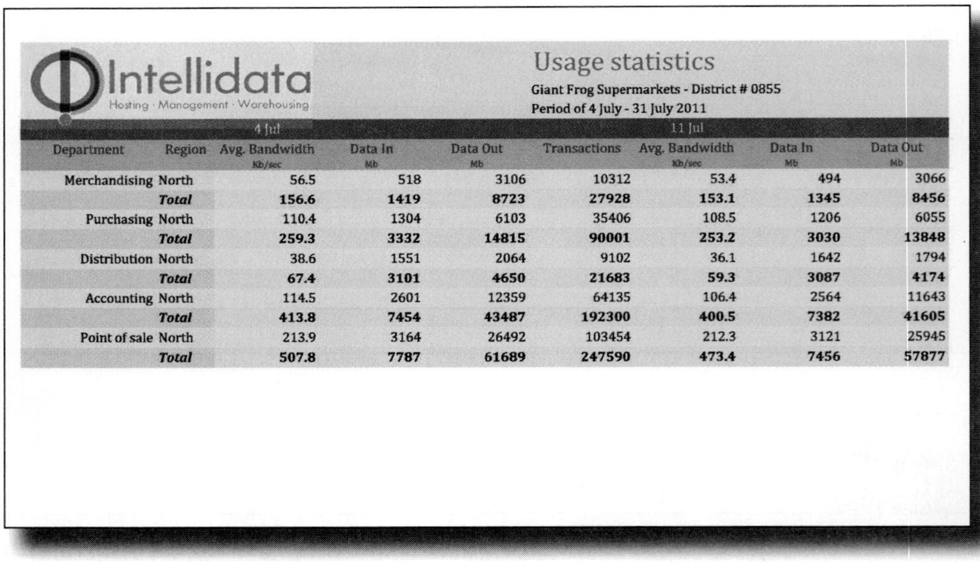

Usage statistics
Giant Frog Supermarkets - District # 0855
Period of 4 July - 31 July 2011

Department	Region	Avg. Bandwidth Kb/sec	Data In Mb	Data Out Mb	Transactions	Avg. Bandwidth kb/sec	Data In Mb	Data Out Mb
		4 Jul				11 Jul		
Merchandising	North	56.5	518	3106	10312	53.4	494	3066
	Total	156.6	1419	8723	27928	153.1	1345	8456
Purchasing	North	110.4	1304	6103	35406	108.5	1206	6055
	Total	259.3	3332	14815	90001	253.2	3030	13848
Distribution	North	38.6	1551	2064	9102	36.1	1642	1794
	Total	67.4	3101	4650	21683	59.3	3087	4174
Accounting	North	114.5	2601	12359	64135	106.4	2564	11643
	Total	413.8	7454	43487	192300	400.5	7382	41605
Point of sale	North	213.9	3164	26492	103454	212.3	3121	25945
	Total	507.8	7787	61689	247590	473.4	7456	57877

Project 6—Apply It

Creating Multiple Views of a Worksheet

DIRECTIONS

1. Start Excel, if necessary, and open **EProj06** from the data files for this lesson.

2. Save the file as **EProj06_studentfirstname_ studentlastname** in the location where your teacher instructs you to store the files for this lesson.

3. Select rows 6 through 26 and unhide them.

   ✓ *Redisplay the row and column headings, if needed.*

4. Create a custom view on the **Usage statistics 0704** worksheet for the **South** offices.

   a. Click cell **B7** and press ⌈CTRL⌉ and click all the places where the words *North* or *Central* appears in column B.

   b. Hide the rows for *North* and *Central*.

   ✓ *If you redisplayed the row and column headings so you could select the rows to hide, be sure to rehide the headings prior to creating each view.*

   c. View the worksheet in Custom View.

   d. Click **Add** and type **South** in the **Name** box.

   e. Ensure that both options are selected and click **OK**.

✓ *Since the department labels appear next to "North" for each group, they disappear in the views for the South and Central offices. This is the kind of problem we'll address in Lesson 6.*

5. Create a custom view on the **Usage statistics 0704** worksheet for the Central offices.

   a. Press ⌈CTRL⌉ and click all the places where the words *North* or *South* appears in column B.

   b. Hide the rows for *North* and *Central*.

   c. View the worksheet in Custom View.

   d. Click **Add** and type **Central** in the **Name** box.

   e. Ensure that both options are selected and click **OK**.

6. Unhide all the rows and test switching to a custom view by showing the South view.

7. Unhide all rows and redisplay the row and column headings again.

8. **With your teacher's permission**, print each of the three custom views. Your worksheet should look similar to Figure 3-2.

9. Close the document, saving all changes, and exit Excel.

Figure 3-2

Intellidata
Hosting · Management · Warehousing

Usage statistics
Giant Frog Supermarkets - District # 0855
Period of 4 July - 31 July 2011

		4 Jul				11 Jul	
Department	Region	Avg. Bandwidth Kb/sec	Data In Mb	Data Out Mb	Transactions	Avg. Bandwidth Kb/sec	Data In Mb
	Central	51.6	495	2943	9103	49.6	487
	Total	**156.6**	**1419**	**8723**	**27928**	**153.1**	**1345**
	Central	89.1	1064	3946	29431	84.5	984
	Total	**259.3**	**3332**	**14815**	**90001**	**253.2**	**3030**
	Central	12.4	674	943	4121	9.8	584
	Total	**67.4**	**3101**	**4650**	**21683**	**59.3**	**3087**
	Central	214.7	3169	21661	81355	205.6	3024
	Total	**413.8**	**7454**	**43487**	**192300**	**400.5**	**7382**
	Central	109.9	1974	15464	65467	97	1821
	Total	**507.8**	**7787**	**61689**	**247590**	**473.4**	**7456**

Lesson 4

Customizing Styles and Themes

WORDS TO KNOW

Excel table
Data arranged in columns and specially formatted with column headers that contain commands that allow you to sort, filter, and perform other functions on the table.

➤ What You Will Learn

Customizing a Workbook Theme
Creating a Custom Table Style

Software Skills   To make a worksheet look more professional, you might want to customize the standard themes Excel provides by choosing company-style fonts and colors. You'll also learn how to create a custom table style.

Application Skills   The worksheet you designed to track accessories sold each day at your PhotoTown store has proven very helpful, and the corporate headquarters may adopt it throughout the company. You need to create a custom theme that includes company standards. As an alternative, you will also create a custom table style for their review.

What You Can Do

Customizing a Workbook Theme

- A theme is a collection of fonts, colors, and effects, saved as a collection that can be applied in a single click.
- You can select a different set of existing fonts, colors, and effects and save these new choices together in a new theme.
- You can also create your own custom set of colors or fonts for use with a theme.
- Themes you create are automatically added to the Themes list on the Page Layout tab.

Try It! **Modifying an Existing Set of Theme Colors**

1 Start Excel and open ETry04 file from the data files for this lesson.

2 Save the file as ETry04_studentfirstname_studentlastname in the location where your teacher instructs you to store the files for this lesson.

3 Click Page Layout > Colors ▣ and select Create New Theme Colors.

4 Click the Accent 6 button and select Light Blue, Text 2.

5 Click the Accent 2 button and select Light Blue, Text 2, Darker 50%.

6 Click the Hyperlink down arrow and select Teal, Accent 5, Darker 50%.

7 Type your name in the Name box and click Save.

✓ *If you don't want to save this new set of colors, click Reset to reset them to the original theme colors.*

8 Save changes and leave the file open to use in the next Try It.

The Create New Theme Colors dialog box

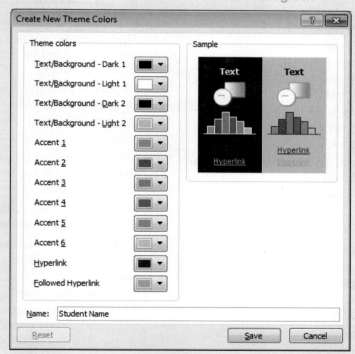

Try It! **Modifying an Existing Set of Theme Fonts**

1 In the ETry04_studentfirstname_studentlastname file, click Page Layout > Fonts 🅰 .

2 Click Create New Theme Fonts.

3 Click the Heading font down arrow and select Verdana.

4 Click the Body font down arrow and select Tahoma.

5 Type your name in the Name box and click Save.

6 Save changes and leave the file open to use in the next Try It.

Try It!   Saving a New Theme

1 In the **ETry04_studentfirstname_studentlastname** file, click Page Layout > Themes and select Elemental.

2 Click Page Layout > Colors > Student Name.

3 Click Page Layout > Fonts > Student Name.

4 Click Page Layout > Themes.

5 Select Save Current Theme.

6 Type your name in the File name box and click Save.

7 Save changes and leave the file open to use in the next Try It.

Creating a Custom Table Style

- You can convert a list of data in Excel into a table using the Format as Table button on the Home tab.
- You select an overall table format and other formatting settings on the Table Tools Design tab.
- You can use one of Excel's many existing table formats or create a custom table style that will appear in the Table Style gallery. You can then apply that table style to any other table.
- When you create a new table style, you can also set your new table style as the default table quick style to be used in that workbook.
- Using the New Table Quick Style dialog box, you can format the following table elements:
  - **Whole Table**: Applies a formatting choice to the entire table.
  - **First Column Stripe**: Applies a formatting choice to the first column in the table as well as each alternating column.
  - **Second Column Stripe**: Applies a formatting choice to the second column in the table as well as each alternating column.
  - **First Row Stripe**: Applies a formatting choice to the first row in the table as well as each alternating row.
  - **Second Row Stripe**: Applies a formatting choice to the second row in the table as well as each alternating row.
  - **Last Column**: Applies a formatting choice to the last column in a table. The last column usually contains totals.
  - **First Column**: Applies a formatting choice to the first column in a table. The first column usually contains headings.
  - **Header Row**: Applies a formatting choice to the Header row in a table.
  - **Total Row**: Applies a formatting choice to the final totals row in a table.
  - **First Header Cell**: Applies a formatting choice to the first cell in the header row. This cell often contains no data.
  - **Last Header Cell**: Applies a formatting choice to the final cell in the header row in a table.
  - **First Total Cell**: Applies a formatting choice to the first cell in the total row. This cell often contains the heading "Total".
  - **Last Total Cell**: Applies a formatting choice to the final cell in the total row. This cell often holds an overall total number.

Try It!   Formatting a Table

1 In the **ETry04_studentfirstname_studentlastname** file, select the range A2:H7.

2 Click Home > Format as Table.

3 Select Table Style Light 1.

4 Make sure that the data range shown in the Format As Table dialog box reflects the range A2:H7.

5 Select the My table has headers box and click OK.

6 On the Table Tools Design tab, select the following options in the Table Style Options group: Header Row, Total Row, Last Column. Deselect any other options.

7 Save changes and leave the file open to use in the next Try It.

Try It!   **Creating a New Table Style**

1 In the **ETry04_studentfirstname_ studentlastname** file, click Home > Format as Table 📊 > New Table Style.

2 Type your name in the Name box.

3 Select Header Row and click Format.

4 Click the Fill tab and click Black under Background Color, then click the Font tab and select White, Background 1 in the Color palette and click OK.

5 Select Total Row and click Format.

6 Click the Border tab and click Outline and select the double line option in the Style list.

7 Click the Fill tab and click the brighter blue in the middle of the theme colors and click OK.

8 Select the Last Total Cell and click Format.

9 Click the Fill tab and select the Orange color on the Standard colors palette and click OK.

10 Select Whole Table and click Format.

11 Click the Border tab and select Inside, choose the Blue-Gray, Accent 4 color.

12 Click OK and then click OK again.

13 Click inside your table and click Table Tools Design and then select the new style in the Table Styles gallery.

14 Close **ETry04_studentfirstname_ studentlastname**, saving all changes, and exit Excel.

The New Table Quick Style dialog box

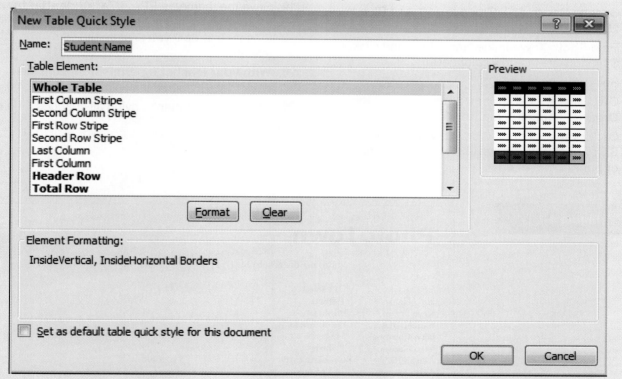

Project 7—Create It

Creating a Custom Theme

DIRECTIONS

1. Start Excel, if necessary, and open **EProj07** from the data files for this lesson.

2. Save the file as **EProj07_studentfirstname_ studentlastname** in the location where your teacher instructs you to store the files for this lesson.

3. Click **Page Layout > Colors** ■ and select **Create New Theme Colors**.

4. Click the **Accent 5** button and select **More Colors**.

5. Set Red to **224**, Green to **183**, and Blue to **119** and click **OK**.

6. Click the **Accent 6** button and select **More Colors**.

7. Change Red to **160**, Green to **113**, and Blue to **255** and click **OK**.

8. Type **Photo Town** in the Name box, and click **Save** to save the new color set.

9. Select the range **A6:C6**.

10. Click **Home > Fill Color** 🖌 and choose **Light Orange, Accent 5, Lighter 40%**.

11. Click **Home > Font Color** **A** and choose **Light Blue, Accent 6, Darker 25% (fifth row, last column)**.

12. Click **Page Layout > Fonts** Ⓐ and select **Create New Theme Fonts**.

13. Click the Heading font down arrow and select **Arial Rounded MT Bold**.

14. Click the Body font down arrow and select **Baskerville Old Face**.

15. Type **Photo Town** in the Name box, and click **Save** to save the new font set.

16. Select the cells **A6:C6**. Press ⌨CTRL and click cell **A2** as well.

17. Click **Home > Font > Arial Rounded MT Bold**.

18. Click **Page Layout > Themes** Ⓐ **> Save Current Theme**.

19. Save the theme as **EProj07a_studentfirstname_ studentlastname** in the location where your teacher instructs you to store the files for this lesson.

20. **With your teacher's permission**, print the worksheet. It should look similar to Figure 4-1.

21. Close the document, saving all changes, and exit Excel.

Figure 4-1

PhotoTown

Photo products sold on 7/22

Employee	Product	No. Sold
Jairo Campos	T-shirts	2
Kere Freed	Photo books	1
Taneel Black	Photo books	2
Jairo Campos	Mugs	4
Jairo Campos	T-shirts	1
Akira Ota	Greeting cards	100
Akira Ota	3-D photos	
Kere Freed	Greeting cards	150
Taneel Black	Photo books	2

Total receipts   214.75

Project 8—Apply It

Creating a Custom Table Style

DIRECTIONS

1. Start Excel, if necessary, and open **EProj08** from the data files for this lesson.
2. Save the file as **EProj08_studentfirstname_ studentlastname** in the location where your teacher instructs you to store the files for this lesson.
3. Click **Home > Format as Table 📊 > New Table Style**.
4. Type your name in the Name box and apply the following formatting to the different table elements:
   a. Whole Table: On the **Border** tab, select both **Inside** and **Outline**.
   b. Header Row: On the **Fill** tab, select the **purple** color in the **Theme** colors area. On the Font tab, select **Bold** and the **Light Blue, Background 2** font color.
   c. Last Total Cell: On the **Fill** tab, select the **gold** color in the **Standard** colors area. On the **Border** tab, select the **thick line** style and select **Outline**.

d. Second Row Stripe: On the **Fill** tab, select the **middle light orange** color in the **Theme** colors area.
e. Last Column: On the **Fill** tab, select the **blue-gray** color in the **Theme** colors area (fourth color from the right). On the **Font** tab, select **Bold**.

5. Select the range **A5:E15** and format this range as a table.
6. Select **Student Name** (your new table style) and then click **OK**.
7. On the Table Tools Design tab, select the following Table Style Options: **Header Row, Total Row, Banded Rows, Last Column**.
8. Adjust column widths as necessary.
9. Add a footer that includes your name.
10. **With your teacher's permission**, print each of the three custom views. Your worksheet should look similar to Figure 4-2.
11. Close the document, saving all changes, and exit Excel.

Figure 4-2

PhotoTown

Photo products sold on 7/22

Employee	Product	No. Sold	Cost per Item	Total Sales
Jairo Campos	T-shirts	2	10	20
Kere Freed	Photo books	1	6.25	6.25
Taneel Black	Photo books	2	6.25	12.5
Jairo Campos	Mugs	4	4	16
Jairo Campos	T-shirts	1	10	10
Akira Ota	Greeting cards	100	0.55	55
Akira Ota	3-D photos	3	2.25	6.75
Kere Freed	Greeting cards	150	0.55	82.5
Taneel Black	Photo books	2	6.25	12.5
Total				221.5

Lesson 5

Using Advanced Sort

WORDS TO KNOW

Ascending order

An arrangement of items in alphabetical order (A to Z) or numerical order (1, 2, 3, and so on). Dates are arranged from oldest to most recent.

Descending order

An arrangement of items in reverse alphabetical order (Z to A) or reverse numerical order (10, 9, 8, and so on). Dates are arranged from newest to oldest.

Key

One level within a sort. For example, you might sort a list by last name (one key) and then sort duplicate last names by first name (another key).

> **What You Will Learn**

Sorting Excel Items
Understanding the Rules for Advanced Sorting
Sorting on Multiple Columns
Removing a Sort

Software Skills   Entering data in random order might make the job a bit easier, but trying to find information in a disorganized spreadsheet is time consuming. So, after entering data into a list, the first order of business is ordering (sorting) the data.

Application Skills   When you add a new patient to the list of cats and dogs in the Wood Hills Animal Clinic patients list, it appears at the end of that list, which ruins the alphabetical order. Luckily, Excel can sort entries for you extremely easily and quickly.

What You Can Do

Sorting Excel Items

- After entering data into an Excel list or table, you can arrange the items in any order: alphabetically (for example, a list of names), or numerically (a price list), or date order (a list of employees and their hire dates).
- Lists can be sorted in **ascending** order or **descending** order.
  - Ascending order will arrange labels alphabetically (A to Z), numbers from smallest to largest, and dates from oldest to most recent.
  - Descending order is simply the reverse of ascending order.

- You can sort any contiguous data in the worksheet; it doesn't have to be a list or table. For example, you might want to sort an expense report to list all the expenses in order by account number.

- You can sort data by using the sort buttons on the Data tab, the Home tab or with the down-arrow button that appears beside the field names in the top row of an Excel table.

  - The sort buttons change names depending on the type of data you're trying to sort.

  - If you're sorting text, the buttons are called Sort A to Z and Sort Z to A.

  - If you're sorting numbers, the buttons are called Sort Smallest to Largest and Sort Largest to Smallest.

  - If you're sorting dates, the buttons are called Sort Oldest to Newest and Sort Newest to Oldest.

Understanding the Rules for Advanced Sorting

- Excel sorts data based on the actual cell content, not the displayed results.

- If you choose to sort in ascending order, items are arranged as follows:

  - Numeric sort—Numbers are sorted from the largest negative number to the largest positive number. For example, -3, -2, -1, 0, 1, 2, and so on.

  - Alphanumeric sort—Labels (text or text/number combinations) are sorted first by symbols, then by letters.

  - Hyphens (-) and apostrophes (') are ignored in alphanumeric sorts, however, if the cell's contents are identical apart from a hyphen or apostrophe in which case the cell containing the symbol is placed last.

  - If names in the list contain spaces (de Lancie), the sort results may differ from what you expect. Because spaces sort to the top of the list, de Lancie lands above Dean and Debrazzi.

- When number/text combinations are sorted alphanumerically, combinations like 1Q through 11Q, for example, sort like this 10Q, 11Q, 1Q, 2Q, 3Q, and so on.

- Dates are sorted chronologically. For example, 1/10/09 would come before 2/12/09.

- If a cell in the sort column is blank, that record is placed at the end of the list.

- As an example of sorted records, consider this list:

  - Jay's Grill   1256 Adams Ave.
  - CompuTrain   12 Brown Street
  - Central Perk
  - Carriage Club   Carriage Center
  - Giving Tree   Mark Building

- If the list is sorted by address (ascending order), you'll end up with:

  - Compu Train   12 Brown Street
  - Jay's Grill   1256 Adams Ave.
  - Giving Tree   Mark Building
  - Carriage Club   Carriage Center
  - Central Perk

- Notice that the record that doesn't contain an address is placed last when you sort by address.

- Using the Sort Options dialog box, you can sort left to right (across a row) rather than top to bottom (down a column). This option is useful if your list is organized with a horizontal rather than a vertical orientation.

- You also can sort with case sensitivity. In a case sensitive sort, capital letters are sorted after lowercase letters, so kit appears above Kit.

Try It!   Sorting a List in Ascending or Descending Order

1 Start Excel and open **ETry05** from the data files for this lesson.

2 Save the file as **ETry05_studentfirstname_ studentlastname** in the location where your teacher instructs you to store the files for this lesson.

3 Click cell F8.

4 Click Data > Sort Smallest to Largest ↓.

5 Click Data > Sort Largest to Smallest ↓.

6 Save changes and leave the file open to use in the next Try It.

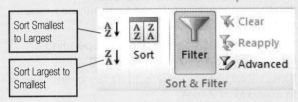

The Sort & Filter Group

Sort Smallest to Largest

Sort Largest to Smallest

Try It!   Sorting in a Table in Ascending or Descending Order

1 In **ETry05_studentfirstname_ studentlastname**, click the arrow next to the First Name column heading.

2 Click Sort A to Z.

3 Click the arrow next to the Hire Date column heading.

4 Click Sort Newest to Oldest.

5 Save changes and leave the file open to use in the next Try It.

Try It!   Sorting in a Table by Formatting

1 In **ETry05_studentfirstname_ studentlastname**, click the arrow next to the Last Name column heading.

2 Select Sort by Color.

3 Select the Green fill color.

4 Save changes and leave the file open to use in the next Try It.

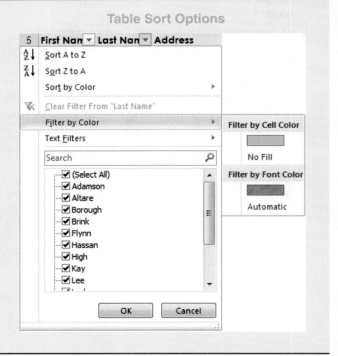

Table Sort Options

Sorting on Multiple Columns

■ Data can be sorted using one or more **keys**.

■ For example, an employee listing could be sorted by ZIP code. Employees with duplicate Zip codes are then sorted by surname (last name), and those with duplicate surnames are sorted by given name (first name) for a total of three keys.

■ You can use the Sort dialog box to create a custom sort that contains multiple sort levels.

Try It!   **Creating a Custom Sort**

1   In ETry05_studentfirstname_studentlastname, click cell B9.

2   Click Data > Sort 🔲.

✓ Notice that the last sort appears as the first sort level. You can keep it or change it.

3   Click the Add Level button and then click the Column Then by down arrow and select Last Name.

4   Click the Sort On down arrow and select Font Color.

5   Click the Automatic down arrow and select the Red font color.

6   Click the Add Level button and then click the next Column Then by down arrow and select Start Time.

7   Click OK.

8   Save changes and leave the file open to use in the next Try It.

The Sort dialog box

Sort		? ✕

🔼 Add Level	✕ Delete Level	📋 Copy Level	▲ ▼	Options...	☑ My data has headers

Column		Sort On		Order	
Sort by	Last Name ▼	Cell Color ▼		▼	On Top ▼
Then by	Last Name ▼	Font Color ▼		▼	On Top ▼
Then by	Start Time ▼	Values ▼		Smallest to Largest ▼	

OK	Cancel

Removing a Sort

- You can undo a sort if you click the Undo button immediately after completing the sort.

- If you don't undo a sort immediately, the original sort order is lost.

- To protect your data, always save the workbook prior to sorting.

    ✓ *If something goes wrong, simply close the workbook without saving changes, and open the previously saved version.*

- If you want to keep your original sort order as well as the new, sorted list, copy the original list to another sheet in the workbook and then sort.

- Another way to restore the original record order at any time is to include a unique field in every record.

    - For example, you could include a field called Record Number, and fill in unique numbers for each record. (Make sure all numbers are the same length.)

    - To restore the original order, simply sort by the Record Number column.

Try It!   **Removing a Sort**

1. In **ETry05_studentfirstname_ studentlastname**, right-click the column F heading and select Insert.

2. In cell F5, type **Record Number**.

3. In cell F6, type **1**. In cell F7 type **2**.

4. Select cells F6 and F7 and drag the bottom right corner down to cell F20 so that AutoFill completes the record number list.

5. Click cell A11 and click Data > Sort A to Z ↓ .

6. Click the arrow next to the Hire Date column heading.

7. Click Sort Oldest to Newest.

8. Click Undo ↺ .

9. Click cell F8 and click Data > Sort Smallest to Largest ↓ .

10. Close **ETry05_studentfirstname_ studentlastname**, saving all changes, and exit Excel.

Project 9—Create It

Sort a Patient List

DIRECTIONS

1. Start Excel, if necessary, and open **EProj09** from the data files for this lesson.

2. Save the file as **EProj09_studentfirstname_ studentlastname** in the location where your teacher instructs you to store the files for this lesson.

3. Click the arrow next to the Breed field name and click **Sort A to Z**.

4. Divide cats from dogs by sorting:
   a. Click cell **B8**.
   b. Click **Data > Sort A to Z**.

✓ Notice that the cat breeds and the dog breeds are still sorted alphabetically as well, by virtue of the sort you performed earlier.

5. Add a footer with your name in it.

6. **With your teacher's permission**, print the worksheet. It should look similar to Figure 5-1.

7. Close the document, saving all changes, and exit Excel.

Figure 5-1

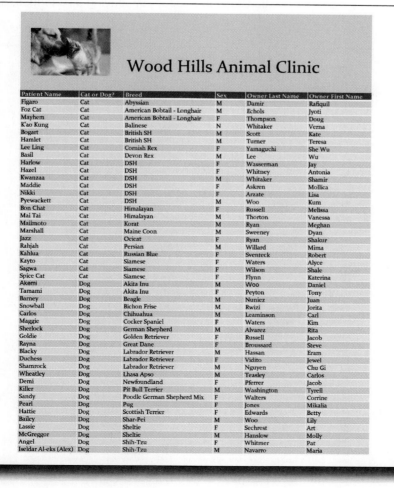

Wood Hills Animal Clinic

Patient Name	Cat or Dog?	Breed	Sex	Owner Last Name	Owner First Name
Figaro	Cat	Abyssian	M	Damir	Rafiquil
Foz Cat	Cat	American Bobtail - Longhair	M	Echols	Jyoti
Mayhem	Cat	American Bobtail - Longhair	F	Thompson	Doug
K'ao Kung	Cat	Balinese	N	Whitaker	Verna
Bogart	Cat	British SH	M	Scott	Kate
Hamlet	Cat	British SH	M	Turner	Teresa
Lee Ling	Cat	Cornish Rex	F	Yamaguchi	She Wu
Basil	Cat	Devon Rex	M	Lee	Wu
Harlow	Cat	DSH	F	Wasserman	Jay
Hazel	Cat	DSH	F	Whitney	Antonia
Kwanzaa	Cat	DSH	M	Whitaker	Shamir
Maddie	Cat	DSH	F	Askren	Mollica
Nikki	Cat	DSH	F	Arzate	Lisa
Pyewackett	Cat	DSH	M	Woo	Kum
Bon Chat	Cat	Himalayan	F	Russell	Melissa
Mai Tai	Cat	Himalayan	M	Thorton	Vanessa
Maiimoto	Cat	Korat	M	Ryan	Meghan
Marshall	Cat	Maine Coon	M	Sweeney	Dyan
Jazz	Cat	Ocicat	F	Ryan	Shakur
Rahjah	Cat	Persian	M	Willard	Mima
Kahlua	Cat	Russian Blue	F	Sventeck	Robert
Kayto	Cat	Siamese	F	Waters	Alyce
Sagwa	Cat	Siamese	F	Wilson	Shale
Spice Cat	Cat	Siamese	F	Flynn	Katerina
Akemi	Dog	Akita Inu	M	Woo	Daniel
Tamami	Dog	Akita Inu	F	Peyton	Tony
Barney	Dog	Beagle	M	Nuniez	Juan
Snowball	Dog	Bichon Frise	M	Rwizi	Jorita
Carlos	Dog	Chihuahua	M	Leaminson	Carl
Maggie	Dog	Cocker Spaniel	F	Waters	Kim
Sherlock	Dog	German Shepherd	M	Alvarez	Rita
Goldie	Dog	Golden Retriever	F	Russell	Jacob
Rayna	Dog	Great Dane	F	Broussard	Steve
Blacky	Dog	Labrador Retriever	M	Hassan	Eram
Duchess	Dog	Labrador Retriever	F	Vidito	Jewel
Shamrock	Dog	Labrador Retriever	M	Nguyen	Chu Gi
Wheatley	Dog	Lhasa Apso	M	Teasley	Carlos
Demi	Dog	Newfoundland	F	Pferrer	Jacob
Killer	Dog	Pit Bull Terrier	M	Washington	Tyrell
Sandy	Dog	Poodle German Shepherd Mix	F	Walters	Corrine
Pearl	Dog	Pug	F	Jones	Mikalia
Hattie	Dog	Scottish Terrier	F	Edwards	Betty
Bailey	Dog	Shar-Pei	M	Woo	Lily
Lassie	Dog	Sheltie	F	Sechrest	Art
McGreggor	Dog	Sheltie	M	Hanslow	Molly
Angel	Dog	Shih-Tzu	F	Whitmer	Pat
Iseldar Al-eks (Alex)	Dog	Shih-Tzu	M	Navarro	Maria

Project 10—Apply It

Custom Sort a Patient List

DIRECTIONS

1. Start Excel, if necessary, and open **EProj10** from the data files for this lesson.

2. Save the file as **EProj10_studentfirstname_studentlastname** in the location where your teacher instructs you to store the files for this lesson.

3. Sort the table by cat or dog, then sex (males first), then breed (see Figure 5-2):

   a. Click anywhere inside the table.

   b. Click **Data > Sort**.

   c. Select **Cat or Dog** from the **Sort by** list.

   d. Select **Values** from the **Sort On** list.

   e. Select **A to Z** from the **Order** list.

   f. Click **Add Level**.

   g. Select **Sex** from the **Column Then** by list.

   h. Select **Values** from the **Sort On** list.

   i. Select **Z to A** from the **Order** list.

   j. Click **Add Level**.

   k. Select **Breed** from the **Then** by list.

   l. Select **Values** from the **Sort On** list

   m. Select **A to Z** from the **Order** list.

   n. Click **OK**.

4. Add a header with your name in it.

5. **With your teacher's permission**, print the worksheet.

6. Close the document, saving all changes, and exit Excel.

Figure 5-2

Wood Hills Animal Clinic

Patient Name	Cat or Dog?	Breed	Sex	Owner Last Name	Owner First Name
Figaro	Cat	Abyssian	M	Damir	Rafiquil
Fez Cat	Cat	American Bobtail - Longhair	M	Echols	Jyoti
K'so Kung	Cat	Balinese	M	Whitaker	Verna
Bogart	Cat	British SH	M	Scott	Kate
Hamlet	Cat	British SH	M	Turner	Teresa
Basil	Cat	Devon Rex	M	Lee	Wu
Kwanzaa	Cat	DSH	M	Whitaker	Shamir
Pyewackett	Cat	DSH	M	Woo	Kum
Mai Tai	Cat	Himalayan	M	Thorton	Vanessa
Maimoto	Cat	Korat	M	Ryan	Meghan
Marshall	Cat	Maine Coon	M	Sweeney	Dyan
Rahjah	Cat	Persian	M	Willard	Mirna
Mayhem	Cat	American Bobtail - Longhair	F	Thompson	Doug
Lee Ling	Cat	Cornish Rex	F	Yamaguchi	She Wu
Harlow	Cat	DSH	F	Wasserman	Jay
Hazel	Cat	DSH	F	Whitney	Antonia
Maddie	Cat	DSH	F	Askren	Mollica
Nikki	Cat	DSH	F	Arzate	Lisa
Bon Chat	Cat	Himalayan	F	Russell	Melissa
Jazz	Cat	Ocicat	F	Ryan	Shakur
Kahlua	Cat	Russian Blue	F	Sventeek	Robert
Kayto	Cat	Siamese	F	Waters	Alyce
Sagwa	Cat	Siamese	F	Wilson	Shale
Spice Cat	Cat	Siamese	F	Flynn	Katerina
Akemi	Dog	Akita Inu	M	Woo	Daniel
Barney	Dog	Beagle	M	Nunez	Juan
Snowball	Dog	Bichon Frise	M	Rwizi	Jorita
Carlos	Dog	Chihuahua	M	Leaminson	Carl
Sherlock	Dog	German Shepherd	M	Alvarez	Rita
Blacky	Dog	Labrador Retriever	M	Hassan	Eram
Shamrock	Dog	Labrador Retriever	M	Nguyen	Chu Gi
Wheatley	Dog	Lhasa Apso	M	Teasley	Carlos
Killer	Dog	Pit Bull Terrier	M	Washington	Tyrell
Bailey	Dog	Shar-Pei	M	Woo	Lily
McGreggor	Dog	Sheltie	M	Hanslow	Molly
Iseldar Al-eks (Alex)	Dog	Shih-Tzu	M	Navarro	Maria
Kidlak	Dog	Siberian Husky	M	Sweares	Lucy
Kodiak	Dog	Siberian Husky	M	Wilson	Opal
Luddie	Dog	Yorkie	M	Eccles	Nyla
Gizmo	Dog	Yorkshire Terrier	M	Hu	Joi
Tamami	Dog	Akita Inu	F	Peyton	Tony
Maggie	Dog	Cocker Spaniel	F	Waters	Kim
Goldie	Dog	Golden Retriever	F	Russell	Jacob
Rayna	Dog	Great Dane	F	Broussard	Steve
Duchess	Dog	Labrador Retriever	F	Vidito	Jewel
Demi	Dog	Newfoundland	F	Pferrer	Jacob
Sandy	Dog	Poodle German Shepherd Mix	F	Walters	Corrine

Lesson 6

Using Advanced Filtering

> ## What You Will Learn

Using AutoFilter to Filter Tables

Using AutoFilter to Filter by Custom Criteria

Filtering Items without Creating a Table

Filtering by Using Advanced Criteria

Removing an In-Place Advanced Filter

Extracting Filtered Rows

Using Sum, Average, and Count in a Filtered Table

Software Skills   When you're looking for particular records in a long list, you can use a filter to reduce the number of records to just the ones you want to view right now. You can use an advanced filter to extract the matching records and then format, sort, and make other changes to them without affecting the records in the list. This is handy when you want to print or format a subset of the list. In addition, advanced filters let you create complex criteria using formulas, multiple conditions applied to a single field, and so on, to filter the list.

Application Skills   You're continuing to put together the inventory tracking sheet for Wood Hills Animal Clinic, and it's looking pretty good. It's your job now to make some sense of all this data. You plan to use filtering to organize the information and make printouts based on particular data the boss has requested.

WORDS TO KNOW

Criteria range
Area of the worksheet in which you specify the criteria for selecting records from the list or table.

Extract
Copy records that match specified criteria to another place in the worksheet where they can be changed, sorted, formatted, printed, and so on.

Extract range
Area where Excel copies the list or table records that match the specified criteria.

Calculated column
A special column that can be added to a table, in which a single formula is automatically applied to each row.

Excel table
A special column that can be added to a table, in which a single formula is automatically applied to each row.

Filter
Reduce the total number of records displayed on the screen to a selected group.

List
A range of Excel data organized primarily in columns.

Total row
A row that can be displayed at the bottom of an Excel table, which provides functions for calculating the values in each column selectively.

What You Can Do

Using AutoFilter to Filter Tables

- You can use the new AutoFilter feature to find pertinent information in a worksheet quickly.
- You can use AutoFilter to **filter** the data in multiple columns.

- When you use AutoFilters, the AutoFilter dropdowns take the place of the column headers when scrolling through long lists so that you can easily see what you're categories are.
- You can access the AutoFilter search settings by clicking the AutoFilter dropdowns.

Try It! Using AutoFilter to Filter Tables

1. Start Excel and open **ETry06** from the data files for this lesson.

2. Save the file as **ETry06_studentfirstname_studentlastname** in the location where your teacher instructs you to store the files for this lesson.

3. Scroll down to cell B23.

4. Click the arrow ▼ next to the Salesperson heading.

5. Deselect (Select All) and then select Alice Harper. Click OK.

6. Hover on the Filter indicator for the Salesperson column to see the ScreenTip.

7. Save changes and leave the file open to use in the next Try It.

Use the Filter Indicator to see your filter criteria

Salesperson	Cost	Sales Ince
Alice Harper	Salesperson: Equals "Alice Harper"	0.28
Alice Harper	$ 11.50 $	0.35
Alice Harper	$ 34.75 $	1.04
Alice Harper	$ 17.75 $	0.53

Using AutoFilter to Filter by Custom Criteria

- In Excel 2010, you can search for specific criteria within an AutoFilter. This allows you to quickly jump to the information you want without having to scroll through a long list of values.

- You can set up an AutoFilter based on specific numeric or text values, formatting, or based on specific custom criteria.

Try It! Using AutoFilter to Filter by Custom Criteria

1. In **ETry06_studentfirstname_studentlastname**, select cell A1.

2. Click the arrow next to the Cost heading.

3. Point to Number Filters and select Greater Than from the list.

4. In the box to the right of the is greater than box, type **15**. Click OK.

5. Click the arrow next to the Description heading.

6. Point to Text Filters and select Custom Filter from the list.

7. In the first box, click does not contain and in the second box, type **puppy**.

8. Click And. Then, in the first box of the second row, select *does not end with*.

(continued)

Try It!   **Using AutoFilter to Filter by Custom Criteria** *(continued)*

9 In the second box, type **n**. Click OK.

10 Click the arrow next to the *Product Type* heading.

11 Point to Filter by Color and select the blue fill color.

12 Save changes and leave the file open to use in the next Try It.

The Custom AutoFilter dialog box

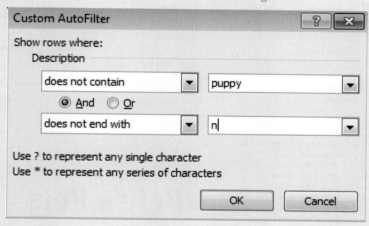

Filtering Items without Creating a Table

■ As mentioned earlier, you do not need to convert a **list** into an **Excel table** in order to filter its data.

■ A **table**, however, does give you several advantages. With a table, you can:

• Create formulas that reference the columns in the table by their name.

• Format the table with a single click.

• Add a **total row** that allows you to select from a range of functions that sum, average, count, or perform other operations on the data in a column.

• Add a **calculated column** that allows you to enter a formula and have that formula copied instantly throughout the column. For example, you could link to Microsoft Excel data during a presentation.

Try It!   **Filtering Items without Creating a Table**

1 In **ETry06_studentfirstname_ studentlastname**, click the Pet Supplies Inventory worksheet tab.

2 Click anywhere in the range A5:H32 and click Data > Filter ▼ .

✓ *Arrow buttons appear next to each column name.*

3 Click the arrow next to the Current Inventory heading.

4 Point to Number Filters and select Less Than Or Equal To from the list.

5 In the second box of the first row, type **10**. Click OK.

(continued)

Try It!   **Filtering Items without Creating a Table** *(continued)*

6 Click the arrow next to the *Description* heading.

7 Deselect the (Select All) option.

8 Type **Collar** in the Search box. Click OK.

9 Save changes and leave the document open to use in the next Try It.

A List Offers Most of the Same Filter Features as a Table

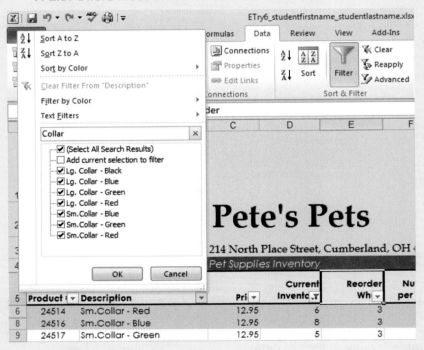

Try It!   **Removing a Filter from a List**

✓ *This process will redisplay all records and remove the filter arrows from a list, but not a table.*

1 In **ETry06_studentfirstname_studentlastname**, in the Pet Supplies worksheet, click any cell in the list.

2 Click Data > Filter .

3 Save changes and leave the file open to use in the next Try It.

Filtering by Using Advanced Criteria

- With an advanced filter, you can filter records to hide records that do not match the criteria you specify—in much the same way as with a regular filter.

- An advanced filter allows you to enter more complex criteria than a regular filter:

- Instead of selecting criteria from a drop-down list, you enter it in a special area in the workbook—perhaps a worksheet unto itself—set aside for that purpose.

- In the marked cells of this **criteria range**, you enter the items you want to match from the list, or expressions that describe the type of comparison you wish to make.

- You then open a dialog box in which you specify the range where the list or table is contained, the range containing the criteria, and the range to which you want records copied/extracted (if applicable).

■ To set up the criteria range, you simply copy the field names from the top of the list to another area of the worksheet, or to a separate worksheet in the same workbook.

  ✓ *The labels in the criteria range must exactly match the labels used in the list, which is why you should copy them rather than typing them.*

Guidelines for Entering Criteria

■ After the criteria range is established, you enter criteria in the criteria range, below the field names you copied.

  ✓ *The following examples are strictly for purposes of demonstration; the field names and contents of your list or table will likely differ from those shown here.*

- For example, to display only records belonging to Smith, you might type Smith under the Last Name field name in the criteria range you've established.

■ If you want to establish an AND condition, where two or more criteria must be true for a record to match, then type the criteria under their proper field names in the same row.

  - For example, to display records where the quantity on hand is over 25 AND the cost is less than $10, type both criteria in the same row, each in their respective column.

■ If you want to establish an OR condition, where any of two or more criteria will qualify a record as a match, then type the criteria under their proper field names, but in separate rows.

■ When you enter text, Excel looks for any match beginning with that text. For example, typing Sam under the First Name label would match records such as Sam, Samuel, and Samantha.

■ You can use wildcards when entering text criteria.

  - A question mark (?) can be used to replace a single character in a specific position within the text. For example, type Sm?th under the Last Name label to get Smith and Smyth.

  - An asterisk (*) can be used to replace one or several characters within the text. For example, type Sm*th under the Last Name label to get Smith, Smyth, Smouth, and Smaningfith.

- Because ? and * are assumed to be wildcards, if you want to find records that actually contain those characters, you must precede them with a tilde (~). For example, type RJ4~?S2 to get RJ4?S2.

■ You can use operators to compare text, numbers, or dates.

  - Operators include < (less than), > (greater than), <= (less than or equal to), >= (greater than or equal to), <> (not equal to), and = (equal to). For example, type >256000 under the Annual Salary label to get all records that contain an annual salary over $256,000.

  - You can use operators with dates as well. For example, type >=01/01/08 under the Hire Date label to get all records with a hire date on or after January 1, 2008.

  - You can also use operators with text, as in <M, which will display all records beginning with the letters A through L.

■ You can use formulas to specify criteria.

  - For example, to display only records where the total sale (stored in column G) is greater than the average of column G, you could enter something like this for cell G5: =G5>AVERAGE($G$5:$G$21).

    ✓ *G5 in this example is the first cell in the list or table in column G.*

  - You could also use the label cell (G4) or the label itself, as in this formula: ="Total Sales">AVERAGE($G$5:$G$21).

  - The comparison cell address uses relative cell addressing, while the rest of the formula must use absolute cell addresses (preceded by $).

■ To use a formula to specify criteria, type it in a cell that doesn't have a label above it.

  ✓ *For this reason, it's usually best to type a formula in the first column to the right of the criteria range you originally established.*

  - Be sure to redefine the criteria range to include the cell that contains the formula and the blank cell above it.

  - You can use more than one formula by typing the second formula in the next column, and adjusting the criteria range again.

  ✓ *If you need to use two formulas, and either one may be true in order to get a match, then type them in the same column in different rows.*

  ✓ *See examples in the next section for placement of formulas in the criteria range.*

Examples of Advanced Criteria

■ To display records for Smith and Jones from the sample shown here, type these criteria, in two rows, under the Name field:

Name	Computer	Sale Amt.
Smith		>1300
Jones		

✓ As on the preceding pages, the following examples show typical list or table field names. Be sure to copy the actual field names from your own list/table to the criteria range.

■ To display records for Jones where the total sale amount is over $1,300, type these criteria in one row under the appropriate field names:

Name	Computer	Sale Amt.
Jones		>1300

✓ You could also display these records with the proper selections from two columns in filtered list or table.

Figure 6-1

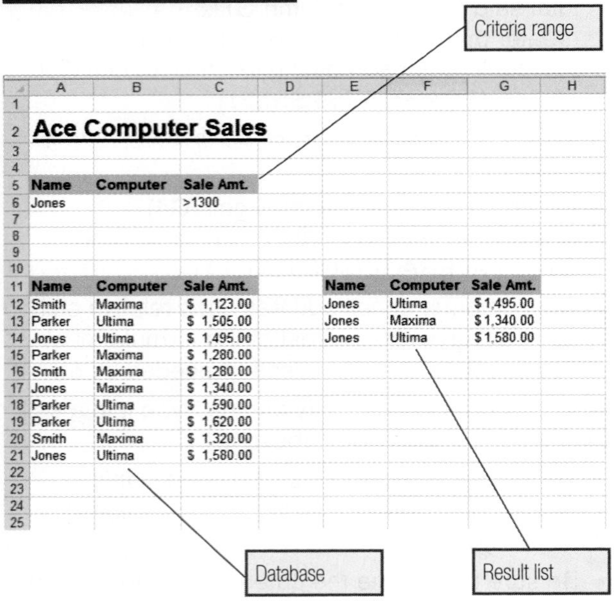

Criteria range

Database

Result list

■ To display Smith's sales records of Maxima computers with a total sales amount more than $1,250, type this in one row:

Name	Computer	Sale Amt.
Smith	Maxima	>1250

✓ Again, you could display these records using a regular filter.

■ To display records for both Smith and Jones that have a sale amount over $1,250, type this in two rows:

Name	Computer	Sale Amt.
Smith		>1250
Jones		>1250

■ To display records that have a sale amount over $1,250 or that involve Maxima computers (no matter what amount), type this in two rows:

Name	Computer	Sale Amt.
	Maxima	
		>1250

■ To display records of sales of Maxima computers over $1,250, type this in one row:

Name	Computer	Sale Amt.
	Maxima	>1250

■ To display records of sales of Maxima or Ultima computers over $1,250, type this in two rows:

Name	Computer	Sale Amt.
	Maxima	>1250
	Ultima	>1250

■ To display records whose sale amount is greater than or equal to the average, type this in a cell without a label:

Sale Amt.

=C2>AVERAGE($C$2:$C$17)

✓ Be sure to include the cell in which you type the formula and the blank cell above it, within the criteria range.

✓ The formula includes an expression of comparison, featuring the > operator, and which evaluates to TRUE or FALSE.

■ To display records whose sale amounts are between $1,250 and $2,000, type this in two cells without a label in the same row, but in different columns:

Computer	Sale Amt.
=C2>1250	=C2<2000

✓ Don't type this in the cell below the Sale Amt. label—it won't work.

■ To display records whose total sale is greater than the average OR over $2,000, type this in two rows, but in the same column:

Sale Amt.

=C2>AVERAGE($C$2:$C$17)

=C2>2000

Try It! — Setting Up a Criteria Range

✓ Prior to using Advanced Filter, you must first set up your criteria range.

1 In **ETry06_studentfirstname_studentlastname**, in the Pet Supplies worksheet, select the range A5:H5.

2 Click Home > Copy 📋.

✓ Typically, you create a criteria range above or to the right of the list or table, separated from it by a few rows or columns, although you can create a separate Criteria worksheet if you like.

3 Click cell J5 and press `CTRL` + `V`.

4 Adjust the column widths as necessary.

5 When ready, you'll enter the criteria in row(s) directly below the appropriate criteria labels.

✓ Remember that formulas, if you use them, must be entered in cells that don't have a label above them.

6 Save changes and leave the file open to use in the next Try It.

Try It! — Setting Up an Advanced Filter

1 In **ETry06_studentfirstname_studentlastname**, create a criteria range, if necessary.

2 Type the following criteria.

Cell	Type
K7	Cat*
M6	<10
N6	<10
P7	>1.00

3 Click any cell within the table or list and click Data > Advanced 🔽.

4 If necessary, select Filter the list, in-place.

5 In the List range text box, type $A$6:$H$32 or select the range containing the list or table.

6 Click Criteria Range and select the range J5:Q7.

✓ Include the criteria label(s) with the criteria.

✓ If the criteria includes a formula, include the blank cell(s) above the cell(s) containing the formula.

7 Click OK.

8 Save changes and leave the file open to use in the next Try It.

Setting Up an Advanced Filter

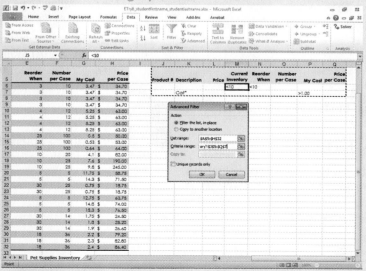

Removing an In-Place Advanced Filter

- Unlike a regular filter, an advanced filter applied in-place to a list or table (rather than copied to another area of the worksheet) isn't easily detectable.

- If the row numbers in the list or table are blue and the filter down-arrow buttons aren't visible, an advanced filter is in place.

- To remove an in-place advanced filter, click in the list/table and click the Clear button on the Data tab.

Try It!   Removing an In-Place Advanced Filter

1 In **ETry06_studentfirstname_ studentlastname**, click any cell in the list.

2 Click Data > Clear 🔽.

3 Save changes and leave the file open to use in the next Try It.

Extracting Filtered Rows

- With an advanced filter, you can **extract** (copy) records to another place in the worksheet.

- The extract records are copied to another area of the worksheet (called the results list.) You can edit them as needed.

- The results list must appear in the same worksheet as the source list from which its records were copied.

- You can change, format, print, sort, delete, and otherwise manipulate the extracted records as you like.

- Even if you alter the extracted records, it won't affect the original records in the list or table.

- This allows you to create a customized, professional-looking report with the extracted records.

- You can even delete some of the extracted records if you don't want to work with them; again, this does not affect the original data.

Try It!   Extracting Filtered Rows

1 In **ETry06_studentfirstname_ studentlastname**, click in the Pet Supplies Inventory worksheet.

   ✓ For this example, you'll use the same criteria and range as before.

2 Click any cell within the table or list and click Data > Advanced 🔽.

3 Select Copy to another location.

4 In the Copy to text box, type **$A$40** or select the location for your results list.

   ✓ The destination range must be located in the same worksheet as the list or table.

   ✓ If you indicate a single cell as the Copy to range, Excel copies the filtered results to cells below and to the right of the cell, overwriting existing data without warning.

5 Click OK.

6 Save changes and leave the file open to use in the next Try It.

Using Sum, Average, and Count in a Filtered Table

- Using tables provides a lot of flexibility when it comes to managing columnar data.

  - For example, it's easy to add totals and perform other calculations on the columns in a table by simply adding a total row.

  - Once a total row is added, click in the total row at the bottom of a column you want to calculate, and choose an available function such as SUM, AVERAGE, or MIN.

  - You can select a different function for each column, or none at all.

  - You can also enter text in the total row if needed.

- You can temporarily hide the total row when needed.

- Another easy way to add calculations to a table is to use calculated columns.

  - A calculated column can be located in a blank column inserted between existing table columns, or simply in the first blank column to the right of a table.

  - To create a calculated column, just type a formula in the blank column you've inserted in the table, or in a blank column just to the right of the table.

  - The formula is instantly copied down the column.

  - If new rows are added to the table, the formula is copied to that new row automatically.

Try It!   **Using Sum, Average, and Count in a Filtered Table**

1. In **ETry06_studentfirstname_ studentlastname**, click the Sept Sales worksheet tab.

2. Click in the list and then click Table Tools Design > Total Row.

3. Click cell F46 and click the down arrow. Select Sum, if necessary.

4. Click cell E46 and click the down arrow. Select Average.

5. Click cell D46 and click the down arrow. Select Count.

6. Close **ETry06_studentfirstname_ studentlastname**, saving all changes, and exit Excel.

Working with a Total Row in a filtered table

September Sales Figures					
Item #	Description	Product Type	Salesperson	Cost	Sales Incentive
51478	Scratch pole	Accessory	Alice Harper	$ 78.95	$ 2.37
53496	Pump	Accessory	Alice Harper	$ 34.85	$ 1.05
50199	30 Gal. Aquarium	Accessory	Alice Harper	$ 78.65	$ 2.36
50432	Blue Day-Glo Rocks	Accessory	Alice Harper	$ 15.65	$ 0.47
51299	Light	Accessory	Alice Harper	$ 32.95	$ 0.99
Total				5	$ 48.21	$ 7.23

None
Average
Count
Count Numbers
Max
Min
Sum
StdDev
Var
More Functions...

Sales Recap

Dogs sold   0

Project 11—Create It

Filtering a Large Data Table

DIRECTIONS

1. Start Excel, if necessary, and open **EProj11** from the data files for this lesson.

2. Save the file as **EProj11_studentfirstname_studentlastname** in the location where your teacher instructs you to store the files for this lesson.

3. Display only the heart medications:

   a. Click the arrow next to **For use on** in cell **B7**, deselect **(Select All)**, select **Heart**, and click **OK**.

   b. Sort the records by price by clicking the arrow next to **Item Cost**, and choosing **Sort Smallest to Largest**.

4. **With your teacher's permission**, print the worksheet.

5. Display only items with 100 or more units remaining in inventory:

   a. Clear the filter by clicking **Data > Clear**.

   b. Click the arrow next to **Total Items2**, and point to **Number Filters**.

c. Select **Greater Than Or Equal To** from the list.

d. Enter **100** in the box immediately to the right. Click **OK**.

6. Add a total row:

   a. Click anywhere in the table, then click **Table Tools Design > Total Row**.

   b. Click at the bottom of the **Total Items2** column, click the arrow, and choose **Average**.

   c. Click at the bottom of the **Total Items** column, click the arrow, and choose **Sum**.

7. Display the top **15** selling items:

   a. Clear the filter by clicking **Data > Clear**.

   b. Click the arrow next to **Total Sales** heading, point to **Number Filters**, and choose **Top 10**.

   c. In the center box, choose **15**, then click **OK**.

8. Select **A1:K95** and click **Page Layout > Print Area > Set Print Area**.

9. **With your teacher's permission**, print the worksheet. It should look similar to Figure 6-2.

10. Close the document, saving all changes, and exit Excel.

Figure 6-2

Wood Hills Animal Clinic
August Drug Sales

Drug	For use on	To treat	No. of Cases	Items per Case	Loose Items	Total Items
Droncit Tapewormer	De-wormer	Dog or Cat	6	100	88	688
Enacard	Heart	Dog or Cat	12	22	20	284
Enacard	Heart	Dog or Cat	14	30	3	423
Anipryl	Endocrine	Dog	12	20	19	259
Enacard	Heart	Dog or Cat	10	30	14	314
Bomazeal Senior	Arthritis	Dog	14	50	42	742
Proin	Incontinence	Dog	15	35	33	558
Tapazole	Hyperthyroidism	Cat	15	30	29	479
Heartgard Plus Blue	Heartworm	Dog	18	75	42	1,392
Soloxine	Hyperthyroidism	Dog or Cat	18	20	17	377
Revolution	Heartworm	Dog	21	32	6	678
Soloxine	Hyperthyroidism	Dog or Cat	21	20	4	424
Advantage Green	Flea	Dog	22	25	14	564
Heartgard Plus Green	Heartworm	Dog	22	75	36	1,686
Heartgard Plus Brown	Heartworm	Dog	30	75	19	2,269
Total						11,137

Project 12—Apply It

Using an Advanced Filter on a Large Data Table

DIRECTIONS

1. Start Excel, if necessary, and open **EProj12** from the data files for this lesson and save the file as **EProj12_studentfirstname_studentlastname** in the location where your teacher instructs you to store the files for this lesson.

2. Set up a criteria range for an advanced filter:

   a. Click the **Insert Worksheet** button. Name the new worksheet **Criteria**.

   b. Copy cells **A7:K7** and paste them in the Criteria worksheet in the same position.

   c. Adjust columns widths as necessary to be readable.

3. Use the Criteria worksheet to select the records from the Drug Sales for Dogs worksheet, featuring only those medications for dogs with sales over $2000 and where less than 150 items are left in inventory:

   a. In the Criteria worksheet, in the cell under **To treat**, type **Dog**.

   b. In the cell under **Total Items2**, type **<150**.

   c. In the cell under **Total Sales**, type **>2000**.

   d. Switch to the **Drug Sales** for Dogs worksheet, and click any cell in the list range.

   e. Click **Data** > **Advanced**.

   ✓ *Under List range, the range $A$7:$K$94 should already appear.*

f. Next to Criteria range, click the **Collapse Dialog Box** button.

g. Switch to the Criteria worksheet, select the range **A7:K8**.

   ✓ *The criteria range should always include the entire field names row, plus as many rows beneath it that include criteria values or expressions, in their entirety.*

h. Click the **Restore Dialog Box** button, then choose **Copy to another location**.

i. Next to **Copy to**, click the **Collapse Dialog Box** button.

j. Select cell **O8** in the Drug Sales for Dogs worksheet.

k. Click the **Restore Dialog Box** button to return to the dialog box. Click **OK**.

   ✓ *Excel will copy all records that match the given criteria, including field names, and will format these records exactly as they appear in their original cells, except for their column width.*

l. Adjust column widths as necessary.

4. Select the range **O1:Y17** and click **Page Layout** > **Print Area** 🖼 > **Set Print Area**.

5. **With your teacher's permission**, print the worksheet. It should look similar to Figure 6-3.

6. Close the workbook, saving all changes, and exit Excel.

Figure 6-3

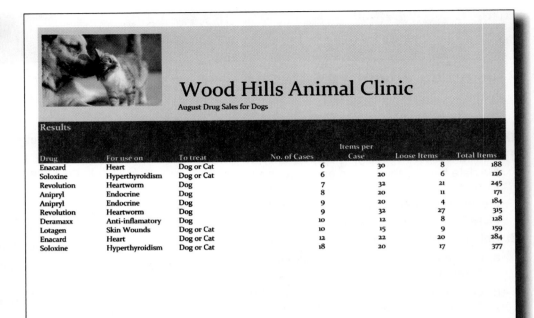

Wood Hills Animal Clinic

August Drug Sales for Dogs

Results

Drug	For use on	To treat	No. of Cases	Items per Case	Loose Items	Total Items
Enacard	Heart	Dog or Cat	6	30	8	188
Soloxine	Hyperthyroidism	Dog or Cat	6	20	6	126
Revolution	Heartworm	Dog	7	32	21	245
Anipryl	Endocrine	Dog	8	20	11	171
Anipryl	Endocrine	Dog	9	20	4	184
Revolution	Heartworm	Dog	9	32	27	315
Deramaxx	Anti-inflamatory	Dog	10	12	8	128
Lotagen	Skin Wounds	Dog or Cat	10	15	9	159
Enacard	Heart	Dog or Cat	12	22	20	284
Soloxine	Hyperthyroidism	Dog or Cat	18	20	17	377

Lesson 7

Customizing Data Entry

➤ What You Will Learn

Entering Labels on Multiple Lines
Entering Fractions and Mixed Numbers

Software Skills   When entering labels, especially long ones, you may want to display them on more than one line so the column will not need to be as wide. Entering fractions, on the other hand, requires a special technique so they display properly.

Application Skills   As Junior Manager for a local PhotoTown store, you have been asked to create a weekly payroll tracker that will calculate the total weekly hours worked for each clerk.

What You Can Do

Entering Labels on Multiple Lines

- If you have long column labels, you can adjust the column width to fit them.
  - This doesn't always look pleasing, however, especially when the column label is much longer than the data in the column.
  - For example, the two columns shown here are much larger than their data:

Unit Number	Total Annual Sales
2	$125,365.97

- One of the easiest ways to fix this problem is to enter the column label with **line breaks**.
- Entering line breaks between words in a cell enables you to place several lines of text in the same cell, like this next example.

Unit Number	Total Annual Sales
2	$125,365.97

- The height of the row adjusts automatically to accommodate the multiple-line column label.

Try It! Entering Labels on Multiple Lines

1 Start Excel and open **ETry07** from the data files for this lesson.

2 Save the file as **ETry07_studentfirstname_studentlastname** in the location where your teacher instructs you to store the files for this lesson.

3 Click cell C11 and type **Cases**.

4 Press ALT + ENTER to insert a line break.

5 Type **Ordered**.

6 Type the labels **Price per Case**, and **Product Total Sales** in cells D11:E11.

7 Click cell E11 and click Home > Wrap Text.

8 Click cell E11 and click Home > Format Painter and then click cell D11.

9 Press ALT + ENTER and then press ENTER.

10 Save changes and leave the file open to use in the next Try It.

Enter a line break within a cell

	B	C	D	E
		Daily Sales Worksheet		
	Date:	9/21/2011		
	Customer:	3829992		
	Salesperson:	Alice Harper		
		Cases Ordered	**Price per Case**	**Total Sales**
	Chew Toys, asst.			
	Med. Bonie			
	Food bowl			

Entering Fractions and Mixed Numbers

- If you type the value 1/3 into a cell, Excel thinks that it's a date (in this case, January 3).

- To enter a fraction, you must precede it with a zero (0) and a space, which tells Excel that the data is a number. For example, to enter 1/3, type 0 1/3.

- A fraction appears as a decimal value in the Formula bar. The fraction 1/3 appears as 0.333333333333333 in the Formula bar.

- You don't need to add the preceding zero when you're entering a mixed number (a number and a fraction, as in 4 1/2).

- To enter a mixed fraction, simply type it: Type 4, a space, then the fraction, 1/2.

- You can **format** existing data to look like fractions. To do this, use the Format Cells command.

Try It!   **Entering Fractions and Mixed Numbers**

1. In the **ETry07_studentfirstname_ studentlastname** file, select the Sales Tracker worksheet.

2. Click cell C12 and type 0.

3. Press SPACE and type 3/4.

4. Press ENTER.

5. In cell C13 type 0 1/2.

6. Press ENTER.

7. Select cell C14.

8. Type 1 1/8 and press ENTER.

9. In cell C15 type 5 1/2 and press ENTER.

10. Save changes to **ETry07_studentfirstname_ studentlastname** and close Excel.

Working with Fractions and Mixed Numbers

Date:	9/21/2011			
Customer:	3829992			
Salesperson:	Alice Harper			
	Cases Ordered	Price per Case	Product Total Sales	
Chew Toys, asst.	3/4	$ 18.75	$ 14.06	
Med. Bonie	1/2	$ 53.00	$ 26.50	
Leash	1 1/8	$ 190.00	$ 213.75	
Puppy Food	5 1/2	$ 24.50	$ 134.75	
		Grand Total	$ 389.06	

Project 13—Create It

Weekly Payroll Tracker

DIRECTIONS

1. Start Excel, if necessary, and open **EProj13** from the data files for this lesson.
2. Save the file as **EProj13_studentfirstname_studentlastname** in the location where your teacher instructs you to store the files for this lesson.
3. In cell **E6** type **Hourly** and press [ALT] + [ENTER].
4. In cell **D6** type **Regular Weekly Hours** and press [ENTER].
5. In cell **C6** type **Full or Part Time** and press [ENTER].
6. Select cells **C6:E6** and click **Home > Center** ≡.
7. Select cell **C6** and click **Home > Wrap Text** 🗗.

8. Click **Home > Format Painter** and click cell **D6**.
9. Select cell **C6** and click the formula bar. Move the insertion point to just before the **P** and press [ALT] and press [ENTER].
10. Click cell **H24** and type **Weekly Payroll** and press [ENTER].
11. Click cell **H24** and click **Home > Align Text Right**.
12. **With your teacher's permission**, print the worksheet. It should look similar to Figure 7-1.
13. Close the workbook, saving all changes, and exit Excel.

Figure 7-1

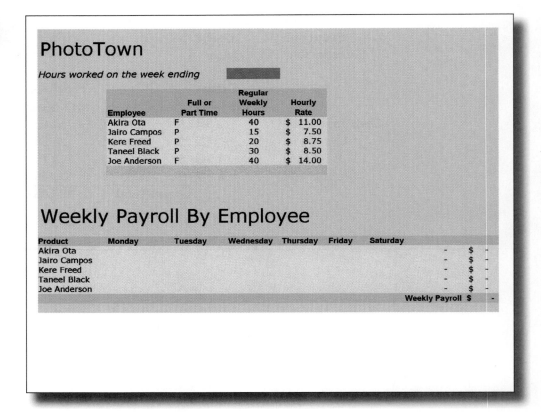

Project 14—Apply It

Weekly Payroll Tracker

DIRECTIONS

1. Start Excel, if necessary, and open **EProj14** from the data files for this lesson and save the file as **EProj14_studentfirstname_studentlastname** in the location where your teacher instructs you to store the files for this lesson.

2. In cell **H18** type **Total Hours This Week** and press `ENTER` .

3. In cell **I18** type **Weekly Income** and press `ENTER` .

4. Select cells **H18:I18**. Click **Home** > **Wrap Text**.

5. Change the column width for row H to **11**.

6. In cell **D4**, enter the fraction **8/15**.

   ✓ *Notice that Excel automatically interprets this as a date.*

7. Enter the following hours for the employees:

Employee	Day	Hours
Kere Freed	Monday	3/4
Taneel Black	Tuesday	4 1/2
Taneel Blac	Thursday	5 1/2
Joe Anderson	Thursday	6 1/2

   ✓ *When entering the Monday hours, remember to type a zero followed by a space before typing the fraction.*

8. Click **Insert** > **Header & Footer** > **Footer** and then select the file name from the list.

9. **With your teacher's permission**, print the document. It should look similar to Figure 7-2.

10. Close the document, saving all changes, and exit Excel.

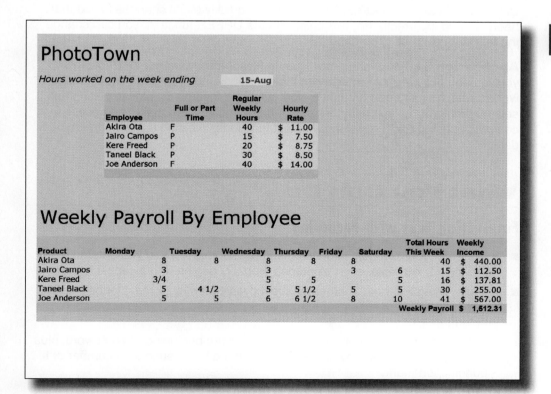

Figure 7-2

PhotoTown

Hours worked on the week ending   15-Aug

Employee	Full or Part Time	Regular Weekly Hours	Hourly Rate
Akira Ota	F	40	$ 11.00
Jairo Campos	P	15	$ 7.50
Kere Freed	P	20	$ 8.75
Taneel Black	P	30	$ 8.50
Joe Anderson	F	40	$ 14.00

Weekly Payroll By Employee

Product	Monday	Tuesday	Wednesday	Thursday	Friday	Saturday	Total Hours This Week	Weekly Income
Akira Ota	8	8	8	8	8		40	$ 440.00
Jairo Campos	3		3		3	6	15	$ 112.50
Kere Freed	3/4		5	5		5	16	$ 137.81
Taneel Black	5	4 1/2	5	5 1/2	5	5	30	$ 255.00
Joe Anderson	5	5	6	6 1/2	8	10	41	$ 567.00
						Weekly Payroll	$	1,512.31

Lesson 8

Using Find and Replace

> **What You Will Learn**

Formatting Text with Formulas
Replacing Text

Software Skills   Using a series of simple text functions, such as PROPER, UPPER, LOWER, and SUBSTITUTE, you can quickly effect changes to text that's been entered incorrectly. For example, with the UPPER function, you can change the text in a cell to all uppercase.

Application Skills   As the new Human Resources Manager for PhotoTown, you've been busy getting familiar with their various employee and benefit related worksheets. It's just been brought to your attention that the Employee Listing has several problems, all text related. It's your hope that you can make the necessary corrections using Excel's vast array of text functions, avoiding the need to retype data.

What You Can Do

Formatting Text with Formulas

- If you enter your own text into a worksheet, chances are that you entered it correctly. For example, every sentence probably begins with a capital letter.
- If you're using text from another source, however, it may or may not be properly capitalized. Excel provides some functions that might be able to solve such a problem:
  - PROPER (*text*)—Capitalizes the first letter at the beginning of each word, plus any letters that follow any character that's not a letter, such as a number or a punctuation mark.
  - UPPER (*text*)—Changes all letters to uppercase.
  - LOWER (*text*)—Changes all letters to lowercase.

Try It!   **Formatting Text Using the PROPER Function**

1 Start Excel and open **ETry08** from the data files for this lesson.

2 Save the file as **ETry08_studentfirstname_studentlastname** in the location where your teacher instructs you to store the files for this lesson.

3 Click cell C33 as the location where the result should appear.

4 Click Formulas > Text 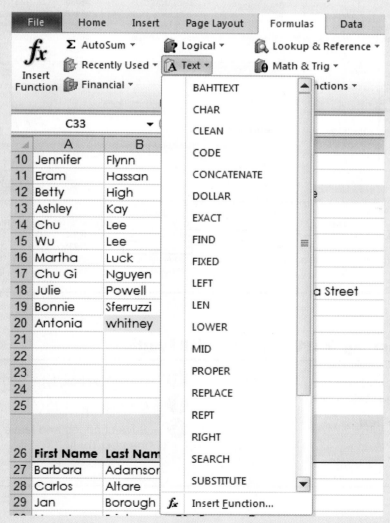.

5 Click PROPER.

6 In the Text box, type **C12** (the source data).

7 Click OK.

8 Save changes and leave the file open to use in the next Try It.

The Text Function in the Functions Library

Try It! **Formatting Text Using the UPPER Function**

① In **ETry08_studentfirstname_studentlastname**, select cell D28.

② Click Formulas > Text 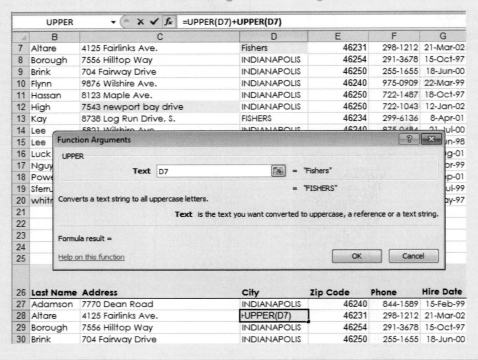.

③ Click UPPER.

④ In the Text box, type **D7** (the source data).

⑤ Click OK.

⑥ Save changes and leave the file open to use in the next Try It.

The Function Arguments dialog box

	B	C	D	E	F	G
	UPPER ▼ ⊙ X ✓ *fx*	=UPPER(D7)+UPPER(D7)				
7	Altare	4125 Fairlinks Ave.	Fishers	46231	298-1212	21-Mar-02
8	Borough	7556 Hilltop Way	INDIANAPOLIS	46254	291-3678	15-Oct-97
9	Brink	704 Fairway Drive	INDIANAPOLIS	46250	255-1655	18-Jun-00
10	Flynn	9876 Wilshire Ave.	INDIANAPOLIS	46240	975-0909	22-Mar-99
11	Hassan	8123 Maple Ave.	INDIANAPOLIS	46250	722-1487	18-Oct-97
12	High	7543 newport bay drive	INDIANAPOLIS	46250	722-1043	12-Jan-02
13	Kay	8738 Log Run Drive, S.	FISHERS	46234	299-6136	8-Apr-01
14	Lee	5821 Wilshire Ave.	INDIANAPOLIS	46240	975-0484	21-Jul-00

Function Arguments

UPPER

Text D7 = "Fishers"

= "FISHERS"

Converts a text string to all uppercase letters.

Text is the text you want converted to uppercase, a reference or a text string.

Formula result =

Help on this function   OK   Cancel

	B	C	D	E	F	G
26	**Last Name**	**Address**	**City**	**Zip Code**	**Phone**	**Hire Date**
27	Adamson	7770 Dean Road	INDIANAPOLIS	46240	844-1589	15-Feb-99
28	Altare	4125 Fairlinks Ave.	=UPPER(D7)	46231	298-1212	21-Mar-02
29	Borough	7556 Hilltop Way	INDIANAPOLIS	46254	291-3678	15-Oct-97
30	Brink	704 Fairway Drive	INDIANAPOLIS	46250	255-1655	18-Jun-00

Try It! **Formatting Text Using the LOWER Function**

① In **ETry08_studentfirstname_studentlastname**, select cell B41.

② Click Formulas > Text 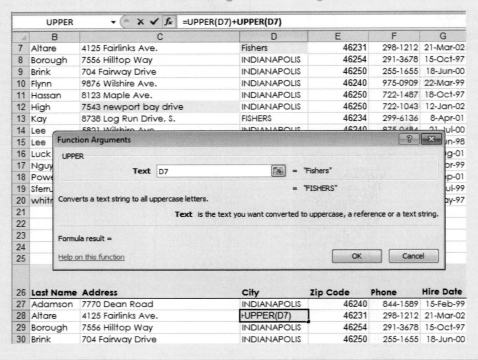.

③ Click LOWER.

④ In the Text box, type **B20** (the source data).

⑤ Click OK.

⑥ Save changes and leave the file open to use in the next Try It.

Replacing Text

- Sometimes, all an old worksheet needs in order to be useful again is an update.

- One way in which you can update data (such as department names, cost codes, or old dates) is to substitute good text for the outdated text.

  - SUBSTITUTE (*text, old_text,new_text, instance_num*)—Replaces *old text* with *new_text* in the cell you specify with the text argument. If you specify a particular *instance* of *old_text*, such as instance 3, then SUBSTITUTE replaces only that specific instance—the third instance—of *old_text* and not all of them.

  - REPLACE (*text, start_num,num_chars, new_text*)—Replaces *old_text* with *new_text*, beginning at the position (*start_num*) you specify. The argument *num_chars* tells Excel how many characters to replace. This allows you to replace 4 characters with only 2 if you want.

Try It!   Changing Text Using the SUBSTITUTE Function

1. In **ETry08_studentfirstname_studentlastname**, select cell K27.

2. Click Formulas > Text 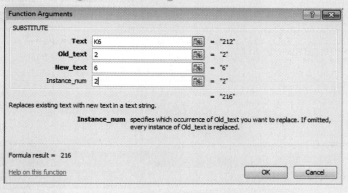.

3. Click SUBSTITUTE.

4. In the Text box, type **K6** (the source data).

5. In the Old_Text box, type **2** (the item being substituted).

6. In the New_Text box, type **6**.

7. In the Instance_num box, type **2** (indicating that only the second 2 in the cell will be changed).

8. Click OK.

9. Save changes and leave the file open to use in the next Try It.

The Function Arguments dialog box for the Substitute Function

Function Arguments	? ✕
SUBSTITUTE	
Text	K6 = "212"
Old_text	2 = "2"
New_text	6 = "6"
Instance_num	2 = "2"
	= "216"

Replaces existing text with new text in a text string.

         Instance_num specifies which occurrence of Old_text you want to replace. If omitted, every instance of Old_text is replaced.

Formula result = 216

Help on this function   OK   Cancel

Try It!   Changing Text Using the REPLACE Function

1. In **ETry08_studentfirstname_studentlastname**, select cell Q27.

2. Click Formulas > Text .

3. Click REPLACE.

4. In the Text box, type **P27** (the source data).

5. IIn the Start_num box, type **4** (to indicate that the change should begin at the fourth digit from the left).

6. In the Num_chars box, type **2** (to indicate that 2 digits should be changed).

7. In the New_text box, type **50** (indicating that the Adjusted Rate should end in .50).

8. Click OK.

9. Save changes, close it, and close Excel.

Project 15—Create It

Updating the Employee Listing

DIRECTIONS

1. Start Excel, if necessary, and open **EProj15** from the data files for this lesson.

2. Save the file as **EProj15_studentfirstname_ studentlastname** in the location where your teacher instructs you to store the files for this lesson.

3. All the department numbers beginning with a 6 must be changed so they begin with a 9 instead. You'll make this change using SUBSTITUTE:

   a. Click cell **J8**, and press [DEL] to clear its contents.

   b. Click **Formulas** > **Text** and click **SUBSTITUTE**.

   c. In the Text box, type **E8**.

   d. In the Old_text box, type **6**.

   e. In the New_text box, type **9**.

   f. In the Instance_num box, type **1** and click **OK**.

4. Copy this formula down the range **J9:J37**.

   a. In cell **J8**, click **Home** > **Copy** .

   b. Select the range **J9:J37**.

   c. On the **Home** tab, click the **Paste** down arrow and select **Formulas** .

5. Transfer these new values to the range **E8:E37**:

   a. Select the range **J8:J37**.

   b. Click **Home** > **Copy** .

   c. On the **Home** tab, click the **Paste** down arrow and select **Values** .

6. Click **Insert** > **Header & Footer** > **Header** and then select **Prepared by Jennifer Fulton [Today's Date] Page 1** from the list.

7. Replace the name Jennifer Fulton in the header with your name.

8. **With your teacher's permission**, print the worksheet. It should look similar to Figure 8-1.

9. Close the document, saving all changes, and exit Excel.

Figure 8-1

PhotoTown Employee Listing
Miller Rd
Unit #2166

Employee ID Number	Title	First Name	Last Name	Department Number	Department Name	Rate	Soc Sec No.	
63778	Mr.	Carlos	Altare	910412pr	processing	$6.30	504-12-3131	910412pr
71335	Mr.	Taneed	Black	218975am	asst. manager	$7.00	775-15-1315	218975am
31524	Mrs.	Jan	Borough	911748qc	quality control	$6.50	727-25-6981	911748qc
18946	Mr.	Shakur	Brown	482178ca	cashier	$7.00	505-43-9587	482178ca
22415	Mr.	Jairo	Campos	914522in	inker	$7.20	110-56-2897	914522in
20965	Mrs.	Rafiquil	Damir	911748qc	quality control	$6.15	102-33-5656	911748qc
64121	Mrs.	Diana	Dogwood	918796so	special orders	$6.20	821-55-3262	918799so
30388	Mrs.	Lucy	Fan	910412pr	processing	$6.55	334-25-6959	910412pr
44185	Mrs.	Jennifer	Flynn	482178ca	cashier	$7.00	221-32-9585	482178ca
32152	Ms.	Katerina	Flynn	271858kc	kiosk control	$7.10	107-45-9111	271858kc
31885	Ms.	Kere	Freed	910412pr	processing	$7.10	222-15-9484	910412pr
33785	Mr.	Eram	Hassan	271858kc	kiosk control	$6.85	203-25-6984	271858kc
55648	Mr.	Tyrell	Johnson	218975am	asst. manager	$6.50	468-25-9684	218975am
60219	Ms.	Verna	Latinz	911748qc	quality control	$6.30	705-85-6352	911748qc
28645	Mr.	Wu	Lee	918796so	special orders	$7.00	255-41-9784	918799so
67415	Mr.	Shamir	Lewis	910412pr	processing	$7.10	112-42-7897	910412pr
27995	Mrs.	Maria	Navarro	910412pr	processing	$6.30	302-42-8465	910412pr
32151	Mr.	Tony	Navarro	271858kc	kiosk control	$6.35	401-78-9855	271858kc
28499	Mr.	Chu Gi	Nguyen	911748qc	quality control	$6.85	823-55-6487	911748qc
17564	Mr.	Juan	Nuniez	914522in	inker	$7.00	208-65-4932	914522in
14558	Mr.	Akira	Ota	911748qc	quality control	$7.25	285-68-9853	911748qc
31022	Mrs.	Meghan	Ryan	910412pr	processing	$7.00	421-85-6452	910412pr
41885	Mrs.	Kate	Scott	482178ca	cashier	$6.85	489-55-4862	482178ca
25448	Mr.	Jyoti	Shaw	911748qc	quality control	$6.50	389-24-6567	911748qc
23151	Ms.	Jewel	Vidito	911748qc	quality control	$6.55	885-63-7158	911748qc
37785	Mrs.	Corrine	Walters	918796so	special orders	$6.65	622-34-8891	918799so
58945	Mrs.	Antonia	Whitney	271858kc	kiosk control	$6.75	312-86-7141	271858kc
57445	Mr.	Shale	Wilson	482178ca	cashier	$7.00	375-86-3425	482178ca
36684	Mrs.	Shiree	Wilson	482178ca	cashier	$7.10	415-65-6658	482178ca
55412	Mrs.	Su	Yamaguchi	910412pr	processing	$6.30	324-75-8021	910412pr

Project 16—Apply It

Updating the Employee Listing

DIRECTIONS

1. Start Excel, if necessary, and open **EProj16** from the data files for this lesson and save the file as **EProj16_studentfirstname_studentlastname** in the location where your teacher instructs you to store the files for this lesson.

2. Delete the data in the range **J8:J37**.

3. The letters at the end of each department number should be capitalized; correct this by using UPPER:

   a. Click cell **J8**. Click **Formulas** > **Text** and click **UPPER**.

   b. In the Text box, type **E8** and click **OK**.

   c. Copy this formula down the range **J9:J37**.

   d. Copy the range **J8:J37**.

   e. Click cell **E8**, and paste only the values.

4. The department names should be capitalized as well. You can correct this problem using PROPER:

   a. Delete the data in the range **J8:J37**.

   b. Click cell **J8**. Click **Formulas** > **Text** and click **PROPER**.

   c. In the Text box, type **F8** and click **OK**.

   d. Copy this formula down the range **J9:J37**.

   e. Copy the range **J8:J37**.

   f. Click cell **F8**, and paste only the values.

5. Delete the data in the range **J8:J37**.

6. Adjust column widths as needed.

7. Click **Insert** > **Header & Footer** 📄 > **Footer** and then select the file name from the list.

8. **With your teacher's permission**, print the document. It should look similar to Figure 8-2.

9. Close the document, saving all changes, and exit Excel.

Figure 8-2

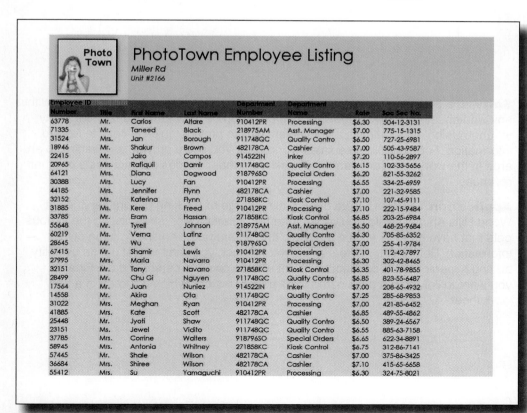

PhotoTown Employee Listing
Miller Rd
Unit #2166

Employee ID Number	Title	First Name	Last Name	Department Number	Department Name	Rate	Soc Sec No.
63778	Mr.	Carlos	Altare	910412PR	Processing	$6.30	504-12-3131
71335	Mr.	Taneed	Black	218975AM	Asst. Manager	$7.00	775-15-1315
31524	Mrs.	Jan	Borough	911748QC	Quality Contro	$6.50	727-25-6981
18946	Mr.	Shakur	Brown	482178CA	Cashier	$7.00	505-43-9587
22415	Mr.	Jairo	Campos	914522IN	Inker	$7.20	110-56-2897
20965	Mrs.	Rafiquil	Damir	911748QC	Quality Contro	$6.15	102-33-5656
64121	Mrs.	Diana	Dogwood	918796SO	Special Orders	$6.20	821-55-3262
30388	Mrs.	Lucy	Fan	910412PR	Processing	$6.55	334-25-6959
44185	Mrs.	Jennifer	Flynn	482178CA	Cashier	$7.00	221-32-9585
32152	Ms.	Katerina	Flynn	271858KC	Kiosk Control	$7.10	107-45-9111
31885	Ms.	Kere	Freed	910412PR	Processing	$7.10	222-15-9484
33785	Mr.	Eram	Hassan	271858KC	Kiosk Control	$6.85	203-25-6984
55648	Mr.	Tyrell	Johnson	218975AM	Asst. Manager	$6.50	468-25-9684
60219	Ms.	Verna	Lafinz	911748QC	Quality Contro	$6.30	705-85-6352
28645	Mr.	Wu	Lee	918796SO	Special Orders	$7.00	255-41-9784
67415	Mr.	Shamir	Lewis	910412PR	Processing	$7.10	112-42-7897
27995	Mrs.	Maria	Navarro	910412PR	Processing	$6.30	302-42-8465
32151	Mr.	Tony	Navarro	271858KC	Kiosk Control	$6.35	401-78-9855
28499	Mr.	Chu Gi	Nguyen	911748QC	Quality Contro	$6.85	823-55-6487
17564	Mr.	Juan	Nuniez	914522IN	Inker	$7.00	208-65-4932
14558	Mr.	Akira	Ota	911748QC	Quality Contro	$7.25	285-68-9853
31022	Mrs.	Meghan	Ryan	910412PR	Processing	$7.00	421-85-6452
41885	Mrs.	Kate	Scott	482178CA	Cashier	$6.85	489-55-4862
25448	Mr.	Jyoti	Shaw	911748QC	Quality Contro	$6.50	389-24-6567
23151	Ms.	Jewel	Vidito	911748QC	Quality Contro	$6.55	885-63-7158
37785	Mrs.	Corrine	Walters	918796SO	Special Orders	$6.65	622-34-8891
58945	Mrs.	Antonia	Whitney	271858KC	Kiosk Control	$6.75	312-86-7141
57445	Mr.	Shale	Wilson	482178CA	Cashier	$7.00	375-86-3425
36684	Mrs.	Shiree	Wilson	482178CA	Cashier	$7.10	415-65-6658
55412	Mrs.	Su	Yamaguchi	910412PR	Processing	$6.30	324-75-8021

Lesson 9

Working with Hyperlinks

WORDS TO KNOW

Hyperlink
Text or graphics linked to related information in the same workbook, another workbook, or another file.

Internet
A global collection of interconnected networks.

Intranet
A private Internet-like network, typically used to link the various parts of a company.

URL
Short for Uniform Resource Locator. The address or location of the page or file on the Internet.

Web pages
Documents (frequently including multimedia elements) that can be accessed with a Web browser.

> **What You Will Learn**

Using a Hyperlink in Excel
Creating a Hyperlink in a Cell
Modifying Hyperlinks
Modifying Hyperlinked Cell Attributes
Removing a Hyperlink

Software Skills   A hyperlink can connect a worksheet to specific locations within any worksheet in any workbook, or to information on the Internet or the company intranet. Using a hyperlink is a convenient way to provide quick access to related information. For example, in a sales worksheet, you could provide a hyperlink to an area in the workbook (or in another workbook) that provides product costs or other revenues.

Application Skills   You've been put in charge of tracking patient services at Wood Hills Animal Clinic. You've put together a patient worksheet listing the various pets that have recently visited the clinic and a separate worksheet listing owner information. Before you get too far on your project, you want to test out its usability, adding hyperlinks that connect each pet with its owner's personal data. Finally, you want to link from a pet's name to its patient history, which is stored in a third worksheet.

What You Can Do

Using a Hyperlink in Excel

- A **hyperlink** is text or a graphic that, when clicked, displays related information elsewhere in the worksheet or in another file.
  - You can link to information in the same worksheet, another worksheet in the same workbook, another workbook, or anywhere on the Internet.
  - You can also link to any other file, such as a Word document, sound file, graphic image, movie, as shown in Figure 9-1.
  - These files may be located on your hard disk, the company network, the **Internet** or an **intranet**.
  - You can link to your e-mail address, to help the user send you an e-mail message.
  - You can also create a new workbook to link to.
- When you move the mouse pointer over a hyperlink, it changes to a pointing hand 👆 .
  - This change helps you distinguish hyperlinks from regular text, and hyperlink graphics from regular pictures.
  - Because the mouse pointer changes to a hand when over a hyperlink, you must use special techniques to select the link for editing.
- When a mouse pointer moves over a hyperlink, a ScreenTip appears, displaying the **URL** of the linked file or e-mail address.
  - You can override this default ScreenTip with a short description of the linked file or e-mail address.
- Text hyperlinks are typically formatted in a different color and underlined.

- When you click a text hyperlink and then later return to it, you'll probably notice that it has changed to purple underlined text.
  - This change helps you quickly identify the links you've used (and those you haven't).
- Clicking a hyperlink moves you to the associated location.
  - If the hyperlink involves another file, that file is opened automatically.
  - If you want the user to move to a particular place within a worksheet, you might want to create a range name so that you can use that name in the link.
  - ✓ *If you don't want to create a range name, you can still link to a specific place within a worksheet by typing its cell address.*
  - If you don't want to create a range name, you can still link to a specific place within a worksheet by typing its cell address.
- You can create hyperlinks that connect a user to data in the current workbook or workbooks located on a company intranet.
- You can also connect to data on the Internet.
  - You can connect to Excel files or to HTML/ MHTML files, since Excel can display either.
  - This capability allows you to include links to related **Web pages** (since they're coded in HTML or MHTML) within your worksheets.
- You can include hyperlinks in ordinary Excel worksheets or in workbooks that you have converted to HTML format.

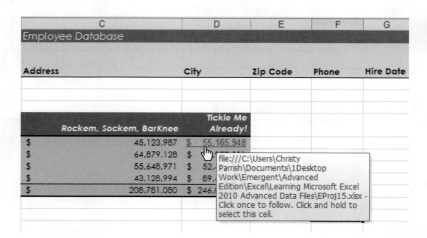

Figure 9-1

Creating a Hyperlink in a Cell

- If you want to create a hyperlink, enter the text or graphic image before you follow the steps to create the hyperlink.

- Normally, you insert a hyperlink using the Insert Hyperlink dialog box.

- If you want to create a hyperlink to a Web page or an intranet document, you can bypass the Insert Hyperlink dialog box and simply type the Web page address (URL) or intranet location into a cell.

  - Excel will instantly recognize the address as a URL, and create a hyperlink from it automatically.
  - A Web address might look like this: http://www. fakeco.com/augsales.html

- You can also type an e-mail address directly in a cell and Excel will convert it to a hyperlink. When a user clicks this type of hyperlink, an e-mail message is automatically created, with the recipient's address included.

Try It!   **Creating a Hyperlink to Another File**

① Start Excel and open **ETry09** from the data files for this lesson.

② Save the file as **ETry09_studentfirstname_ studentlastname** in the location where your teacher instructs you to store the files for this lesson.

③ Click cell B8 and click Insert > Hyperlink 🔍 .

④ Click Existing File or Web Page.

⑤ Click **ETry09a** from the data files for this lesson.

⑥ Click OK.

⑦ Save changes and leave the file open to use in the next Try It.

The Insert Hyperlink dialog box

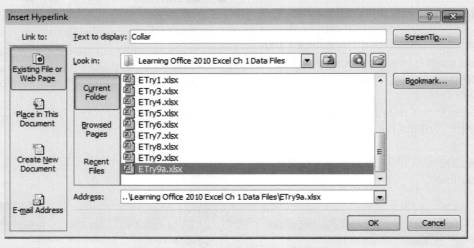

Try It!   **Creating a Hyperlink to a Web Page**

① In **ETry09_studentfirstname_ studentlastname**, click cell D7.

② Click Insert > Hyperlink 🔍 .

③ Click Existing File or Web Page.

④ Type http://www.akc.org/ in the Address box.

⑤ Click OK.

⑥ Save changes and leave the file open to use in the next Try It.

Try It! **Inserting a Hyperlink to a Location in the Current Workbook**

1 In **ETry09_studentfirstname_
studentlastname**, click cell B6.

2 Click Insert > Hyperlink 🌐 .

3 Click Place in This Document.

4 Select Customers in the Or select a place in this
document section.

5 Click OK.

6 Save changes and leave the file open to use in
the next Try It.

Creating a hyperlink to a location in the current workbook

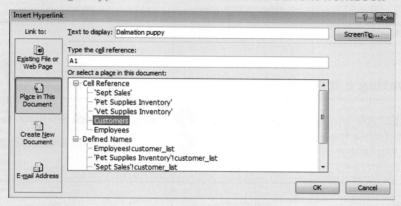

Try It! **Inserting a Hyperlink to a New Workbook**

1 In **ETry09_studentfirstname_
studentlastname**, click cell B10.

2 Click Insert > Hyperlink 🌐 .

3 Click Create New Document.

4 Type **ETry09b_studentfirstname_
studentlastname** in the Name of the new
document box.

5 Click Change, if necessary, and select the
location your teacher instructs you to store files
for this lesson. Click OK.

6 Save changes to **ETry09_studentfirstname_
studentlastname**, and leave the file open to
use in the next Try It.

Creating a hyperlink to a new workbook

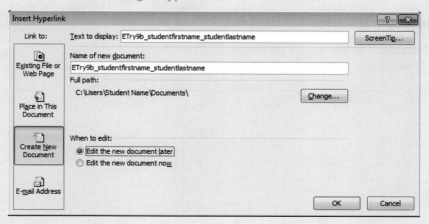

Try It! Inserting a Hyperlink to an E-mail Address

1. In the Excel file **ETry09_studentfirstname_studentlastname**, click cell C4.

2. Click Insert > Hyperlink 🖳 .

3. Click E-mail Address.

4. In the E-mail address box, type **accounting@petes_pets.com**.

5. In the Subject box, type **Request for additional sales information**.

6. Click OK.

7. Save changes and leave the file open to use in the next Try It.

Try It! Activating a Hyperlink

1. In the Excel file **ETry09_studentfirstname_studentlastname**, click the hyperlink in cell B6. The Customers worksheet is displayed.

2. Click the Sept Sales worksheet tab.

3. Save changes and leave the file open to use in the next Try It.

Modifying Hyperlinks

■ You can modify a hyperlink by providing a custom ScreenTip, by changing the destination for the link, or by editing the screen text.

Try It! Modifying a Hyperlink

1. In **ETry09_studentfirstname_studentlastname**, select cell C8 and press ⌫ one time.

2. Type **Collar**.

3. Right-click cell D7 and select Edit Hyperlink.

4. Change the destination of the link by clicking Place in This Document.

5. Click Employees in the destination list and type **A6** in the Type the cell reference box. Click OK.

6. Save changes and leave the file open to use in the next Try It.

Try It! Creating a Custom ScreenTip for a Hyperlink

1 In **ETry09_studentfirstname_studentlastname**, click cell C4.

2 Select Edit Hyperlink.

3 Click Screen Tip.

4 Type **E-mail us for more information**.

5 Click OK two times.

6 Save changes and leave the file open to use in the next Try It.

Creating a custom ScreenTip for a hyperlink

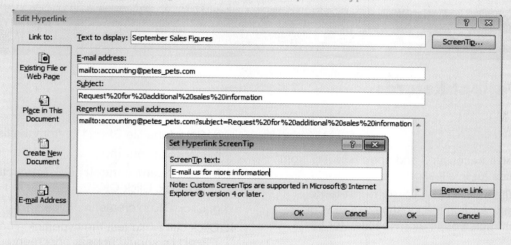

Modifying Hyperlinked Cell Attributes

- When you add a hyperlink to a cell, you might find that the resulting link colors do not look good with the existing formatting of the worksheet.

- You can modify the appearance of hyperlinked cells using the Cell Styles button on the Home tab. You can also manually change your worksheet's formatting, including theme and font colors and other text attributes.

Try It! Modifying Hyperlinked-Cell Attributes

1 In **ETry09_studentfirstname_studentlastname**, select cells A4:F4.

2 Click Home > Cell Styles 🔲.

3 In the Cell Styles gallery, select Accent1 in the Themed Cell Styles.

4 Save changes and leave the file open to use in the next Try It.

Removing a Hyperlink

- There are many ways to remove a hyperlink from a worksheet depending on whether you want to eliminate the hyperlink itself or remove the cell contents as well.

Try It!   **Removing a Hyperlink**

1 In **ETry09_studentfirstname_ studentlastname**, select cell B6.

2 Select Remove Hyperlink.

3 Save the changes to **ETry09_ studentfirstname_studentlastname** and close the workbook. Exit Excel.

Project 17—Create It

Linking Patient Records

DIRECTIONS

1. Start Excel, if necessary, and open **EProj17** from the data files for this lesson.

2. Save the file as **EProj17_studentfirstname_ studentlastname** in the location where your teacher instructs you to store the files for this lesson.

3. Create a link to Akemi's medical history:

   a. With cell **A6** selected, click **Insert > Hyperlink** 🔍 .

   b. **Click the Existing File or Web Page** button on the Link to bar.

   c. Select the folder where the data files for this lesson are stored from the Look in list.

   d. Select the file **EProj17a** from the list.

   e. Click **ScreenTip**.

   f. Type **Akemi's medical history** in the ScreenTip text box. Click **OK**.

   g. Click **OK** to create the hyperlink.

4. Click cell **A6** to test the hyperlink. The file **EProj17a** should appear onscreen.

   ✓ *Remember that when you click a link, only the linked workbook appears on the screen, unless you arrange the view so you can see both.*

5. Close both workbooks, saving all changes, and exit Excel.

Project 18—Apply It

Linking Patient Records

DIRECTIONS

1. Start Excel, if necessary, and open **EProj18** from the data files for this lesson and save the file as **EProj18_studentfirstname_studentlastname** in the location where your teacher instructs you to store the files for this lesson.

2. Create a hyperlink to information about Akemi's owner:

   a. With cell **E6** selected, click **Insert > Hyperlink** 🔍 .

   b. Click the **Existing File or Web Page** button on the Link to bar.

c. Select the folder where data files for this lesson are stored from the Look in list.

d. Select the file **EProj18b** from the list.

e. Create a ScreenTip that says **View owner information**.

f. Click the **Bookmark** button.

g. Select the range name **woo_daniel**. Click **OK**.

h. Click **OK** to create the hyperlink.

3. Test both hyperlinks on the worksheet. See Figure 9-2.

✓ *The linked workbooks have been arranged onscreen so you can see how they are linked. To do the same click View > Arrange All > Cascade.*

4. Close the two linked workbooks.

5. Create a footer using your name.

6. Close the workbook, saving all changes, and exit Excel.

Figure 9-2

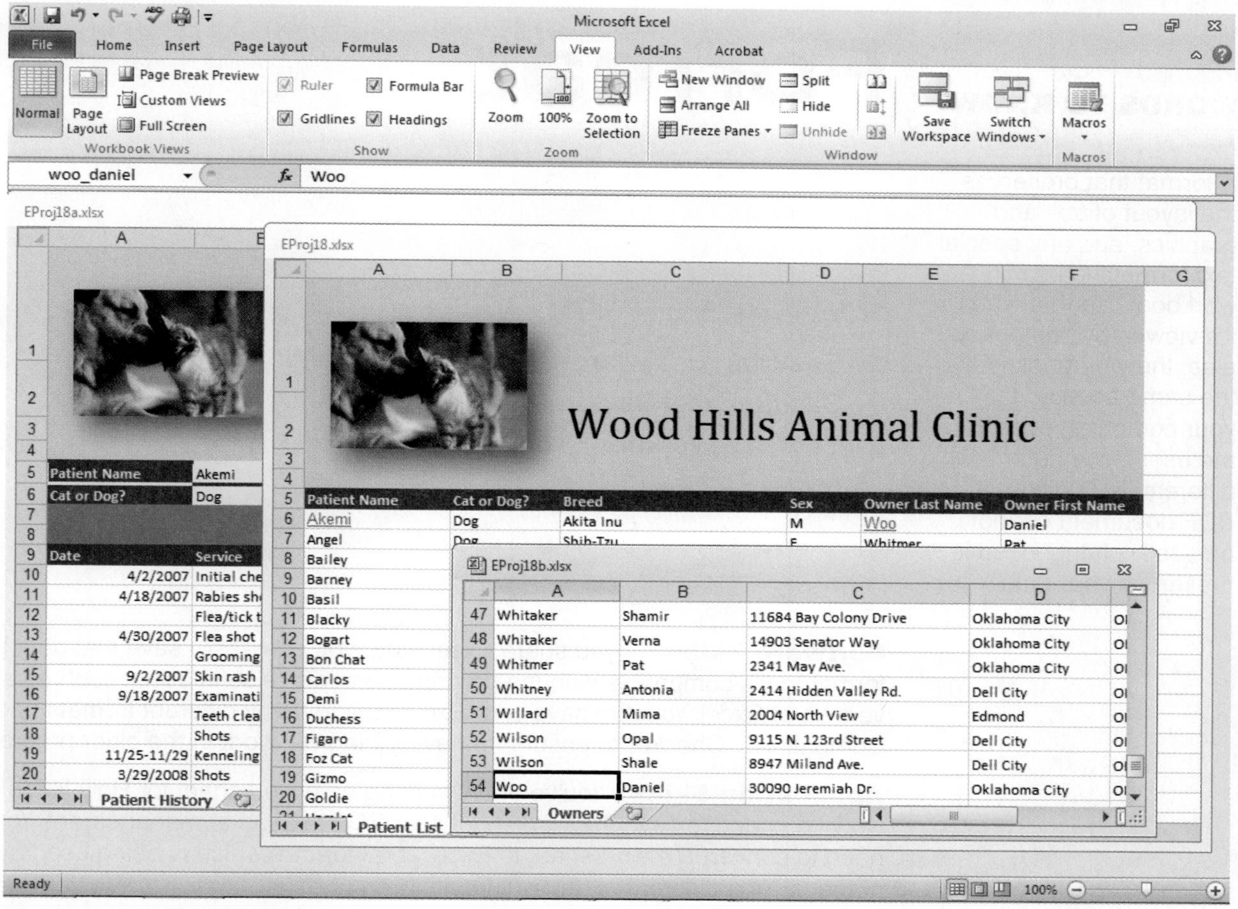

Lesson 10

Saving Excel Data in a Different File Format

➤ What You Will Learn

Ensuring Backward-Compatibility in a Workbook
Saving Excel Data in CSV File Format
Saving a Workbook as a PDF or XPS File

Software Skills If you share Excel data, you can easily save that data in a format that's compatible with the program someone else is using, such as an older version of Excel. You can save your Excel data in many different formats and use the Compatibility Checker to ensure that everything will work in the older program.

Application Skills You've been working on a worksheet for Holy Habañero. Now you need to save the worksheet as a PDF to send to management. You'll also need to convert the worksheet to Excel 2003 format, which is being used by the manager of a different restaurant location.

What You Can Do

Ensuring Backward-Compatibility in a Workbook

- Sometimes saving your workbook in a different format will result in a loss of some data—typically formatting changes.
- You can see which features might be lost before resaving a workbook in an older version of Excel by running Check Compatibility first.

- Check Compatibility scans the workbook and lists any incompatibilities, and the number of occurrences of that incompatibility.
  - Incompatibilities are grouped by severity.
  - You can copy this list of incompatibilities to a sheet in the workbook for further review if you want.

Try It!　　**Using the Compatibility Checker**

1 Start Excel and open ETry10 from the data files for this lesson.

2 Save the file as ETry10_studentfirstname_studentlastname in the location where your teacher instructs you to store the files for this lesson.

3 Click File > Info > Check for Issues.

4 Select Check Compatibility.

5 Excel will display a list of potential problems. Scroll through the issues.

✓ *You can click the Find link to have Excel show you where the problem is.*

6 Click OK.

7 Save changes and leave the file open to use in the next Try It.

The Compatibility Checker Report

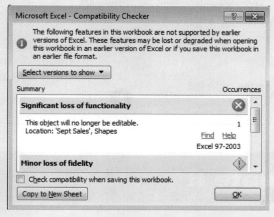

Saving Excel Data in CSV File Format

- Although many programs can open Excel files, you may occasionally need to save your workbook in a different format.
- For example, you might need to save a workbook in Excel 2003 format so that a colleague using an older version of Excel can open it.

- Besides converting a workbook to an earlier version of Excel, you can also convert your data to the popular CSV format, which is compatible with almost every kind of spreadsheet or database software.
- The CSV file format maintains the functionality of your data, but the formatting is lost.

Try It!   Saving Excel Data in CSV File Format

1 In the **ETry10_studentfirstname_ studentlastname** file, click File > Save As 🖼️ .

2 Select CSV (Comma delimited) from the Save as file type list.

✓ *Notice that there are two other CSV formats: one for Macintosh and one for MS-DOS. Choose the correct one for your computer.*

3 Save the file as **ETry10_studentfirstname_ studentlastname** in the location where your teacher instructs you to store files for this lesson.

4 When Excel warns that features might not be compatible with CSV, click Yes to save the file as is.

5 Close the CSV file.

Saving a Workbook as a PDF or XPS File

■ Besides converting a workbook to another spreadsheet format, you can also convert the file to PDF format and XPS format.

■ In order to view a workbook saved in PDF format, you need Adobe Reader or Adobe Acrobat software.

● To make changes to a workbook saved as PDF, you can use Adobe Acrobat, or simply open the original file in Excel, make your changes, and then resave the file in PDF format

■ To view a worksheet saved in XPS format, you need an XPS viewer, available free from Microsoft.

● To make changes to a workbook saved in XPS, open the original file in Excel, make your changes, and resave the file.

Try It!   Saving a Workbook as a PDF or XPS File

1 Reopen the **ETry10_studentfirstname_ studentlastname.xls** file from your solution files, click File > Save As 🖼️ .

2 Click Other Formats.

3 Select PDF from the Save as file type list.

OR

Select XPS from the Save as file type list.

4 Save the file as **ETry10a_studentfirstname_ studentlastname** in the location where your teacher instructs you to store files for this lesson.

5 Close Excel and the new file viewer.

Project 19—Create It

Checking Compatibility

DIRECTIONS

1. Start Excel, if necessary, and open **EProj19** from the data files for this lesson.

2. Save the file as **EProj19_studentfirstname_ studentlastname** in the location where your teacher instructs you to store the files for this lesson.

3. Use Check Compatibility to see if any features are incompatible with Excel 2003 format. Click **File > Info**.

4. Click **Check for Issues**.

5. Select **Check Compatibility**.

6. Review the Compatibility Checker report.

a. Click **Select Versions to Show** and click **Excel 2007** to turn off that version of Excel.

b. Note that some of the formatting (themes) are not compatible with the older version of Excel.

c. Click **OK**.

✓ *Despite the warning, in most case this formatting issue is not really a big concern. The worksheet will function properly in Excel 2003; it just might look a bit different. But it's always best to test the converted workbook to make sure that it looks and works as you want it to before you send it to your colleague.*

7. Resave the workbook as **EProj19a_studentfirstname_studentlastname** in the Excel 97-2003 workbook format in the location where your teacher instructs you to store the files for this lesson.

8. The Compatibility Checker opens again. Click **Continue**.

9. Close the document, saving all changes, and exit Excel.

Project 20—Apply It

Saving a Worksheet in Different Formats

DIRECTIONS

1. Start Excel, if necessary, and open **EProj20** from the data files for this lesson and save it as **EProj20_studentfirstname_studentlastname** in the location where your teacher instructs you to store the files for this lesson.

2. **File > Save & Send > Create PDF/XPS Document**.

3. Save the file as **EProj20a_studentfirstname_studentlastname** in the location where your teacher instructs you to store the files for this lesson.

4. Select **Open file after publishing** and click **Publish**.

5. Look at the PDF file that opens and notice that the print settings are not correct for the file. Close the PDF.

6. Select the range **A1:J28** and click **Page Layout > Print Area** 🗐 **> Set Print Area**.

7. Click **Page Layout > Orientation** 🗐 **> Landscape**.

8. Click **File > Print and click No Scaling > Fit Sheet on One Page**.

9. Save the file again as a PDF, replacing the previous PDF file. Look over the PDF that appears and then close the PDF file.

10. Click **File > Save As** 🗐 and select **CSV (MS-DOS)** from the **Save as type** list.

11. Save the file as **EProj20b_studentfirstname_studentlastname** in the location where your teacher instructs you to store the files for this lesson. Click **Save**.

12. Click **Yes** at the prompt to continue saving in the CSV format.

13. Close all Excel files, saving the changes.

14. Open the **EProj20b_studentfirstname_studentlastname** to see what the CSV file looks like.

✓ *Remember the CSV format maintains the data but eliminates all formatting.*

15. Close the document, saving all changes, and exit Excel.

Lesson 11

Working with Subtotals

WORDS TO KNOW

Database function
A specialized type of function for databases/lists. For example, the DSUM function totals the values in a given range, but only for the database records that match criteria you supply.

Function
A preprogrammed calculation. For example, the SUM function totals the values in a specified range.

➤ **What You Will Learn**

Using Go To and Go To Special
Creating Subtotals
Creating Nested Subtotals
Hiding or Displaying Details
Removing a Subtotal
Manually Outlining and Adding Subtotals

Software Skills   You can use the Go To command to instantly jump to any cell in a worksheet. With the Subtotals feature, you can create automatic totals within the records of a database to help you perform more complex analyses. For example, if the database contains sales records for various stores, you can create totals for each store or each salesperson. With the Subtotals feature, you can total numeric data instantly without having to insert rows, create formulas, and copy data. Instead, it all happens with a few simple clicks.

Application Skills   August has come and gone, and the usage statistics for Giant Frog Supermarkets' leased network space have been added to Intellidata's ongoing usage logs. With so much new data to keep track of, the workbook now needs to be reorganized so managers can view meaningful summaries of the data.

What You Can Do

Using Go To and Go To Special

- Go To is a feature that allows you to tell Excel the exact address of the cell that you want to be the current active cell.
- Using Go To changes the location of the active cell.
- If your goal is not to locate data, but to find particular kinds of cells quickly and then select them, then you need a different kind of Find command—Go To Special.
- Using Go To Special, you can locate cells that contain:
  - Comments
  - Constants
  - Formulas
  - Row differences, Column differences
  - Precedents, Dependents
  - Blanks
  - Conditional formats
  - Data validation
- You can also locate:
  - Cells in the current region
  - Cells in the current array
  - Objects
  - The last cell with data
  - Visible (non-hidden) cells
- Some of these commands are accessible from the Find & Select menu on the Home tab; others are accessed through the Go To Special dialog box.

Try It!   **Using Go To and Go To Special**

1. Start Excel and open **ETry11** from the data files for this lesson.

2. Save the file as **ETry11_studentfirstname_studentlastname** in the location where your teacher instructs you to store the files for this lesson.

3. Click Home > Find & Select 🔍 .

4. Select Go To.

    OR

    Press [F5].

5. Type **A1** in the Reference text box.

6. Click OK.

    ✓ *If you want to select a group of related cells using Go To, click the Special button in the Go To dialog box; then choose the type of cells you want to select and click OK.*

7. Click Home > Find & Select 🔍 > Go to Special.

8. Select Formulas and click OK.

9. Save changes and leave the file open to use in the next Try It.

The Go To Special dialog box

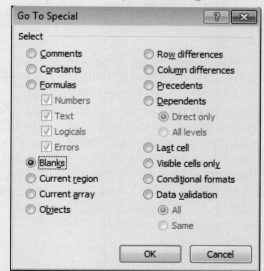

Creating Subtotals

■ With the Subtotal feature, you can quickly insert subtotals between similar rows in an Excel list without having to create custom functions.

   ✓ *You cannot use the Subtotal feature with an Excel table.*

   • Instead of entering DSUM formulas to total a field for particular rows, you can use the Subtotal feature. For example, you can subtotal a sales list to compute the amount sold by each salesperson on a given day.

   • You can also use the Subtotal feature to insert other database functions, such as DCOUNT, DAVERAGE, and so on.

   ✓ *To learn more about using database functions, see Chapter 4.*

■ The Subtotal feature does the following:

   • Calculates subtotals for all rows that contain the same entry in one column. For example, if you select the field Salesperson, Excel will create subtotals for each salesperson.

   • Inserts the totals in a row just below that group of data.

   • Calculates a grand total.

   • Inserts a label for each group totaled/subtotaled.

   • Displays the outline controls.

   ✓ *The outline controls allow you to control the level of detail displayed.*

■ For the Subtotal feature to work, all records containing values that contribute to that subtotal (or other calculation) must be sorted together.

   • Before applying the subtotal feature, sort the list so that all records that are to be calculated together, are grouped together. This way, for example, all of the "Sacramento" entries will be in a group.

   • Excel inserts a subtotal line whenever it detects a change in the value of the chosen field—for instance, a change from "Sacramento" to "San Francisco."

   • Also, if the subtotal line is to show the average pledge amount for all callers to the Sacramento office, then each pledge must contain "Sacramento" in one column—preferably one with a meaningful field name, such as "Office."

■ When you click the Subtotal button on the Data tab, a dialog box displays, from which you can make several choices:

   • *At each change in*—Select the field name by which you want to total.

   • *Use function*—Select a database function.

   • *Add subtotal to*—Select one or more fields to use with the database function you selected.

   • *Replace current subtotals*—Select this option to create a new subtotal within a database, removing any current subtotals. Deselect this option to retain current subtotals.

   • *Page break between groups*—Places each subtotaled group on its own page.

   • *Summary below data*—Inserts the subtotals/ grand total below each group, rather than above it.

   • *Remove All*—Removes all subtotals.

■ Subtotals act just like any other formula; if you change the data, the total will recalculate automatically.

■ You can use the Subtotal feature on a filtered list.

   • The totals are calculated based only on the displayed data.

   ✓ *To learn more about filtering a list, see Lesson 6.*

■ As mentioned previously, you cannot use the Subtotals feature on an Excel table.

   • To enable a table to use subtotals, first convert it back to a list.

Try It!   Creating Subtotals

1   In the **ETry11_studentfirstname_studentlastname** file, you need to sort the list before you add subtotals.

2   Select range A5:G29 and click Home > Sort & Filter ⧩ .

3   Select Sort A to Z.

4   Click Data > Subtotal ⊞ .

5   In the At each change in drop-down list, select Item Type, if necessary.

   ✓ *A new subtotal will be calculated at each change within the column you choose here.*

6   In the Use function box, select Sum.

7   In the Add Subtotal to box, select Items Sold and Value Sold.

8   Select Summary below data (Places a Grand Total row at the bottom of the list).

9   If desired, you can choose the additional options:
- Replace current subtotals (use when you've made changes to the data and need to refresh the subtotals).

- Page break between groups (use when you want to create individual printouts for each subtotal).

10   Click OK. Save changes and leave the file open to use in the next Try It.

The Subtotal dialog box

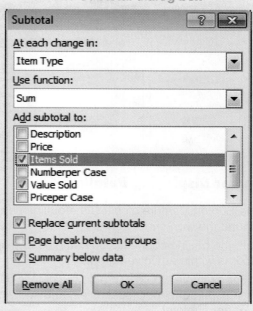

Creating Nested Subtotals

- You can create subtotals within subtotals (nested subtotals).
- To create nested subtotals, sort the list by both of the fields you wish to total.

Try It!   Creating Nested Subtotals

1   In the **ETry11_studentfirstname_studentlastname** file, select the range A5:G37, if necessary.

   ✓ *You need to subtotal the list before you can create a nested subtotal.*

2   Click Data > Subtotal ⊞ .

3   In the At each change in box, select Description. Leave the current options in the Use function and Add subtotal to boxes.

4   Select Summary below data (Places a Grand Total row at the bottom of the list).

(continued)

Try It! 　Creating Nested Subtotals (continued)

5 Make sure that the Replace current subtotals option is deselected. Click OK.

6 Save changes and leave the file open to use in the next Try It.

Nested subtotals

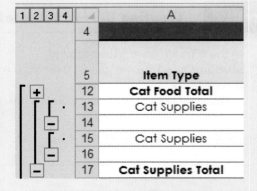

Hiding or Displaying Details

- The Subtotal feature displays the outline controls around the worksheet frame.

- With the outline controls, you can hide or display the records within any given group.
  - For example, you could hide the details of each salesperson's individual sales, and show only his or her subtotal.
  - You could also show details for some salespeople while hiding the details for others.

- The first subtotal added to a worksheet subdivides it into *three* levels of data.
  - The highest detail number always represents the view with *all* the data.
  - Detail level 1 always represents grand totals only.
  - Intermediate detail levels represent summaries of detail levels.

- Each subtotal added to a worksheet that already contains subtotals, adds one detail level.

Try It! 　Hiding or Displaying Details

1 In the **ETry11_studentfirstname_studentlastname** file, select cell C12.

2 Click Data > Hide Detail and notice that all the rows in the Cat Food type are hidden.

3 Click the plus sign in the 2nd column of row 12.

4 Click the number 1 outline symbol to hide the entire list.

5 Click the number 3 outline symbol to show the subtotals.

6 Click Data > Show Detail to show the entire list.

7 Save changes and leave the file open to use in the next Try It.

The Outline Controls

Removing a Subtotal

- You can remove the subtotals from a list by clicking the Remove All button in the Subtotal dialog box.

- You can also remove subtotals by creating new subtotals that replace old ones.

- If you just created the subtotals and you don't like the results, click the Undo button on the Quick Access Toolbar to remove the subtotals, and then start over.

Try It!　Removing Automatic Subtotals

1. In the **ETry11_studentfirstname_ studentlastname** file, click anywhere in the list.

2. Click Data > Subtotal ▦.

3. Click Remove All.

4. Save changes and leave the file open to use in the next Try It.

Outlining and Adding Subtotals Manually

- Even with the Subtotal feature, you might still want to manually outline (group) a list.

  - For example, you might use the Group feature to manually group particular rows together.

  - Using Group, you can also create a list that contains totals for multiple fields in the same row.

- Group also allows you to manually group columns together, in a situation where your data is arranged mainly in rows (rather than mainly in columns).

- Another reason to use the Group feature is to add subtotals to an Excel table.

  - You can also use the Group feature to add the outlining controls to an Excel table.

Try It!　Outlining and Adding Subtotals Manually

1. In the **ETry11_studentfirstname_ studentlastname** file, right-click the heading for row 13 and select Insert.

2. Select the range A6:G12.

3. Click Data > Group ➡. Click Rows and click OK.

4. Click Home > Sum Σ.

5. Click Data > Ungroup ➡. Click Rows and click OK.

6. Save changes, and close Excel.

Project 21—Create It

Organizing Usage Statistics

DIRECTIONS

1. Start Excel, if necessary, and open **EProj21** from the data files for this lesson.
2. Save the file as **EProj21_studentfirstname_ studentlastname** in the location where your teacher instructs you to store the files for this lesson.
3. Select the **Forecasts** worksheet.
4. Click **Home** > **Find & Select** 🔍 > **Go To**.
5. Type **G74** in the Reference box and click **OK**.
6. Click **Home** > **Find & Select** 🔍 > **Go To Special**.
7. Select **Comments** and click **OK**. Click **Review** > **Edit Comment** to read the comment.
8. Click cell **D38** to close the comment.
9. Click **Review** > **Delete Comment** and type **1974** in cell **D38**.
10. Go to the **Usage statistics 0804** worksheet to create subtotals for each Sunday that begins a measurement period:
    a. Select the range **A5:G140**.
    b. Click the **Data** > **Subtotal** 📊 .
    c. From the **At each change in** list, click **Date**.
    d. From the **Use function** list, click **Sum**.

    e. From the **Add subtotal to** list, select **Avg. Bandwidth**, **Data In**, **Data Out**, and **Transactions**.
    f. Clear the **Replace current subtotals** check box.
    g. Clear the **Page break between groups**.
    h. Select the **Summary below data** check box.
    i. Click **OK**.

    ✓ *There are now three levels of detail. Level 3 shows all the data; level 2 shows just the subtotals for each week; and level 1 shows only the grand totals.*

11. Adjust column widths as necessary.
12. Click the 2 [2] Outline group button to see all the subtotals.
13. Select **A1: G150** and click **Page Layout** > **Print Area** 📋 > **Set Print Area**.
14. Add a footer with your name.
15. **With your teacher's permission**, print the worksheet. It should look similar to Figure 11-1.
16. Close the workbook, saving all changes, and exit Excel.

Figure 11-1						

Intellidata
Hosting · Management · Warehousing

Usage statistics
Giant Frog Supermarkets - District # 0855
Period of 4 July - 4 September 2011

Date	Department	Region	Kb/sec Avg. Bandwidth	Mb Data In	Mb Data Out	Transactions
7/4/2011 Total			1404.9	23093	133364	579502
7/11/2011 Total			1339.5	22300	125960	555785
7/18/2011 Total			1377.7	23944	129681	566206
7/25/2011 Total			1464.4	25935	139778	586438
8/1/2011 Total			1439.5	24978	142019	578358
8/8/2011 Total			1400.8	23830	139363	572934
8/15/2011 Total			1406.2	24204	139935	487461
8/22/2011 Total			1410.9	27659	149379	577563
8/29/2011 Total			1433.6	28952	158298	605427
Grand Total			12677.5	224895	1257777	5109674

Project 22—Apply It

Organizing Usage Statistics

DIRECTIONS

1. Start Excel, if necessary, and open **EProj22** from the data files for this lesson and save the file as **EProj22_studentfirstname_studentlastname** in the location where your teacher instructs you to store the files for this lesson.

2. Go to the **Usage statistics 0804** worksheet, if necessary.

3. Calculate the average bandwidth for each department:

   a. Select the range **A5:G150**, and click **Data > Subtotal**.

   b. From the **At each change in** list, click **Department**.

   c. From the **Use function** list, click **Average**.

   d. From the **Add subtotal to** list, click **Avg. Bandwidth**. Then clear **Data In**, **Data Out**, and **Transactions**.

   e. Click **OK**.

   ✓ *There are now four levels of detail. Level 1 is the grand total (plus the "grand average" bandwidth). Level 2 summarizes each week, and level 3 summarizes each department. Level 4 contains the complete data.*

4. Create subtotals for each department:

   a. With the range still selected, click the **Subtotal** button again.

   b. From the **At each change in** list, click **Department**.

   c. From the **Use function** list, click **Sum**.

   d. From the **Add subtotal to** list, click **Avg. Bandwidth**, **Data In**, **Data Out**, and **Transactions**.

   e. Click **OK**.

   ✓ *There are now five levels of detail.*

5. Click outline level button **3** to display only the department averages, weekly totals, and grand totals. **With your teacher's permission**, print the worksheet.

6. Display the detail rows for the Accounting department for the week of August 22. **With your teacher's permission**, print the worksheet.

7. Click outline level button **2** to display just weekly totals.

8. Expand the outline to show all the department averages for the week of August 29.

9. Expand the outline to show the Point of sale department's detail for that week, as shown in Figure 11-2.

10. Manually add a new group:

    a. Insert a new row above row **236**.

    b. Type **POS North and South Total** in cell **C236**.

    c. Apply Bold, Right alignment to cell **C236**.

    d. In cell **D236**, insert a formula that totals the average bandwidths for **Point of sale North** and **Point of sale South**.

    e. Select rows **234** to **236**, then click **Data > Group** 🗎 to group the three rows. See Figure 11-2.

    ✓ *There are now six levels of detail.*

11. **With your teacher's permission**, print the worksheet. It should look similar to Figure 11-2.

12. Close the workbook, saving all changes, and exit Excel.

Figure 11-2

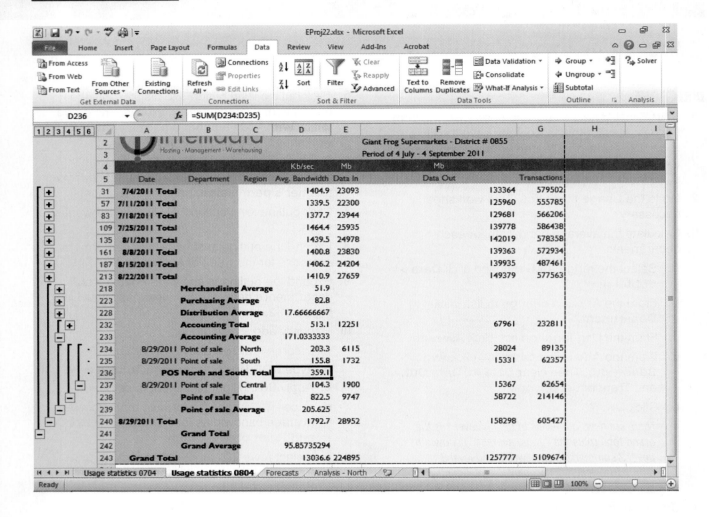

Chapter Assessment and Application

Project 23—Make It Your Own

Payroll Calculations

You are the corporate payroll clerk at PhotoTown, and you've been calculating payroll checks manually ever since you were hired a month ago. Now that you're familiar with Excel, however, you want to use it to complete this weekly task more easily.

DIRECTIONS

1. Start Excel, if necessary, and open **EProj23** from the data files for this project, Save the file as **EProj23_studentfirstname_studentlastname** in the location where your teacher instructs you to store the files for this project.

2. Type several two-line column labels:
   a. In cell **A7**, type **Check Number** (enter the column label on two lines).
   b. In cell **B7**, type **Employee ID Number** on two lines.
   c. In cell **E7**, type **Hours Worked** on two lines.
   d. Adjust column widths as needed.

3. Separate the **Name** column into **First Name** and **Last Name**:
   a. Insert a column to the right of column D.
   b. After selecting the range **D8:D37**, click **Data > Text to Columns**.
   c. Choose the **Delimited, Space** options.
   d. Format both columns as text, and save the result in the range beginning in cell D8.
   e. Type **First Name** in cell **D7** and **Last Name** in cell **E7**.
   f. Correct the one error by typing **Chu Gi** in cell **D26**, and **Nguyen** in cell **E26**.

4. Enter the hours everyone has worked as mixed fractions, as shown in Illustration A.

5. Use **Go To** to jump to the cell that displays the total cost of the payroll this week:
   a. Click the **Find & Select** button on the **Home** tab, and choose **Go To**.
   b. Choose **Payroll_Total** from the list, and click **OK** to jump to cell **L41**.

6. Enter today's date in cell **H3**, and apply the Short Date format.

7. Type **Click here to view employee tax data** in cell **G2**:
   a. Select the range **G2:H2**.
   b. Use this text to create a hyperlink to **EProj23a** from the data files for this lesson.
   c. Use the ScreenTip **Employee Database**.
   d. Change the point size of the hyperlink text to **11 point**.
   e. Format cells **G2:J2** and use the Cell Styles gallery to apply the **60% Accent 5** style.

8. Fill all cells in the worksheet with the color, **Gold, Accent 5, Lighter 60%** (see Illustration A):
   a. Select rows 1-6, and fill them with **Lighter 40%**.
   b. Select **A7:L7**, and apply a **Red, Accent 2** fill color.

9. Create two custom views:
   a. Save the current settings as a custom view called **Full View**.
   b. Hide columns **C-G**, and call that view **Payroll Checks**.
   c. Adjust columns as needed and, **with your teacher's permission**, print the worksheet.

10. Change back to **Full View**.

11. Widen columns as needed.

12. Click **Insert > Header & Footer** and then type your name.

13. **With your teacher's permission**, print the worksheet in **Full View** horizontal in landscape orientation.

14. Close the workbook, saving all changes, and exit Excel.

Illustration A

PhotoTown

Miller Rd
Unit #2166

Click here to view employee tax data

Date   11/14/2011

Check Number	Employee ID Number	Title	First Name	Last Name	Hours Worked	Rate	Gross Pay	Fed	SS	State	Net Pay
41289	63778	Mr.	Carlos	Altare	12	$6.30	$75.60	$14.36	$5.86	$4.16	$51.22
41290	31524	Mrs.	Jan	Borough	22	$6.50	$143.00	$27.17	$11.08	$7.87	$96.88
41291	18946	Mr.	Shakur	Brown	40	$7.00	$280.00	$53.20	$21.70	$15.40	$189.70
41292	71335	Mr.	Taneed	Black	38 1/2	$7.00	$269.50	$51.21	$20.89	$14.82	$182.59
41293	22415	Mr.	Jairo	Campos	21 3/4	$7.20	$156.60	$29.75	$12.14	$8.61	$106.10
41294	20965	Mrs.	Rafiquil	Damir	10 1/2	$6.15	$64.58	$12.27	$5.00	$3.55	$43.75
41295	64121	Mrs.	Diana	Dogwood	19 3/4	$6.20	$122.45	$23.27	$9.49	$6.73	$82.96
41296	30388	Mrs.	Lucy	Fan	31 1/4	$6.55	$204.69	$38.89	$15.86	$11.26	$138.68
41297	44185	Mrs.	Jennifer	Flynn	30	$7.00	$210.00	$39.90	$16.28	$11.55	$142.28
41298	32152	Mrs.	Katerina	Flynn	30	$7.10	$213.00	$40.47	$16.51	$11.72	$144.31
41299	31885	Ms.	Kere	Freed	32 1/2	$7.10	$230.75	$43.84	$17.88	$12.69	$156.33
41300	33785	Mr.	Eram	Hassan	27 1/2	$6.85	$188.38	$35.79	$14.60	$10.36	$127.62
41301	55648	Mr.	Tyrell	Johnson	22	$6.50	$143.00	$27.17	$11.08	$7.87	$96.88
41302	60219	Ms.	Verna	Latinz	12 1/2	$6.30	$78.75	$14.96	$6.10	$4.33	$53.35
41303	28645	Mr.	Wu	Lee	10 3/4	$7.00	$75.25	$14.30	$5.83	$4.14	$50.98
41304	67415	Mr.	Shamir	Lewis	20	$7.10	$142.00	$26.98	$11.01	$7.81	$96.21
41305	27995	Mrs.	Maria	Navarro	20	$6.30	$126.00	$23.94	$9.77	$6.93	$85.37
41306	32151	Mr.	Tony	Navarro	18 3/4	$6.35	$119.06	$22.62	$9.23	$6.55	$80.66
41307	28499	Mr.	Chu Gi	Nguyen	23 1/2	$6.85	$160.98	$30.59	$12.48	$8.85	$109.06
41308	17564	Mr.	Juan	Nuniez	39 1/4	$7.00	$274.75	$52.20	$21.29	$15.11	$186.14
41309	14558	Mr.	Akira	Ota	14 1/2	$7.25	$105.13	$19.97	$8.15	$5.78	$71.22
41310	31022	Mrs.	Meghan	Ryan	31 3/4	$7.00	$222.25	$42.23	$17.22	$12.22	$150.57
41311	41885	Mrs.	Kate	Scott	23	$6.85	$157.55	$29.93	$12.21	$8.67	$106.74
41312	25448	Mr.	Jyoti	Shaw	32 1/4	$6.50	$209.63	$39.83	$16.25	$11.53	$142.02
41313	23151	Ms.	Jewel	Vidito	35	$6.55	$229.25	$43.56	$17.77	$12.61	$155.32
41314	37785	Mrs.	Corrine	Walters	35 1/2	$6.65	$236.08	$44.85	$18.30	$12.98	$159.94

Project 24—Master It

Women and Children First

In American History, your class is studying the Titanic. Questions have been raised as to whether the rule of the sea, "women and children first," was followed. You and your classmates hope to analyze the data and come up with an analysis of who was most likely to survive.

DIRECTIONS

1. Start Excel, if necessary, and open **EProj24** from the data files for this project. Save the file as **EProj24_studentfirstname_studentlastname** in the location where your teacher instructs you to store the files for this project.

2. First thing you've noticed is that the data is not as readable as it might be. Use **Find & Replace** to replace the numbers with text: **Yes** and **No**:

    a. Select the range C6:C1318 and click **Home > Find & Select** 🔍 **> Replace**.

    b. Replace 1 with Yes and 0 with **No**.

    c. Close the Find and Replace dialog box.

3. Next, sort the database into two groups—those who survived and those who did not:

    a. Select the range A5:K1318 and click **Data > Filter** 🔽.

    b. Click **Data > Sort** 📶 and create a custom sort.

    c. Set up a sort of the following:

Survived?	Z to A
Class	A to Z
Sex	Z to A
Age	Smallest to largest

4. Add subtotals that count the survivors (or non-survivors):

    a. Create an initial subtotal based on count of the records based on Survived?

    b. Add a page break between groups.

    c. Create a nested subtotal that calculates the average age based on class.

    d. Add another nested subtotal that counts the number of survivors (or non-survivors) by sex

5. Use the outline controls to display only the totals, then adjust column widths as needed to display data. **With your teacher's permission**, print the worksheet.

6. Redisplay all data and remove the subtotals.

7. Now you'll set up a criteria range to do some further analysis on the survivors. Use **DCOUNT** to total the female survivors, male survivors, and child survivors:

    a. For female and male survivors, count only people older than 18.

    b. You'll need to set up two criteria ranges for females, and subtract those people 18 and under from the total number of females.

    c. Repeat this process for male passengers.

    d. For children, count people 18 and younger (male or female).

8. Create a similar criteria range to calculate the total non-survivors. See Illustration A.

9. Adjust column widths as needed to display data and, **with your teacher's permission**, print the worksheet.

10. Close the workbook, saving all changes, and exit Excel.

Illustration A

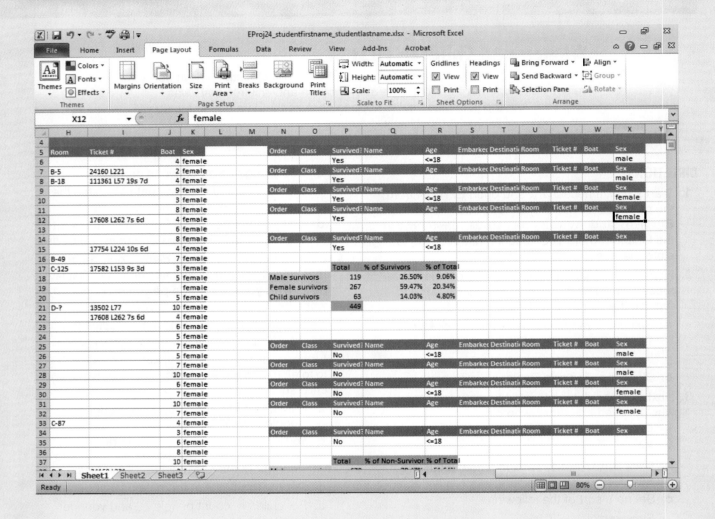

Chapter 2

Creating Charts, Shapes, and Templates

Lesson 12
Formatting Chart Elements
Projects 25-26

- Changing Chart Elements
- Setting Data Label Options
- Setting Data Table Options
- Formatting a Data Series

Lesson 13
Formatting the Value Axis
Projects 27-28

- Creating a Stock Chart
- Modifying the Value Axis
- Formatting Data Markers
- Formatting a Legend
- Adding a Secondary Value Axis to a Chart

Lesson 14
Creating Stacked
Area Charts
Projects 29-30

- Creating a Stacked Area Chart
- Formatting the Chart Floor and Chart Walls
- Displaying Chart Gridlines
- Applying a Chart Layout and Chart Styles

Lesson 15
Working with Sparklines
Projects 31-32

- Inserting a Line, Column, or Win/Loss Sparkline
- Formatting a Sparkline
- Inserting a Trendline

Lesson 16
Drawing and Positioning
Shapes
Projects 33-34

- Drawing Shapes
- Resizing, Grouping, Aligning, and Arranging Shapes

Lesson 17
Formatting Shapes
Projects 35-36

- Formatting Shapes
- Adding Shape Effects

Lesson 18
Enhancing Shapes with
Text and Effects
Projects 37-38

- Adding Text to a Text Box, Callout, or Other Shape
- Adding 3-D Effects
- Rotating Shapes
- Inserting a Screen Capture

Lesson 19
Working with Templates
Projects 39-40

- Changing Cell Borders
- Filling Cells with a Color or a Pattern
- Adding a Watermark or Other Graphics
- Formatting the Worksheet Background
- Creating a Workbook Template

Lesson 20
Protecting Data
Projects 41-42

- Locking and Unlocking Cells in a Worksheet
- Protecting a Range
- Protecting a Worksheet
- Protecting a Workbook

End-of-Chapter Assessments
Projects 43-44

Lesson 12

Formatting Chart Elements

WORDS TO KNOW

Categories
For most charts, a category is information in a worksheet row. If you select multiple rows of data for a chart, you'll create multiple categories, and these categories will be listed along the x-axis.

Data series
For most charts, a data series is the information in a worksheet column. If you select multiple columns of data for a chart, you'll create multiple data series. Each data series is then represented by its own color bar, line, or column.

Data table
This optional table looks like a small worksheet, and displays the data used to create the chart.

Legend key
Symbol in a legend that identifies the color or pattern of a data series in a chart.

Plot area
The area that holds the data points on a chart.

➤ **What You Will Learn**

Changing Chart Elements
Setting Data Label Options
Setting Data Table Options
Formatting a Data Series

Software Skills   A chart presents complex numerical data in a graphical format. Because a chart tells its story visually, you must make the most of the way your chart looks. There are many ways in which you can enhance a chart; for example, you can add color or pattern to the chart background, and format the value and category axes so that the numbers are easier to understand.

Application Skills   You're keeping the books for Special Events, the premiere party planners in your local area, and you've been asked to produce a couple of different sales charts based on last month's sales figures. The owner will choose one to use in a presentation for her bank so the stakes are high.

What You Can Do

Changing Chart Elements

■ A chart may include some or all of the parts shown in Figure 12-1.

■ You can format various chart elements such as the data labels, data table, plot area, legend, chart title, axis titles and the data series.

■ As you move your mouse pointer over a chart, the name of the chart element appears in the ScreenTip.

■ You can select specific chart elements for formatting from the Current Selection group of the Chart Tools Layout tab.

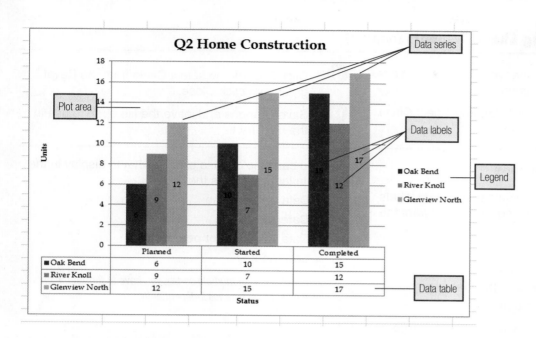

Figure 12-1

- A chart title describes the purpose of the chart. You can change the font, color, and size of the chart title as with any other text.

- The **plot area** of a chart is the element that holds the data points on a chart. You can change the plot area of the chart by modifying the border color or style, or applying a shadow or pattern to the background. You could also apply 3-D formatting effects to the plot area if a chart has a background.

Try It! Changing Chart Elements

1. Start Excel, if necessary, and open **ETry12** from the data files for this lesson.

2. Save the file as **ETry12_studentfirstname_ studentlastname** in the location where your teacher instructs you to store the files for this lesson.

3. Click the Country Antiques Q3 Sales Chart tab, if necessary.

4. Click Chart Tools Layout > Chart Title in the Labels group. Choose Above Chart.

5. Type **Third Quarter Sales** and press ENTER.

6. Move the mouse pointer over the chart and click when you see the ScreenTip for Plot Area.

7. With the plot area selected, click Chart Tools Layout > Plot Area in the Background group. Select More Plot Area Options.

8. Click Fill, then select Gradient fill.

The Format Plot Area dialog box

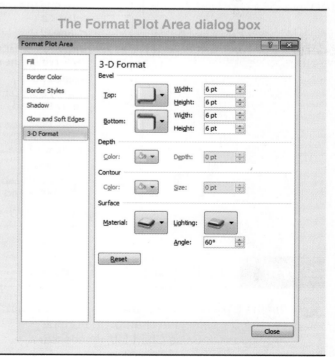

(continued)

Try It!　　**Changing Chart Elements** *(continued)*

9　Click 3-D Format, then type **60** in the Angle text box in the Surface group.

10　In the Bevel group, click Top and select Circle from the Bevel group.

11　Click Bottom and select Circle from the Bevel group and click Close.

12　Save changes and leave the file open to use in the next Try It.

Setting Data Label Options

■ As shown in Figure 12-2, you can add data labels to a chart by simply choosing where you want the labels placed.

- Centered on the data point(s)
- Inside the end of the data point(s)
- Inside the base of the data point(s)
- Outside the end of the data point(s)

✓ *Data labels are only valuable if they are legible. Data labels can overlap if you aren't careful.*

■ You can also choose exactly what to display in the data label, such as the:

- Data series name
- **Category** name
- Data value and/or percentage
- **Legend key**

✓ *For charts with multiple series, you have to format the data labels for each series independently.*

Figure 12-2

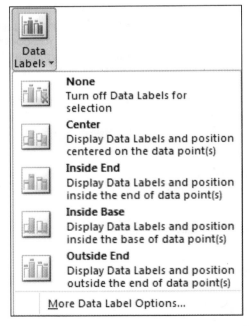

Try It!　　**Setting Data Label Options**

1　In the **ETry12_studentfirstname_studentlast name** file, select the chart on the Country Antiques Q3 Sales Chart tab, if necessary.

2　Click Chart Tools Layout > Data Labels . Select Inside Base.

(continued)

Try It!   **Setting Data Label Options** *(continued)*

3 Observe the data labels. By default, Excel uses the data value as the data label. In this instance, the dollar values overlap, making them illegible.

4 Click Chart Tools Layout > Data Labels 📊 > None to clear the labels.

5 Click Chart Tools Layout > Data Labels 📊 > Center. All of the data labels are centered within the data points.

6 Click one of the August data labels. All of the August data labels are selected.

7 Click Chart Tools Layout > Data Labels 📊 > More Data Label Options. The Format Data Labels dialog box opens.

8 Click Inside End in the Label Position group and click Close.

9 Click one of the September data labels. All of the September data labels are selected.

10 Click Chart Tools Layout > Data Labels 📊 > More Data Label Options. Click Series Name in the Label Contains group.

11 Click Include legend key in label and click Close.

12 Observe the September data labels. The yellow-green legend key and the name September appear beside the data value.

13 Click Chart Tools Layout > Data Labels 📊 > More Data Label Options. Deselect Series Name and deselect Include legend key in label, click Inside End, and click Close.

14 Save changes and leave the file open to use in the next Try It.

Data Label Options

Setting Data Table Options

- You can add a data table to the bottom of a chart.
- The **data table** looks like a small worksheet, and it lists the data used to create the chart.
- Adding a data table to a chart allows a viewer to easily understand the values plotted on the chart.
- Data tables have only a few basic options beyond normal formatting such as the fill and border colors.
  - You can add a border around the cells in the data table—horizontally, vertically, or around the table's outline.
  - You can also choose whether or not to display the legend keys as part of the table.

Try It!   **Setting Data Table Options**

1 In the **ETry12_studentfirstname_studentlastname** file, select the chart on the Country Antiques Q3 Sales Chart tab, if necessary.

2 Click Chart Tools Layout > Data Table 📊 and click More Data Table Options.

3 Accept the default options and click Close. A data table appears below the chart with the legend key displayed next to the data series name.

(continued)

Try It!   Setting Data Table Options *(continued)*

4 Click Chart Tools Layout > Data Table 📊 and click More Data Table Options.

5 Click Fill, and then click Solid fill and click Color in the Fill Color group. Select Light Green from the Standard Colors group and click Close.

  ✓ *Data table formatting options, such as fill and shadow, are applied to the data inside the cells of the table, not to the table itself.*

6 Click Chart Tools Layout > Data Table 📊 and click More Data Table Options.

7 Click Fill, click No fill, and click Close.

8 Save changes and leave the file open to use in the next Try It.

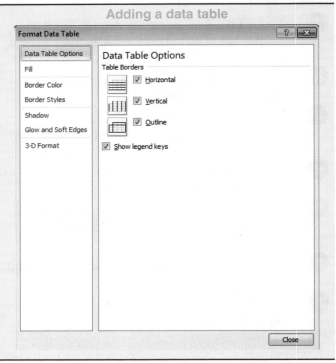

Adding a data table

Formatting a Data Series

- When you create a chart, Excel automatically assigns a color to each **data series** in the chart.
- That color appears as the bars of a column chart, the slices of a pie chart, and the legend key.
  - You may want to change the color of a particular data series to coordinate with your other business documents, or simply because you don't like the default color.
  - Even if you're printing the chart in black and white, you may want to change the color of a data

series to better distinguish it from other colors in the chart that translate to a similar gray tone.

- In certain chart types such as bar and column charts, you can adjust the amount of space between each series in a group or between each category by changing the Series Options.
- In line charts, you can change the type and look of the markers used to plot each data point.
- In pie charts, you can change the position of the first slice within the pie, and the amount of separation between the remaining slices.

Try It!   Formatting a Data Series

1 In the **ETry12_studentfirstname_studentlast name** file, select the chart on the Country Antiques Q3 Sales Chart tab, if necessary.

2 Click Chart Tools Format > Chart Elements [Chart Area ▾] in the Current Selection group.

3 Select Series "July" from the Chart Elements drop-down list.

4 Click Format Selection ⚙ Format Selection in the Current Selection group. The Format Data Series dialog box appears.

5 Type -30% in the Separated text box of the Series Overlap group.

6 Type 30% in the Gap Width text box. Click Close.

7 Close **ETry12_studentfirstname_studentlast name**, saving all changes, and exit Excel.

Project 25—Create It

Formatting a Sales Column Chart

DIRECTIONS

1. Start Excel, if necessary, and open **EProj25** from the data files for this lesson.

2. Save the file as **EProj25_studentfirstname_ studentlastname** in the location where your teacher instructs you to store the files for this lesson.

3. Select the chart on the **Chart-July Party Sales** tab, if necessary.

4. Click **Chart Tools Layout > Data Table** 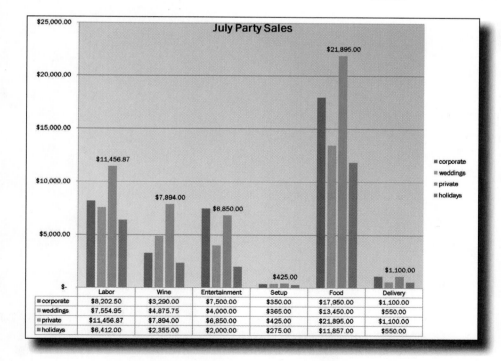 **> Show Data Table with Legend Keys**.

5. Click **Chart Tools Layout > Chart Title**. Choose **Centered Overlay Title**.

6. Type **July Party Sales** and press ENTER.

7. Click **Chart Tools Format** and select **Plot Area** from the Chart Elements drop-down menu.

8. Click **Chart Tools Format > Shape Fill > Gradient**, then select **Linear Diagonal – Top Right to Bottom Left**.

9. Click one of the columns in the private data series. The private data series is selected.

10. Click **Chart Tools Layout > Data Labels > Outside End**.

11. With the series still selected, click **Format Selection** in the Current Selection group to select the data series.

12. Type **-25%** in the Separated text box of the Series Overlap group.

13. Type **200%** in the Gap Width text box.

14. **With your teacher's permission**, print the chart. Your chart should look like Figure 12-3.

15. Close the workbook, saving all changes, and exit Excel.

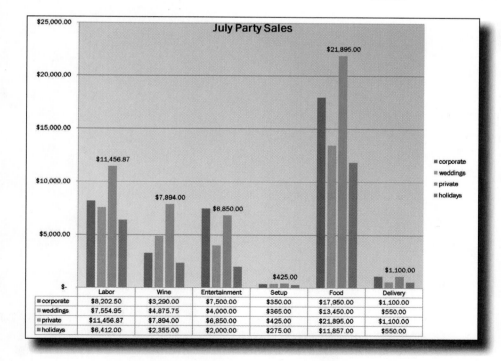

July Party Sales

	Labor	Wine	Entertainment	Setup	Food	Delivery
corporate	$8,202.50	$3,290.00	$7,500.00	$350.00	$17,950.00	$1,100.00
weddings	$7,554.95	$4,875.75	$4,000.00	$365.00	$13,450.00	$550.00
private	$11,456.87	$7,894.00	$6,850.00	$425.00	$21,895.00	$1,100.00
holidays	$6,412.00	$2,355.00	$2,000.00	$275.00	$11,857.00	$550.00

Figure 12-3

Project 26—Apply It

Formatting a Sales Chart

DIRECTIONS

1. Start Excel, if necessary, and open **EProj26** from the data files for this lesson.

2. Save the file as **EProj26_studentfirstname_ studentlastname** in the location where your teacher instructs you to store the files for this lesson.

3. Select the chart on the July Party Sales tab, if necessary.

4. Add a centered overlay chart title, **July Party Sales**, above the chart.

5. Format the chart elements as follows:
   a. Add a Data Table and show the legend keys in the table.
   b. Apply a Solid fill to the Plot Area.
   c. Change the Fill Color to **Turquoise, Accent 3, Lighter 80%**.

6. Add Data Labels outside the end of your data points.

7. Format the Data Series as follows:
   a. Set the Series Overlap to **0%**.
   b. Set the Gap Width to **200%**.

8. **With your teacher's permission**, print the chart. Submit the printout or file for grading as required.

9. Close the workbook, saving all changes, and exit Excel.

Lesson 13

Formatting the Value Axis

➤ What You Will Learn

Creating a Stock Chart
Modifying the Value Axis
Formatting Data Markers
Formatting a Legend
Adding a Secondary Value Axis to a Chart

Software Skills   Because Excel is used every day by thousands of investors—many of whom invest as a profession—it has to be capable of producing charts specifically tailored to the needs and expectations of those users. A stock chart is no ordinary graphical rendering, since it often has to show several related values (such as opening and closing values) on a single chart.

Application Skills   You work in the Communications department of Midwest Pharmaceutical and the annual shareholders' meeting is scheduled for next week. Your job is to put together a stock chart for the CFO's presentation.

WORDS TO KNOW

Data marker
The symbol that appears on a stock chart to mark a specific data point.

Legend
An optional part of the chart, the legend displays a description of each data series included in the chart.

Value axis
The vertical scale of a chart on which the values from each category are plotted, sometimes called the Y axis.

What You Can Do

Creating a Stock Chart

- Charting stock data requires a special type of chart designed to handle standard stock information.
- Excel offers four different kinds of stock charts:
  - High-Low-Close
  - Open-High-Low-Close
  - Volume-High-Low-Close
  - Volume-Open-High-Low-Close

- Each chart handles a different set of data taken from this standard set of stock information:
  - Volume: the number of shares of a particular stock traded during the market day.
  - Open: the value of the stock at the time when the market opened for the day.
  - High: the highest value at which the stock was traded that day.
  - Low: the lowest value at which the stock was traded that day.
  - Close: the value of the stock when the market closed for the day.

- To create a stock chart, you must enter the data in columns or rows in the order specified by the type of stock chart you want.

  ✓ *For example, if you select the Open-High-Low-Close chart, you must enter the data in four columns (or rows) in that order: open, high, low, close.*

  - As row (or column) labels, you can use the stock symbol or name, if you are going to track more than one type of stock, or the date, if you're tracking one stock's trading pattern over several days.

- A stock chart is also ideal for charting certain kinds of scientific data, such as temperature changes throughout the day.

Try It!   Creating a Stock Chart

1 Start Excel, if necessary, and open **ETry13** from the data files for this lesson.

2 Save the file as **ETry13_studentfirstname_ studentlastname** in the location where your teacher instructs you to store the files for this lesson.

3 Select the range A5:F258.

4 Create a Volume-Open-High-Low-Close stock chart:

a. Click the Insert tab and click the Other Charts button ⊙ Other Charts ▾.

b. Choose the Volume-Open-High-Low-Close from the Stock group in the gallery.

c. Click Chart Tools Design > Move Chart 📊 from the Location group to open the Move Chart dialog box.

d. Click New sheet and type **Stock Chart** in the New sheet text box.

e. Click OK to move the chart to its own worksheet page.

5 Add a title **Midwest Pharmaceutical Stock Tracking** above the chart.

6 Save changes and leave the file open to use in the next Try It.

The Volume-Open-High-Low-Close stock chart

Modifying the Value Axis

- The vertical, or **value axis**, provides a scale for the values of the data for most chart types.

  ✓ *For bar charts, the horizontal and vertical axes are reversed.*

- You can change the font, size, color, attributes, alignment, and placement of text or numbers along the axis.

- Click Chart Tools Layout > Axis Titles 📊 to add a title to the axis.

- Use the Chart Tools Layout > Axes 📊 submenus to control whether either axis should be displayed.

  - In addition, you can adjust the scale used along either axis so that the numbers are easy to read.

Try It!   Modifying the Value Axis

1 In the **ETry13_studentfirstname_studentlast name** file, select the chart on the Stock Chart tab, if necessary.

2 Click Chart Tools Layout > Axis Titles 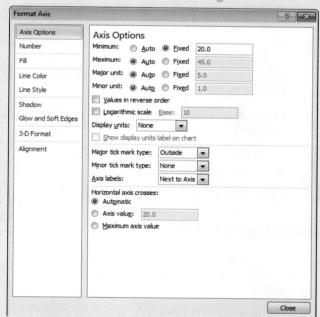 > Primary Vertical Axis Title > Rotated Title.

3 Type **Volume (in millions)** and press ENTER.

4 Click Chart Tools Layout > Axis Titles > Secondary Vertical Axis Title > Rotated Title.

5 Type **Value** and press ENTER.

6 Select the primary vertical axis (the vertical axis on the left) and click Chart Tools Layout > Axes > Primary Vertical Axis.

7 Click Show Axis in Millions.

8 Click Chart Tools Layout > Axes > Primary Vertical Axis > More Primary Vertical Axis Options.

9 Click Axis Options in the Format Axis dialog box. Click Fixed in the Minimum group and type **10,000,000** in the text box. Deselect the Show display units label on chart check box.

10 Click Number in the left pane of the Format Axis dialog box. Click Number in the Category list, type **0** in the Decimal places text box, and click Close.

✓ *Because the stock exchange is not operating every day of the year, there are points along the horizontal axis with no data because Excel assumes that all dates should be included in the axis, not just the dates in your data table. You will need to modify the horizontal axis.*

11 Click Chart Tools Layout > Axes > Primary Horizontal Axis > More Primary Horizontal Axis Options.

12 Click Axis Options on the Format Axis dialog box. Click Text axis under Axis Type and click Close.

13 Click Chart Tools Layout > Axes > Secondary Vertical Axis > More Secondary Vertical Axis Options.

14 Click Number in the left pane of the Format Axis dialog box. Click Currency in the Category list to convert the stock values.

15 Click Axis Options in the left pane. Click Fixed in the Minimum group and type **20.0** in the text box and click Close.

16 Save changes and leave the file open to use in the next Try It.

The Format Axis dialog box

Formatting Data Markers

- When you create a stock chart, Excel uses a series of standard **data markers** for the open, close, high-low, volume, close up, and close down values.

- Some of these markers may be too small, too dark, or too light to appear clearly on a printout.

- To improve the appearance of your chart, you may want to adjust the data markers used by Excel.

- To do that, select a series to change, and click Marker Options in the Format Data Series dialog box.

- You can change the fill color, size, shape, outline color, and outline style of each data marker used in a stock chart.

  ✓ *You can also change the data markers used in line, xy (scatter), and radar charts.*

- You can also choose to hide the data markers by selecting None in the Marker Options area of the Format Data Series dialog box.

Try It!   Formatting Data Markers

1 In the **ETry13_studentfirstname_studentlast name** file, select the chart on the Stock Chart tab, if necessary.

2 Click the Chart Tools Layout tab, select the chart element Series "High" in the Current Selection group, and click Format Selection to open the Format Data Series dialog box.

3 Click Marker Options and click Built-in from the Marker Type group.

4 From the Type drop-down list, choose the triangle and enter **4** in the Size text box.

5 Click Marker Fill and then click Solid fill.

6 Click the Color button in the Fill Color group and select Light Green from the Standard Colors palette and click Close.

   ✓ *The green triangle data marker has been added to the legend.*

7 Click the Chart Tools Layout tab, select the chart element Series "Low" in the Current Selection group, and click Format Selection to open the Format Data Series dialog box.

8 Click Marker Options and click Built-in from the Marker Type group.

9 From the Type drop-down list, choose the circle and enter **3** in the Size spin box.

10 Click Marker Fill and click Solid fill.

11 Click the Color button in the Fill Color group and select Red from the Standard Colors palette and click Close.

   ✓ *The red circle data marker has been added to the legend.*

12 Save changes to the file and leave it open to use in the next Try It.

Formatting data markers

Formatting a Legend

- Though a **legend** is automatically displayed when you create a chart, you can choose where you want to place it.

- Use the Chart Tools Format > Legend to place the legend at the top, left, bottom, or right of the chart. The legend can also be overlaid at the left or right edge of the chart as shown in Figure 13-1.

- In addition, you can change the fill color, size, border color, and outline style.

Figure 13-1

Try It! **Formatting a Legend**

1 In the **ETry13_studentfirstname_ studentlastname** file, select the chart on the Stock Chart tab, if necessary.

2 Select the legend and click Chart Tools Layout > Legend ≡ > None to delete the legend.

3 Click Chart Tools Layout > Legend ≡ > Show Legend at Top.

4 Select the legend and click the Chart Tools Layout tab and click Format Selection in the Current Selection group to open the Format Legend dialog box.

5 Deselect the Show the legend without overlapping the chart option.

6 Click Fill and Solid fill.

7 Click the Color button in the Fill Color group and select Aqua, Accent 1, Lighter 80% from the Theme Colors palette.

8 Click Border Color and then click Solid line.

9 Click the Color button and select Black, Text 1 from the Theme Colors palette and click Close.

10 Save changes and leave the file open to use in the next Try It.

Adding a Secondary Value Axis to a Chart

- To track two related but different values, use two value axes in the chart.

- The value axes appear on opposite sides of the chart.

- For example, Excel uses two value axes for a stock chart that includes both the volume of stock trading and the value of the stock.

- One axis plots the stock's trading volume.
- The other axis plots the stock's value at open, close, high, and low points in the day.

- Secondary value axes are most common on stock charts and will appear automatically when Excel determines that two value axes are needed, but you can manually add a secondary axis to other types of charts as well.

Try It! **Adding a Secondary Value Axis to a Chart**

1 In the **ETry13_studentfirstname_student lastname** file, select the YTD Table tab, if necessary.

2 Select the range E5:E258 and click Home > Copy ᯳.

3 Switch to the YTD Average Table chart sheet and press CTRL + V.

4 Right-click the yellow line and select Format Data Series.

5 Click Series Options and then select Secondary Axis. Click Close.

6 On the Chart Tools Format tab, select Secondary Vertical (Value) Axis in the Chart Elements box.

7 Click Chart Tools Format > Format Selection ᯳.

8 Click Axis Options and then click Fixed in the Maximum group and type **100.00** in the text box. Click Close.

9 Save the changes to **ETry13_student firstname_studentlastname** and close Excel.

A chart with a Secondary Axis

Project 27—Create It

Formatting a Stock Chart

DIRECTIONS

1. Start Excel, if necessary, and open **EProj27** from the data files for this lesson.
2. Save the file as **EProj27_studentfirstname_ studentlastname** in the location where your teacher instructs you to store the files for this lesson.
3. Select the range **A3:E66**.
4. Create a **Volume-High-Low-Close** stock chart on its own sheet tab:
   a. Click **Insert > Other Charts** button ⃝ and choose the **Volume-High-Low-Close**.
   b. Click **Chart Tools Design > Move Chart** 📊 to open the Move Chart dialog box.
   c. Click **New sheet** and type **Q1 Stock Chart** in the New sheet text box.
   d. Click **OK** to move the chart to its own worksheet page.
5. Click **Chart Tools Layout > Chart Title** 📊 > **Above Chart** and type **Midwest Pharmaceutical First Quarter Stock** and press [ENTER].
6. Click **Chart Tools Layout > Axis Titles** 📊 > **Primary Vertical Axis Title > Rotated Title**.
7. Type **Volume (in millions)** and press [ENTER].
8. Click **Chart Tools Layout > Axis Titles** 📊 > **Secondary Vertical Axis Title > Rotated Title**.
9. Type **Stock Price (USD)** and press [ENTER].

10. Select the primary vertical axis (the vertical axis on the left) and click **Chart Tools Layout > Axes** 📊 > **Primary Vertical Axis > Show Axis in Millions**.
11. Click **Chart Tools Layout > Axes** 📊 > **Primary Vertical Axis > More Primary Vertical Axis Options**.
12. Click **Axis Options**. Click **Fixed** in the Minimum group and type **12,500,000** in the text box. Deselect the Show display units label on chart check box. Click **Close**.
13. Click **Chart Tools Layout > Axes** 📊 > **Primary Horizontal Axis > More Primary Horizontal Axis Options**.
14. Click **Axis Options**. Click **Text axis** in the Axis Type group and click **Close**.
15. Click **Chart Tools Layout > Axes** 📊 > **Secondary Vertical Axis > More Secondary Vertical Axis Options**.
16. Click **Number** and then click **Currency** in the Category list to convert the stock values.
17. Click **Axis Options** in the Format Axis dialog box. Click **Fixed** in the Minimum group, type **25.0** in the text box, and click **Close**.
18. **With your teacher's permission**, print the chart. The chart should look like Figure 13-2.
19. Close the workbook, saving all changes, and exit Excel.

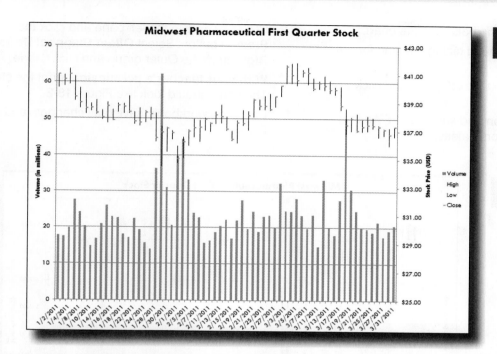

Figure 13-2

Project 28—Apply It

Formatting a Stock Chart

DIRECTIONS

1. Start Excel, if necessary, open **EProj28** from the data files for this lesson, and save the file as **EProj28_studentfirstname_studentlastname** in the location where your teacher instructs you to store the files for this lesson.

2. Click the Q1 Stock Chart tab, if necessary. Add formatting to the "High" data series.

   a. Click the **Chart Tools Layout** tab, select the chart element **Series "High"** in the Current Selection group. Click **Format Selection** to open the Format Data Series dialog box.

   b. Click **Marker Options** and click **Built-in** from the Marker Type group.

   c. From the Type drop-down list, choose the triangle and enter **4** in the Size spin box.

   d. Click **Marker Fill** and click **Solid fill**.

   e. Click the **Color** button in the Fill Color group, select **Light Green** from the Standard Colors palette, and click **Close**.

3. Add formatting to the "Low" data series.

   a. Click the **Chart Tools Layout** tab, and select the chart element **Series "Low"** in the Current Selection group. Click **Format Selection** to open the Format Data Series dialog box.

   b. Click **Marker Options** and click **Built-in** from the Marker Type group.

   c. From the Type drop-down list, choose the circle and enter **3** in the Size spin box.

   d. Click **Marker Fill** and click **Solid fill**.

   e. Click the **Color** button in the Fill Color group, select **Red** from the Standard Colors palette, and click **Close**.

4. Add formatting to the "Volume" data series.

   a. Click the **Chart Tools Layout** tab, select the chart element **Series "Volume"** in the Current Selection group, and click **Format Selection** to open the Format Data Series dialog box.

   b. Click **Fill** and click **Solid fill**.

   c. Click the **Color** button in the Fill Color group and select **Gold, Accent 5** from the Theme Colors palette; click **Close**.

5. Show the legend at the bottom of the chart.

6. Open the Format Legend dialog box and format the legend.

7. Click **Border Color** in the left pane and click **Solid line**.

8. Click the **Color** button and select **Gold, Accent 5** from the Theme Colors palette.

9. Click **Shadow** in the left pane and click the **Presets** button. Select **Offset Diagonal Bottom Right** from the Outer group and click **Close**.

10. **With your teacher's permission**, print the chart. The chart should look like Figure 13-3.

11. Close the workbook, saving all changes, and exit Excel.

Figure 13-3

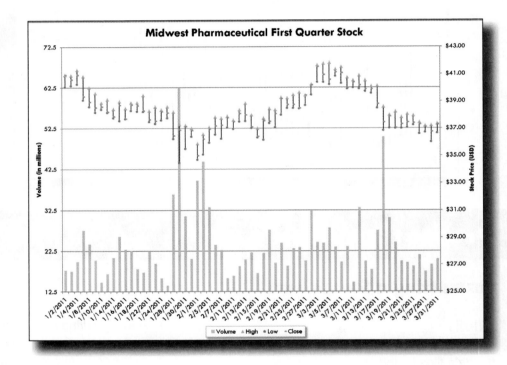

Lesson 14

Creating Stacked Area Charts

> ➤ **What You Will Learn**

Creating a Stacked Area Chart
Formatting the Chart Floor and Chart Walls
Displaying Chart Gridlines
Applying a Chart Layout and Chart Styles

Software Skills   Whether you're creating a chart for a big presentation or a printed report, you want that chart to look as good as possible. Using a 3-D chart adds a high-tech look to an otherwise ordinary presentation of the facts. 3-D charts contain two new chart elements: the chart wall and chart floor.

As with other chart elements, basic formatting can enhance the look of your chart. You also may want to display or hide gridlines to make the values on the axes easier to read.

Application Skills   You've just been hired by Premiere Formatting. The company hires recent graduates with an expertise in Excel to help local businesses with their spreadsheet requirements. Your first assignment is to produce stacked area charts for two companies. Midwest Pharmaceutical is looking to see a breakdown of their first quarter expenses.

What You Can Do

Creating a Stacked Area Chart

- In a **stacked area chart**, the values in each data series are stacked on top of each other, creating a larger area.

WORDS TO KNOW

Chart floor
The horizontal floor below the data on a 3-D chart.

Chart wall
The vertical wall behind the data on a 3-D chart.

Gridlines
In the worksheet, gridlines are the light gray outline that surrounds each cell. In charts, gridlines are the lines that appear on a chart, extending from the value or category axes.

Stacked area chart
A special type of area chart in which the values for each data series are stacked on one another, creating one large area.

- Whereas a line chart would show the relative positions of multiple series compared to one another, a stacked area chart shows their cumulative position.
  - Each entry is stacked on top of the previous one, forming a peak that represents the sum of all series' entries together.
- Use a stacked area chart to emphasize the difference in values between two data series, while also illustrating the total of the two.

✓ A stacked area chart can be used to track the relative contribution of each item in the data series to the cumulative total.

- In a 100% stacked area chart, for each category, all of the series combine to consume the entire height of the chart.
- Both stacked area and 100% stacked area charts come in 2-D and 3-D versions.

Try It!   Creating a Stacked Area Chart

1 Start Excel, if necessary, and open **ETry14** from the data files for this lesson.

2 Save the file as **ETry14_studentfirstname_ studentlastname** in the location where your teacher instructs you to store the files for this lesson.

3 Select the Patient care breakdown sheet, if necessary.

4 Select the range A9:G18.

5 Click Insert > Area 🔺 in the Charts group and click Stacked Area in 3-D from the gallery.

6 Click Chart Tools Design > Move Chart 📊 from the Location group and move the chart to a New sheet titled **Patient Care Chart**.

7 Save changes and leave the file open to use in the next Try It.

Formatting the Chart Floor and Chart Walls

- Three-dimensional charts include a **chart wall**, which forms the side and back of the chart, and the **chart floor**, which forms the bottom of the chart.

  ✓ Because 3-D pie charts are not plotted on vertical and horizontal axes, they do not include chart walls and a floor.

- You can format or remove the chart wall and the chart floor from the options in the Background group of the Chart Tools Layout tab.
- You can apply standard formatting options, such as fill color, borders, shadows, and glows to the chart walls and floors.

Try It!   Formatting the Chart Floor and Chart Walls

1 In the **ETry14_studentfirstname_studentlast name** file, select the chart on the Patient Care Chart tab, if necessary.

2 Click Chart Tools Layout > Chart Wall 📊 and choose More Walls Options to open the Format Walls dialog box.

3 Click Fill, click Gradient fill, and click Close.

4 Select the chart area and click Chart Tools Layout > Chart Floor 📊 and choose More Floor Options to open the Format Floor dialog box.

5 Click Fill, and then click Solid fill. Click the Color button in the Fill Color group and select Blue, Accent 1, Lighter 40% from the Theme Colors palette and click Close.

6 Save changes and leave the file open to use in the next Try It.

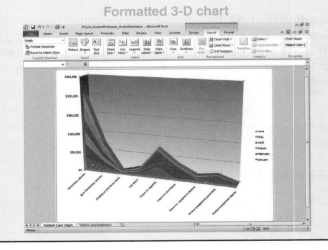

Formatted 3-D chart

Displaying Chart Gridlines

- On Excel charts, **gridlines** can help guide the eye along a given axis.

- You can increase the number of major gridlines by changing the point at which the gridlines recur.
- You can also display minor gridlines, which fall between major gridlines.

Try It!   **Displaying Chart Gridlines**

1 In the **ETry14_studentfirstname_studentlastname** file, select the chart on the Patient Care Chart tab, if necessary.

2 Click Chart Tools Layout > Gridlines. Point to Primary Vertical Gridlines and click Major Gridlines.

3 Click Chart Tools Layout > Gridlines. Point to Primary Horizontal Gridlines and click Major Gridlines.

4 Save changes and leave the file open to use in the next Try It.

Applying a Chart Layout and Chart Styles

- When you create a chart, Excel adds a legend and assigns default colors to each series in the chart.

- As you've already seen, you can manually adjust the colors and placements of many items on a chart.

- Excel includes two built-in formatting features: Chart Styles and Chart Layout. These features work together to help you quickly format charts.

- Use Chart Tools Design > Chart Styles to quickly apply one of 48 different color schemes, as shown in Figure 14-1.

- These styles include several grayscale, monotone, and multi-colored options, and even 3-D formatting.

- Use Chart Tools Design > Chart Layouts to format the placement of chart elements such as the legend, chart title, and the data labels.

  ✓ *The number of chart layout options available depends on the type of chart you are formatting.*

- Once these formatting features have been applied, you may still manually adjust any chart element as desired.

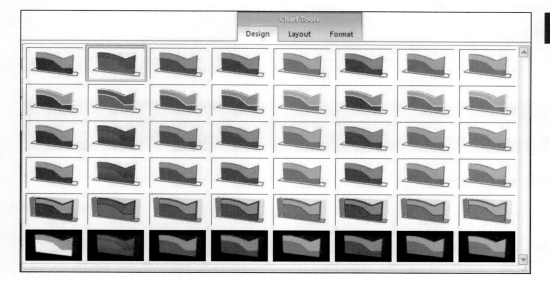

Figure 14-1

Try It!   Applying a Chart Layout and Chart Styles

1 In the **ETry14_studentfirstname_studentlast name** file, select the chart on the Patient Care Chart tab, if necessary.

2 Click Chart Tools Design > Layout 2 ⬛ from the Chart Layouts group to position the chart elements.

3 Click the Chart Tools Design tab and select Style 42 from the Chart Styles gallery.

4 Select the chart title, type **Wood Hills Patient Care Expenses** and press ENTER.

5 On the Home tab, click the Increase Font Size button A⁺ twice to increase the font size of the chart title to 24 points.

6 On the Home tab, click Font Color A⁻ and select Orange, Accent 6 from the Theme Colors palette.

7 Click Chart Tools Design > Switch Row/Column ⬛.

8 Click Chart Tools Layout > Axes ⬛ > Primary Horizontal Axis and then select Show Right to Left Axis.

9 Select the chart area and click Chart Tools Layout > Chart Wall ⬛ and choose More Walls Options to open the Format Walls dialog box.

10 Click Fill, click Gradient fill, and click Close.

11 Select the chart area and click Chart Tools Layout > Chart Floor ⬛ and choose More Floor Options to open the Format Floor dialog box.

12 Click Fill, and click Solid fill. Click the Color button in the Fill Color group and select Blue, Accent 1, Lighter 40% from the Theme Colors palette and click Close.

13 Close **ETry14_studentfirstname_studentlast name**, saving all changes, and exit Excel.

Final stacked chart

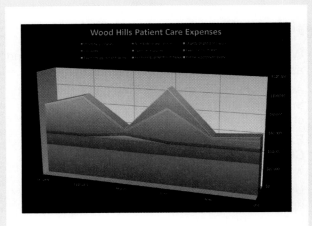

Project 29—Create It

Formatting a Budget Chart

DIRECTIONS

1. Start Excel, if necessary, and open **EProj29** from the data files for this lesson.

2. Save the file as **EProj29_studentfirstname_ studentlastname** in the location where your teacher instructs you to store the files for this lesson.

3. Select the range **A3:E10**.

4. Click **Insert > Area** ⬛ **> Stacked Area in 3-D** from the gallery.

5. Click **Chart Tools Design > Move Chart** ⬛.

6. Select **New sheet** and type **Budget Chart** in the New sheet text box and click **OK**.

7. Click **Chart Tools Design > Layout 5** to position the chart elements.

8. Select the chart title, type **First Quarter Budget** and press [ENTER].
9. Click **Home** > **Font Color** ![A].
10. Select **Light Blue, Background 2, Darker 75%** from the Theme Colors palette.

11. Click **Home** > **Increase Font Size A˙** to increase the font size of the chart title to **20 points**.
12. **With your teacher's permission**, print the chart. The chart should look like Figure 14-2.
13. Close the workbook, saving all changes, and exit Excel.

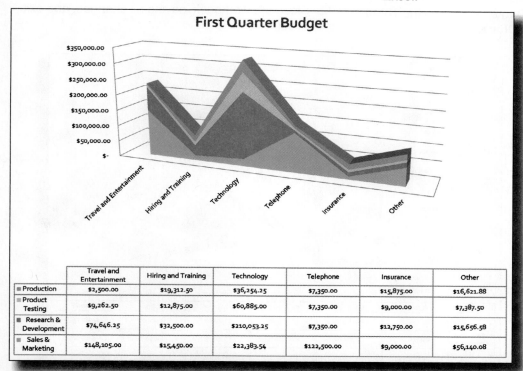

Figure 14-2

	Travel and Entertainment	Hiring and Training	Technology	Telephone	Insurance	Other
■ Production	$2,500.00	$19,312.50	$36,254.25	$7,350.00	$15,875.00	$16,621.88
■ Product Testing	$9,262.50	$12,875.00	$60,885.00	$7,350.00	$9,000.00	$7,387.50
■ Research & Development	$74,646.25	$32,500.00	$210,053.25	$7,350.00	$12,750.00	$15,656.58
■ Sales & Marketing	$148,105.00	$15,450.00	$22,383.54	$122,500.00	$9,000.00	$56,140.08

Project 30—Apply It

Formatting a Budget Chart

DIRECTIONS

1. Start Excel, if necessary, and open **EProj30** from the data files for this lesson.
2. Save the file as **EProj30_studentfirstname_ studentlastname** in the location where your teacher instructs you to store the files for this lesson.
3. On the Chart Tools Design tab, click **More** to open the Chart Styles gallery. Select **Style 34**.
4. Format a chart wall for the budget chart.
   a. Select the chart area and click **Chart Tools Layout** > **Chart Wall** ![icon] > **More Walls Options** to open the Format Walls dialog box.

   b. Click **Fill**, click **Gradient fill** and click **Close**.
5. Format a chart floor for the budget chart.
   a. Select the chart area and click **Chart Tools Layout** > **Chart Floor** ![icon] > **More Floor Options** to open the Format Floor dialog box.
   b. Click **Fill**, and then click **Solid fill**. Click the **Color** button in the Fill Color group.
   c. Select **Light Blue, Background 2, Darker 25%** from the Theme Colors palette and click **Close**.
6. Click **Chart Tools Layout** > **Gridlines** ![icon] > **Primary Vertical Gridlines** > **Minor Gridlines**.

7. Click **Chart Tools Layout** > **Gridlines** > **Primary Horizontal Gridlines** > **Major Gridlines**.

8. Click **Chart Tools Layout** > **Data Table** > **More Data Table Options**.

9. Click **Border Color** and **Solid line**. Click the **Color** button in the Fill Color group and select **Light Blue, Background 2, Darker 25%** from the Theme Colors palette and click **Close**.

10. Format the horizontal axis.

   a. Select the horizontal, category, axis.
   b. Click **Home** > **Decrease Font Size A˅** to decrease the font size to **8 point**.

11. **With your teacher's permission**, print the chart. Your chart should look like Figure 14-3.

12. Close the workbook, saving all changes, and exit Excel.

Figure 14-3

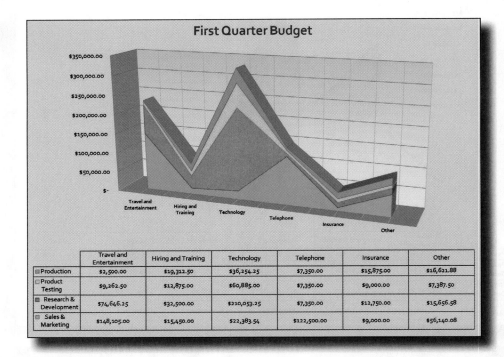

	Travel and Entertainment	Hiring and Training	Technology	Telephone	Insurance	Other
Production	$2,500.00	$19,312.50	$36,254.25	$7,350.00	$15,875.00	$16,621.88
Product Testing	$9,262.50	$12,875.00	$60,885.00	$7,350.00	$9,000.00	$7,387.50
Research & Development	$74,646.25	$32,500.00	$210,053.25	$7,350.00	$12,750.00	$15,656.58
Sales & Marketing	$148,105.00	$15,450.00	$22,383.54	$122,500.00	$9,000.00	$56,140.08

Lesson 15

Working with Sparklines

➤ What You Will Learn

Inserting a Line, Column, or Win/Loss Sparkline
Formatting a Sparkline
Inserting a Trendline

Software Skills   Sometimes the most valuable information found on a chart is the data you don't keep records of. Trendlines can help you determine what your data means: are your sales going up all year long or do they only go up in the summer? On a worksheet, a Sparkline can save you the effort of creating a chart at all since it is like adding a mini chart right in your worksheet.

Application Skills   As the manager of PhotoTown, you are concerned that sales have fallen off lately. You decide to track each individual's gross sales for a week and try to identify a trend. In addition, you think the employees should be selling more T-shirts than they are, so you decide to track their sales and talk to anyone you feel is underperforming.

What You Can Do

Inserting a Line, Column, or Win/Loss Sparkline

- **Sparklines** are like mini charts placed in the worksheet itself.
- Sparklines can show trends in data, or highlight maximum and minimum values.
- Excel will automatically update the Sparkline as your data changes.
- Charts are objects that sit on top of the worksheet and can be moved independent of the data. Sparklines appear as a cell background. You can add descriptive text on top of the Sparkline, if desired.
- Excel includes three distinct Sparkline types:
  - Line ⊠ : this Sparkline type tracks the data using a solid line.
  - Column ⊞ : this Sparkline type tracks the data using vertical bars.

WORDS TO KNOW

Sparkline
Tiny charts within a worksheet cell that represent trends in a series of values.

Trendline
A line that helps determine the trend, or moving average, of your existing data.

- Win/Loss : this Sparkline type tracks the positive (win) or negative (loss) change in the data.

  ✓ *A data value equal to zero is treated as a gap in the Win/Loss Sparkline.*

- Delete a Sparkline by selecting Clear Selected Sparklines from the Sparklines group in the shortcut menu.

Try It!   Inserting a Line, Column, or Win/Loss Sparkline

1 Start Excel, if necessary, and open **ETry15** from the data files for this lesson.

2 Save the file as **ETry15_studentfirstname_ studentlastname** in the location where your teacher instructs you to store the files for this lesson.

3 Select the cell H9 and click the Insert tab.

4 In the Sparklines group, click Line.

5 Select cells E9:G9 to fill the Data Range box in the Create Sparklines dialog box, and click OK.

6 Expand the width of column H.

  ✓ *The Sparkline will expand to fill the column width.*

7 Drag the AutoFill Handle ⅂ of the Sparkline cell down to H14 to add a Sparkline to the remaining cells.

8 Save changes and leave the file open to use in the next Try It.

Formatting a Sparkline

- When Sparkline are inserted, the Sparkline Tools Design tab is automatically displayed on the Ribbon.

  - Use the Sparkline Color button to format the color of the Sparkline's line.

- Use the Marker Color button to format the color of the data markers on a Sparkline.

- Use the options in the Style gallery to choose one of the theme's formats.

- You can also determine which data points, such as the high point, low, first, last, or negative values, to highlight on a Sparkline.

Try It!   Formatting a Sparkline

1 In the **ETry15_studentfirstname_studentlast name** file, select the cells H9:H14 and click the Sparkline Tools Design tab.

2 Click High Point in the Show group to add a data marker at the highest point of each Sparkline.

3 Click the Sparkline Color button and select Light Blue from the Standard colors palette.

4 Click the More button on the Style gallery and select Sparkline Style Accent 2, Lighter 40% from the gallery.

5 Save changes and leave the file open to use in the next Try It.

Sparklines in place on the worksheet

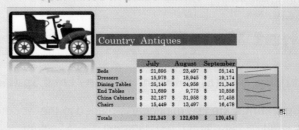

		July	August	September	
Beds	$	21,895	$ 23,497	$ 25,141	
Dressers	$	15,978	$ 18,945	$ 19,174	
Dining Tables	$	25,145	$ 24,958	$ 21,345	
End Tables	$	11,689	$ 9,775	$ 10,858	
China Cabinets	$	32,187	$ 31,958	$ 27,458	
Chairs	$	15,449	$ 13,497	$ 16,478	
Totals	$	122,343	$ 122,630	$ 120,454	

Inserting a Trendline

- **Trendlines** can be inserted in any unstacked, 2-D, non-pie chart.

- Trendlines can be used to show trends in your recorded data, or to suggest a forecast of future data.

- Excel provides 6 different Trendline options from the Format Trendline dialog box, as shown in Figure 15-1:

  - Linear trendline—a trendline that can be plotted in a straight line, indicating that the trend is increasing or decreasing at a steady rate.

  - Logarithmic trendline—a trendline that can be plotted in a gentle curve, indicating that the trend increased sharply and then levels out over time.

- Polynomial trendline—a trendline that curves following data that fluctuates in highs and lows over time.

- Power trendline—a trendline that curves upward, indicating that the trend is increasingly moving up.

- Exponential trendline—a trendline that is a gentle curve downward, indicating that the values rise or fall at constantly increasing rates.

- Moving average trendline—a trendline that smoothes out fluctuations over time; it determines the average of a specified number of values at each point on the line.

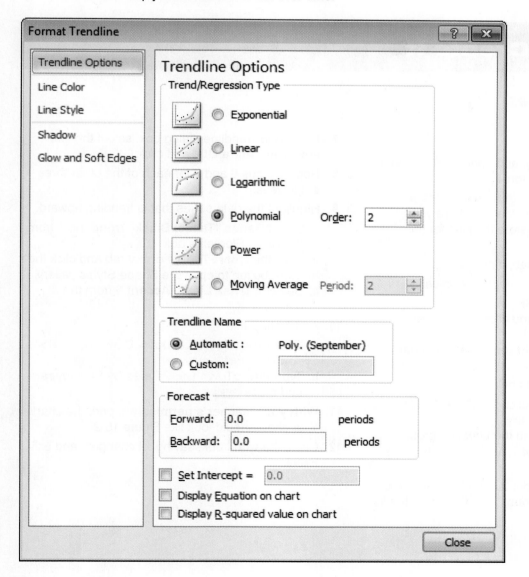

Figure 15-1

Try It!   **Inserting a Trendline**

1 In the **ETry15_studentfirstname_ studentlastname** file, select cells D8:G14.

2 Click Insert > Column 📊 in the Charts group and Click Clustered Column Chart. Drag the chart below the worksheet data.

3 Click Chart Tools Layout > Trendline 📈 and select a Linear Trendline from the list.

4 In the Add Trendline dialog box, select September from the Add a Trendline based on Series box and click OK.

5 Select the Trendline on the chart and click Chart Tools Layout > Trendline 📈 > More Trendline Options.

6 Click Polynomial in the Trend/Regression Type group and click Close to change the Trendline type.

7 Close **ETry15_studentfirstname_student lastname**, saving all changes, and exit Excel.

Project 31—Create It

Inserting Trendlines

DIRECTIONS

1. Start Excel, if necessary, and open **EProj31** from the data files for this lesson.

2. Save the file as **EProj31_studentfirstname_ studentlastname** in the location where your teacher instructs you to store the files for this lesson.

3. Select the **Daily Sales** tab, if necessary.

4. Create a scatter chart for employee sales.
   a. Select the cells **A4:G8**.
   b. Click the **Insert** tab and click the **Scatter** button ⊹ Scatter ▾ .
   c. Select the **Scatter with only Markers** chart from the list.

5. Move the new chart to its own tab.
   a. Select the chart and click the **Chart Tools Design** tab, if necessary.
   b. Click **Move Chart** from the Location group.
   c. In the New Sheet box, type **Employee Sales Chart** and click **OK**.

6. On the Chart Tools Layout tab, click **Trendline** 📈 and select **Linear Forecast Trendline** from the list.

7. In the Add Trendline dialog box, select the first employee, **Akira Ota**, and click **OK**.

8. Repeat steps 6 and 7 for each of the other three employees.

9. Highlight the data series that is trending upward.
   a. Select **Series "Taneel Black" Trendline 1** from the Chart Elements box.
   b. Click the **Chart Tools Format** tab and click the **More** button to open the Shape Styles gallery.
   c. Select **Intense Line – Accent 6** from the gallery.

10. Add a chart title.
    a. Click **Chart Tools Layout > Chart Title** 📊 > **Above Chart**.
    b. Type **PhotoTown Daily Sales by Employee** and press ENTER.

11. **With your teacher's permission**, print the chart. Your chart should look like Figure 15-2.

12. Close the workbook, saving all changes, and exit Excel.

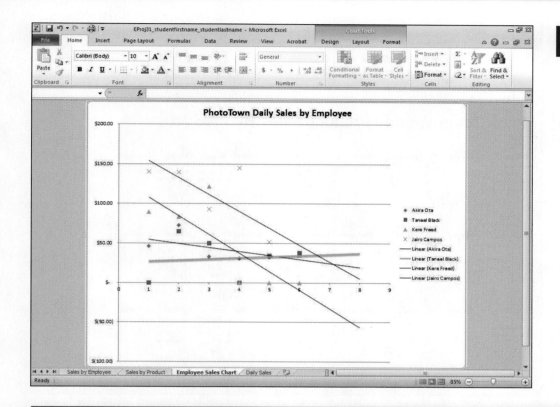

Figure 15-2

Project 32—Apply It

Adding Sparklines

DIRECTIONS

1. Start Excel, if necessary, and open **EProj32** from the data files for this lesson.

2. Save the file as **EProj32_studentfirstname_ studentlastname** in the location where your teacher instructs you to store the files for this lesson.

3. Select the **Sales by Product** tab, if necessary.

4. Add Sparklines to the T-shirt sales.

   a. Select cell **J5**.

   b. Click **Insert** > **Line** from the Sparklines group.

   c. Select cells **B5:G5** to fill the Data Range box of the Add Sparkline dialog box and click **OK**.

   d. Select cell **J5**, if necessary, and drag the AutoFill Handle down to cell **J8**.

5. With the cells still selected, click **Sparklines Tools Design** tab and click the **Ungroup** button from the Group group.

6. Format the Sparklines based on performance.

   a. Select cell **J5** and click the **Sparkline Tools Design** tab.

   b. Click the **Sparkline Color** button and select **Red** from the Standard Colors palette.

   c. Select cell **J6** and click **Sparkline Tools Design** tab.

   d. Click **Sparkline Color** and select **Green** from the Standard Colors palette.

   e. Select cells **J7:J8**.

   f. Click **Sparkline Color** and select **Yellow** from the Standard Colors palette.

7. Select cells **J5:J8** and click **Sparkline Tools Design** > **High Point** to add a data marker at the point of each employee's highest sales.

8. **With your teacher's permission**, print the worksheet. Your worksheet should look like Figure 15-3.

9. Close the workbook, saving all changes, and exit Excel.

Figure 15-3

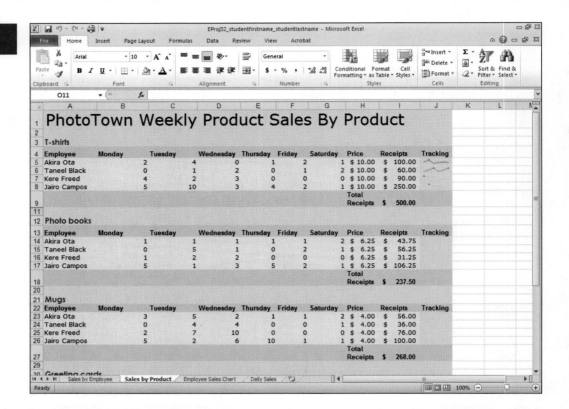

Lesson 16

Drawing and Positioning Shapes

➤ **What You Will Learn**

Drawing Shapes

Resizing, Grouping, Aligning, and Arranging Shapes

Software Skills   After putting all that hard work into designing and entering data for a worksheet, of course you want it to look its best. You already know how to add formatting, color, and borders to a worksheet to enhance its appeal.

To make your worksheet stand out from all the rest, you may need to do something "unexpected," such as adding your own art. You can insert predesigned shapes (such as stars or arrows) or combine them to create your own designs.

Application Skills   You're the accountant at Sydney Crenshaw Realty and you need to compile a year-to-date spreadsheet showing the total sales and commissions paid. You want to add your company logo and call attention to some record sales figures.

What You Can Do

Drawing Shapes

- With the Shapes button in the Illustration group of the Insert tab, you can create many **shapes**.
- Add lines, rectangles, arrows, equation shapes, stars and banners, and callouts as shown in Figure 16-1 to highlight important information in your worksheet.
- You can also add a text box or a callout—a shape in which you can type your own text.

WORDS TO KNOW

Adjustment handle
A yellow diamond-shaped handle that appears with some objects. You can drag this handle to manipulate the shape of the object, such as the width of a wide arrow, or the tip of a speaking bubble's pointer.

Group
Objects can be grouped together so they can act as a single object. Grouping makes it easier to move or resize a drawing that consists of several objects.

Order
The position of an object with respect to other objects that are layered or in a stack.

Shape
A predesigned object (such as a banner or star) that can be drawn with a single dragging motion.

Sizing handles
Small white circles that appear around the perimeter of the active drawing object. You can resize an object by dragging one of these handles.

Stack
A group of drawing objects layered on top of one another, possibly partially overlapping. Use the Order command to change the position of a selected object within the stack.

Figure 16-1

- A text box or callout, like other shapes, can be placed anywhere on the worksheet.
- The Shapes button ⬚ Shapes ▾ presents you with a palette of shapes sorted by category that makes it easy for you to select the shape you want to insert.

- To insert a shape, simply select the shape you want, and then drag in a cell to create it—no actual drawing skills are needed.
- After inserting a shape, you can format it as needed.

Try It!   Drawing Shapes

1 Start Excel, if necessary, and open **ETry16** from the data files for this lesson.

2 Save the file as **ETry16_studentfirstname_ studentlastname** in the location where your teacher instructs you to store the files for this lesson.

3 Select the P&L sheet, if necessary.

4 Click Insert > Shapes ⬚ and select the Rounded Rectangle from the Rectangles group.

5 Click at the upper-left corner of cell H6, then drag downward to the lower-right corner of cell J8.

✓ *All shapes will appear using a default style and color.*

6 Click Insert > Shapes ⬚ and select Rectangle from the Rectangles group, to add a second shape from the upper-left corner of cell G14 to the lower-right corner of cell I16.

7 Save changes and leave the file open to use in the next Try It.

Resizing, Grouping, Aligning, and Arranging Shapes

- A shape can also be resized, moved, and copied, like any other object, such as clip art.
  - To resize an object, drag one of the **sizing handles**.
  - To manipulate the shape of an object, drag the **adjustment handle** if one is available with that particular object.
- You can move shapes so that they partially cover other shapes.
  - To move a shape, drag it.
  - To move a shape more precisely, use Snap to Grid. When you drag a shape, it snaps automatically to the closest gridline or half-gridline.
  - The Snap to Shape command is similar, but it snaps a shape to the edge of a nearby shape when you drag the first shape close enough.
- Shapes can be aligned in relation to each other automatically.

- For example, you might align objects so that their top edges line up.
  - Shapes can be aligned along their left, right, top, or bottom edges.
  - Shapes can also be aligned horizontally through their middles.
- When needed, you can change the **order** of objects that are layered (in a **stack**) so that a particular object appears on top of or behind another object.
- To select an object, you simply click it.
  - Sometimes, selecting one object in a stack is difficult because the objects overlap and even obscure other objects below them in the stack.
  - The Selection and Visibility Pane makes it easy to select a specific object because all the objects on a worksheet appear in a list. To select one, click it.
  - The Selection Pane also makes it easy to rearrange objects in the stack.
- You can **group** two or more objects together so they act as one object.

Try It!   Resizing, Grouping, Aligning, and Arranging Shapes

1 In the ETry16_studentfirstname_studentlastname file, select the P&L tab, if necessary.

2 Select the rounded rectangle and drag it into place fitting the area between cells F14 and I17.

3 Select the rectangle and drag it inside the rounded rectangle, as shown in the figure.

4 To draw a third shape, select the Right Arrow from the Block Arrows category of the Insert > Shapes 🖳 drop-down list. Click anywhere in the worksheet to insert the shape.

5 Move and resize the right arrow shape to fit inside the rounded rectangle, as shown in the figure.
  a. Drag the arrow inside the rounded rectangle.
  b. Drag the center-top sizing handle to stretch the arrow's height to fit just inside the top and bottom border of the rounded rectangle.

6 Click Page Layout > Selection Pane 🖳 Selection Pane in the Arrange group.

7 Press CTRL and click the Right Arrow, Rectangle, and Rounded Rectangle shape names in the Shapes on this Sheet group.

8 Click Drawing Tools Format > Align 🖳 Align ▾. Choose Align Middle from the drop-down list.

9 With the shapes still selected, click Drawing Tools Format > Group 🖳 Group ▾. Select Group from the drop-down list.

10 Click Page Layout > Selection Pane 🖳 to close the Selection Pane.

11 Close ETry16_studentfirstname_student lastname, saving all changes, and exit Excel.

Arranging shapes

Project 33—Create It

Drawing and Arranging Shapes

DIRECTIONS

1. Start Excel, if necessary, and open **EProj33** from the data files for this lesson.
2. Save the file as **EProj33_studentfirstname_studentlastname** in the location where your teacher instructs you to store the files for this lesson.
3. Select the **Year to Date Sales** sheet, if necessary.
4. Click **Page Layout > Themes** 🔠 **> Solstice**.
5. Click **Insert > Shapes** 🔷 and select the **Rectangle** from the Rectangles group.
6. Click at the upper-left corner of cell **B2**, then drag downward and to the right to form a rectangle about the height of the title text.
7. Resize the new rectangle.
   a. Click **Drawing Tools Format > Shape Height** 🔲 and type **.28**.
   b. Click **Drawing Tools Format > Shape Width** 🔳 and type **.48**.
8. Click **Insert > Shapes** 🔷 and select **Isosceles Triangle** from the Basic Shapes group, to add a second shape in cell **B1** to about the size of the previously inserted rectangle.

9. Resize the new triangle.
   a. Click **Drawing Tools Format > Shape Height** 🔲 and type **.22**.
   b. Click **Drawing Tools Format > Shape Width** 🔳 and type **.48**.
10. Drag the triangle over the top of the rectangle to form the shape of a house.
11. Arrange the house shape.
    a. Press ⌨CTRL and click the rectangle shape.
    b. Click **Drawing Tools Format > Align** ▣ **> Align Center**.
    c. Click **Drawing Tools Format > Group** ▣ **> Group**.
    d. Drag the right edge of the "house" even with the right edge of column B.
    e. Align the top edge of the house to just below the column header, as shown in Figure 16-2.
12. Close the workbook, saving all changes, and exit Excel.

Project 34—Apply It

Drawing and Arranging Shapes

DIRECTIONS

1. Start Excel, if necessary, and open **EProj34** from the data files for this lesson.
2. Save the file as **EProj34_studentfirstname_studentlastname** in the location where your teacher instructs you to store the files for this lesson.
3. Insert the **Right Brace** shape from the Basic Shapes group.

4. Click at the upper-left corner of the **G21** cell and drag downward to the lower-left corner of the **G23** cell to add a brace that visually groups the data from the month of May.
5. Insert the **Left Arrow** from the Block Arrows group.
6. Click at the upper-left corner of the **H21** cell and drag downward to the lower-right corner of the **I23** cell.

7. Align the brace and arrow together.
   a. Drag the arrow closer to the right brace, press CTRL and select both the left arrow and the right brace.
   b. Click **Drawing Tools Format > Align ▯ > Align Middle**.
   c. With both shapes still selected, click **Drawing Tools Format > Group ▯ > Group**.
8. Insert the **12-Point Star** from the Stars and Banners group.
9. Click at the upper-left corner of the **F1** cell and drag downward to the lower-right corner of the **F3** cell.

10. With the shape still selected, type **.76** in the Shape Height text box of the Size group and type **.93** in the Shape Width box.
11. With the shape still selected, open the Selection Pane.
12. Press CTRL and select the house shape as well.
13. Click **Drawing Tools Format > Align ▯ > Align Middle**.
14. **With your teacher's permission**, print the worksheet. Your worksheet should look like Figure 16-2.
15. Close the workbook, saving all changes, and exit Excel.

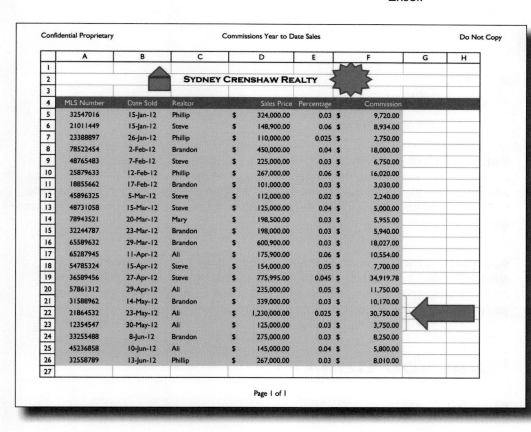

Figure 16-2

Lesson 17

Formatting Shapes

➤ What You Will Learn

Formatting Shapes
Adding Shape Effects

Software Skills   When shapes such as rectangles, block arrows, and banners
are added to a worksheet, they originally appear in the default style—a shape with
a black outline filled with the Accent 1 color. You can change both the color and the
outline style of any shape easily. You can also add special effects such as shadows
and soft edges.

Application Skills   As the accountant for Sydney Crenshaw Realty, you've
already created a spreadsheet to track year-to-date sales and commissions with
some basic shapes. Now you'd like to spend a little time formatting the shapes
you've added. You want to add some color and dimension to them.

What You Can Do

Formatting Shapes

- When a shape is selected, the Drawing Tools Format tab automatically appears
  on the Ribbon in anticipation of your need to edit it.
- Since all new shapes appear in the default style, you might want to change:
  - Shape Styles: A set of formats that include the outline color and style, edge
    style, and fill.
  - Shape Fill: The color, picture, gradient, or texture that fills a shape.

    ✓ *A line shape cannot be filled. A line's color is determined by the Shape Outline settings.*

  - Shape Outline: The color, weight, and style of the border that outlines a shape.

    ✓ *You can change the color, weight, and style of a line. You can also add arrows at one or both
    ends.*

- Shape Effects: Complex formats applied with a single click.

■ When changing any color on a shape, either the fill or the outline, you can use the Colors dialog box to create a custom color, and even to add transparency if desired.

Try It!   Formatting Shapes

1 Start Excel, if necessary, and open **ETry17** from the data files for this lesson.

2 Save the file as **ETry17_studentfirstname_studentlastname** in the location where your teacher instructs you to store the files for this lesson.

3 Click Page Layout > Selection Pane.

4 In the Selection and Visibility Pane, select Rectangle and click the Drawing Tools Format tab.

5 Click the Shape Fill button in the Shape Styles group and select Orange, Accent 6, Lighter 60% from the palette.

6 Click the Shape Outline button and click Red, Accent 2, Lighter 60% from the palette.

7 In the Selection and Visibility Pane, click Right Arrow and click the Drawing Tools Format tab, if necessary.

8 Click Shape Fill > Gradient > More Gradients.

9 Click Fill, if necessary, and click Gradient fill. From the Preset colors list, select Gold.

10 From the Type list, select Linear, if necessary.

11 From the Direction list, select the first option: Linear Diagonal-Top Left to Bottom Right. Click Close.

12 Click Line Color in the left pane. From the Color list, select Olive Green, Accent 3, Lighter 40% and click Close.

13 In the Selection Pane, click Rounded Rectangle and click the Drawing Tools Format tab, if necessary.

14 Click the More button in the Shape Styles group, and select Moderate Effect-Red Accent 2.

15 Save changes and leave the file open to use in the next Try It.

The Selection and Visibility Pane

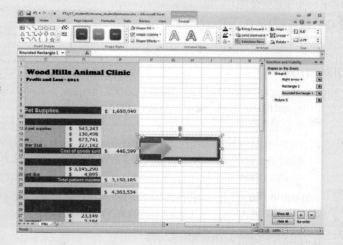

Adding Shape Effects

■ Shape **effects** that you can apply to a selected shape include:
- Shadows
- Reflections
- Glows
- Soft edges
- Beveled edges
- 3-D rotations

■ Each shape effect style comes with options that allow you to customize the effect to get the look you want.

■ The Preset category on the Shape Effects drop-down menu displays a set of common effects, with the options already pre-selected for you.

■ Choose one of the Preset effects to quickly change the look of a selected shape.

Try It!   **Adding Shape Effects**

1 In the **ETry17_studentfirstname_studentlast name** file, select the P&L tab, if necessary.

2 Click Page Layout > Selection Pane ⬚, if necessary.

3 In the Selection and Visibility Pane, select Rectangle and click the Drawing Tools Format tab.

4 Click the Shape Effects button ⬚, click Glow, then Orange, 8 pt glow, Accent color 6.

5 In the Selection and Visibility Pane, click Rounded Rectangle and click the Drawing Tools Format tab, if necessary.

6 Click Shape Effects ⬚ > Reflection > Tight Reflection, 4 pt offset.

7 Close the Selection Pane.

8 Close **ETry17_studentfirstname_studentlast name**, saving all changes, and exit Excel.

Project 35—Create It

Formatting Shapes

DIRECTIONS

1. Start Excel, if necessary, and open **EProj34_ studentfirstname_studentlastname** created in Project 34.

   ✓ *If* **EProj34_studentfirstname_studentlastname** *is not available, you can use* **EProj35** *from the data files for this lesson.*

2. Save the file as **EProj35_studentfirstname_ studentlastname** in the location where your teacher instructs you to store the files for this lesson.

3. Click **Page Layout** > **Selection Pane** ⬚ to open the Selection Pane.

4. In the Selection Pane, select **Isosceles Triangle**.

5. On the Drawing Tools Format tab, click the **More** button to open the Shape Styles gallery.

6. Select **Moderate Effect, Red Accent 3**.

7. In the Selection Pane, select **Rectangle**.

8. On the Drawing Tools Format tab, click the **More** button to open the Shape Styles gallery.

9. Select **Moderate Effect, Red Accent 3**.

10. Click **Shape Effects** ⬚ > **Reflection** and select **Tight Reflection, touching** from the Reflection Variations group.

11. Close the Selection Pane.

12. **With your teacher's permission**, print the worksheet. Your worksheet should look like Figure 17-1.

13. Close the workbook, saving all changes, and exit Excel.

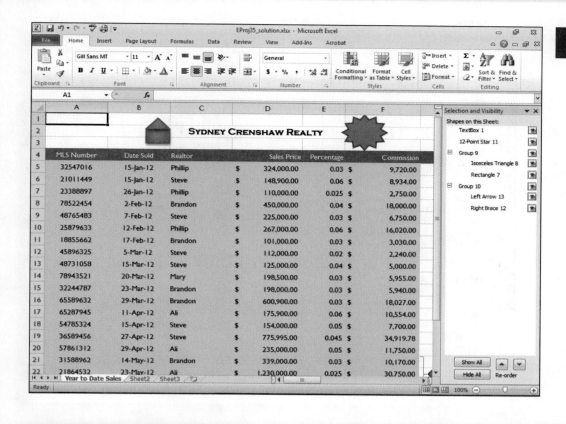

Figure 17-1

Project 36—Apply It

Formatting Shapes

DIRECTIONS

1. Start Excel, if necessary, and open **EProj36** from the data files for this lesson.

2. Save the file as **EProj36_studentfirstname_studentlastname** in the location where your teacher instructs you to store the files for this lesson.

3. Click **Page Layout > Selection Pane** to open the Selection Pane.

4. In the Selection Pane, select the Group that includes the Left Arrow and the Right Brace.

5. Open the Shape Styles and select **Intense Effect-Red Accent 3**.

6. In the Selection Pane, select the Right Brace.

7. Open the Shape Styles and select **Subtle Line-Accent 3**.

8. In the Selection Pane, select the **12-Point Star**.

9. Open the Shape Styles and select **Moderate Effect-Gold, Accent 2**.

10. With the shape still selected, click **Shape Effects > Shadow** and select **Offset Diagonal Top Left** from the Outer group, as shown in Figure 17-2.

11. Close the Selection Pane.

12. **With your teacher's permission**, print the worksheet. Your worksheet should look like Figure 17-2.

13. Close the workbook, saving all changes, and exit Excel.

Figure 17-2

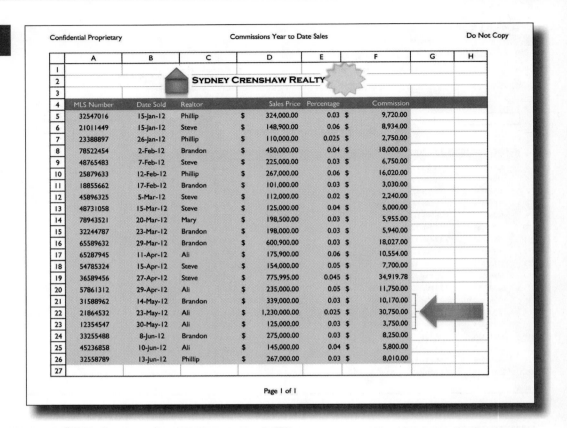

Commissions Year to Date Sales

	A	B	C	D	E	F	G	H
1								
2			SYDNEY CRENSHAW REALTY					
3								
4	MLS Number	Date Sold	Realtor	Sales Price	Percentage	Commission		
5	32547016	15-Jan-12	Phillip	$ 324,000.00	0.03	$ 9,720.00		
6	21011449	15-Jan-12	Steve	$ 148,900.00	0.06	$ 8,934.00		
7	23388897	26-Jan-12	Phillip	$ 110,000.00	0.025	$ 2,750.00		
8	78522454	2-Feb-12	Brandon	$ 450,000.00	0.04	$ 18,000.00		
9	48765483	7-Feb-12	Steve	$ 225,000.00	0.03	$ 6,750.00		
10	25879633	12-Feb-12	Phillip	$ 267,000.00	0.06	$ 16,020.00		
11	18855662	17-Feb-12	Brandon	$ 101,000.00	0.03	$ 3,030.00		
12	45896325	5-Mar-12	Steve	$ 112,000.00	0.02	$ 2,240.00		
13	48731058	15-Mar-12	Steve	$ 125,000.00	0.04	$ 5,000.00		
14	78943521	20-Mar-12	Mary	$ 198,500.00	0.03	$ 5,955.00		
15	32244787	23-Mar-12	Brandon	$ 198,000.00	0.03	$ 5,940.00		
16	65589632	29-Mar-12	Brandon	$ 600,900.00	0.03	$ 18,027.00		
17	65287945	11-Apr-12	Ali	$ 175,900.00	0.06	$ 10,554.00		
18	54785324	15-Apr-12	Steve	$ 154,000.00	0.05	$ 7,700.00		
19	36589456	27-Apr-12	Steve	$ 775,995.00	0.045	$ 34,919.78		
20	57861312	29-Apr-12	Ali	$ 235,000.00	0.05	$ 11,750.00		
21	31588962	14-May-12	Brandon	$ 339,000.00	0.03	$ 10,170.00		
22	21864532	23-May-12	Ali	$ 1,230,000.00	0.025	$ 30,750.00		
23	12354547	30-May-12	Ali	$ 125,000.00	0.03	$ 3,750.00		
24	33255488	8-Jun-12	Brandon	$ 275,000.00	0.03	$ 8,250.00		
25	45236858	10-Jun-12	Ali	$ 145,000.00	0.04	$ 5,800.00		
26	32558789	13-Jun-12	Phillip	$ 267,000.00	0.03	$ 8,010.00		
27								

Page 1 of 1

Lesson 18

Enhancing Shapes with Text and Effects

➤ **What You Will Learn**

Adding Text to a Text Box, Callout, or Other Shape
Adding 3-D Effects
Rotating Shapes
Inserting a Screen Capture

Software Skills   If you need to place text in some spot within the worksheet that doesn't correspond to a specific cell, you can "float" the text over the cells by creating a text box or by adding a callout. A text box or callout can be placed anywhere in the worksheet, regardless of the cell gridlines. You can add text to any shape you choose. Add 3-D effects or rotation to shapes to really make them stand out.

Application Skills   The year-to-date sales and commission report that you've been working on for Sydney Crenshaw Realty is coming along nicely, but you think that adding some additional text or callouts might make the information you are tracking easier to understand.

What You Can Do

Adding Text to a Text Box, Callout, or Other Shape

- A **callout** is basically a **text box** with a shape, such as a cartoon balloon, with an extension that points to the information you wish to write about.
  - When a callout shape is selected, a yellow diamond indicates the **extension point**.
    - ✓ *On other shapes, this yellow diamond handle is called an adjustment handle, because it lets you adjust the outline of the shape itself.*

WORDS TO KNOW

Callout
Text that's placed in a special AutoShape balloon. A callout, like a text box, "floats" over the cells in a worksheet—so you can position a callout wherever you like.

Extension point
The yellow diamond handle that indicates the position where a callout can be resized or extended.

Rotation handle
A green circular handle that appears just over the top of most objects when they are selected. Use this handle to rotate the object manually.

Screenshot
A screenshot is a picture of all or part of an open window, such as another application or a Web page.

Text box
A small rectangle that "floats" over the cells in a worksheet, into which you can add text. A text box can be placed anywhere you want.

- Drag this yellow extension point to make the callout point precisely to the data you wish to talk about.
- Text boxes do not have these extensions, but you can easily add an arrow or line shape to a text box to accomplish the same thing.

■ You can use a callout like a text box, to draw attention to important information, or to add a comment to a worksheet.

■ You can add text to any shape.

✓ *If the shape already contains text, the text you type will be added to the end of the existing text. You can replace text by selecting it first, then typing new text.*

■ The border of a selected shape changes to indicate whether you're editing the object itself (solid border) or the text in the object (dashed border).

- To move, resize, copy, or delete the object, the border must be solid.
- To edit or add text in a text box or shape, the border must be dashed.

Try It!   Adding Text to a Text Box, Callout, or Other Shape

1 Start Excel, if necessary, and open **ETry18** from the data files for this lesson and open the P&L tab, if necessary.

2 Save the file as **ETry18_studentfirstname_ studentlastname** in the location where your teacher instructs you to store the files for this lesson.

3 Click Page Layout > Selection Pane 🖫.

4 In the Selection Pane, select Rectangle and type **This cost is down because of better inventory management**.

5 Select the text in the shape and click the Home tab.

6 Click the Font Color button and select Dark Red from the Standard Colors palette.

7 With the text still selected, click the Decrease Font button four times to change the font size to 10 points.

8 Click the Align Center button ≡ on the Alignment group.

9 With the rectangle still selected, right-click the rectangle and select Format Text Effects from the shortcut menu to open the Format Text Effects dialog box.

10 Type **.3** in the Left box of the Internal margin group, type **.1** in the Top box, and click Close.

11 Create a callout:

a. Click Insert > Shapes and choose Rectangular Callout from the Callouts group.
b. Draw a callout in the area of F34:I36.
c. Type **Next year's purchases should be much lower than this.**

d. Click the Home tab and click the Decrease Font button three times to change the font size to 9.
e. Click the Center text button in the Alignment group.
f. Click the border of the callout shape.

✓ *Clicking the border allows you to change the format of the whole text box, not just the text.*

g. On the Drawing9 Tools Format tab, click the More button in the Shape Styles group and select Moderate Effect-Red, Accent 2.

12 Click the yellow extension point and drag until the callout tip points to cell E38.

13 Save changes and leave the file open to use in the next Try It.

The Format Text Effects dialog box

Adding 3-D Effects

- When you add 3-D effects to an object, that object appears to have depth.
- You can add 3-D effects to any object, even grouped objects.
- Select the 3-D rotation style you want first, from the 3-D Rotation palette, located on the Shape Effects button.
  - If you choose 3-D Rotation Options instead, the Format Shape dialog box appears where you can customize the settings.
  - Here you can set the exact degree of rotation and other options such as whether you want the text in the shape (if any) to be rotated with the shape.

- Objects are rotated along three axes—the X (horizontal), Y (vertical), and Z (depth dimension).
- In the Format Shape dialog box, shown in Figure 18-1, you can also adjust the format of the 3-D shape, selecting the depth, surface texture, and other options.
  - Here you can adjust the style of the edge of your 3-D shape. You can also change the color and contour of this third dimension.
  - You can also select a surface texture—such as the apparent material used.
  - You can also change how the surface is lit (both the color of the light and the angle at which it shines on the 3-D object).

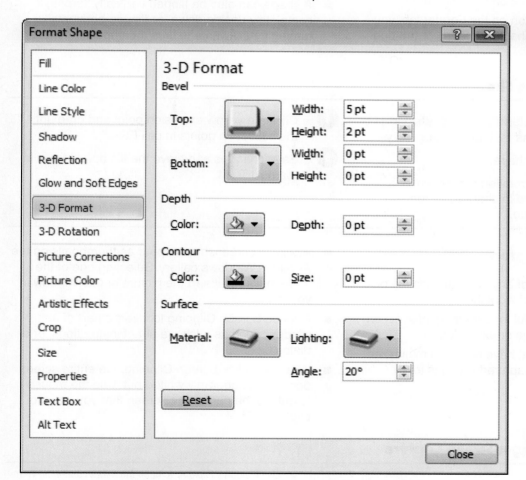

Figure 18-1

Try It!   Adding 3-D Effects

1 In the **ETry18_studentfirstname_studentlast name** file, select the P&L tab, if necessary.

2 Select the callout shape and click the Drawing Tools Format tab.

3 Click Shape Effects ⬎ > Bevel and select Circle from the Bevel group.

4 Click Shape Effects ⬎ > 3-D Rotation and select Oblique Top Right from the Oblique group.

5 Click the yellow extension point until the callout tip points to cell E38, if necessary.

6 Save changes and leave the file open to use in the next Try It.

Rotating Shapes

■ A shape can be rotated around an invisible pin holding its center in place on the worksheet.

  • Using the Rotate button on the Format tab, you can quickly rotate a shape to the left or the right, by 90 degrees.

• You can also rotate a shape by a custom amount.

• Shapes can be manually rotated, using the **rotation handle**.

■ A shape can also be flipped vertically, turning it completely upside down, or flipped horizontally, turning it backwards to face the opposite direction.

Try It!   Rotating Shapes

1 In the **ETry18_studentfirstname_studentlast name** file, select the P&L tab, if necessary.

2 Select the callout shape.

3 Click and hold the rotation handle while dragging the mouse to change the rotation amount of the shape.

4 Click the yellow extension point and drag until the callout tip points to cell E38.

5 Save changes and leave the file open to use in the next Try It.

Inserting a Screen Capture

■ You can add a picture of any open application or Web page to your Excel worksheet.

■ **Screenshots** are helpful for capturing information that is subject to change or expiration.

■ Only open windows that have not been minimized to the taskbar can be captured with this tool.

■ Available screenshots appear as thumbnails on the Available Windows gallery. Selecting one of the thumbnails will insert the picture of that window in your file.

■ Choose Screen Clipping to insert a part of a window, such as a logo, a set of instructions, or a dialog box.

■ When you click Screen Clipping, the entire screen becomes temporarily whited out. Use the mouse to outline the part of the screen that you want to capture.

Try It!   Inserting a Screen Capture

1 In the **ETry18_studentfirstname_studentlast name** file, select the P&L tab, if necessary.

2 Open **ETry18a.jpg** from the data files for this lesson.

✓ *Use Windows Explorer to open the folder containing your data files. Double-click on* **ETry18a.jpg** *file to open it in your image viewer.*

3 Minimize all open windows except Excel and your image viewer.

(continued)

Try It!   **Inserting a Screen Capture** *(continued)*

4 In Excel, click Insert > Screenshot 📷 in the Illustrations group to view your Available Windows gallery.

5 Click Screen Clipping and drag your mouse over the picture in your image viewer to select only the picture.

✓ *Screen Clipping whites out your screen. Dragging the mouse over the desired area of the screen restores the color to that area and highlights the portion of your screen that will be inserted into Excel.*

6 Once the screen clipping has been added to your worksheet, drag the picture to the open area of your spreadsheet between the two text boxes.

7 With the screen clipping still selected, click Picture Tools Format > Picture Border button 🖼 Picture Border ▾.

8 Click Automatic to add a border around your screenshot.

9 Save the changes to **ETry18_studentfirst name_studentlastname**, close the workbook, and exit Excel.

Using Screen Clipping

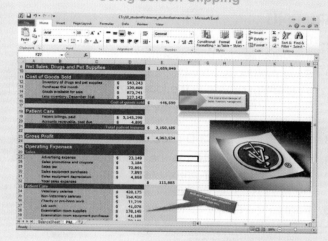

Project 37—Create It

Adding Text Effects

DIRECTIONS

1. Start Excel, if necessary, and open **EProj37** from the data files for this lesson.

2. Save the file as **EProj37_studentfirstname_ studentlastname** in the location where your teacher instructs you to store the files for this lesson.

3. Add text to the yellow star shape:
   a. Right-click the star and select **Edit Text**.
   b. Type **Rated # 1**.
   c. Select the text **# 1** and click **Home** > **Increase Font Size** A˄ four times.

4. Add text to the red arrow shape:
   a. Right-click the arrow and select **Edit Text**.
   b. Type **Best Month**.

5. Insert a callout to bring attention to the highest commission figure.
   a. Click **Insert** > **Shapes** 🗯 and select **Rectangular Callout** from the callouts group.
   b. Click the upper-left corner of the **H16** cell and drag downward to the right to the lower-left corner of **I18** to add a callout to the worksheet.

6. **With your teacher's permission**, print the worksheet.

7. Close the workbook, saving all changes, and exit Excel.

Project 38—Apply It

Enhancing Shapes

DIRECTIONS

1. Start Excel, if necessary, and open **EProj38** from the data files for this lesson.

2. Save the file as **EProj38_studentfirstname_studentlastname** in the location where your teacher instructs you to store the files for this lesson.

3. Add the **Preset 4** 3-D effect to the star shape.

4. Add the following text to the callout shape: **Largest commission ever paid by our firm. Record this number for year-end award.** Set the font size to **10**.

5. Format the shape as follows:
   a. Shape height **0.93"**.
   b. Shape width **1.31"**.
   c. Apply the **Subtle Effect, Gold, Accent 2**.
   d. Apply the **Gold, Accent 2** style to the shape outline.

6. Click the callout's yellow extension point and position on the line between F19 and G19 to indicate the larger commission figure.

7. Click **Drawing Tools Format > Shape Effects > Bevel** and select the **Circle** option.

8. Grab the shape's rotation handle and rotate so that it looks similar to Figure 18-2.

9. Click **Page Layout Gridlines** and then clear the **Print** check box to print without gridlines.

10. **With your teacher's permission**, print the worksheet. Your worksheet should look like Figure 18-2.

11. Close the workbook, saving all changes, and exit Excel.

Figure 18-2

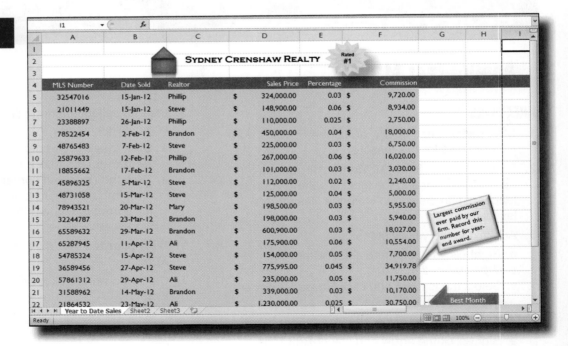

Lesson 19

Working with Templates

➤ **What You Will Learn**

Changing Cell Borders
Filling Cells with a Color or a Pattern
Adding a Watermark or Other Graphics
Formatting the Worksheet Background
Creating a Workbook Template

Software Skills   Each worksheet tells a story—of lost profits, increased costs, or skyrocketing sales. To help your worksheet tell its "story," you can add shading, border, or conditional formatting to highlight or separate important information in a complex worksheet.

To make a worksheet look more professional, you might want to customize the standard themes Excel provides by choosing company-style fonts and colors, adding a watermark, or applying a custom worksheet background.

Application Skills   The worksheet you designed to track sales each day at Pete's Pets has proven very helpful, and the corporate headquarters may adopt it throughout the company. Before you send it off for their review, you want to add some professional formatting touches.

What You Can Do

Changing Cell Borders

- To outline or separate data, you can include a variety of line styles that border the edge (top, bottom, left, or right) of a cell or range of cells.
- **Borders** can be set with the Border tab in the Format Cells dialog box or by using the Borders button on the Formatting toolbar.

   ✓ *You can vary the border style and color as well.*

- If you prefer, you can "draw" borders along cell edges rather than selecting a pattern from a list or dialog box.

WORDS TO KNOW

Border
An outline applied to the sides of a cell.

Pattern
A cell can be filled with a plain color and/or a pattern. A pattern is laid on top of the cell in your choice of layouts, such as a vertical stripe or a thin crosshatch. You can also select a pattern of dots, which has the effect of muting the fill color so that it's less intense.

Reverse type
Normal type is typically black on a light background; reverse type is white text on a black or dark background.

Template
A workbook designed for a specific purpose, complete with formatting, formulas, text, and row and column labels that you can customize.

Watermark
A faint image embedded in paper that identifies its maker. This faint image appears behind text when it's printed.

Try It!   Changing Cell Borders

1 Start Excel, if necessary, and open the ETry19 file from the data files for this lesson, and select the July 22 tab, if necessary.

2 Save the file as ETry19_studentfirstname_ studentlastname in the location where your teacher instructs you to store the files for this lesson.

3 Select the cells A6:C6.

4 Click the Home tab and click the Borders button ⊞ ▾ in the Font group.

5 From the list, select Top and Double Bottom Border.

6 Save changes and leave the file open to use in the next Try It.

Filling Cells with a Color or a Pattern

■ Cells in a worksheet can be filled with a background color and/or **pattern**.

  ✓ Even if you're using a black-and-white printer, you can still achieve an interesting look by applying a fill color to the cells. Depending on the color you choose, the cell may appear light, medium, or dark gray when printed.

■ To apply a sold fill color, select one from the Fill Color palette, located on the Home tab.

■ If you want to apply a color using a pattern, such as stripes, use the Fill tab of the Format Cells dialog box.

■ You can also combine solid colors to create a new color using the Fill tab of the Format Cells dialog box.

  ● To do this, you select a main color from the Background Color palette, choose a % Gray pattern such as the 25% Gray in the Pattern

Style list, and then choose a pattern color in the Pattern Color list.

  ● For example, if you choose an aqua from the Background Color palette, and yellow from the Pattern Color palette, then open the Pattern Style list and select the 25% Gray pattern style, you would end up with a light green with just a hint of yellow—the result of blending 75% aqua with 25% yellow.

  ● If you switched to a 75% Gray pattern, the result color would look more yellow, since the ratio would then be 25% aqua and 75% yellow.

■ When changing the fill color of a cell, you may also wish to change the font color of the data inside.

■ It's possible to display and print data in white against a black, or dark colored, background. This is sometimes called **reverse type**.

Try It!   Filling Cells with a Color or a Pattern

1 In the ETry19_studentfirstname_ studentlastname file, select the July 22 tab, if necessary.

2 Select the cells A6:C14 and click the Home tab.

3 Click Format ▤ Format ▾ in the Cells group and select Format Cells from the list.

4 Click the Fill tab and select Light Yellow from the Background Color list (third from the left in the first row below the divider line). Click OK.

5 Select the cells A6:C6 and click Home > Format ▤ Format ▾ > Format Cells.

6 Click the Fill tab and select Fill Effects.

7 From the Color 1 list, select More Colors and click the Custom tab.

8 In the Red box, type: 255, in the Green box, type: 163, in the Blue box, type: 165 and click OK.

9 From the Color 2 list, select Red from the Standard Colors palette.

10 In the Variants group, click Horizontal in the Shading styles group, if necessary, and then select the second gradient option in the first row. Click OK and then click OK again.

11 Save changes and leave the file open to use in the next Try It.

(continued)

Try It!   **Filling Cells with a Color or a Pattern** *(continued)*

Fill Effects dialog box

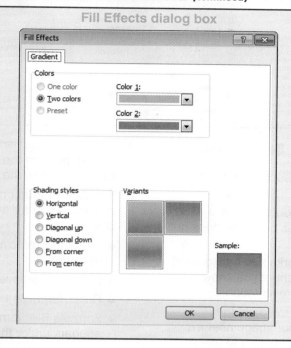

Adding a Watermark or Other Graphics

- You can recreate the look of a **watermark** by placing the graphic behind your Excel data.
  - You add the watermark graphic to either the header or footer of every page.
  - This graphic begins within either the header or footer area, and depending on its size, extends into the data area to act as a watermark.

- After inserting the graphic, you can adjust the size so that it fills the page.
- You can also adjust the inserted graphic's brightness and contrast in order to make the worksheet data, which appears on top of the watermark, easier to read.
- Watermarks appear only on the worksheet on which they were added, and not every worksheet within a workbook.

Try It!   **Adding a Watermark or Other Graphics**

1 In the **ETry19_studentfirstname_ studentlastname** file, select the July 22 tab, if necessary.

2 Click the Insert tab and click Header & Footer 📄 from the Text group.

3 Click in the middle section of the header, then click the Picture button 🖼 from the Header & Footer Elements group.

✓ *A watermark picture can be added in any of the three header sections depending on your desire to add other header elements to your page.*

4 Select **ETry19a.jpg** from the data files for this lesson and click Insert.

5 Click the Format Picture 🖼 button and type **75** in the Height box of the Scale group.

6 Click the Picture tab and type **60** in the Brightness box of the Image Control group.

7 Next, type **20** in the Contrast box of the Image Control group and click OK.

8 Save changes and leave the file open to use in the next Try It.

(continued)

Try It!   **Adding a Watermark or Other Graphics** *(continued)*

Header & Footer Tools Design tab

Header & Footer Tools
Design

Header Footer | Page Number Current Current File File Sheet Picture Format | Go to Go to | ☐ Different First Page ☑ Scale with Document
            Number of Pages Date Time Path Name Name   Picture | Header Footer | ☐ Different Odd & Even Pages ☐ Align with Page Margins
Header & Footer | Header & Footer Elements | Navigation | Options

Formatting the Worksheet Background

- You can add a graphic to the background of the worksheet, behind the data.

- Unlike a watermark, a background image is used for on-screen display purposes only, and does not print.

  - You might want to add a worksheet background graphic to enhance a worksheet you know will only be used in onscreen presentations.

  - Because you won't be able to adjust the brightness or contrast of your image after it's inserted, for the best effect, be sure to use a graphic that's very light in color, so that your data can still be read.

    ✓ *After inserting a graphic for use as a worksheet background, if you have trouble reading your data, you can apply a fill color to just the data cells so that the data can be more easily read.*

- The background isn't included when you create a Web page from the sheet, unless you create the Web page from the whole workbook.

- The Show group on the View tab includes a number of options to alter the version of the worksheet you see.

  - Headings: removes the row and column headings.

  - Gridlines: removes the cell gridlines.

  - Ruler: removes the horizontal and vertical rulers.

  - Formula Bar: removes the formula bar that appears under the Ribbon.

    ✓ *The options on this tab affect only the onscreen view of the worksheet and do not affect how the file prints.*

Try It!   **Formatting the Worksheet Background**

1. In the **ETry19_studentfirstname_studentlast name** file, select the July 23 tab and click Normal in the status bar.

2. Click the Page Layout tab and click the Background button 🖼 in the Page Setup group.

3. Select **ETry19a.jpg** from the data files for this lesson and click Insert.

   ✓ *The background image cannot be sized or recolored. A small image will be tiled to fill the background.*

4. Select the cells A5:C16 and click the Home tab.

5. Click the Fill Color button 🎨 ▾ and select Light Yellow, Background 2 from the Theme Colors palette.

6. Click Page Layout > Delete Background 🖼 to remove the background image.

7. Save changes and leave the file open to use in the next Try It.

Page Setup group

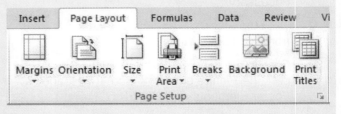

| Insert | Page Layout | Formulas | Data | Review | Vi |

Margins Orientation Size Print Area Breaks Background Print Titles
        Page Setup

Creating a Workbook Template

- If you create workbooks with a lot of similar elements—a company name and logo, similar column and row labels, and so on—create one workbook and save it as a **template**.
  - You can create a new workbook based on any existing workbook without creating a template from it first.
  - However, if you often base new workbooks on a particular workbook, you can save time by creating a template.
  - For example, with a template, you won't have to delete the data from the copied workbook before you can enter new data.
- With a template, you can quickly create new workbooks that contain the same elements.

- In the New dialog box, you can browse through the templates you've created.
- By default, templates are saved in the Templates folder, and then appear on the Personal Templates tab of the New dialog box.
- You can create a subfolder off the Templates folder; that subfolder will appear as its own tab in the New dialog box.
- You can edit and modify templates that you create as well as any existing templates.
  - When saving a template, you can save it as read-only to prevent any accidental changes.

    ✓ *Template files have .xltx file name extensions. Macro-enabled template files have .xltm file extensions.*

Try It! **Creating a Workbook Template**

1 In **ETry19_studentfirstname_studentlastname**, double-click the July 22 tab and type **Products Sold**.

2 Make a couple of changes to the worksheet.
  a. Edit cell B3 to remove the date.
  b. Switch to Sheet3 and select cells B2:C21 and click Home > Copy.
  c. Switch to the July 22 sheet and select A7. Click Home > Paste.
  d. Select cell E4 and click Home > Borders > Bottom border.
  e. Deselect the Gridlines option on the View tab.

3 Click File > Save As and then select Excel Template in the Save as type list.

4 Click the New folder button, and name the new folder **Class**.

5 Type **ETry19_studentfirstname_studentlastname** in the File name box and click Save.

6 Close the template.

7 Create a new workbook using the new template:
  a. Click File > New.
  b. Click My templates and click the Class tab.
  c. Select the **ETry19_studentfirstname_studentlastname** template and click OK.

8 Type **July 24** in cell E4.

9 Type **10** in cell C7, type **5** in cell C12, type **4** in cell C17, and type **2** in cell C22.

10 Save the file as **ETry19a_studentfirstname_studentlastname** file in the location where your teacher instructs you to store the files for this lesson.

11 Close **ETry19_studentfirstname_studentlastname**, and exit Excel.

(continued)

Try It!   **Creating a Workbook Template** *(continued)*

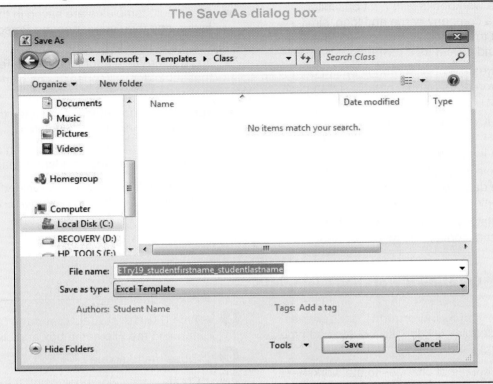

The Save As dialog box

Project 39—Create It

Formatting the Worksheet

DIRECTIONS

1. Start Excel, if necessary, and open **EProj39** from the data files for this lesson.

2. Save the file as **EProj39_studentfirstname_ studentlastname** in the location where your teacher instructs you to store the files for this lesson.

3. Add a watermark:

   a. Change to the **Watermark** sheet, if necessary.
   b. Click **Insert > Header & Footer** 🖼.
   c. Click in the middle section of the header, then click **Header & Footer Tools Design > Picture** button.
   d. Select and insert **EProj39a.jpg**.
   e. Click the **Header & Footer Tools Design > Format Picture** button.

   f. Click the **Size** tab, and select the **Lock aspect ratio** check box, if necessary.
   g. Set the Scale Height to **75%**. (The Scale Width will automatically change to 75%.)
   h. Click the **Picture** tab, and set the Brightness to **75%**.
   i. Set the Contrast to **25%**, and click **OK**.

4. Click in the worksheet and then click **View > Gridlines** to hide gridlines.

5. Select the range **E15:L15**.

6. Click **Home > Fill Color** 🎨 **> Orange, Accent 6, Lighter 40%**.

7. Select the range **E14:L14**.

8. Click **Home > Fill Color** 🎨 **> Orange, Accent 6, Lighter 80%**.

9. Widen columns as needed.

10. **With your teacher's permission**, print the worksheet. Your worksheet should look like Figure 19-1.

11. Close the workbook, saving all changes, and exit Excel.

Project 40—Apply It

Creating a Workbook Template

DIRECTIONS

1. Start Excel, if necessary, and open **EProj40** from the data files for this lesson.

2. Save the file as **EProj40_studentfirstname_studentlastname** in the location where your teacher instructs you to store the files for this lesson.

3. Switch to the **Background** sheet, if necessary.

4. Insert **EProj39a.jpg** as the background on the Background sheet.

5. Apply the **Accent 6, 40%** color fill to the range **E15:L15**.

6. Hide the gridlines.

7. Add borders to the column labels:
   a. Select the range **E15:L15**.
   b. Click **Home > Border**.
   c. Select **Top and Double Bottom Border**.

8. Select the range **F16:K20** and press DEL.

9. Adjust column widths as necessary and save your changes.

10. Create a template from the workbook and save it in the location where your teacher instructs you to store the files for this lesson. Name the template file **EProj40a_studentfirstname_studentlastname**.

11. Close the workbook, saving all changes, and exit Excel.

Lesson 20

Protecting Data

WORDS TO KNOW

Lock
Cells that, if the worksheet is later protected, cannot be changed.

Protect
To prevent changes to locked or protected areas or objects.

Unlock
To enable changes in particular cells of a worksheet you want to later protect.

Unprotect
To remove protection from a worksheet or workbook.

➤ **What You Will Learn**

Locking and Unlocking Cells in a Worksheet
Protecting a Range
Protecting a Worksheet
Protecting a Workbook

Software Skills　If you design worksheets for others to use, or if you share a lot of workbooks, you may wish to protect certain areas of a worksheet from changes. You can protect any cell you want to prevent it from accepting new data or changes. You can also protect an entire worksheet or workbook so that others may only view its contents and not make changes.

Application Skills　You are the payroll manager for Marcus Furniture and you've just created the monthly earnings report used for generating commission checks. You need to have the data checked before the checks can be issued, but you want to ensure that no one can change the data in the file without notifying you. You decide to protect certain areas of the worksheet, while still allowing you full access later.

What You Can Do

Locking and Unlocking Cells in a Worksheet

■ To prevent changes to selected cells or ranges in a worksheet, you can **protect** the worksheet.

- All cells in an Excel worksheet are **locked** by default.
- When you turn on worksheet protection, the locked cells cannot be changed.
- To allow changes in certain cells or ranges, unlock just those cells before protecting the worksheet.
- If you **unlock** a cell that contains a formula, an Error Options button appears to remind you that you might not want to allow other people to change your formulas.

✓ *You can choose to ignore these errors when they appear, or tell Excel to lock the cell again.*

- If necessary, you can **unprotect** a protected worksheet so that you can change the data in locked cells.

- You can protect charts and other objects in a worksheet by using this same process.

- If someone tries to make a change to a protected cell, a message indicates that the cell is protected and considered read-only.

- Users move between the unlocked cells of a protected worksheet by pressing TAB.

  ✓ *However, if ranges were locked using the Allow Users to Edit Ranges dialog box as explained in the next section, the Tab key does not work.*

- Users can copy the data in a locked cell, but they can't move or delete it.

- Data can't be copied to a part of the worksheet that's protected.

Try It!   **Locking and Unlocking Cells in a Worksheet**

1 Start Excel, if necessary, and open **ETry20** from the data files for this lesson and select the Order Form tab, if necessary.

2 Save the file as **ETry20_studentfirstname_ studentlastname** in the location where your teacher instructs you to store the files for this lesson.

3 Unlock the areas of the worksheet that customers will use to enter data:

  a. Select the range B8:B9.
  b. Click Home > Format.
  c. Click Lock Cell from the list.
  d. Unlock the following cells in the same manner: E9, G9, I9, B12:B28, G12:G28, B35:B49, D35:D49, B53, and G36.

4 Save changes and leave the file open to use in the next Try It.

The Cells group

Protecting a Range

- When you unlock cells to allow changes, you can tell Excel to allow changes from anyone, or just selected individuals.

- To unlock cells for everyone, remove the Lock Cell protection format.

- To allow changes to selected individuals, use the Allow Users to Edit Ranges dialog box, shown in Figure 20-1.

- When protecting ranges within a worksheet, you can tell Excel to create a workbook with the details of the permissions you've granted—the range addresses and passwords you've specified.

Figure 20-1

Try It!   Protecting a Range

1. In the **ETry20_studentfirstname_student lastname** file, select the Product Listing tab, if necessary.

2. Select the range name Products from the Name box, as shown in the figure.

3. Click the Review tab and click the Allow Users to Edit Ranges button ![Allow Users to Edit Ranges].

4. Click New in the Allow Users to Edit Ranges dialog box.

5. In the New Range dialog box, type **Product Listing** in the Title box.

6. In the Range Password box, type **supersecret** and click OK.

7. Type **supersecret** again to confirm the password, and click OK.

8. Click Protect Sheet.

9. Type **supersecret** in the Password to unprotect sheet box.

10. Turn on the Select locked cells, Select unlocked cells, Insert rows, and Sort options and click OK.

11. Confirm the password and click OK again.

12. Save changes and leave the file open to use in the next Try It.

The Name box

Protecting a Worksheet

- Even if you activate worksheet protection, the cells you have unlocked are not protected.

    ✓ Changes can still be made to those cells.

- You can also prevent changes to objects, such as clip art or shapes, hyperlinks, PivotTables, and scenarios, which are stored variations of a worksheet.

- Use the options on the Protect Sheet dialog box to prevent certain actions, such as formatting, inserting columns and rows, deleting columns and rows, sorting, and filtering.

- You can password-protect the sheet so that no one can unprotect the worksheet accidentally.

    • If you forget the password, you will not be able to unprotect the worksheet later on.

    • However, you can copy the data to another, unprotected worksheet, to start over.

    • Passwords are case sensitive.

Try It! Protecting a Worksheet

1 In the ETry20_studentfirstname_ studentlastname file, select the Order Form tab, if necessary.

2 Click the Review tab and click the Protect Sheet button 📖.

3 Type **mysecret** in the Password to unprotect sheet box.

4 Make sure that the Select unlocked cells option is the only one turned on in the Allow all users of this worksheet to section, then click OK.

5 Type **mysecret** again to confirm the password and click OK.

6 Save changes and leave the file open to use in the next Try It.

Protect Sheet dialog box

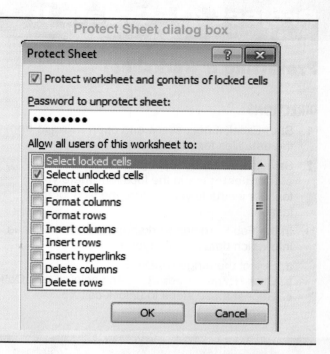

Protecting a Workbook

■ You can protect an entire workbook against certain kinds of changes.

■ By applying this protection, you can prevent worksheets from being added, moved, hidden, unhidden, renamed, or deleted.

■ You can also prevent a workbook's window from being resized or repositioned.

■ You can add a password from the Protect Structure and Windows dialog box. A password will prevent users from changing the protection level of a workbook.

■ If you want to share a workbook with others, and track the changes they make, you can still protect the workbook so that they can't erase the change history.

✓ Note: You will learn how to protect a workbook's structure in Lesson 33.

Try It! Protecting a Workbook

1 In the ETry20_studentfirstname_studentlast name file, select the Order Form tab, if necessary.

2 Click the Review tab and click the Protect Workbook button 📖.

3 To protect the workbook's window, select Windows.

4 Type **secret** in the Password box and click OK.

5 Type **secret** again to confirm the password and click OK.

6 Close ETry20_studentfirstname_studentlast name, saving all changes, and exit Excel.

Project 41—Create It

Protecting a Worksheet

DIRECTIONS

1. Start Excel, if necessary, and open **EProj41** from the data files for this lesson.
2. Save the file as **EProj41_studentfirstname_ studentlastname** in the location where your teacher instructs you to store the files for this lesson.
3. In the Feb Earnings worksheet, unlock the areas into which data may be typed:
   a. Select the range **D9:D23**.
   b. Click **Home** > **Format** 🔳 and select **Lock Cell**.
   c. Repeat these steps to unlock cell **A5**.

4. Protect the Feb Earnings worksheet so that only you can make changes:
   a. Click **Review** > **Protect Sheet** 🔳.
   b. Type **protection** in the Password to unprotect sheet box.
   c. Make sure that the Select unlocked cells option is the only one turned on in the Allow all users of this worksheet to section, then click **OK**.
   d. Confirm the password by typing **protection** again and click **OK**.
5. Click cell **C11** and try typing **$850**.
6. Click **OK** to close the warning box.
7. Close the workbook, saving all changes, and exit Excel.

Project 42—Apply It

Protecting Data

DIRECTIONS

1. Start Excel, if necessary, and open **EProj42** from the data files for this lesson.
2. Save the file as **EProj42_studentfirstname_ studentlastname** in the location where your teacher instructs you to store the files for this lesson.
3. In the Feb Earnings worksheet, unprotect the worksheet.
   a. Click **Review** > **Unprotect sheet** 🔳.
   b. Type **protection** in the Password box and click **OK**.
4. Edit the worksheet.
   a. Click cell **C11** and type **$850**.
   b. Click cell **B17** and type **Mary Williams**.
   c. Click cell **C17** and type **$750**.
5. Protect the worksheet again; this time turn off the **Select locked cells** option and do not set a password.

6. Type the sales amounts in column D that are shown in Figure 20-2.
7. Copy the **Feb Earnings** worksheet, place it before the **Comm-Bonus** worksheet, and name it **Mar Earnings**.
8. Change the text in cell **A5** to **March Earnings Report**.
9. Try to make an entry in any cell in the table other than in the Sales column to see if the cells are still locked.
10. Make an entry in the Sales column to see if the cells are unlocked, and then delete all the entries in the Sales column.
11. **With your teacher's permission**, print the Feb Earnings worksheet.
12. Close the workbook, saving all changes, and exit Excel.

Figure 20-2

Marcus Furniture

January Earnings Report

ASSOCIATE	BASE SALARY	SALES	COMM. RATE	COMM. AMT.	BONUS	TOTAL EARNINGS
Bob Walraven	$1,000.00	$7,437.52	5%	$371.88	$0.00	$1,371.88
Mike Davis	$1,000.00	$11,265.93	9%	$1,013.93	$350.00	$2,363.93
Bill Mergenthal	$700.00	$4,768.06	2%	$95.36	$0.00	$795.36
Pete Sanger	$850.00	$9,872.14	7%	$691.05	$250.00	$1,791.05
Dorothy Bishop	$750.00	$5,194.58	3%	$155.84	$0.00	$905.84
Mary La Rue	$1,100.00	$10,615.00	8%	$849.20	$300.00	$2,249.20
Ernest Dedmon	$1,000.00	$7,920.19	5%	$396.01	$0.00	$1,396.01
Karen Frisch	$750.00	$4,050.03	2%	$81.00	$0.00	$831.00
Pat Kawalski	$900.00	$3,596.00	1%	$35.96	$0.00	$935.96
Mike McCutcheon	$750.00	$13,250.00	11%	$1,457.50	$450.00	$2,657.50
Lorna Myers	$900.00	$8,560.00	6%	$513.60	$0.00	$1,413.60
James Neely	$950.00	$6,520.30	4%	$260.81	$0.00	$1,210.81
Scott Gratten	$850.00	$11,255.60	9%	$1,013.00	$350.00	$2,213.00
Betty Miller	$925.00	$12,481.35	10%	$1,248.14	$400.00	$2,573.14
Fillard Willmore	$1,000.00	$5,280.45	3%	$158.41	$0.00	$1,158.41

Chapter Assessment and Application

Project 43—Make It Your Own

Cash Flow Projection

You are the founder of a public relations firm called Jones PR. You are looking for additional capital from angel investors and other local seed capital sources, and will need to make presentations to investors soon.

One important set of data you need to present is a Cash Flow Projection. The cash flow project will forecast your company's future performance based on data you have captured from past performance. You need to embellish the raw data you'll present with some charts that show comparisons and trends.

DIRECTIONS

1. Start Excel, if necessary, and open the **EProj43** file from the data files for this project.
2. Save the file as **EProj43_studentfirstname_studentlastname** in the location where your teacher instructs you to store the files for this project.
3. Adjust worksheet formatting as you prefer.
4. Enter **16000** in cell **B4**. Notice that previously applied formatting rules make the entries in cells B7:C7 turn red.
5. Select the range **A12:N12** and insert a **Line with Markers** chart.
   a. Move the chart to its own sheet called **Comparison**.
   b. Return to the Cash Flow worksheet, and select and copy the range **A38:N38**.
   c. Return to the Comparison worksheet and paste the copied data into the chart.
   d. With the chart selected, click **Chart Tools Design > Layout 1**.
   e. Add **Receipts vs. Cash Out** as a centered overlay title for the chart.
   f. Edit the chart series so that the ranges **C12:N12** and **C38:N38** on the Cash Flow sheet are charted, omitting the blank cells in column B.
   g. Specify the range **C6:N6** on the Cash Flow sheet for the X axis labels. The resulting chart should resemble Illustration A.

6. Return to the Cash Flow worksheet and select the range **A38:N38** again and insert a **Scatter with Only Markers** chart.
   a. Move the chart to its own sheet called **Trend**.
   b. Edit the chart series so that the range **C38:N38** on the Cash Flow sheet is charted, omitting the blank cell in column B.
   c. Specify the range **C6:N6** on the Cash Flow sheet for the X axis labels, making sure that cell **A38** is specified as the series name, and hide the Y axis label.
   d. Add **Cash Out Trend** as a centered overlay title for the chart.
   e. Make sure that data labels appear to the right of the data points on the chart.
   f. Add a Linear trendline to the chart to show the trend for cash out over time. The finished chart should look like Illustration B.

      ✓ Use the Trendline button drop-down list in the Analysis group of the (Chart Tools) Layout tab to add predefined trendlines in a chart.

7. Apply a coordinating chart style to each of the charts.
8. Lock all cells on the Cash Flow sheet.
9. Protect the Cash Flow worksheet, preventing the selection of locked cells, with the password **trend**.
10. **With your teacher's permission**, print the chart sheet.
11. Close the workbook, saving all changes, and exit Excel.

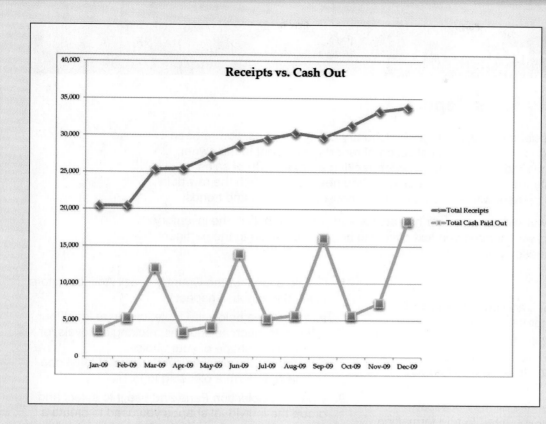

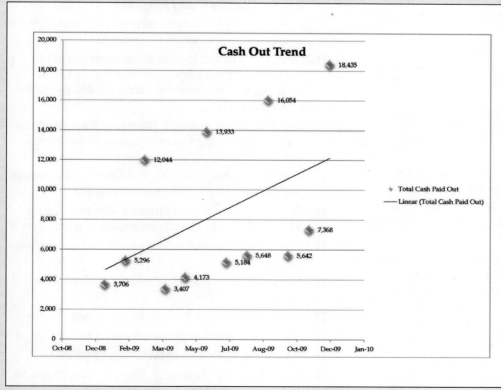

Project 44—Master It

Daily Sales Report

As assistant sales manager for Country Crazy Antiques, you've been asked to put together a collection of reports to present to the owner. You need to create a template for tracking a day's worth of sales. You update the third quarter sales data. You need to embellish the raw data you'll present with some charts that show comparisons and trends.

The warehouse manager has also asked you to embellish the inventory report with shapes and text effects to help call attention to the pertinent information before the next meeting.

DIRECTIONS

1. Start Excel, if necessary, and open the **EProj44** file from the data files for this lesson.

2. Save the file as **EProj44_studentfirstname_ studentlastname** in the location where your teacher instructs you to store the files for this project.

3. The existing worksheet has all the necessary columns and totals, but you need to add formatting.

   a. Add the **Green, Accent 1, Lighter 80%** fill to cells A1:O50.

   b. Select rows 1-4 and fill with **Gold, Accent 3, Lighter 60%**.

   c. Select cell **E2**, and apply the **Consolas** font, size **20**, in bold.

   d. Select range **B8:K8** and apply the **Gold, Accent 3, Lighter 80%** fill. With the range selected, use format painter to apply the formats to range **B9:K33**.

   e. Select range **B7:K7** and increase the font size, then add a border of your choice.

4. Adjust column widths as necessary and save your changes. The completed worksheet should look similar to Illustration A.

5. Create a template from the workbook and save it in the location where your teacher instructs you to store the files for this lesson. Use the file name **EProj44a_studentfirstname_studentlastname**.

6. Open **EProj44a** from the data files for this lesson.

7. Save the file as **EProj44a_studentfirstname_ studentlastname** in the location where your teacher instructs you to store the files for this project.

8. Create a logo for the Country Crazy Antiques store using the various shapes:

   a. In the area below the table, create at least four objects, such as squares, rectangles, ovals, or any other shape of your choice.

   b. Combine the objects, overlapping at least one object, to form a pleasing logo.

9. Open the Selection Pane and use it to select and group the individual shapes you used to create a logo for Country Crazy Antiques.

10. Apply various fill, outline, and shape effect styles to create a logo you feel represents the business.

11. Move the finished logo to the area at the left of the Country Crazy Antiques title and resize as necessary to fit within the range A1:A6, as shown in Illustration B.

12. Insert a banner from the Stars and Banners group under the Country Crazy Antiques title in rows 4 and 5.

13. Add the text **Inventory as of 6/10/11** to the banner you created. Format the text as you like.

14. Select the banner and format it with the **Subtle Effect-Green, Accent 1**, as shown in Illustration B.

15. Insert a **Rounded Rectangular Callout** from the callouts group.

16. Add the following text to the callout: **End table sale was held 6/1–6/3**.

17. Apply the **Subtle Effect-Green, Accent 1**.

18. Apply the **Preset 2** shape effect.

19. Rotate the callout as shown in Illustration B.

20. Apply the **Gold, Accent 3, Lighter 40%** shape fill.

21. Adjust column widths as necessary.

22. **With your teacher's permission**, print the chart sheet.

23. Close the workbook, saving all changes, and exit Excel.

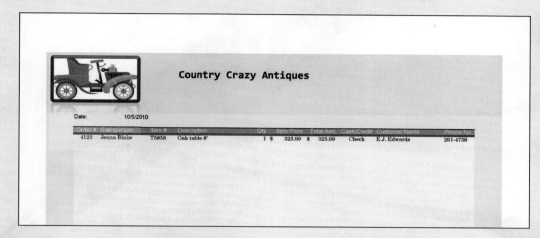

Illustration A

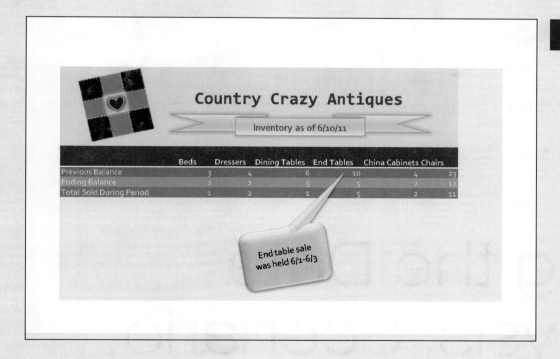

Illustration B

Chapter 3

Using the Data Analysis, Scenario, and Worksheet Auditing Features

Lesson 21
Inserting Functions and
Using Logical Functions
Projects 45-46

- Using Insert Function
- Creating an IF Function
- Creating SUMIF and AVERAGEIF Functions
- Creating SUMIFS and AVERAGEIFS Functions

Lesson 22
Working with Absolute
References and Using
Financial Functions
Projects 47-48

- Using Absolute, Relative, and Mixed References
- Using Financial Functions

Lesson 23
Creating and Interpreting
Financial Statements
Projects 49-50

- Loading the Analysis Toolpak Add-On
- Calculating a Moving Average
- Calculating Growth Based on a Moving Average
- Using Trendlines
- Charting the Break-Even Point with a Line Chart

Lesson 24
Creating Scenarios
and Naming Ranges
Projects 51-52

- Creating a Scenario Using the Scenario Manager
- Naming a Range
- Creating a Scenario Summary

Lesson 25
Finding and Fixing
Errors in Formulas
Projects 53-54

- Using Formula Error Checking
- Understanding Error Messages
- Showing Formulas
- Evaluating Individual Formulas
- Using the Watch Window
- Tracing Precedents and Dependents

Lesson 26
Ensuring Data Integrity
Projects 55-56

- Turning Off AutoComplete
- Controlling Data Entry with Data Validation
- Circling Invalid Data
- Copying Validation Rules
- Removing Duplicate Data

End-of-Chapter Assessments
Projects 57-58

Lesson 21

Inserting Functions and Using Logical Functions

➤ What You Will Learn

Using Insert Function
Creating an IF Function
Creating SUMIF and AVERAGEIF Functions
Creating SUMIFS and AVERAGEIFS Functions

Software Skills   Excel includes logical functions that enable you to set up conditions where a calculation is performed only if the conditions are met, such as IF, SUMIF, AVERAGEIF, and so on. Such functions are somewhat more complex to set up than other functions, so you may prefer to construct them using Insert Function, a built-in utility in Excel that prompts you for the necessary arguments.

Application Skills   Your boss at Wood Hills Animal Clinic has asked you to modify the monthly sales report and create an analysis of sales based on several factors such as animal type (cat versus dog, for example) and purpose (ear infection versus flea control, for example).

What You Can Do

Using Insert Function

■   The **Insert Function** feature can help you construct functions in cases where either you don't know which function to use or you don't remember what arguments it takes.

■ Insert Function helps in two ways:

- It allows you to look up functions based on what they do.

● It prompts you for the arguments needed for the chosen function.

Try It! Inserting a Function

1 Start Excel and open **ETry21** from the data files for this lesson.

2 Save the document as **ETry21_ studentfirstname_studentlastname** in the location where your teacher has instructed you to save your work.

3 On the IF worksheet tab, type **Total** in cell A13.

4 Click cell B13, and click the Insert Function button **𝑓𝑥** on the formula bar. The Insert Function dialog box opens.

Click the Insert Function button

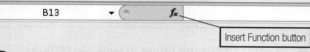

| B13 | ▼ | 𝑓𝑥 | |

Insert Function button

5 In the Search for a Function box, type **addition** and press ENTER or click Go.

✓ We actually already know that we want the SUM function in this case; step 5 is just for practice.

6 In the list of functions that appears, click SUM, and read the description of it at the bottom of the dialog box.

7 Click OK. The Function Arguments dialog box opens. There are text boxes for each of the arguments.

✓ The SUM function has only one required argument. The labels for required arguments appear bold.

8 Confirm that the Number1 argument displays B5:B12.

✓ If Excel guessed at the range incorrectly, you could manually correct it, or you could select the range yourself. You can click the Collapse Dialog Box button to the right of the argument to get the dialog box out of the way, select the desired range, and then click the Expand Dialog Box button or press Enter to bring the dialog box back.

Fill in the arguments for the SUM function

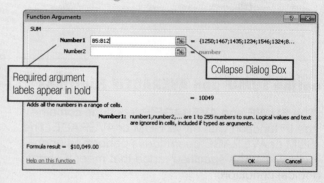

9 Click OK. The formula result appears in the cell. Save changes and leave the workbook open to use in the next Try It.

Creating an IF Function

■ **Logical functions** enable you to set up yes/no questions, and then perform one action or another based on the answer

■ **IF** is the simplest of the logical functions. It has three arguments:

- The logical condition
- What to do if it is true
- What to do if it is false

■ For example, suppose that if cell A1 contains 100, you want cell B1 to show "Perfect Score." Otherwise B1 should show "Thanks for Playing." To achieve this, you would place the following function in B1:

IF(A1=100,"Perfect Score","Thanks for Playing")

■ Notice that the text strings are enclosed in quotation marks, and that commas separate the arguments.

■ You can use Insert Function to enter the arguments instead of typing them manually if you prefer.

Try It!   Inserting an IF Function

1 In ETry21_studentfirstname_studentlastname, on the IF worksheet tab, click cell C5.

2 Click Insert Function.

3 In the Select a Function list, click IF.

4 Click OK. The Function Arguments dialog box opens.

5 In the Logical test box, type **B5>=1000**.

6 In the Value_if_true box, type **B5*0.05**.

7 In the Value_if_false box, type **B5*0.02**.

8 Click OK. The function is placed in cell C5.

9 Copy the function from cell C5 to the range C6:C12. Save changes and leave the workbook open to use in the next Try It.

✓ Use any copy method you like. You can drag the fill handle or use the Copy and Paste commands.

Enter the arguments for the IF function

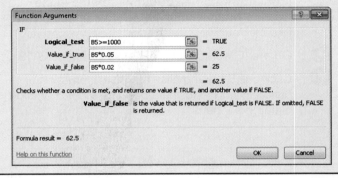

Creating SUMIF and AVERAGEIF Functions

■ The **SUMIF** and **AVERAGEIF** functions combine the IF function with either SUM or AVERAGE. The SUM or AVERAGE operation is performed upon cells within the specified range that meet a certain logical condition.

■ The syntax is:

=SUMIF(range,criteria,sum_range)

■ In some cases the range to evaluate (*range*) and the range to calculate (*sum_range*) are the same. In that case, you can omit the *sum_range* argument.

■ To specify that a criterion not be a certain value, precede the value with <>. For example, to exclude records where the value is 500, you would use <>500 as the criterion.

■ AVERAGEIF works the same way, with the same types of arguments.

Try It!   Inserting a SUMIF Function

1 In ETry21_studentfirstname_studentlastname, click the SUMIF tab.

2 Click cell B15, and click Insert Function.

3 Type **SUMIF** and click Go.

4 Click SUMIF in the list of functions, if necessary, and click OK.

5 In the Range box, type **D4:D13**.

6 In the Criteria box, type **Yes**.

✓ Quotation marks around the criteria are required, even if the criteria are numeric. Insert Function automatically puts quotation marks around the criteria for you.

7 In the Sum Range box, type **C4:C13**.

8 Click OK. The result ($802.00) appears in cell B15. Save changes and leave the workbook open to use in the next Try It.

Enter the arguments for the SUMIF function

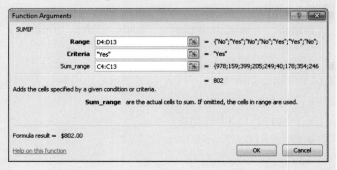

Creating SUMIFS and AVERAGEIFS Functions

- The **SUMIFS** and **AVERAGEIFS** functions are the same as SUMIF and AVERAGEIF except they allow multiple criteria.

- For the function to be evaluated as true, all the criteria must be met.

Try It!   Inserting an AVERAGEIFS Function

1 In ETry21_studentfirstname_studentlast name, in cell A17 in the SUMIF worksheet, type **Avg Due for Dog Items**.

2 Click cell B17, and click Insert Function.

3 Type **AVERAGEIFS** and click Go.

4 Click AVERAGEIFS in the function list, if necessary, and click OK.

5 In the Average_range box, type **C4:C13**.

6 In the Criteria_range1 box, type **D4:D13**.

7 In the Criteria1 box, type **No**.

8 In the Criteria_range2 box, type **E4:E13**.

9 In the Criteria2 box, type **Dog**.

10 Click OK. The function appears in the cell.

11 Close the workbook, saving all changes, and exit Excel.

Enter the arguments for the AVERAGEIFS function

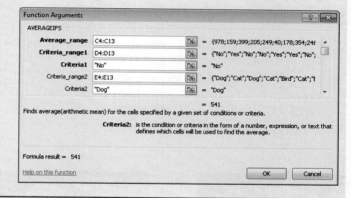

Project 45—Create It

Pet Drug Sales

DIRECTIONS

1. Start Excel, if necessary, and open EProj45 from the data files for this lesson.

2. Save the file as **EProj45_studentfirstname_ studentlastname** in the location where your teacher instructs you to store the files for this lesson.

3. Open the header area (**Insert > Header & Footer** 🖼) and type your full name on the left and today's date on the right. Click below the header, and then click **View > Normal** ▦ to return to Normal view of the worksheet.

4. In cell D99, type the formula, **=SUM(K8:K94)** to compute the total sales revenues.

5. Use Insert Function to create a formula in cell D100 to sum the sales from dog products:

   a. Click cell **D100**.

   b. Click **Insert Function** on the formula bar. The Insert Function dialog box opens.

   c. Click **SUMIF** and click **OK**.

   ✓ Scroll down in the list of functions if necessary to find SUMIF.

   d. In the Function Arguments dialog box, for the Range argument, type **C8:C94**.

   e. In the Criteria argument, type **"Dog"**.

   ✓ Typing the quotation marks is optional; if you do not type them, Excel will add them for you automatically.

   f. In the Sum_range argument, type **K8:K94**.

   g. Click **OK**. Cell D100 displays $157,691.75.

6. Use the same process as in step 5 to sum the sales of cat products in cell D101.

✓ *The function to be placed in cell D101 is identical to the one in cell D100 except it uses Cats rather than Dogs.*

7. Use Insert Function to create a formula in cell D103 to sum the sales from flea products:

   a. Click cell **D103**.
   b. Click **Insert Function** on the formula bar. The Insert Function dialog box opens.
   c. Click **SUMIF** and click **OK**.
   d. In the Function Arguments dialog box, for the Range argument, type **B8:B94**.
   e. In the Criteria argument, type **"Flea"**.
   f. In the Sum_range argument, type **K8:K94**.
   g. Click **OK**. Cell D103 displays $18,630.10.

8. Complete the functions for cells **D104** and **D105** the same way as in step 7. For cell D104, use **"Flea and Tick"** as the Critieria argument. For cell D105, use **"Heartworm"** as the Criteria argument.

9. Complete the functions for cells **D108:D114** using the same methods as in steps 5–8 except use **AVERAGE** and **AVERAGEIF** functions.

10. In cell **D106**, type **=D99-SUM(D103:D105)**.

11. In cell **D115**, enter an **AVERAGEIFS** function that averages the values that are not Flea, Flea and Tick, or Heartworm:

    a. Click cell **D115**.
    b. Click **Insert Function** on the formula bar. The Insert Function dialog box opens.
    c. Type **AVERAGEIFS** and click **Go**.
    d. Click **AVERAGEIFS** in the function list and click **OK**.
    e. In the Average_range argument, type **K8:K94**.
    f. In the Criteria_range1 argument, type **B8:B94**.
    g. In the Criteria1 argument, type **"<>Flea"**.

    ✓ *Make sure you put the <> inside the quotation marks.*

    h. In the Criteria_range2 argument, type **B8:B94**.
    i. In the Criteria2 argument, type **"<>Flea and Tick"**.
    j. In the Criteria_range3 argument, type **B8:B94**.
    k. In the Criteria3 argument, type **"<>Heartworm"**.
    l. Click **OK**.

12. **With your teacher's permission**, print cells **A98:E117**.

13. Close the workbook, saving all changes, and exit Excel.

Figure 21-1

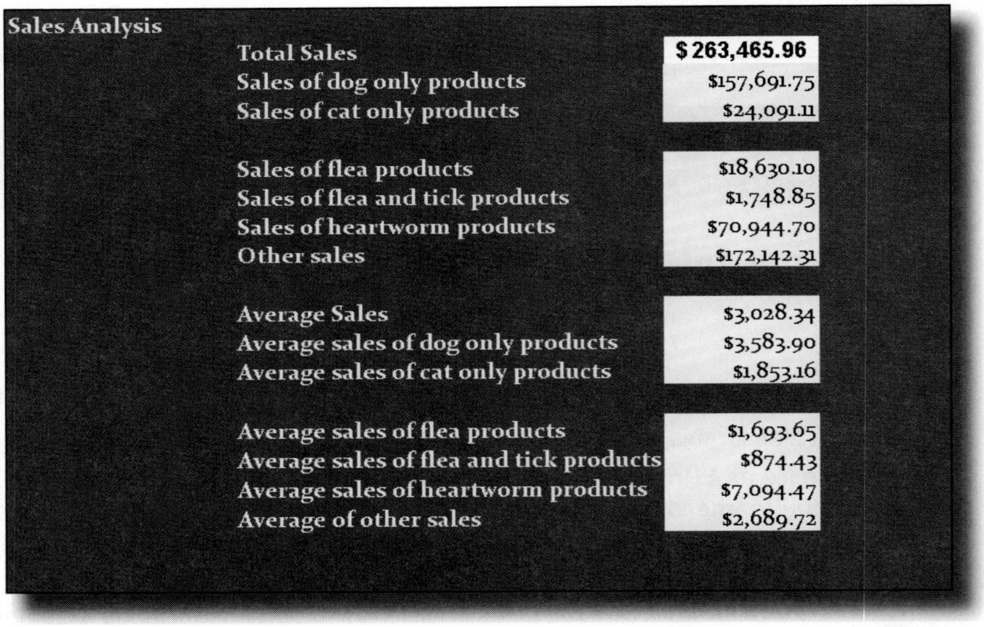

Sales Analysis

Total Sales	$263,465.96
Sales of dog only products	$157,691.75
Sales of cat only products	$24,091.11
Sales of flea products	$18,630.10
Sales of flea and tick products	$1,748.85
Sales of heartworm products	$70,944.70
Other sales	$172,142.31
Average Sales	$3,028.34
Average sales of dog only products	$3,583.90
Average sales of cat only products	$1,853.16
Average sales of flea products	$1,693.65
Average sales of flea and tick products	$874.43
Average sales of heartworm products	$7,094.47
Average of other sales	$2,689.72

Project 46—Apply It

Pet Store Sales

DIRECTIONS

1. Start Excel, if necessary, and open **EProj46** from the data files for this lesson.

2. Save the file as **EProj46_studentfirstname_ studentlastname** in the location where your teacher instructs you to store the files for this lesson.

3. Open the header area and type your full name on the left and insert today's date on the right.

4. In cell **D62**, use the **SUMIF** function to compute the total sales for **Alice Harper**.

5. In cell **D63**, use the **SUMIF** function to compute the total sales for **Bob Cook**.

6. In cell **E62**, use the **AVERAGEIF** function to compute the average sale for **Alice Harper**.

7. In cell **E63**, use the **AVERAGEIF** function to compute the average sale for **Bob Cook**.

8. In cell **D66**, use **SUMIFS** to compute the total fish sales for **Alice Harper**.

9. In cell **D67**, use **SUMIFS** to compute the total fish sales for **Bob Cook**.

10. In cell **E66**, use **SUMIFS** to compute the total accessory sales for **Alice Harper**.

11. In cell **E67**, use **SUMIFS** to compute the total accessory sales for **Bob Cook**.

12. In cell **D70**, use **AVERAGEIFS** to calculate the average fish sale for **Alice Harper**.

13. In cell **D71**, use **AVERAGEIFS** to calculate the average accessory sale for **Bob Cook**.

14. Apply **Accounting Format** with two decimal places to all the functions you created.

15. Adjust column widths as needed.

16. **With your teacher's permission**, print cells **B52:E71**. The printout should look similar to Figure 21-2.

17. Close the workbook, saving all changes, and exit Excel.

Figure 21-2

Sales Recap			
Dogs sold		3	
Cats sold		2	
Fish sold		9	
Pet sales	$	1,696.37	
Feed sales	$	200.71	
Accessories	$	464.16	
	Total Sales		**Average Sales**
Alice Harper	$	1,059.37	$ 48.15
Bob Cook	$	1,301.87	$ 72.33
	Total Fish Sales		**Total Accessories Sales**
Alice Harper	$	135.15	$ 297.96
Bob Cook	$	17.22	$ 166.20
	Average Fish Sales		**Average Accessories Sales**
Alice Harper	$	22.53	$ 27.09
Bob Cook	$	5.74	$ 18.47

Lesson 22

Working with Absolute References and Using Financial Functions

➤ What You Will Learn

Using Absolute, Relative, and Mixed References
Using Financial Functions

Software Skills   Usually when you create a function, the cell references are relative. When you copy the function to another cell, the cell references change in relation to the new location. Sometimes, though, you may not want the cell reference to change. In cases like that, you need an absolute reference. Excel enables you to create relative, absolute, or mixed references as needed. Absolute references come in handy when you are creating functions that calculate interest rates, payments, loan periods, and other financial information.

Application Skills   The manager at Sally's shoes wants to analyze the potential revenue from various sales scenarios per month. She knows that ladies want to purchase shoes for a lower price, but a few people want the high end style and are willing to pay the price for a unique designer shoe. Should the manager focus on more customers purchasing lower priced shoes, or on fewer customers purchasing higher priced shoes? You have been tasked with creating a worksheet to analyze the potential revenue from these scenarios. You will use financial functions to analyze some loan scenarios for expanding the business.

What You Can Do

Using Absolute, Relative, and Mixed References

- When you create a formula and then copy or move the formula, a **relative reference** changes to reflect the new position.

- For example, in Figure 22-1, cell D3 contains the formula =B3+C3. If you copy that formula to cell D4, it will automatically change to =B4+C4. It increments the row number by one because the copy is being placed one row below the original.

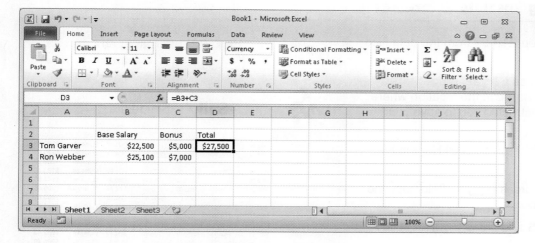

Figure 22-1

- Cell references are relative by default in Excel; you do not need to do anything special to create a relative cell reference.

- An **absolute reference** to a cell locks the cell's reference when the formula is moved or copied. Absolute references are created by placing a dollar sign ($) before both the row and the column of the cell reference, like this: $B$3.

- For example, in Figure 22-2, in cell C5, the following formula appears: =B5+$B$1. If you copy that formula to cell C6, the reference to B5 will change because it is relative, but the reference to B1 will not because it is absolute. The resulting formula in cell C6 will be =B6+$B$1.

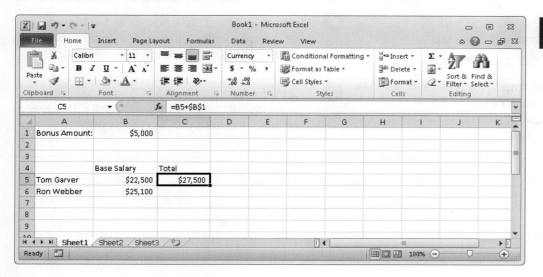

Figure 22-2

- A **mixed reference** is one in which only one dimension is absolute. For example, $B1 locks the column but not the row, and B$1 locks the row but not the column.

- To create absolute or mixed references, you can manually type the dollar signs into the formulas in the appropriate places.

- You can also toggle a cell reference among all the possible combinations of absolute, relative, and mixed by pressing F4 when the insertion point is within the cell reference.

Try It!   Creating Absolute References

1. Start Excel and open **ETry22** from the data files for this lesson.

2. Save the document as **ETry22_studentfirstname_studentlastname** in the location where your teacher has instructed you to save your work.

3. On the Taxes worksheet, click cell H3 and type =G3*$A$18.

4. Select cell H3 and press CTRL + C to copy the formula to the Clipboard.

5. Select cells H4:H15 and press CTRL + V to paste the formula into those cells.

6. Browse the contents of several of the pasted cells to confirm that the reference to A18 remained absolute. Save changes and leave the workbook open to use in the next Try It.

The reference to the Total is relative; the reference to the Tax rate is absolute

	H15		fx	=G15*$A$18			
	A	B	C	D	E	F	G	H
1				Sally's Shoes				
2		Clarks	Easy Spirit	Converse	Bali	Sketchers	Total	Total Taxes
3	January	$865.00	$657.00	$357.00	$456.00	$321.00	$2,656.00	$232.40
4	February	$561.00	$358.00	$159.00	$789.00	$654.00	$2,521.00	$220.59
5	March	$891.00	$159.00	$456.00	$321.00	$789.00	$2,616.00	$228.90
6	April	$236.00	$753.00	$789.00	$159.00	$159.00	$2,096.00	$183.40
7	May	$458.00	$159.00	$321.00	$357.00	$357.00	$1,652.00	$144.55
8	June	$695.00	$456.00	$582.00	$159.00	$456.00	$2,348.00	$205.45
9	July	$498.00	$987.00	$471.00	$753.00	$258.00	$2,967.00	$259.61
10	August	$285.00	$123.00	$693.00	$852.00	$123.00	$2,076.00	$181.65
11	September	$795.00	$951.00	$214.00	$741.00	$852.00	$3,553.00	$310.89
12	October	$125.00	$357.00	$236.00	$369.00	$456.00	$1,543.00	$135.01
13	November	$952.00	$458.00	$785.00	$196.00	$951.00	$3,342.00	$292.43
14	December	$159.00	$852.00	$985.00	$852.00	$528.00	$3,376.00	$295.40
15	Total	$6,520.00	$6,270.00	$6,048.00	$6,004.00	$5,904.00	$30,746.00	$2,690.28
16								

Try It!   Creating Mixed References

1. In **ETry22_studentfirstname_studentlastname**, click the Area worksheet tab.

2. In cell C5, type =$B5*C$4.

3. Select cell C5 and drag the fill handle down to fill cells C6:C9 with that formula.

4. Click in any filled cell and look at the formula bar. Notice that the relative references changed and that the absolute references remained the same.

5. Copy the formula from cell C5 into the remainder of the range (through cell F9). Save changes and leave the workbook open to use in the next Try It.

Using Financial Functions

- Excel includes a set of financial functions that can calculate variables in a loan or investment equation.

- They are considered a set because each function solves for a particular variable, and the other pieces of information are arguments within that function.

Function	Purpose	Required Arguments	Optional Arguments
PMT	Calculates a loan payment	RATE, NPER, PV,	FV, TYPE
RATE	Calculates a loan rate	NPER, PMT, PV	FV, TYPE, GUESS
NPER	Calculates the number of periods in a loan	RATE, PMT, PV	FV, TYPE
PV	Calculates the present value (beginning balance)	RATE, NPER, PMT	FV, TYPE
FV	Calculates the future value (ending balance)	RATE, NPER, PMT	PV, TYPE

- For example, if you know the loan length (60 months), the loan rate (5.9% per year), and the loan amount ($20,000), you can calculate your monthly payment with the PMT function:

$$=PMT(.059/12,60,20000)$$

✓ Note that you divide the interest rate by 12 because the interest rate is per year, and a payment is made monthly.

- Alternatively, suppose you want to know how much money you can afford to borrow at 7% interest for 60 months if you can pay $250 a month:

$$=PV(0.07/12,60,250)$$

- To find out how much an investment made now will be worth later, such as buying a savings bond, use the FV function. For example, suppose you buy a $10,000 savings bond that pays 5% interest, compounded monthly, and matures in 20 years:

$$=FV(0.05/12,20*12,0,10000)$$

✓ The third argument (PMT) is 0 because you don't make any payments after the initial investment of $10,000.

- In actual usage, you would probably want to put those values into cells, and then reference the cells in the functions rather than hard-coding the actual numbers in. That way, you could change the variables and see different results without modifying the functions themselves.

Try It!   **Using Financial Functions**

1 In the **ETry22_studentfirstname_studentlastname** file, click the Functions worksheet tab.

2 In cell B3, type **60,000**.

3 In cell B4, type **.065**.

4 In cell B5, type **1**.

5 In cell B6, type **60**.

6 In cell B8, type **=PMT(B4/12,-B6,B3)**.

✓ Notice the − preceding B6; this is to make the value negative, so the result in B* will be positive.

7 In cell B12, type **=PV(B13/12,B15,-B17)**. B17 is referred to as a negative so the formula result will be positive. The same is true for B26 in the next step, too. In cell B32, type **=FV(B35,B28*B29,,-B26)**.

✓ Notice that there are two commas in a row in this function, because the PMT argument is blank.

8 Close the workbook, saving all changes, and exit Excel.

Project 47—Create It

Shoe Sales Evaluation

DIRECTIONS

1. Start Excel, if necessary, and open **EProj47** from the data files for this lesson. Save the file as **EProj47_studentfirstname_studentlastname** in the location where your teacher instructs you to store the files for this lesson.

2. Open the header area and type your full name on the left and insert today's date on the right. Click below the header, and then click **View > Normal** to return to normal viewing.

3. In cell **C5**, type =$B5*C$4.

4. Use the Fill feature to fill in the rest of the chart, down to cell **F9**.

5. Select cells **A3:F19** and press CTRL + C to copy.

6. Click in cell **A13** and press CTRL + V to paste.

7. Change the values in cells **C14:F14** to **35**, **50**, **75**, and **100**, from left to right.

8. Edit the formula in cell **C15** to =$B15*C$14.

9. Copy the formula from cell **C15** into the rest of the chart, replacing the previous values in each cell.

10. **With your teacher's permission**, print one copy of the worksheet. See Figure 22-3.

11. Close the workbook, saving all changes, and exit Excel.

Figure 22-3

Sally's Shoes

	Price Points			
	$45	**$65**	**$85**	**$125**
50	2,250.00	3,250.00	4,250.00	6,250.00
75	3,375.00	4,875.00	6,375.00	9,375.00
100	4,500.00	6,500.00	8,500.00	12,500.00
125	5,625.00	8,125.00	10,625.00	15,625.00
150	6,750.00	9,750.00	12,750.00	18,750.00

Number of Sales

	Price Points			
	$35	**$50**	**$75**	**$100**
50	1,750.00	2,500.00	3,750.00	5,000.00
75	2,625.00	3,750.00	5,625.00	7,500.00
100	3,500.00	5,000.00	7,500.00	10,000.00
125	4,375.00	6,250.00	9,375.00	12,500.00
150	5,250.00	7,500.00	11,250.00	15,000.00

Number of Sales

Project 48—Apply It

Loan and Investment Analysis

DIRECTIONS

1. Start Excel, if necessary, and open **EProj48** from the data files for this lesson. Save the file as **EProj48_studentfirstname_studentlastname** in the location where your teacher instructs you to store the files for this lesson.

2. Open the header area and type your full name on the left and insert today's date on the right. Then return to Normal view.

3. In the Payment Calculation grid, calculate what the payment would be on a four-year loan of **$30,000** with a monthly interest rate of **5.25%**. Fill the numbers for the calculation into cells **B4:B6** and then reference those cells in a function in cell **B7**.

   ✓ *Make the reference to the present value negative, so that the amount in cell B7 is positive.*

4. In the Present Value Calculation grid, calculate the present value of a loan with **$800** in monthly payments at **4.35%** interest rate for **360** months.

   ✓ *Make the reference to the payment amount negative, so that the amount in cell B11 is positive.*

5. In the Compound Interest Calculation grid, calculate the future value (FV) of an investment of **$4,000** with a **3.25%** interest rate, compounded monthly, for **5** years.

   ✓ *Make the reference to the present value amount negative, so that the amount in cell B23 is positive.*

   ✓ *The Periodic interest rate is the annual interest rate (B19) divided by the number of compounding periods per year (B20).*

6. **With your teacher's permission**, print the worksheet. It should look similar Figure 22-4.

7. Close the workbook, saving all changes, and exit Excel.

Figure 22-4

Payment Calculation

Loan Amount:	$30,000
Annual Interest Rate:	5.25%
Number of Periods:	48
Payment per Period:	$694.28

Present Value Calculation

Loan Amount:	$160,703.30
Annual Interest Rate:	4.35%
Number of Periods:	360
Payment per Period:	$800.00

Compound Interest Calculation

Investment amount:	$4,000.00
Annual interest rate:	3.25%
Compounding periods/year	12
Term (years)	5
Periodic interest rate:	0.27%
Investment value at end of term:	$4,704.76
Total interest earned:	
Annual yield:	

Lesson 23

Creating and Interpreting Financial Statements

WORDS TO KNOW

Break-even point
The number of units, or individual items, you must sell to begin making a profit, given your fixed costs for the unit, cost per unit, and revenue per unit.

Moving average
A sequence of averages computed from parts of a data series. In a chart, a moving average corrects for the fluctuations in data, showing the pattern or trend more clearly.

Trendline
A graphic representation of trends in a data series, such as a line sloping upward to represent increased sales over a period of months. Trendlines are used to make predictions based on past trends; this is also called *regression analysis.*

> ➤ **What You Will Learn**

> Loading the Analysis Toolpak Add-On
> Calculating a Moving Average
> Calculating Growth Based on a Moving Average
> Using Trendlines
> Charting the Break-Even Point with a Line Chart

Software Skills   Excel contains more financial capabilities than just simple loan and investment calculation. You can use Excel to create and analyze financial statements and scenarios that include moving averages, growth calculations, and income and expense projections.

Application Skills   The owner of several small businesses has asked you to create financial statements so that he can make decisions about his main business and some of his investment accounts, as well as a side seasonal business he has. In this lesson you will set up a worksheet using Excel functions to calculate a moving average of mutual fund values. You will show growth based on a moving average. You will help the owner project income and expenses, and then show the break-even point for his seasonal side business.

What You Can Do

Loading the Analysis Toolpak Add-On

■ This lesson requires you to use the Analysis Toolpak in Excel, which is not loaded by default.

■ If you are working on a PC in a lab that is regularly used for computer classes, it may have already been loaded by a previous student.

Try It!   Determining Whether the Analysis Toolpak Add-On Is Loaded

1 Start Excel, and click the Data tab.

2 Look for a Data Analysis command. If you don't see one, the Analysis Toolpak is not loaded.

Try It!   Loading the Analysis Toolpak Add-On

1 In Excel, click File > Options.

2 Click the Add-Ins category.

3 Confirm that Manage (at the bottom of the dialog box) is set to Excel Add-ins, and click Go. The Add-Ins dialog box opens.

4 Click to place a check mark next to Analysis Toolpak.

5 Click OK.

6 Click the Data tab, and confirm that there is now an Analysis group, with a Data Analysis command in it. Leave Excel open for the next Try It.

Calculating a Moving Average

■ A **moving average** is considered more accurate than a simple average of a set of numbers in predicting future trends. A moving average is used with data that represents changes over time to smooth out short-term fluctuations and highlight the long-term trends.

■ To calculate a moving average, start with a subset of the data (for example, items 1–20 in a 100-item list) and calculate their average. That average becomes the first a data point. Then you calculate the average of items 2–21 on the list, and that average becomes the second data point. You progress through the entire list until you have a complete set of data points.

■ Calculating a moving average would be very labor-intensive by hand, so it makes sense to use a program like Excel to do the calculations.

■ Excel's Moving Average data analysis tool makes the process easy. You can specify how many numbers to use in the averaging calculation.

Try It!   Calculating a Moving Average

1 Open ETry23 from the data files for this lesson. Save the file as ETry23_studentfirstname_studentlastname in the location where your teacher instructs you to store the files for this lesson.

2 Click the Moving Average worksheet tab.

✓ This data represents the share price of mutual funds for a month.

3 Click Data > Data Analysis. The Data Analysis dialog box opens.

4 Click Moving Average and click OK. The Moving Average dialog box opens.

5 In the Input Range box, type A2:A31.

✓ You can also click the Collapse Dialog Box button next to Input Range and select the desired range.

(continued)

Try It!   **Calculating a Moving Average** *(continued)*

6 In the Interval box, type 5. This tells Excel how many numbers to average for one output.

7 In the Output Range box, type B2:B31.

✓ *You can also click the Collapse Dialog button next to Output Range and select the desired range.*

8 Select the Chart Output check box.

9 Click OK. A line chart is generated from the raw data and the moving average data.

10 Click in the chart area to select it and drag a corner to make the chart larger.

11 To see how the moving average works, click cell B8. The formula, =AVERAGE(A4:A8), shows that the average is of the data in cells A4, A5, A6, A7, and A8.

12 Save your work. Leave the workbook open to use in the next Try It.

Enter the specifications for the moving average calculation

Moving Average	? ✕
Input	
Input Range:	A2:A31	OK
☐ Labels in First Row	Cancel
Interval:	5	Help
Output options	
Output Range:	B2:B31	
New Worksheet Ply:	
New Workbook	
☑ Chart Output ☐ Standard Errors	

Calculating Growth Based on a Moving Average

■ When you have historical data, it is possible to predict what might happen in the future. You can use the GROWTH function to analyze a pattern of data from the past and create a new pattern of data for the future.

■ The GROWTH function creates a statistical prediction for the future that can be used to compare actual data with what you predicated.

✓ *It is best to base the predictions you create with the GROWTH function on stable and reliable known data.*

■ The GROWTH function arguments are [known-y], [known-x], [new known-x].
  • Known-x is the known original data.
  • Known-y is the past output based on the known-x values.
  • New known-x is the known new data.
■ Given that information, it will predict the future output based on the new known-x values.

Try It!   **Calculating Growth Based on a Moving Average**

1 In the ETry23_studentfirstname_studentlastname file, click on the Growth worksheet tab.

2 Examine the data in the worksheet and note the following:

  • The data in column A represents days of the month. Range A2:A16 is the first half of the month (the known-x), and range A19:A33 is the second half of the month (the new known-x).

  • The data in range B2:B16 is moving average data for the first half of the month (the known-y).

  • The GROWTH function will be used to predict the moving averages to be placed in cells B19:B33.

3 Click cell B19. Type =GROWTH(.

4 For the first argument, drag across cells B2:B6 to select that range. Then type a comma (,) to separate the arguments.

Try It!   **Calculating Growth Based on a Moving Average** *(continued)*

5 For the second argument, drag across cells A2:A6. Then type a comma (,) to separate the arguments.

6 For the third argument, drag across cells A19:A23. This represents 5 days that will be used to predict future growth. Then press ENTER to complete the function. The final function in cell B19 should be =GROWTH(B2:B6,A2:A6,A19:A23).

7 Copy the formula in cell B19 into cells B20:B33.

✓ Notice that starting at cell B30 an error message displays, #VALUE!. That's because the GROWTH formula in cell B30 refers to data in cell A34, and there is no data in cell A34.

8 Select B30:B33 and press DEL to clear the content of those cells. Save changes and leave the workbook open to use in the next Try It.

✓ Based on the mutual funds moving average growth experienced from the first of the month to the fifteenth of the month, you can predict that by the end of the month the mutual fund will be at the value shown in cell B29.

Using Trendlines

■ Use **trendlines** to chart the trends of a set of data and to project into the future based on the slope of the curve. Trendlines can deal with any data over time. Income and expense reports are a good example of this type of data.

Try It!   **Projecting Income and Expenses with Trendlines**

1 In the **ETry23_studentfirstname_studentlast name** file, click the Income-Expense tab.

2 Select the data range C2:D38.

3 Click Insert > Line 〰 > Line (the first chart type under 2-D). A chart displays showing the trend.

4 With the chart selected, click Chart Tools Layout > Trendline 〰 > Linear Forecast Trendline. The Add Trendline dialog box opens.

5 Click Income and click OK.

6 Click Chart Tools Layout > Trendline 〰 > Linear Forecast Trendline. Click Expense and click OK.

7 Save your work. Leave the workbook open to use in the next Try It.

Trendlines added to the chart

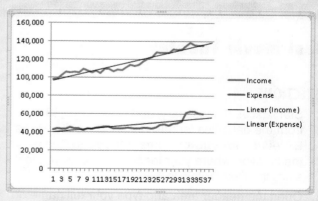

Charting the Break-Even Point with a Line Chart

- You can enter your known costs and your projected income from sales to calculate when your revenue will exceed your costs, the **break-even point**. You can create a break-even line chart based on known expenses and projected income.

- This calculation can help you analyze finances to know how much you need to sell in order to make a profit, as well as how much more you need to sell in order to make a pre-determined profit amount.

Try It!   **Charting the Break-Even Point with a Line Chart**

1 In **ETry23_studentfirstname_studentlastname**, click the Break-Even worksheet tab.

2 In cell B1, type **100**.

3 In cell B2, type **1**.

4 In cell B3, type **6**.

5 In cell B6, type **=A6*$B$2+$B$1**.

  ✓ *Notice the absolute references to cells B1 and B2.*

6 Copy the formula in cell B6 to cells B7:B30. Cell B30 should show $125.00.

7 In cell C6, type **=A6*$B$3**.

8 Copy the formula in cell C6 to cells C7:C30. Cell C30 should show $150.00.

9 In cell D6, type **=C6-B6**.

10 Copy the formula in cell D6 to cells D7:D30. Cell D30 should show $25.00

11 Select the range B5:D30 and click Insert > Line > Stacked Line (the second chart in the 2-D section).

12 Close the workbook, saving all changes, and exit Excel.

  ✓ *The point where the Profit and Revenue lines cross is the break-even point.*

Project 49—Create It

Best Movie Theater

DIRECTIONS

1. Start Excel, if necessary, and open **EProj49** from the data files for this lesson. Save the file as **EProj49_studentfirstname_studentlastname** in the location where your teacher instructs you to store the files for this lesson.

2. Open the header area and type your full name on the left and insert today's date on the right. Then return to Normal view.

3. Select **Data** > **Data Analysis** 📊. The Data Analysis dialog box opens.

  ✓ *If the Data Analysis command is not on the Data tab, see the exercise earlier in this lesson for enabling the Analysis Toolpak.*

4. Click **Moving Average** and click **OK**.

5. In the Input box, type **A2:A31**.

6. In the Interval box, type **7**.

7. In the Output box, type **B2:B31**.

8. Click the **Chart Output** check box.

9. Click **OK**. A chart appears.

10. Drag the lower right corner of the chart frame to enlarge the chart so it is more readable.

  ✓ *You can delete the function from cells B2:B7 when finished; they show an #N/A error rather than a value. This is expected.*

11. **With your teacher's permission,** print the chart. It will look similar to Figure 23-1.

12. Close the workbook, saving your changes, and exit Excel.

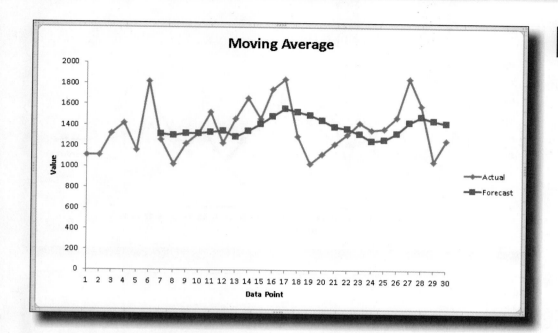

Figure 23-1

Project 50—Apply It

Rowdy Cowboy Hats

DIRECTIONS

1. Start Excel, if necessary, and open **EProj50** from the data files for this lesson. Save the file as **EProj50_studentfirstname_studentlastname** in the location where your teacher instructs you to store the files for this lesson.

2. Open the header area and type your full name on the left and insert today's date on the right. Then return to Normal view.

3. On the **Moving Average** worksheet tab, redo the moving average calculations in column B to change the interval from **7** data points to **5** data points, and to create a line chart showing the moving average.

   ✓ *You can delete the function from cells B3:B6 when finished; they show an #N/A error rather than a value. This is expected.*

4. On the **Growth** worksheet tab, in cells **B19:B33**, use the **GROWTH** function to use 5 days to predict future growth based on the moving averages in range **B2:B16**.

   ✓ *You can delete the function from B30:B33 when finished; they show a #VALUE error rather than a value. This is expected.*

5. On the **Income-Expense** worksheet tab, create a **Line** chart from the data in range **B2:D26**. Include linear trendlines for both **Income** and **Expenses**.

6. On the **Break-Even** worksheet tab, fill in the **Cost**, **Revenue**, and **Profit** columns (range **B6:D105**) with formulas that include absolute references to cells **B1**, **B2**, and **B3**.

7. Create a **Stacked Line** chart from range **B5:D105** showing the break-even point.

8. **With your teacher's permission**, print the charts from the Moving Average, Income-Expense, and Break-Even workbooks. See Figure 23-2.

9. Close the workbook, saving all changes, and exit Excel.

Figure 23-2

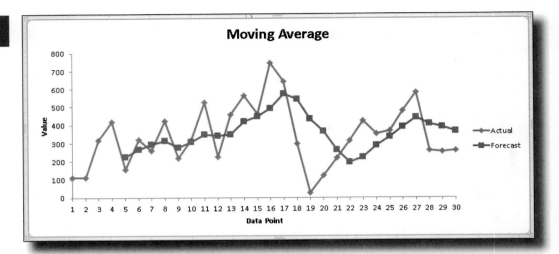

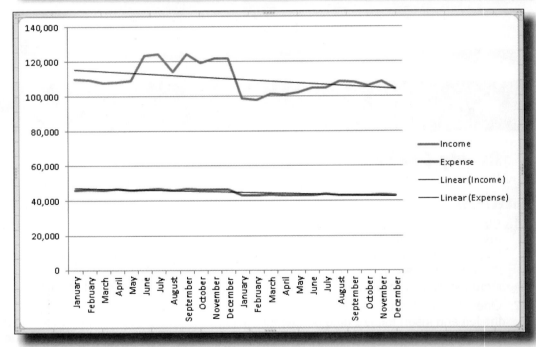

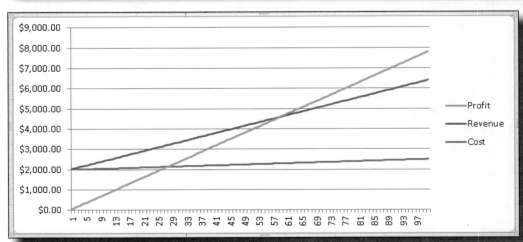

Lesson 24

Creating Scenarios and Naming Ranges

> ## What You Will Learn

Creating a Scenario Using the Scenario Manager
Naming a Range
Creating a Scenario Summary

Software Skills   With scenarios, you can create and save several versions of a worksheet based on "what-if" data. For example, you can create a best case, probable case, and worst case scenario for your company's annual sales. After you create your scenarios, you can use Report Manager to print the various versions of your data quickly.

Application Skills   A customer of Breakaway Bike Shop is in a dilemma about some bike work he would like to have done. Some work is needed right away, while other parts that are showing wear could conceivably be put off until after the winter holidays. The only problem is that your labor charge is going up in January, so the customer needs help deciding between several scenarios—doing some of the work now and putting off the rest indefinitely, doing all of the work now, or waiting until after the winter holidays to do the work. Using scenarios, you will quickly create the reports he needs to compare the costs and make his decision.

What You Can Do

Creating a Scenario Using the Scenario Manager

- Scenarios help you see possible outcomes of an unpredictable future. You can create and save versions of your worksheet data based on changing variables.
- With the Scenario Manager in Excel, you can plug in the most likely values for several possible situations, and save the scenarios with the resulting worksheet data. You can print and compare scenarios, save them, and switch between them.

WORDS TO KNOW

Scenario
A what-if analysis tool you can use to create several versions of a worksheet, based on changing variables.

Scenario Manager
Creates named scenarios and generates reports that use outlines or pivot tables. The scenario manager can create a report that summarizes any number of input cells and result cells.

Variable
An input value that changes depending on the desired outcome.

■ When you switch to a particular scenario, Excel plugs the saved values into the appropriate cells in your worksheet that represent variables and then adjusts formula results as needed.

Try It!   Creating a Scenario Using the Scenario Manager

1 Start Excel, if necessary, and open **ETry24** from the data files for this lesson.

2 Save the file as **ETry24_studentfirstname_ studentlastname** in the location where your teacher instructs you to store the files for this lesson.

3 Examine the formulas in cells B9:D13 to see how the bike cost data was determined.

✓ *Notice that named ranges have been defined for cells B2 and B3, and the names are used in the formulas in range B9:D9.*

4 Click Data > What-If Analysis > Scenario Manager.

5 Click Add.

6 In the Scenario name text box, type **Worst Case**.

7 In the Changing cells box, type **B2:B3**.

8 In the Comment section, type **Worst case scenario**, replacing the default comment.

✓ *These are the cells where you will change the input data that causes the scenario to change the value in the results cells. If the hourly rate goes up, then the cost of modifying the bikes goes up.*

9 Click OK. The Scenario Values dialog box opens. The current contents of cells B2 and B3 appear there.

10 In the 1: Hourly_labor_cost field, type **58**.

11 In the 2: Material_and_supplies_cost field, type **75**.

12 Click OK. The Scenario Manager dialog box reappears.

13 Click Show to see the results of the change.

✓ *Notice the negative profit.*

14 Add two more scenarios the same way, viewing each scenario's result after creating it:

● Add a Most Likely case in which the Hourly_labor_cost is 45 and the Material_and_supplies cost is 57.

● Add a Best Case scenario in which the Hourly_labor_cost is 37 and the Material_and_supplies cost is 52.

15 Click Close to close the Scenario Manager dialog box. Save changes and leave the workbook open to use in the next Try It.

Specify the scenario's name and the cells that will change

Specify the values to use in the cells that will change

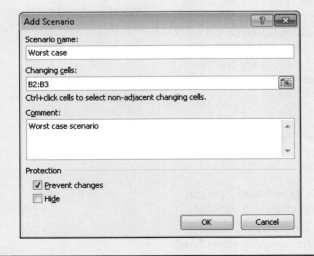

Naming a Range

- As you saw in the preceding exercise, it is sometimes helpful to give ranges descriptive names. A range can be a single cell or multiple cells.

- When a range has a name, you can use the name in formulas and functions in place of the row-and-column cell references.

- You can manually name each range by typing in the Name box on the formula bar, or you can use the naming tools on the Formulas tab. For example, to name cells based on the labels in adjacent cells, you can use Create from Selection.

Try It!   **Naming Ranges**

1 In **ETry24_studentfirstname_ studentlastname**, select cell B13.

2 Click in the Name box (on the far left end of the formula bar) and type **Beach_cruzer_profit**.

Name the selected range

Beach_cruzer_profit ▾	*fx*	=B11*B12

> Type the range name here

3 Click cell C13 and type **Off_road_profit** in the Name box.

4 Click cell D13 and type **Iron_man_profit** in the Name box.

5 Select cells A15:B15.

6 Click Formulas > Create from Selection 📋.

7 Select the Left Column check box and click OK. The name Total_Profit is assigned to cell B15. Save changes and leave the workbook open to use in the next Try It.

Creating a Scenario Summary

- If you have created many scenarios on many different sheets, the best way to view the multiple results is to create a summary sheet of all your scenarios.

- You can create a scenario summary as a worksheet or as a PivotTable. In this lesson you will create the summary as a worksheet.

Try It!   **Creating a Scenario Summary**

1 In **ETry24_studentfirstname_studentlast name**, click Data > What-If Analysis 📊 > Scenario Manager. The Scenario Manager dialog box opens.

2 Click Summary. The Scenario Summary dialog box opens.

3 In the Result cells box, type **B13,C13,D13,B15**.

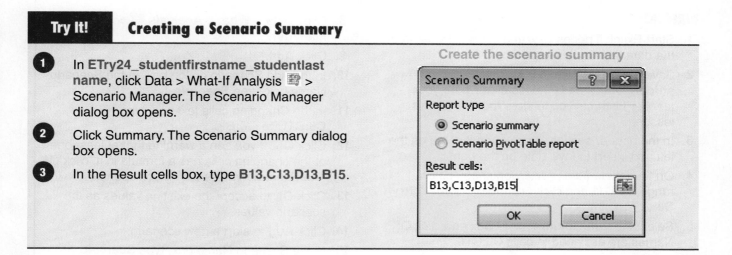

Create the scenario summary

(continued)

Try It!   **Creating a Scenario Summary** *(continued)*

4 Click OK.

✓ *A comparison summary chart appears on a new tab. Here you can view each scenario and analyze the numbers to help you decide what business decisions to make. Your summary report may look like this example.*

5 Close the workbook, saving all changes, and exit Excel.

Scenario Summary

	Current Values	Worst Case	Most Likely	Best Case
Scenario Summary				
Changing Cells:				
Hourly_labor_cost	58	58	45	37
Material_and_supplies_cost	75	75	57	52
Result Cells:				
Beach_cruzer_profit	-$1,305	-$1,305	$8,235	$12,465
Off_road_profit	-$2,024	-$2,024	$5,544	$8,998
Iron_man_profit	-$3,211	-$3,211	$4,121	$7,527
Total_profit	-$6,540	-$6,540	$17,900	$28,990

Notes: Current Values column represents values of changing cells at time Scenario Summary Report was created. Changing cells for each scenario are highlighted in gray.

Project 51—Create It

Theater Profits

DIRECTIONS

1. Start Excel, if necessary, and open **EProj51** from the data files for this lesson.

2. Save the file as **EProj51_studentfirstname_ studentlastname** in the location where your teacher instructs you to store the files for this lesson.

3. In the header section, type your full name on the left and insert today's date on the right.

4. On the **Glass Menagerie** worksheet, select range **B6:C11** and click **Formulas > Create from Selection** .

5. Select the **Left Column** check box and click **OK**. Names are assigned to cells C6:C11.

6. Select range **F6:G7** and click **Formulas > Create from Selection** .

7. Select the **Left Column** check box and click **OK**.

8. Click **Data > What If Analysis** **> Scenario Manager**.

9. Click **Add**.

10. In the Add Scenario dialog box, in the Scenario Name box, type **Scenario 1**.

11. In the Changing cells text box, type **C6:C11,E5,G6:G7**.

12. Click **OK**. If you see a warning that at least one of the changing cells has a formula in it, click **OK**. The Scenario Values dialog box opens.

13. Click **OK** to accept the existing values as the scenario values.

14. Click **Add** to start a new scenario.

15. In the Scenario Name box, type **Scenario 2**.

16. Click **OK**. If you see a warning that at least one of the changing cells has a formula in it, click OK. The Scenario Values dialog box opens.

17. Change the Ticket_price to $9.00 and click OK.
18. Click Show to show Scenario 2.
19. Click Close to close the Scenario Manager dialog box.

20. **With your teacher's permission**, print A2:H15. It should look similar to Figure 24-1.
21. Close the workbook, saving all changes, and exit Excel.

Figure 24-1

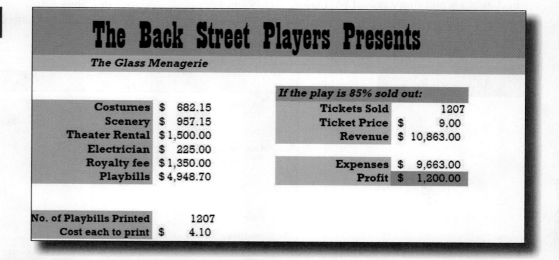

Project 52—Apply It

Repair Scenarios

DIRECTIONS

1. Start Excel, if necessary, and open EProj52 from the data files for this lesson. Save the file as EProj52_studentfirstname_studentlastname in the location where your teacher instructs you to store the files for this lesson.

2. In the header section, type your full name on the left and insert today's date on the right. Then return to Normal view.

3. Create a scenario called Minimum Replacements in which the values in the following ranges are saved as they currently appear:
   - B26:F26
   - B28:F28
   - B37:F38
   - G3

4. Create another scenario called Recommended Replacements in which these values change.
   - B26   RPL
   - C26   2
   - D26   Aurens BR321

   - E26   1
   - F26   39.25
   - B28   RPL
   - C28   2
   - D28   Aurens BI321
   - E28   .10
   - F28   4.95
   - B37   RPL
   - C37   1
   - D37   Road Warrior 18F
   - E37   .15
   - F37   25.75
   - B38   RPL
   - C38   1
   - D38   Road Warrior 18R
   - E38   .25
   - F38   28.95

5. Create another scenario called All Work After January that is identical to the Recommended Replacements scenario from step 4 except that cell G3 changes to 50.00.

✓ *The simplest way to accomplish this is to first display the changed values in the worksheet—so use the Scenario Manager to display the values associated with the Recommended Replacements scenario. Then create the new scenario, and the only value you have to edit is G3.*

6. Create a summary report with **G3** as the result cell.

7. On the Scenario Summary tab, in the header section, type your full name on the left and insert today's date on the right. Then return to Normal view.

8. **With your teacher's permission**, print the Scenario Summary worksheet. It should look similar to Figure 24-2.

9. Close the workbook, saving all changes, and exit Excel.

Figure 24-2

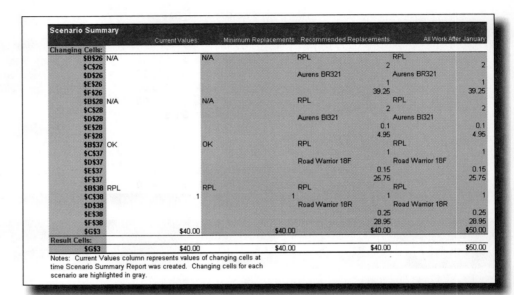

Lesson 25

Finding and Fixing Errors in Formulas

➤ **What You Will Learn**

Using Formula Error Checking
Understanding Error Messages
Showing Formulas
Evaluating Individual Formulas
Using the Watch Window
Tracing Precedents and Dependents

Software Skills If you have a problem with formulas in a large or complex worksheet, working through each formula to locate the values in the cells it references and to verify that everything is all right can be a tedious, complex job unless you use Excel's error and formula auditing features.

Application Skills It looks like the sale of your old building and the purchase of a new headquarters for the Wood Hills Animal Clinic is going to go through. Before you can get final approval for your loan, however, you must prepare a balance sheet and a profit and loss statement. You've been working on the profit and loss statement, and there's just something wrong with the numbers. Your hope is that Excel's powerful formula auditing tools can help you sort out the problem. You'll also create the commission, bonuses and earnings for Old Southern Furniture.

WORDS TO KNOW

Circular reference
A reference in a formula to the cell in which the formula resides. For example, the formula =C5 placed in C5 would be circular.

Dependents
Formulas whose results depend on the value in a cell.

Evaluate
To view the intermediate results step-by-step, as Excel solves a formula.

Error Checking
An information button on a cell. Error Checking options can contain information about an error in the cell contents.

Precedent
A cell referenced in a formula.

Watch Window
A floating window that allows you to watch the results of formulas change as you change data.

What You Can Do

Using Formula Error Checking

- When background error checking is enabled in Excel, a small triangle in the upper left corner of a cell indicates a possible error. When you select the cell, an **Error Checking** button appears. Click the Error Checking button to see a message explaining what the potential error is. See Figure 25-1.

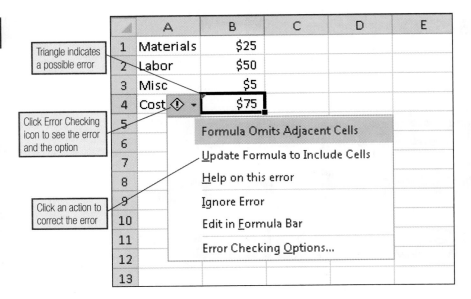

Figure 25-1

Triangle indicates a possible error

Click Error Checking icon to see the error and the option

Click an action to correct the error

✓ *If errors do not appear in Error Checking options, the feature may not be enabled. Click File > Options, click Formulas, and select the Enable background error checking check box.*

- Excel checks for the following errors:
  - Formulas that result in an error value, such as #DIV/0.
  - Formulas containing a text date entered using a two-digit year, such as =YEAR("02/20/27"), because it is not clear which century is being referenced.
  - Numbers stored as text rather than actual numbers, because this can cause sorting and other errors.
  - Formulas that are inconsistent with formulas in surrounding cells.
  - For example, if Excel notices the pattern =SUM(A2:A10), =SUM(B2:B10) in two adjacent cells, and then sees the formula =SUM(C2:C4) in another adjacent cell, it will flag it as a possible mistake because it doesn't fit the pattern of the other formulas.
  - Formulas that omit adjacent cells, as in Figure 25-1.
  - An unprotected formula, if worksheet protection is enabled.

    ✓ *If you turn on worksheet protection, all cells are protected against changes by default. You can selectively unprotect the cells you want to allow others to enter data into. However, if you unprotect a cell with a formula, Excel will see that as a possible error, because it's unusual that you would want someone else to change your formulas.*

  - A formula that refers to empty cells.
  - Invalid data entered into a cell.
  - An inconsistent formula in a calculated table column.

- When you find an error in a formula, one way in which you might need to correct it is to change the cell(s) that the formula references. For example, you might need to change the formula =SUM(D2:D10) so that it reads =SUM(D2:D12).

- When you click a cell with a formula, and then click in the formula bar, the cells referenced by the formula are outlined with colored borders. You can drag these colored borders and drop them on different cells, in order to change the cells used in the formula. You can also resize a colored border to make the formula reference more or fewer cells in that range.

Understanding Error Messages

- The following is a list of some error messages you might get if you enter data or formulas incorrectly:
  - **####** The cell contains an entry that's wider than the cell can display. In most cases, you can just widen the column to correct the problem.
  - **#VALUE!** The wrong type of data was used in a formula. Possible causes are entering text when a formula requires a number or logical value, or entering a range in a formula or function that requires a single value.

- **#DIV/0!** A formula is attempting to divide a value by zero. For example, if the value in cell B5 in the formula =A5/B5 is zero, or if cell B5 is empty, the result will be the #DIV/0! error.

- **#NAME?** Excel doesn't recognize text in the formula. Possible causes include a misspelling or using a nonexistent range name, using a label in a formula if the Accept labels in formulas option is turned off, or omitting a colon (:) in a range reference.

- **#N/A** No **value** is available to the formula or function. Possible causes include omitting a required argument in a formula or function or entering an invalid argument in a formula or function.

- **#REF!** A cell reference is invalid. Possible causes include deleting cells referred to by formulas.

- **#NUM** Indicates a problem with a number in a formula or function. Possible causes include using a nonnumeric argument in a function that requires a numeric argument, or entering a formula that produces a number too large or too small for Excel to represent.

- **#NULL!** The formula contains incorrect operators or cell references using ranges in formulas. For example, if you left the comma out of the following formula, a #NULL! error would occur: SUM(A1:A6,C1:C6).

- A **circular reference** is a special kind of error that's caused when a formula references itself. For example, if you're adding the values of a group of cells and include the cell that contains the formula, you are creating an endless loop, which generates a circular reference error.

  When a circular reference occurs, an error message appears, followed by a Help screen filled with tips to help you correct the error.

- Until you correct a circular reference, the status bar displays the words "Circular References" and if the worksheet with the error is displayed, the address of the cell(s) with the Circular Reference error appears after "Circular References" in the status bar.

- You can also locate any cell(s) that contain circular references by using the Circular References option on the Error Checking button on the Formulas toolbar.

Try It!   Correcting Formula Errors

1 Start Excel and open **ETry25** from the data files for this lesson. If you see a circular reference warning, click OK to close it.

2 Save the file as **ETry25_studentfirstname_ studentlastname** in the location where your teacher instructs you to store the files for this lesson.

3 On the Office Items worksheet, click cell B8. An Error Checking button appears to its left.

4 Click the Error Checking button. A menu opens.

5 Click Update Formula to Include Cells.

6 Click Formulas > Error Checking ◆. A dialog box appears pointing out the error in C8.

7 Click Copy Formula from the Left. A message appears that error checking is complete.

8 Click OK.

9 Use Format Painter to copy the formatting from C7 to C8.

10 Click the Sales Tax worksheet tab.

11 Click cell B12. An Error Checking button appears to its left.

12 Click the Error Checking button. A menu opens.

13 Click Convert XX to 20XX.

14 Examine the formulas in column D to figure out why there is such a large value in cell D3 and zero values in cells D4:D7.

> ✓ The formula for calculating tax is correct in cell D2. However, the formula was filled down with relative references instead of absolute references. Every row needs to reference the sales tax rate in cell B11. Fix this by making cells D3:D7 have an absolute reference to B11.

15 Change the formula in cell D2 to =B2*C2*$B$11.

> ✓ Instead of retyping the formula in cell D2, you could click in the B11 reference in the formula bar and then press F4 to cycle through the relative/absolute reference combinations until you arrive at $B$11.

16 Copy the formula in cell D2 to cells D3:D7.

17 Save your work. Leave the workbook open to use in the next Try It.

Showing Formulas

- Sometimes it can be helpful to view the actual formulas in the cells, rather than the formula results. To do this, you can either press `CTRL` + `` ` `` (the accent mark above the Tab key, not an apostrophe) or you can click Formulas > Show Formulas. Repeat the command to switch back to viewing the worksheet normally.

Try It!   Showing Formulas

1 In **ETry25_studentfirstname_studentlast name**, click Formulas > Show Formulas. The worksheet view changes to show the formulas.

2 Click Formulas > Show Formulas again to return to normal. Leave the worksheet open to use in the next Try It.

Evaluating an Individual Formula

- When a formula has multiple calculations in it, it can be helpful to **evaluate** each part of the formula step-by-step.

Try It!   Evaluating a Formula

1 In **ETry25_studentfirstname_studentlast name**, click the Sales Tax worksheet tab.

2 Click cell E2.

3 Click Formulas > Evaluate Formula. The Evaluate Formula dialog box opens, showing the following:

(B2*C2)+D2

4 Click Evaluate. The value of the first reference appears in italic, and the second reference is underlined:

(20*C2)+D2

5 Click Evaluate. The value of the second reference appears in italic, and the portion of the formula that is in parentheses is underlined:

(20*245)+D2

6 Click Evaluate. The portion of the formula in parentheses is calculated:

(4900)+D2

7 Click Evaluate. The parentheses are removed and D2 becomes underlined:

4900+D2

8 Click Evaluate. The value of D2 appears:

4900+416.5

9 Click Evaluate. The final result of the formula appears:

$5316.50

10 Click Close. Leave the worksheet open to use in the next Try It.

Using the Watch Window

- Using the **Watch Window**, you can watch the results of your formulas change as you change other data, even if that formula is located in a cell that's out of view, on another worksheet, or located in another open workbook.

- You can watch multiple cells and their formulas if you like.

Try It!   Using the Watch Window

1 In **ETry25_studentfirstname_studentlast name**, click Formulas > Watch Window 📖.

2 Click Add Watch.

3 On the Sales Tax worksheet, select cell E3. An absolute reference to that cell appears in the Add Watch dialog box.

4 Click Add. That cell reference appears in the Watch Window.

5 Change the value in cell B3 to 20. Notice that the result for E3 changes in the Watch Window.

6 Change the value in cell B3 back to 16.

7 Click the watch item in the Watch Window to select it.

8 Click Delete Watch. The watch is removed.

9 Close the Watch Window. Leave the worksheet open to use in the next Try It.

Tracing Precedents and Dependents

■ With the Trace Precedents button, you can trace a formula's **precedents**—cells referred to by the formula. This can help you find and fix errors that have to do with wrong cell references.

■ If you are concerned about changing the value in a cell, you can trace its **dependents** with the Trace Dependents button. A dependent is a cell whose value depends on the value in another cell.

■ When you trace precedents or dependents, arrows point to the related cells.

Try It!   Tracing Precedents and Dependents

1 In **ETry25_studentfirstname_studentlast name**, click the Office Items worksheet tab.

2 Click cell D2.

3 Click Formulas > Trace Precedents 💠. A line appears from cells B2 through D2 with blue dots in each field that contributes to the value in D2.

4 Click Formulas > Remove Arrows 🔍.

5 Click cell D5 and click Formulas > Trace Precedents 💠. Lines appear that show cell D5's precedents.

6 Click Formulas > Trace Dependents 💠. A line appears that shows cell D5's dependents.

7 Click Formulas > Remove Arrows 🔍.

8 Close the file, saving all changes, and exit Excel.

Project 53—Create It

Wood Hills Animal Clinic

DIRECTIONS

1. Start Excel, if necessary, and open **EProj53** from the data files for this lesson. Click OK if the file opens with a warning notice about a circular error.

2. Save the file as **EProj53_studentfirstname_studentlastname** in the location where your teacher instructs you to store the files for this lesson.

3. On the P&L worksheet, in the header section, type your full name on the left and insert today's date on the right. Then click **View > Normal** 🔲 to return to Normal view.

4. Repeat step 3 on the Balance Sheet worksheet.

5. Look over both tabs to see areas where there might be errors in formulas because data is missing or data doesn't look as expected.

✓ *Notice that when you are on the Balance Sheet worksheet, the status bar shows there is a circular reference, but no cell reference is given. Move to the P&L worksheet. Notice that the status bar now shows there is a circular reference in cell E57.*

6. Click cell **E57** in the P&L worksheet. The formula in this cell is =SUM(E32,E43,E56,E57).

7. Edit this circular reference error by removing **E57** from the formula. The new formula should read =SUM(E32,E43,E56).

✓ *Be sure to remove the last comma. If not, you will receive an error message.*

8. Click cell **E64** and see what formula is in the formula bar.

✓ *Cell E64 should have a calculation in it to show the earnings per share of common stock. The formula to calculate earnings per share of common stock is to divide net income by common stock shares outstanding. However, the current formula in cell E64 references E62, a blank cell.*

9. In cell **E64**, type =E61/E63.

10. **With your teacher's permission**, print both worksheets.

11. Close the workbook, saving all changes, and exit Excel.

Project 54—Apply It

Earnings

DIRECTIONS

1. Start Excel, if necessary, and open **EProj54** from, the data files for this lesson.

2. Save the file as **EProj54_studentfirstname_ studentlastname** in the location where your teacher instructs you to store the files for this lesson.

3. In the header section, type your full name on the left and insert today's date on the right.

4. Create formulas that calculate the commission and bonuses for each salesperson.

   a. In cell **C13**, create a formula that multiplies cell **B13** by an absolute reference to cell **B9**.

   b. Copy the formula from cell **C13** to cells **C14:C24**.

   c. In cell **D13**, use an **IF** function to show the value of cell **B10** if the value of cell **B13** is greater than $40,000, and otherwise to show $0. Refer to B10 with an absolute reference.

   d. Copy the formula from cell **D13** to cells **D14:D24**.

   e. Use **Format Painter** to copy the formatting from cell **C13** to range **D13:D24**.

5. Create formulas that calculate the total earnings, which is the total of commissions and bonuses.

   a. In cell **E13**, use a **SUM** function to add cells **B13:D13**.

   b. Copy the function from cell **E13** to cells **E14:E24**.

6. Click any cell in the **Comm.** column and trace the precedents. Remove the arrows.

7. Click any cell in the **Bonus** column and trace the precedents. Remove the arrows.

8. Click any cell in the **Total Earnings** column and trace the precedents. Remove the arrows.

9. Type **0.06** in cell **B9** and type **$200** in cell **B10**. Apply the percentage format, zero decimal places, to cell **B9**.

10. Click cell **B9** and trace its dependents. Remove the arrows.

11. Click cell **B10** and trace its dependents. Remove the arrows.

12. Click any cell in the **Sales** column and trace its dependents. Remove the arrows.

13. Evaluate a formula in column **B**.

14. Show the formulas in all cells. Adjust column widths as necessary so that all formulas are fully visible and the worksheet fits on a single page across.

15. **With your teacher's permission**, print the range **A9:E24** with the formulas showing. It should look similar to Figure 25-2.

16. Return to viewing formula results in the cells, and readjust column widths as needed so nothing is truncated and the worksheet fits on a single page across.

17. Close the workbook, saving all changes, and exit Excel.

				Total
9	Commission Rate	0.06		
10	on sales over $40K	200		
11				
12	**Salesperson**	**Sales**	**Comm.**	**Bonus**	**Earnings**
13	Carl Jackson	44202	=B13*$B$9	=IF(B13>40000,$B$10,0)	=SUM(B13:D13)
14	Ni Li Yung	41524	=B14*$B$9	=IF(B14>40000,$B$10,0)	=SUM(B14:D14)
15	Tom Wilson	43574	=B15*$B$9	=IF(B15>40000,$B$10,0)	=SUM(B15:D15)
16	Jill Palmer	39612	=B16*$B$9	=IF(B16>40000,$B$10,0)	=SUM(B16:D16)
17	Rita Nuez	39061	=B17*$B$9	=IF(B17>40000,$B$10,0)	=SUM(B17:D17)
18	Maureen Baker	38893	=B18*$B$9	=IF(B18>40000,$B$10,0)	=SUM(B18:D18)
19	Kim Cheng	31120	=B19*$B$9	=IF(B19>40000,$B$10,0)	=SUM(B19:D19)
20	Lloyd Hamilton	41922	=B20*$B$9	=IF(B20>40000,$B$10,0)	=SUM(B20:D20)
21	Ed Fulton	45609	=B21*$B$9	=IF(B21>40000,$B$10,0)	=SUM(B21:D21)
22	Maria Alvarez	30952	=B22*$B$9	=IF(B22>40000,$B$10,0)	=SUM(B22:D22)
23	Katie Wilson	31472	=B23*$B$9	=IF(B23>40000,$B$10,0)	=SUM(B23:D23)
24	Tim Brown	44783	=B24*$B$9	=IF(B24>40000,$B$10,0)	=SUM(B24:D24)

Figure 25-2

Lesson 26

Controlling Data

WORDS TO KNOW

Input message
A message that appears when a user clicks in a cell providing information on how to enter valid data.

Paste Special
A variation of the Paste command that allows you to copy part of the data relating to a cell—in this case, the validity rules associated with that cell—and not the data in the cell itself.

Validation
A process that enables you to maintain the accuracy of the database by specifying acceptable entries for a particular field.

> ## What You Will Learn

Turning Off AutoComplete
Controlling Data Entry with Data Validation
Circling Invalid Data
Copying Validation Rules
Removing Duplicate Data

Software Skills   When adding, changing, and deleting records, it is all too easy to enter incorrect information. This is especially true when several people maintain a database. Since the accuracy of your data is often critical—especially if the data tells you what to charge for a product or what to pay someone—controlling the validity of the data is paramount. Anything you can do to control data entry and identify errors will contribute to the quality of your work.

Application Skills   As an employee of PhotoTown, one of your assignments is to make the photo product order form easier to use. The boss also wants all the empty space to be sewn up whenever an order contains only a few items, and he also wants all forms to contain only information that matches up with the inventory and product listings.

What You Can Do

Turning Off AutoComplete

- Excel's AutoComplete feature can complicate data entry in an Excel worksheet, because AutoComplete can alter the case of an entry or complete an entry in a manner the user doesn't intend. For example, if a previous entry in the field is Westlane and the user is entering only West, AutoComplete will nonetheless fill in Westlane.

Try It! — Turning Off AutoComplete

1. Start Excel, if needed, and click File > Options 📄.

2. Click Advanced.

3. Clear the Enable AutoComplete for cell values check box.

4. Click OK.

Controlling Data Entry with Data Validation

- With data **validation**, you can control the accuracy of the data entered into a worksheet.

- By specifying the type of entries that are acceptable, you can prevent invalid data from being entered. For example, you could create a list of valid department numbers, and prevent someone from entering a department number that wasn't on the list.

- You can set other rules as well, such as whole numbers only; numbers less than or greater than some value; or data of a specific length, such as five characters only.

- After entering the criteria for what constitutes a valid entry, you can also specify a particular error message to appear when an incorrect entry is typed.

- In addition, you can create an input message that displays when a user clicks a cell to help that user enter the right type of data.

  The types of validation criteria that are possible are:

  - Any value
  - Whole number
  - Decimal
  - List
  - Date
  - Time
  - Text length—limit the number of characters that can be entered
  - Custom—requires the use of logical formulas

    ✓ With the Custom option, you can enter a formula that compares the entry value with a value in another column. For example, you could set up a rule that if the Rented column contains the word Yes, then the Number of Occupants field must have a value greater than zero.

- If you restrict entries to a specified list, a down-arrow button appears when the cell is selected. Clicking the button displays a drop-down list of the acceptable entries, from which you can select.

  ✓ Entries in a restricted list are case-sensitive. If the list specifies Yes and the user instead types yes, for example, Excel will reject the entry. Whenever possible, use lowercase letters for list entries to prevent case-sensitivity problems and speed up data entry.

- Data validation is designed to check against data entered directly into cells in the worksheet. Data validation doesn't apply if the cell entry is the result of:
  - Data copied there using the fill handle.
  - Data pasted or moved from another location.
  - Data that is the result of a formula.

Try It! — Setting Up a Simple Data Validation Rule

1. Open **ETry26** from the data files for this lesson.

2. Save the file as **ETry26_studentfirstname_ studentlastname** in the location where your teacher instructs you to store the files for this lesson.

3. On the Office Items worksheet, select the range C4:C15.

4. Select Data > Data Validation 📇. The Data Validation dialog box opens.

5. On the Settings tab, open the Allow drop-down list and click Whole number.

6. Open the Data drop-down list and click greater than.

7. In the Minimum text box, type **0**.

8. On the Error Alert tab, click in the Error message text box and type **Positive whole numbers only**.

9. Click OK.

(continued)

Try It!   Setting Up a Simple Data Validation Rule *(continued)*

10 Click cell C11 and type **0**, then press ENTER .
The error message appears.

11 Click Cancel to close the error message box.
Leave the workbook open to use in the next
Try It.

✓ *Clicking Cancel removes the number you entered from
cell C11. If you were to click Retry, the number would
remain in the cell, highlighted black, and the cell active,
waiting for you to retry your entry.*

Set up a validation rule that allows
positive whole numbers only

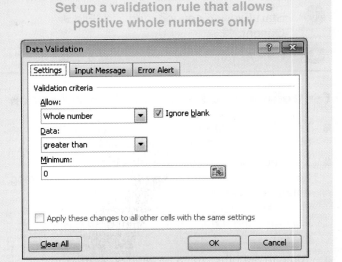

Try It!   Setting Up Custom Validation

1 In **ETry26_studentfirstname_studentlast
name**, on the Office Items worksheet, select
the range A4:A15.

2 Select Data > Data Validation ⊞. The Data
Validation dialog box opens.

3 On the Settings tab, open the Allow drop-down
list and click Custom.

4 In the Formula text box, type **=ISTEXT(A4)**.

✓ *This formula refers to the first cell in the range; the
validation formulas for the other cells in the range will
be for those cells because Excel considers this a relative
reference.*

5 On the Input Message tab, in the Title box, type
Item Name.

6 In the Input message box, type **Enter only the
item name from the catalog**.

7 Click the Error Alert tab, open the Style drop-
down list, and click Stop if it is not already
selected.

8 In the Title text box, type **Verify Item Name**.

Set up the Input Message tab like this

(continued)

Try It!   **Setting Up Custom Validation** *(continued)*

9 In the Error message text box, type **The item name must be text only.**

10 Click OK. The dialog box closes.

11 Click cell A4 and notice the message that appears. Click each of the cells in the range A5:A15; the message appears for them too.

12 Click cell B4. No message appears because there is no validation set up for that cell.

13 Click cell A12 and type **12345** and press ENTER. An error message appears.

14 Click Cancel to clear the error message. Save changes and leave the workbook open to use in the next Try It.

Try It!   **Turning Off Notification of Errors**

1 In **ETry26_studentfirstname_studentlast name**, click cell A4 and click Data > Data Validation.

2 On the Input Message tab, clear the Show input message when cell is selected check box.

3 On the Error Alert tab, clear the Show error alert after invalid data is entered check box.

4 On the Settings tab, select the Apply these changes to all other cells with the same settings check box.

5 Click OK.

6 Click A12. Type **12345** and press ENTER. No warning appears. Save changes and leave the workbook open with the invalid data in place to use in the next Try It.

Circling Invalid Data

■ Even with data validation rules in effect, sometimes invalid data can still be recorded. Data entered by copying and pasting, by using the fill handle, or as the result of a formula all bypass Excel's validation rules, for example.

■ With the Circle Invalid Data command, data that violates specified validation rules is identified quickly with a red circle.

■ As you correct the data, the circle in that cell automatically disappears.

■ You can remove any remaining circles (for errors you want to ignore) with the Clear Validation Circles command.

Try It!   **Circling Invalid Data**

1 In **ETry26_studentfirstname_studentlast name**, click the Data tab, click the Data Validation drop-down list, and click Circle Invalid Data. Cell A12 shows a red circle, indicating the validation rule is violated.

2 Select cell A12 and press DEL. The red circle remains.

3 Select cell A12, type **Product**, and press ENTER. The red circle goes away.

4 Select cell A12 and press DEL. Save changes and leave the workbook open to use in the next Try It.

Try It!   Turning On Notification of Errors

1 In **ETry26_studentfirstname_studentlast name**, select the range A4:A15 and click Data > Data Validation 🔲.

2 On the Error Alert tab, select the Show error alert after invalid data is entered check box.

3 Click OK. Save changes and leave the workbook open to use in the next Try It.

Copying Validation Rules

■ You can copy validation rules between cells using the Clipboard. This enables you to reuse a rule without having to recreate it from scratch.

■ To copy a validation rule, you use the **Paste Special** feature of the Clipboard. This enables you to specify what aspect of the copied range you want to paste.

Try It!   Copying Validation Rules

1 In **ETry26_studentfirstname_studentlast name**, on the Office Items worksheet, select the range A4:A11.

2 Press CTRL + C to copy.

3 Switch to the Sales Tax worksheet by clicking its tab.

4 On the Sales Tax worksheet, select the range A4:A11.

5 Click CTRL + V to paste. (The two lists are identical, so it's okay to overwrite the content.) The content is copied, and also the validation rule.

6 Switch to the Office Items worksheet and select cell C4. Then press CTRL + C to copy.

7 Switch to the Sales Tax worksheet and select the range B4:B14.

8 On the Home tab, click the down arrow under the Paste button 🔲, opening a menu.

9 At the bottom of the Paste button's menu, click Paste Special. The Paste Special dialog box opens.

10 In the Paste Special dialog box, click Validation.

11 Click OK. Only the validation rule is copied. Save changes and leave the workbook open to use in the next Try It.

Removing Duplicate Data

■ Another type of invalid data that might be entered into a worksheet is a duplicate entry.

■ Sometimes, duplicates are valid. For example, if two people happen to make $18.45 an hour, that might be perfectly normal. However, if the worksheet contains a database, such as a list of employees or customers, duplicates may indicate an error.

■ To remove duplicate entries from a range, use the Remove Duplicates command. When you remove duplicate entries this way, Excel identifies what it considers duplicates, and automatically removes them for you.

✓ You cannot remove duplicates from data that is outlined or subtotaled. To remove duplicates, remove the outlining/subtotaling.

Try It!   **Removing Duplicate Data**

1 In **ETry26_studentfirstname_studentlast name**, switch to the Office Items worksheet.

2 Click Data > Remove Duplicates. The Remove Duplicates dialog box opens.

3 Under Columns, clear all the check boxes except Catalog Item Number.

4 Click OK. A message appears that a duplicate has been removed. Click OK.

5 Close the workbook, saving all changes, and exit Excel.

Choose which fields must contain identical values for a record to be considered a duplicate

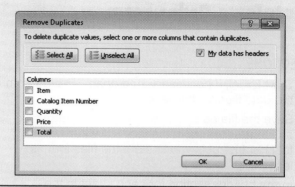

Project 55—Create It

PhotoTown Order Form

DIRECTIONS

1. Start Excel, if necessary, and open **EProj55** from the data files for this lesson.

2. Save the file as **EProj55_studentfirstname_ studentlastname** in the location where your teacher instructs you to store the files for this lesson.

3. In the header section, enter your full name on the left and insert today's date on the right. Then return to Normal view.

4. Click the Order Form worksheet tab. Test the list-based order form:

   a. Click cell **B12**.
   b. Type **PZ101** and press TAB. The Description field shows Photo puzzle.
   c. Click cell **G12** and type **1**.

5. Add a validation rule for the Item # field that permits only valid item numbers:

   a. Select the range **B12:B28**.
   b. Click **Data > Data Validation**.

   c. On the **Settings** tab, under **Allow**, choose **List**.
   d. Click the **Collapse Dialog** button next to the **Source** text box.
   e. Click the **Product Listing** worksheet tab.
   f. Select the range **A9:A68** and press ENTER to return to the dialog box.
   g. Click **OK** to create the rule.
   h. Click in **B13**. A drop-down list arrow appears to its right.

6. Click the arrow to open a menu, and click **GC075**. The information about the product is filled in.

7. Click cell **C13** and look at the formula in the formula bar, to see how the worksheet is constructed.

   ✓ *An IF function evaluates B13 and then looks up data from the Product Listing sheet with VLOOKUP.*

8. Click in **G13** and type **2**.

9. Close the workbook, saving all changes, and exit Excel.

Project 56—Apply It

PhotoTown Order Form

DIRECTIONS

1. Start Excel, if necessary, and open **EProj56** from the data files for this lesson.

2. Save the file as **EProj56_studentfirstname_ studentlastname** in the location where your teacher instructs you to store the files for this lesson.

3. In the header section for each sheet in the workbook, type your full name on the left and insert today's date on the right. Then return to Normal view.

4. On the Order Form worksheet, add a validation rule for the Qty field (range **G12:G28**) that permits only whole positive numbers and shows a Stop type error message that explains the rule when it is violated.

5. Test the validation rule and make any corrections needed.

6. Add a validation rule for the Greeting card text box (merged cell **G36**) that permits a maximum of 180 characters. Set an input message of **Enter up to 180 characters**. If the rule is violated, an error message should appear: **Please enter a message of no more than 180 characters.**

7. To test the validation rule, attempt to enter the following text into cell G36. (Use ⌐ALT¬ + ⌐ENTER¬ to insert line breaks.)

   Wheaten's Glenn Apple Orchard
   First Annual Harvest Festival
   September 12th to 28th
   10:00 A.M. to 6:00 P.M.

   Hay rides, apple picking, cider tasting, corn maze, and more!
   Take NC-7 to R.R. 12, west 10 miles.

8. When the error message appear, click Retry, and edit the entry to fewer than 180 characters:

   Wheaten's Glenn Apple Orchard
   Harvest Festival
   Sept. 12th to 28th
   10 A.M. to 6 P.M.

   Hay rides, apple picking, cider tasting, corn maze, and more!
   NC-7 to R.R. 12, west 10m.

9. Select **G36** and click Home > Top Align ☰ to top-align the text in G36.

10. Use **Remove Duplicates** to remove any duplicate items in rows **B12:I28**.

    ✓ *This has the effect of removing all of the blank rows from the order form except two. However, it does not completely delete the rows; it only deletes their content and formatting.*

11. Select the unformatted rows (the ones in the space where the duplicates were removed) and click **Home > Delete** ☒.

12. **With your teacher's permission,** print the worksheets.

13. Close the workbook, saving all changes, and exit Excel.

Chapter Assessment and Application

Project 57—Make It Your Own

Analyzing a Business Opportunity

You are interested in purchasing a business, and you want to analyze the financial numbers of the business from the past 2 years to see if it is a profitable, growing company. You will analyze the raw data that the current owner has provided to make sure the business would be a good investment.

If you do purchase the business, you will need to get a small business loan. You are considering two different loans, each with different terms. You will use what you know about financial functions to determine which loan is a better deal.

DIRECTIONS

1. Start Excel and open **EProj57** from the data files for this project. Save the file as **EProj57_ studentfirstname_studentlastname** in the location where your teacher instructs you to store the files for this project.

2. On each of the sheets in the workbook, open the header area and type your full name on the left and insert today's date on the right. Close the header and return to Normal view.

3. On the **Expenses** worksheet, in cell **G5**, create a **SUMIF** function that sums the values from **D5:D124** where "Facility Rental" appears in column C.

4. Enter the appropriate **SUMIF** functions in columns **G** and **I** that summarize the data in the ways described by the labels in columns **F** and **H**. Illustration A shows the totals that should appear in the cells when the functions are correctly created.

✓ *If you apply absolute references to all the cells in the function in G5, it makes it easier to copy and paste the function into other cells and then modify the copies to meet the new criteria. For example, you can copy the function into G6 and change Facility Rental to Loan Payment.*

Illustration A

2-Year Total of Expenses		2-Year Total Expenses by Type	
Facility Rental	$19,200	Fixed	$48,000
Loan Payment	$28,800	Variable	$6,268,911
Materials	$5,567,857		
Payroll	$694,826	**2010 Expenses by Type**	
Utilities	$6,228	Fixed	$24,000
		Variable	$3,626,809
2010 Expenses			
Facility Rental	$9,600	**2011 Expenses by Type**	
Loan Payment	$14,400	Fixed	$24,000
Materials	$2,344,531	Variable	$3,626,809
Payroll	$294,522		
Utilities	$3,049		
2011 Expenses			
Facility Rental	$9,600		
Loan Payment	$14,400		
Materials	$3,223,326		
Payroll	$400,304		
Utilities	$3,179		

5. On the **Summary** tab, examine the **SUMIFS** functions in cells **C5** and **D5**.

   ✓ *Notice that in both functions, the date Jan-2010 is being referenced as a general number: 40179. To determine the numeric equivalent of a date, temporarily set the cell's number format to General.*

6. Using **C5** and **D5** as examples, complete the rest of the functions for **C6:D28**.

   ✓ *Because the cell references are absolute, you can copy and paste the functions from cells C5 and D5 into the remaining cells and then edit each copy.*

   ✓ *You may want to set all the dates in column A temporarily to General format to make it easier to see what numbers to use for the dates. Don't forget to set them back to the custom Date format of MMM-YY when you are finished.*

   ✓ *Another shortcut: after completing column C's functions, copy them to column D and then use Find and Replace to replace all instances of "Fixed" with "Variable".*

7. Copy the formula from cell **E5** to cells **E6:E28**.

8. Create a line chart from the values in column **E**, using the dates in column **A** as labels.

9. Add an exponential trend line to the chart.

10. Place the chart on its own sheet in the workbook. Name the sheet **Net Profit**.

   ✓ *To place the chart on its own sheet, right-click the chart border and click Move Chart.*

11. On the **Loans** sheet, use the **PMT** function to calculate the monthly payments on two different loans, both for **$2 million**:

    Loan 1: **6% APR for 60 months**
    Loan 2: **5% APR for 48 months**

12. On the **Loans** worksheet, in cell **B10**, create a formula that evaluates whether the amount in cell **B9** is less than the smallest value in column **E** of the **Summary** worksheet (hint: use the =MIN function). If it is less, display **OK**. If it is not less, display **No**. Copy the formula to cell **C10**, changing any cell references as needed.

13. Create a scenario for the current values on the **Loans** sheet, with cell **B4** as the changing cell. Name the scenario **2 Million Loan**.

14. Create another scenario in which the loan amount is **$2,500,000**. Name it **2.5 Million Loan**. Show that scenario; then show the **2 Million Loan** scenario.

15. **With your teacher's permission**, print the **Loans** worksheet and the **Net Profit** chart.

16. Close the workbook, saving all changes, and exit Excel.

Project 58—Master It

Projecting Business Scenarios

The purchase of the business seems to be a good decision. However, the net profit per month seems to fluctuate quite a bit, making it difficult to predict how much money you can safely borrow to purchase the business. You can be more confident by calculating a moving average of the monthly profits, and by setting up several scenarios with varying degrees of optimism, ranging from worst case to best case.

DIRECTIONS

1. Start Excel and open **EProj58**. Save the file as **EProj58_studentfirstname_studentlastname** in the location where your teacher instructs you to store the files for this project.

2. On the **Summary** worksheet, in the **F** column, create a 5-interval moving average of the values in the **E** column and chart the output.

3. Move the chart to its own sheet. Name the sheet **Profit Moving Average**.

4. On the **Summary** sheet, in the range **B29:B40**, use the **GROWTH** function to predict the future monthly gross revenues for 2012.

5. Copy the formula from cell **E28** to range **E29:E40**.

6. In cell **C29**, enter **$1,500**. Copy that value to range **C30:C40**.

7. In cell **D29**, enter **$370,000**. Copy that value to range **D30:D40**.

8. Use **Format Painter** to copy the formatting from cell **B29** to range **C29:E40**.

9. Type **$1500** in cell I29. Enter **$200,000** in cell I30.

10. In cell **C29**, enter a formula that provides an absolute reference to I29.

11. In cell **D29**, enter a formula that provides an absolute reference to I30.

12. Copy the formulas from range **C29:D29** to range **C30:D40**.

13. Create a new scenario called **Best Case** that allows I29 and I30 to change, and uses the current values of those cells.

14. Create another scenario called **Most Likely** that sets cell I29 to **$1750** and cell I30 to **$300,000**.

15. Create another scenario called **Worst Case** that sets cell I29 to **$2000** and cell I30 to **$400,000**.

16. Show the **Most Likely** scenario.

17. **With your instructor's permission**, print the range **A29:E40** on the **Summary** worksheet, and print the **Profit Moving Average** chart.

18. Close the workbook, saving all changes, and exit Excel.

Chapter 1

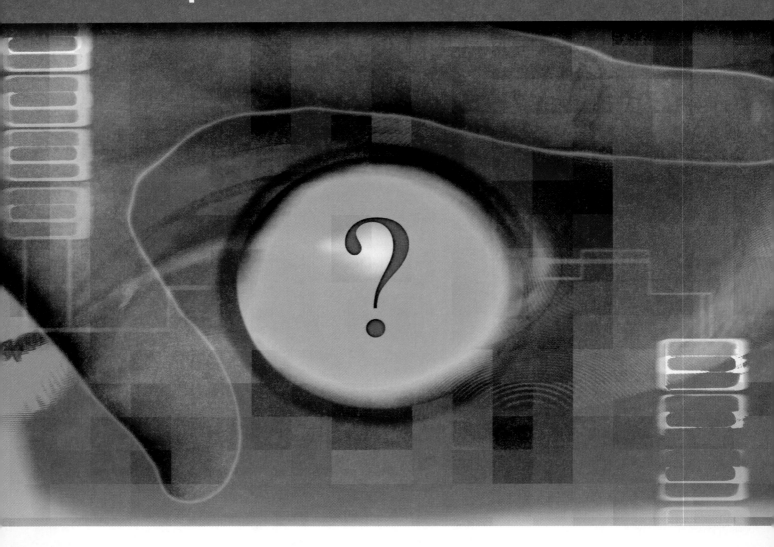

Enhancing Queries

Lesson 1
Creating Crosstab Queries
Projects 1-2

- Using the Crosstab Query Wizard
- Creating a Crosstab Query in Design View

Lesson 2
Creating Queries That Find Unmatched or Duplicate Records
Projects 3-4

- Using the Find Unmatched Query Wizard
- Using the Find Duplicates Query Wizard
- Enforcing Referential Integrity in a Table Relationship

Lesson 3
Creating Queries That Prompt for Input
Projects 5-6

- Understanding Parameter Queries
- Creating Criteria-Based Prompts
- Showing All Records If No Parameter Is Entered
- Creating a Field Prompt

Lesson 4
Creating Action Queries
Projects 7-8

- Understanding Action Queries
- Backing Up a Table
- Creating a Make Table Query
- Creating an Update Query
- Creating an Append Query
- Creating a Delete Query

Lesson 5
Working with Advanced Query Options
Projects 9-10

- Identifying Which Table to Draw a Field from in a Multi-Table Query
- Creating Ad-Hoc Joins
- Changing the Join Type
- Changing Field Properties in Query Design View
- Showing Top Values

End-of-Chapter Assessment
Projects 11-12

Lesson 1

Creating Crosstab Queries

WORDS TO KNOW

Column heading
The field that provides labels for the columns in a crosstab query.

Crosstab Query
A query that summarizes one field by two or more other category fields. The category fields display in row and column headings. At the intersection of each row and column is a summary (sum, average, count) of the value.

Row heading
One or more fields that label each row of a crosstab query.

Value
The field that provides the data to summarize for the intersection of each column and row of a crosstab query.

➤ **What You Will Learn**

Using the Crosstab Query Wizard
Creating a Crosstab Query in Design View

Software Skills   Crosstab queries are a rather "special purpose" item. Instead of presenting just summary data, or just detail data, they allow you to combine summary and detail in specific ways to deliver information you need. In this way, they are somewhat like PivotTables.

Application Skills   You are helping a company called Bookseller Source that offers large quantities of textbooks to bookstores at 50 percent off retail prices. They have already set up the database for this business, and they have three days' worth of sales data entered. Now the owners would like to look at the data for these first few days to evaluate what items are selling well and which salespeople are performing the best. You will use crosstab queries to produce this data.

What You Can Do

Using the Crosstab Query Wizard

■ A crosstab query summarizes data in a very specific way that you set up yourself to fit a specialized information need.

■ For example, in Figure 1-1, each product is listed along with its price per unit, and a sum of the quantity of that product ordered appears, first totaled (Total Of Quantity), and then broken out by salesperson's last name.

   ✓ *If the fields that you want to summarize are in more than one table, create a query first that joins those tables before you use the Crosstab Query Wizard and base the crosstab query on that query.*

■ The Crosstab Query Wizard leads you through the steps to create a crosstab query.

■ The Wizard first asks for a table or query on which to base the new query. Then it asks you to choose which field will be the source for **row headings** in the left column of the query. All like values from the row heading field are grouped together, and each unique value in the row heading field becomes a heading for each row of the query. You can choose up to three fields for row headings.

■ The Wizard then asks you to choose which field will be the source for **column headings** along the top of the query. All like values from the column heading field are grouped together and each unique value in the column heading field becomes a heading for the data columns of the query. You can choose only one field for a column heading.

   ✓ *If you choose a field that is a Date data type for a row or column heading, you will be asked how you want to group the dates on the next step of the wizard. You can choose Year, Month, or another date category.*

■ The next step of the Wizard enables you to choose which field you are going to summarize. Generally this field is a number that you can sum. Sometimes this field is a text or other type of field that you may want to count. You choose both the field and the function you want to perform on it.

■ Table 1-1 on the next page summarizes the functions you can use. The available functions change depending on whether the value data field is a number or other data type. In this step of the wizard, you can also choose if you want a total for each row. (This will total all column values for each row.)

Figure 1-1

qryOrderInfo_Crosstab								
ProductName	PricePerUnit	Total Of Quantity	Bastilla	Jackson	Sanchez	Serino	Wakasuki	Wendtworth
4" zinc tealight wicks	$3.45	2					2	
6" zinc votive wicks	$3.45	21	10			10	1	
Container wax, 10lb	$13.80	6		1	3			2
Mold sealant	$2.30	1					1	
Pillar mold 9"x3"	$28.75	1		1				
Stearic acid	$6.90	4			2			2
Tealight candle	$1.20	24					24	
Votive mold, square	$5.75	6			6			
Votive/pillar wax, 10lb	$13.80	3	1	2				
Vybar 103	$5.75	2						2

Table 1-1	Functions in the Crosstab Query Wizard
Avg	Sum the numeric values and divide by the number of values.
Count	Count the number of records.
First	Show the field value for the first record.
Last	Show the field value for the last record.
Max	Show the highest value (if a number), the last alphabetic value (if a text string), or the latest date (if a date).
Min	Show the lowest value (if a number), the first alphabetic value (if a text string), or the earliest date (if a date).
StDev	Calculate the standard deviation, which is used to see how close all values are to the average.
Sum	Sum numeric values.
Var	Calculate the variance of the number, which is another way to see how close values are to the average.

Try It!   Using the Crosstab Query Wizard

1 Start Access and open **ATry01** from the data files for this lesson. Click Enable Content if the information bar appears.

2 Save the file as **ATry01_studentfirstname_ studentlastname** in the location where your teacher instructs you to store the files for this lesson.

3 Click Create > Query Wizard 🗾. The New Query dialog box opens.

4 Click Crosstab Query Wizard and click OK.

5 In the Crosstab Query Wizard dialog box, click the Queries option button.

6 Click qryOrderInfo on the list of queries.

7 Click Next.

Select the qryOrderInfo query as the basis for the crosstab query

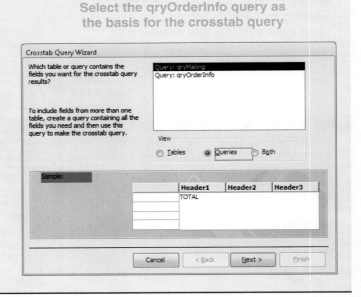

(continued)

Try It!   **Using the Crosstab Query Wizard** *(continued)*

8 Click ProductName and click Add > .

9 Click PricePerUnit and click Add > .

10 Click Next.

Choose ProductName and PricePerUnit as the rows

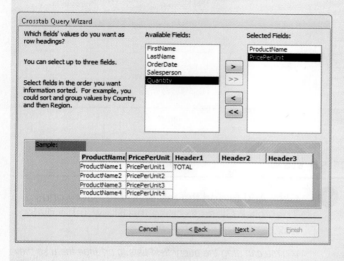

11 Click LastName to select it for a column heading and click Next.

12 On the Fields list, click Quantity.

13 On the Functions list, click Sum.

Choose to sum the Quantity field

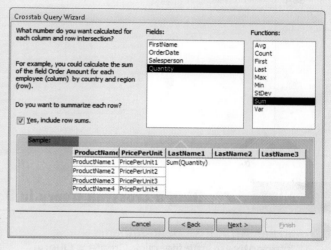

14 Click Next.

15 Leave the default name and click Finish. The query results appear. Leave them open for the next exercise.

Creating a Crosstab Query in Design View

- In a Crosstab query, a Crosstab row appears in the Query Design grid. Figure 1-2 on the next page shows the query design grid for the query you created in the preceding steps. You can switch to Datasheet view or click the Run button to see the results of the Crosstab query.

- The choices in the Crosstab row are Row Heading, Column Heading, and Value. You must have at least one of each.

    ✓ *You can make any query into a Crosstab query by clicking the Crosstab button on the Design tab.*

- You can have more than one Row Heading field, but not more than one Column Heading or Value field.

- The Total row for the Row Heading and Column Heading fields shows Group By.

- If you choose to display row totals, the Crosstab row also shows Row Heading, but the Total row shows the Sum (or other) function.

- The Total row for the Value field shows the function you want to apply, such as Sum.

- If you want to include only certain records, choose Where in the Total row and type the filtering criteria in the Criteria row.

Figure 1-2

Field:	[ProductName]	[PricePerUnit]	[LastName]	[Quantity]	Total Of Quantity: [Quantity]
Table:	qryOrderInfo	qryOrderInfo	qryOrderInfo	qryOrderInfo	qryOrderInfo
Total:	Group By	Group By	Group By	Sum	Sum
Crosstab:	Row Heading	Row Heading	Column Heading	Value	Row Heading
Sort:					
Criteria:					
or:					

Try It!   Creating a Crosstab Query in Design View

1 In the **ATry01_studentfirstname_ studentlastname** file, click Create > Query Design 📄.

2 In the Show Table dialog box, click the tblCustomers table. Hold down the CTRL key and click the tblOrderDetails, tblOrders, and tblProducts tables, too.

3 Click Add to add the tables to the query grid. Then click Close to close the Show Table dialog box.

✓ *You can drag the query field lists to arrange them so they are more readable if desired.*

4 Double-click the LastName field in tblCustomers to add it to the query grid.

Create a crosstab query from scratch in Query Design view

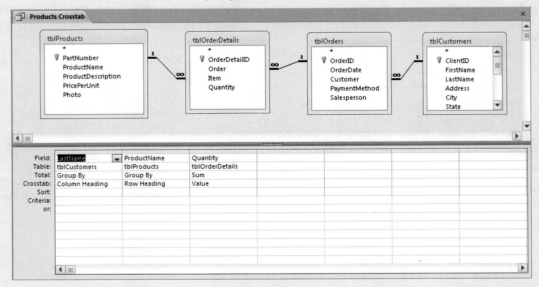

Try It!   **Creating a Crosstab Query in Design View** *(continued)*

5 Double-click the ProductName field in tblProducts.

6 Double-click the Quantity field in tblOrderDetails.

✓ *You needed to add the tblOrders table to the query in step 3 to get the linkage between the other tables; however, none of its fields are used directly in this query.*

7 Click Query Tools Design > Crosstab ▦. A Crosstab row appears in the grid.

8 In the LastName column, open the Crosstab drop-down list and click Column Heading.

9 In the ProductName column, open the Crosstab drop-down list and click Row Heading.

10 In the Quantity column, open the Crosstab drop-down list and click Value.

11 In the Quantity column, open the Total drop-down list and click Sum.

12 Click Query Tools Design > Run ❗ to see the results.

13 Right-click the Query1 tab and click Close. When prompted to save changes, click Yes.

14 In the Save As dialog box, type **Products Crosstab** and click OK.

15 Close **ATry01_studentfirstname_ studentlastname**, saving all changes, and exit Access.

Project 1—Create It

Bookseller Database

DIRECTIONS

1. Start Access, if necessary, and open **AProj01** from the data files for this lesson.

2. Save the file as **AProj01_studentfirstname_ studentlastname** in the location where your teacher instructs you to store the files for this lesson.

3. Click **Enable Content** on the information bar to enable all content.

4. Click **Create > Query Wizard** 🔍.

5. Click **Crosstab Query Wizard** and click **OK**.

6. Click the **Queries** option button.

7. Click **qryOrdersWithDetails** and click **Next**.

8. Click the **Salesperson** field, and click the **Add** button ▸ to move it to the Selected Fields list. Then click **Next**.

9. Click the **OrderDate** field and click **Next**.

10. Click **Date** and click **Next**.

11. In the **Fields** column, click **Total**.

12. In the Functions column, click **Sum**. Make sure the **Yes, include row sums** check box is marked.

13. Click **Next**.

14. Replace the default name with **qrySalesValuePerDay-Crosstab**, as shown in Figure 1-3, and click **Finish**.

15. In the query results, double-click the dividers between each set of column headers, expanding the column widths as needed to fit the contents.

16. **With your teacher's permission**, print the query results.

17. Close the database, and exit Access.

Figure 1-3

qrySalesValuePerDay-Crosstab				
Salesperson ▾	Total Of Total ▾	1/15/2012 ▾	1/16/2012 ▾	1/17/2012 ▾
Christine Cutler ▾	$12,338.00	$7,498.50		$4,839.50
Julie Burrow	$80,291.38	$61,109.00	$14,184.38	$4,998.00
Marjorie Hopper	$108,652.00	$74,420.00	$29,607.50	$4,624.50
Melissa Louks	$53,493.00	$21,495.50		$31,997.50

Project 2—Apply It

Bookseller Database

DIRECTIONS

1. Start Access, if necessary, and open **AProj02** from the data files for this lesson.

2. Save the file as **AProj02_studentfirstname_ studentlastname** in the location where your teacher instructs you to store the files for this lesson.

3. Click **Enable Content** on the information bar to enable all content.

4. Open the **qrySalesValuePerDay-Crosstab** query in Design view.

5. Change the column name of the Total Of Total column to **Total All Days**.

   ✓ To do this, edit the text in the Field row to read Total All Days:Total.

6. Run the query. Then save and close it.

7. Make a copy of the query, and name the copy **qrySalesQuantityPerDay-Crosstab**.

   ✓ To do this from the navigation pane, select the query, press CTRL + C , and then press CTRL + V . You will be prompted for the new name.

8. Open the **qrySalesQuantityPerDay-Crosstab** query in Design view, and edit the query so that it shows the total number of books sold, rather than the value of the books sold, per salesperson per day.

   ✓ To do this, change the references to the Total field to the Quantity field in the last two columns of the query grid.

9. Save and run the query. It should look like Figure 1-4.

Figure 1-4

qrySalesQuantityPerDay-Crosstab				
Salesperson ▾	Total All Days ▾	1/15/2012 ▾	1/16/2012 ▾	1/17/2012 ▾
Christine Cutler ▾	600	300		300
Julie Burrow	2675	1600	675	400
Marjorie Hopper	2875	2050	675	150
Melissa Louks	2000	1000		1000

10. Start a new query in Design view based on **qryOrdersWithDetails**. Choose **Crosstab query** as the query type.

11. Enter the appropriate fields and settings to produce the results shown in Figure 1-5.

- The order dates are the row headings.
- The salespeople are the column headings.
- The average price of the books sold (Our Price field) is the value.

12. Run the query, and widen the columns as needed so that no text is truncated.

13. Save the new query as **qryAvgPricePerDay-Crosstab**.

14. **With your teacher's permission**, print the results for all three queries.

15. Close the database, and exit Access.

Figure 1-5

qryAvgPricePerDay-Crosstab				
Order Date ▾	Christine Cutler ▾	Julie Burrow ▾	Marjorie Hopper ▾	Melissa Louks ▾
1/15/2012	$27.50	$36.71	$32.92	$20.00
1/16/2012		$18.50	$31.93	
1/17/2012	$17.10	$12.50	$35.00	$32.00

Lesson 2

Creating Queries That Find Unmatched or Duplicate Records

> **What You Will Learn**

Using the Find Unmatched Query Wizard
Using the Find Duplicates Query Wizard
Enforcing Referential Integrity in a Table Relationship

Software Skills   The Find Unmatched Query Wizard and the Find Duplicates Query Wizard are two special-purpose query types for specific tasks. They do just what their names suggest. The Find Unmatched Query Wizard compares two tables and reports records from one that do not have a corresponding entry in the other. The Find Duplicates query lists records that have the same value for one or more specified fields.

Application Skills   You are continuing work for Bookseller Source, and you just learned that they have not set up referential integrity in the relationships between their tables; this means there may be some errors in the database. Your next task is to check their database to make sure that all the records in tblOrderDetails have valid entries in tblOrders and also to ensure that there are no duplicate entries for the bookstores with different contact people entered. You will use queries to track down this information.

What You Can Do

Using the Find Unmatched Query Wizard

- The Find Unmatched Query Wizard leads you through the steps needed to create a query that will show records that do not match up with corresponding values in another table.

- Suppose, for example, that you have separate tables for Orders and OrderDetails. Every record in OrderDetails should refer to a valid order number in the Orders table. If there are detail records that do not, they are unmatched.

✓ This type of error would not occur if you were enforcing referential integrity in the relationship between the two tables. This illustrates the importance of referential integrity.

- The results appear in a datasheet, just like a select query. You can print it to use as a reference when fixing the problems.

- You can also use this type of query in cases where there aren't any errors, but you just want information. For example, in the following steps, you'll use it to find payment methods that no customers have used.

Try It!   **Using the Find Unmatched Query Wizard**

1. Start Access and open **ATry02** from the data files for this lesson. Click Enable Content if the information bar appears.

2. Save the file as **ATry02_studentfirstname_ studentlastname** in the location where your teacher instructs you to store the files for this lesson.

3. Click Create > Query Wizard 📇.

4. Select Find Unmatched Query Wizard and click OK.

5. Click Table:tblPaymentMethods and click Next.

Select the table from which to display unmatched records

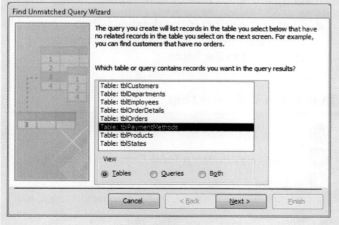

6. Click Table:tblOrders and click Next.

7. The field matching should already be set correctly, as shown below. Click Next to accept it.

Access guesses the field matching correctly in this case

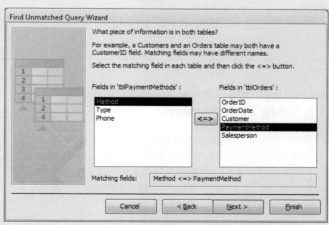

8. Click the All Fields button `>>` to select all the fields to include in the query results. Then click Next.

9. Replace the default query name with **qryUnusedPaymentMethods**.

10. Click Finish. Access finds four unmatched records.

11. Right-click the query's tab, and click Close.

12. Leave the database open to use in the next Try It.

Using the Find Duplicates Query Wizard

- The Find Duplicates Query Wizard is like a super "search" that helps ferret out duplication in your data.

- For example, suppose you want a single record in your Customers table for each business, but you have ended up with some businesses entered multiple times with different contact people in each record. You could find the duplicates with the Find Duplicates Query Wizard.

✓ This error would not occur if you set up the business name field to not allow duplicates. Setting its Indexed setting to Yes (No Duplicates) would prevent the problem from happening in the future.

- In the following exercise, you will find products that have the same name in a product table. You could then examine the duplicate products to make sure they were indeed different products and, if they were not, you could delete or combine the duplicates.

Try It!   **Using the Find Duplicates Query Wizard**

1 In the **ATry02_studentfirstname_studentlastname** file, click Create > Query Wizard.

2 Click Find Duplicates Query Wizard, and click OK.

3 Click Table:tblProducts and click Next.

4 Click the ProductName field, and click the Add button **>** . Then click Next.

5 Click the ProductDescription field, and click the Add button **>** .

6 Click Next.

7 Replace the default query name with **qryProductDuplicates**.

8 Click Finish. Query results appear showing product with duplicate names.

9 Right-click the query's tab, and click Close.

10 Leave the database open to use in the next Try It.

Enforcing Referential Integrity in a Table Relationship

- Referential integrity in a relationship between two tables helps prevent errors in the database such as situations where there are order details without a corresponding order, or orders without a corresponding customer.

- In a well-constructed database, referential integrity will already be enforced in the appropriate relationships. However, if you are working with a database that someone else has constructed, you may need to enable it.

- First fix the errors in the database; then enforce referential integrity to prevent the errors from happening in the future.

Try It!   **Enforcing Referential Integrity in a Table Relationship**

1 In the **ATry02_studentfirstname_studentlastname** file, click Database Tools > Relationships.

2 Double-click the line between tblOrders and tblOrderDetails. The Edit Relationship dialog box opens.

3 Mark the Enforce Referential Integrity check box.

4 Click OK.

5 Click Relationship Tools Design > Close ⊠ .

6 Close **ATry02_studentfirstname_studentlastname**, saving all changes, and exit Access.

Project 3—Create It

Bookseller Database

DIRECTIONS

1. Start Access, if necessary, and open **AProj03** from the data files for this lesson.

2. Save the file as **AProj03_studentfirstname_ studentlastname** in the location where your teacher instructs you to store the files for this lesson.

3. Click **Create > Query Wizard** 🐦.

4. Click **Find Unmatched Query Wizard** and click **OK**.

5. Click **Table:tblOrderDetails** and click **Next**.

6. Click **Table:tblOrders** and click **Next**.

7. The field matching should already be set correctly. Click **Next** to accept it.

8. Click the **All Fields** button `>>` to select all the fields to include in the query results, then click **Next**.

9. Replace the default query name with **qryUnmatchedOrders**.

10. Click **Finish**. Access finds five unmatched records.

11. **With your teacher's permission**, print the query results. See Figure 2-1.

12. Close the database, and exit Access.

Figure 2-1

qryUnmatchedOrders			
OrderDetailI ▾	Order ▾	ISBN ▾	Quantity ▾
12	7	Computer Networks, 4th Edition	650
13	7	Computer Science: An Overview 7th Edition	700
32	19	The Web Wizard's Guide to Freeware and Shareware	200
33	19	Authentication: From Passwords to Public Keys	100
34	19	Internet Visual Reference Basics	100
*	(New)		

Project 4—Apply It

Bookseller Database

DIRECTIONS

1. Start Access, if necessary, and open **AProj04** from the data files for this lesson.

2. Save the file as **AProj04_studentfirstname_ studentlastname** in the location where your teacher instructs you to store the files for this lesson.

3. Create a **Find Duplicates** query that locates all records in the **tblCustomers** table with a duplicate value in either **Store** or **Phone**. Name the query **qryDuplicateCustomers**.

4. Fix the records in the table so that each store exists only once. You can delete either of the duplicate records to achieve this.

5. Close the query, and then reopen it in Datasheet view to run it again. This time it should produce no results. Close the query window.

6. Open **tblCustomers** in Design view and set the **Store** and **Phone** fields' Indexed properties to **Yes (No Duplicates)** so the problem will not happen again.

7. Run the **qryUnMatchedOrders** query. In the query results, change all references to order 7 to 8. Change all references to order 19 to 18.

8. Close the query and then reopen it to confirm that there are no more unmatched orders.

9. Open the Relationships for the database, and enforce referential integrity between the **tblOrders** and **tblOrderDetails** tables.

10. Close the database, and exit Access.

Lesson 3

Creating Queries That Prompt for Input

➤ **What You Will Learn**

Understanding Parameter Queries
Creating Criteria-Based Prompts
Showing All Records If No Parameter Is Entered
Creating a Field Prompt

Software Skills Instead of creating many similar queries, you can create one query that will prompt you for different possibilities. For example, if you use the same query to look up addresses in different states and you have a version of the query for each state, you can create a single query that prompts you for the state each time you run it.

Application Skills You are working for a company called The Textbook Exchange, which buys and sells individual copies of textbooks. The company managers would like to be able to target people and books in the database that have specific properties, but the desired properties may change each time they run the query. For example, they might want to see all the people in a certain state or city. In this exercise, you will create parameter queries that will prompt you to include the criteria values.

WORDS TO KNOW

Parameter
A value that is required to run a query (or other object). The parameter is entered in a dialog box.

Query Parameters dialog box
A dialog box that displays all parameters and their data types for a query.

SQL (Structured Query Language)
A computer language common to database programs that is generally used for selecting or managing data.

What You Can Do

Understanding Parameter Queries

- **Parameter** queries allow you to use the same query to extract data that meets different criteria.

- For example, suppose you want one query to show all customers in a specific city and another to show customers in a different city. You can place a parameter in the Criteria row of the City field in the query design. When you run the query, you are prompted to enter the desired city.

- You can run parameter queries as a select query or change the query type to an action query. For example, you could prompt the user for which records to delete every month.

  ✓ *Action queries are covered in Lesson 4.*

- A parameter query can also be the source for a report or form. For example, you could request a date range for a report or choose a state for printing mailing labels.

- The parameter can be in a stand-alone query or can be part of the **SQL** statement in a form or report's Record Source property.

Creating Criteria-Based Prompts

- Perhaps the most common type of parameter occurs in the Criteria row of a query's design.

- Place the message you want for the prompt in square brackets. In Figure 3-1, the criteria box shows [What state?].

- When you run the query, a dialog box displays with the message and a text box for your input, as shown in Figure 3-2.

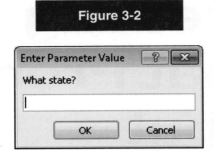

Figure 3-2

- Access takes the value the user types in the message box and places it in the Criteria row in place of the prompt to select the records.

- If you want to re-run the prompt from Datasheet view without returning to Design view, press SHIFT + F9.

- The prompt can be combined with other criteria to permit a variety of responses. Suppose, for example, you were prompting for a particular state:

Entry in Criteria	Permissible Responses
[What state?]	Entire state abbreviation
Like [What state?]	Entire state abbreviation
	Any portion of field contents with a wildcard; for example, c* displays CA, CO, CN. *A displays CA, IA, PA, WA.

Figure 3-1

Field:	FirstName	LastName	Address	City	State	ZIP
Table:	tblCustomers	tblCustomers	tblCustomers	tblCustomers	tblCustomers	tblCustomers
Sort:						Ascending
Show:	✓	✓	✓	✓	✓	✓
Criteria:					[What state?]	
or:						

Like [What state?] or Is Not Null	Entire state abbreviation
	Any portion of field contents with a wildcard
	Nothing (press Enter or click OK) displays all records
Like [What state?] & "*"	Same as above except wildcard displays all entries with the letter in any position. For example, *A displays AR, CA, and so on.

- You can have multiple prompts in one query, or even in one box within one query.
- For example, if you have an invoice date, you could type
  Between [Enter State Date] and [Enter End Date]
  to create two prompts to give you a date range to select specific invoices.

Try It!   **Creating a Criteria-Based Prompt**

1. Start Access and open **ATry03** from the data files for this lesson. Click Enable Content if the information bar appears.

2. Save the file as **ATry03_studentfirstname_ studentlastname** in the location where your teacher instructs you to store the files for this lesson.

3. In the navigation pane, right-click qryMailing and click Design View ✎.

4. In the State column in the Criteria row, type **[What state?]**.

5. Click Query Tools Design > Run ❗. The prompt appears.

6. Type **IN** and click OK. The query results display only people who live in Indiana.

7. Click the Save button 🖫 on the Quick Access toolbar.

8. Press SHIFT + F9 to redisplay the prompt.

9. Type **NJ** and click OK. The results display only people who live in New Jersey.

10. Right-click the query's tab and click Close.

11. Leave the database open to use in the next Try It.

Showing All Records If No Parameter Is Entered

- One minor issue with parameter queries is that if the user does not enter anything for the parameter, no records will show.

- In fact, what you probably want is for ALL records to show if the user enters no parameter.

- To accomplish this, add **& "*"** at the end of the parameter, and if it is a text field, add **Like** at the beginning. (Do not add Like if it is a numeric field.)

- This extra code allows all records to show if the parameter returns a null value.

Try It!   Showing All Records If No Parameter Is Entered

1 In **ATry03_studentfirstname_ studentlastname**, in the navigation pane, double-click qryMailing. In the Enter Parameter dialog box, click OK without entering a value.

✓ *The query results show no records.*

2 Right-click the query's tab, and click Design View ⬈.

✓ *Close the Property Sheet pane if it is in your way.*

3 In the Criteria row in the State column, change the entry to:

Like [What state?]& "*"

4 Click Run ❗. The Enter Parameter dialog box opens.

5 Click OK without entering a parameter. The query results show all records.

6 Press ⬚SHIFT⬚ + ⬚F9⬚ to reopen the Enter Parameter dialog box.

7 Type **IN** and click OK. Only the records from Indiana appear.

8 Click the Save button 💾 on the Quick Access toolbar.

9 Right-click the query tab, and click Close.

10 Leave the database open to use in the next Try It.

Creating a Field Prompt

■ You can also place a parameter in the Field row of the query design, creating a new field column in the query results.

■ Generally, the purpose of a field parameter is to create a calculation using the same value in every record.

■ For example, you may want to see the value of a variable price decrease for every record.

New Price: [AskingPrice]- ([AskingPrice]*[Percentage Decrease?]/100)

✓ *Note that running this query does not actually change the prices in the database; to do that, you would need to run an action query, as described in Lesson 4.*

■ Here's an explanation of that example:

● [Asking Price] is a field name. For example, suppose a record's asking price was $30.

● The rest of the expression is in parentheses, indicating that it should be performed first, before being subtracted from the [AskingPrice] amount.

● [Percentage Decrease?] is a prompt, not a field name.

● [Percentage Decrease?] is divided by 100 to create a percentage (such as 0.10) when a whole number is entered (such as 10). If you wanted to make that clearer, to avoid entry errors you could include a more verbose instruction, such as:

New Price: [AskingPrice]-([AskingPrice]* [Enter the desired percentage of decrease as a whole number]/100)

Try It!	**Creating a Field Prompt**

1 In **ATry03_studentfirstname_studentlastname**, click Create > Query Design.

2 In the Show Table dialog box, double-click tblProducts and then click Close.

3 Double-click ProductName and PricePerUnit to add those fields to the query grid.

4 In the first empty column in the Field row, type **New Price:[PricePerUnit]+([PricePerUnit]*[Enter the markup percentage as a whole number]/100)**

5 Right-click the text you just entered and click Properties.

6 In the Property Sheet, open the Format drop-down list and click Currency.

7 Click **Query Tools Design > Run** . A prompt appears.

8 Type **20** and click OK. New prices in the query results show with a 20% markup.

The query results

ProductName	▾	PricePerUnit	▾	New Price	▾
Votive mold, round		$1.00		$1.20	
Votive mold, square		$5.00		$6.00	
Pillar mold 9"x3"		$25.00		$30.00	
Pillar mold 6"x6"		$32.00		$38.40	
Mold sealant		$2.00		$2.40	
Votive/pillar wax, 10lb		$12.00		$14.40	
Container wax, 10lb		$12.00		$14.40	
Stearic acid		$6.00		$7.20	
Vybar 103		$5.00		$6.00	

9 Right-click the query tab and click Save.

10 In the Save As dialog box, type **qryMarkup** and click OK.

11 Right-click the query tab, and click Close.

12 Close the database, and exit Access.

Project 5—Create It

Textbook Database

DIRECTIONS

1. Start Access, if necessary, and open **AProj05** from the data files for this lesson.

2. Save the file as **AProj05_studentfirstname_studentlastname** in the location where your teacher instructs you to store the files for this lesson.

3. In the navigation pane, select **qryBooksForSale**.

4. Press CTRL + C to copy it, and then CTRL + V to paste the copy.

5. In the Paste As dialog box, type **qryBooksByDiscount** and click OK.

6. Right-click **qryBooksByDiscount** and click **Design View**.

7. In the Criteria row for the Discount field, enter the following:

   >([Minimum discount?]/100)

   ✓ *This parameter enables the user to enter a whole number for the minimum percentage of discount to show.*

8. Click **Query Tools Design > Run** . A prompt appears.

9. Type **60** and click OK.

   ✓ *Only records with at least 60% discount appear.*

10. **With your teacher's permission**, print the query results.

11. Click **Home > View** to return to Design view.

12. In the Criteria row for the Discount field, change the parameter so that leaving the parameter value empty will display all records:

    >([Minimum discount?]/100)&"*"

13. Click **Query Tools Design** > **Run** ❗. A prompt appears.

14. Click **OK** to bypass the prompt. All the records appear.

15. Click **Save** 🖫 on the Quick Access toolbar.

16. Close the database, and exit Access.

Project 6—Apply It

Textbook Database

DIRECTIONS

1. Start Access, if necessary, and open **AProj06** from the data files for this lesson.

2. Save the file as **AProj06_studentfirstname_ studentlastname** in the location where your teacher instructs you to store the files for this lesson.

3. Create a query based on **tblBooks** (all fields) that will show only the books that begin with a certain string of numbers in their ISBN field. Name the query **qryBooksByISBN**.

    ✓ For example, you might use this parameter: **Like [ISBN begins with:] & "*"**

4. Test the query using **1** as the parameter value.

5. **With your teacher's permission**, print one copy of the result in Landscape orientation.

6. Retest the query (⌷SHIFT⌷ + ⌷F9⌷) using **02** as the parameter value.

7. Retest the query by leaving the parameter value prompt blank.

    ✓ Leaving the parameter prompt blank should display all records.

8. Save and close the query.

9. Create a new query called **qryCustomersByLocation** that uses all the fields from **tblCustomers**.

10. Add parameter criteria for both the **City** and **State** fields that prompt the user to enter the desired city or state.

    ✓ Don't forget to add Like at the beginning and &"*" at the end of the parameter statements so that if the user enters nothing, all records will be included.

    ✓ For example, for the city, you might use **Like [What city?]&"*"**

11. Run the query, specifying **Macon** as the city name and not entering a state name.

12. **With your teacher's permission**, print one copy of the results in landscape orientation.

13. Save the query.

14. Close the database, and exit Access.

Lesson 4

Creating Action Queries

➤ What You Will Learn

Understanding Action Queries

Backing Up a Table

Creating a Make Table Query

Creating an Update Query

Creating an Append Query

Creating a Delete Query

Software Skills   Action queries can save a significant amount of time if you need to change a number of records at once. You may want to delete or update records based on criteria. You can also create a new table or add records to an existing table.

Application Skills   The owners of The Textbook Exchange have decided to start a new spin-off company called The Textbook Place that will sell only new books, but at 20% off retail prices. They have started a new database file with some of the old data plus some new data. You will use action queries to further prepare this data for use.

WORDS TO KNOW

Action query
A query that changes the value of one or more records.

Append query
A query that adds records to another table.

Delete query
A query that removes records from a table.

Make Table query
A query that creates a new table using records from another table.

Update query
A query that changes the entry in one or more fields in multiple records at once.

What You Can Do

Understanding Action Queries

■ **Action queries** modify records based on criteria you add.

■ A good starting point for an action query is to begin with a regular query, and to view the datasheet to make sure the selection is what you want to change. Then modify the query in Design view to apply the action functionality.

■ Be careful with action queries. Each time you run them they make permanent changes to the table.

■ There are four kinds of action queries: **Make Table query**, **Update query**, **Append query**, and **Delete query**.

✓ *Any of these queries can optionally have parameters in the Criteria, Field, or Update To rows (see Lesson 3).*

Backing Up a Table

■ Before running an action query, you should back up the original table, especially if you have not run that query before and are not certain what it will do.

■ To back up a table, copy it and then paste the copy. You will be prompted for a name.

■ You will also be prompted to copy either the structure only or the structure and the data. Make sure you choose to copy both the structure and the data; otherwise you won't get any of the records in the copy.

Try It!   **Backing Up a Table**

1 Start Access and open **ATry04** from the data files for this lesson. Click Enable Content if the information bar appears.

2 Save the file as **ATry04_studentfirstname_studentlastname** in the location where your teacher instructs you to store the files for this lesson.

3 In the navigation pane, click tblCustomers and press `CTRL` + `C`.

4 Press `CTRL` + `V`. The Paste Table As dialog box opens.

5 In the Table Name box, type tblCustomers Backup.

6 Make sure the Structure and Data option button is selected.

7 Click OK.

Create a backup copy of a table before running an action query

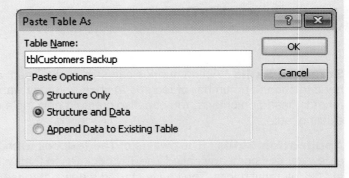

8 Leave the database open to use in the next Try It.

Creating a Make Table Query

- Whereas the backup procedure you just learned makes a copy of the entire table, a Make Table query makes a copy of only specific fields or records you specify.

- Create a select query first (that is, a normal query), and display the results in Datasheet view to make sure you have the right fields and records. Then change the query type to a Make Table query and run it.

  ✓ *For select queries, clicking the Run button and switching to Datasheet view do the same thing. For action queries, however, they do not. The Run button performs the action; switching to Datasheet view does not.*

| **Try It!** | **Creating a Make Table Query** |

1 In **ATry04_studentfirstname_studentlastname**, click Create > Query Design 🔲 to start a new query. The Show Table dialog box opens.

2 Double-click tblCustomers to add it to the query, and then click Close.

3 Select all the fields on the tblCustomers field list and drag them to the grid, adding all fields to the query.

4 In the Criteria row for the State field, type **Like "IN"**.

5 Click Query Tools Design > Run ❗ to run the query. Only records from Indiana should appear.

6 Click Home > View 🖺 to return to Design view.

7 Click Query Tools Design > Make Table 🔲❗. The Make Table dialog box opens.

8 In the Table Name box, type **tblIndianaCustomers**.

9 Click OK.

  ✓ *Note that the new table is not yet created at this point. You must run the query.*

Specify the name of the new table to create

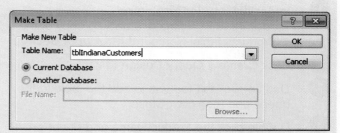

10 Click Query Tools Design > Run ❗. A confirmation message appears.

11 Click Yes. The new table is created.

12 Click the Save button 🖫 on the Quick Access toolbar.

13 In the Save As dialog box, type **qryMakeTableIndianaCustomers** and click OK.

14 Right-click the query's tab and click Close.

15 In the navigation pane, double-click tblIndianaCustomers to view the new table in Datasheet view.

16 Right-click the table's tab and click Close.

17 Leave the database open to use in the next Try It.

Creating an Update Query

- An Update query enables you to change the value of one or more fields in the records you select.

- Create a Select query first, and display it in Datasheet view to make sure you have the fields and records you want.

- Then, in Query Design view, switch it to an Update query. The query grid changes to add an Update To row. In the Update To row for the field to be modified, type an expression that describes the updated data. For example, to decrease the value in the [Price] field by 20%, you might use **=[Price]*.8**.

- To preview the records to be changed by the update, switch to Datasheet view. The records display but they do not show the update values. You can switch to datasheet view for any action query to review results without changing the database objects. To actually update the records, click Run.

Try It!   Creating an Update Query

1. In **ATry04_studentfirstname_studentlastname**, make a backup copy of the tblProducts table. Name it **tblProducts Backup**.

2. Click Create > Query Design 🔲.

3. Double-click tblProducts to add the table to the query, and then click Close.

4. Double-click the ProductName and PricePerUnit fields to add them to the grid.

5. In the Criteria row for the ProductName field, type **Like "Tealight candle"**.

6. Click Query Tools Design > Run ❗ to view the results. The results should show only Tealight candles.

7. Click Home > View 🔲 to return to Design View.

8. Click Query Tools Design > Update 🔺. An Update To row appears in the grid.

9. In the Update To row for the PricePerUnit field, type **$2.00**.

10. Click Query Tools Design > Run ❗. A confirmation message appears.

11. Click Yes. The query is run. You will not see the results onscreen.

12. Click the Save button 🔲 on the Quick Access toolbar.

13. In the Save As dialog box, type **qryUpdateTealightPrices** and click OK.

14. Right-click the query tab and click Close.

15. In the navigation pane, double-click tblProducts and check that the Tealight prices were updated.

16. Right-click the table tab and click Close.

17. Leave the database open to use in the next Try It.

Creating an Append Query

- An Append query copies certain records from one table to another. It does not remove the records from the original table.

  ✓ *To move records from one table to another, you might use an Append query to copy certain records into another table and then use a delete query to remove them from the original table.*

- Before you start, make sure you have another table prepared with the fields to which you want to add. If necessary, use a Make Table query or copy the table to create the table first.

- Start a select query with the fields you want to add to the other table, and then display the result in Datasheet view to make sure you have the right data. Then, in Query Design view, switch to an Append query design.

- If the two tables do not have exactly the same fields, you may need to match them up manually. You can do this by selecting the appropriate field in the Append To row of the query grid.

Try It!   Creating an Append Query

Choose the tblTealightProducts
table as the destination

1 In ATry04_studentfirstname_
studentlastname, select tblProducts in the
navigation pane. Press CTRL + C to copy it, and
then CTRL + V to paste it.

2 In the Paste Table As dialog box, in the Table
Name field, type **tblTealightProducts**.

3 Click the Structure Only option button and
click OK.

4 Click Create > Query Design.

5 Double-click tblProducts, and then click Close.

6 Select all the fields on the field list, and drag
them to the grid to add them to the query.

7 In the Criteria row for the ProductName field,
type **Like "Tealight" & "*"**.

8 Click Query Tools Design > Run ! to check the
results. Nine records should appear.

9 Click Home > View to return to Design view.

10 Click Query Tools Design > Append +!. The
Append dialog box opens.

11 Open the Table Name drop-down list and click
tblTealightProducts.

12 Click OK.

13 Check the Append To row in the query grid to
make sure that all fields are matched up with the
corresponding field in the destination table.

✓ *They will be in this example because the destination file
is based on the original. However, they may not always
be. You can change the match-up by opening the drop-
down list for the Append To row in that column and
selecting a different field to match.*

14 Click Save on the Quick Access
toolbar. In the Save As dialog box, type
qryAppendProducts and click OK.

15 Click Query Tools Design > Run !.
A confirmation box appears.

16 Click Yes.

17 Right-click the query's tab and click Close.

18 In the navigation pane, double-click
tblTealightProducts to confirm that the records
were appended there.

19 Right-click the table's tab and click Close.

20 Leave the database open to use in the next
Try It.

Creating a Delete Query

■ An Append query and a Delete query are often run
together. For example, first you append old records
to an archive table for storage, and then you delete
them from the current table.

✓ *If you get a message about key violation when you
are deleting records with a Delete query, check the
relationships. If referential integrity is enforced between two
tables, such that deleting records will cause a violation of
the rules, Access won't let you run the Delete query until you
turn off referential integrity for the relationship.*

Try It!   **Creating a Delete Query**

1 In **ATry04_studentfirstname_studentlastname**, click Create > Query Design ▦.

2 Double-click tblProducts and then click Close.

3 Double-click the ProductName field to add it to the query grid.

4 Click Query Tools Design > Delete ✕!.

5 In the Criteria row, type **Like "Tealight" & "*"**.

6 Click Query Tools Design > View ▦ to switch to Datasheet view and preview the results. Nine records should appear.

7 Click Home > View ◣ to return to Design view.

8 Right-click the query tab and click Save. In the Save As dialog box, type **qryDeleteProducts** and click OK.

9 Click Query Tools Design > Run !. A confirmation message appears.

10 Click Yes.

11 Right-click the query tab and click Close.

12 In the navigation pane, double-click tblProducts and confirm that the Tealight records have been deleted.

13 Close the database file, and exit Access.

Project 7—Create It

Textbook Place Database

TDIRECTIONS

1. Start Access, if necessary, and open **AProj07** from the data files for this lesson.

2. Save the file as **AProj07_studentfirstname_studentlastname** in the location where your teacher instructs you to store the files for this lesson.

3. In the navigation pane, select **tblBooks** and press `CTRL` + `C` to copy it.

4. Press `CTRL` + `V` to paste the copy. Type **tblBooksBackup** as the new table name, and click **OK**.

5. Click **Create** > **Query Design** ▦ to start a new query. Double-click **tblMoreBooks**, and click **Close**.

6. Select all the fields except Out of Print from the **tblMoreBooks** field list and drag them to the grid, adding them to the query.

7. Click **Query Tools Design** > **Append** ⊹!.

8. In the Table Name box, type **tblBooks**. Click **OK**. An Append To row appears in the query grid.

   ✓ *Notice that there is no entry in the Append To row for the Retail Price column.*

9. In the Retail Price column, open the **Append To** row's drop-down list and click **Retail Price**.

10. Click **Query Tools Design** > **Run** !.

11. Click **Yes** to confirm.

12. Click the **Save** button ▣ on the Quick Access toolbar.

13. Type **qryAppendBooks** and click **OK**.

14. Close the database, and exit Access.

Project 8—Apply It

Textbook Place Database

DIRECTIONS

1. Start Access, if necessary, and open **AProj08** from the data files for this lesson.
2. Save the file as **AProj08_studentfirstname_studentlastname** in the location where your teacher instructs you to store the files for this lesson.
3. Start a select query based on **tblBooks** using all the fields.
4. Enter criteria that will include only books that were published prior to 01/01/2008.
5. Test the query by running it, and return to Design view.
6. Change the query to a Make Table query that creates a new table called **tblOldBooks** based on the criteria entered earlier. Run the query to make the new table.
7. Save the query as **qryPre2008** and close it.
8. Open **tblOldBooks** in Datasheet view to confirm that it contains six records, and then close it.
9. Open **qryPre2008** in Design view.
10. Change the query to a Delete query that deletes the records that have dates before 01/01/2008.
11. Run the query.
12. Save the query as **qryDeletePre2008** and close it.

13. Open **tblBooks** in Datasheet view to confirm that it contains no records with dates before 01/01/2008, and then close it.
14. Open **tblBooks** in Design view, and add a new field called **Our Price**. Set its type to **Currency**, with two decimal places, and place it immediately after the Retail Price field.
15. Save and close the table.
16. Create a select query based on **tblBooks**. Include only the ISBN, Retail Price, and Our Price fields.
17. Change the query to an Update query that sets the value in the Our Price field to 80% of the Retail Price field's value.
18. Run the query and save it as **qryOurPrice**.
19. Modify **qryOurPrice** so instead of multiplying the Retail Price by 80%, it multiplies it by a percentage that the user enters when prompted. Use a parameter for this, as you learned earlier in this chapter.
20. Run the query, and when prompted, specify **50** as the percentage of discount.
21. Save and close the query.
22. Open **tblBooks** and confirm that the values in Our Price are 50% of the values in Retail Price.
23. Close the database, and exit Access.

Lesson 5

Working with Advanced Query Options

WORDS TO KNOW

Ad-hoc join
A relationship between two tables that exists only within the query in which it is created.

Inner join
A join that includes only records that have corresponding matches in a related table.

Outer join
A join that includes all the records in one table, but only the records in a related table that have a corresponding record in the original table.

Top values
Property of a query that shows the first set number of records in a query. When sorted descending, the query shows the top values in the list. When sorted ascending, the query shows the bottom values in the list.

➤ **What You Will Learn**

Identifying Which Table to Draw a Field from in a Multi-Table Query
Creating Ad-Hoc Joins
Changing the Join Type
Changing Field Properties in Query Design View
Showing Top Values

Software Skills A query is a great way of tying multiple tables together for use as a single data source on which to base other objects like forms or reports. In this lesson, you will learn how create ad-hoc joins that establish temporary relationships within a query and manage the join types for those relationships. You will also learn how to format fields in a query design and how to show top values in a summary query.

Application Skills The Textbook Exchange would like to get some additional information from the database, but the information needed is scattered among several unconnected tables. You will create some queries that bring the needed data together to answer some specific questions they have.

What You Can Do

Identifying Which Table to Draw a Field from in a Multi-Table Query

- In a multi-table query, it is possible that the same field, with the same name, exists in two or more queries. When that happens, you must make sure that you have identified from which table the field should be drawn.

✓ If the Table row does not appear in the lower part of the grid, make sure the Table Names button is selected on the Design tab.

Try It!   **Changing the Table from Which a Field Is Drawn**

1. Start Access and open **ATry05** from the data files for this lesson. Click Enable Content if the information bar appears.

2. Save the file as **ATry05_studentfirstname_ studentlastname** in the location where your teacher instructs you to store the files for this lesson.

3. In the navigation pane, right-click qryOrdersbySalesperson and click Design View ☑.

4. In the query design grid's first column, open the Table drop-down list and click tblEmployees. This changes which table the field is being drawn from.

5. Click Query Tools Design > Run ❗ to see the query results.

6. Click the Save button 🖫 on the Quick Access toolbar to save the query.

7. Right-click the query's tab, and click Close.

8. Leave the database open to use in the next Try It.

Choose a different table as a source for the field

Field:	LastName	OrderID	OrderDate	LastName
Table:	tblCustomers ▾	tblOrders	tblOrders	tblCustomers
Sort:	tblCustomers			
Show:	tblOrders	☑	☑	☑
Criteria:	tblEmployees			
or:				

Creating Ad-Hoc Joins

- An **ad-hoc join** is a connection between two tables that exists only within the query in which you create it. Access provides an opportunity for you to create temporary, informal relationships between data sources for the purpose of building the query without those relationships persisting outside the query.

- To create an ad-hoc join, drag from a field in one field list (in the upper portion of query design grid) to the equivalent field in another table's field list.

- Unlike in the Relationships window, you cannot enforce referential integrity in an ad-hoc join.

Try It!   Creating an Ad-Hoc Join

1 In **ATry05_studentfirstname_ studentlastname**, in the navigation pane, right-click qryIndianaOrders and click Design View.

2 Click Query Tools Design > Run ! to see the results prior to the join.

✓ *Access (inappropriately) matches up every instance from one table with every instance from the other. Creating the join will fix that.*

3 Click Home > View to return to Design view.

4 Drag the ClientID field from the tblIndianaCustomers table to the Customer field in tblOrders. A line appears connecting them.

5 Click Query Tools Design > Run ! to see the results.

✓ *This time the records are appropriately matched up.*

6 Click Home > View to return to Design view.

7 Click the Save button on the Quick Access toolbar.

A join line appears between the tables

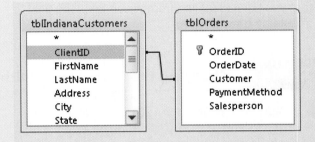

8 Leave the database open to use in the next Try It.

Changing the Join Type

- When you create queries that pull fields from multiple related tables, join type becomes important. Join type determines which records will be included when compiling a list of records by pulling information from both tables. For example, you might want to allow records from one table to be included in the results only if they have a valid corresponding record in the other table.

- You can force each table to contain only records for which there is a corresponding record in the other table. This is called an **inner join**.

- You can allow all records to appear from one table, even if there is no match in the joined table. This is called an **outer join.**

- You can change the join type either for an ad-hoc join, or for a regular (permanent) relationship between two tables in the Relationships window.

✓ *You cannot change the join type for a relationship that has enforced referential integrity unless it is a one-to-one relationship. That is not an issue for an ad-hoc join because you can't have enforced referential integrity for an ad-hoc join anyway.*

Try It!   Changing the Join Type

1 In **ATry05_studentfirstname_ studentlastname**, open the qryIndianaOrders query in Design view if it is not already open.

2 Double-click the join line between the two tables. The Join Properties dialog box opens.

3 Click the third join option.

(continued)

Try It!   Changing the Join Type (continued)

Select a join type for an ad hoc join

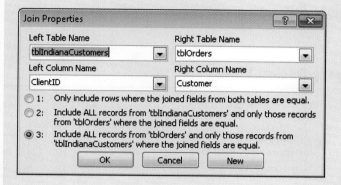

4 Click OK.

5 Click Query Tools Design > Run ❗ to see the query results.

✓ *Notice that the results have changed since you checked them in the previous exercise.*

6 Click Home > View 🖳 to return to Design view.

7 Double-click the join line between the two tables.

8 Click the second join option.

9 Click OK.

10 Click Query Tools Design > Run ❗ to see the query results.

✓ *Notice that the results are different because of the different join type.*

11 Click the Save button 💾 on the Quick Access toolbar.

12 Right-click the query tab, and click Close.

13 Leave the database open to use in the next Try It.

Try It!   Changing the Join Type for a Relationship

1 In **ATry05_studentfirstname_studentlastname**, click Database Tools > Relationships 🖾.

2 Double-click the line between tblProducts and tblOrderDetails.

3 Click Join Type.

4 In the Join Properties dialog box, click the first option.

5 Click OK.

6 In the Edit Relationships dialog box, click OK.

7 Click Relationship Tools Design > Close ⊠.

8 Leave the database open to use in the next Try It.

Changing Field Properties in Query Design View

- You can change the way a field looks in the query results by changing its field properties in Query Design view in the Property Sheet pane.

- In the Property Sheet, the Format property displays options in the drop-down list depending on the data type. Text fields do not have any drop-down choices in the Format property.

✓ *You can type a custom format in the Format property, such as m/d/yyyy to display the four-digit year along with the month and day. For more details on custom formats, click in the Format property and press F1.*

- Type > (greater than) in the Format property to force a text field to be all uppercase or < (less than) to force the field to display in lowercase.

- The Description property allows you to add a note to help you remember what the field does. The description will appear on the status bar in Datasheet and Form views when you are in the field.

- The Input Mask property validates each character as you type it in the field and displays parentheses, dashes, or other characters. Click the Build button to the right of the field and choose a build option in the Input Mask Wizard, just as you do when working in a table's Design view.

- By default, Yes/No fields appear as check boxes. If you want them to display Yes or No, click on the Lookup tab in the Property Sheet and change the Display Control property from Check Box to Text Box.

Try It!   **Changing Field Properties in Query Design View**

1. In **ATry05_studentfirstname_ studentlastname**, in the navigation pane, double-click qryOrderInfoSummary. Notice that the amounts in the Total field are formatted as plain numbers.

2. Right-click the query's tab, and click Design View ✎.

3. Click in the Total field's column.

4. Click Query Tools Design > Property Sheet ☞.

5. In the Property Sheet pane, click in the Format text box. A drop-down list arrow appears.

6. Open the Format drop-down list and click Currency.

7. Click in the Decimal Places field. Open its drop-down list, and click 2.

8. Click Query Tools Design > Run ❗. The query results appear. Notice that the amounts are formatted as currency.

Choose Currency as the field format

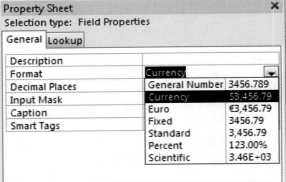

9. Click the Save button 🖫 on the Quick Access toolbar to save the query.

10. Right-click the query's tab, and click Close.

11. Leave the database open to use in the next Try It.

Showing Top Values

- The **top values** property of a query allows you to see the top (or bottom) values of your list.

- You can use top values in conjunction with a summary query to see a summary of the highest categories, or use it without Totals turned on to see the individual records with the lowest or highest values.

- The top values depend on the sort order of the records. If you want to see the highest values, first sort the field in descending order. If you want to see the lowest values, first sort the field in ascending order.

- Choose a value in the Top Values box, or type a value or percent.

- If you choose or type a percent, the number of values depends on the total number of records. If there are 50 records, 10% will show 5 records.

- If there is a tie on the last record, the query will show all ties. For example, if the 10th, 11th, and 12th record had the same value, you would see all 12 records even though 10 was input in Top Values.

Try It!   Showing Top Values

1 In **ATry05_studentfirstname_studentlastname**, in the navigation pane, right-click qryTopProducts and click Design View ☒.

2 In the Quantity field's column, open the Sort drop-down list and click Descending.

3 On the Query Tools Design tab, open the Return drop-down list and click 5.

4 Click Query Tools Design > Run ! to see the top five products.

5 Click Home > View ☒ to return to Design view.

6 Open the Return drop-down list and click 25%.

7 Click Query Tools Design > Run ! to see the top 25% products.

8 Click Home > View ☒ to return to Design view.

9 Click in the Return drop-down list's text box and type 3.

10 Click Query Tools Design > Run ! to see the top 3 products.

✓ *Notice that it actually shows 5 products, not 3, because there is three-way tie for the third product.*

11 Right-click the query tab, and click Close. Click Yes to confirm saving your work.

12 Close the database file, and exit Access.

Project 9—Create It

Textbook Database

DIRECTIONS

1. Start Access, if necessary, and open **AProj09** from the data files for this lesson.

2. Save the file as **AProj09_studentfirstname_studentlastname** in the location where your teacher instructs you to store the files for this lesson.

3. Click **Create > Query Design** ☐.

4. Double-click the following tables to add them to the query: **tblBooks, tblMoreBooks**. Then click **Close**.

5. Drag the **ISBN** field in **tblBooks** to the **ISBN** field in **tblMoreBooks**, creating an ad-hoc join.

6. Double-click the join line between the two tables, opening the Join Type dialog box.

7. Click option **3** (*Include ALL records from 'tblMoreBooks' and only those records from 'tblBooks' where the joined fields are equal*).

8. Click **OK**.

9. Double-click the following fields to add them to the query grid:

   From **tblBooks: ISBN, Title, Our Price**

   From **tblMoreBooks: Out of Print**

10. Open the **Table** drop-down list for the **ISBN** column in the query grid and click **tblMoreBooks**.

11. Click **Query Tools Design > Run** ! to check the query results. See Figure 5-1 on the next page. Then click **Home > View** ☒ to return to Query Design view.

12. Right-click the query's tab and click **Close**. Click **Yes** when prompted to save.

13. In the Save As dialog box, type **qryCrossCheckBooks** and click **OK**.

14. Close the database, and exit Access.

Figure 5-1

ISBN	Title	Our Price	OOP
020133466X			☐
0201741244	Introduction To Data Security	$21.00	☐
0805346332	Lectures in Design Technique	$37.00	☐
201237368	Understanding Web Publishing	$20.00	☐
201402894			☐
201615993	Public Key Encryption	$25.00	☐
201700028			☐
201702733	Network Administration for All	$27.50	☐
201730598	The HTML Companion	$22.50	☐
201736279	Understanding Broadband Technologies	$20.00	☐
201746717	The Web Wizard's Guide to PHP	$14.20	☐
201751686	Visual Basic from the Ground Up	$35.00	☐
201758791	Nitty Gritty HTML	$15.00	☐

Project 10—Apply It

Textbook Database

DIRECTIONS

1. Start Access, if necessary, and open **AProj10** from the data files for this lesson.

2. Save the file as **AProj10_studentfirstname_ studentlastname** in the location where your teacher instructs you to store the files for this lesson.

3. Create a new query in Design View. Add **qryBooksForSale** and **tblMoreBooks** as the data sources.

4. Add the following fields to the query grid:

   From **tblMoreBooks**: **ISBN, Author**

   From **qryBooksForSale**: **Condition, AskingPrice, RetailPrice**

5. If **qryBooksForSale** and **tblMoreBooks** are not already joined by their ISBN numbers, join them.

6. Edit the join type for the relationship so that all books from **tblMoreBooks** appear in the results and only the records from **qryBooksForSale** where the joined fields are equal.

7. Save the query as **qryMoreBooksForSale** and run it to check your work. See Figure 5-2 on the next page. Then close the query.

8. Open **qryBooksByDiscount** in Design view.

9. Using the Property Sheet, set the format for the **Discount** column to **Percent** with **0** decimal places.

10. Run the query to confirm that the Discounts show up as percentages. Then save and exit the query.

11. Copy **qryBooksByDiscount** and name the copy **qryTopBargains**.

12. Open **qryTopBargains** in Design view. Set it up to be sorted in **Descending** order by the **Discount** column.

13. Set up the query to show only the top **10** records.

14. Run the query to confirm that only 10 records show. Then save and close the query.

15. Close the database, and exit Access.

qryMoreBooksForSale

ISBN	Author	Condition	Asking Price	Retail Price
020133466X	Cheswick			
0201741244	Roeger			
0805346332	Crane			
1562438115	Ashford	Good	$10.00	$30.00
1562438115	Ashford	Like New	$15.00	$30.00
1585770884	Stevenson	Good	$22.00	$30.00
1585770884	Stevenson	Like New	$21.00	$30.00
201237368	Robertson			
201402894	Salvage			
201615993	Smith			
201700028	Budd			
201702733	Limoncelli			
201730598	Bradley			
201736279	Smith			
201746717	Lehnert			
201751686	Skansholm			
201758791	Stein			

Figure 5-2

Chapter Assessment and Application

Project 11—Make It Your Own

Music Database

A friend who is trying to organize her CDs has asked for your help with her database. She has created several tables, but because she did not enforce referential integrity, there are some problems with inconsistencies between them. In addition, the database still contains records for some CDs that she has given away or sold. You will help her out by using queries to tidy up her database.

DIRECTIONS

1. Start Access, if necessary, and open **AProj11** from the data files for this chapter.

2. Save the file as **AProj11_studentfirstname_studentlastname** in the location where your teacher instructs you to store the files for this chapter.

3. Using a Find Unmatched Query, find any recordings from **tblRecordings** that have no tracks listed in **tblTracks**, and delete them from **tblRecordings**. Keep the query; name it **qryFindUnmatchedRecordings**.

4. Enforce referential integrity between **tblRecordings** and **tblTracks** so the problem will not occur in the future.

5. Create a query called **qryMinimumPrice** that prompts the user to enter a minimum purchase price to display, and then displays a list of all recordings that cost at least that amount. Show all available fields from the **tblRecordings** table for each recording.

6. Use an Append query to add the records from **tblMoreArtists** to **tblArtists**. Save the Append query as **qryAppendArtists**.

7. Create a query that shows the last 5 recordings purchased using Top Values. Name the query **qryLastFive**.

8. Close the database, and exit Access.

Project 12—Master It

Tutoring Center Database

You are a consultant for The Tutoring Center, a company that offers academic test preparation and tutoring. You will create some queries that will help the office staff get information from their database.

DIRECTIONS

1. Start Access, if necessary, and open **AProj12** from the data files for this chapter.

2. Save the file as **AProj12_studentfirstname_ studentlastname** in the location where your teacher instructs you to store the files for this chapter.

3. Using a Make Table query, create a new table that contains the first and last names of students who have registered for an Algebra class. Name the new table **tblAlgebraStudents**. Save the query as **qryMakeTableAlgebra**.

4. Using the Crosstab Query Wizard, create a new query based on **qryEnrollment** that counts the number of enrollments for each course offered, with separate columns for each year as in Illustration A. Name the query **qryEnrollmentSummary**.

5. Make a copy of **qryEnrollment**, and name the copy **qryFutureEnrollment**.

6. Modify **qryFutureEnrollment** to create a parameter prompt that asks the user for today's date and then shows enrollments only for classes that begin after the current date. Test it by entering several different dates before and after the start dates in the unfiltered query results.

7. Create a query that deletes the inactive records from the **tblClasses** table and run it. Save the query as **qryDeleteInactiveClasses**.

8. In **qryClassesAndInstructors**, format the **Class** field so that all class names appear in all uppercase.

9. Using any method, create a query that lists the names of the top 3 most expensive courses offered and their prices. Name it **qryTop3Prices**.

10. Close the database, saving all changes, and exit Access.

Illustration A

qryEnrollmentSummary			
Class	Total Of EnrollmentID	2011	2012
ACT Prep	11	11	
Algebra I	6		6
SAT Prep	6		6

Chapter 2

Customizing Forms and Reports

Lesson 6
Working with Report Layouts
Projects 13-14

- Viewing a Report in Layout View
- Switching Between Layout Types
- Adjusting Control Margins and Control Padding
- Changing Column Width
- Adding, Deleting, and Reordering Fields
- Inserting a Title
- Changing the Page Setup

Lesson 7
Working with Controls
Projects 15-16

- Understanding Controls
- Inserting Text Box Controls
- Binding a Record Source to a Form
- Binding and Unbinding Fields to Controls
- Inserting List Boxes and Combo Boxes
- Inserting Labels
- Renaming a Control
- Inserting Check Boxes
- Inserting Option Button Groups

Lesson 8
Formatting Controls
Projects 17-18

- Formatting Controls on Forms and Reports
- Using Conditional Formatting
- Concatenating Fields

Lesson 9
Grouping, Sorting, and Filtering Report Data
Projects 19-20

- Grouping Report Data
- Sorting Report Data
- Adding Statistics
- Filtering Form or Report Data

Lesson 10
Creating Special Forms and PivotTables
Projects 21-22

- Using Datasheet Forms
- Using Multi-Item Forms
- Creating a Split Form Using the Split Form Tool
- Setting a Form's Default View
- PivotTable Basics
- Filtering a PivotTable View
- Creating a PivotTable Form

Lesson 11
Working with Subforms and Subreports
Projects 23-24

- Understanding Subforms and Subreports
- Creating a Form and Subform with the Form Wizard
- Creating a Subform with the Subform Wizard
- Creating a Subreport with Drag-and-Drop
- Editing a Subform or Subreport

Lesson 12
Working with Charts
Projects 25-26

- Inserting a Chart in a Report
- Editing a Chart
- Creating a PivotChart

Lesson 13
Creating Switchboards
Projects 27-28

- Opening the Switchboard Manager
- Managing Switchboard Pages
- Editing a Switchboard Page's Content
- Formatting the Switchboard
- Activating or Deactivating the Switchboard

Lesson 14
Creating Navigation Forms
Projects 29-30

- About Navigation Forms
- Creating a Navigation Form
- Adding Command Buttons to a Form
- Tying a Navigation Form into the Switchboard

End-of-Chapter Assessments
Projects 31-32

Lesson 6

Working with Report Layouts

➤ **What You Will Learn**

Viewing a Report in Layout View
Switching Between Layout Types
Adjusting Control Margins and Control Padding
Changing Column Width
Adding, Deleting, and Reordering Fields
Inserting a Title
Changing the Page Setup

WORDS TO KNOW

Print layout
The placement of fields on a report page.

Stacked report
A report that arranges data in rows with each field for each record on a separate row.

Tabular report
A report that arranges data in columns with each column representing a field.

Software Skills   The default reports that Access creates are fine for some circumstances, but in many cases you can improve them with a few simple tweaks. For example, you can control the print layout and change the margins, or you can change the page orientation.

Application Skills   Michigan Avenue Athletic Club would like you to improve on a report in their database that lists class enrollments. You will set up a print layout for this report that makes it as attractive as possible. You will also create a new report that shows each instructor's teaching assignments.

What You Can Do

Viewing a Report in Layout View

- **Print layout** refers to the placement of fields on a report page. It can include margin settings, field sizes, spaces between fields, placement of text labels, page orientation, and more.
- You can change the print layout either in Design view or Layout view.

- Layout view enables you to move, resize, and arrange fields in a what-you-see-is-what-you-get environment, unlike in Design view. This exercise focuses on Layout view.

- When you are working in Layout view, four additional tabs appear on the ribbon:
  - **Design:** Contains buttons and commands for grouping controls and for adding more controls to the report. You will learn more about these options in Lesson 7.

- **Arrange:** Enables you to change the overall layout of the report fields and the positioning of individual objects quickly.
- **Format:** Contains buttons and commands for formatting controls and text on the report.
- **Page Setup:** Provides settings that govern the page size and orientation, margins, and number of columns.

Try It!   Viewing a Report in Layout View

1 Start Access and open **ATry06** from the data files for this lesson. Click Enable Content if the information bar appears.

2 Save the file as **ATry06_studentfirstname_studentlastname** in the location where your teacher instructs you to store the files for this lesson.

3 Right-click rptCustomerMailing and click Layout View ▤. Leave the report open to use in the next Try It.

Switching Between Layout Types

- A report can be laid out either in Tabular or Stacked mode.

- A **tabular report** arranges data in columns with each column representing a field. Figure 6-1 shows an example of a tabular report. A **stacked report** arranges data in rows with each field for each record in a separate row, as shown in Figure 6-2.

Figure 6-1

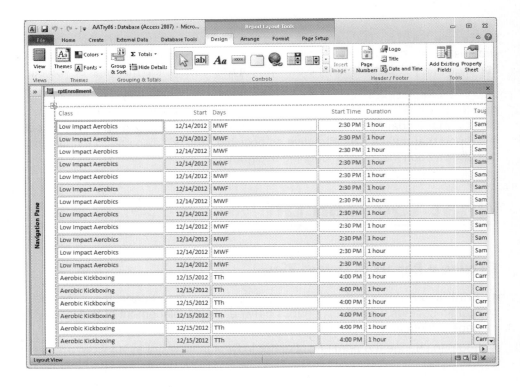

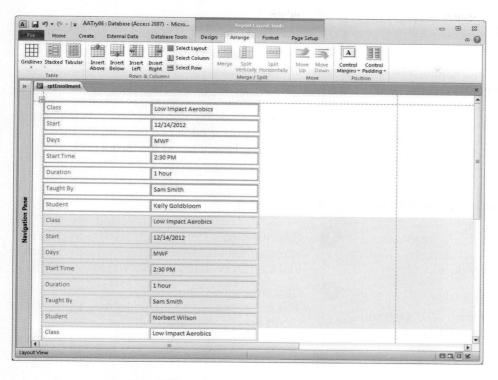

Figure 6-2

- You can select all the fields at once by clicking the Layout Selector icon ⊹ in the upper-left corner of the layout grid.
- To switch between the two modes, select all the fields to affect and then click either Tabular or Stacked on the Arrange tab.

- The reason you must select fields to affect before changing the layout is that it is possible to have a combination report, using tabular layout for some fields and stacked layout for others.
- The Remove command takes a field out of the layout grid, making it a free-floating object on the report. This might be useful to position a field in a precise location, for example.

Try It!   Switching Between Layout Types

1 In the **ATry06_studentfirstname_studentlast name** file, open rptCustomerMailing in Layout view if you did not previously do so.

2 Click the Layout Selector icon ⊹ in the upper corner of the table. All fields appear with an orange border around them indicating that they are selected.

3 Click Report Layout Tools Arrange > Stacked ▦. The layout changes to a stacked layout, as seen in Figure 6-2.

4 Press CTRL + Z to undo the last action, returning the report to a Tabular layout. Leave the report open for the next Try It.

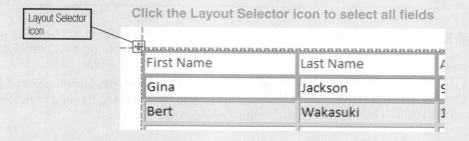

Layout Selector icon

Click the Layout Selector icon to select all fields

Adjusting Control Margins and Control Padding

- Each field and its data appear in a separate tabular cell on the layout. Each of these cells can have its margins and paddings set individually.

- The Control Margins drop-down list on the Arrange tab refers to the internal margins within the cells of the layout, not to the margins for the entire page. The margin setting here determines how much blank space there will be between the inner edge of a cell and the text within it.

  ✓ Note: If you want to change the margins for the entire report, use the Margins button on the Page Setup tab.

- The Control Padding drop-down list sets the space between the outer edge of a cell and the outer edge of an adjacent cell in the layout grid.

Try It!   Adjusting Control Margins and Control Padding

1 In the ATry06_studentfirstname_studentlast name file, open rptCustomerMailing in Layout view if you did not previously do so.

2 Click the first entry in the First Name column.

3 Click Arrange > Control Padding 🔲 > Medium. The padding between the cells increases.

4 Click Arrange > Control Margins 🄰 > Wide. The internal margins in each cell increases so much that the text is no longer fully visible.

5 Click Arrange > Control Margins 🄰 > Narrow. The text appears readable in the cell. Leave the report open for the next Try It.

Changing Column Width

- If a column is not wide enough to accommodate the widest entry in it, you might want to widen the column. You can also decrease a column's width to tighten up wasted space.

Try It!   Changing Column Width

1 In the ATry06_studentfirstname_studentlast name file, with the rptCustomerMailing open in Layout view, click any data row in the First Name column.

2 Position the mouse pointer at the right edge of any record's entry in the First Name column. The mouse pointer shows a double-headed arrow.

3 Drag to the left to decrease the column width so that the longest entry fits with no extra space.

4 Repeat step 3 to shrink the width of all the remaining columns to fit the longest entry in each. Leave the report open to use in the next Try It.

  ✓ Note: Try to shrink the widths enough so that the entire report fits on one page width.

Adding, Deleting, and Reordering Fields

- To add a field to the layout, on the Design tab click Add Existing Fields. A Field List task pane appears. From there you can view a list of fields in the available tables and drag-and-drop a field onto the layout grid.

- You can change the order of the fields by dragging the field to the left or right (in a tabular layout) or up or down (in a stacked layout).

- To remove a field from the layout, select it and press Delete. Any fields to its right or below it move to close up the hole.

Try It!   Deleting a Field

1 In the **ATry06_studentfirstname_studentlast name** file, with the rptCustomerMailing open in Layout view, click in the First Name column.

2 Click Report Layout Tools Arrange > Select Column ⊞.

✓ *Step 2 is necessary to select the entire column, not just the content in it. If you don't do this, you'll be left with an empty but still-present column when you delete.*

3 Press DEL. Leave the report open to use in the next Try It.

Try It!   Adding a Field

1 In the **ATry06_studentfirstname_studentlast name** file, with the rptCustomerMailing open in Layout view, click Report Layout Tools Design > Add Existing Fields ⊞.

2 Drag the First Name field from the Field List to the report layout, and drop it between the Last Name and Address fields. Leave the report open to use in the next Try It.

Try It!   Reordering Fields

1 In the **ATry06_studentfirstname_studentlast name** file, with the rptCustomerMailing open in Layout view, click in the Last Name column.

2 Click Report Layout Tools Arrange > Select Column ⊞.

3 Drag the First Name column to the left one position, and drop it to the left of the Last Name field. Leave the report open to use in the next Try It.

Inserting a Title

- If the report does not already have a label at the top that functions as a title, you can add one by clicking the Title button on the Design tab.

- If the report already has a title, this command moves the insertion point into the title box, so that you can change the title if needed.

Try It!   Inserting a Title

1 In the **ATry06_studentfirstname_studentlast name** file, with the rptCustomerMailing open in Layout view, click Report Layout Tools Design > Title ⊟. A placeholder title appears.

2 Type **Customer Mailing Information**, replacing the placeholder.

3 Click the blank cell to the left of the title.

4 Press DEL. Leave the report open to use in the next Try It.

Changing the Page Setup

■ Page setup includes the paper size, page orientation, page margins, and number of columns. All of these are controlled from the Page Setup tab.

■ On the Page Setup tab, you can:

• Select a paper size from the Size button's list.

• Select a margin preset from the Margins button's list.

• Mark or clear the Show Margins check box to show margins in Layout view or not.

• Mark or clear the Print Data Only check box to print data only or not. You might do this, for example, if filling out a pre-printed form. You would want to see the pre-printed labels and headings onscreen, but not on the hard copy.

• Click Portrait or Landscape to change page orientation.

• Select a number of columns from the Columns button's list.

• Click Page Setup to open a Page Setup dialog box in which you have greater control over many of these settings, such as the ability to specify exact margin amounts.

Try It! Changing the Page Setup

1 In the **ATry06_studentfirstname_studentlast name** file, with the rptCustomerMailing open in Layout view, click Report Layout Tools Page Setup > Margins 🔲 > Normal.

2 Click Size 🔲 > 8x10in.

3 Click Landscape 🔲.

4 Click Page Setup 🔲. The Page Setup dialog box opens.

5 On the Print Options tab, enter 1 in the Left text box, replacing the current value.

6 Enter 1 in the Right text box, replacing the current value.

7 Click OK.

8 Close the report, saving all changes.

9 Close the database, and exit Access.

Project 13—Create It

Michigan Avenue Athletic Club Database

DIRECTIONS

1. Start Access, if necessary, and open **AProj13** from the data files for this lesson.

2. Save the file as **AProj13_studentfirstname _studentlastname** in the location where your teacher instructs you to store the files for this lesson.

3. Click **Enable Content** on the information bar to enable all content.

4. In the Navigation Pane, click **qryTeachingAssignments** once to select it.

5. Click **Create > Report** 🖼️. A new report appears in Layout view.

6. Double-click the report title to select it. Type **Teaching Assignments**, replacing the default title.

7. Click the **Layout Selector** icon to select all fields and records.

8. Click **Report Layout Tools Arrange > Stacked** 🔲.

9. Click **Report Layout Tools Page Setup > Margins** 🔲 **> Wide**.

10. Click **Report Layout Tools Page Setup > Landscape** 🔲.

11. Click **Report Layout Tools Arrange > Control Padding** 🔲 **> None**.

12. **With your teacher's permission**, print the report.

13. Press CTRL + S to save the report.

14. In the Save As dialog box, type **rptTeaching Assignments** and click **OK**.

15. Close the database, and exit Access.

Project 14—Apply It

Michigan Avenue Athletic Club Database

DIRECTIONS

1. Start Access, if necessary, and open **AProj14** from the data files for this lesson.

2. Save the file as **AProj14_studentfirstname _studentlastname** in the location where your teacher instructs you to store the files for this lesson.

3. Click **Enable Content** on the information bar to enable all content.

4. Open **rptEnrollment** in Layout view.

5. Add a title to the top of the report. Title it **Enrollment Information**.

6. Use Page Setup to change the report margins to **0.5"** on all sides.

7. Set the control padding for the entire report to **Medium**.

8. Adjust the column widths for all columns so that all the fields fit across one page horizontally.

9. At the bottom left of the report, delete the record count field (37).

10. At the bottom right of the report, delete the **Page 1 of 1** text.

11. **With your teacher's permission**, print the report.

12. Save and close the report.

13. Close the database, and exit Access.

Lesson 7

Working with Controls

➤ What You Will Learn

Understanding Controls
Inserting Text Box Controls
Binding a Record Source to a Form
Binding and Unbinding Fields to Controls
Inserting List Boxes and Combo Boxes
Inserting Labels
Renaming a Control
Inserting Check Boxes
Inserting Option Button Groups

Software Skills   For more control over a form or report's appearance, you can create it in Design view. In Design view, you can insert various types of controls such as check boxes, option buttons, and drop-down lists that enhance the form or report's appearance and functionality.

Application Skills   Michigan Avenue Athletic Club would like a form that the office manager can use to enter and look up class offerings. You will create this form using a variety of control types.

What You Can Do

Understanding Controls

- A **control** is any object on a form or report. Controls can include text boxes, labels, drop-down list boxes, hyperlinks, and many other object types.
- Some types of controls display data from a table or query. For example, fields can appear as text boxes, list boxes, check boxes, or other control types.

- Other types of controls provide visual aids that make the form or report easier to understand, such as labels that identify the title of the report or a tab or grouping that provides a logical structure in which you place fields.

- Some text boxes and labels can be placed in Layout view, but most work involving controls is typically done in Design view. In Design view you can move, format, insert, and delete all types of controls.

✓ *Most controls can be used on either forms or reports, but many of them make more sense on a form. For example, a list box on a report would not be very useful because it would show only one value when printed; it would not be functionally any different from a text box.*

- Figure 7-1 shows some of the most common types of controls you can use.

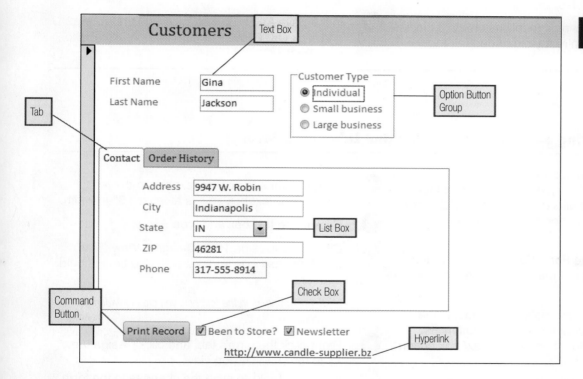

Figure 7-1

Inserting Text Box Controls

- Text boxes can be placed on forms and reports in either of two ways, based on whether or not they are bound or unbound. A **bound control** is connected to a field in a table or query. For example, when you place a field on a form, you are actually placing a bound text box on that form.

- An **unbound control** is not linked to one particular field. You might place an unbound text box on a form and then type a formula in it that calculates values from multiple fields, for example.

Try It! | **Inserting a Bound Text Box and Label on a Form**

1. Start Access and open **ATry07** from the data files for this lesson. Click Enable Content if the information bar appears.

2. Save the file as **ATry07_studentfirstname_ studentlastname** in the location where your teacher instructs you to store the files for this lesson.

(continued)

Try It!   **Inserting a Bound Text Box and Label on a Form** *(continued)*

3 Click Create > Form Design ⬚ . A blank form opens, with the Property Sheet pane open.

4 If the Field List pane does not appear, click Form Design Tools Design > Add Existing Fields ⬚ .

5 If a list of tables does not appear in the field list, click Show All Tables.

6 Click the plus sign next to tblCustomers if the list of its fields is not already expanded.

7 Double-click the FirstName field. A text box (for the field itself) and a label (containing the field's caption) appear on the form.

8 Double-click the LastName, Address, City, State, and ZIP fields to add them to the form.

9 Click the Save button ⬚ on the Quick Access Toolbar.

10 In the Save As dialog box, type **frmCustomers2** and click OK. Leave the form open to use in the next Try It.

Try It!   **Inserting an Unbound Text Box and Label on a Form**

1 In the frmCustomers2 form in the **ATry07_ studentfirstname_studentlastname** database, right-click the Detail section bar, and click Form Header/Footer. The form header and footer areas open up.

2 Scroll down to the Form Footer area, and drag the bottom border of the footer down, enlarging the footer by 0.5".

3 On the Form Design Tools Design tab, in the Controls group, click the Text Box button ⬚ . The mouse pointer changes to a text box button symbol.

4 Click in the Form Footer section, near the 4" mark on the horizontal ruler. A new unbound text box is placed in the form footer.

5 Click the label associated with the new text box and press ⬚DEL⬚. The label is deleted; the text box remains.

6 Drag the left edge of the text box to the left to enlarge the text box so it is at least 1.5" in width.

7 Click in the text box and type **=now( )**.

8 Click Form Design Tools Design > View ⬚ to check the text box. Today's date and time should appear in it.

✓ *If #### appears in the text box, you did not widen it enough in step 6.*

9 Right-click the form's tab, and click Design View ⬚ to return to Design view.

10 Press ⬚CTRL⬚ + ⬚S⬚ to save the changes to the form. Leave it open to use in the next Try It.

(continued)

Try It!   **Inserting an Unbound Text Box and Label on a Form** *(continued)*

Place a new unbound text box in the footer of the form

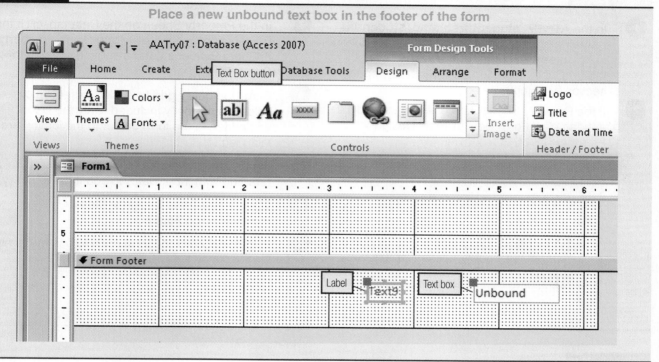

Binding a Record Source to a Form

- A form that you create from scratch using the Create > Form Design command does not have a record source assigned. In other words, there is no table or query associated with it by default.

- As you add fields to the form, those individual fields become part of its record source. However, any fields from that same table/query that are not added to the form are not part of the record source and therefore not available for binding to controls that you manually insert.

- For this reason, it may be useful to bind a table or query to the report before you start adding controls other than field text boxes. You can bind individual additional fields, as shown in the following exercise, or you can bind an entire table or query, as shown in the exercise that follows it.

Try It!   Editing the Record Source for the Form

1 In the **ATry07_studentfirstname_studentlast name** database, click the Form Selector button in the upper-left corner of the form to select the frmCustomers2 form itself (not any specific section or object).

2 If the Property Sheet pane does not already appear, click Form Design Tools Design > Property Sheet 🖼.

Click the form selector to select the entire form.

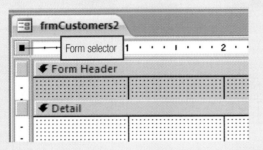

3 In the Property Sheet, on the Data tab, click the Build button ⋯ for the Record Source property. A Query Builder interface appears, similar to Query Design view.

4 Scroll the query grid to the left to see which fields are currently included. Only the fields you added to the form earlier in the lesson are included.

5 On the field list, double-click each missing field (starting with Input Date) to add it to the query.

6 Click Query Tools Design > Close ☒. A confirmation appears.

7 Click Yes. Leave the form open to use in the next Try It.

Try It!   Assigning an Entire Table as a Record Source

1 In the **ATry07_studentfirstname_studentlast name** database, click the Form Selector button in the upper-left corner of the form to select the frmCustomers2 form itself (not any specific section or object).

2 In the Property Sheet, on the Data tab, open the drop-down list for the Record Source property.

3 Click tblCustomers. Leave the form open to use in the next Try It.

Binding and Unbinding Fields to Controls

- You can create an unbound control and then bind a field to it later if you prefer.
- A control's binding is controlled from the Control Source property in its Property Sheet. The Control Source property can be found on both the Data and the All tabs.
- When you click in the Control Source box, a drop-down list appears of the fields in the currently selected data source (table or query). You can select one of these to avoid potential typing errors from manually typing the field name.

- If you know the exact names of the table and field you want to reference in the control, you can manually type them in as an expression; you do not have to go through the Expression Builder. If the field is from the same table or query as the primary record source for the form, you can type its name directly into the text box in Design view.

- If you want to reference a field from a different (related) table or query, you can write an expression that references the table name and the field name, like this: =**[tblEmployees]![Notes]**.

  ✓ *Alternatively you can click the Build button ⋯ to open the Expression Builder. From here you can pick fields from other data sources or create more complex expressions.*

- To unbind a control from the data source, clear the value in the Control Source box.

Try It!   Binding a Control to a Field

1 In the **ATry07_studentfirstname_studentlast name** database, with frmCustomers2 open in Design view, insert an unbound text box immediately below the ZIP field's text box.

    ✓ *Refer to the steps provided earlier in the lesson.*

2 If the Property Sheet is not already displayed, click Form Tools Design > Property Sheet 🗒.

3 Click the Data tab in the Property Sheet pane.

4 Open the Control Source property's drop-down list and click Phone.

5 Edit the Phone field's label to display Phone.

6 Insert another unbound text box immediately below the Phone field's text box.

7 Click in the new text box, and type **InputDate**. Change the new text box's label to Input Date.

8 Right-click the form's tab, and click Form View 🗒 to preview the form and confirm that the Phone and Input Date fields appear correctly.

9 Right-click the form's tab, and click Design View 🖎 to return to Design view. Leave the form open to use in the next Try It.

Try It!   Unbinding a Control

1 In the **ATry07_studentfirstname_studentlast name** database, with frmCustomers2 open in Design view, click in the InputDate text box to select it.

2 In the Property Sheet pane, clear the Control Source text box. *Unbound* appears in the text box.

3 Select the text box and press ⌨DEL⌨, removing it from the form.

4 Press ⌨CTRL⌨ + ⌨S⌨ to save the changes to the form. Leave the form open to use in the next Try It.

Inserting List Boxes and Combo Boxes

- **List boxes** and **combo boxes** are alternatives to text boxes for entering and displaying data. Both are text boxes with drop-down list capability, and both are used to allow users to select a value from a list rather than having to type a value.

- A list box restricts the user to only the values you present on the list. A combo box allows users to enter their own values (for example, if none of the list's values are appropriate).

Try It!   Inserting a List Box on a Form

1 In the **ATry07_studentfirstname_studentlast name** database, with frmCustomers2 open in Design view, on the Form Design Tools Design tab, in the Controls group, click the More button ⏷ to open a palette of available controls.

2 Click the List Box button ▤. The mouse pointer changes to a crosshair.

Click the List Box button in the Controls palette

3 Position the crosshair about 2" to the right of the State field's text box, and click. The List Box Wizard appears.

4 Click Next to accept the default value (I want the list box to get values from another table or query).

5 Click Table:tblStates and click Next.

6 Click the ▣ button to move the State field to the Selected Fields list. Then click Next.

7 When prompted for sorting, open the drop-down list and click State. Then click Next.

8 Click Next to accept the default width of the list column.

9 Click the Store that value in this field option button.

10 Open the drop-down list and click State. Then click Next.

Select State as the field in which to store the values

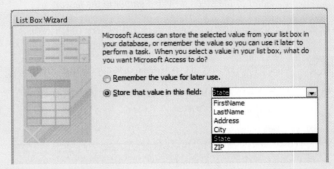

11 Type **State** in the text box, replacing the default label for the control.

12 Click Finish.

13 Click the original State field (not the list box you just created) and press ⌴DEL⌴.

14 Drag the ZIP and Phone fields down on the form to make enough space that the new State list box fits in the space formerly occupied by the old State text box.

15 Drag the State list box into the spot formerly occupied by the deleted State field.

16 Click Form Design Tools Design > View ▤ to view the form. Open the State list and confirm that it works.

17 Click the Save button 💾 on the Quick Access Toolbar.

18 Right-click the form's tab, and click Design View ⬚ to return to Design view. Leave the form open to use in the next Try It.

Inserting Labels

■ When you add bound controls to a field, such as a field text box, the associated caption for it automatically appears in a label.

■ You can also create unbound labels for titles or explanatory notes as well.

■ If you click on the form after selecting the Label button, a label box appears that automatically expands as you type. To create line breaks, press ⌴SHIFT⌴ + ⌴ENTER⌴.

■ If you drag on the form after selecting the Label button, a label box appears that is the size and shape of the area you dragged. Text automatically wraps to the next line as needed as you type in it.

Try It!   **Inserting a Label on a Form**

1 In the **ATry07_studentfirstname_studentlast name** database, with frmCustomers2 open in Design view, on the Form Design Tools Design tab, in the Controls group, click the Label button **Aa**.

2 Click in the empty area to the right of the form fields in the Detail section.

3 Type the following: **Note: This form is for residential**

4 Press **SHIFT** + **ENTER** to start a new line.

5 Type the following: **customers only**.

6 Leave the form open to use in the next Try It.

Try It!   **Associating a Label with a Control**

1 In the **ATry07_studentfirstname_studentlast name** database, with frmCustomers2 open in Design view, on the Form Design Tools Design tab, in the Controls group, click the Label button **Aa**.

2 Click on the form to the right of the Phone text box.

3 Type **Please include area code**.

4 Click the warning icon to the left of the new label. A menu appears.

5 Click Associate Label with a Control.

6 Click Text26 and click OK.

   ✓ *The number following Text may be something other than 26. There should only be one item that starts with Text on the list.*

The warning icon opens a menu

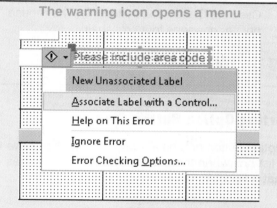

7 Press **CTRL** + **S** to save the form. Leave the form open to use in the next Try It.

Renaming a Control

■ In the preceding exercise, the text box for the Phone field had a generic name, such as Text26, because it was originally an unbound text box when created. Text boxes that start out bound to fields have names assigned that match the field names automatically.

■ You can rename a control on its Property Sheet.

Try It!   **Renaming a Control**

1 In the **ATry07_studentfirstname_studentlast name** database, with frmCustomers2 open in Design view, select the Phone text box.

2 If the Property Sheet pane is not open, click Form Design Tools Design > Property Sheet.

3 Click the Other tab.

4 In the Name property, change the name to **Phone**. Leave the form open to use in the next Try It.

Inserting Check Boxes

- When you place a Yes/No field on a form, it automatically appears as a check box control with an associated label.

- You can also place an unbound check box on a form and then bind it to a field as you learned earlier in the lesson. The following exercise demonstrates how to do that.

Try It!   Inserting Check Boxes

1 In the **ATry07_studentfirstname_studentlast name** database, with frmCustomers2 open in Design view, on the Form Design Tools Design tab, in the Controls group, click the More button ▼ to open a palette of available controls.

2 Click the Check Box button ☑ . The mouse pointer changes to a crosshair.

3 Click on the form, immediately beneath the Phone field text box. A check box and generic label appear.

4 On the Property Sheet, on the Data tab, open the Control Source property's drop-down list and click Newsletter.

5 Click in the label associated with the check box and type **Newsletter**, replacing the placeholder. Leave the form open to use in the next Try It.

Inserting Option Button Groups

- Option button groups are used as an alternative to a list box when there are only a few valid values that a field can have.

- In an option button group, when one button is selected, the previously-selected button becomes deselected. This exclusivity is what distinguishes option buttons from check boxes, which can each individually have their own on/off state.

Try It!   Inserting Option Button Groups

1 In the **ATry07_studentfirstname_studentlast name** database, with frmCustomers2 open in Design view, select the Country field's text box and press DEL , removing it from the form.

2 On the Form Design Tools Design tab, in the Controls group, click the More button ▼ to open a palette of available controls.

3 Click the Option Group button ⬚.

4 Click in the blank area to the right of the Address text box on the form. The Option Group Wizard opens.

5 Type the following label names, each on their own row:
United States
Canada
Mexico

Enter the values for the option buttons

6 Click Next.

7 Click Next to accept the default choice of United States.

8 Click Next to accept the default number assignments for the options.

(continued)

Try It!   **Inserting Option Button Groups** *(continued)*

9 Click Store the value in this field.

10 Open the drop-down list and click Country. Then click Next.

11 Click Next to accept the default button type.

12 Type **Country**, replacing the default caption text.

13 Click Finish.

14 Press ⌨CTRL⌨ + ⌨S⌨ to save the form.

15 Right-click the form's tab and click Form View 🖼 to display the form in Form view.

16 Save and close the form.

17 Close the database, and exit Access.

Project 15—Create It

Class Offerings Form

DIRECTIONS

1. Start Access, if necessary, and open **AProj15** from the data files for this lesson.

2. Save the file as **AProj15_studentfirstname_ studentlastname** in the location where your teacher instructs you to store the files for this lesson.

3. Click **Enable Content** on the information bar to enable all content.

4. Click **Create** > **Form Design** 🖼 . A new form appears in Design view.

5. If the Property Sheet does not appear, click **Form Design Tools Design** > **Property Sheet** 📈 .

6. In the Record Source property, open the drop-down list and click **tblClassOfferings**.

7. Click ☒ to close the Property Sheet.

8. Click **Form Design Tools Design** > **Add Existing Fields** 🗔 . A list of fields in tblClassOfferings appears.

9. Double-click the **ClassOfferingID** field. It is added to the form.

10. On the Form Design Tools Design tab, in the Controls group, click the **More** button ⊡, opening a palette of control types.

11. Click the **Combo Box** button 🖵.

12. Click on the form, immediately below the ClassOfferingID field. The Combo Box Wizard appears.

13. Leave the default selected (I want the list box to get values from another table or query) and click **Next**.

14. Click **Table:tblClasses** and click **Next**.

15. Click the **ClassName** field and click ▷ to move it to the Selected Fields list. Then click **Next**.

16. Open the drop-down list and click **ClassName** to set the sort field. Then click **Next**.

17. Double-click the right edge of the **Class** heading in the dialog box to auto-widen the column to fit the longest entry. Then click **Next**.

18. Click **Store that value in this field**.

19. Open the drop-down list, and click **Class**. Then click **Next**.

20. Type **Class**, replacing the default label for the control. Then click **Finish**.

21. Drag the right edge of the new control to the right to increase its width to **2"**.

22. Click the **Save** button 🖫 on the Quick Access Toolbar.

23. Type **frmClassOfferings** and click **OK**.

24. Right-click the form's tab and click **Form View** 🖼 to display the form in Form View.

25. **With your teacher's permission**, print the form. See Figure 7-2.

26. Close the database, and exit Access.

Figure 7-2	
ClassOfferingID	1
Class	Low Impact Aerobics ▼

Project 16—Apply It

Class Offerings Form

DIRECTIONS

1. Start Access, if necessary, and open **AProj16** from the data files for this lesson.

2. Save the file as **AProj16_studentfirstname_ studentlastname** in the location where your teacher instructs you to store the files for this lesson.

3. Open **frmClassOfferings** in Design view.

4. Delete the **Notes** field.

5. Beneath the Size Limit field, add a combo box for the **Instructor** field.

   - Set it to look up the first and last names from tblInstructors.
   - Sort the list by **Last Name**.
   - Store the value in the **Instructor** field.
   - Name the combo box **Instructor**.

6. Add an option group that provides buttons for selecting a location:

   - Use the following list: **Gym, Pool, Upstairs Studio**.
   - Do not set a default.
   - Use the default values for each option.
   - Store the value in **Location**.
   - Use **Option buttons**.
   - Use **Shadowed** as the group style.
   - Name the group **Location**.

7. Move the option group's label to the left, to align with the other labels on the form.

8. Save the form, and view it in Form View.

9. In Form View, enter a new record:

   Start: **11/26/2012 08:00 AM**
   Days: **MWF**
   Duration: **6 weeks**
   Size Limit: **20**
   Instructor: **Carrie Anderson**
   Location: **Upstairs Studio**

10. To the right of the Start fields, create a new label with the following text:

    Enter a date and time. You can use the Calendar button to select a date if desired.

11. Associate the label with the **StartTime** control.

    ✓ *Click the icon to the left of the unbound label, and on the menu that appears, click Associate label with a control, and click StartTime.*

12. **With your instructor's permission,** print one copy of the form with the new record displayed. See Figure 7-3.

13. Close the database, and exit Access.

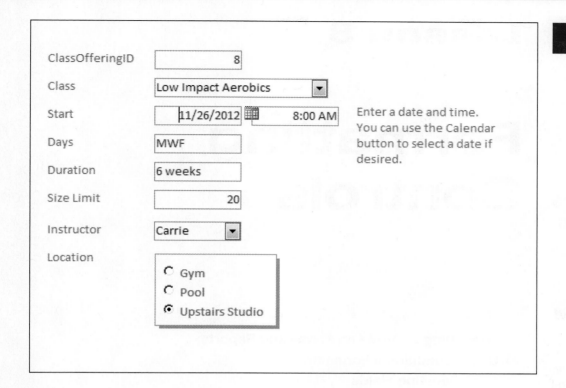

Figure 7-3

Lesson 8

Formatting Controls

WORDS TO KNOW

Concatenate
To join two separate
entities into a single one,
such as combining a first
and last name to form a
full name.

Conditional formatting
Formatting that is applied
only when a condition is
met.

Expression
A logical condition
including comparison
operators such as greater
than (>), less than (<), or
equals (=).

➤ What You Will Learn

Formatting Controls on Forms and Reports
Using Conditional Formatting
Concatenating Fields

Software Skills   Forms and reports are very similar in terms of the formatting
you can apply to them. Both enable you to position fields and labels for optimal
viewing; the main difference is that a form is designed for onscreen use whereas a
report is designed to be printed. In this exercise, you will learn some tips and tricks
for formatting and concatenating controls on forms and reports.

Application Skills   Michigan Avenue Athletic Club would like the Teaching
Assignments report in their database to show the instructors' full names on a single
line, rather than a separate line for first and last names. You will make this change
by creating a concatenated control in that report. You will also modify a form that
shows class offerings such that if a particular class is on sale, the sale price is
reflected onscreen and is marked with special formatting.

What You Can Do

Formatting Controls on Forms and Reports

- You can apply the same types of formatting to controls on forms and reports
  that you would apply in any word processing program. For example, you
  can change the font, size, color, attributes such as bold and italic, and text
  alignment (left, right, or center).

- You can also apply a background fill to the control that applies color behind the
  text in that control's frame.

- To copy formatting between controls, use Format Painter. Select the control that is already formatted correctly, and then click the Format Painter button. Then click the control to receive the formatting.

- All these formatting features are found on the Format tab when in Layout or Design view.

✓ *To paint the formatting onto multiple destinations without having to re-select the source each time, double-click instead of single-clicking the Format Painter button.*

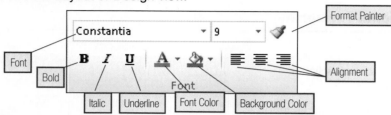

Figure 8-1

Try It!   Formatting Controls

1   Start Access and open **ATry08** from the data files for this lesson. Click Enable Content if the information bar appears.

2   Save the file as **ATry08_studentfirstname _studentlastname** in the location where your teacher instructs you to store the files for this lesson.

3   In the Navigation pane, right-click rptEmployeesByBuilding and click Layout View.

4   Click the Building column heading to select it.

5   Hold down CTRL and click the Department column heading.

6   Click Report Layout Tools Format > Bold **B**.

7   Open the Font Size drop-down list and click 11.

8   Open the Font Color button's **A** menu and click bright yellow.

9   Click the Building column heading so that only that heading is selected.

✓ *Format Painter works only when a single object is selected.*

10   Double-click the Format Painter button.

11   Click the First Name and Last Name headings.

12   Press ESC to cancel Format Painter.

13   Right-click the report's tab and click Close. Click Yes when asked to save changes. Leave the database open to use in the next Try It.

Using Conditional Formatting

- **Conditional formatting** sets up special formatting conditions that should apply if the value in a field or other control meets certain criteria.

- Some examples: You could color items with low sales (under a certain dollar amount) in red to indicate a problem, or you could underline the names of students who have not yet paid for a class.

- Conditional formatting can be applied to both forms and reports, in both Design and Layout views.

- Conditional formatting conditions can be set either by the field's value, as in the preceding steps, or by an expression. An **expression** is a formula. It can reference field names (enclosed in square brackets).

- [Quantity] * [Unit Price] > 1000 is an example of an expression. In this case, the conditional formatting would apply if multiplying the values from the quantity and unit price fields resulted in a value of less than 1,000.

- You must use an expression if you want to format a control (or multiple controls) based on the value of another control, or based on the result of a calculation.

- You must also use an expression to apply conditional formatting to an unbound control (that is, a control that is not connected to a field in an underlying table, query, or SQL statement). The date in a report's footer is an example of an unbound control.

- You do not have to type an equals sign at the beginning of a function in the Conditional Formatting dialog box.

✓ *You can use almost all of the functions from Microsoft Excel in expressions in Access. For example, suppose you want the date at the bottom of the report to print in bold if the report is being printed on a Monday because it is the first report of the week. Excel has a WEEKDAY function that* converts *a date to a number representing the day of the week (starting with Sunday as 1). Excel also has a NOW function that returns today's date and time. You can combine these to make an expression for conditional formatting: WEEKDAY(NOW)=2.*

Try It!   Using Conditional Formatting

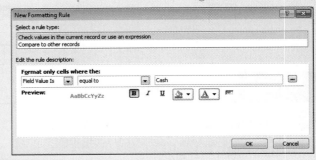

Set up the new formatting condition

1. In **ATry08_studentfirstname_studentlast name**, in the Navigation Pane, right-click frmOrders and click Layout View.

2. Click the Payment Method text box (not its label) to select it.

3. Click Form Layout Tools Format > Conditional Formatting. The Conditional Formatting Rules Manager dialog box opens.

4. Click New Rule. The New Formatting Rule dialog box opens.

5. Open the second drop-down list (currently showing between) and click equal to.

6. In the text box to the right of the drop-down list, type **Cash**.

7. Click the Bold button **B** in the dialog box.

8. Open the Font Color button's **A** menu in the dialog box and click a green square.

9. Click OK.

10. Click OK to close the Formatting Rules Manager dialog box.

11. Click the Next Record button ▸ to move to record 2, which has Cash as the payment type. Note the formatting applied.

12. Click the Save button on the Quick Access toolbar to save the changes. Then right-click the form's tab and click Close. Leave the database open to use in the next Try It.

Try It!   Using an Expression in Conditional Formatting

1. In **ATry08_studentfirstname_studentlast name**, in the Navigation pane, right-click rptOrderInfo and click Layout View.

2. Click the first entry in the ProductName column.

3. Click Report Layout Tools Format > Conditional Formatting.

4. Click New Rule.

5. Open the first drop-down list (currently set to Field Value Is) and click Expression Is.

6. Click the Build button to open the Expression Builder.

7. In the middle pane (Expression Categories), double-click Quantity. It appears in the text box at the top of the dialog box.

8. Type >1.

9. Click OK.

✓ *You can type the expression directly into the New Formatting Rule dialog box if you prefer; the Expression Builder's use is optional. When typing field names, enclose them in square brackets, like this: [Quantity].*

(continued)

Try It! | **Using an Expression in Conditional Formatting** *(continued)*

Create an expression with the Expression Builder

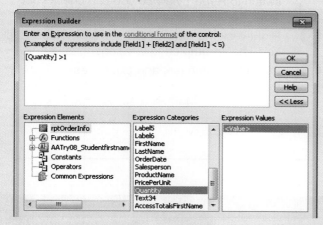

10 Open the Font Color button's ![A] drop-down list and click Automatic.

11 Open the Background Color button's ![icon] drop-down list and click a bright blue square.

12 Click OK.

13 Click OK to close the Conditional Formatting Rules Manager. In all records where the Quantity is more than 1, the product name now appears with a bright blue background.

14 Right-click the report's tab and click Close. When prompted to save changes, click Yes. Leave the database open to use in the next Try It.

Concatenating Fields

■ On some reports it may look better if multiple fields are combined in a single control, such as first and last name.

■ To **concatenate** (combine) fields, first delete their original individual fields from the report. Then, in Design view, add a new text box with the Text Box tool. (You cannot do this from Layout view.) In the new text box, type an expression that begins with an equal sign and then contains the field names in square brackets, separated by ampersand signs (&).

■ To include spaces or fixed text or punctuation between the fields, enclose it in quotation marks.

■ For example, to combine FirstName and LastName fields:
=[FirstName]&" "&[LastName]

■ To combine City, State, and ZIP fields:
=[City]&", "&[State]&" "&[ZIP]

Try It! | **Concatenating Fields**

1 In **ATry08_studentfirstname_studentlast name**, in the Navigation Pane, right-click rptCustomerDirectory and click Design View ![icon].

2 In the Detail section, select FirstName and press [DEL].

3 In the Detail section, select LastName and press [DEL].

4 On the Report Design Tools Design tab, in the Controls group, click the Text Box button [abl].

5 Click in the Detail area in the blank spot. A new blank text box appears.

6 Type =[FirstName]" "&[LastName].

7 Click away from the text box to deselect it.

8 Click the label to the left of the new text box and press [DEL] to remove it.

9 Drag the right border of the new text box to the right to widen it to fill the available space.

✓ *The expression you typed in the text box will appear truncated; that's okay. It will still work.*

10 In the Page Header section, select the First Name label and press [DEL].

11 In the Page Header section, in the Last Name label, delete *Last* so the label reads Name.

(continued)

Try It!   **Concatenating Fields** *(continued)*

Create an expression that concatenates
the values of two fields

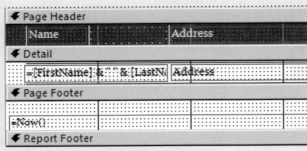

12 Click Report Design Tools Design > View ▥ to switch to Report view so you can check your work.

13 Right-click the report's tab and click Close. Click Yes when prompted to save changes.

14 Close the database, and exit Access.

Project 17—Create It

Teaching Assignments Report

DIRECTIONS

1. Start Access, if necessary, and open **AProj17** from the data files for this lesson.

2. Save the file as **AProj17_studentfirstname_ studentlastname** in the location where your teacher instructs you to store the files for this lesson.

3. Click **Enable Content** on the information bar to enable all content.

4. In the Navigation pane, right-click **rptTeaching Assignments** and click **Layout View** ▤.

5. Click the **Class** label for the first record if it is not already selected.

6. Click **Report Layout Tools Format > Bold** ▣.

7. Right-click the report's tab and click **Design View** ◪.

8. Click the **FirstName** text box and press DEL.

9. Click the **LastName** text box and press DEL.

10. Click **Report Design Tools Design > Text Box** abl.

11. Click in the space formerly taken by the FirstName field to place an unbound text box there.

12. Click in the text box and type =[FirstName] &" "& [LastName].

13. Double-click the label associated with the new text box and change its text to **Instructor**.

14. Drag the text box and label to align with the other text boxes and labels on the form.

   ✓ *Because the form uses a layout, you can make the text box and label snap to the layout. Drag the text around slightly until an orange box lights up behind it, indicating that if you drop it, it will drop into the layout. Then release the mouse button. Doing this not only positions it in the layout but also automatically adjusts its width to match the other fields.*

   Figure 8-2 shows the completed design.

15. Right-click the report's tab, and click **Report View**.

16. **With your teacher's permission**, print the report.

17. Right-click the report's tab and click **Close**. When prompted, click **Yes** to save your work.

18. Close the database, and exit Access.

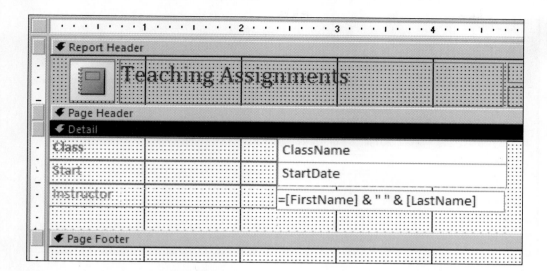

Figure 8-2

Project 18—Apply It

Class Offerings Form

DIRECTIONS

1. Start Access, if necessary, and open **AProj18** from the data files for this lesson.

2. Save the file as **AProj18_studentfirstname_studentlastname** in the location where your teacher instructs you to store the files for this lesson.

3. Open **frmClassOfferings** in Layout view.

4. Create a conditional formatting rule that makes the price of the class appear in red if the Sale check box is marked.

5. Using the Text Box tool, place a new text box below the Sale check box.

6. In the new text box, enter =**"On Sale Now."**

7. Delete the label associated with the new text box.

8. Format the new text box to use pale gray font color, so the text disappears into the background.

9. Click **Form Design Tools Format** > **Shape Outline** ⬔ and click **Transparent** to remove the border from the new text box.

10. Check your work in Form view to make sure the new text box border does not appear on the form.

11. Set up a conditional format for the new text box so that if the Sale check box is marked, the text in it appears in bright red.

12. Check your work in Form view, viewing several records, to make sure the *On Sale Now* text appears only when the class is on sale. See Figure 8-3.

13. Close the database, and exit Access.

Figure 8-3

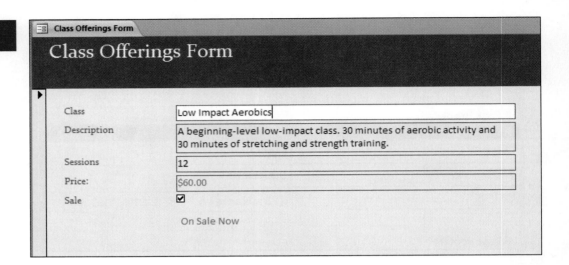

Lesson 9

Grouping, Sorting, and Filtering Report Data

> ## What You Will Learn

Grouping Report Data

Sorting Report Data

Adding Statistics

Filtering Form or Report Data

WORDS TO KNOW

Totals
Statistics that summarize report data, such as sum, count, or average.

Software Skills   One way in which reports are better than datasheets for printouts is that you can group, sort, and filter the data that appears and add summary statistics. All these tools make it possible to highlight the important trends in the information being presented.

Application Skills   The Textbook Exchange would like some reports that will help them understand their sales data better. You will create some grouped, filtered, and summarized reports that will provide quick and accurate information about sales trends.

What You Can Do

Grouping Report Data

- When records are grouped, one field serves as a sub-heading in the report, and records are placed under the appropriate sub-heading depending on their value for that field. See Figure 9-1.

Figure 9-1

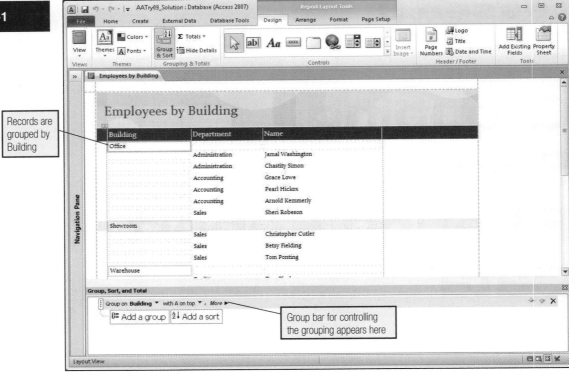

Records are grouped by Building

Navigation Pane

Group bar for controlling the grouping appears here

- A grouping has a default sort order, which you can change from the group bar in the Group, Sort, and Total pane.

- For more options to define the group operation, click the word *More* on the bar. The options will vary depending on the field type.

- One of the options you can select there is whether or not to keep a group together on one page.

Try It!   Grouping Report Data

1 Start Access and open **ATry09** from the data files for this lesson. Click Enable Content if the information bar appears.

2 Save the file as **ATry09_studentfirstname_ studentlastname** in the location where your teacher instructs you to store the files for this lesson.

3 In the Navigation pane, right-click rptEmployees ByBuilding and click Layout View .

4 Click Report Layout Tools Design > Group & Sort . The Group, Sort, and Total pane appears at the bottom of the report.

5 In the Group, Sort, and Total pane, click Add a Group.

6 On the field list that pops up, click Building. The report changes so that records are grouped by Building, and a group bar for the Building field appears in the Group, Sort, and Total pane. Leave the report open to use in the next Try It.

A group bar appears for the Building field

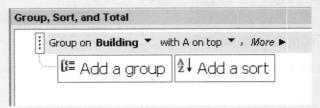

Try It! — Changing Group Options

1 In the rptEmployeesByBuilding report in the **ATry09_studentfirstname_studentlastname** file, click With A on top in the Group, Sort, and Total pane. On the pop-up menu that appears, click With Z on top.

2 Click More. Additional options appear.

3 Click the drop-down arrow to the right of Do not keep group together on one page, opening a menu.

4 Click Keep whole group together on one page. Leave the report open to use in the next Try It.

You can keep a group together on a page when the report is printed

Group, Sort, and Total

Group on **Building** ▼ with Z on top ▼ , by entire value ▼ ,
do not keep group together on one page ▼ , Less ◄
   do not keep group together on one page
   keep whole group together on one page
   keep header and first record together on one page

Sorting Report Data

- Use sorting only if you just want to sort, not group. Grouping includes sorting.

- To sort the records in a report, click Add a sort. A sort bar appears, with a drop-down list from which to select the field by which to sort. Click the desired field.

- The bar shows a default sort order that Access defines for you. The exact wording depends on the type of field. For example, for a date field, it might be "from oldest to newest." You can click this to select an alternate order if you prefer.

- In the event of a duplicate value in the sort field for two or more records, you might want to specify a second-level sort field. To do this, click the Add a sort button beneath the first sort. You can do this beneath a group too if you want additional sorting levels besides the default one that comes with the grouping.

Try It! — Sorting Report Data

1 In the rptEmployeesByBuilding report in the **ATry09_studentfirstname_studentlastname** file, click Add a sort under the Group on Building bar in the Group, Sort, and Total pane.

2 On the pop-up menu that appears, click Department.

3 Click the drop-down arrow to the right of From smallest to largest, opening a menu.

4 Click From largest to smallest.

✓ In this example, From largest to smallest is the same as With Z on top. Both sort in alphabetical descending order.

5 Click the Save 🖫 button on the Quick Access toolbar. Leave the report open to use in the next Try It.

Adding Statistics

- Report statistics are called **totals** in Access.

- After clicking More for a grouping, you can click *with no totals* for a Totals box in which you can specify the statistics you want to display for each group. You can choose the field on which to total, the function to use (such as Sum or Average), whether or not to show grand totals, and whether to show totals in the group header or group footer.

- When you specify totals, the expressions needed to create them are inserted automatically in the proper section(s).

- You can also manually enter your own expressions in placed text boxes in any section. Click the Text Box tool on the Design tab, and then click in a footer or header section and type in any of the following:
  - =SUM([fieldname]) to total the values in the *fieldname* field.
  - =AVG([fieldname]) to average the values in the *fieldname* field.

- =COUNT([fieldname]) to return the number of items in the *fieldname* field.
- =MAX([fieldname]) to return the largest value in the *fieldname* field.
- =MIN([fieldname]) to return the smallest value in the *fieldname* field.

✓ *If you just want to show the statistics and not the records themselves, click the Hide Details button on the Design tab.*

Try It!   **Adding Statistics with the Totals Panel**

1 In the rptEmployeesByBuilding report in the **ATry09_studentfirstname_studentlastname** file, click More under the Group on Building bar in the Group, Sort, and Total pane.

2 Click the down arrow to the right of With no totals. A Totals panel opens.

3 Open the Total On drop-down list and click Building.

4 Click the Show subtotal in group footer check box. The Totals panel closes, and the report changes to show the number of values in each group.

5 Right-click the report's tab and click Close. Click Yes when prompted to save your changes.

6 Leave the database open to use in the next Try It.

Add a subtotal by group

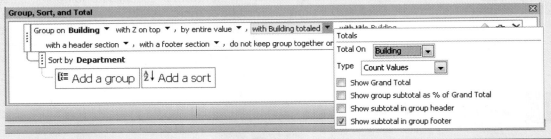

Try It!   **Adding Statistics with a Function**

1 In **ATry09_studentfirstname_studentlast name**, in the Navigation pane, right-click rptOrderInfo and click Design View.

2 In the Group, Sort, and Total pane, click More.

3 Click the drop-down arrow to the right of Without a footer section, and click With a footer section.

4 Click Report Design Tools Design > Text Box.

5 Click in the Report Footer section, approximately 1.5" from the right edge. An unbound text box appears. Drag the text box to make its right edge align with the right edge of the Quantity text box above it.

6 Click in the text box and type =SUM([Quantity]).

7 Double-click the text in the label associated with the text box to select the label text and type **Total:**.

8 Click the Total: label to select it, and then drag it (by its upper-left corner selection handle) closer to the text box.

✓ *Dragging a label by its upper-left corner selection handle enables you to move the label separately from its associated text box.*

9 Right-click the report's tab, and click Report View to preview your work.

10 Right-click the report's tab and click Close. Click Yes when prompted to save your work.

11 Leave the database open to use in the next Try It.

Filtering Form or Report Data

- You can set up filtering for a form or report from Layout view.
- To filter by example, right-click a field and then choose one of the filter commands on the shortcut menu. This submenu provides Boolean options such as equals, does not equal, and so on.

✓ It is often just as easy to create a query that filters the data, and then base the form or report on that query, as it is to set up record filtering on the form or report layout itself.

- You can also set up custom filters that enable you to use wildcard characters such as * for any number of characters or ? for single characters.

Try It!   Filtering Report Data by Example

1. In **ATry09_studentfirstname_studentlast name**, in the Navigation pane, right-click rptCustomerDirectory and click Layout View ▦.

2. Right-click the State field column, on any record that shows IL in that field. A shortcut menu opens.

3. Click Equals "IL." The report changes to show only the two records where the state is IL.

4. Right-click the State column again.

5. Click Clear filter from State. Leave the report open to use in the next Try It.

Try It!   Filtering Report Data with a Custom Filter

1. In the rptCustomerDirectory report in the **ATry09_studentfirstname_studentlastname** file, right-click anywhere in the Phone field's column. A shortcut menu opens.

2. Point to Text Filters. A submenu opens.

3. Click Begins With. A Custom Filter dialog box opens.

4. Type **317** and click OK. The report shows only records where the area code is 317.

5. Right-click the Phone column again.

6. Click Clear filter from Phone.

7. Right-click the report's tab and click Close. Click No if prompted to save changes.

8. Close the database and exit Access.

Project 19—Create It

Book Discount Report

DIRECTIONS

1. Start Access, if necessary, and open **AProj19** from the data files for this lesson.

2. Save the file as **AProj19_studentfirstname_ studentlastname** in the location where your teacher instructs you to store the files for this lesson.

3. Click **Enable Content** on the information bar to enable all content.

4. In the Navigation pane, right-click **rptBooksByDiscount** and click **Layout View** ▦.

5. If the Group, Sort, and Total pane does not already appear, click **Report Design Tools Design > Group & Sort** ▦.

6. In the Group, Sort, and Total pane, click **Add a group**.

7. In the list of fields that appears, click **Discount**.

8. Click the drop-down arrow to the right of From smallest to largest, and click **From largest to smallest**.

9. Click **Add a sort**.
10. In the list of fields that appears, click **Title**.
11. In the Discount column on the report layout, select 50%.
12. Right-click **50%** and click **Greater than or equal to 50%**.

13. Select the text in the Books by Discount label at the top of the report, and type **Books by Discounted 50% or More**
14. **With your teacher's permission**, print one copy of the report. Figure 9-2 shows the first page of the report.
15. Save and close the report, then close the database, and exit Access.

Figure 9-2

Books Discounted by 50% or More

Discount	ISBN	Title	Author	Condition	Retail Price	Asking Price	Last
85%							
	936862114	Touch 'N' Type, 25 Words to Success	Hall	Like New	$20.00	$17.00	Stevenson
80%							
	0201440997	Computer Security: Art and Science	Bishop	Like New	$74.99	$60.00	Hallan
73%							
	1585770884	Learning the Internet for Business	Stevenson	Good	$30.00	$22.00	Hickox
72%							
	0201976994	Computer Networking: A Top-Down Approach Featuring the Internet	Kurose	Like New	$97.00	$70.00	Nelson
70%							
	1585770884	Learning the Internet for Business	Stevenson	Like New	$30.00	$21.00	Shlaer
67%							
	0201648598	Computer Systems Architecture	Brookshire	Good	$89.00	$60.00	Hallan
67%							
	1585771368	Learning FrontPage 2002	Kemmerly	Good	$30.00	$20.00	Burmeister
	1562438638	Learning Medical Word Processing Projects and Exercises	Ditmeyer	Good	$30.00	$20.00	Anderson
	1303641186	Learning Microsoft Office XP Spanish Edition (Aprendiendo Microsoft Office XP)	Brown	Good	$30.00	$20.00	Reisner
63%							

Page 1 of 3

Project 20—Apply It

Order Summary Report

DIRECTIONS

1. Start Access, if necessary, and open **AProj20** from the data files for this lesson.
2. Save the file as **AProj20_studentfirstname _studentlastname** in the location where your teacher instructs you to store the files for this lesson.
3. Open **rptOrderSummaryByCustomer** in Layout view.
4. Group the report by the **Last** field.

5. Set the group options so that each group stays together on one page.
6. Within each group, sort the records by **ISBN** in ascending order (**with A on top**).
7. Remove the grand total at the bottom of the report.
8. Add a sum of the **Quantity** field in a group footer for each customer.
9. Delete the **First** field from the report.
10. Add the **Title** field to the report, between **ISBN** and **Quantity**.

11. Widen the **Title** field so that all titles appear on single lines.

    ✓ *Make sure that the report does not widen so much that it will not fit on a single portrait-orientation page.*

12. Delete the date and time codes from the top of the report.

13. Add a label to the report header that displays your full name, in a 12 point font, right-aligned.

14. Right-align the page numbering code in the page footer. Move the page numbering code to the left enough that it does not overflow the right margin of the page.

15. Save the changes to the report and view it in Report view.

16. **With your teacher's permission**, print one copy of the report. Figure 9-3 shows the first page.

17. Close the database, and exit Access.

| | | Order Summary by Customer | | Student Name |

Figure 9-3

Last	ISBN	Title		Quantity
Abraham				
	201721686	C++ From the Beginning		100
	201738279	Broadband Internet Connections		200
				300
Anderson				
	0321219139	Applied Computer Forensics: Handling Cybercrime Evidence		150
	201615991	Authentication: From Passwords to Public Keys		100
				250
Balto				
	201721686	C++ From the Beginning		1000
				1000
Beal				
	201700026	Classic Data Structures in Java		500
				500
Betts				
	0130153907	Computer Graphics with OpenGL, 4th Edition		250
	0130921203	Computer Confluence Business, 3rd Edition		250
				500
Bhimani				
	0130153907	Computer Graphics with OpenGL, 4th Edition		100
	0201976994	Computer Networking: A Top-Down Approach Featuring the Internet		400
	1562438115	Computer Literacy Generic Edition for PC and Mac		50
				550
Braswell				
	020163466X	Firewalls and Internet Security		400
	1585771716	Learning Microsoft Publisher 2010		100
				500

Page 1 of 3

Lesson 10

Creating Special Forms and PivotTables

➤ What You Will Learn

Using Datasheet Forms
Using Multi-Item Forms
Creating a Split Form Using the Split Form Tool
Setting a Form's Default View
PivotTable Basics
Filtering a PivotTable View
Creating a PivotTable Form

Software Skills   Access offers a variety of form views. In this exercise, you will try your hand at using several types of form views that differ from the traditional default layout, and you will learn how to create PivotTables and use a form in PivotTable view.

Application Skills   You have been asked by a friend who works at Sycamore Knoll Bed and Breakfast for suggestions on improving their database. You will set up their database's forms to use various views that demonstrate the power of forms in Access, and you will show them how to use a PivotTable form to analyze their data.

What You Can Do

Using Datasheet Forms

■   A datasheet form is not an actual type of form, but rather a **view** of a form. Rather than viewing the form in Form view (the default), you view it in Datasheet view. Datasheet view is commonly used to display subforms, which you will learn about in Lesson 11.

- You can display any form in Datasheet view, regardless of its default view. Figure 10-1 shows a form in Datasheet view.

- If you know from the start that you would like the form to appear in Datasheet view as its default, you can specify that when you create the form.

tblOrders

OrderID	OrderDate	Customer	PaymentMethod	Salesperson
1	4/1/2012	2	Visa	1
2	4/15/2012	5	Cash	3
3	4/20/2012	6	American Express	7
4	7/22/2012	1	Visa	8
5	7/26/2012	3	Mastercard	9
6	7/31/2012	3	Mastercard	7
7	8/2/2012	2	Visa	2
8	8/2/2012	5	American Express	1
9	8/5/2012	4	Visa	1
* (New)		0		

Figure 10-1

Try It!   Displaying a Form in Datasheet View

1. Start Access and open **ATry10** from the data files for this lesson. Click Enable Content if the information bar appears.

2. Save the file as **ATry10_studentfirstname_studentlastname** in the location where your teacher instructs you to store the files for this lesson.

3. In the Navigation pane, double-click frmCustomers. It opens in Form view.

4. Right-click the form's tab, and note the available views.

   ✓ Datasheet view is not available.

5. Click Design View.

6. Click Form Design Tools Design > Property Sheet.

7. In the Property Sheet pane, on the Format tab, set the Allow Datasheet View property to Yes.

8. Press CTRL + S to save the changes to the form.

9. Right-click the form's tab, and click Datasheet View.

10. Right-click the form and click Close.

11. Leave the database open for the next Try It.

Try It!   Creating a New Form in Datasheet View

1. In **ATry10_studentfirstname_studentlastname**, in the Navigation pane, click tblOrders to select it.

2. Click Create > More Forms > Datasheet. A new datasheet form appears based on the selected table.

3. Right-click the form's tab and click Close. Click No when prompted to save changes. Leave the database open to use in the next Try It.

Using Multi-Item Forms

- Like the datasheet form, a **multi-item form** is also not actually a form type, but rather a view of a form (also called Continuous Forms view). In this view, multiple records are displayed at once. The form can use any arrangement (tabular or stacked). Figure 10-2 shows a multi-item form.

- You can also create a new multi-item form from any table, query, or form. This results in a tabular layout form.

Figure 10-2	Customer Contact Information

First Name	Chris
Last Name	Jackson
Address	9947 W. Robin
City	Indianapolis
State	IN
ZIP	46281
Phone	3175558914
First Name	Bert
Last Name	Wakasuki
Address	16 Evans Pkwy.
City	Indianapolis
State	IN
ZIP	46240
Phone	3175551473

Record: ◄ ◄ 1 of 15 ► ►I ►⊞ ☒ No Filter   Search

Try It!   Displaying a Form in Continuous Forms View

1. In **ATry10_studentfirstname_studentlast name**, in the Navigation pane, right-click frmCustomerContact and click Design View ☒ .

2. If the Property Sheet is not already open, click Form Design Tools Design > Property Sheet ☒ .

3. On the Property Sheet, on the Format tab, open the Default View property's list and click Continuous Forms.

4. Right-click the report's tab, and click Form View ☒ . The form appears as a multi-item (continuous) form.

5. Right-click the form's tab and click Close. Click No when prompted to save changes.

6. Save changes and leave the database open for the next Try It.

Try It! **Creating a New Multi-Item Form**

1 In **ATry10_studentfirstname_studentlast name**, in the Navigation pane, click tblDepartments to select it.

2 Click Create > More Forms 🗔 > Multiple Items. A multi-item form appears based on the selected table.

3 Right-click the form's tab and click Close. Click No when prompted to save changes. Leave the database open to use in the next Try It.

Creating a Split Form Using the Split Form Tool

■ A **split form** is one that displays a Datasheet view on half the screen and a Form view on the other half. It is useful in cases where you want to browse the data records easily, as with a datasheet, but you also want the ease of data entry that Form view provides. Figure 10-3 shows an example.

■ As with the other views discussed so far in this lesson, Split view is just a view, not an actual type of form. Any form can be viewed as a Split form by setting its Default View to Split Form (in Design view) and then closing and reopening the form.

■ You can also create a new split form from any table, query, or form.

Figure 10-3

First Nan ▾	Last Name ▾	Address ▾	City ▾	ZIP ▾	Phone ▾	State ▾
Chris	Jackson	9947 W. Robin	Indianapolis	46281	3175558914	IN
Bert	Wakasuki	16 Evans Pkwy.	Indianapolis	46240	3175551473	IN
Leeza	Sanchez	566 W. Main	Indianapolis	46274	3175559411	IN
Shelby	Serino	1711 Tacoma Dr.	Noblesville	46060	3175557488	IN
Pasha	Bastilla	8377 Barker Way	Pendleton	19831	5845559821	NJ
George	Wendtworth	1817 Dusty Trail	Archie	87487	8045558741	CO
Stephen	Chekov	665 Pine Tree Road	Noblesville	46060	3175557149	IN
Beverly	Kincaid	1818 Wilmington	Moweaqua	62550	2175557687	IL
John	Wempen	768 Leopold Drive	Macon	62544	2115554984	IL
Jim	Beasley	444 Washington Boulevard	Indianapolis	46244	3175558488	IN
Margaret	Colvin	982 Cisco Trail	Indianapolis	46240	3175552424	IN
Cindy	Wilson	9820 Berry Road	Beverly	88988	3035553342	CO
Alice	Nelson	491 Brahman Lane	Indianapolis	46291	3175559738	IN

Customer Contact Information

First Name	Chris
Last Name	Jackson
Address	9947 W. Robin
City	Indianapolis
State	IN
ZIP	46281
Phone	3175558914

Record: I◄ ◄ 1 of 15 ► ►I ►☐ ☒ No Filter Search

View

Try It!   **Displaying a Form in Split View**

1 In **ATry10_studentfirstname_studentlast name**, in the Navigation pane, right-click frmCustomerContact and click Design View.

2 If the Property Sheet is not already open, click Form Design Tools Design > Property Sheet.

3 On the Property Sheet, on the Format tab, open the Default View property's list and click Split Form.

4 Right-click the report's tab, and click Form View. The form appears as a split form.

5 Right-click the form's tab and click Close. Click No when prompted to save changes.

6 Leave the database open for the next Try It.

Try It!   **Creating a New Split Form**

1 In **ATry10_studentfirstname_studentlast name**, in the Navigation pane, click tblOrders to select it.

2 Click Create > More Forms > Split Form. A split form appears based on the selected table.

3 Right-click the form's tab and click Close. Click No when prompted to save changes. Leave the database open to use in the next Try It.

Setting a Form's Default View

■ If you decide later that you want a form to default to a different view than you chose when you created it, you can edit its properties to make that happen. Change the Default View property to the desired view.

Try It!   **Setting a Form's Default View**

1 In **ATry10_studentfirstname_studentlast name**, in the Navigation pane, right-click frmCustomers and click Design View.

2 If the Property Sheet pane does not appear, click Form Design Tools Design > Property Sheet.

3 On the Property Sheet, on the Format tab, set the Default View property to Datasheet.

4 Right-click the form's tab and click Close. Click Yes when prompted to save changes.

5 In the Navigation pane, double-click frmCustomers. It opens in Datasheet view.

6 Right-click the form's tab, and click Design View.

7 On the Property sheet, set the Default View property to Single Form.

8 Right-click the form's tab and click Close. Click Yes when prompted to save changes. Leave the database open to use in the next Try It.

PivotTable Basics

- **PivotTable** is a view, available for tables and queries. A PivotTable is essentially an empty grid, into which you drag-and-drop field names. The positions in which you drop them determine how the data will be summarized and presented.

- Figure 10-4 shows an empty PivotTable.

- In PivotTable view, the fields from the table or query appear in a field list, shown in Figure 10-4. If the field list does not automatically appear, you can click the Field List button ▦.

- To create the PivotTable, drag fields from the field list onto one of the placeholder areas on the grid.

  ✓ *The PivotTable feature originated in Excel. It is included in Access because of its data analysis benefits.*

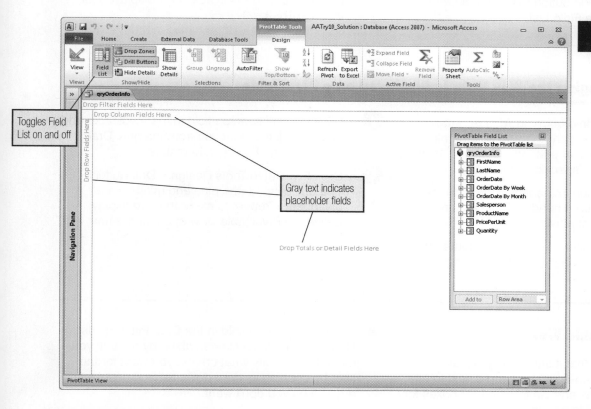

Figure 10-4

- PivotTables are remarkably flexible. You can:
  - Click a plus sign to expand an area or click a minus sign to collapse it. These plus and minus signs are called **drill buttons**.
  - Select a field and press ⌊DEL⌋ to remove it from the grid.
  - Drag other fields from the Field List to the grid to include them.
  - Filter to show only certain values (covered later in this lesson).

Try It!   **Switching to PivotTable View**

1 In **ATry10_studentfirstname_studentlast name**, in the Navigation pane, double-click qryOrderInfo to display it in Datasheet view.

2 Right-click the query's tab, and click PivotTable View 🗔. Leave PivotTable view displayed for use in the next Try It.

Try It!   Adding Fields to a PivotTable

1 In the qryOrderInfo query in **ATry10_ studentfirstname_studentlastname**, drag the Salesperson field to the Drop Column Fields Here placeholder (along the top edge of the grid).

2 Click the plus sign button to the left of OrderDate by Month on the Field List.

3 Drag Months from the expanded list to the Drop Row Fields Here placeholder (along the left edge of the grid).

4 Drag the Quantity field to the Drop Total or Detail Fields Here placeholder (in the center of the grid). Leave PivotTable view displayed for the next Try It.

Try It!   Changing the Way Data Is Displayed on a PivotTable

1 In the qryOrderInfo query in **ATry10_student firstname_studentlastname**, click the plus sign to the left of Apr in the Months column. The view expands to show specific dates in April.

2 Click the plus sign immediately beneath the Grand Total column header. That column becomes populated with totals.

3 Drag the ProductName field to the center of the grid and drop it. That field becomes part of the data shown.

4 Click the Salesperson field in the PivotTable and press DEL. It is removed from the grid. Drag it back from the Field List to restore it.

5 Click PivotTable Tools Design > Drill Buttons. The drill buttons (the plus and minus signs) disappear. Repeat to make them redisplay. Leave the PivotTable view open for the next Try It.

Filtering a PivotTable View

- To filter the data so that it shows only certain values, click the down-pointing triangle next to one of the column names and clear the check boxes for the values you want to exclude.

- If you want to filter by a field that is not one of the column headings, drag it to the Drop Filter Fields Here area.

- The presence of a field in the Drop Filter Fields Here area does not filter anything by default; you must then specify what criteria you want for the filter by opening its drop-down list and deselecting any values you don't want.

  ✓ *The down-pointing triangle on a field name turns blue when a filter is applied to remind you that the column is being filtered.*

- You can quickly turn a filter on/off by clicking the AutoFilter button on the Design tab.

Try It!   Filtering a PivotTable View

1 In the qryOrderInfo query in **ATry10_student firstname_studentlastname**, click the drop-down arrow next to the Salesperson field. A list of salesperson numbers appears, each with a check box.

2 Clear the check boxes for 3 and 7.

3 Click OK. The PivotTable changes to exclude those two salespeople.

4 Click PivotTable Tools Design > AutoFilter. The filter is removed.

5 Drag the PricePerUnit field to the Drop Filter Fields Here placeholder.

(continued)

Try It!   **Filtering a PivotTable View** *(continued)*

Filter a field by deselecting certain values

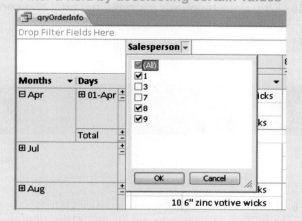

6 Click the drop-down arrow next to the PricePerUnit field. A list of prices appears.

7 Clear the check boxes for $12.00 and $25.00 and click OK. The PivotTable changes to exclude those two prices.

8 Click the drop-down arrow again next to PricePerUnit.

9 Click the All check box to re-select all values, and click OK. This is an alternate way of removing the filter.

10 Right-click the query's tab and click Close. Click Yes when prompted to save your changes. Leave the database open for the next Try It.

Creating a PivotTable Form

■ You can have only one PivotTable view for each table or query when you enter PivotTable view via the table or query datasheet.

■ However, you can create PivotTable forms that are just like PivotTable views for tables or queries, and you can have as many different forms that refer to a specific table or query as you like.

Try It!   **Creating a PivotTable Form**

1 In **ATry10_studentfirstname_studentlastname**, in the Navigation pane, click qryOrderInfo.

2 Click Create > More Forms 🖼 > PivotTable.

3 If the Field List does not appear, click PivotTable Tools Design > Field List 📇 twice: once to turn it off and once to turn it back on again.

4 Drag the ProductName field to the Drop Row Fields Here placeholder.

5 Drag the Quantity field to the Drop Totals or Detail Fields Here placeholder.

6 Right-click the form's tab and click Close. Click Yes when prompted to save changes.

7 In the Save As dialog box, type **frmProductSalesPivot** and click OK.

8 Close the database, and exit Access.

Project 21—Create It

Sycamore Knoll Database

DIRECTIONS

1. Start Access, if necessary, and open **AProj21** from the data files for this lesson.

2. Save the file as **AProj21_studentfirstname_studentlastname** in the location where your teacher instructs you to store the files for this lesson.

3. In the Navigation pane, click **frmReservations** and press CTRL + C to copy it.

4. Press CTRL + V to paste it. In the Paste As dialog box, type **frmReservationsDatasheet** and click OK.

5. Right-click **frmReservationsDatasheet** and click **Design View**.

6. If the Property Sheet pane does not appear, click **Form Design Tools Design > Property Sheet** 📇.

7. On the Format tab in the Property Sheet pane, open the drop-down list for the **Default View** property and click **Datasheet** 🗇.

8. Right-click the form's tab and click **Close**. Click **Yes** when prompted to save changes.

9. In the Navigation pane, double-click **frmReservationsDatasheet**. It opens in Datasheet view.

10. **With your teacher's permission**, print one copy of the form.

11. Close the database, and exit Access.

Project 22—Apply It

Sycamore Knoll Database

DIRECTIONS

1. Start Access, if necessary, and open **AProj22** from the data files for this lesson.

2. Save the file as **AProj22_studentfirstname_studentlastname** in the location where your teacher instructs you to store the files for this lesson.

3. Create a new split form based on **frmReservations** and save it as **frmReservationsSplit**.

4. Create a new PivotTable form based on **tblReservations**.

5. Drag the **Nights** field to the **Drop Row Fields Here** area.

6. Click the plus sign by **ReservationDate by Month** and drag **Quarters** to the **Drop Column Fields Here** area.

7. Drag the **TotalDue** field to the **Drop Totals or Detail Fields Here** area.

8. Drag the **Suite** field to the **Drop Filter Fields Here** area.

9. Exclude all suites except S1.

10. Save the form as **frmPivotS1**. The finished PivotTable should resemble Figure 10-5.

11. Close all open objects, saving your changes, and exit Access.

Figure 10-5

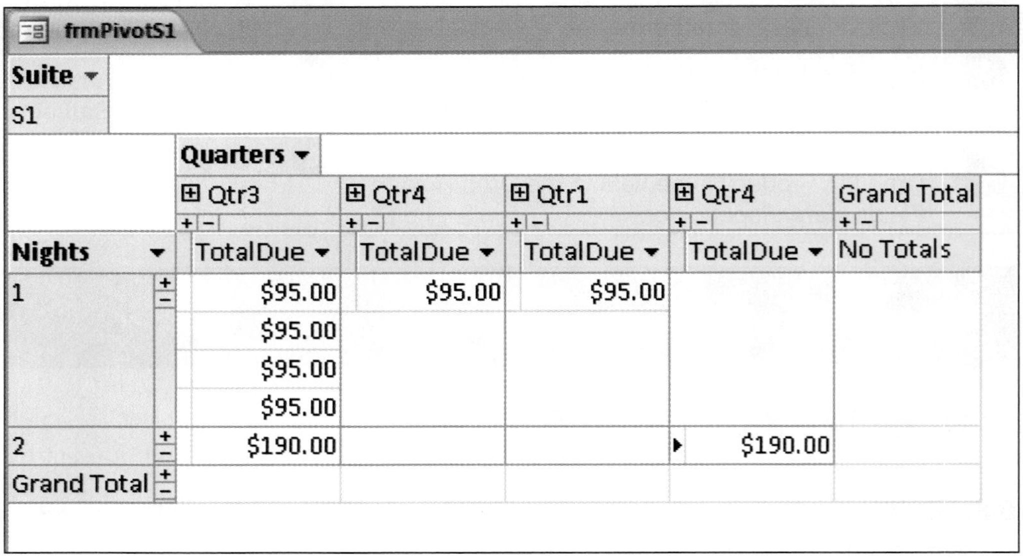

🔳 frmPivotS1					
Suite ▾					
S1					
	Quarters ▾				
	⊞ Qtr3	⊞ Qtr4	⊞ Qtr1	⊞ Qtr4	Grand Total
	+ –	+ –	+ –	+ –	+ –
Nights ▾	TotalDue ▾	TotalDue ▾	TotalDue ▾	TotalDue ▾	No Totals
1	$95.00	$95.00	$95.00		
	$95.00				
	$95.00				
	$95.00				
2	$190.00			▸ $190.00	
Grand Total					

Lesson 11

Working with Subforms and Subreports

➤ **What You Will Learn**

Understanding Subforms and Subreports
Creating a Form and Subform with the Form Wizard
Creating a Subform with the Subform Wizard
Creating a Subreport with Drag-and-Drop
Editing a Subform or Subreport

Software Skills   When you have one set of records that is related to another, it is much easier to input new records when you can see the main record and the records that are related to it. For example, if you have an order record that could be related to one or more order detail items, the top half of the form might show the order information in general and the bottom half might show the items within the order.

Application Skills   Working for The Textbook Exchange, you will set up a form with a subform that helps salespeople see at a glance the details of each book being offered for sale.

What You Can Do

Understanding Subforms and Subreports

- **Subforms** and **subreports** allow you to see values related to a main record.
- You can go ten levels deep with a subform within a subform within the **main form**. However, one subform level deep is probably plenty in most circumstances; otherwise your forms get too complicated.

WORDS TO KNOW

Main form
In a form with a main form and subform, the part of the form that is on the parent side of a parent-to-child relationship.

Subform
In a form with a main form and subform, the part of the form that is on the child side of a parent-to-child relationship.

Subreport
Similar to a subform. A report can have a subreport that is the child side of a parent-to-child relationship.

- A subform can be displayed in any view (Form view, Datasheet view, and so on). However, most subforms are displayed in Datasheet view by default because it is the most efficient view for packing a lot of information into a small space, and subforms are usually limited in the amount of space they occupy.

  ✓ *There must be a relationship between the table or query that comprises the main form and the one that comprises the subform. You must create that relationship before creating the form.*

- In a form with a subform, there are two sets of record-navigation controls. The subform has its own set, as does the main form. Figure 11-1 shows a main form and subform.

  ✓ *Once created, a subform also exists outside of the main form, as a separate form in the object list for your database. You can open and use it as a separate form whenever you*

like. It is customary to include "subform" in the names you assign to subforms so that you will remember what they were created for.

- To create a subform, you can do any of the following:
  - Use the Form Wizard to create both the main form and the subform at the same time.
  - Create the main form and then use the Subform button's wizard to build the subform.
  - Drag-and-drop another form onto an existing form in Design view to place it there as a subform.

- You will learn about each of these methods in this lesson.

- A subreport is much like a subform; the main difference is that it's on a report. There is no wizard for creating subreports; you must set them up manually.

Figure 11-1	

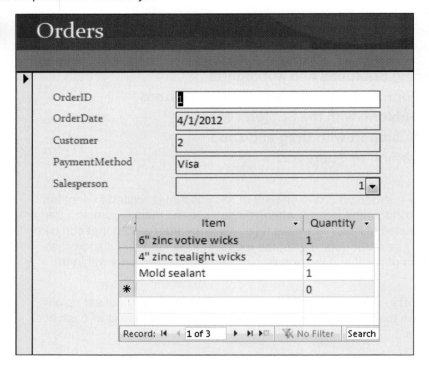

Creating a Form and Subform with the Form Wizard

- If you create the form and subform at the same time using the Wizard, Access does all the work for you.

- When you select fields from more than one table or query, the Wizard automatically offers to set up the subform.

Try It!   Creating a Form and Subform with the Form Wizard

1 Start Access and open **ATry11** from the data files for this lesson. Click Enable Content if the information bar appears.

2 Save the file as **ATry11_studentfirstname_ studentlastname** in the location where your teacher instructs you to store the files for this lesson.

3 Click Create > Form Wizard 📄. The Form Wizard opens.

4 Open the Tables/Queries drop-down list and click tblOrders.

5 Click the **>>** button to add all the fields to the form.

6 Open the Tables/Queries drop-down list and click tblOrderDetails.

7 Click the **>>** button to add all the fields to the form. Then click Next.

8 When prompted for how you want to view your data, click Next to accept the default of by tblOrders.

✓ *The Linked forms option places a button on the main form instead of displaying the subform there. Users can click the button to open the subform separately.*

9 Click Next to accept the default of Datasheet for the subform layout.

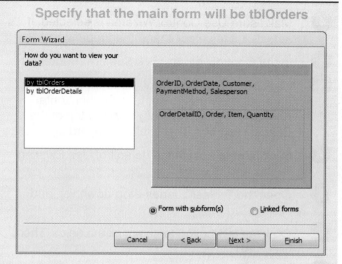

Specify that the main form will be tblOrders

10 In the Form text box, replace the default name with **frmOrderForm**.

11 In the Subform text box, replace the default name with **frmOrderDetailsSubform**.

12 Click Finish. The new form and subform appear.

13 Right-click the form tab and click Close. You are not prompted to save changes because the Wizard saved the forms. Leave the database open for the next Try It.

Creating a Subform with the Subform Wizard

■ When you add a subform or subreport to an existing report in Design view by using the Subform or Subreport button (in the Controls group), a Subform or Subreport Wizard runs to guide you through the process.

Try It!   Creating a Subform with the Subform Wizard

1 In **ATry11_studentfirstname_studentlast name,** right-click frmCustomers and click Design View 📐.

2 Drag the right border of the form to the 7.5" mark on the horizontal ruler, expanding the form width.

3 On the Form Design Tools Design tab, click the More button 🔽 for the Controls group.

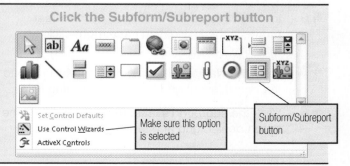

Click the Subform/Subreport button

Make sure this option is selected

Subform/Subreport button

(continued)

Try It!   Creating a Subform with the Subform Wizard *(continued)*

4 Make sure Use Control Wizards is selected. If it's not, click it to select it, and then repeat step 3.

5 In the Controls group, click Subform/Subreport.

6 Click on the blank area of the form, at approximately the 4" mark on the horizontal ruler and aligned vertically with the top of the ClientID text box. The Subform Wizard opens.

7 Click Next to accept the default of Use Existing Tables and Queries.

8 Open the Tables/Queries drop-down list, and click tblOrders.

9 Click the ⮞⮞ button to select all the fields. Then click Next.

10 When prompted to define which fields link the forms, click Next to accept the default.

11 Replace the default name with **frmOrdersSubform** and click Finish. The subform appears on the form.

12 Click the subform's label to select it, and press DEL to delete the label.

✓ *Do not worry that the subform appears in Single Item form view rather than Datasheet view. It will appear correctly in Layout and Form views.*

Define which fields link the forms

13 Right-click the form's tab and click Form View to view your work. Click Next Record ▶ a few times to move through the records in the main form and confirm that the records shown in the subform change.

14 Right-click the form's tab and click Close. Click Yes when prompted to save changes. Leave the database open for the next Try It.

Creating a Subreport with Drag-and-Drop

■ The easiest way to create a subform on a form, or a subreport on a report, is if you have already created both of them separately. You can then drag the subform or subreport onto the main one in Design view from the Navigation pane.

■ You can also drag a table directly onto a form or report in Design view, and a wizard will ask you to verify the relationship.

Try It!   Creating a Subreport with Drag-and-Drop

1 In **ATry11_studentfirstname_studentlast name,** in the Navigation pane, right-click rptMailerMain and click Design View ⬓.

2 From the Navigation pane, drag rptMailerSub to the report layout grid, below the existing fields.

3 Click the subreport's label (rptMailerSub) on the report design grid and press DEL.

4 Click the Save button 🖫 on the Quick Access toolbar.

5 Right-click the report's tab, and click Report View ▦ to check your work.

6 Right-click the report's tab and click Close. Click Yes when prompted to save. Leave the report open to use in the next Try It.

Try It!   Creating a Subreport with Drag-and-Drop (continued)

Drag the subreport onto the main report directly from the Navigation pane

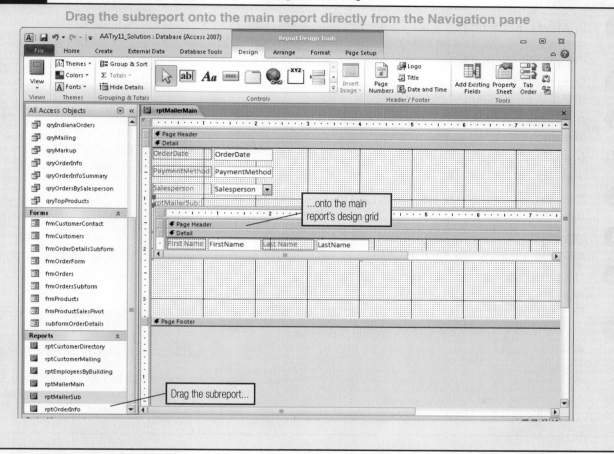

Editing a Subform or Subreport

- You can change the size of the subform or subreport like any other object by selecting it and then dragging its borders.

- When you save the form, both the main form and the subform are saved (or the main report and subreport).

- When using a preexisting form or report as your subform or subreport, there may be fields that you do not want to be included on the subform. You can hide them from Layout view by right-clicking the unwanted field and choosing Hide Columns.

Try It!   **Editing a Subform and Subreport**

1 In **ATry11_studentfirstname_studentlast name**, with rptMailerMain still open, right-click the report's tab and click Design View ✎.

2 Drag the right border of the subreport to the left until it does not overlap the page margin line.

3 Right-click the report's tab and click Close. Click Yes when prompted to save changes.

4 In the Navigation pane, right-click frmOrderForm and click Design View ✎.

5 Click the subform's label and press DEL to remove it.

6 Drag the subform to the left to align with the left edges of the labels on the main form.

7 Drag the right edge of the subform to the right to align with the right edge of the Salesperson field in the main form.

8 On the subform, click the OrderDetailID text box and press DEL.

Adjust the position of the subform in Design view

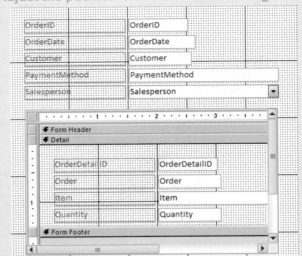

9 Right-click the main form's tab and click Form View ▦.

✓ *Note that OrderDetailID does not appear in the subform.*

10 Right-click the form's tab and click Close. Click Yes when prompted to save changes. Exit the database and close Access.

Project 23—Create It

Textbook Exchange Database

DIRECTIONS

1. Start Access, if necessary, and open **AProj23** from the data files for this lesson.

2. Save the file as **AProj23_studentfirstname_ studentlastname** in the location where your teacher instructs you to store the files for this lesson.

3. In the Navigation pane, right-click **frmMembers** and click Design View ✎.

4. Drag **frmForSale** from the Navigation pane to the empty area at the bottom of the **frmMembers** form, making it a subform.

5. Right-click the main form's tab, and click **Form View** ▦.

6. Notice that this does not look very good because of the large form header on the frmForSale form. It is clear that a new subform should be created, rather than trying to use an existing form as a subform.

7. Right-click the main form's tab, and click **Design View** ✎.

8. Select the subform, and press DEL to remove it.

9. Click **Form Design Tools Design** > **More** ▾ to open the palette of controls you can insert.

10. Click **Subform/Subreport**.

11. Click on the main form, below the label of the bottommost field. The Subform Wizard opens.

12. Click **Next** to accept the default (Use Existing Tables and Queries).

13. Open the **Tables/Queries** drop-down list and click **Table:tblForSale**.

14. Click the **ListingDate** field and click [>] to add it to the form. Do the same for **Book**, **Condition**, and **Asking Price**. Then click **Next**.

15. Click **Next** to accept the default field associations.

16. Replace the default name with **frmForSaleSubform** and click **Finish**.

17. Click the **frmForSaleSubform** label on the form and press [DEL].

18. Right-click the form's tab and click **Form View** [image].

19. Right-click the form's tab and click **Close**. When prompted to save changes, click **Yes**.

20. Close the database, and exit Access.

Project 24—Apply It

Textbook Exchange Database

DIRECTIONS

1. Start Access, if necessary, and open **AProj24** from the data files for this lesson.

2. Save the file as **AProj24_studentfirstname_studentlastname** in the location where your teacher instructs you to store the files for this lesson.

3. Open **frmMembers** in Layout view.

4. Resize columns in the subform, and the subform itself, so that all data is visible in the subform. See Figure 11-2.

5. Close the form, saving changes to both the form and the subform.

6. Open **frmBookInformation** in Design view and add a subform to it showing which members are selling each book. Name the subform **frmSalesSubform**.

   ✓ Use any method and settings you wish, but make sure that for each book, the user viewing the form will be able to see who is selling a copy (the member number) and what is the condition and asking price of each book. Check your work in Layout view and make adjustments to the subform's columns and overall width as needed.

7. Save and close all forms.

8. Use the Form Wizard to create a new form/subform combo called **frmBooks2**. The main form should use all the fields from **tblBooks** and the subform should show all fields from **tblForSale** and should open in a linked form. The subform should be named **frmSaleSubform2**.

9. Try out the button for the linked form in Form view. It doesn't work because the form title is covering it.

10. In Design view, move the form's title (in the Form Header) to the right so it does not overlap the button.

11. Switch to Form view, and try the button again. This time it works. The subform opens in a separate tab.

12. Return to Design view and make the following changes:

   a. Change the text on the button to **Copies for Sale**.

   b. Change the form title label to **Books**.

13. Close the form, saving changes.

14. Display **frmSaleSubform2** in Layout view, and delete the form title.

15. Resize columns as needed so all text fits.

   ✓ Because the fields are not part of a layout, the fields to the right don't adjust automatically when you drag the ones to their left. Because of this, resizing the fields is a little more work. One technique is to drag the right edge of the rightmost field to the right, then drag its left edge, and work your way across the fields from right to left to expand them as needed into the extra space.

16. Save your changes, and close the form.

17. Open **frmBooks2** in Form view again, and test the button.

   ✓ The subform opens showing only the records that are associated with the record that was showing in the main form.

18. Close all open objects, saving all changes, and exit Access.

Figure 11-2

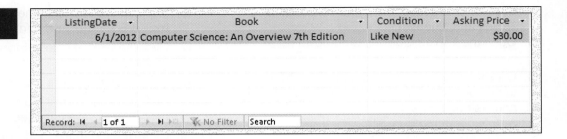

Lesson 12

Working with Charts

> **What You Will Learn**

Inserting a Chart in a Report
Editing a Chart
Creating a PivotChart

Software Skills Although Access is not known for its powerful charting capabilities like Excel, you can still produce attractive and useful charts using Access data.

Application Skills The manager of The Textbook Exchange has asked about charting in Access and would like to see some examples of what can be created. You will create a chart that summarizes the sales by salesperson to illustrate the value of charts.

WORDS TO KNOW

Legend
A color-coded key that tells what each color in a chart represents.

Microsoft Graph
A charting tool that creates embedded charts in applications such as Access.

What You Can Do

Inserting a Chart in a Report

- There are two ways to create charts in Access:
  - You can place a Microsoft Graph chart on a report or form.
  - You can create a PivotChart form.
- Microsoft Graph charts use a somewhat awkward user interface from earlier versions of Microsoft Office, but can be placed on any report or form.
- PivotCharts (also called PivotTable Charts) are more flexible and easier to work with, but can't be used on reports. However, you can print a PivotChart, so it's similar to a report in some ways.
- Access uses **Microsoft Graph** to create chart objects on reports and forms.

- To create a chart report, first create a blank report using the Blank Report button ⬜ on the Create tab. Then, in Design view, use the Chart button 🏛 on the Design tab to start a new chart.
- The Chart Wizard runs, prompting you to select the table or query from which you want to pull data.

✓ *Do not be alarmed that the chart does not show the data from your selected data source in Design view. This is one of the quirks of Microsoft Graph. It does not show the actual chart data in Design view. Switch to Layout view or Report view to see your data.*

Try It!   Inserting a Chart in a Report

1 Start Access and open **ATry12** from the data files for this lesson. Click Enable Content if the information bar appears.

2 Save the file as **ATry12_studentfirstname_studentlastname** in the location where your teacher instructs you to store the files for this lesson.

3 Click Create > Blank Report ⬜. A blank report appears in Layout view.

4 Right-click the report's tab, and click Design View ◣.

✓ *Some of the controls can be inserted from Layout view, but a chart is not one of them.*

5 On the Report Design Tools Design tab, in the Controls group, click the More button ▼ to display a palette of available tools.

6 Click the Chart button 🏛, and click on the report in the Detail section. The Chart Wizard opens.

7 Click Table: tblOrderDetails and click Next.

8 Click Item and click ⊳ to select it.

9 Click Quantity and click ⊳ to select it. Then click Next.

10 Click Pie Chart (in bottom-left of dialog box) and click Next.

11 Click Next to accept the default placement of the fields.

12 Replace the default name with **chtOrderDetails** and click Finish. The chart appears on the report layout. The actual data does *not* appear at this point.

13 Click on the report background, away from the chart. Microsoft Graph closes.

14 Right-click the report's tab, and click Report View ▦ to see the actual chart.

15 Click the Save button 💾 on the Quick Access toolbar. In the Save As dialog box, type **rptOrderChart** and click OK. Leave the report open to use in the next Try It.

Editing a Chart

- If the chart is the wrong size, you can drag the chart object's border to resize it. You can do this in either Design or Layout view.
- To edit the chart's content, you must return to Design view and double-click the chart. This opens Microsoft Graph. Notice that Microsoft Graph uses a traditional menu and toolbar system of navigation, unlike Office 2010. See Figure 12-1.
- When you are working in Microsoft Graph, the chart displays dummy data, except for the chart title. You can format the labels, **legends**, axes, and so on, and those formatting settings will be passed on to the actual chart that is generated when you are in Layout or Report view.

- The small floating spreadsheet is called the datasheet. You can close it by clicking the View Datasheet button on the toolbar. It does not contain the actual data for the chart; it is only for the sample chart.

✓ *The two toolbars in Microsoft Graph appear on a single line, which means both are truncated. You can access hidden buttons on a toolbar by clicking the More button at the right end, or you can click More and then click Show Buttons on Two Rows to separate them so all buttons are visible.*

Figure 12-1

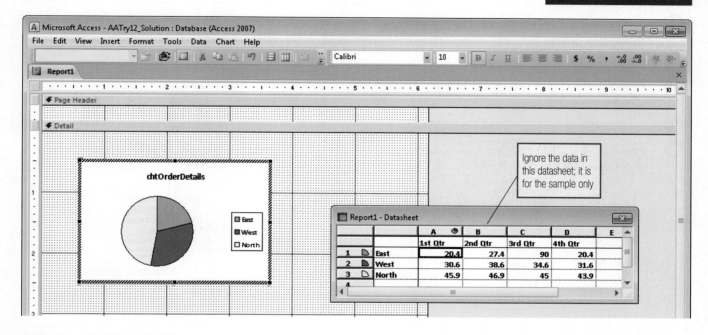

Changing the Chart Type

- You can change the chart's type without having to recreate it entirely.

- To change the chart's type, open it in Microsoft Graph and then click the drop-down arrow next to the Chart Type button. From the palette of types, click the one you want.

✓ *If you have a chart that uses three fields, such as a bar chart, and you switch to a chart that uses only two fields, such as the pie chart, only the first series will show (that is, the first color of bar from the legend).*

- For additional chart types, open the Chart menu and click Chart Type. From the Chart Type dialog box, you can select a type and a subtype. There is also a Custom Types tab that has some interesting preset formatting types on it.

Try It!   Editing a Chart

1 In **ATry12_studentfirstname_studentlast name**, right-click the rptOrderChart tab and click Design View .

2 Double-click the chart to reopen Microsoft Graph.

3 Click the drop-down arrow on the Chart Type button to open a palette of chart types.

4 Click 3-D Bar Chart .

Select a different chart type

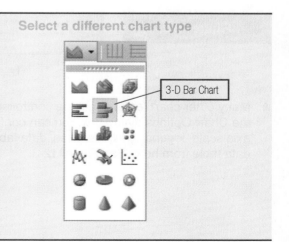

3-D Bar Chart

(continued)

Try It!   **Editing a Chart** *(continued)*

5 Click Chart > Chart Type 📊. The Chart Type dialog box opens.

6 Click Column in the list of chart types.

7 Click the Clustered Column subtype (first sample in the top row).

8 Click OK.

9 Press [CTRL] + [S] to save your work. Leave the chart open for the next Try It.

The Chart Type dialog box contains more chart subtype options

Changing Chart Options

■ Sometimes a chart can convey a different message if you display its data by row versus by column. To switch between the two on a two-axis chart such as a bar, line, column, or area chart, use the By Row 📋 and By Column 🏛 buttons on the toolbar. (This is not applicable to pie charts.)

■ You can toggle certain optional elements on/off on the chart by clicking the buttons on the toolbar. Some of these buttons are available only for certain chart types. See Figure 12-2.

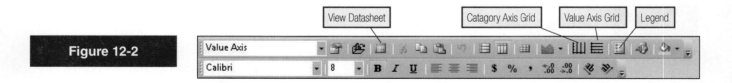

Figure 12-2

■ Many other chart features can be controlled from the Chart Options dialog box. You can control the axis scale, legend, gridlines, titles, data labels, and data table from here. See Figure 12-3.

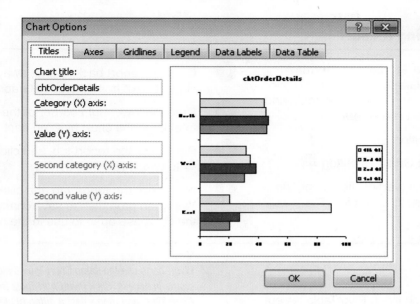

Figure 12-3

■ You can use the character formatting buttons on the Formatting toolbar to format any of the text objects on the chart, such as the title, legend, and axes. Select any of these and then choose a different font, font size, attributes (such as bold and italic), and so on. These work just like they do in any other Office application. See Figure 12-4.

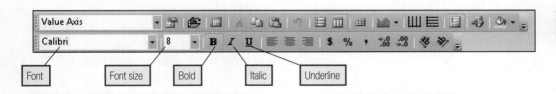

Figure 12-4

■ There are also buttons on the Formatting toolbar for applying formatting to numbers, such as making numbers appear as currency or percentages and changing the number of decimal places. These work just like in Excel. See Figure 12-5.

■ There are also buttons on the Formatting toolbar for aligning the text horizontally within its text box and slanting the text diagonally. See Figure 12-5.

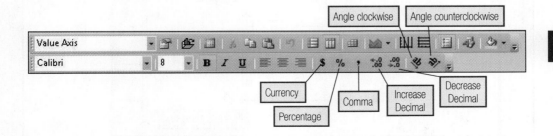

Figure 12-5

Try It!   Formatting a Chart

1 In **ATry12_studentfirstname_studentlast name**, in Microsoft Graph, click the chart title (chtOrderDetails) on the chart to select it, and press DEL. The chart title is removed.

2 Click the By Row button .

3 Click the Value Axis Gridlines button ▤.

4 Click the vertical axis (vertical line along the left edge of the chart) to select it.

5 Click the Italic button *I*.

6 Click the report background, away from the chart, to exit from Microsoft Graph.

7 Drag the lower-right corner of the chart frame to enlarge the chart by 2" in each direction.

8 Right-click the report tab, and click Report View ▣ to check your work.

9 Right-click the report tab and click Close. Click Yes when prompted to save changes, and keep the database open to use in the next Try It.

Creating a PivotChart

- A PivotChart is very much like a PivotTable except it displays the data graphically rather than in a row and column format.

- You can view a table or query in PivotChart view to create a PivotChart (only one per table or query), or you can create a PivotChart form to hold the PivotChart (as many different forms as you need).

- A PivotChart is an empty chart space into which you drag-and-drop field names to create the chart. The positions in which you drop them determine how the data will be presented.

✓ *PivotCharts use the same Chart Type dialog box as regular charts in Access. Click PivotChart Tools Design > Change Chart Type, and then select a different chart type, the same as you learned earlier in this lesson.*

- Figure 12-6 shows an empty PivotChart.

- Depending on which fields you add to the PivotChart, Access may set them up to be calculated fields on-the-fly. For example, if you add a text-based field to the data area (where numeric values would be plotted), Access automatically creates a COUNT function for it.

- You can change the calculation used for the field by right-clicking it in the chart placeholder, pointing to AutoCalc, and selecting a different function.

Figure 12-6

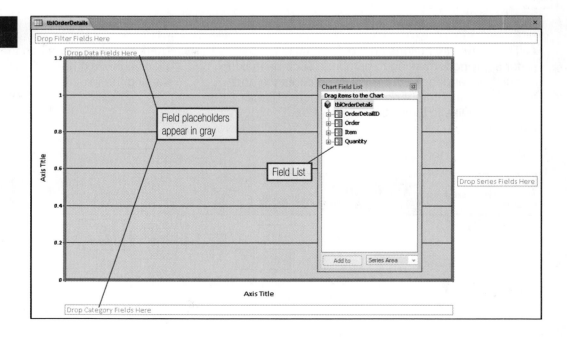

Try It!   Switching to PivotChart View

1 In **ATry12_studentfirstname_studentlast name**, in the Navigation pane, double-click tblOrderDetails to display it in Datasheet view.

2 Right-click the table's tab, and click PivotChart View 📊.

3 Right-click the table's tab and click Close. Leave the database open to use in the next Try It.

Try It!   Starting a New PivotChart Form

1 In **ATry12_studentfirstname_studentlast name**, in the Navigation pane, click qryOrderInfo to select it.

2 Click Create > More Forms 📑 > PivotChart. A new PivotChart opens.

3 Click PivotChart Tools Design > Field List 📊 twice, to toggle it off and on again, so the field list appears.

4 Click the Save button 💾 on the Quick Access toolbar.

5 In the Save As dialog box, type **frmOrdersPivotChart** and click OK. Leave the form open to use in the next Try It.

Try It!   Adding and Removing Fields on a PivotChart

1 In the frmOrdersPivotChart chart in **ATry12_studentfirstname_studentlastname**, drag the Salesperson field to the Drop Series Fields Here placeholder (at the right side of the chart).

2 Drag the ProductName field to the Drop Category Fields Here placeholder (at the bottom of the chart).

3 Drag the Quantity field to the center of the chart (the gray area).

4 Click the ProductName field's placeholder at the bottom of the chart and press DEL.

5 Click the Salesperson field's name at the right side of the chart and press DEL.

6 Drag the Salesperson field to the Drop Category Fields Here placeholder.

7 Click the plus sign to expand the Order Date by Month list in the Field List, and drag Quarters to the Drop Series Fields Here placeholder.

The chart should look like this when you are finished

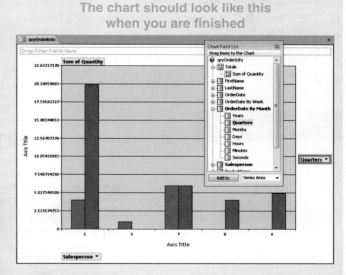

8 Click the Save button 💾 on the Quick Access toolbar.

9 Close the database, and exit Access.

Project 25—Create It

Textbook Exchange Database

DIRECTIONS

1. Start Access, if necessary, and open **AProj25** from the data files for this lesson.
2. Save the file as **AProj25_studentfirstname_ studentlastname** in the location where your teacher instructs you to store the files for this lesson.
3. Click **Create** > **Blank Report** .
4. Right-click the report's tab, and click **Design View** .
5. Click Report **Design Tools Design** > **More** (in the Controls group).
6. Click the **Chart** button .
7. Click in the Detail area of the report layout. The Chart Wizard opens.
8. Click the **Queries** button.
9. Click **qryTopFiveExtended** and click **Next**.
10. Click **Last** and click .
11. Click **Condition** and click .
12. Click **AskingPrice** and click . Then click **Next**.
13. Click **3-D Column Chart** and click **Next**.
14. Click the **Preview Chart** button. A preview appears in its own window. Close the preview window.

15. In the Preview area, swap the positions of the **Condition** and **Last** fields. To do this:
    a. Drag the **Condition** field from the sample area to the list at the right. It is removed from the sample.
    b. Drag the **Last** field from the sample area to the list at the right.
    c. Drag the **Condition** field from the list to the **Axis** placeholder.
    d. Drag the **Last** field from the list to the **Series** placeholder.
16. Click the **Preview Chart** button. A preview appears in its own window. Close the preview window.
17. Click **Next**.
18. Replace the default name with **chtTop5ByCondition** and click **Finish**.
19. Drag the lower-right selection handle on the chart frame to approximately double the height and width of the chart.
20. Right-click the report tab and click **Save**. In the Save As dialog box, type **rptTop5Chart** and click **OK**.
21. Right-click the report tab, and click **Report View** to check your work. It should look like Figure 12-7.
22. Close the database, and exit Access.

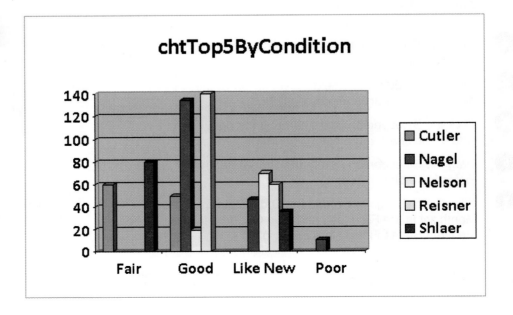

Figure 12-7

Project 26—Apply It

Textbook Exchange Database

DIRECTIONS

1. Start Access, if necessary, and open **AProj26** from the data files for this lesson.

2. Save the file as **AProj26_studentfirstname_ studentlastname** in the location where your teacher instructs you to store the files for this lesson.

3. Open **rptTop5Chart** in Design view.

4. Open the chart in Microsoft Graph and make the following edits:
   - Remove the chart title.
   - Change to a **By Row** layout.
   - Change the chart type to **Stacked Bar with a 3-D Visual Effect**.
   - Add a data table.
   - Change the font size in the data table to **10**.
   - Change the font size for the chart's vertical and horizontal axes to **10**.
   - Change the font size for the chart's legend to **10**.

5. Switch to Layout view and enlarge the chart as much as needed to make it readable and attractive.

6. View the chart in Report view to check your work. See Figure 12-8.

7. Close the report, saving your changes.

8. Create a new PivotChart form based on **qry BooksForSale**. Save the new form as **frmBook SalePivotChart**.

9. Drag the **Last** field to the **Drop Category Fields Here** placeholder.

10. Drag the **Title** field to the data area at the center of the chart.

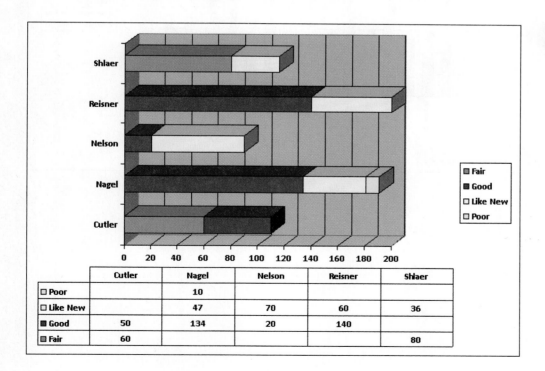

Figure 12-8

	Cutler	Nagel	Nelson	Reisner	Shlaer
☐ Poor		10			
☐ Like New		47	70	60	36
■ Good	50	134	20	140	
▥ Fair	60				80

11. Delete the Title field from the chart.

12. Drag the Retail Price and Asking Price fields into the data area at the center of the chart.

   ✓ *A multi-series chart results when you drag more than one field into the data area.*

13. Display the legend for the chart.

   ✓ *A legend is useful when you have a multi-series chart to tell you what the different colors mean.*

14. Right-click Sum of Retail Price on the chart and choose AutoCalc > Average.

15. Right-click Sum of Asking Price on the chart and choose AutoCalc > Average. The finished chart appears in Figure 12-9.

16. Click PivotChart Tools Design > Drop Zones to turn off the placeholder display on the chart.

17. **With your teacher's permission**, print one copy of the chart.

18. Save your work.

19. Close the database, and exit Access.

Figure 12-9

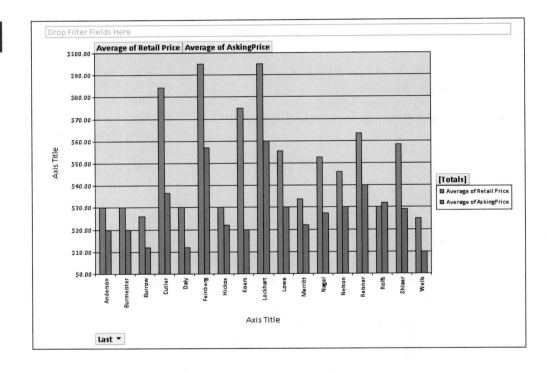

Lesson 13

Creating Switchboards

➤ **What You Will Learn**

Opening the Switchboard Manager

Managing Switchboard Pages

Editing a Switchboard Page's Content

Formatting the Switchboard

Activating or Deactivating the Switchboard

Software Skills   All the powerful queries, reports, and other objects you create are perhaps a little intimidating for a beginning user. If you are going to allow other people to access the database, it might be a good idea to create a friendlier interface than the standard Navigation pane. Access has a built-in system for this purpose called the Switchboard.

Application Skills   The Textbook Exchange has asked you to create a user-friendly interface from which employees can access the database's objects. You will create a Switchboard system that does so.

What You Can Do

Opening the Switchboard Manager

- The **Switchboard** is a set of forms that Access generates for navigation among database objects.
- The Switchboard is not just a single form, but a whole system of interconnected forms. The menu buttons in Figure 13-1 open other forms, which are also part of the Switchboard.

WORDS TO KNOW

Switchboard
A set of system-generated forms that help less-experienced users access database objects.

Figure 13-1

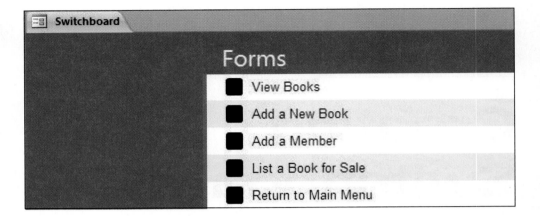

■ In Access 2010, the Switchboard Manager command is not available on the Ribbon by default. You can add it to the Ribbon, or you can add it to the Quick Access Toolbar.

■ When you click the Switchboard Manager button, if you have not yet created the Switchboard, a message appears that the Switchboard Manager was unable to find a valid Switchboard, offering to create one. The Switchboard Manager lists each page of the switchboard. By default, there is just one Main page.

■ Once you have created the Switchboard, the Main Switchboard page always exists; you cannot delete it. (You can change its content, however.)

Try It!   Adding the Switchboard Manager to the Quick Access Toolbar

1 Start Access and open **ATry13** from the data files for this lesson. Click Enable Content if the information bar appears.

2 Save the file as **ATry13_studentfirstname_studentlastname** in the location where your teacher instructs you to store the files for this lesson.

3 Click File > Options 📄 .

4 Click Quick Access Toolbar.

5 Open the Choose Commands From the drop-down list and click Commands Not in the Ribbon.

6 On the list of commands that appears, click Switchboard Manager.

7 Click Add to add the command to the Quick Access Toolbar.

8 Click OK. A button for the Switchboard Manager appears on the Quick Access Toolbar. Leave the database open to use in the next Try It.

Try It!   Creating the Switchboard

1 In **ATry13_studentfirstname_studentlast name**, click the Switchboard Manager button on the Quick Access toolbar.

2 When prompted to create a switchboard, click Yes. The Switchboard Manager window opens.

3 Close the Switchboard Manager window. Leave the database open to use in the next Try It.

Try It!   **Opening the Switchboard**

1 In **ATry13_studentfirstname_studentlast name**, click the Switchboard Manager button on the Quick Access Toolbar.

The Switchboard Manager opens. Leave the Switchboard Manager open to use in the next Try It.

Managing Switchboard Pages

- Add a new Switchboard page if you want additional pages to be available from the Main page.

- You can change which page appears first by clicking the desired page in the Switchboard Manager and then clicking Make Default.

Try It!   **Adding a Switchboard Page**

1 In **ATry13_studentfirstname_studentlast name**, in the Switchboard Manager window, click New.

2 In the Create New dialog box, type **Forms** and click OK.

3 Click New.

4 Type **Reports** and click OK.

5 Click New.

6 Type **Master** and click OK. Leave the database open to use in the next Try It.

Try It!   **Changing the Default Switchboard Page**

1 In **ATry13_studentfirstname_studentlast name**, in the Switchboard Manager window, click Master.

2 Click Make Default. The Master page moves to the top of the list, and (Default) appears next to it. Leave the database open to use in the next Try It.

Try It!   **Deleting a Switchboard Page**

1 In **ATry13_studentfirstname_studentlast name**, in the Switchboard Manager window, click Main Switchboard.

2 Click Delete.

3 Click Yes. Leave the database open to use in the next Try It.

Editing a Switchboard Page's Content

- By default, a Switchboard page is empty. You add entries that correspond to an action that the user will be able to select, such as opening a form or a report.

✓ *The list of items on each level of the Switchboard is stored in a table called Switchboard Items. You can edit the records in this table to edit the item names on the Switchboard menus.*

- When at least one Switchboard page exists, a Switchboard form appears in the list of database forms in the Navigation pane.

Try It!   Adding a Link to Another Page

1 In **ATry13_studentfirstname_studentlast name**, in the Switchboard Manager window, click Master (Default).

2 Click Edit. The Edit Switchboard Page dialog box opens.

3 Click New.

4 In the Text box, type **Forms Page**.

5 Open the Switchboard drop-down list and click Forms.

6 Click OK.

Create a link to the Forms switchboard page off the main (Master) page

Edit Switchboard Item		
Text:	Forms Page	OK
Command:	Go to Switchboard ▾	Cancel
Switchboard:	Forms ▾	

7 Click Close. Leave the database open to use in the next Try It.

Try It!   Adding a Link to a Form

1 In **ATry13_studentfirstname_studentlast name**, in the Switchboard Manager window, click Forms.

2 Click Edit.

3 Click New.

4 In the Text box, type **Customer Form**.

5 Open the Command drop-down list and click Open Form in Edit Mode.

✓ *When working with form-based commands, you have a choice of Open Form in Edit Mode or Open Form in Add Mode. Edit Mode starts on the first record, whereas Add Mode starts with a new blank record.*

6 Open the Form drop-down list and click frmCustomers.

7 Click OK. Leave the Forms switchboard open for the next Try It.

Try It!   Adding a Link That Returns to the Main Switchboard

1 In **ATry13_studentfirstname_studentlast name**, on the Forms switchboard page, click New. The Edit Switchboard Items dialog box opens.

2 In the Text box, type **Return to Main Form**.

3 Open the Switchboard drop-down list and click Master.

4 Click OK.

5 Click Close.

6 Click Close to close the Switchboard Manager. Leave the database open to use in the next Try It.

Try It!   Testing the Switchboard

1 In **ATry13_studentfirstname_studentlast name**, in the Navigation pane, in the Forms section, double-click Switchboard.

2 Click the Forms Page button.

3 Click the Return to Main Form button.

4 Right-click the form's tab and click Close. Leave the database open to use in the next Try It.

Formatting the Switchboard

- You can open the Switchboard form in Design or Layout view and edit it, much the same as you would edit any other form, including changing the background color.

- One thing that is very different, however, is that in Design view you will see blank placeholders with buttons next to them. These generically represent the text that will appear on each page.

- You can change the font used for the Switchboard text by formatting these blank placeholder boxes. You will not see the results of your formatting in Design view because there is no text to be shown there.

- You format the entire Switchboard as one unit; this keeps its formatting consistent across all pages.

  ✓ *Each page appears as a separate form when you are working with the Switchboard, but you see only a single form for the Switchboard in the Navigation pane. Part of the benefit of the Switchboard system is that it keeps certain formatting features constant among all pages of the Switchboard.*

Try It!   Formatting the Switchboard

1. In **ATry13_studentfirstname_studentlastname**, in the Navigation pane, right-click Switchboard and click Design View ⬈.

2. In the Form Header, click the dark green rectangle.

3. On the Form Design Tools Format tab, click the Shape Fill button's 🎨 drop-down list.

4. Click the dark blue square in the Standard Colors area.

5. In the Detail section, click the dark green rectangle.

6. On the Form Design Tools Format tab, click the Shape Fill button's 🎨 drop-down list.

7. Click the dark blue square in the Standard Colors area.

8. In the Detail area, click Item Text.

9. On the Form Design Tools Format tab, open the Font Size drop-down list and click 10.

10. Right-click the form's tab, and click Form View 🖿 to check your work.

11. Right-click the form's tab and click Close. Click Yes when prompted to save changes. Leave the database open to use in the next Try It.

Activating or Deactivating the Switchboard

- To make the Switchboard load automatically when the database is opened, set it up as the default display form.

- To do this, set the Display Form value to Switchboard in the Current Database category in the Access Options dialog box.

- You might also want to hide the Navigation pane so that users are limited to the commands provided on the Switchboard.

Try It!   Activating the Switchboard

1. In **ATry13_studentfirstname_studentlastname**, click File > Options 📄.

2. Click the Current Database category.

3. Click the Display Form drop-down list and click Switchboard.

4. Click OK.

5. Click OK.

6. Close and reopen the database file. The Switchboard loads automatically. Leave the database open to use in the next Try It.

Try It!	**Deactivating the Switchboard**

1 In **ATry13_studentfirstname_studentlast name**, click File > Options 📄.

2 Click the Current Database category.

3 Click the Display Form drop-down list and click (none).

4 Click OK.

5 Close the database, and exit Access.

Project 27—Create It

Textbook Exchange Database

DIRECTIONS

1. Start Access, if necessary, and open **AProj27** from the data files for this lesson.

2. Save the file as **AProj27_studentfirstname_ studentlastname** in the location where your teacher instructs you to store the files for this lesson.

3. Click the **Switchboard Manager** button on the Quick Access toolbar.

   ✓ *If you did not already put the Switchboard Manager button on the Quick Access toolbar earlier in this lesson, go back and do so now by completing the first Try It exercise in this lesson.*

4. Click **Yes** to create a new switchboard. The Switchboard Manager opens.

5. Click **New**. In the Create New dialog box, type **Reports** and click **OK**.

6. Click **New**. In the Create New dialog box, type **Forms** and click **OK**.

7. Click **Main Switchboard (Default)** and click **Edit**. The Edit Switchboard Page dialog box opens.

8. Click **New**. In the Edit Switchboard Item dialog box, in the Text box, type **Forms**.

9. Open the **Switchboard** drop-down list and click **Forms**. Then click **OK**.

10. Click **New**. In the Edit Switchboard Item dialog box, in the Text box, type **Reports**.

11. Open the **Switchboard** drop-down list and click **Reports**. Then click **OK**.

12. Click **Close**.

13. Close the database, and exit Access.

Project 28—Apply It

Textbook Exchange Database

DIRECTIONS

1. Start Access, if necessary, and open **AProj28** from the data files for this lesson.

2. Save the file as **AProj28_studentfirstname _studentlastname** in the location where your teacher instructs you to store the files for this lesson.

3. Open the Switchboard Manager.

4. On the Main Switchboard page, create a **Close the Database** option that calls the **Exit Application** command.

5. On the Reports page, create the following items:

Text	Command	Object
Books Report	Open Report	rptBooks
Members Report	Open Report	rptMembers
Return to Main Menu	Go to Switchboard	Main Switchboard

6. On the Forms page, create the following items:

Text	Command	Object
View Books	Open Form in Edit Mode	frmBooks
Add a New Book	Open Form in Add Mode	frmBooks
Add a Member	Open form in Add Mode	frmMembers
List a Book for Sale	Open form in Add Mode	frmForSale
Return to Main Menu	Go to Switchboard	Main Switchboard

7. Click the Switchboard Manager, and view the Switchboard in Form view. Then close it.

8. Open the Switchboard Items table and change Main Switchboard in record 1 to **The Textbook Exchange**.

9. Reopen the Switchboard form, and confirm that the change you just made appears.

10. Switch to Layout view, and format the text next to the buttons as **10 pt Arial**.

11. Switch to Form view, and check each button to make sure you can navigate between all three forms using the buttons and that each form or report button opens the appropriate object.

12. Close the database, and exit Access.

Lesson 14

Creating Navigation Forms

WORDS TO KNOW

Command button
A button on a form that, when clicked, performs some action or command, such as opening a form or report.

Navigation form
An unbound form that exists to provide command buttons that move the user between other objects in a database.

Unbound form
A form that is not associated with any specific table or query.

➤ What You Will Learn

About Navigation Forms
Creating a Navigation Form
Adding Command Buttons to a Form
Tying a Navigation Form into the Switchboard

Software Skills   The Switchboard is the easiest way of creating user navigation forms, but there are some limitations. Each page of the Switchboard is formatted the same way, for example. Although it's a lot more work, you might want to create your own user navigation forms and tie them together into a Switchboard-like system that you develop yourself.

Application Skills   The Switchboard that you created for The Textbook Exchange in Lesson 13 is working well, but you wonder whether it would be better to have each page of the menu system appear in a different color background. Since this isn't possible with the Switchboard, you decide to try creating your own navigation forms.

What You Can Do

About Navigation Forms

■ An **unbound form** is a form that has no data source (no table or query providing records to it). An unbound form can serve a variety of purposes, including creating your own dialog boxes and menus.

- A **navigation form** is a special type of unbound form that serves the same purpose as a Switchboard page, as shown in Figure 14-1. It displays various options for opening and editing data in forms and reports and contains command buttons for selecting those options.

- You can create your own navigation forms whenever the Switchboard's default offering does not meet your needs for some reason.

- You can create an entirely separate navigation system, or you can tie forms for specific pages into the Switchboard.

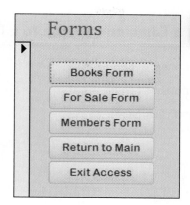

Figure 14-1

Creating a Navigation Form

- To create a navigation form, start a new form without specifying a table or query on which it should be based.

Try It!   Creating a Navigation Form

1   Start Access and open ATry14 from the data files for this lesson. Click Enable Content if the information bar appears.

2   Save the file as ATry14_studentfirstname_ studentlastname in the location where your teacher instructs you to store the files for this lesson.

3   Click Create > Blank Form . The form opens in Layout view.

4   Close the Field List pane.

5   Click the Save button on the Quick Access toolbar.

6   In the Save As dialog box, type **Custom Menu** and click OK. Leave the form open for the next Try It.

Adding Command Buttons to a Form

- The heart of a navigation form is a set of **command buttons**—buttons that the user will click to open objects.

- When you place a command button on a form in Design view, the Command Button Wizard runs, prompting you step-by-step to set up the button.

  ✓ *If you are creating a command button that will open another form, you must create that form before setting up that command button.*

Try It!   Adding a Command Button to a Form

1   In the ATry14_studentfirstname_studentlast name database, with the Custom Menu form open in Layout view, click the Form Layout Tools Design tab.

2   On the Controls group's palette of buttons, click the Button button .

3   Click on the form. The Command Button Wizard opens.

(continued)

Try It!   **Adding a Command Button to a Form** *(continued)*

4 Click Form Operations.

5 Click Open Form and click Next.

6 Click frmOrders and click Next.

7 Click Next.

Use the Command Button Wizard to set up the button

8 Click Text.

9 Replace the default label (Open Form) with **Order Form**. Click Next.

10 Replace the default button name (command1) with **cmdOpenOrderForm**.

11 Click Finish. The Order Form button appears on the form.

12 Right-click the Custom Menu form tab, and click Form View ⊟.

13 Click the button to test it. The Orders form opens.

14 Right-click the Orders form tab and click Close.

15 Right-click the Custom Menu form tab, and click Layout View ▦. Leave the form open for the next Try It.

Tying a Navigation Form into the Switchboard

■ You can use your own navigation forms as part of the Switchboard by creating an item on the Main Switchboard or any of the subordinate switchboards that opens the desired form.

■ Set up the Switchboard item as if you were opening a form in Edit mode, and specify the navigation form's name as the form to open.

✓ *If you want to use your own navigation form instead of the Switchboard, use the Display Form drop-down list in the Access Options dialog box to select your navigation form, just as you did with the Switchboard in Lesson 13.*

■ Make sure you include an item on your custom form that links back to the Switchboard so the user can return to it. The following exercise shows how to do that; it's just the same as creating an item for any other form on the Switchboard.

Try It!   **Creating a Button That Links Back to the Switchboard**

1 In the **ATry14_studentfirstname_studentlast name** database, with the Custom Menu form open in Layout view, click the Form Layout Tools Design tab.

2 On the Controls group's palette of buttons, click the Button ▭.

3 Click on the form, immediately below the Order Form button. The Command Button Wizard opens.

4 Click Form Operations.

5 Click Open Form. Then click Next.

6 Click Switchboard and click Next.

7 Click Next to accept the default of Open the form and show all the records.

8 Click Text, and replace the default label (Open Form) with **Return to Main Menu**. Then click Next.

(continued)

Try It! **Creating a Button That Links Back to the Switchboard** (continued)

9 Replace the default button name with **cmdSwitchboard**.

10 Click Finish. The button appears, but the text in it is truncated.

11 Drag the right edge of the button to the right to enlarge the button so the text fits.

12 Right-click the form's tab and click Close. Click Yes when prompted to save changes and leave the database open to use in the next Try It.

Try It! **Adding a Custom Navigation Form to the Switchboard**

1 In the **ATry14_studentfirstname_studentlast name** database, click the Switchboard Manager button on the Quick Access toolbar.

✓ *If the button does not appear there, return to Lesson 13 and use the first exercise to add it.*

2 Click Master (Default) and click Edit.

3 Click New. The Edit Switchboard Item dialog box opens.

4 In the Text box, type **Custom Page**.

5 Open the Command drop-down list, and click Open Form in Edit Mode.

6 Open the Form drop-down list and click Custom Menu.

7 Click OK.

8 Click Close.

9 Click Close.

Project 29—Create It

Textbook Exchange Database

DIRECTIONS

1. Start Access, if necessary, and open **AProj29** from the data files for this lesson.
2. Save the file as **AProj29_studentfirstname _studentlastname** in the location where your teacher instructs you to store the files for this lesson.
3. Click **Create** > **Blank Form** ▢.
4. On the Form Layout Tools Design tab, click the **Button** ⬛.
5. Click on the blank form. The Command Button Wizard runs.
6. Click **Report Operations**.
7. Click **Open Report**. Then click **Next**.
8. Click **rptBooks** and click **Next**.
9. Click the **Text** button.
10. Replace the default text (Open Report) with **Books Report**. Then click **Next**.
11. Replace the default button name with **cmdBooksReport**.
12. Click **Finish**.
13. On the Form Layout Tools Design tab, click the **Button** ⬛.
14. Click on the blank form. The Command Button Wizard runs.
15. Click **Application**.
16. Click **Quit Application**. Then click **Next**.
17. Click the **Text** button.
18. Replace the default text (Quit App) with **Exit Access**. Then click **Next**.
19. Replace the default button name with **cmdExit**.
20. Click **Finish**.
21. Click the **Save** 💾 button on the Quick Access Toolbar. Type **Reports Form** as the name, and click **OK**.
22. Test the form by viewing it in Form view and clicking the Books Report button.
23. Close the database, and exit Access.

Project 30—Apply It

Textbook Exchange Database

DIRECTIONS

1. Start Access, if necessary, and open **AProj30** from the data files for this lesson.
2. Save the file as **AProj30_studentfirstname _studentlastname** in the location where your teacher instructs you to store the files for this lesson.
3. Open the **Forms** form in Layout view, and add the following command buttons to it , as shown in Figure 14-2:
   - Add a **Members Form** button that opens **frmMembers**
   - Add a **Return to Main** button that opens the **Main Form**.
   - Add an **Exit Access** button that exits the application.

4. Format the three forms as desired (**Main Form, Forms Form**, and **Reports Form**). At the minimum, change the background color and the font used on the buttons. Make all forms and buttons identical in design.
5. Delete the **Forms** and **Reports** pages from the Switchboard, and edit the default page of the Switchboard so that your new navigation forms can be accessed from it.
6. Save your work, and try all the options in the Switchboard to make sure everything works.
7. Set the database so that the **Main Form** opens automatically when the database opens.
8. Close and reopen the database, and test all buttons on the Switchboard and on the forms.
9. Close the database, and exit Access.

Figure 14-2

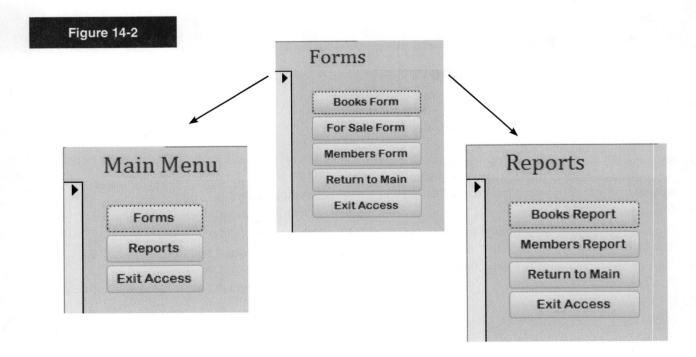

Forms

- Books Form
- For Sale Form
- Members Form
- Return to Main
- Exit Access

Main Menu

- Forms
- Reports
- Exit Access

Reports

- Books Report
- Members Report
- Return to Main
- Exit Access

Chapter Assessment and Application

Project 31—Make It Your Own

Frog Activity Data

In Biology class, you are learning how to analyze data samples collected from field research. You have a database that contains a table of data collected about frog activity in Vermont from 2009 through 2011, and you will create some reports and charts that summarize the data.

DIRECTIONS

1. Start Access, if necessary, and open **AProj31** from the data files for this lesson.

2. Save the file as **AProj31_studentfirstname_ studentlastname** in the location where your teacher instructs you to store the files for this lesson.

3. Create a PivotChart form that shows the overall trend of whether the frog activity is going up or down over time. Choose the best chart type to use for this. Name the form **Activity Trend**.

   ✓ *If you are grouping data by month or quarter, make sure your chart shows the average for that time period (Average of Average Intensity), and not the sum. Showing sum would skew data in periods that have more samples collected than others.*

4. Create a PivotTable form that examines the average intensities for each individual date and excludes dates where the number of visits is 1. Save the form as **Multi-Visit PivotTable**.

5. Create a new report based on the **FrogActivity** table where the records are grouped by year. Include group averages in the footer of each group (**Average of Average Intensity**). Format the group averages as **Standard** number type with **1** decimal place. Name the report **Grouped By Year**.

6. Create a new form that includes the **Date** and **Average Intensity** fields as text boxes and the **Number of Visits** field as a combo box. Name the form **Data Entry**. Add a title of **Data Entry** to the form header.

7. Close the database, and exit Access.

Project 32—Master It

Computers for Seniors

The Computers for Seniors donation program has a basic database in which donors and donations are being tracked. You will improve this database by adding some additional forms and reports to it, so that the organization's management can analyze and use the data more effectively.

DIRECTIONS

1. Start Access, if necessary, and open **AProj32** from the data files for this lesson.

2. Save the file as **AProj32_studentfirstname _studentlastname** in the location where your teacher instructs you to store the files for this lesson.

3. Copy **frmDonors** and name the copy **frmDonorsAndDonations**.

4. Place the **frmDonors** form as a subform at the bottom of **frmDonorsAndDonations** that shows the individual donations in Datasheet view.

5. Change the default view of **frmDonors** to **Continuous Forms**.

6. In **frmDonations**, set up conditional formatting so that if no thank-you note has been sent, the donor name appears in bright red.

   ✓ *Hint: Use the expression ThankYouNote Is Null.*

7. Create a **PivotTable** form called **frmDonationsPivot** that uses **DonationDate by Year** as the column headings, **DonorID** as the row headings, and **Donation Value** as the detail data. Filter the data so that only donations where the **ThankYouNote** field is blank appear in the table.

8. Display the form footer for the **frmDonors** form and place a code there in an unbound text box that shows today's date.

   ✓ *Hint: Use the =NOW( ) function. In the Property Sheet for the unbound text box, set the Format to Short Date.*

9. Create a new query called **qryDonorsAndDonations** that combines all the fields from **tblDonations** and **tblDonors**.

10. Create a pie chart on a report called **rptDonationPieChart** that shows each donor's last name and the total value of what they have donated. Use the query you just created as the data source.

11. Format the chart attractively, using whatever chart options you think are appropriate. Use data labels for category name and value, and do not use a legend. Format the numbers as currency.

   ✓ *Turn on data labels from the Chart Options dialog box.*

12. Set up a Switchboard that accesses all forms and reports (except the PivotTable), and set it to load at startup.

13. Close the database, and exit Access.

Chapter 3

Enhancing Tables and Working with Macros

Lesson 15

Normalizing and Analyzing Tables

WORDS TO KNOW

1NF (First Normal Form)
A normalization standard that dictates that the table must contain no duplicate records.

2NF (Second Normal Form)
A normalization standard that dictates that all other fields must be fully dependent on the primary key.

3NF (Third Normal Form)
A normalization standard that dictates that every field must be directly dependent on the primary or composite key fields, not just indirectly dependent.

Composite key
A key that consists of two or more fields, the unique combination of which forms the key.

Normalized
A table that has been structured so that it conforms to 1NF, 2NF, and 3NF.

Primary key
The unique identifying field for each record, such as an ID number.

> **What You Will Learn**

Normalizing Table Structure
Copying a Table
Renaming a Table
Deleting a Table
Splitting a Table Using the Table Analyzer
Identifying Object Dependencies

Software Skills   Databases developed by beginners can sometimes suffer from structural problems that make the database prone to problems with inconsistencies, excess duplication, and so on. By normalizing a database, you can make it both easier to use and less prone to errors.

Application Skills   A friend is starting up a lawn care service called Green Designs, and he has created a single-table database in Access to hold his business records to date. He would like your help in improving the database's structure before he goes any further.

What You Can Do

Normalizing Table Structure

■ The choices you make as you design Access tables play a big part the database's usability and effectiveness.

■ In an effective database, tables will:

   • Calculate values when more appropriate than storing the raw data

   • Link to external sources when required

   • Use the appropriate field types and formats

   • Apply data normalization rules to all tables

- This lesson focuses on the last of those items: applying data normalization rules.
- A database is said to be **normalized** if it follows certain structural rules for avoiding repeated and redundant data.
- Normalization addresses problems such as:
  - Logical inconsistencies from the same information appearing differently in multiple records (such as a customer's address being different in two different orders)
  - Deletion of important data that should be retained when all records of a certain type are deleted (such as tax ID information about an instructor being removed if he is no longer actively teaching)
- Database designers rely on three main criteria for determining a table's degree of vulnerability to logical inconsistencies and abnormalities: **1NF (first normal form)**, **2NF (second normal form)**, and **3NF (third normal form)**.

First Normal Form

- A table is in 1NF if it does not allow duplicate rows or null values. A table with a unique **primary key** or **composite key** (either of which, by definition, prevents two records from being complete duplicates of one another) and without any null values, is in 1NF.

Second Normal Form

- A table is in 2NF if it is in 1NF and if all of the other fields are fully dependent on the primary key.
- For example, suppose you have a table with the following fields: Employee ID, Employee Name, Employee Address, and Skill.
- The combination of Employee ID and Skill is the composite key (that is, each record has a unique combination of those two values, but individual records might have the same value as one or the other of those fields).
- The table in Figure 15-1 is NOT in 2NF because there is the possibility for the same employee ID to have two different addresses in this table, which would be in error.

- To normalize that table, you would need to create two separate tables: one with Employee ID and Skill in it, and another with Employee ID, Employee Name, and Employee Address in it. See Figure 15-2.

Figure 15-2

Employee ID	Skill
1	Typing
1	Filing
2	Typing
2	Spreadsheets

Employee ID	Employee Name	Employee Address
1	Bob Smith	123 Main Street
2	Sharon Jones	370 East Warren

Third Normal Form

- A table is in 3NF if it is in 2NF and if every field is *directly* dependent on the primary or composite key fields, not just indirectly dependent.
- For example, suppose you want to keep track of departments and their managers. Each department has only one manager, and each manager has only one department.
- You have a Departments table with these fields: Department, Manager, and Hire Date. See Figure 15-3.

Figure 15-3

Department	Manager	Hire Date
Sales	Bruce Duncan	12/7/2007
Operations	Jan Roth	5/15/2008
Accounting	Judy Braswell	8/1/2005
Marketing	Riley O'Malley	2/16/2002

Employee ID	Employee Name	Employee Address	Skill
1	Bob Smith	123 Main Street	Typing
1	Bob Smith	123 Main Street	Filing
2	Sharon Jones	370 East Warren	Typing
2	Sharon Jones	370 East Warren	Spreadsheets

Figure 15-1

- The Department field is the primary key. The Hire Date is only indirectly related to the Department field. It is directly related to the Manager field. The manager's hire date is irrelevant to the department.

- In this example, these two things should not be in the same table. You should have separate tables for Managers and Departments.

Figure 15-4

Department	Manager
Sales	Bruce Duncan
Operations	Jan Roth
Accounting	Judy Braswell
Marketing	Riley O'Malley

Manager	Hire Date
Bruce Duncan	12/7/2007
Jan Roth	5/15/2008
Judy Braswell	8/1/2005
Riley O'Malley	2/16/2002

- Whenever possible, you should try to use ID numbers for primary keys rather than text, even if it means adding another field to the table. This is because it is much easier to make typos when typing text, so relying on the accuracy of text-based fields to be the primary key can be risky.

- The Managers and Departments tables can further be improved by adding Department and Manager ID fields. See Figure 15-5.

Figure 15-5

Department ID	Department	Manager
D01	Sales	M01
D02	Operations	M02
D03	Accounting	M03
D04	Marketing	M04

Manager ID	Manager	Hire Date
M01	Bruce Duncan	12/7/2007
M02	Jan Roth	5/15/2008
M03	Judy Braswell	8/1/2005
M04	Riley O'Malley	2/16/2002

A Normalization Example

- Now let's take a look at an example to reinforce the concepts you just learned further.

- The table in Figure 15-6 is not normalized.

- This table could be problematic to use in the following ways:

  - What if a position is described differently for the same individual? For example, what if Edith's title is entered as Executive Secretary in some records?

  - What if a person gets promoted into another position?

  - What if there are data-entry errors because of the unnecessary retyping of certain data, like Position, Department Name, and Training?

  - What if an employee quits and you delete his entries, but he was the only person to have taken a particular training class? Does that class's information get deleted from the system entirely?

- To normalize it to 3NF, it needs to be split up into four separate tables. The primary key fields are shown in italics here. Notice that the Training Completed table has a composite key consisting of a unique combination of Class ID and Employee ID.

Employees
Employee ID
First
Last
Position
Department

Training Classes
Class ID
Class Name

Departments
Department ID
Department Name

Training Completed
Class ID
Employee ID
Date

Figure 15-6

Employee ID	First	Last	Position	Dept. ID	Dept. Name	Training	Date
1	John	Bell	Accountant	D1	Accounting	Orientation	4/15/2010
1	John	Bell	Accountant	D1	Accounting	Time Cards	4/16/2010
1	John	Bell	Accountant	D1	Accounting	Supervision	4/20/2010
2	Edith	O'Reilly	Secretary	D2	Operations	Orientation	6/1/2011
2	Edith	O'Reilly	Secretary	D2	Operations	Time Cards	6/2/2011

■ You would then need to create relationships between the tables, as in the following illustration:

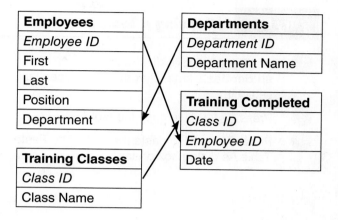

Employees
Employee ID
First
Last
Position
Department

Departments
Department ID
Department Name

Training Completed
Class ID
Employee ID
Date

Training Classes
Class ID
Class Name

Try It! — Normalizing a Database for First Normal Form (1NF)

1 Start Access and open **ATry15** from the data files for this lesson. Click Enable Content if the information bar appears.

2 Save the file as **ATry15_studentfirstname_studentlastname** in the location where your teacher instructs you to store the files for this lesson.

3 In the Navigation pane, double-click Employees to open it in Datasheet view.

✓ *Note that there is no primary key field; this is a violation of 1NF. This table has two records that are exact duplicates (8 and 9); this would not have happened if the table had a primary key field.*

4 In the Navigation pane, right-click the Employees table and click Design View .

5 Click Table Tools Design > Insert Rows . A new row appears at the top of the field list.

6 Type **ID** and press TAB to move to the Data Type column.

7 Open the Data Type drop-down list and click Number.

8 Click Table Tools Design > View . When prompted to save, click Yes.

9 In Datasheet view, select the last record and press DEL, removing the duplicate record. Click Yes to confirm the deletion.

10 Drag the ID column from the leftmost position in the datasheet to the rightmost position.

11 Number the remaining records consecutively by entering unique numbers in the ID column for each one, starting with 1.

12 Right-click the table's tab, and click Design View .

13 Click Table Tools Design > Primary Key . The table is now normalized to 1NF.

14 Right-click the table's tab and click Close. Click Yes when prompted to save changes. Leave the database open to use in the next Try It.

Copying a Table

■ Often normalizing a database involves making copies of tables and then modifying the copies.

■ To copy a table, first close it. Then you can either use the standard shortcut keys for copying and pasting in Windows (CTRL + C and CTRL + V respectively) or use the Copy and Paste buttons on the Home tab.

■ You have a choice of pasting the structure only, pasting the structure and data, or appending the data to an existing table.

Try It!   Copying a Table

1 In **ATry15_studentfirstname_ studentlastname**, click the Employees table to select it.

2 Press CTRL + C to copy the table.

3 Press CTRL + V to paste the table. The Paste Table As dialog box opens.

4 In the Click OK to accept the default name and the default setting of pasting both the structure and the data. Leave the database open to use in the next Try It.

The Paste Table As dialog box

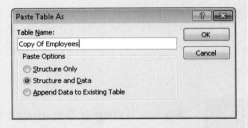

Renaming a Table

■ As you fine-tune your database's table designs, you may decide that you need to rename a certain table.

■ When you rename a table, all instances of that table name are automatically changed (for example, in relationships, and in queries, forms, and reports). However, any labels within those objects that reported the table's name do not change. For example, if the report's title had the old name in it, the old name will continue to appear until you manually edit it in Design view.

Try It!   Renaming a Table

1 In **ATry15_studentfirstname_ studentlastname**, right-click the Copy of Employees table.

2 Click Rename.

3 Type **Duties** and press ENTER . Leave the database open to use in the next Try It.

Try It!   Normalizing a Database for Second Normal Form (2NF)

1 In **ATry15_studentfirstname_ studentlastname**, double-click the Employees table to open it in Datasheet view.

  ✓ *Notice that there are many records for which almost all the fields are duplicated. This is a violation of 2NF.*

2 Right-click the table's tab and click Close.

3 Make another copy of the Employees table, the same way you did earlier in the chapter in Copying a Table. Name the copy **Employees Backup**.

4 Open the Employees table in Datasheet view again, and delete records 8, 6, 5, 3, and 2. One record for each employee remains.

(continued)

Locating the Default Save Options *(continued)*

5 Renumber the ID field entries for the remaining records 1, 2, and 3.

6 Switch to Design view. Select the Duty field, and click Table Tools Design > Delete Rows ⯈✕.

7 Switch to Datasheet view to check your work. Then close the table, saving changes when prompted.

Each employee has only 1 record now, and the Duty field is gone

ID ▾	First ▾	Last ▾	Address ▾	City ▾	State ▾	ZIP ▾	Phone ▾	Position ▾	Wage ▾
1 Jan		Smith	233 W. 38th Street	Indianpolis	IN	46242	317-555-8822	Custodian	$8.25
2 Tony		Emerson	5211 E. State Street	Noblesville	IN	46060	317-555-1498	Custodian	$7.75
3 Lois		Lowe	720 E. Warren	Macon	IL	62544	217-555-5576	Receptionist	$9.00

(Table titled **Employees**)

8 Open the Duties table in Datasheet view, and delete records 4 and 5 so that each remaining record has a unique value in the Duty column.

9 Switch to Design view, and delete all the fields *except* ID and Duty, the same way you deleted the Duty field in step 6.

10 Change the ID field's Data Type setting to Text. Then switch to Datasheet view, saving changes when prompted.

11 Change the entries in the ID column to be consecutively numbered D1 through D6. Then close the table.

Each duty is unique, and has a unique ID that begins with D

Duties

ID ▾	Duty ▾
⊞ D1	Mop Floors
⊞ D2	Wash Windows
⊞ D3	Empty Trash
⊞ D4	Set Up Lunchroom
⊞ D5	Answer Phones
⊞ D6	Greet Visitors

✓ *The ID numbers are changed to include "D" to help avoid confusing the ID numbers in this table with the ID numbers in the Employees table.*

12 Click Create > Table Design 🖫 to start a new table in Design view. Create the following fields:

Field Name	Data Type
ID	Text
Employee	Number
Duty	Text

13 Select the ID field, and click Table Tools Design > Primary Key 🔑 to set that field as the primary key.

14 Switch to Datasheet view. When prompted to save, click Yes. Type **Assignments** as the table name and click OK.

15 Enter the following records into the Assignments table:

ID	Employee	Duty
A1	1	D1
A2	1	D2
A3	1	D3
A4	2	D3
A5	2	D1
A6	2	D4
A7	3	D5
A8	3	D6

16 Close all tables, and click Database Tools > Relationships ▣.

(continued)

| **Try It!** | **Locating the Default Save Options** *(continued)* |

17 In the Show Table window, click Assignments, Duties, and Employees and click Add. Then click Close.

18 Drag the ID field from the Duties table to the Duty field in the Assignments table. In the Edit Relationships dialog box, mark the Enforce Referential Integrity check box and click OK.

19 Drag the ID field from the Employees table to the Employee field in the Assignments table. In the Edit Relationships dialog box, mark the Enforce Referential Integrity check box and click Create.

20 Click Relationship Tools Design > Close
☒ . When prompted to save changes, click Yes. Leave the database open to use in the next Try It.

✓ *This database is now normalized to 2NF.*

Relationships created between the tables connect their data

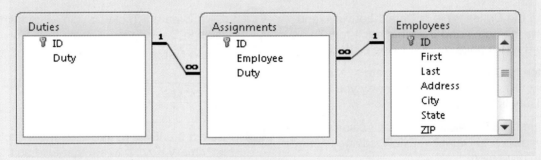

Deleting a Table

■ After manually normalizing a database, as you did in the preceding exercise, you may find yourself with unwanted extra copies of some tables.

■ To delete a table, first close it. Then from the Navigation pane, right-click the table and choose `DEL`, or select it and then press the `DEL` key on the keyboard. If prompted to confirm, click Yes.

✓ *Deleting a table permanently deletes all the data in it.*

| **Try It!** | **Deleting a Table** |

1 In **ATry15_studentfirstname_ studentlastname**, right-click Employees Backup in the Navigation pane.

2 Click Delete.

3 Click Yes.

4 Click File > Close Database ☐ to close the database file.

Splitting a Table Using the Table Analyzer

■ The Table Analyzer offers a point-and-click interface that looks for normalization problems in your tables. If you are having trouble seeing the normalization issues intuitively, you may find this tool helpful.

■ It works by looking at the table to identify repeated data, which could indicate 1NF or 2NF issues, and splits the table to solve the problem. It creates new tables; the original is left alone. You can then delete the original if desired.

Try It!   **Running the Table Analyzer**

1 Reopen **ATry15** from the data files for this lesson. Click Enable Content if the information bar appears.

2 Save the file as **ATry15A_studentfirstname_ studentlastname** in the location where your teacher instructs you to store the files for this lesson. Click Enable Content if a security warning appears.

✓ *Note: You are reopening the original data file and saving it under a different name so you can keep the previous changes you made in earlier exercises.*

3 Click Database Tools > Analyze Table 🔲.

4 Read the introductory information and click Next to continue. Then read the additional information and click Next again.

5 Click Next to accept the default of Employees as the table to analyze.

6 Click Yes, let the Wizard decide and click Next.

7 Examine the divisions that the Wizard suggested. Then click Back to go back to the previous screen.

8 Click No, I want to decide, and click Next.

9 Drag the Duty field out of the field list. A Table Analyzer Wizard dialog box opens.

✓ *(Optional) Drag the field lists to resize or rearrange them if they are difficult to see.*

10 In the Table Name box, replace the default entry with **Duties** and click OK.

11 Click the Table1 field list and click the Add Generated Key button 🔳. A Generated Unique ID field appears in that field list.

12 Select all the fields in the Table1 list *except* Generated Unique Key and Lookup to Duties, and drag them out of the list. The Table Analyzer Wizard dialog box opens.

13 In the Table Name box, replace the default entry with **Employee Info** and click OK.

14 Double-click the Table1 field list heading. The Table Analyzer Wizard dialog box opens.

15 In the Table Name box, replace Table1 with **Assignments** and click OK.

16 In the Assignments table's field list, drag the Lookup to Employee Info field above the Lookup to Duties field.

The finished redesign of the database structure

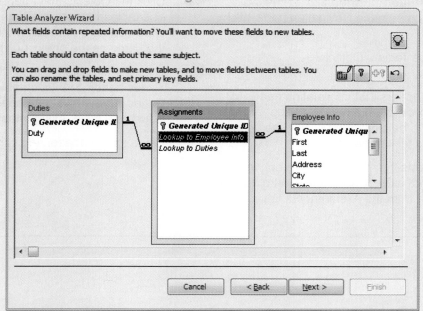

(continued)

Try It!   **Running the Table Analyzer** *(continued)*

17 Click Next, and then click Finish. The tables are split and a query is created that replicates the original table. The query opens in Datasheet view.

18 Right-click the query's tab and click Close.

19 Open the Assignments, Duties, and Employee Info tables in Datasheet view to examine them; then close them when finished.

20 Delete the Employees_OLD table, as you learned earlier in the lesson. Leave the database open to use in the next Try It.

Identifying Object Dependencies

■ Because Access is a relational database system with relationships between objects, many times the changes you make in one object affects another object.

■ This is true not only between related tables, but also between tables and the forms, reports, and queries that are based on them. For example, if you change the name of a field in a table design, you might need to edit the label for that field manually on a report.

■ In a complex database, it can be difficult to recall what objects rely on what others. To help with this, the Object Dependencies task pane can be used.

■ When the Object Dependencies task pane is open, you can select an object from the Navigation Pane and see its dependencies. The Object Dependencies task pane has two buttons: Objects that depend on me, and Objects that I depend on. Click one or the other to see the forward or backward dependencies.

■ If you select a different object in the Navigation Pane, the Object Dependencies task pane does not immediately update. Click its Refresh button to make it update.

Try It!   **Identifying Object Dependencies**

1 In **ATry15A_studentfirstname_ studentlastname**, in the Navigation pane, click Assignments.

2 Click Database Tools > Object Dependencies.

3 If a warning appears that information needs to be updated, click OK. If a message appears that objects need to be closed, click Yes. The Object Dependencies task pane opens.

4 Click the Objects that depend on me option button if it is not already selected. A list of tables that draw data from the Assignments table appears.

5 Click the Objects that I depend on option button. The tables that provide data to the Assignments table appear on the list. (In this case, they are the same as the ones shown before.)

6 Click the plus sign next to Duties under the Tables heading. A list of tables from which the Duties table draws data appears. In this case, it is just one table: Assignments.

7 Close the database, and exit Access.

Project 33—Create It

Green Designs Database

DIRECTIONS

1. Start Access, if necessary, and open **AProj33** from the data files for this lesson.
2. Save the file as **AProj33_studentfirstname_ studentlastname** in the location where your teacher instructs you to store the files for this lesson.
3. Click **Enable Content** on the information bar to enable all content.
4. Double-click the **Business** table to open it in Datasheet view, and evaluate its current structure.
   - ✓ *Look for violations of 1NF, 2NF, and 3NF.*
5. Right-click the table's tab and click **Close**.
6. Click **Database Tools** > **Analyze Table** 🗔. The Table Analyzer Wizard dialog box opens.
7. Click **Next** twice to skip the informational screens.
8. Click **Next** to accept the Business table as the table to analyze.

9. Click **Yes, let the Wizard decide**, and click **Next**.
10. Drag the **City** field from **Table4** to **Table2**, positioning it immediately before State.
    - ✓ *Table4 disappears.*
11. Double-click the **Table1** heading. Type **Sales** and press [ENTER].
12. Double-click the **Table2** heading. Type **Clients** and press [ENTER].
13. Double-click the **Table3** heading. Type **Services** and press [ENTER]. Then click **Next**.
14. Click **Next** to accept the default choices for the primary keys for each table.
15. Click **No, don't create the query**.
16. Click **Finish**.
    - ✓ *Note: If you get a message "The command to tile horizontally isn't available now," click OK to bypass it.*
17. Close the database, and exit Access.

Project 34—Apply It

Green Designs Database

DIRECTIONS

1. Start Access, if necessary, and open **AProj34** from the data files for this lesson.
2. Save the file as **AProj34_studentfirstname_ studentlastname** in the location where your teacher instructs you to store the files for this lesson.
3. Click **Enable Content** on the information bar to enable all content.
4. Create new tables (or copy existing ones) and copy/modify tables to split the information from the **Business** table into the following three tables. Make the first field in each table the primary key:
   Services table: **Service ID, Service**
   Sales table: **Sales ID, Client, Service, Service Date**
   Clients table: **Client ID, Client First Name, Client Last Name, Address, City, State, ZIP, Phone**
   - ✓ *Set the data type for all fields in all tables to Text (except the Service Date field, which should be a Date/Time field).*

   - ✓ *Make up ID numbers for the records in each table. Add an S prefix to the Service IDs, an A prefix to the Sales IDs, and a C prefix to the Clients IDs.*
5. In the Relationships window, create the relationships between the tables that will enable the database to function. Enforce referential integrity for all relationships.
   Service ID in the **Service** table > **Service** in the **Sales** table
   Client ID in the **Clients** table > **Client** in the **Sales** table
6. Check the relationships using the **Object Dependencies** task pane.
7. After you have copied all the data needed from the Business table, delete the **Business** table.
8. Close the database, and exit Access.

Lesson 16

WORDS TO KNOW

Attachment field
A field type that enables the user to insert and store data files from other programs in the database. The attachments can then be saved to disk outside the database whenever needed, or opened in their native application.

Index
A feature of Access that allows you to speed up searches and sorts and can require that a field contain unique values for each record.

Allow Zero Length
A property for a text, hyperlink, or memo field that enables that field to be non-blank but still contain zero characters.

Required
A property for a field (except AutoNumber type) that, when set to Yes, forces the user to make an entry in the field for each record.

Rich text formatting
A widely accepted file format for text documents that includes basic character, paragraph, and document formatting.

Using Advanced Field and Table Properties

> **What You Will Learn**

Requiring an Entry and Allowing Zero-Length Entries
Indexing a Field
Working with Memo Fields
Creating and Using Attachment Fields
Working with Table Properties

Software Skills   After defining the table structures for your database and creating the relationships between them, you may want to tweak the internal properties of one or more tables, including setting up special field types such as Memo and Attachment and setting options for the table as a whole.

Application Skills   The database for Ace Learning needs some additional work. Managers would like to be able to attach data files to the records in tblInstructors, and they would like to have memo fields in some of the tables where the history is tracked.

What You Can Do

Requiring an Entry and Allowing Zero-Length Entries

■ There are two settings that determine whether or not a field must contain data: **Required** and **Allow Zero Length**. They are different in these ways:

● Required can be set for all field types except AutoNumber (because AutoNumber is by definition a required field). Fields are set to No by default for this property. If you set Yes for the Required property, and then try to save a record that contains no entry for that field, an error appears.

- Allow Zero Length is set specifically for text, hyperlink, or memo fields. It allows you to enter a text string with zero characters in it to indicate that the field does not apply to that record, such as a middle initial entry for someone who has no middle initial.

- Access allows these two field properties to be set independently, so the possibility exists for having a field that is required and yet that allows zero length. If both of those conditions exist, Access stores a zero-length text string instead of a null value in the field when you leave it blank.

Try It!   **Setting the Required and Allow Zero-Length Properties**

1. Start Access and open **ATry16** from the data files for this lesson. Click Enable Content if the information bar appears.

2. Save the file as **ATry16_studentfirstname_ studentlastname** in the location where your teacher instructs you to store the files for this lesson.

3. Right-click the Assignments table and click Design View ☑.

4. Click the Employee field.

5. On the General tab at the bottom of the window, set the Required property to Yes.

6. Click the Duty field.

7. On the General tab at the bottom of the window, set Allow Zero Length to No.

8. Set the Required property to Yes.

9. Right-click the table's tab and click Datasheet View ▥. Click Yes when prompted to save changes. Click Yes when prompted that data integrity rules have changed.

Set the Duty field to be required and not to allow zero length

General	Lookup
Field Size	255
Format	
Input Mask	
Caption	
Default Value	
Validation Rule	
Validation Text	
Required	Yes
Allow Zero Length	No
Indexed	No
Unicode Compression	Yes
IME Mode	No Control
IME Sentence Mode	None
Smart Tags	

10. Try to create a new record that leaves the Employee field blank.

11. Try to create a new record that leaves the Duty field blank.

12. Press Esc to clear the attempt at the new record.

13. Right-click the table's tab and click Close. Leave the database open to use in the next Try It.

Indexing a Field

- An **index** makes searching, sorting, and grouping go faster. The speed improves when you use the Find and Sort commands in tables, queries, and forms; the sort and criteria rows in queries; and the sorting and grouping options in reports.

- A minor drawback of indexing comes when you add or delete records. If you are adding one record at a time, you won't see a difference. However, appending many records at once may take longer if you have many indexes.

- When you create a primary key, the field is automatically indexed. You can index other fields by changing the Indexed property of the field to Yes (No Duplicates) or Yes (Duplicates OK).

- Index as many fields as you need, but you cannot index memo, OLE object, attachment, or hyperlink fields.

- Each index has a name, a field (or fields) that makes up the index, a sort order, and three properties:
  - Primary: This identifies which index is the primary key. You can set this by assigning a primary key in Table Design view. Only one index can be the primary index.
  - Unique: When you set the Indexed property to Yes (No Duplicates) this property changes to Yes.
  - Ignore Nulls: If you expect to have lots of blanks, change this to Yes to exclude null values from the index and speed up the searches.

Try It!   **Indexing a Field**

1 In ATry16_studentfirstname_ studentlastname, in the Navigation pane, right-click Employees and click Design View.

2 Click the ZIP field.

3 On the General tab at the bottom of the window, set the Indexed property to Yes (Duplicates OK). Leave the database and Employees table open to use in the next Try It.

Try It!   **Viewing and Modifying Indexes**

1 In ATry16_studentfirstname_ studentlastname, with the Employees table open in Design view, click Table Tools Design > Indexes.

2 Click the ZIP field in the Index Name column.

3 Click in the Ignore Nulls property.

4 Open the drop-down list for Ignore Nulls and click Yes.

5 Click the Close button to close the Indexes:Employees window. Leave the table open in Design view to use in the next Try It.

Working with Memo Fields

- On the surface, a memo field might appear simply to be a text field with a larger size limit. A memo field can contain up to 65,536 characters (whereas a Text field is limited to 255 characters in length).

- However, the Memo field type has some other differences as well. For example, you can't index on a memo field.

- You can apply **rich text formatting** to the text in a memo field. For example, you can make certain text bold or underlined, and you can apply different fonts and colors.

- To apply rich text formatting to text in a memo field, you must first set the Text Format property for that field to Rich Text. By default it is Plain Text.

   ✓ *The Font group and Rich Text group on the Home tab contain the buttons for formatting text. If you apply formatting to text in some field type other than Memo, or if you have not yet set the Text Format property for that memo field to Rich Text, the formatting applies to the entire datasheet.*

- Another feature of the Memo field type is the ability to set a memo field to Append Only. This is one of the field's properties; when it is set to Yes, history will be collected on this field. This enables the Memo field to be used for ongoing note-taking for records, without worrying that an untrained or careless worker will accidentally delete something that should be retained.

- The phrase "append only" is somewhat misleading in that it does not prevent you from deleting or changing the content of the field. Instead, it makes a Show Column History command available for that field when you right-click it. When you choose that command, you see a History dialog box that contains the versions of the field's content over time.

- If you want to clear the history for the field, you must set Append Only to No in the field properties in Table Design view, and then save the table. This clears the history from all records. You can then toggle Append Only to Yes if desired.

Try It!   **Using Rich Text Formatting in a Memo Field**

1 In ATry16_studentfirstname_ studentlastname, with Employees open in Design view, click the Notes field.

2 On the General tab at the bottom of the window, set the Text Format property to Rich Text.

(continued)

Try It! Using Rich Text Formatting in a Memo Field *(continued)*

3 At the confirmation prompt, click Yes.

4 Right-click the table's tab, and click Datasheet View ▦. Click Yes when prompted to save changes.

5 Drag the right border of the Notes field's column header to the right to widen the field.

> ✓ *This gives you more room to enter and format text.*

6 Click in the Notes field for the first record and type **Winner of Staff Performance Award**.

7 Select Staff Performance Award, and press ⌑CTRL⌑ + ⌑I⌑ to italicize that text.

8 With Staff Performance Award still selected, on the Home tab, click the down arrow next to the Font Color button ⌑A ▾⌑ , and click a red square. Leave the table open to use in the next Try It.

Try It! Experimenting with Append Only

1 In **ATry16_studentfirstname_ studentlastname**, right-click the Employees table's tab and click Design View ⬧.

2 Click the Notes field.

3 On the General tab, set the Append Only property to Yes.

> ✓ *You may need to scroll down to find that property, depending on your window size and display resolution.*

4 Right-click the table's tab, and click Datasheet View ▦. Click Yes when prompted to save changes.

5 In the Notes field for the first record, replace the current entry with **Received Safety Training 9/12** and press ⌑ENTER⌑ to move away from the field, saving the new entry.

6 Right-click the field, and click Show Column History. A History for Notes dialog box appears listing the column history.

> ✓ *Notice that the entry you made earlier in that field is not on the list. That's because you made it prior to turning on the Append Only feature.*

7 Click OK to close the dialog box. Leave the table open to use in the next Try It.

Creating and Using Attachment Fields

- **Attachment fields** enable you to attach data files from word processing programs, spreadsheets, graphics editing programs, and so on. Attachments cannot be edited directly from within Access; the native application launches to edit them.

- Create an attachment field in Table Design view by setting the field type to Attachment. You cannot change a field's type to Attachment; you can select the Attachment type only when you first create the field.

- When you click the paper clip icon for an attachment field in a datasheet or form, the Attachments dialog box opens. From here you can add or remove attachments, open an attachment in its native program, or save an attachment to a separate file.

Try It! Creating and Using Attachment Fields

1 In ATry16_studentfirstname_ studentlastname, right-click the Employees table's tab, and click Design View ⬚.

2 Click in the first empty row of the field list, and type Photo in the Field Name column.

3 Open the Data Type drop-down list and click Attachment.

4 Right-click the table's tab, and click Datasheet View ⬚. Click Yes when prompted to save changes.

5 Double-click the paperclip icon in the Photo column for the first record. The Attachments dialog box opens.

6 Click Add.

7 Navigate to the folder containing the data files for this lesson, and double-click JanSmith.jpg. The file becomes attached, and it appears in the Attachments dialog box.

8 Click OK. The dialog box closes and a (1) appears next to the paperclip icon for that record. Leave the database open to use in the next Try It.

Try It! Saving and Removing an Attachment

1 In ATry16_studentfirstname_ studentlastname, in the Employee table, double-click the paperclip icon for the first record. The Attachments dialog box opens. One attachment is listed.

2 Click JanSmith.jpg and click Save As.

3 Navigate to the folder where you are storing your completed work for this lesson.

4 Change the file name in the File Name box to ATry16pic.jpg.

5 Click Save. The file is saved as a separate file.

6 In the Attachments dialog box, click JanSmith. jpg.

7 Click Remove.

8 Click OK to close the dialog box.

9 Right-click the table's tab and click Close.

Working with Table Properties

■ Just as each field in a table has field properties, the table itself has table properties. These apply to the entire table.

■ Here are the properties you can set for a table:

✓ *To get more space to enter or edit a property, click in the property and press Shift + F2.*

● Read Only When Disconnected: Specifies whether the table can be modified when it is disconnected from its data source. This is applicable only to remotely-stored databases, not to databases created and used on a single PC.

● Subdatasheet Expanded: Specifies whether or not any subdatasheets appear expanded by default when the table opens. If the subdatasheet is not expanded, a plus sign appears next to each record, and you can click that plus sign to expand the subdatasheet manually for a particular record.

● Subdatasheet Height: If the subdatasheet is set to be expanded, this setting controls how large it will be.

● Orientation: Set the view orientation for left-to-right or right-to-left, depending on your language. (English is left-to-right.)

● Description: Text you enter here will appear in tooltips for the table.

- Default View: Set Datasheet, PivotTable, or PivotChart as the default view when the table is opened.

- Validation Rule: You can enter an expression here that must be true whenever you add or change a record. You can also add validation rules to individual fields, of course; this box is mainly for multi-field validation rules, such as for setting up conditions where one field's value must be greater than another (like end time must come after start time).

- Validation Text: If you create a validation rule (see above), this specifies the message that is displayed when a record violates the rule.

- Filter: Here you can define criteria so that only rows matching it will appear in the datasheet. It's kind of like creating a query that filters records without actually creating the query.

- Order By: You can select one or more fields by which the data should be sorted by default.

- Subdatasheet Name: Here you can choose which subdatasheet should appear (if any). This is useful if the table has relationships with more than one other table and the wrong one is showing in the subdatasheet.

- Link Child Fields: This lists the fields in the table that are used for the subdatasheet that match the Link Master Fields property (see below).

- Link Master Fields: This lists the fields in the table that match the Link Child Fields property (see above).

- Filter on Load: If you defined criteria in the Filter field, you can set that criteria to be applied or not when the table opens. This is useful to turn the filtering off temporarily without erasing what you have put in the Filter field.

- Order By On Load: If you entered anything in the Order By field, you can turn it on or off here so that the sort order is applied when the table opens or not.

Try It! Working with Table Properties

1 In **ATry16_studentfirstname_studentlastname**, right-click Employees and click Design View.

2 Click Table Tools Design > Property Sheet.

3 Set the Subdatasheet Expanded property to Yes.

4 Right-click the table's tab, and click Datasheet View. Click Yes when prompted to save changes. The table appears with all the subdatasheets expanded.

5 Right-click the table's tab, and click Design View.

6 Set the Subdatasheet Expanded property back to No.

7 Right-click the table's tab and click Close. Click Yes when prompted to save changes.

8 Close the database, and exit Access.

Project 35—Create It

Ace Learning Database

DIRECTIONS

1. Start Access, if necessary, and open **AProj35** from the data files for this lesson.

2. Save the file as **AProj35_studentfirstname_studentlastname** in the location where your teacher instructs you to store the files for this lesson.

3. Click **Enable Content** on the information bar to enable all content.

4. Right-click **tblInstructors** and click Design View.

5. Click in the first empty row of the field list in the Field Name column and type **Documentation**.

6. In the Data Type column for the new field, open the drop-down list and click **Attachment**.

7. Click **Table Tools Design** > **Property Sheet** 📇 .

8. Set the **Order By** property to **LastName**.

9. Right-click the table's tab, and click **Datasheet View** ▦ . Click **Yes** when prompted to save changes.

10. Confirm that instructors are sorted by last name.

11. Close the database, and exit Access.

Project 36—Apply It

Ace Learning Database

DIRECTIONS

1. Start Access, if necessary, and open **AProj36** from the data files for this lesson.

2. Save the file as **AProj36_studentfirstname_ studentlastname** in the location where your teacher instructs you to store the files for this lesson.

3. Open **tblInstructors** in Datasheet view.

4. For the entry for instructor **Wendy Reynolds**, attach the file **Reynolds.txt** in the **Attachment** field.

5. Open the attachment from within Access, and change the year of her degree from 1990 to **1991**. Close the file, saving your changes.

6. Use **Save As** to save the attachment **Reynolds.txt** to your hard disk as **AProj36Reynolds_Studentfirstname_ Studentlastname.txt**.

7. Close **tblInstructors**.

8. Open **tblStudents** in Design view.

9. Add a memo field called **Notes**, and set its **Append Only** property to **Yes**.

10. Set the **Notes** field's **Text Format** property to **Rich Text**.

11. Switch to **Datasheet** view, saving all changes.

12. In the record for **Sean Gartner**, enter the following note into the Notes field:

    10/1/11: Nominated for Student of the Year.

13. Format the Words **Student of the Year** in bold and italics.

14. Edit the entry to read:

    10/1/11: Nominated for Student of the Year. 12/1/11 Dean's List

15. View the field's history.

16. Close the database, and exit Access.

Lesson 17

Formatting and Correcting Datasheets

➤ **What You Will Learn**

Formatting Datasheets
Checking Spelling

Software Skills   Datasheets are not the most glamorous venue for presenting data to users because they are not usually formatted attractively. The column widths may be too large or small, the fonts may be difficult to read, and so on. This isn't by necessity, though; you can apply a variety of formatting changes to a datasheet that make it easier and more interesting to read. You can also run a spell check on a datasheet to clean up any errors that may have been made in data entry.

Application Skills   The Ace Learning database has been in use for several weeks now, and the staff has been complaining that the datasheet is hard to read and that there are some spelling errors in the data. You will fix these problems.

What You Can Do

Formatting Datasheets

- You can apply most of the same types of formatting to datasheets that you can apply in a spreadsheet application like Excel.
- The main difference is that the character formatting you apply to a datasheet applies equally to *all* of the datasheet; you cannot format specific records or fields separately.
- Character formatting includes font, font size, attributes like bold and italic, and font color.

✓ *The exception to that limitation is the Memo type field which, as you learned earlier in this lesson, can be set to Rich Text Format and then the text within it can be separately formatted.*

■ Paragraph formatting applies to entire columns. For example, you can set a certain column to be horizontally aligned a certain way (left, centered, or right).

■ The formatting tools are located on the Home tab.

Try It!   Formatting a Datasheet

1 Start Access and open **ATry17** from the data files for this lesson. Click Enable Content if the information bar appears.

2 Save the file as **ATry17_studentfirstname_studentlastname** in the location where your teacher instructs you to store the files for this lesson.

3 Double-click the Employees table to open it in Datasheet view.

4 On the Home tab, click the Font drop-down list, and click Century Schoolbook (or any other font if you do not have that one).

5 Open the Font Size drop-down list and click 10.

6 Click the arrow on the Font Color button ▣▾ and click a dark red square.

7 Click in the ID column, and click the Center button ▤ .

8 Click the Gridlines button ▦▾ and, on its menu, click None.

9 Click the arrow on the Fill Color button ▣▾ and click a yellow square.

10 Click the arrow on the Alternate Row Color ▦▾ button and click an orange square.

11 Right-click the table's tab and click Close. Click No when prompted to save changes. Leave the database open to use in the next Try It.

Checking Spelling

■ Access includes a Spell Check feature. It is not as robust as the Spell Check feature included in Word, but it uses the same dictionaries (including any custom dictionaries you have created). See Figure 17-1.

■ When a word is found that is not in the dictionary, a list of suggestions appears. Click the word that represents the correct spelling. Or, if none of the suggestions are right, make a correction directly in the Not in Dictionary text box.

■ After selecting or typing the correct spelling, you can click Change to change only the found instance of a word or Change All to change all instances of that word in the table with the same misspelling.

■ If the word is actually spelled correctly, you can click Ignore to ignore only this instance, Ignore All to ignore all instances in this table, or Add to add the word to the custom dictionary stored on your PC.

Figure 17-1

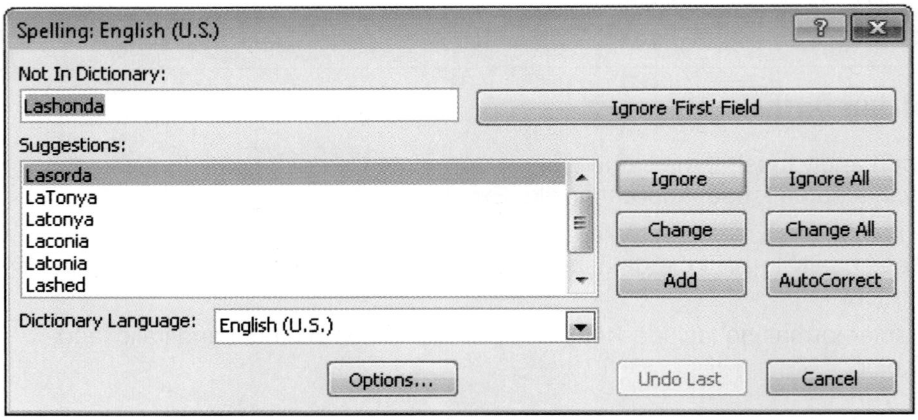

Spelling: English (U.S.)

Not In Dictionary:

Lashonda   Ignore 'First' Field

Suggestions:

Lasorda
LaTonya
Latonya
Laconia
Latonia
Lashed

Ignore   Ignore All
Change   Change All
Add   AutoCorrect

Dictionary Language: English (U.S.)

Options...   Undo Last   Cancel

Try It!   Checking Spelling

1 In **ATry17_studentfirstname_ studentlastname**, in the Navigation pane, double-click the Duties table to open it in Datasheet view.

2 Click Home > Spelling. The Spelling dialog box opens.

✓ *The first misspelled word found is identified in the Not in Dictionary box. On the Suggestions list, Wash is already selected.*

3 Click Change. The next misspelling appears.

4 Click Change. The word is corrected and a message appears that the spelling check is complete.

5 Click OK. Leave the database open to use in the next Try It.

Try It!   Adding a Word to the Dictionary

1 In **ATry17_studentfirstname_ studentlastname**, double-click the Employees table to open it in Datasheet view.

2 Click Home > Spelling.

✓ *A proper name appears as misspelled, but it is actually correct.*

3 Click Add. A message appears that the spell check is complete.

4 Click OK.

5 Close the database, and exit Access.

Project 37—Create It

Ace Learning Database

DIRECTIONS

1. Start Access, if necessary, and open **AProj37** from the data files for this lesson.

2. Save the file as **AProj37_studentfirstname_ studentlastname** in the location where your teacher instructs you to store the files for this lesson.

3. Click **Enable Content** on the information bar to enable all content.

4. In the Navigation pane, double-click **tblClasses** to open it in Datasheet view.

5. Click **Home** > **Spelling**.

6. Click **Change** to change the first misspelled word.

7. Click **Change** to change the second misspelled word.

8. Click **Change** to change the third misspelled word.

9. Click **OK**.

10. Click in the **ID** column.

11. Click the **Align Left** button.

12. Right-click the table's tab and click **Close**. Click **Yes** when prompted to save changes.

13. Close the database, and exit Access.

Project 38—Apply It

Ace Learning Database

DIRECTIONS

1. Start Access, if necessary, and open **AProj38** from the data files for this lesson.

2. Save the file as **AProj38_studentfirstname_ studentlastname** in the location where your teacher instructs you to store the files for this lesson.

3. Open **tblInstructors** and run a spell check. Ignore all possible spelling errors that are found in the Address field. Correct any other errors found.

4. Open **tblStudents** and run a spell check. Ignore all possible spelling errors that are found in the **FirstName**, **LastName**, and **Address** fields. Correct any other spelling errors found.

5. In **tblStudents**, change the alternate row color to **pale green**.

6. In **tblStudents**, change the font to **12-point Times New Roman**.

7. In **tblStudents**, widen all the columns as needed so that the content fits (except the Notes field, which can stay truncated).

   ✓ *To widen a column, position the mouse pointer at the right edge of the column header and double-click.*

8. Set the **Gridlines** setting to **Horizontal**.

9. Close the table, saving the changes.

10. Close the database, and exit Access.

Lesson 18

Creating Macros

➤ **What You Will Learn**

Creating and Running a Standalone Macro
Creating an Embedded Macro
Printing Macro Details

Software Skills   Macros enable you to automate groups of steps so that they can be executed in a single action, such as pressing a key combination or clicking a button. Writing a simple macro requires no programming experience; the interface for creating a macro is point-and-click. More sophisticated macros can also be written in Visual Basic.

Application Skills   The Ace Learning database has a Main Menu from which users can open various forms, but the menu doesn't close when a form is open, and it doesn't reappear when a form closes. You will use macros to set up those actions to occur automatically.

What You Can Do

Creating and Running a Standalone Macro

- A **standalone macro** is a macro that is saved as a separate object. You can run the macro from the Navigation pane, activate it with a shortcut key combination you assign, or start it with a button that you add to the Quick Access toolbar.

- Macros are created in Macro Design view. You select commands from a series of drop-down lists, so no typing of programming code is required.

- You can run macros by double-clicking them in the Navigation pane or by using the Database Tools > Run Macro command. You can also run a macro from Design view, which is useful for testing the macro as you are constructing it.

- If you aren't sure which command to add to the macro, you can browse for an action by category using the Action Catalog, a task pane that appears on the right side of Macro Design view.

- The Action Catalog also includes some Program Flow options that add special sections to the macro (Comment, Group, If, and Submacro).

WORDS TO KNOW

Embedded macro
A macro that is stored in another database object, such as a table, query, form, or report.

Macro
A sequence of steps that are automatically performed when a specific trigger is activated.

Standalone macro
A macro that exists as a separate object in the database from any other table, query, form, or report.

User Interface (UI) macro
An embedded macro.

Try It!   Starting a New Macro

1 Start Access and open **ATry18** from the data files for this lesson. Click Enable Content if the information bar appears.

2 Save the file as **ATry18_studentfirstname_ studentlastname** in the location where your teacher instructs you to store the files for this lesson.

3 Click Create > Macro 📜. A new Macro object opens, ready for you to enter commands.

4 Open the Add New Action drop-down list, and click OpenTable. Additional drop-down list boxes appear that are specific to that command.

5 Open the Table Name drop-down list and click Assignments.

6 Open the second Add New Action drop-down list, and click OpenTable. A second set of drop-down list boxes appears for the new command.

7 Open the Table Name drop-down list and click Employees.

8 Click the Save button 💾 on the Quick Access toolbar.

9 In the Save As dialog box, type **Open Assignments and Employees** and click OK. Leave the macro open to use in the next Try It.

A command added to the macro

⊟ OpenTable		✕
Table Name	Assignments	▾
View	Datasheet	▾
Data Mode	Edit	▾
➕	Add New Action	▾

Try It!   Running a Macro (Macro Open)

1 In the **ATry18_studentfirstname_ studentlastname** database, with the macro open, click Macro Tools Design > Run ❗. Both of the tables referenced in the macro open.

2 Right-click any open object's tab and click Close All. Leave the database open to use in the next Try It.

Try It!   Running a Macro (Macro Not Open)

1 In the **ATry18_studentfirstname_ studentlastname** database, from the Navigation pane, double-click Open Assignments and Employees.

2 Right-click any open object's tab and click Close All. Leave the database open to use in the next Try It.

Try It!   **Selecting Commands from the Action Catalog**

1   In **ATry18_studentfirstname_ studentlastname**, click Create > Macro.

2   In the Action Catalog, double-click Comment in the Program Flow section.

3   In the comment box that appears, type **This macro closes the current database without exiting Access.**

4   In the Actions section of the Action Catalog pane, click the plus sign next to System Commands.

5   Double-click Close Database. The command is added to the macro.

6   Click the Save button on the Quick Access toolbar. In the Save As dialog box, type **Close Database** and click OK.

7   Click Macro Tools Design > Run. The macro runs, and the database closes.

8   Reopen the **ATry18_studentfirstname_ studentlastname** database.

Add a command from the Action Catalog

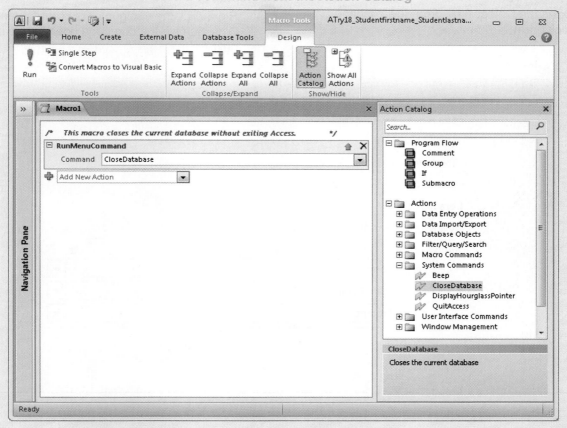

Creating an Embedded Macro

- An **embedded macro**, also called a **User Interface (UI) macro**, is one that is associated with a particular control. For example, a macro can be assigned to a command button, so that when you click the button a series of actions execute.

- When you created command buttons in Chapter 2, you were actually creating embedded macros for the buttons through the Command Button Wizard. You can edit these macros to add or change the actions assigned.

- You can also embed macros in any database object. For example, you can specify that a certain action occurs when an object opens or closes.

Try It!   Editing an Embedded Macro

1 In **ATry18_studentfirstname_ studentlastname**, in the Navigation pane, right-click Main Form and click Layout View ▦.

2 Click the Assignments Form button, and click Form Layout Tools Design > Property Sheet ▦.

3 In the Property Sheet, click the Event tab.

4 In the On Click property, click the Build button ▦. The macro design interface opens. It is the same interface as with a standalone macro.

5 Open the Add New Action drop-down list and click Close Window.

6 Open the Object Type drop-down list and click Form.

7 Open the Object Name drop-down list and click Main Form.

8 Click Macro Tools Design > Close ✕. Click Yes when prompted to save changes.

9 Click the Save button ▦ on the Quick Access toolbar to save the changes to Main Form.

10 Click Form Layout Tools Design > View ▦ to switch to Form view.

11 Click the Assignments Form button. The Assignments Form opens and the Main Form closes.

12 Right-click the Assignments Form tab and click Close. Leave the database open to use in the next Try It.

Add another action to the embedded macro

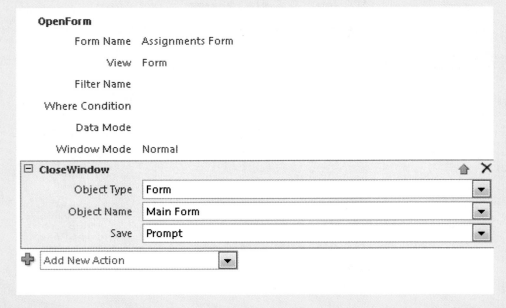

Try It!   Creating an Embedded Macro

1 In **ATry18_studentfirstname_ studentlastname**, in the Navigation pane, right-click Assignments Form and click Layout View.

2 If the Property Sheet is not already open, click Form Layout Tools Design > Property Sheet ▦.

(continued)

Try It!   **Creating an Embedded Macro** *(continued)*

3 At the top of the Property Sheet, open the Selection Type drop-down list and click Form.

4 In the Property Sheet, click the Event tab.

5 Click in the On Close property box.

6 Click the Build button ⬚.

7 Click Macro Builder and click OK.

8 Open the Add New Action drop-down list and click Open Form.

9 Open the Form Name drop-down list and click Main Form.

10 Click Macro Tools Design > Close ⊠. Click Yes when prompted to save changes.

11 Click Save ⬚ on the Quick Access toolbar to save the changes to the Assignments Form.

12 Right-click the form's tab and click Close. The Main Form opens.

13 Right-click the Main Form tab and click Close. Leave the database open to use in the next Try It.

Printing Macro Details

■ To keep track of the macros in your database, you may wish to document each macro in printed form. When you print a macro, a variety of information about it also prints in addition to the macro commands.

Try It!   **Printing Macro Details**

1 In **ATry18_studentfirstname_ studentlastname**, in the Navigation pane, right-click the Open Assignments and Employees macro and click Design View ⬚.

2 Click File > Print > Print Preview. The Print Macro Definition dialog box opens.

3 Click OK to accept all the additional information to be printed.

  ✓ *The report appears in Print Preview.*

4 Click Close Print Preview.

5 Close the database, and exit Access.

Project 39—Create It

Ace Learning Database

DIRECTIONS

1. Start Access, if necessary, and open **AProj39** from the data files for this lesson.

2. Save the file as **AProj39_studentfirstname_ studentlastname** in the location where your teacher instructs you to store the files for this lesson.

3. Click **Enable Content** on the information bar to enable all content.

  ✓ *Enabling all content is especially important when working with macros, as macros are one of the content types that are otherwise blocked.*

4. Right-click **frmClasses** and click **Layout View** ▦.

5. Click **Form Layout Tools Design > Property Sheet** ☞.

6. Open the **Selection Type** drop-down list in the **Property Sheet** pane and click **Form**.

7. Click in the **On Open** property box.

8. Click the **Build button** ⬓.

9. Click **Macro Builder** and click **OK**.

10. Open the **Add New Action** drop-down list and click **Close Window**.

11. Open the **Object Type** drop-down list and click **Form**.

12. Open the **Object Name** drop-down list and click **frmMenu**.

13. Click **Macro Tools Design > Close** ⊠. Click **Yes** when prompted to save changes.

14. Click in the **On Close** property box.

15. Click the **Build** button ⬓.

16. Click **Macro Builder** and click **OK**.

17. Open the **Add New Action** drop-down list and click **Open Form**.

18. Open the **Form Name** drop-down list and click **frmMenu**.

19. Click **Macro Tools Design > Close** ⊠. Click **Yes** when prompted to save changes.

20. Right-click the **frmClasses** tab and click **Close**. Click **Yes** when prompted to save changes.

21. On the **frmMenu** form in Form view, click the **Classes** button. The **frmClasses** form opens, and the **frmMenu** form closes.

22. Right-click the **frmClasses** tab and click **Close**. The **frmClasses** form closes, and the **frmMenu** form opens.

23. Close the database, and exit Access.

Project 40—Apply It

Ace Learning Database

DIRECTIONS

1. Start Access, if necessary, and open **AProj40** from the data files for this lesson.

2. Save the file as **AProj40_studentfirstname_ studentlastname** in the location where your teacher instructs you to store the files for this lesson.

3. Open **frmVolunteers** in Layout view and set its **On Open** property so that **frmMain** closes when **frmVolunteers** opens.

4. Set the **On Close** property so that **frmMain** opens when **frmVolunteers** closes.

5. Save and close **frmVolunteers**. The **frmMain** form opens automatically.

6. Test each of the buttons on **frmMain** to confirm that each button opens a form and closes **frmMain**, and that closing each of the opened forms causes **frmMain** to reappear.

7. Create a new macro that opens all the tables in the database. Name it **mcrOpenAll**.

8. Run **mcrOpenAll** to test it, and then close all tabs.

   ✓ *Right-click any tab and click* **Close All**.

9. Open the **frmClasses** form in Layout view and select the **Notes** text box.

10. Open the **Property Sheet** for the Note text box and click in the **On Got Focus** property.

11. Open the **Macro Builder**, and create a **MessageBox** action with the following properties:

    Message: **Please enter notes about classes whenever possible.**

    Beep: **No**

    Type: **Information**

    Title: **Notes Requested**

12. Save and close the macro.

13. Test the new macro by viewing the **Classes** form in Form view and clicking the **Notes** field for a record.

14. Close the database, and exit Access.

Chapter Assessment and Application

Project 41—Make It Your Own

Bugs Be Gone Database

You have been hired by Bugs Be Gone, a pest control company, to develop a database for their business records. The initial meeting with the general manager resulted in the notes shown in Illustration A.

Your job is to develop a working, multi-table database that accomplishes the key goals identified in the notes.

DIRECTIONS

1. Referring to the notes in Illustration A, make a list (on paper or in a word processing program) of the tables you will create, the fields in each table, the primary key field for each table, and how the tables will be related.

   ✓ *Make sure that your tables are normalized to 3NF.*

2. Start Access, if necessary, and create a new blank database called **AProj41_Studentfirstname_ Studentlastname**.

3. Create the needed tables. Use Memo fields set to accept Rich Text Formatting for the Notes fields in each table.

   ✓ *When creating fields that will have relationships to the primary key values in other tables, make sure you use the right data type. For example, if the Badge Number field in Employees is Number, make sure that the Employee field in the Schedule table is also set to Number. Otherwise you won't be able to create the relationships.*

4. Create the needed relationships between the tables, and enforce referential integrity where it is helpful to do so.

5. Arrange and size the field lists in the Relationships window so that they are all fully visible and the relationship lines are clear.

6. **With your teacher's permission,** print a Relationships report showing the relationship window.

7. Create reports that deliver the information described in the Most Important Information Retrieval Goals in Illustration A.

8. Enter one record in each table, for example purposes. (Make up the data.) Check your spelling in each table to make sure you have not made any typos.

9. Close the database, and exit Access.

Notes from Meeting

Data to include, at a minimum:
- About the customers: contact information (mailing address, phone number, e-mail), notes
- About the services we offer: name, description, cost, time interval between treatments, notes
- About the employees: Badge number, name, job title, hire date, notes
- The service schedule: date, time, customer, service being performed, employee performing the service, whether or not the service has been performed yet, notes

Most important information retrieval goals:
- A list of services that have been scheduled but not yet performed, sorted by date
- A list of services scheduled for a particular day, grouped by employee

Project 42—Master It

Marketing Database

Marketing Concepts Inc. has started a database in Access, but they have made the mistake of combining too much information into a single table. In this exercise, you will split the table into multiple tables, thereby normalizing the database and improving its functionality. You will also improve some of the tables by formatting them, adjusting properties, and creating macros.

DIRECTIONS

1. Start Access, if necessary, and open **AProj42** from the data files for this lesson.

2. Save the file as **AProj42_studentfirstname_ studentlastname** in the location where your teacher instructs you to store the files for this lesson.

3. Either using the **Table Analyzer Wizard** or creating tables manually, split the database's single table into multiple tables, resulting in the database being normalized to at least 2NF.

4. Delete the **Marketing Concepts** table after you have extracted all the information you need from it.

5. Open the **Staff** table in Datasheet view, and change its font to **10-point Arial**. Do the same for the **Clients** and **Promotions** tables.

6. Create a form for each of the tables by doing the following:

   a. Click the table name in the Navigation pane.

   b. Click **Create > Form** .

   c. Save the form with the same name as the table name, but with frm at the beginning. For example, the form for **Clients** would be **frmClients**.

7. Open **frmPromotions** in Layout view.

8. Delete the **In-House Contact** label.

9. In the position formerly occupied by the deleted label, create a command button. Click **Cancel** to close the Command Button Wizard when it appears.

10. Change the text on the button face to **In-House Contact**.

11. Create an embedded macro for the command button that opens **tblStaff** in Datasheet view whenever the button is clicked.

12. Save the form, and test the button in Form view.

13. Close all open tabs.

14. Close the database, and exit Access.

Chapter 1

Working with Masters, Comments, Handouts, and Pictures

Lesson 1

Advanced Slide Master Features

➤ **What You Will Learn**

Inserting a New Slide Master
Inserting a Picture on the Slide Master
Inserting a Shape on the Slide Master
Customizing Placeholders on the Slide Master

Software Skills   You can add variety to presentations by inserting additional slide masters, which allows you to have additional options within the same theme. For example, you have one slide master in which you've inserted a shape and one without it. You can also customize a slide master by adding a shape or picture or by modifying the placeholder arrangement. Use the Master Layout dialog box to restore master elements that have been removed.

Application Skills   You will work on a presentation for Yesterday's Playthings. In this lesson, you add and customize a new slide master and add a graphic element to the slide master.

What You Can Do

Inserting a New Slide Master

- You can add themes to a presentation by adding slide masters in Slide Master view.
- Clicking Insert Slide Master in the Edit Master group on the Slide Master tab adds a new slide master in the slide thumbnail pane.
- The new master displays the default Office theme and is designated as 2, indicating it is the second master in the presentation. The new master includes all the standard layouts below the slide master. You can use the Rename command to give the new slide master a more meaningful name.

- A small pushpin symbol appears below the new slide master. This symbol indicates the master is being preserved for use even though no slide currently uses this master. If a slide master that you add does not automatically display this symbol, you can click the Preserve button in the Edit Master group to preserve the master.

- You can also add a new slide master with a theme other than the Office theme using the Themes button in the Edit Themes group.

- You can add as many masters as you want, but keep in mind that using many themes in a presentation will compromise your presentation's visual consistency.

- When adding multiple slide masters to a presentation, you can add completely distinct themes, or you can add another instance of the same theme. Using multiple versions of the same theme allows you to apply different background or color formatting to slides while maintaining the same fonts and layouts for a consistent appearance.

- The Master Layout group of the Slide Master tab contains several commands that help you work more efficiently with slide masters.

Try It!   Inserting a New Slide Master

1 Start PowerPoint and open **PTry01** from the data files for this lesson.

2 Save the file as **PTry01_studentfirstname_studentlastname** in the location where your teacher instructs you to store the files for this lesson.

3 Click View > Slide Master 🔲.

4 Click the Insert Slide Master button 🔲.

5 With the new slide master selected, click Slide Master > Themes 🔲.

6 Right-click on the Tradeshow 🔲 theme and select Apply to Selected Slide Master.

✓ *If you do not have Tradeshow available on your PC, you can use the PTry01_Tradeshow.thmx file in the data files for this lesson.*

OR

- Click View > Slide Master 🔲.

- Click Slide Master > Themes 🔲.

- Right click on the Tradeshow 🔲 theme and select Add as New Slide Master.

7 Save changes, and leave the file open to use in the next Try It.

Insert a New Slide Master in a Second Theme

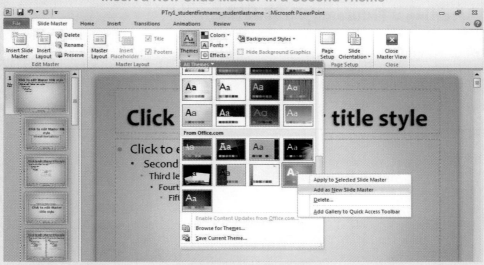

Inserting a Shape on the Slide Master

■ You can save time by adding a shape to a slide master so that it will appear whenever that slide layout is used.

■ Use the shapes on the Home tab or Drawing Tools tab to draw basic objects, such as lines, rectangles, and circles, as well as more complex shapes such as stars, banners, and block arrows on a slide master.

■ You control the size and shape of most shapes as you draw. Some shapes also have a yellow diamond adjustment handle that you can use to modify the appearance of the shape.

Try It!　　Inserting a Shape on the Slide Master

❶ With **PTry01_studentfirstname_ studentlastname** open in Slide Master view, go to the Tradeshow Slide Master.

❷ Click Insert > Shapes 🔲.

❸ Select the Rounded Rectangle shape.

❹ Draw and position the shape to enable text to be entered.

❺ Right-click the shape and select Edit Text.

❻ Type **Helping Hands**.

❼ Save changes, and leave the file open to use in the next Try It.

Inserting a Picture on the Slide Master

■ The easiest way to have a picture appear on multiple slides is to insert it on the slide master.

■ You can use the Insert Picture from File icon in any content placeholder or the Picture button on the Insert tab to place your own picture file on a slide. This command opens the Insert Picture dialog box so you can navigate to and select the picture you want to insert.

■ If you want to insert a picture on a slide master that doesn't contain a content placeholder, use the Insert Picture button on the Insert tab.

Try It!　　Inserting a Picture on the Slide Master

❶ With **PTry01_studentfirstname_ studentlastname** open in Slide Master view, click the Trade Show Slide Master.

❷ Click Insert > Insert Picture from File 🔲.

❸ Navigate to the data files for this lesson, select the **PTry01_soup** image, and click Insert

---

(continued)

Try It!   **Inserting a Picture on the Slide Master** *(continued)*

4 Drag the picture to the position shown in the figure.

5 Save changes, and leave the file open to use in the next Try It.

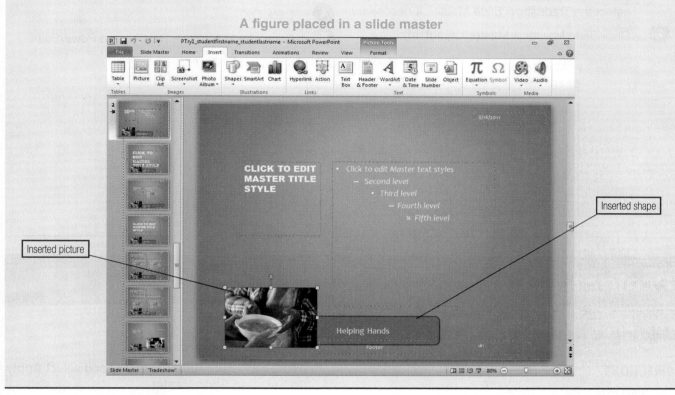

A figure placed in a slide master

Customizing Placeholders on the Slide Master

■ When a slide layout master is selected (rather than the slide master), the Title and Footers check boxes are active. Deselect either or both to remove the title or the date, footer, and slide number placeholders from the master. Display these placeholders again by selecting the appropriate check box.

■ You can also select and delete any default placeholder on a master.

■ You can restore deleted placeholders using the Master Layout dialog box. This command is active when the slide master is selected.

■ By default, the dialog box shows all placeholders selected and unavailable for change. Only deleted placeholders are active in the Master Layout dialog box so that you can select it to restore it.

Try It!   **Customizing Placeholders on the Slide Master**

1 With **PTry01_studentfirstname_studentlastname** open in Slide Master view, select the Tradeshow Slide Master, if necessary.

2 Click the border of the footer placeholder under the inserted shape.

3 Press .

4 Save changes, and leave the file open to use in the next Try It.

Try It!   Restoring Master Layout Placeholders

1 With **PTry01_studentfirstname_ studentlastname** open in Slide Master view, select the Tradeshow Slide Master, if necessary.

2 Click Slide Master > Master Layout 🔲 .

3 Select check boxes of the footer placeholder to restore.

4 Click OK.

5 Save changes, close the file, and PowerPoint.

The Master Layout dialog box

Project 1—Create It

Adding a New Slide Master

DIRECTIONS

1. Start PowerPoint, if necessary, and open **PProj01** from the data files for this lesson.

2. Save the presentation as **PProj01_ studentfirstname_studentlastname** in the location where your teacher instructs you to store the files for this lesson.

3. Click **View** > **Slide Master** 🖻 .

4. Click the **Insert Slide Master** button 🖼 .

5. Select the new slide master and click **Slide Master** > **Themes** 🔠 .

6. Right-click on the **Module** theme and select **Apply to Selected Slide Master**.

7. Click **Slide Master** > **Rename** 🖼 .

8. Type **Light Module** in the Layout Name box and click **Rename**.

9. Click **Slide Master** > **Close Master View**.

10. Save the changes to the document.

11. Close the document, and exit PowerPoint.

Project 2—Apply It

Enhancing a New Slide Master

DIRECTIONS

1. Start PowerPoint, if necessary, and open **PProj02** from the data files for this lesson.

2. Save the file as **PProj02_studentfirstname_ studentlastname** in the location where your teacher instructs you to store the files for this lesson.

3. Create a footer that includes your full name and today's date.

4. Display the **Light Module** slide master in the Slide Master View.

   a. Click **View** > **Slide Master**.

   b. In the pane that contains the slide masters and layouts, scroll down the thumbnails using ScreenTips to help you locate the Light Module slide master.

   c. Click the **Light Module** slide master thumbnail.

5. Display the Background Styles gallery and select **Style 6**.

6. Apply a shape style to the black bar at the top of the slide.

   a. Select the black shape at the top of the slide behind the title placeholder.

   b. Click **Drawing Tools Format** > **More** to open the Shape Styles gallery.

   c. Select **Subtle Effect – Aqua, Accent 2** Quick Style.

7. Select the thin gray horizontal shape below the shape you just reformatted and apply a fill of **Orange, Accent 5, Darker 25%**.

8. Click the **Title** placeholder. Click **Drawing Tools Format** > **Text Fill** > **Gray 25%, Background 1, Darker 25%**.

9. Change the size of first-level bulleted text to **20** and second-level bulleted text to **25**.

10. Click the title slide layout below the **Light Module** slide master, change the background style to **Style 7**.

11. Select the black shape that takes up the top third of the slide and apply the **Moderate Effect – Aqua, Accent 2** Quick Style shape style to the black shape.

12. Select the thin white horizontal shape below the shape you just reformatted and apply a fill of **Gold, Accent 1**.

13. Change the title font color to **Black, Text 1, Lighter 50%**.

14. Close Slide Master view. Display **Slide 6** and apply the **Light Module Title and Content** layout. Your slide should look similar to Figure 1-1.

15. **With your teacher's permission**, print slide 6. It should look similar to Figure 1-1.

16. Close the document, saving all changes, and exit PowerPoint.

Figure 1-1

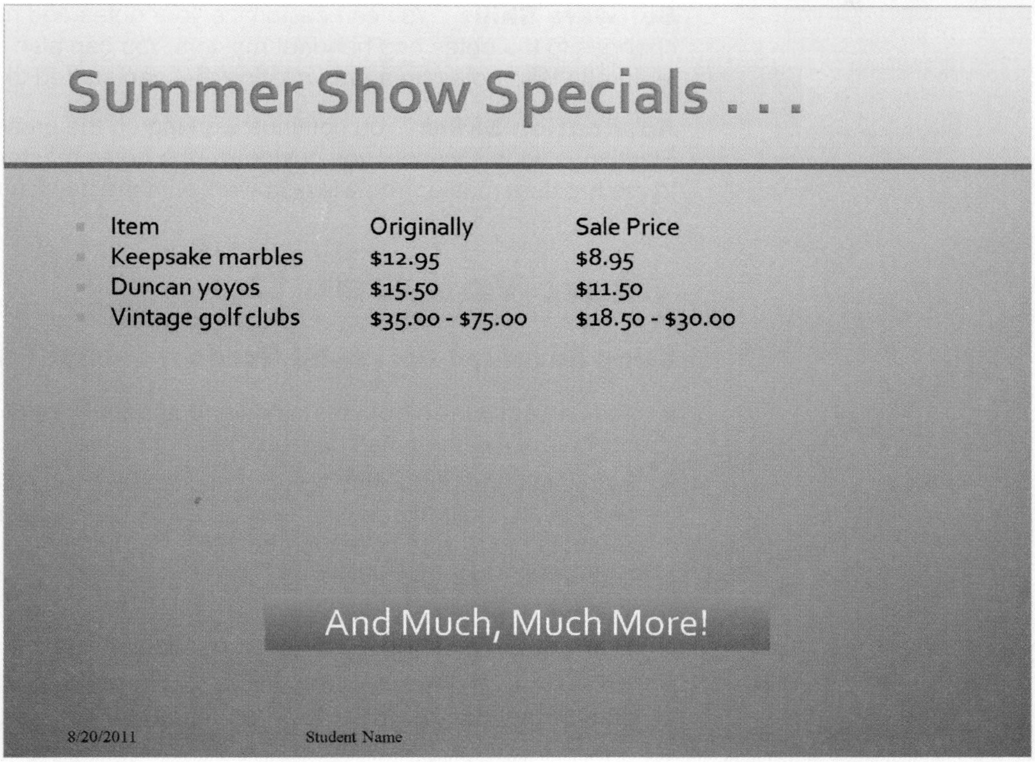

Summer Show Specials . . .

Item	Originally	Sale Price
Keepsake marbles	$12.95	$8.95
Duncan yoyos	$15.50	$11.50
Vintage golf clubs	$35.00 - $75.00	$18.50 - $30.00

And Much, Much More!

8/20/2011   Student Name

Lesson 2

Working with Notes and Handouts

➤ **What You Will Learn**

Using Advanced Notes and Handout Master Formats
Working with Linked Notes (OneNote 2010)

Software Skills　You can customize your notes and handouts by making changes to the notes and handout masters. You can also use the new Linked Notes feature to take notes on a presentation that can shared to help when collaborating.

Application Skills　You continue working on the presentation for Yesterday's Playthings. In this lesson, you customize the notes master and apply custom formats to the handout master. You will also work with the new Linked Notes feature.

What You Can Do

Using Advanced Notes and Handout Master Formats

- You can customize both the notes and handout masters to improve visual appearance when notes pages or handouts are printed.
- By default, the notes and handout masters use the Office theme colors, fonts, and effects, no matter what theme is applied to the slides in the presentation. Changing fonts and colors to match the current theme can give your notes pages consistency with the slides.
- You can apply graphic formats such as Quick Styles or fills, borders, and effects to any placeholder on the notes or handout master.
- You can also add content to the handout master, such as a new text box or a graphic that will then display on all pages.

■ When adding content such as a text box to the handout master, consider that your added content must be positioned so it doesn't interfere with the slide image placeholders for layouts other than the one you are currently working with.

■ If you insert a text box above the slide image on the one-slide-per-page layout, for example, it will obscure the slide images for other handout layouts.

■ You can, however, use the Colors, Fonts, and Effects buttons to apply theme formatting to your masters.

✓ *Note that even though the Themes button appears on the Notes Master tab and the Handout Master tab, you cannot use it to apply a theme.*

■ Use the Background Styles option in the Background group to apply a background that will fill the entire notes page or handout. Background colors are controlled by the theme colors you have applied to the master.

Try It!   **Applying Notes Master Formats**

1 Start Word and open **PTry02** file from the data files for this lesson.

2 Save the file as **PTry02_studentfirstname_ studentlastname** in the location where your teacher instructs you to store the files for this lesson.

3 Click on slide 8.

4 Click View > Notes Master 📄 .

5 Click Theme > Theme Fonts 🅰 and select the Austin theme font.

6 Click the Notes placeholder, then click Drawing Tools Format > Colored Outline – Blue Accent 1 🔲 in the Shape Styles gallery.

7 Click Theme > Background Styles 🔳 and select Style 6.

8 Save changes, and leave the file open to use in the next Try It.

Applying custom formats to the notes master

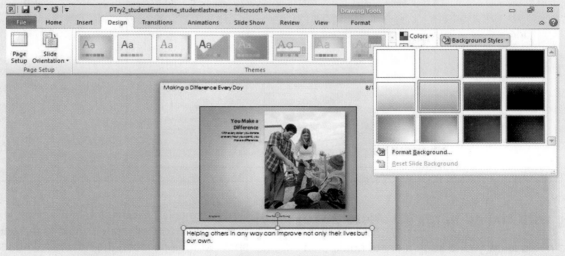

Try It!   **Applying Handout Master Formats**

1 In **PTry02_studentfirstname_ studentlastname**, click View > Handout Master 🔳 .

2 Click Handout Master > Theme Colors 🔲 .

(continued)

Try It!   **Applying Handout Master Formats** *(continued)*

3 Select the Origin theme color.

4 Click Insert > Shapes 🔲 > Rectangle.

5 Draw a rectangle that covers the top of the page, as shown in the figure.

6 Right click the shape and select Send to Back.

7 Select the Header and Date placeholders, then click Home > Font Color **A ·** and select White.

8 Click File > Print and click Full Page Slides and select 1 Slide Handout to see how the new handout will look.

9 Save changes, and leave the file open to use in the next Try It.

A formatted handout

Working with Linked Notes (OneNote 2010)

■ Linked notes allow you to keep a set of notes on a presentation that retain the context of the original slides.

■ You can create Linked Notes using the Linked Notes button 🔲 on the Review tab.

■ If you have OneNote installed, but don't see the Linked Note button on your Review tab, you can add it Backstage View using the Options page.

■ OneNote attaches a note-taking dock to the desktop beside the PowerPoint window.

■ When you take linked notes in the dock, a PowerPoint icon will appear next to the dock to show what application the note is linked to.

■ To see the subject of the note, hover over the icon. To review the original presentation, just click on the icon.

■ You can tag a note as a To Do item using the keyboard shortcut CTRL + 1.

■ When you use shared OneNote notebooks to store your Linked Notes, team members can see and respond to each other's notes.

Try It!   Adding the Linked Notes Button to the Ribbon

1 In **PTry02_studentfirstname_ studentlastname**, click File > Options > Customize Ribbon.

   ✓ *Remember that OneNote 2010 must be installed on your computer in order to use this feature.*

2 On the Customize Ribbon page, select All Tabs in the Choose commands from: drop menu.

3 Click the ⊞ button next to Review in the Main Tabs list on the left to expand the Review tab options and select OneNote.

4 Select the Review tab in the Main Tabs list on the right as the location for the button.

5 Click the Add button and click OK.

6 Save changes, and leave the file open to use in the next Try It.

Try It!   Working with Linked Notes (OneNote 2010)

1 In **PTry02_studentfirstname_ studentlastname**, select slide 6.

2 Click Review > Linked Notes .

Select Location in OneNote dialog box

(continued)

Try It! **Working with Linked Notes (OneNote 2010)** *(continued)*

③ Select Academic in the All Notebooks area and click OK.

④ In the header box, type your name and press ENTER.

⑤ In the note box, type **Find out when the MS Walk and AIDS Awareness Week will take place.**

⑥ Switch to slide 8.

⑦ Hover your mouse over the PowerPoint icon ⓟ next to the note box to see the original slide.

⑧ Close the OneNote dock and close **PTry02_ studentfirstname_studentlastname**, saving all changes, and exit PowerPoint.

A Linked Note

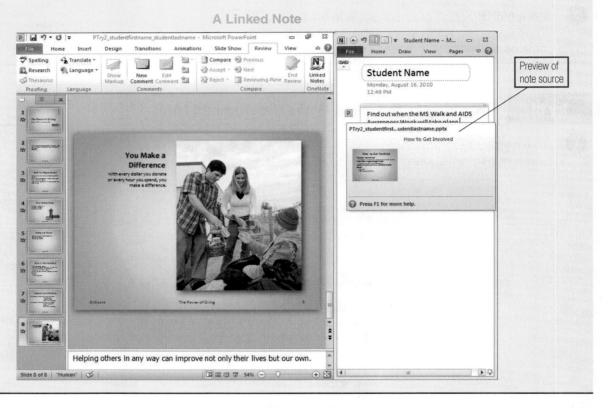

Project 3—Create It

Formatting Notes

DIRECTIONS

1. Start PowerPoint, if necessary, and open **PProj03** from the data files for this lesson.

2. Save the file as **PProj03_studentfirstname_ studentlastname** in the location where your teacher instructs you to store the files for this lesson.

3. Click **View > Notes Master** 🖿.

4. Click **Notes Master > Background Styles > Style 6**.

5. Click **Notes Master > Colors** ▉.

6. Select **Austin**.

7. Click **Notes Master > Fonts > Aspect**.

8. Click **Notes Master > Close Master View**.

9. Insert a header on the Notes and Handouts that includes your full name and today's date.

10. Save the changes to the document. Your presentation should look similar to Figure 2-1.

11. Close the document, and exit PowerPoint.

Figure 2-1

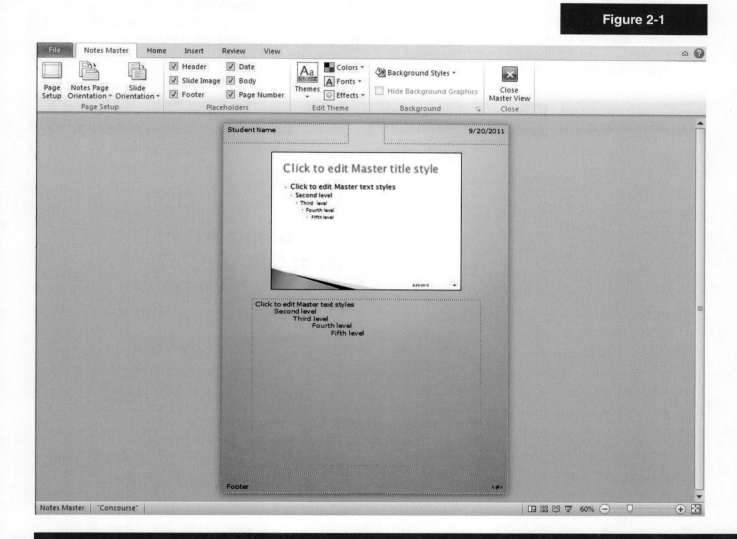

Project 4—Apply It

Formatting Notes

DIRECTIONS

1. Start PowerPoint, if necessary, and open **PProj04** from, the data files for this lesson.

2. Save the file as **PProj04_studentfirstname_ studentlastname** in the location where your teacher instructs you to store the files for this lesson.

3. Display the presentation in Notes Master View.

4. Insert a **Rectangle** shape at the top of the page the same height as the header and date placeholders.

5. Use the Shape Style gallery to apply a **Moderate Effect – Black, Dark 1** and send it to the back.

6. Change the size of the header and date text to **14 point**, apply **bold**, and change the color if desired to contrast better with the shape behind the text.

7. Select the content placeholder and apply the **Colored Outline – Olive Green, Accent 4** shape style.

8. Close Notes Page Master view and switch to Notes Page view. Figure 2-2 shows a sample of one of the presentation's slides in this view.

9. Type **Going green can help save the planet, but it is also a great way to save you real green in your wallet!** in the content placeholder.

10. Save the changes to the document.

11. **With your teacher's permission**, print the Notes page for slide 1. It should look similar to Figure 2-2.

12. Close the document, saving all changes, and exit PowerPoint.

| Figure 2-2 | Student Name | 9/20/2011 |

Going Green: What Can You Do?

Presented by Planet Earth

Going green can help save you the planet, but it is also a great way to save you real green in your wallet!

1

Lesson 3

Working with Comments in a Presentation

> ➤ **What You Will Learn**

Compare Presentations
Review Comments
Delete Comments

Software Skills   You can use the Compare feature to quickly see any changes made to your presentation after it has been reviewed by others. When you're working with others on a project, comments are a great way to communicate ideas. After a presentation has been reviewed by coworkers, you need to review the presentation to resolve and delete any comments you find.

Application Skills   In this lesson, you will work on a presentation you created for Restoration Architecture. The presentation has been reviewed by the marketing department and you need to resolve any comments and review the presentation for changes.

What You Can Do

Comparing Presentations

- You can use the Compare feature in PowerPoint 2010 to instantly see any changes to a presentation that you've sent out for review.

- Reviewers often make small changes to a presentation without bothering to add comments. The best way to spot these changes is using the compare feature to merge the presentations.

- When comparing presentations you can choose whether to keep a reviewer's changes.

Try It!   **Comparing and Merging Presentations**

1 Start PowerPoint and open the PTry02_studentfirstname_studentlastname file that you worked with in the Try Its for Lesson 2.

2 Save the file as PTry03_studentfirstname_studentlastname in the location where your teacher instructs you to store the files for this lesson.

3 Click Review > Compare 🗌.

4 In the Choose File to Merge with Current Presentation window, select PTry03 from the data files for this lesson and click Merge.

✓ Note that the presentation skips to slide 2 (the first one with a change) and that a Revisions pane opens along the right of the PowerPoint window showing changes.

5 Save changes and leave PTry03_studentfirstname_studentlastname open to use in the next Try It.

Merging two presentations

Revisions pane explains all of the differences between the presentations

Try It!   **Reviewing Changes to a Presentation**

1 In PTry03_studentfirstname_studentlastname, click the Slides tab in the Revisions pane to see changes to the slides. Notice the difference in the alignment of the content on slide 2.

2 Click the change indicator 🗋 on the slide to see a description of the changes. Select the third option to see that change on your slide.

(continued)

Try It!   **Reviewing Changes to a Presentation** *(continued)*

3 On the Review tab, click the Reject down arrow. Select Reject All Changes to the current slide.

4 Click Next in the Compare group to see the next change.

5 Click Review > Accept to keep the color change and click Next.

6 Click the change indicator to see the inserted content and click the box to see the change on your slide.

7 Click Review > Accept to keep the color change and click Next.

8 Click Cancel when PowerPoint asks if you want to start reviewing changes from the beginning.

9 Click Review > End Review. When prompted, click Yes.

10 Save changes, and leave the file open to use in the next Try It.

Rejecting changes to a slide

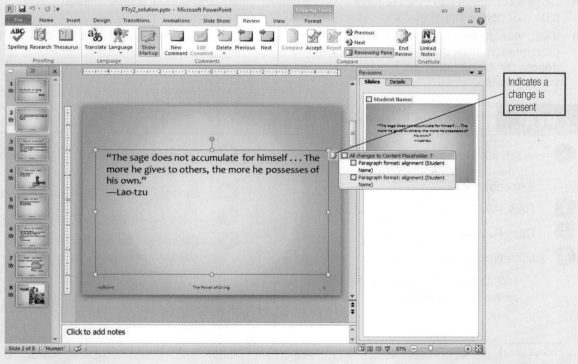

Reviewing Comments

- You use the Comments group on the Review tab to work with comments and markup.
- When you open a presentation that contains comments, the comment markers display on the slides by default, and the Show Markup button is active on the Review tab.
- The name and initials that display on each comment are those of the current user. The date displayed is the current date.

- To read a comment that is not open, point to the comment marker to open the comment box.
- If you have a number of comments in a presentation, the Previous and Next buttons allow you to move quickly from comment to comment, opening each so you can read it.

Try It!   Reviewing Comments

1 In **PTry03_studentfirstname_ studentlastname**, select slide 6 and click Review > Next Comment 🗨.

2 Move to the end of the text in the content placeholder and press `ENTER`.

3 Type **For the food bank**. Press `TAB`. Type **Pantry staples**.

4 Click Review > Next Comment 🗨 twice.

5 After you've read the comment on slide 5, press `ENTER` at the end of the first line in the content placeholder.

6 Press `TAB` and type **The foundation has an immediate need for a Webmaster**.

7 Save changes, and leave the file open to use in the next Try It.

Deleting Comments

- Once a comment has been resolved you can either hide it or delete it.
- If you want to hide comments as you review a presentation, click the Show Markup button to deactivate it. The comment markers then disappear from the slides.

- The Delete button allows you to remove a single comment, all comments on a slide, or all comments throughout a presentation.
- Before you complete a presentation, you should make sure you've resolved and deleted every comment.

Try It!   Deleting Comments

1 In **PTry03_studentfirstname_ studentlastname**, click the comment on slide 5, if necessary.

2 Click Review > Next Comment 🗨.

3 Click Review > Delete 🗨.

4 Click Next Comment 🗨.

  ✓ Click Continue when PowerPoint asks whether to continue from the beginning.

5 On the Review tab, click the Delete down arrow 🗨.

6 Select Delete All Markup in this Presentation.

7 Click Yes to confirm the deletion.

8 Close **PTry03_studentfirstname_ studentlastname**, saving all changes, and exit PowerPoint.

Deleting all the comments in a presentation

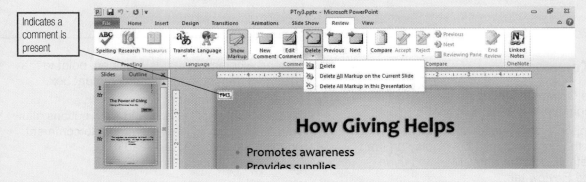

Project 5—Create It

Resolving Comments

DIRECTIONS

1. Start PowerPoint, if necessary, and open **PProj05** from the data files for this lesson.

2. Save the file as **PProj05_studentfirstname_ studentlastname** in the location where your teacher instructs you to store the files for this lesson.

3. Click **Review > Next Comment** in the Comments group to see the first change.

4. Read the comment.

5. Click **Design > Colors** and right-click on **Couture**.

6. Select **Apply to Selected Slides**.

7. Select the comment again and click **Review > Delete Comment**.

8. Click **Review > Next Comment** and read the comment.

9. Double-click the table on the slide to open the Excel Ribbon commands.

10. Click cell **A8** and type **Total**.

11. Click cell **B8** and click **Home > Sum** and press ENTER.

12. Click cell **C8** and repeat.

13. Select cells **A8:C8** and click **Home > Fill Color**. Select **Olive Green – Accent 3, Lighter 40%**.

14. Click outside of the table to return to the PowerPoint ribbon.

15. On the Review tab, click the **Delete Comment** down arrow and select **Delete All Markup in this Presentation**.

16. Save the changes to the document.

17. **With your teacher's permission**, print slide 7. It should look similar to Figure 3-1.

18. Close the document, saving all changes, and exit PowerPoint.

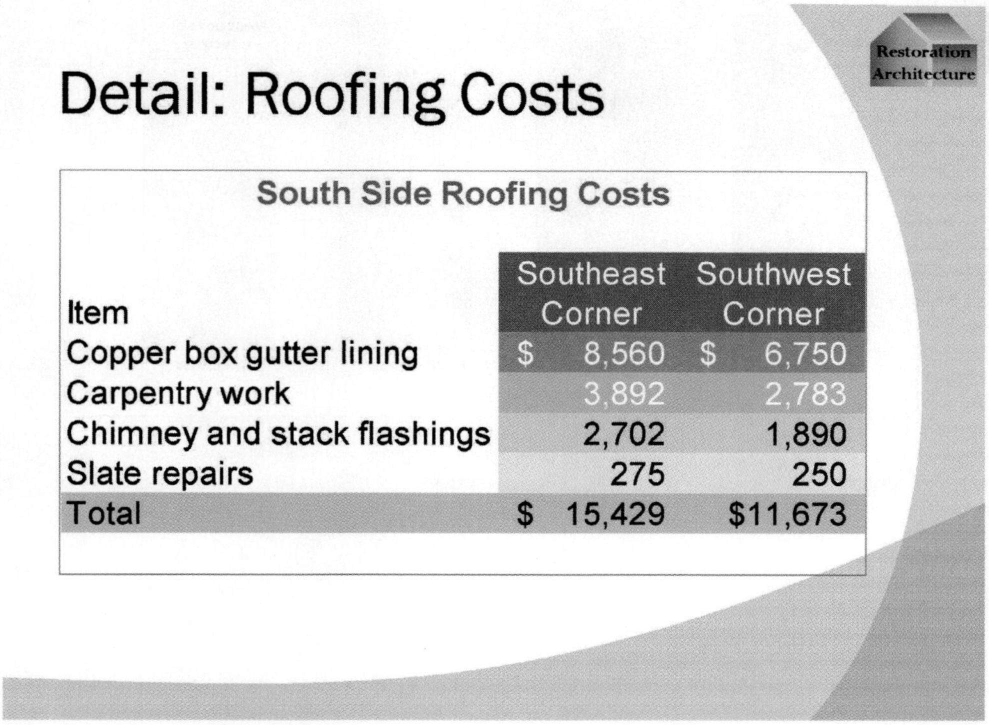

Figure 3-1

Restoration Architecture

Detail: Roofing Costs

South Side Roofing Costs

Item	Southeast Corner	Southwest Corner
Copper box gutter lining	$ 8,560	$ 6,750
Carpentry work	3,892	2,783
Chimney and stack flashings	2,702	1,890
Slate repairs	275	250
Total	$ 15,429	$11,673

Project 6—Apply It

Comparing Presentations

DIRECTIONS

1. Start PowerPoint, if necessary, and open **PProj06** from the data files for this lesson.
2. Save file as **PProj06_studentfirstname_studentlastname** in the location where your teacher instructs you to store the files for this lesson.
3. Click **Review** > **Compare** 🗋.
4. Select the file **PProj06_Reviewed** from the data files for this lesson.
5. Click **Merge**.
6. Click **Slides** in the Revisions pane.

7. Click **Review** > **Next Change** repeatedly to view each change until you return to slide 2.
8. Reject the change on slide 2.
9. Accept the changes on slides 3 and 4.
10. Reject the changes on slides 6 and 7.
11. Accept the change on slide 8.
12. Click **Review** > **End Review**.
13. Spell check the presentation.
14. **With your teacher's permission**, print slide 4. It should look similar to Figure 3-2.
15. Close the document, saving all changes, and exit PowerPoint.

Figure 3-2

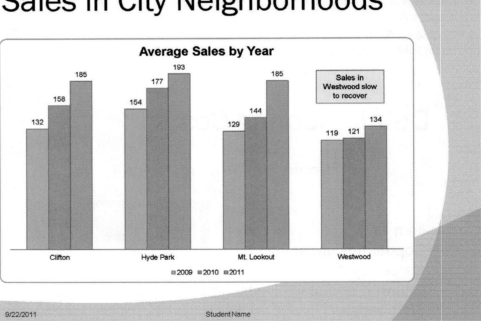

Lesson 4

Exporting Slide Handouts to Word

> ## ➤ What You Will Learn

Exporting Handouts to Word
Linking Presentations to Word

Software Skills   Send presentation materials to Microsoft Word to take advantage of Word's formatting options. You can also choose to link the presentation materials to a Word document. Handouts linked to a presentation will change automatically when the presentation is updated.

Application Skills   You will work with the presentation for Holmes Medical Center. In this lesson, you send the presentation data to Microsoft Word and create linked handouts.

What You Can Do

Exporting Handouts to Word

- You can send presentation data to Microsoft Word to create handouts or an outline. Exporting a presentation to Microsoft Word gives you the option of using Word's tools to format the handouts.

- You can modify the size of the slide images, format text, and add new text as desired to customize your handouts.

- Use the Create Handouts command on the Save and Send page in Backstage View to begin the process of sending materials to Word.

- The Send To Microsoft Word dialog box opens to allow you to select an export option.

- You have two options for positioning slide notes relative to the slide pictures and two options for placing blank lines that your audience can use to take their own notes.

- You can also choose to send only the outline. The exported outline retains the font used in the presentation and displays at a large point size.

Try It!   Exporting Handouts to Word

1 Start Word and open **PTry04** file from the data files for this lesson.

2 Save the file as **PTry04_studentfirstname_ studentlastname** in the location where your teacher instructs you to store the files for this lesson.

3 Click File > Save & Send.

4 Click Create Handouts under File Types, and then click Create Handouts in the right pane.

5 Select Blank lines next to slides and Paste under Add slides to Microsoft Word document.

6 Click OK.

7 View the newly created Microsoft Word document to see how the handouts look. Close Microsoft Word without saving changes.

8 Save **PTry04_studentfirstname_ studentlastname**, and leave the file open to use in the next Try It.

The Send to Microsoft Word dialog box

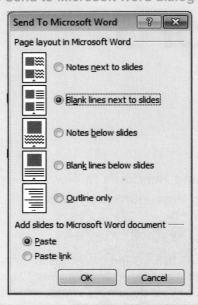

Linking Presentations to Word

- If the presentation might change over time, the best option is to maintain a link between the handouts in Word and the material displayed on a slide.

- When you choose the Paste link option, you create a link between the Word document and the PowerPoint presentation. Any changes you save to the slides in PowerPoint will appear in the Word document.

✓ You do not have the paste/paste link options when exporting an outline.

- To create a link between your presentation and the handouts choose the Paste Link option in the Send to Microsoft Word dialog box.

Try It!   Linking Presentations to Word

1 In **PTry04_studentfirstname_ studentlastname**, click File > Save & Send.

2 Click Create Handouts under File Types, and then click Create Handouts in the right pane.

(continued)

Try It!   **Linking Presentations to Word** *(continued)*

3 Select Notes next to slides and Paste Link under Add slides to Microsoft Word document.

4 Click OK.

5 View the newly created Microsoft Word document to see how the handouts look.

6 Return to **PTry04_studentfirstname_studentlastname** and click Design > Colors ▣ > Pushpin.

7 Close **PTry04_studentfirstname_studentlastname**, saving all changes, and exit PowerPoint.

8 Return to the Microsoft Word document and click File > Print.

9 Save the file as **PTry04a_studentfirstname_studentlastname** in the location where your teacher instructs you to store the files for this lesson.

10 Close Microsoft Word.

Updated linked handouts

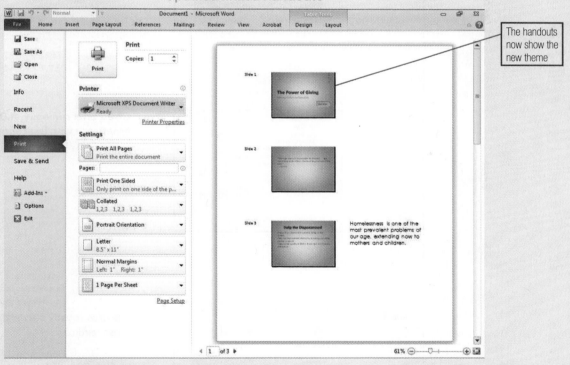

The handouts now show the new theme

Project 7—Create It

Creating Presentation Handouts in Word

DIRECTIONS

1. Start PowerPoint, if necessary, and open **PProj07** from the data files for this lesson.

2. Click **File** > **Save & Send**.

3. Click **Create Handouts** under File Types, and then click **Create Handouts** in the right pane.

4. Select Notes next to slides.

5. Select Paste Link under Add slides to Microsoft Word document and click OK.

6. Close PowerPoint without saving any changes.

7. View the newly created Microsoft Word document to see how the handouts look and save the file as PProj07_studentfirstname_studentlastname.

8. **With your teacher's permission**, print the document. It should look similar to Figure 4-1.

9. Close the document, saving all changes, and exit Word.

Figure 4-1

Slide 1

Welcome to Holmes Medical Center!

Slide 2

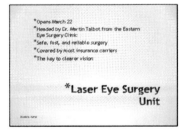

Give a brief summary of Dr. Talbot's experience with laser surgery.

Slide 3

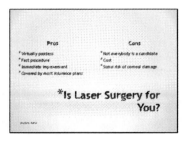

The pros usually outweigh the cons for most candidates.

Project 8—Apply It

Modifying Linked Handouts in Word

DIRECTIONS

1. Start Word, if necessary, and open **PProj07_studentfirstname_studentlastname** from the location where you stored your work for Project 7.

   ✓ *Click Yes when prompted to update the links in the file.*

2. Save the file as **PProj08_studentfirstname_studentlastname** in the location where your teacher instructs you to store the files for this lesson.

3. Double-click on the thumbnail for slide 1 to open the linked presentation.

4. Click **Design** > **Austin** and then press [CTRL] + [A].

5. Click **Home** > **Reset** to ensure the correct placement of elements.

6. Save the file as **PProj08a_studentfirstname_studentlastname** in the location where your teacher instructs you to store the files for this lesson and then close PowerPoint.

7. Return to the Word document. Notice the updated slides.

8. Click **Insert** > **Header** and choose **Tiles** from the list of built-in header styles.

9. Click **[YEAR]** in the header.

10. Click the down arrow and click **Today**.

11. Click **[TYPE THE DOCUTMENT TITLE]** in the header and type your name.

12. Click **Design** > **Close Header and Footer View**.

13. **With your teacher's permission**, print the document. It should look similar to Figure 4-2.

14. Close the document, saving all changes, and exit PowerPoint.

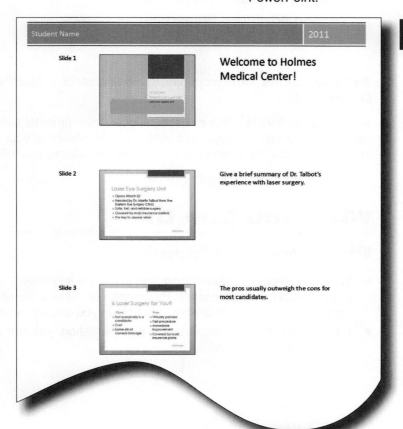

Figure 4-2

| Student Name | | 2011 |

Slide 1 — Welcome to Holmes Medical Center!

Slide 2 — Give a brief summary of Dr. Talbot's experience with laser surgery.

Slide 3 — The pros usually outweigh the cons for most candidates.

Lesson 5

Working with Presentation Properties

➤ What You Will Learn

Viewing Presentation Properties
Entering or Editing Properties
Viewing Advanced Properties

Software Skills   Add properties to a presentation to identify information about the presentation.

Application Skills   Planet Earth, a local environmental action group, has asked you to prepare a presentation that can be shown at your civic garden center to encourage city residents to "go green." In this lesson, you will add presentation properties.

What You Can Do

Viewing Presentation Properties

- When you create a presentation, you can store information about the presentation called properties. Properties can include the author of the presentation, its title, and keywords to help you quickly identify the presentation.
- After you have added properties to a presentation, you can view them on the Info page in Backstage View.

Try It!   **Viewing Document Properties in Backstage View**

1. Start PowerPoint and open **PTry05** file from the data files for this lesson.

2. Save the file as **PTry05_studentfirstname_ studentlastname** in the location where your teacher instructs you to store the files for this lesson.

3. Click File > Info.

4. View the properties listed on in the Document Information pane on the right of the screen.

5. Leave the presentation open to use in the next Try It.

Document properties in Backstage View

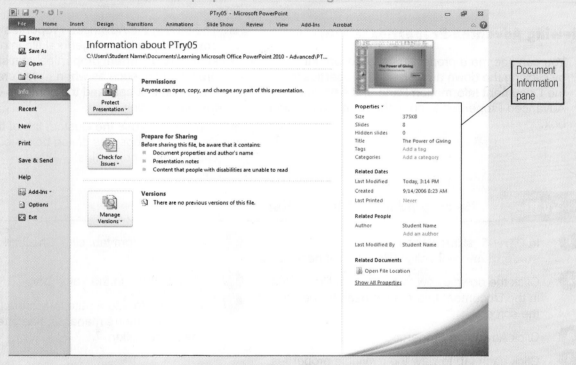

Try It!   **Viewing Document Properties Using the Document Information Panel**

1. In **PTry05_studentfirstname_ studentlastname**, click File > Info.

2. Click the down arrow next to Properties in the Document Information pane.

3. Click Show Document Panel.

4. Leave the presentation open to use in the next Try It.

Entering or Editing Properties

- Document properties, which are sometimes referred to as *metadata*, are also an easy way to organize and locate files that have the same kinds of information. When searching for files, for example, you can use document properties as criteria in the search.

- The Document Information Panel shows information that PowerPoint collects for you, such as the file location, as well as standard properties you supply yourself, such as the author, title, status, and any comments you want to add.

- You can add properties using either the Document Information pane on the Info page in Backstage View or using the Document Information Panel.

Try It!   **Adding Document Properties**

1 In PTry05_studentfirstname_ studentlastname, type your name in the Author box.

2 Type Foundation Fundraiser in the Subject box and Draft in the Status box.

3 Close the Document Information Panel.

4 Click File > Info.

5 Type Promotions in the Tags box in the Document Information pane on the right of the screen.

6 Save changes, and leave the file open to use in the next Try It.

Viewing Advanced Properties

- You can see more properties for a document by clicking the down arrow next to Properties in the Document Information Pane and selecting Advanced Properties to open the Properties dialog box.

- The tabs in the Advanced Properties dialog box allow you to view general file information, a summary of current properties, statistics about the presentation, such as when it was created and how many slides it has, and the contents of all slides in the presentation.

- You can also use the Custom tab of the Advanced Document Properties dialog box to create your own categories of properties.

Try It!   **Viewing Advanced Properties**

1 In PTry05_studentfirstname_ studentlastname, click File > Info, if necessary.

2 Click the down arrow to the right of Properties in the Document Information pane to the right of the screen.

3 Click Advanced Properties.

4 Click each tab to view the available properties.

5 On the Custom tab, click Checked by in the Name list.

6 Type Shirley in the Value box.

7 Click Add to add a note indicating that Shirley, the Foundation's manager, has already reviewed the presentation.

(continued)

Try It! | **Viewing Advanced Properties** *(continued)*

8 Click OK when finished viewing properties.

9 Close **PTry05_studentfirstname_studentlastname**, saving all changes, and exit PowerPoint.

Working with Advanced Properties

Project 9—Create It

Potential Cost Table

DIRECTIONS

1. Start PowerPoint, if necessary, and open **PProj09** from the data files for this lesson.

2. Save the presentation as **PProj09_studentfirstname_studentlastname** in the location where your teacher instructs you to store the files for this lesson.

3. Click **File > Info**.

4. Click **Add an author** in the Document Information pane on the right of the screen.

5. Type your name.

6. Click **Add a title** in the same pane and type **Going Green**.

7. Click **Add a tag** and type **lawn, organic, composting**. Your presentation should look similar to Figure 5-1.

8. Close the document, saving all changes, and exit PowerPoint.

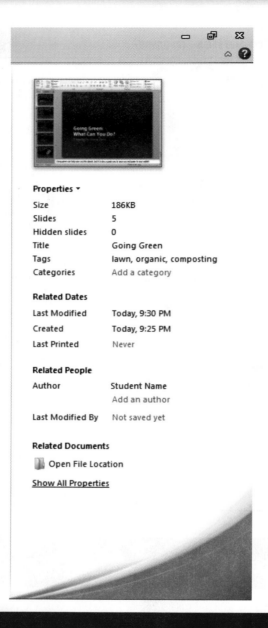

Figure 5-1

Project 10—Apply It

Adding Custom Properties

DIRECTIONS

1. Start PowerPoint, if necessary, and open **PProj10** from the data files for this lesson.

2. Save the file as **PProj10_studentfirstname_ studentlastname** in the location where your teacher instructs you to store the files for this lesson.

3. Click **File** > **Info**.

4. Click the arrow next to the word **Properties** in the pane and select **Show Document Panel**.

5. Type **Green Strategies** in the Subject box.

6. Type **In progress** in the Status box.

7. Type **Public Presentations** in the Category box.

8. Close the Document Information Panel and click **File** > **Info**.

9. Click the arrow next to the word **Properties** in the pane and select **Advanced Properties**.

10. On the Custom tab, click **Checked by** from the Name list, as shown in Figure 5-2.

11. In the Value box, type your name.

12. Click **Add** and then **OK**.

13. Close the document, saving all changes, and exit PowerPoint.

Figure 5-2

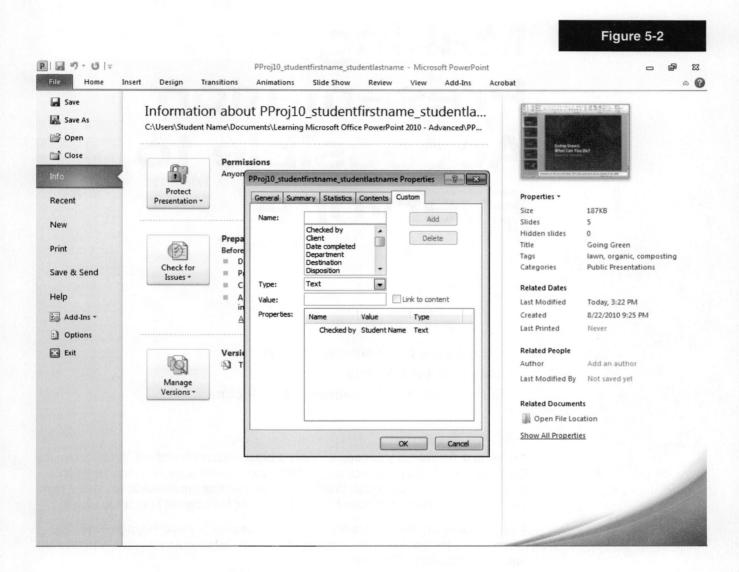

Lesson 6

Making a Presentation Accessible to Everyone

> ➤ **What You Will Learn**
>
> **Running the Compatibility Checker**
> **Checking Accessibility**
> **Saving a Slide or Presentation As a Picture**

Software Skills   If you need to share a presentation with others, you can use the Compatibility Checker to check accessibility and prepare a presentation for its final use. You can also prepare your presentation as a picture presentation to ensure that the recipient won't need to have Microsoft Office or the Internet in order to view it.

Application Skills   In this lesson, you will prepare a PowerPoint picture presentation for a presentation you created for Restoration Architecture. You also will run the Compatibility Checker.

What You Can Do

Running the Compatibility Checker

- The Compatibility Checker is a tool designed to flag features in your current presentation that are not supported in previous PowerPoint versions.
- Always run the Compatibility Checker before saving to an earlier version of PowerPoint, because some of PowerPoint 2010's effects cannot be edited in previous versions of the program.

- When you click Run Compatibility Checker from the Info page in Backstage View, the Compatibility Checker reviews each slide for compatibility issues and then displays a report.

- The report tells you any compatibility issues, such as a SmartArt graphic that cannot be edited in earlier versions of PowerPoint, lets you know how many times the issue occurs, and offers a Help link that provides more information about the issue.

- You'll want to go through each slide listed and look for the compatibility issues.

- In most cases, nothing needs to be done. The compatibility issues will not compromise the look of the slides when they are shown in other versions of PowerPoint.

  ✓ *For example, although you will not be able to edit a SmartArt graphic, its components are saved as pictures that will display the same way they do in PowerPoint 2010.*

- The help files offer advice on how to modify PowerPoint 2010 features to improve compatibility. For example, you can convert a SmartArt graphic to separate shapes so that you can edit them in any version of PowerPoint.

Try It!   **Running the Compatibility Checker**

1 Start PowerPoint and open **PTry06** from the data files for this lesson.

2 Save the file as **PTry06_studentfirstname_studentlastname** in the location where your teacher instructs you to store the files for this lesson.

3 Click File > Info.

4 Under Prepare for Sharing, click Check for Issues > Check Compatibility.

5 Click OK.

6 Look through the slides listed (1, 2, 3, 4, 5, 6, & 7).

  ✓ *Note that on some slides (such as 1 and 3) the compatibility issue is obvious. On other slides there is no visible problem.*

7 Since none of these issues will cause a problem, you decide to leave the presentation as is.

8 Leave the presentation open to use in the next Try It.

The Compatibility Checker dialog box

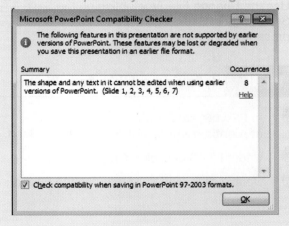

Checking Accessibility

- The Accessibility Checker looks for places in your presentation that could potentially make it difficult for someone with disabilities to view the entire presentation.

- When the Accessibility Checker finds problems, it will open a task pane listing each issue and classifying them as Errors, Warnings, or Tips.

  - Errors are extremely difficult, if not impossible, for someone with disabilities to understand.

  - Warnings are places where the content might be difficult for people with disabilities to understand.

  - Tips are suggestions about places that can be modified to make it easier for someone with disabilities to understand.

- When the Accessibility Checker finds problems, it will provide you with instructions that you can use to eliminate the problems.

- You can choose whether you want to resolve the issues found or leave the presentation as is.

Try It!   Checking Accessibility

1 In **PTry06_studentfirstname_ studentlastname**, click File > Info.

2 Under Prepare for Sharing, click Check for Issues > Check Accessibility.

3 Click on each issue located and read the Additional Information box at the bottom of the task pane.

4 Follow the instructions in the Additional Information box to resolve each issue.

5 Save changes, and leave the presentation open to use in the next Try It.

Saving a Slide or Presentation As a Picture

■ You can save a single slide or an entire presentation in a graphic file format that allows you to insert the slides as pictures in other applications, such as Word documents.

■ By saving a slide or presentation as a picture you can ensure that it is viewable by anyone with a computer regardless of whether they have a Mac or PC computer or what version of software they are using.

■ Use the Change File Type option on the Save & Send page in Backstage View to save a slide or presentation as a picture.

■ You can choose among four picture file formats. PNG and JPEG are listed on the Change File Type page. If you prefer GIF or TIFF, you can use the Save As button at the bottom of the pane and choose either option in the File as Type box.

■ Once you have provided a name for the new file, selected a format, and issued the Save command, PowerPoint displays a dialog box to ask if you want to save only the current slide or every slide in the current presentation.

■ The resulting files can be used just like any other picture file.

Try It!   Saving a Slide As a Picture

1 In **PTry06_studentfirstname_ studentlastname**, click File > Save & Send.

2 Under File Types, click Change file type.

3 Double click JPEG File Interchange Format.

4 Save changes to **PTry06_studentfirstname_ studentlastname** in the location where your teacher instructs you to store the files for this lesson.

5 Select Current Slide Only at the prompt.

6 Save changes to **PTry06_studentfirstname_ studentlastname**, close the file, and exit PowerPoint.

Save a slide as a picture

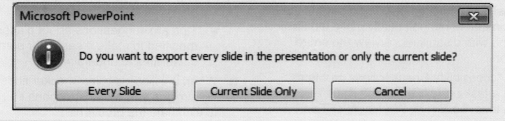

Project 11—Create It

Checking the Compatibility of a Presentation

DIRECTIONS

1. Start PowerPoint, if necessary, and open **PProj11** from the data files for this lesson.

2. Save the presentation as **PProj11_ studentfirstname_studentlastname** in the location where your teacher instructs you to store the files for this lesson.

3. Click **File** > **Info**.

4. Under Prepare for Sharing, click **Check for Issues** > **Check Compatibility**.

5. Read the error and click **OK**.

6. Click on slide 4 to view the SmartArt graphic identified by the compatibility checker.

7. Since the organization chart will not need to be modified in a previous version of PowerPoint you decide to leave it as is.

8. Close the document, saving all changes, and exit PowerPoint.

Project 12—Apply It

Checking the Accessibility of a Presentation

DIRECTIONS

1. Start PowerPoint, if necessary, and open **PProj12** from the data files for this lesson.

2. Save the presentation as **PProj12_ studentfirstname_studentlastname** in the location where your teacher instructs you to store the files for this lesson.

3. Create a slide footer with an automatically updating date and your name.

4. Click **File** > **Info**.

5. Under Prepare for Sharing, click **Check for Issues** > **Check Accessibility**.

6. Click on the first error listed (Picture 3) and right-click the picture on slide 2.

7. Select **Format Picture** and click **Alt Text**.

8. Type **Lilly pond in the garden** in the **Title** box and click **Close**.

9. Click on the next error listed and right-click the object on slide 4.

10. Select **Format Object** and click **Alt Text**.

11. Type **Organizational Chart** in the **Title** box and click **Close**.

12. Click on the tip listed in the Accessibility Checker pane and read the Additional Information.

13. Follow the instructions to organize the reading order as shown in Figure 6-1.

14. Click the ✖ button to close the Accessibility Checker pane.

15. Click **File** > **Save & Send** > **Change File Type** > **JPEG File Interchange Format** > **Save As**.

16. Name the file **PProj12_studentfirstname_ studentlastname**. Choose **CurrentSlide Only**.

17. Close the document, saving all changes, and exit PowerPoint.

Figure 6-1

Opportunity
Knocks

- Money is currently available to fund one or more new features
- New feature(s) should enhance visitor experience; for example, visitors might want to:
  - Learn more about horticulture in a library
  - Purchase high-quality merchandise related to the site in a gift shop
  - Relax and enjoy the atmosphere while eating or drinking

Student Name   4/22/2011

Chapter Assessment and Application

Project 13—Make It Your Own

Reviewing Comments and Finalizing a Presentation

You've been working on a presentation for Voyager Travel Adventures about their newest adventure location, Glacier National Park. You sent the draft of the presentation to your boss, Jan Weeks. In this project, you'll review her comments and make any necessary changes to the presentation so that you can submit the final presentation.

DIRECTIONS

1. Start PowerPoint, if necessary, and open **PProj13** from the data files for this project.

2. Save the presentation as **PProj13a_ studentfirstname_studentlastname** in the location where your teacher instructs you to store the files for this project.

3. Click **Review** > **Next Comment** and read the remarks.

4. Click **Review** > **Next Comment** to read the comment on slide 6 of the presentation.

5. On the slide tab, right-click slide 6 and choose **Duplicate Slide**.

6. Select the comment and click **Review** > **Delete Comment**.

7. Select the slide title and type **Fauna**.

8. Select the first image and click **Picture Tools Format** > **Change Picture** 🖼.

9. Select one of the **PProj13_fauna** pictures from the data files for this lesson.

10. Repeat this process for each picture on this slide. The order of the images is not important.

11. Click **Review** > **Next Comment** and read the next comment.

12. To resolve this comment, click **Insert** > **Picture** and select the **PProj13_glacier** picture from the data files for this lesson.

13. Adjust the size and spacing of the elements on this slide as shown in Illustration A.

14. Click **Review** > **Delete** > **Delete All Markup in this Presentation** to remove all remaining comments.

15. Click **File** > **Save** 💾 and then click the **File** tab again.

16. Click **Check for Issues** and select **Check Compatibility**. Since these graphics and smart art elements won't need to be changed in 97-2003 format you can just click **OK** to close the box.

17. Click **File** > **Save & Send**.

18. Click **Create Handouts** under File Types, and then click **Create Handouts** in the right pane.

19. Select **Blank lines** next to slides and **Paste**. Click **OK**.

20. Add a slide footer that includes a date that updates automatically and your name. Apply the footer to all slides.

21. In the Word document, change the margins to **Narrow**.

23. Insert an **Austere (Odd Page)** header to the Word document with your name as the title. Save the Word document as **PProj13b_studentfirstname_ studentlastname**.

23. **With your teacher's permission**, print the handouts. They should look similar to Illustration B.

24. Close Word and PowerPoint, saving all your changes.

Illustration A

Illustration B

Project 14—Master It

Creating a Kiosk Presentation

Peterson Home Health Care has asked you to create a presentation that can be used at local health fairs to give viewers information about the company's home health care options. You will start work on that presentation in this project.

DIRECTIONS

1. Start PowerPoint, if necessary, and open **PProj14** from the data files for this project.

2. Save the presentation as **PProj14_ studentfirstname_studentlastname** in the location where your teacher instructs you to store the files for this project.

3. Click **View > Slide Master** 🖵.

4. On the slide master make the following changes.

   a. Select the title placeholder and change the font to **Corbel**.

   b. Select the content placeholder and change the font to **Calibri**.

   c. Change the color of headings to **Black, Text 1**.

5. On the title slide master, make the following changes.

   a. Move the subtitle placeholder to the right to align at the right side with the title placeholder.

   b. Change the alignment of both the title and subtitle to right alignment.

   c. Click **Drawing Tools Format > More** and select a Shape Style of your choice to the title placeholder.

   d. Insert an appropriate figure.

6. Add a complementary slide master.

7. On the new slide master's two content master, insert a narrow rectangle shape along the inside edge of the right hand content placeholder. Adjust the position of the shape to leave room between it and the picture, and to be as tall as the content placeholder. Apply a Quick Style of your choice to the rectangle shape. Your slide should look similar to Illustration A.

8. Display the notes page master and make the following changes to the master.

   a. Apply different theme colors and theme fonts that complement the presentation's appearance.

   b. Change the background style to **Style 10**.

   c. Apply a Quick Style of your choice to the Notes placeholder.

   d. Change the size of the text in the placeholder to **14 point**.

9. Apply the new slide master, two content layout to slides 4 and 5. Make any changes necessary to the size and format of the slide contents to suit the new master. Your slides should look similar to Illustration B.

10. Open the Document Information Panel and add the following properties to the presentation.

    Author: Your name

    Title: Our Reputation

    Category: Kiosk presentations

    Status: In progress

11. **With your teacher's permission**, print the presentation.

12. Close and save all files.

Illustration A

Illustration B

Chapter 2

Applying Advanced Graphic and Media Techniques

Lesson 7
Advanced Picture Formatting
Projects 15-16

- Understanding Picture Formats
- Applying Advanced Picture Formatting
- Adding a Border to a Picture

Lesson 8
Advanced Multimedia Features
Projects 17-18

- Understanding Multimedia Presentations
- Embedding a Web Video in a Presentation
- Setting Advanced Video Options
- Setting Advanced Sound Options

Lesson 9
Working with Advanced Photo Album Features
Projects 19-20

- Editing a Photo Album
- Adding Captions
- Compressing Pictures

Lesson 10
Advanced Animation Features
Projects 21-22

- Applying Advanced Animation Effects
- Creating a Motion Path Animation
- Changing the Order of Animation Effects
- Applying Advanced Effect Options
- Adjusting Animation Timing
- Working with the Animation Timeline
- Changing or Removing an Animation

Lesson 11
Finalizing Slide Shows
Projects 23-24

- Creating Presentation Sections
- Adding Narration to a Presentation

Lesson 12
Working with Actions
Projects 25-26

- Using Advanced Hyperlink Settings
- Working with Action Settings

End-of-Chapter Assessments
Projects 27-28

Lesson 7

Advanced Picture Formatting

WORDS TO KNOW

Bitmap image
Graphic created from arrangements of small squares called *pixels.* Also called raster images.

Lossless compression
Compression accomplished without loss of data.

Lossy compression
Compression in which part of a file's data is discarded to reduce file size.

Pixel
Term that stands for picture element, a single point on a computer monitor screen.

Vector image
Drawings made up of lines and curves defined by vectors, which describe an object mathematically according to its geometric characteristics.

➤ **What You Will Learn**

Understanding Picture Formats
Applying Advanced Picture Formatting
Adding a Border to a Picture

Software Skills   Understanding picture formats helps you select an appropriate file type for your presentation. Advanced formatting options such as brightness and contrast adjustments and recoloring options allow you to create sophisticated picture effects.

Application Skills   Thorn Hill Gardens wants to run a presentation on a kiosk at the main entrance advertising the annual Butterfly Show. In this exercise, you add several pictures to a presentation and format pictures according to file type.

What You Can Do

Understanding Picture Formats

- PowerPoint 2010 can accept a number of picture formats, including both **bitmap** and **vector** images.
- Understanding the advantages and disadvantages of these common graphic file formats can help you choose pictures for your presentations.
- The following table lists some of the more common formats that PowerPoint supports, with their file extensions.
- When selecting pictures, consider the following:
  - If you plan on displaying it only on a screen, GIF and JPG files will provide a good-quality appearance.

Table 7-1

Format	Extension	Characteristics
WMF	.wmf	Windows Metafile. Contains both bitmap and vector information and is optimized for use in Windows applications.
PNG	.png	Portable Network Graphics. A bitmap format that supports lossless compression and allows transparency; no color limitations.
BMP	.bmp	Windows Bitmap. Does not support file compression so files may be large; widely compatible with Windows programs.
GIF	.gif	Graphics Interchange Format. A widely supported bitmap format that uses lossless compression; maximum of 256 colors; allows transparency.
JPEG	.jpg	Joint Photographic Experts Group. A bitmap format that allows a tradeoff of lossy compression and quality; best option for photographs and used by most digital cameras.
TIFF	.tif	Tagged Image File Format. Can be compressed or uncompressed; uncompressed file sizes may be very large. Most widely used format for print publishing; not supported by Web browsers.

- If you plan to print your slide materials, you may want to use TIFF images for better-quality printed appearance.
- For small graphics with a limited number of colors, for example, a picture in GIF or PNG format will be perfectly adequate.
- Photographs, on the other hand, should be saved in JPG or TIFF format.
  - ✓ *Remember the higher the picture quality, the larger the presentation's file size.*
- You can modify file size by compressing pictures you have inserted in the presentation.

Applying Advanced Picture Formatting

- The Picture Styles gallery on the Picture Tools Format tab is the easiest way to change the shape and appearance of a picture on a slide.
- Other options on this tab allow you to create interesting and unusual picture effects as well as specify a precise size.

- Use the tools in the Adjust group to modify the appearance of the image. Some of these tools provide menus of preset adjustments; you may also have the option of opening a dialog box for more control over the adjustment.
- Use the Corrections options to adjust the brightness and contrast of the image.
- The Color Option allows you to modify the colors in an image using a variety of different tint options.
- You can also select the Set Transparent Color command on the Color gallery to make one of the image's colors transparent.
- When you click this command, a paintbrush icon attaches to the pointer. Click on the color you want to make transparent and all pixels of that color are removed to allow the background to show through.
- The Change Picture option reopens the Insert Picture dialog box so you can replace the currently selected picture with a different one.
- Use the Reset Picture option to restore a picture's original settings. Clicking this button reverses any changes you have made to size, brightness, contrast, or color.

Try It!   **Making Part of a Graphic Transparent**

 Start PowerPoint and open **PTry07** from the data files for this lesson.

 Save the file as **PTry07_studentfirstname_studentlastname** in the location where your teacher instructs you to store the files for this lesson.

(continued)

Try It!   **Making Part of a Graphic Transparent** (continued)

③ Click on the graphic on slide 2.

④ Click Picture Tools Format > Color 🖾 and then click Set Transparent Color.

✓ *The cursor will change to a pointing wand 🖉. Aim the tip of the wand at the color in the object you want to make transparent.*

⑤ Click the white background on the graphic.

⑥ Save changes, and leave the file open to use in the next Try It.

Making part of a graphic transparent

The Pilot Project
⟶ ℭℨ ⟶

- ℭℨ A goal of our organization is grass-roots participation in strategies to save our planet
- ℭℨ The Eco-Sales Pilot Project was conceived to help our community put green strategies in place
- ℭℨ A survey was conducted to determine which of a number of fairly simple green strategies our neighbors would support

---

Try It!   **Recoloring a Picture**

① In **PTry07_studentfirstname_studentlast name**, click the clip art image on slide 2, if necessary.

② Click Picture Tools Format > Color 🖾.

③ Click Green, Accent color 1, Light from the Recolor group.

④ Save changes, and leave the file open to use in the next Try It.

Changing the color of a graphic

Try It!   **Adjusting Brightness and Contrast**

① In **PTry07_studentfirstname_studentlast name**, click the photo in slide 6.

② On the Picture Tools Format tab, click the Corrections button 🔆.

③ Under Brightness and Contrast, select Brightness: +20% Contrast: +40%.

④ Save changes, and leave the file open to use in the next Try It.

(continued)

Try It!   Adjusting Brightness and Contrast *(continued)*

Correcting the brightness and contrast of a graphic

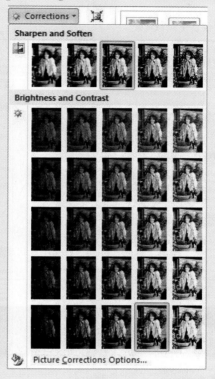

Try It!   Resetting a Graphic to Normal

1 In **PTry07_studentfirstname_studentlast name**, click the clip art image in slide 6, if necessary.

2 Click Picture Tools Format > Reset Picture.

3 Save changes, and leave the file open to use in the next Try It.

Try It!   Applying a Picture Style to a Graphic

1 In **PTry07_studentfirstname_studentlast name**, click the clip art image in slide 6, if necessary.

2 Click Picture Tools Format > More in the Picture Styles group.

3 Select Drop Shadow Rectangle.

✓ *Live Preview enables you to see the effect of a style by hovering over the option.*

4 Save changes, and leave the file open to use in the next Try It.

Adding a Border to a Picture

■ Another way to add emphasis to a graphic is to apply a border to it.

■ Use the Picture Border button on the Picture Tools Format tab to add a border to a graphic.

■ When you use the Picture Border button, a gallery of border colors that coordinate with your theme opens.

■ Alternatively, you can choose More Outline Colors at the bottom of the gallery to open a dialog box that lets you select any possible color.

■ You can also control the weight of the outline and give it a pattern.

Try It!   **Adding a Border to a Picture**

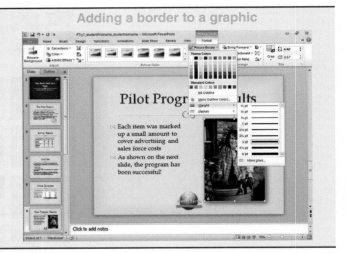
Adding a border to a graphic

1 In **PTry07_studentfirstname_studentlast name**, click the clip art image in slide 6, if necessary.

2 Click Picture Tools Format > Picture Border in the Picture Styles group.

3 Select Light Blue in the Standard group.

4 Click Picture Tools Format > Picture Border > Weight and select 3 pt.

5 Close the file, saving all changes, and exit PowerPoint.

Project 15—Create It

Kiosk Presentation Graphics

DIRECTIONS

1. Start PowerPoint, if necessary, and open **PProj15** from the data files for this lesson.

2. Save the file as **PProj15_studentfirstname_studentlastname** in the location where your teacher instructs you to store the files for this lesson.

3. Select slide 1 and click **Insert** > **Picture**.

4. Open **PProj15a** from the data files for this lesson.

5. With the image selected, click **Picture Tools Format** > **Crop**.

6. Drag the left center cropping handle to the right **1.5** inches until the width is approximately **4.5** inches.

7. Click **Picture Tools Format** > **Crop**.

8. Right-click the image and select **Format Picture** to open the Format Picture dialog box.

9. Click **Size** and then in the **Scale** area, type **75%** in the Height box and press ENTER.

10. With the image selected, click **Picture Tools Format** > **More** ⟱ in the Picture Styles group. Select **Soft Edge Oval**.

11. Click **Picture Tools Format** > **Color** and select **Blue-Grey, Accent Color 6, Dark**.

12. Drag the image to position as shown in Figure 7-1.

13. Insert a footer with your name in it for all slides.

14. **With your teacher's permission**, print the document. It should look similar to Figure 7-1.

16. Close the file, saving all changes, and exit PowerPoint.

Figure 7-1

Project 16—Apply It

Kiosk Presentation Graphics

DIRECTIONS

1. Start PowerPoint, if necessary, and open **PProj16** from the data files for this lesson.

2. Save the file as **PProj16_studentfirstname_ studentlastname** in the location where your teacher instructs you to store the files for this lesson.

3. Select slide 3 and insert the JPEG picture file **PProj16a** in the content placeholder.

4. Format the picture as follows.
   a. Adjust the brightness to make the picture **20%** brighter. Adjust the contrast to **+40%**.
   b. Apply a **Drop Shadow Rectangle** picture style. Your slide should look similar to Figure 7-2.

5. Select slide 4, and insert the JPEG picture file **PProj16b** in the content placeholder.

6. Format the picture as follows.
   a. Apply a correction to sharpen the image **50%**.
   b. Apply a **Drop Shadow Rectangle** picture style.
   c. Increase the contrast by **20%**.
   d. Apply a picture border using the color **Teal, Accent 2, Darker 25%.**

7. Select the clip art on slide 2. Recolor it using **Lime, Accent color 1, Light**.

8. The resulting clip isn't very exciting. Reset the picture to its original appearance, then make the background blue color transparent.

9. Apply the **Teal, Accent color 2, Light** color effect.

10. Add a footer with your name.

11. **With your teacher's permission**, print the document.

12. Close the file, saving all changes, and exit PowerPoint.

Figure 7-2

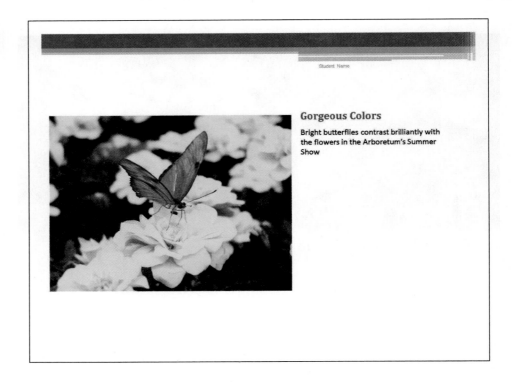

Lesson 8

Advanced Multimedia Features

➤ **What You Will Learn**

Understanding Multimedia Presentations
Embedding a Web Video in a Presentation
Setting Advanced Video Options
Setting Advanced Sound Options

Software Skills   To make a presentation "come alive," use multimedia content such as animation, movies, and sounds. Media clips can add considerable impact to a presentation as well as convey information in ways that other graphic objects cannot.

Application Skills   Voyager Adventure Travel is beginning the task of adding a new hiking package to its list of adventures. The decision-making process requires consideration of both pros and cons for each suggested venue, and you have been asked to prepare a slide show to present the information. In this lesson, you will begin work on the presentation with pros and cons for Glacier National Park.

What You Can Do

Understanding Multimedia Presentations

■ **Multimedia** presentations display information in a variety of media, including text, pictures, movies, animations, and sounds.

- Multimedia content not only adds visual and audio interest to slides but also presents information in ways that plain text cannot. A simple picture can convey an image that would take many words to describe; likewise, a movie can show a process or sequence of events that might take many pictures to convey.

- You can choose how much or how little multimedia content to include in a presentation.

- When deciding on multimedia options for a presentation, you must consider the trade-off between multimedia impact and the presentation's file size. Multimedia files such as videos and sounds can be quite large.

- You also need appropriate computer resources, such as speakers and video or sound cards to play media files successfully.

- Use good research standards when locating multimedia content. Always request permission to use materials you may find on the Internet, or follow directives for crediting persons or agencies.

- When creating a presentation for personal use, you can use CD music tracks for background sound, but you should not use such copyrighted materials if you plan to sell your presentation or publish it on the Web.

- If you decide to include multimedia content in a presentation, you will find that PowerPoint offers a number of options for playing both movies and sounds.

Embedding a Video from the Web in a Presentation

- You have three options for adding a video to your presentation:
  - Insert an animated clip art graphic.
  - Insert a movie file saved in a format such as AVI or MPEG.
  - Insert a movie from the Web.

- You can embed a video from the Web using the Video button on the Insert tab.

- When you insert a video from the Web, the Video Tools Format and Video Tools Playback tabs open.

- When you insert a video, a small star symbol appears next to the slides thumbnail in the slide tab. This symbol signifies the file is animated.

- To see the animation in motion, display the slide in Slide Show view or click Video Tools Format > Play.

Try It!   **Embedding a Web Video in a Presentation**

1 Start PowerPoint and open **PTry08** file from the data files for this lesson.

2 Save the file as **PTry08_studentfirstname_ studentlastname** in the location where your teacher instructs you to store the files for this lesson.

3 Open your Internet browser and navigate to *http://www.youtube.com/ watch?v=vdvksW6RAWs*.

   ✓ *This video is copyright-free. Be sure to only use videos that are copyright-free. If you are unsure, do a search for "copyright-free videos."*

4 Under the video screen, click <Embed> to open a box containing the embed codes for this video.

5 Press CTRL + C to copy the embed codes.

6 In the presentation, select slide 9 and click Insert > Video 🎬 down arrow.

7 Select Video from Web site to open the Insert Video From a Web Site dialog box.

8 In the Insert Video From Web Site box, press CTRL + V .

9 Click Insert.

10 Close the browser window, save the changes to the **PTry08_studentfirstname_ studentlastname** file, and leave it open to use in the next Try It.

Using embed codes to insert a video from a Web site

Setting Advanced Video Options

- You need to understand video formats to determine the quality of video clips you intend to insert. A file in MPEG1 format, for example, is not likely to display with the same quality as an MPEG2 file, but it will be smaller in size.

- Likewise, you need to know that PowerPoint does not support some popular video formats, such as QuickTime or RealMedia files.

Table 8-1

Format	Extension	Characteristics
ASF	.asf	Advanced Streaming Format. Microsoft's streaming format that can contain video, audio, slide shows, and other synchronized content.
AVI	.avi	Audio/Video Interleave. A file format that stores alternating (interleaved) sections of audio and video content; widely used for playing video with sound on Windows systems; AVI is a container (a format that stores different types of data), not a form of compression.
MPEG	.mpg, .mpeg	Moving Picture Experts Group. A standard format for lossy audio and visual compression that comes in several formats, such as MPEG1 (CD quality) and MPEG2 (DVD quality).
WMV	.wmv	Windows Media Video. Microsoft's lossy compression format for motion video; it results in files that take up little room on a system.

- Once you have selected and inserted a video clip, you can use the tools on the Video Tools Playback tab to work with a movie.

- Use the Preview button in the Play group to preview the movie while in Normal view.

- The Video Tools Playback options give you more control over how the movie plays during the presentation.
  - Change the play setting using the Play Movie list. You can play the movie automatically, when clicked, or set the movie to continue playing as you continue to display later slides.

- You can choose to hide the movie during the show, play it at full screen size, loop it (play it over and over) until you stop it by pressing ESC, or return the movie to its first frame after it has finished playing.

- Use the Volume button to control the playback of the individual video clip within the overall presentation.

- The Fade Duration settings allow you to ease into and out of video playback. Depending on the video contents, this can be less jarring to the viewer.

- Using the Video Tools Playback tab you can trim an inserted video so that only a small portion of the video plays.

Try It!   Setting Advanced Video Options

1. In **PTry08_studentfirstname_studentlastname**, select the video on slide 5.

2. On the Video Tools Playback tab, add a timed fade to the beginning of your video by clicking the up arrows to increase the Fade In time to 00.50.

3. Click Video Tools Playback > Start `Start: On Click` down arrow.

4. Select Automatically.

5. Click Video Tools Playback > Play ▶ to watch the video.

6. Save changes, and leave the file open to use in the next Try It.

(continued)

Try It!   **Setting Advanced Video Options** *(continued)*

The Video Tools Playback tab

Try It!   **Trimming a Video**

1. In **PTry08_studentfirstname_studentlast name**, select the video on slide 5.

2. Click Video Tools Playback > Trim Video 🎞.

3. In the Trim Video dialog box, drag the green start indicator ▌ to the right until the Start Time indicates approximately 00:02:50.

   OR

   Click in the Start Time box and type **00:02:50**.

4. Drag the End Time indicator ▌ to the left until the End Time box shows 00:15:00.

   OR

   Click in the End Time box and type **00:15:00**.

5. Click OK.

6. Save changes, and leave the file open to use in the next Try It.

Trimming a video

Setting Advanced Sound Options

■ Use the Sound Tools Playback tab to control sound options.

■ Many of these options look similar to those on the Video Tools Playback tab and operate in the same way. You can use Preview to listen to the sound in Normal view, for example, and use the Sound Options group tools to hide the sound icon, loop the sound, or adjust the play setting.

Try It!   Setting Advanced Sound Options

1 In **PTry08_studentfirstname_student lastname**, select the audio clip on slide 9.

2 On the Audio Tools Playback tab, add a timed fade to the beginning of your audio, by clicking the up arrows to increase the Fade In time to 00.25.

3 Click Audio Tools Playback > Volume 🔊 down arrow and select Medium.

4 Click Audio Tools Playback > Loop until Stopped.

5 Save changes, and leave the file open to use in the next Try It.

The Audio Tools Playback tab

Try It!   Setting a Trigger for an Embedded Sound

1 In **PTry08_studentfirstname_student lastname**, select the audio clip on slide 9, if necessary.

2 Click Audio Tools Playback > Start [Start: On Click] down arrow.

3 Select Automatically.

4 Click Slide Show > From Beginning 🖥 to watch the show.

✓ *Note that because the video on slide 9 is embedded, you will need to click the screen once to open the video controls and then click on the video again to start the playback.*

5 Close the file, saving all changes, and exit PowerPoint.

Project 17—Create It

Multimedia Presentation

DIRECTIONS

1. Start PowerPoint, if necessary, and open **PProj17** from the data files for this lesson. Save the file as **PProj17_studentfirstname_studentlastname** in the location where your teacher instructs you to store the files for this lesson.

2. Select slide 5 and click Insert > Video 📹 > Video from file. The Insert Video dialog box opens.

3. Navigate to the location where the data files for this lesson are stored and select **PProj17a.mpeg**.

4. Click Insert. The video appears in the placeholder.

5. Right-click the video and select **Format Video** to open the Format Video dialog box.

6. Click **Size** and then in the **Scale** area type **75%** in the Height box and press [ENTER]. Click **Close**.

7. Click the **Start** down arrow on the **Video Tools Playback** tab and select **Automatically**.

8. Select slide 6 and click the **Audio** down arrow on the **Insert** tab.

9. Select **Clip Art Audio** to open the Clip Art task pane.

10. Type **helicopter** in the Search for box and click **Go**.

11. Locate a clip that sounds like a helicopter flyover. Rest the mouse pointer on each thumbnail to see file sizes. Click on one that is larger than 100 KB.

12. Close the file, saving all changes, and exit PowerPoint.

Project 18—Apply It

Multimedia Presentation

DIRECTIONS

1. Start PowerPoint, if necessary, and open **PProj18** from, the data files for this lesson.
2. Save the file as **PProj18_studentfirstname_ studentlastname** in the location where your teacher instructs you to store the files for this lesson.
3. Display slide 5, select the video, and click **Video Tools Playback** > **Play Full Screen**.
4. Click **Video Tools Playback** > **Trim Video** 🎞.
5. Trim the beginning of the video clip so that the start time is **00:01**.
6. Apply the **Glow Rounded Rectangle** picture style to the video on slide 5.
7. Display slide 6 and drag the sound icon off the slide so that it won't show during a slide show.

8. Set the sound to play across slides so that it will play from slide 6 to slide 7 and have it play across slides.
   a. Select the audio clip icon.
   b. Click **Audio Tools Playback** > **Start** 📄 drop-down list.
   c. Select **Play across slides**.
9. Display slide 7 and insert the JPEG file **PProj18a** from the data files for this lesson.
10. Format the picture to match the picture on slide 6.
11. View the slide show see the movie and hear the sound. Your presentation should look similar to Figure 8-1.
12. Close the file, saving all changes, and exit PowerPoint.

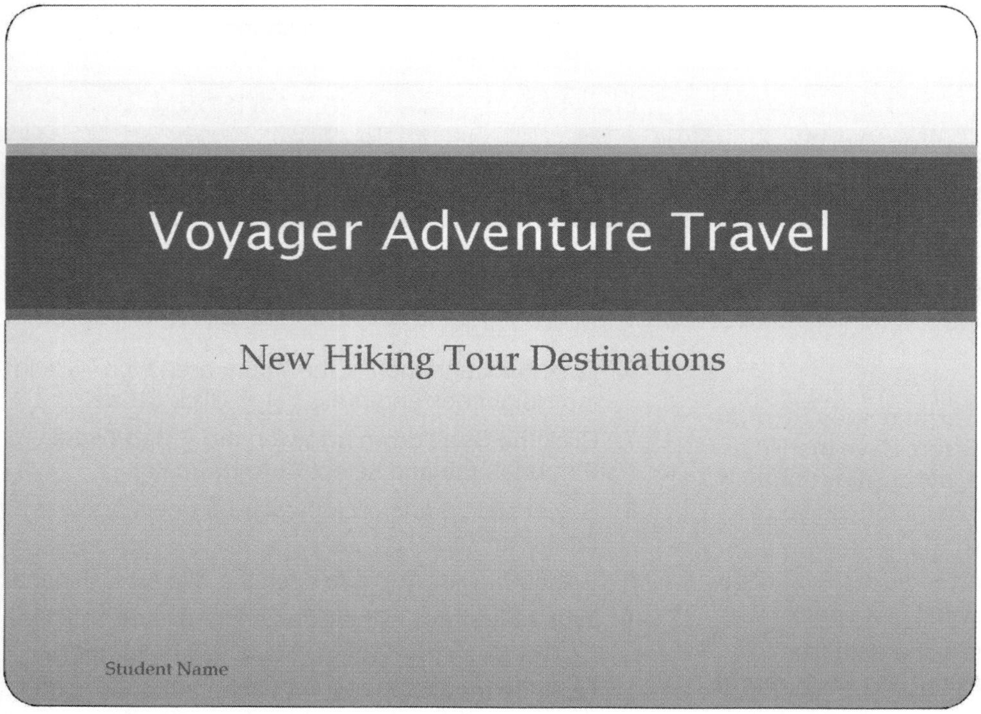

Figure 8-1

Voyager Adventure Travel

New Hiking Tour Destinations

Student Name

Lesson 9

Working with Advanced Photo Album Features

➤ **What You Will Learn**

Editing a Photo Album
Adding Text and Captions
Compressing Pictures

Software Skills   Working with PowerPoint's advanced photo album features makes it easy to modify and enhance a photo album. You can arrange the photos in a number of layouts and apply enhancements such as frames, captions, and other effects. To reduce file size of a presentation, you can also compress the pictures.

Application Skills   Voyager Adventure Travel has decided to approve the Glacier National Park hiking adventure and wants you to create a photo album of Glacier Park images to present at a travel show.

What You Can Do

Editing a Photo Album

- You can edit an existing photo album by displaying it in Normal view and then clicking the down arrow on the Photo Album button. Choosing Edit Photo Album opens the Photo Album dialog box.
- The Photo Album dialog box is where you rearrange pictures in the album and select settings for the way the pictures will display.
- Selected picture file names display in the Pictures in album list in the center of the dialog box. The currently selected picture displays in the Preview area.
- You can adjust the order of pictures or remove a selected picture. Use the buttons below the preview to flip the picture horizontally or vertically, adjust its contrast, or adjust its brightness.
- After you make changes, click the Update button to apply your changes to the album.

WORDS TO KNOW

Resolution
The number of dots or pixels per linear unit of output. For example, a computer monitor's resolution is usually 72 pixels per inch.

Try It!   Removing a Picture from a Photo Album

1 Start PowerPoint and open **PTry09** file from the data files for this lesson.

2 Save the file as **PTry09_studentfirstname_studentlastname** in the location where your teacher instructs you to store the files for this lesson.

3 Click View > Normal 📄, if necessary to show the presentation in Normal view.

4 Right click slide 7 and select Delete Slide from the content menu.

5 Click Insert > Photo Album 📷 down arrow.

6 Click Edit Photo Album.

7 Select Summer River Sun from the Pictures in album list.

8 Click Remove.

9 Leave the dialog box open to use in the next Try It.

Try It!   Changing the Layout Options in a Photo Album

1 In the Edit Photo Album dialog box for presentation **PTry09_studentfirstname_studentlastname**, click the Frame shape down arrow.

2 Select Center Shadow Rectangle from the list.

3 Leave the dialog box open to use in the next Try It.

Try It!   Changing the Order of Pictures in a Photo Album

1 In the Edit Photo Album dialog box for presentation **PTry09_studentfirstname_studentlastname**, click Raccoon Wave in the Pictures in album list.

2 Click the reorder Down 🔽 button three times.

3 Leave the dialog box open to use in the next Try It.

Quickly change the order of pictures in an album

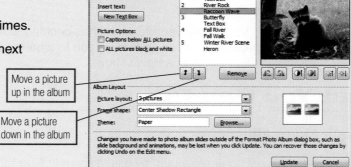

Move a picture up in the album

Move a picture down in the album

Adding Text and Captions

- A PowerPoint photo album is just like a physical photo album in that it is designed primarily to showcase images, but you also can add text in the form of captions or text boxes.

- The Picture Options check boxes allow you to add a caption to each picture or transform all pictures to black and white.

- By default, PowerPoint uses a picture's file name as its caption, but you can replace these captions with more descriptive ones on the slides.

- You can choose to add a text box to the list of pictures. Text boxes display according to the current picture layout, at the same size as the pictures.

■ PowerPoint might insert a text box placeholder for you, if you choose a layout that requires more images on a slide than you've included in your album. To turn on this text box placeholder, select the text box in the Edit Photo Album dialog box and click Update.

Try It!   Inserting a Text Box in a Photo Album

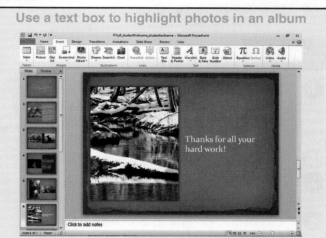
Use a text box to highlight photos in an album

1 In the Edit Photo Album dialog box for presentation **PTry09_studentfirstname_ studentlastname**, select Winter River Scene in the Pictures in album list.

2 Click the New Text Box button in the Album Content area.

3 Click Update and select slide 6.

4 Select the words *Text Box* on slide 6 and type **Thanks for all your hard work!**

5 Save the file, and leave it open to use in the next Try It.

Try It!   Adding Captions to a Photo Album

You can add custom captions to every picture in an album

1 In **PTry09_studentfirstname_studentlast name**, right-click on slide 7.

2 Select Delete slide from the content menu.

3 Click Insert > Photo Album 🖼 > Edit Photo Album.

4 Select Captions below ALL pictures.

5 Click Update.

6 Select the caption below the raccoon picture on slide 3.

7 Type **Wildlife is returning to the park**.

8 Save the file, and leave it open to use in the next Try It.

Compressing Pictures

■ A photo album—or any presentation that contains pictures, movies, or sounds—can turn into a large file that may be a challenge to store or take extra time to open.

■ To streamline a presentation's file size, use the Compress Pictures option on the Picture Tools Format tab to open the Compress Pictures dialog box.

✓ Note that by default PowerPoint compresses pictures automatically when the file is saved.

■ By default, PowerPoint will compress all pictures in the presentation. If you want to compress only a selected picture or pictures, click the Apply to selected pictures only check box.

- The Target output settings allow you to choose a resolution appropriate for the way the pictures will be viewed. Measurements for the resolution are given in ppi, pixels per inch.

- Choose the compression resolution based on how the presentation will be viewed (print, screen, or e-mail).

- If you have cropped pictures to hide areas you don't want to see, you can also choose to delete the cropped portions of the pictures. Keep in mind, of course, you cannot go back and uncrop a picture.

Try It!   Compressing Pictures

1 In **PTry09_studentfirstname_studentlast name**, click File > Info and note the size of the file in the Document Information pane on the right of the window.

2 Click Home and select the picture on slide 2.

3 Click **Picture Tools Format > Compress Pictures** .

4 Deselect Apply only to this picture in the Compression options area.

5 Select Screen (150 ppi); good for Web pages and projectors in the Target output area.

6 Click OK.

7 Click File > Save 💾 and then click Info. Note that the file size in the Document Information pane on the right of the window has gone down significantly.

8 Close **PTry09_studentfirstname_studentlast name** and exit PowerPoint.

The Compress Pictures dialog box

Project 19—Create It

Enhanced Photo Album

DIRECTIONS

1. Start PowerPoint, if neccesary and click **Insert > Photo Album** 🖼️.

2. Click **File/Disk**, select the JPEG files **PProj19a -PProj19e** in the location where the data files are stored for this lesson, and click **Create**.

3. Save the new album as **PProj19_ studentfirstname_studentlastname** in the location where your teacher instructs you to store the files for this lesson.

4. Click **Insert > Photo Album** 🖼️ **> Edit Photo Album**.

5. In the Album Layout area, click the **Picture Layout** down arrow and select **1 picture**.

6. In the Album Layout area, click the **Frame Shape** down arrow and select **Compound Frame, Black**.

7. In the Album Content area, select **Captions below ALL pictures**.

8. Click **Update**.

9. **With your teacher's permission**, print the document. It should look similar to Figure 9-1.

10. Close the file, saving all changes, and exit PowerPoint.

Figure 9-1

PProj19a

Project 20—Apply It

Enhanced Photo Album

DIRECTIONS

1. Start PowerPoint, if necessary, and open **PProj20** from the data files for this lesson.

2. Save the file as **PProj20_studentfirstname_ studentlastname** in the location where your teacher instructs you to store the files for this lesson.

3. View the album as a slide show.

4. Change the title to **Voyager Travel Adventures Presents**.

5. Place your cursor at the beginning of the subtitle text, type **Glacier National Park**, then press ENTER. On the second subtitle line, replace Student Name with your own.

6. Click **Insert** > **Photo Album** 🖼 > **Edit Photo Album**.

7. In the Pictures in album box, move **PProj20b** below figure **PProj20c**.

8. Delete figure **PProj20e** from the album.

9. Turn off the captions since they don't add much to this album.

10. In the Album Layout area, change the frame shape to **Simple Frame, White**.

11. In the Album Layout area, add the **Elemental** theme to the album and click **Update**.

12. Use the **Picture Tools Format** tab to compress all the pictures in the album.

13. Use the Header & Footer dialog box to add a footer that includes your name and a date that updates automatically.

14. Click **Slide Show** > **From Beginning** and view the entire slide show to see your changes.

15. **With your teacher's permission**, print slide 4. It should look similar to Figure 9-2.

16. Close the file, saving all changes, and exit PowerPoint.

Figure 9-2

Lesson 10

Advanced Animation Features

➤ **What You Will Learn**

Applying Advanced Animation Effects
Creating a Motion Path Animation
Changing the Order of Animation Effects
Applying Advanced Effect Options
Adjusting Animation Timing
Working with the Animation Timeline
Changing or Removing an Animation

WORDS TO KNOW

Path
A line or shape on a slide
that an object will follow
when a Motion Path
animation is applied to
the object.

Software Skills   Animating slides is another way to add multimedia interest to
a presentation. Using custom animation options, you can add entrance, emphasis,
and exit effects, as well as move an object along a path. Use advanced features to
trigger animations and delay effects. Change or remove an animation at any time.

Application Skills   Natural Light has asked you to add animations to a
presentation that will be available in the showroom for visitors to browse. In this
lesson, you work with a number of custom animation options.

What You Can Do

Applying Advanced Animation Effects

■ There are many additional animation features available on the Advanced
Animation group of the Animation tab.

■ Options in the Advanced Animation group allow you to select individual parts of an object to animate, to apply special effects, to adjust timing so that an effect occurs just when you want it to, and to set an animation so that it occurs when you click on another object on the slide.

Try It! — Applying Advanced Exit Effects

1 Start PowerPoint and open **PTry10** file from the data files for this lesson.

2 Save the file as **PTry10_studentfirstname_ studentlastname** in the location where your teacher instructs you to store the files for this lesson.

3 Click the title and subtitle placeholders on slide 9.

4 Click Animations > Add Animation ⭐.

5 Select More Exit Effects from the list.

6 Select Preview Effect in the Add Exit Effects dialog box and scroll down to the bottom of the list.

7 Select Contract and watch the preview. Click OK.

8 Save changes, and leave the file open to use in the next Try It.

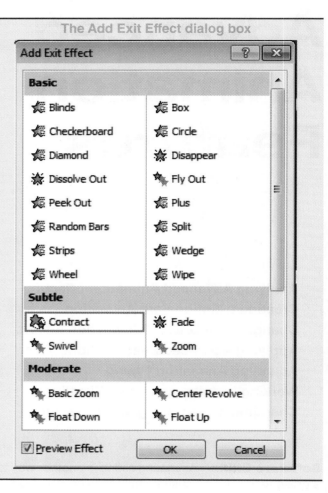

The Add Exit Effect dialog box

Try It! — Applying More Than One Animation Effect to the Same Object

1 In **PTry10_studentfirstname_studentlast name**, select the profit text box on slide 7.

2 Click Animations > Preview ⭐.

3 Click Animations > Add Animation ⭐.

4 Select Pulse from the list.

5 Click Animations > Preview ⭐.

6 Save changes, and leave the file open to use in the next Try It.

Try It!   Animating Separate Parts of an Object

1 In **PTry10_studentfirstname_ studentlastname**, select the chart on slide 8.

2 Click Animation > Add Animation ⭐.

3 Click Shape ☆ from the Animation list.

4 Click Animation > Effect Options 🔆.

5 Select By Category ▮▮.

6 Save changes, and leave the file open to use in the next Try It.

Use the Effect Options button to animate separate parts of an object

Creating a Motion Path Animation

- You can also set a motion path that an object will follow on the slide.

- The path may be one of a number of straight lines, such as Diagonal Down Right, Left, or Up, or you can draw a custom path using the Line, Freeform, Curve, or Scribble tool.

- You can also click More Motion Paths on the Motion Paths submenu to open a dialog box where you can select from many shape options, such as stars, arcs, loops, and spirals.

- After you choose the motion path, a dotted line represents the path, and the red arrow and line represent the end of the path, the point at which animation stops.

- You can adjust the motion path if it is not in the right position or the right duration by dragging the red arrow on the display. It will maintain its direction or shape as you move it.

- To move one end of the path, or to change its length, click on one of the handles at the end of the path.

Try It!   Applying Motion Paths

1 In **PTry10_studentfirstname_studentlast name**, click the earth logo on slide 1.

2 Click Animations > Add Animation ⭐ > Arcs ⌒.

3 Save changes, and leave the file open to use in the next Try It.

Motion path options

Motion Paths

| Lines | Arcs | Turns | Shapes | Loops |

Custom Path

Try It!   Adjusting a Motion Path

1 In **PTry10_studentfirstname_studentlast name**, click the motion path on slide 1, if necessary to select it.

2 Click Animations > Effect Options > Up.

3 Click Animations > Effect Options > Reverse Path Directions.

4 Select the path indicator and drag it to the left so that that green end indicator is placed on the globe.

5 Drag the red end point left to extend the line.

6 Use the rotate handle to adjust the angle of the arc.

7 Make any further modifications to ensure that the end point is centered above the green line.

8 Save changes, and leave the file open to use in the next Try It.

Use the Motion Path lines to adjust the path of the animation

Changing the Order of Animation Effects

■ Each type of animation effect has its own symbol, such as the green star for entrance effects and the red star for exit effects.

■ These symbols help you identify items in the animation pane. The symbols make it easy to check that the effects are in the correct order.

■ If the object you are animating has more than one line or part, such as a text content placeholder or a chart or diagram, a bar displays below the effect with a Click to expand contents arrow. Clicking the arrow displays all the parts of the object.

■ When you have finished animating the parts, use the Click to hide contents arrow to collapse the effect and save room in the animation list.

Try It!   Changing the Order of Animation Effects

1 In **PTry10_studentfirstname_studentlast name**, select slide 6.

2 Click Animations > Preview ⭐.

3 Click Animations > Animation Pane 🔲 Animation Pane.

4 Click on the entrance effect 🟢 item in the Animation Pane.

5 Click the Re-Order Up button ⬆.

6 Click on the exit effect ⭐ item in the Animation Pane.

7 Click the Re-Order Down button ⬇ two times.

8 Save changes, and leave the file open to use in the next Try It.

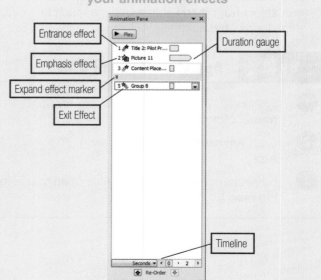

Use the Animation Pane to control your animation effects

Applying Advanced Effect Options

- When you select an animation in the Animation Pane, a down arrow appears containing a number of options that you can use to modify an effect.

- Selecting Effect Options from the content list opens a dialog box. The Effect tab offers a number of special effects that you can apply to an object, depending on the type of object being animated.

- You can adjust the direction of the animation and choose Smooth start and Smooth end to control how the object starts and stops during the animation.

- All animation types allow you to select a sound effect from the Sound list to accompany the effect.

✓ *Use sound effects sparingly; it can be distracting to hear the same sound effect over and over when multiple parts of an object are animated.*

- The After animation palette gives you a number of options for emphasizing or deemphasizing an object after the animation ends. You can hide the object after the animation, hide it the next time you click the mouse, or change its color.

- If the animated object contains text, the Animate text settings become active, allowing you to animate the text all at once, by word, or by letter, and set the delay between words or letters.

Try It!   **Applying Advanced Effect Options**

1   In **PTry10_studentfirstname_studentlast name**, select slide 7.

2   Click on the Entrance animation in the animation pane and then on the down arrow and select Effect Options.

3   On the Effect tab, select Applause in the Sound box.

4   Click OK.

5   Click the first animation in the animation pane and press `CTRL`. Then select the second animation in the animation pane.

6   Click the down arrow that appears and select Effect Options.

7   Select Hide After Animation in the After animation box.

8   Click OK.

9   Save changes, and leave the file open to use in the next Try It.

Set advanced animation effects

Fly In dialog box — Effect | Timing | Text Animation tabs

Settings
- Direction: From Right
- Smooth start: 0 sec
- Smooth end: 0 sec
- Bounce end: 0 sec

Enhancements
- Sound: Applause
- After animation: Don't Dim
- Animate text: All at once
- % delay between letters

Try It!   **Animating Text on a Slide**

1   In **PTry10_studentfirstname_studentlast name**, select slide 1.

2   Click the down arrow on the animation in the Animation Pane and select Effect Options.

3   On the Effect tab, select By word in the Animate text box.

4   Type **20** in the % delay between words box.

5   Click OK.

6   Save changes, and leave the file open to use in the next Try It.

(continued)

Try It!   **Animating Text on a Slide** *(continued)*

The Fade dialog box

Adjusting Animation Timing

■ The Animations tab contains duration, delay, and trigger tools for controlling the timing on your animations.

- Use the Delay setting to control exactly when an animation takes place by specifying the amount of time that must elapse before the animation begins.
- Use the Duration setting to adjust the speed of the animation.
- Use the Trigger setting to control what starts an animation.

■ Using triggers is one way to make a slide show interactive by controlling which object on the slide to click to start the animation.

■ You can also control animation timing using controls on the Timing tab in the Effect Options dialog boxes, such as Repeat and Rewind.

- Use the Repeat setting to replay the animation a specific number of times or until the next click or the next slide displays.
- Use the Rewind when done playing option to return the object to its original position or state. If you have a picture fade into view, for example, the Rewind setting will remove it from the slide after the animation finishes.

Try It!   **Adjusting Timing Using the Animations Tab**

1 In **PTry10_studentfirstname_studentlast name**, select the animation on slide 1, if necessary.

2 Type **02.00** in the Duration box.

3 Type **00.75** in the Delay box.

4 Save changes, and leave the file open to use in the next Try It.

Try It!   Adjusting Timing Using the Effect Options Dialog Box

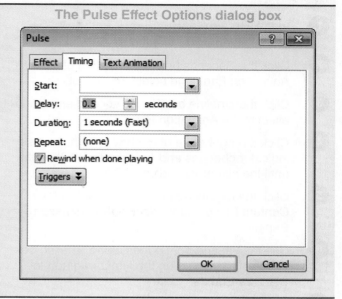

The Pulse Effect Options dialog box

1. In **PTry10_studentfirstname_studentlastname**, select the first two text boxes on slide 7.

2. Click the down arrow on the animation in the Animation Pane and select Effect Options.

3. On the Timing tab, select 1 seconds (Fast) in the Duration box.

4. Select Rewind when done playing.

5. Select 0.5 in the Delay box.

6. Click OK.

7. Save changes, and leave the file open to use in the next Try It.

Try It!   Setting the Start for an Animation

1. In **PTry10_studentfirstname_studentlastname**, select the Profit text box on slide 7.

2. Select After Previous in the Start box on the Animations tab.

3. Save changes, and leave the file open to use in the next Try It.

Try It!   Setting an Animation Trigger

1. In **PTry10_studentfirstname_studentlastname**, select the chart and the three text boxes at the bottom of slide 7.

   ✓ Hint: Press CTRL to enable you to select multiple objects.

2. Click Animations > Float In.

3. Click Animations > Trigger ⚡ > On Click Of > Textbox 7.

4. Save changes, and leave the file open to use in the next Try It.

Working with the Animation Timeline

- The easiest way to fine-tune animation timing is to use the timeline feature in the Animation pane.

- The bars next to the individual effects in the Animation pane indicate the duration of each effect and when it starts relative to other effects.

- The timeline includes a seconds gauge at the bottom of the task pane. You can use this gauge to see the duration of each effect as well as the overall duration of all animations on the slide.

- You can use the timeline to set a delay or adjust the length of an effect or double-click an orange bar to open the Timing dialog box for further adjustments.

Try It!   Adjusting the Duration of an Effect in the Timeline

1 In **PTry10_studentfirstname_ studentlastname**, select slide 6.

2 Click the Seconds box at the bottom of the Animation Pane and select Zoom Out.

3 Click the timeline box for the second animation effect in the Animation Pane.

4 Click the right edge of the box until the mouse indicator changes and drag the line to the left until the screen tip indicates 2.5s.

5 Click the expand contents arrow below the Content Placeholder effect in the Animation Pane.

6 Use the left and right edges of the timeline box to adjust the timing on the first paragraph to Start, 2s End 3s.

7 Adjust the timing of the second paragraph to Start, 3s End 4s.

8 Save changes, and leave the file open to use in the next Try It.

Adjusting the timeline

Try It!   Setting a Delay Using the Timeline

1 In **PTry10_studentfirstname_ studentlastname**, click the Seconds box at the bottom of the Animation Pane and select Zoom In.

2 Select the exit effect and drag the entire timeline box to the right until the indicator shows Start, 4.5s.

3 Save changes, and leave the file open to use in the next Try It.

Set a Delay in the Animation Pane

Changing or Removing an Animation

■ If you find that a particular animation option isn't giving you the effect you want, you can easily change the animation effect using the Animation Pane.

■ You can also click the Remove button to delete the effect entirely.

Try It!   Removing an Animation Effect

1 In **PTry10_studentfirstname_student lastname**, click the globe logo on slide 6.

2 Click the effect down arrow in the Animation Pane.

3 Click Remove.

4 Save changes, and leave the file open to use in the next Try It.

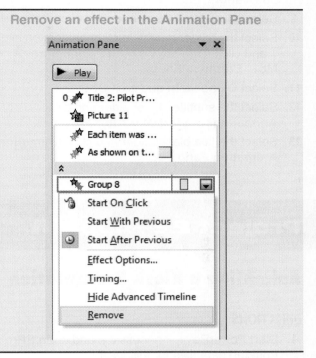

Remove an effect in the Animation Pane

Try It!   Change an Animation

1 In **PTry10_studentfirstname_studentlast name**, click the effect for the picture in the Animation Pane.

2 Click **Animation > More** ⌄ to open the Animation Gallery.

3 Select the Pulse ☆ emphasis effect.

4 Click Play ▶ Play in the Animation Pane to see the changes to the slide.

5 Close the file, saving all changes, and exit PowerPoint.

Project 21—Create It

Animating a Kiosk Presentation

DIRECTIONS

1. Start PowerPoint, if necessary, and open **PProj21** from the data files for this lesson.

2. Save the file as **PProj21_studentfirstname_ studentlastname** in the location where your teacher instructs you to store the files for this lesson.

3. On slide 1, select the **Star** object.

4. Click **Animations > Add Animation** 🌟 **> Color Pulse** 🌟.

5. Click **Animations > Effect Options** and select the last color on the top row.

6. Click **Animations > Start** ▶ **> After Previous**.

7. Click **Animations > Animation Pane** 🎬 and then click the emphasis animation down arrow in the Animation Pane.

8. Select **Timing** from the menu and click the **Repeat** down arrow.

9. Select **Until Next Click** and then click **OK**.

10. Select the title and subtitle placeholders on slide 1 and click **Animations** > **Add Animation** ★ > **More Entrance Effects**.

11. Select **Dissolve In** and click **OK.**

12. Select the subtitle placeholder and click **Animations** > **Start** 🗗 > **After Previous**.

13. Select the title placeholder and click **Animations** > **Animation Pane** 🌠.

14. Click the title animation down arrow and select **Effect Options**.

15. On the Effect tab, click the **After animation** down arrow and select the black square.

16. Click the Animate text box, and select **By word.**

17. On the Timing tab, click the **Start** down arrow and select **With Previous**.

18. Click **OK**.

19. Close the Animation Pane and click **Animations** > **Preview** 🌟 to see your changes.

20. Close the file, saving all changes, and exit PowerPoint.

Project 22—Apply It

Animating a Kiosk Presentation

DIRECTIONS

1. Start PowerPoint, if necessary, and open **PProj22** from the data files for this lesson.

2. Save the file as **PProj22_studentfirstname_ studentlastname** in the location where your teacher instructs you to store the files for this lesson.

3. Display slide 4 and apply animation effects as follows:

   a. Set the **Sales** placeholder to **Fly In** from the left, **After Previous, Fast**.

   b. Select the **Sales** animation in the Animation pane and then change the effect to a **Fade** entrance effect.

   c. Select the content placeholder below the Sales object and fade the text into view **After Previous**.

   d. Animate the **Service** placeholder to **Fly In** from the right, **After Previous**.

   e. Select the **Sales** content placeholder and then click **Animations** > **Animation Painter**.

   f. Click the **Service** content placeholder to apply the same settings to the Service content placeholder that you applied to the Sales content placeholder.

   g. Delay the start of the Service placeholder by **1.5** seconds.

4. Display slide 5 and apply a **Fly In** entrance animation to the SmartArt graphic, **After Previous, Fast From Left**. Then modify the animation effects as follows:

   a. Change the SmartArt Animation option in the Effect Options dialog box to **One by one**, then expand the effect to see all the shapes that make up the diagram.

   b. Using the timeline, adjust the duration and delay of each shape so that a viewer has time to read the Step 1 shape before the first bulleted shape appears, read the text in this shape before the Step 2 shape appears, and so on.

   c. Use the **Play** button and the **Slide Show** button to test your delays until you are satisfied with the results.

5. On slide 6, set a trigger to animate the picture with a **Wipe** entrance effect, **From Top, Fast**, when the slide title is clicked. Then animate the picture description with a **Fade** effect so it displays after the picture.

   ✓ *Hint: You might need to reorder the effects to get the animation right.*

6. On slide 7, apply to the WordArt object the **Fade** entrance effect, the **Grow/Shrink** emphasis effect, and the **Fade** exit effect. Apply the following settings.

   a. **After Previous** to all of the effects.

   b. Change the timing of the entrance effect to **Slow**.

   c. Change the timing of the emphasis effect to **Medium**.

   d. Change the timing of the exit effect to **Slow**.

7. On slide 7, add a motion path to the **Star** object so that it moves to the center of the slide after the WordArt object exits. Then apply a **Grow/Shrink** emphasis effect and use the Effect Options dialog box to increase the size of the object **200%**. Apply **After Previous** to both. The motion path should look similar to Figure 10-1.

8. View the slide show to see the effects. Make any adjustments necessary.

9. After viewing the slide show, you decide that the title animation on the first slide is unnecessary. Remove the animation from the title and subtitle.

10. Close the file, saving all changes, and exit PowerPoint.

Figure 10-1

Lesson 11

Finalizing Slide Shows

WORDS TO KNOW

Narration
A recording of your voice that describes or enhances the message in each slide.

➤ What You Will Learn

Creating Presentation Sections
Adding Narration to a Presentation

Software Skills   You can add narration to a presentation so that you don't have to be present to get your main points across. Explore all options in the Set Up Show dialog box to present your slides in the most effective way. Save the presentation as a Show so that it opens directly in Slide Show view.

Application Skills   In this lesson, you will add narration to a presentation designed to convince Peterson Home Healthcare to update their IT equipment. You'll then add that presentation to the Peterson Healthcare Annual Board Meeting presentation and use sections to organize the slide show.

What You Can Do

Creating Presentation Sections

- Sections are used to organize large presentations into more manageable groups.
- You can also use presentation sections to assist in collaborating on projects. For example, each colleague can be responsible for preparing slides for a separate section.
- You can apply unique names and effects to different sections.
- You can also choose to print by section.

Try It!   Creating Presentation Sections

1 Start PowerPoint and open **PTry11** file from the data files for this lesson.

2 Save the file as **PTry11_studentfirstname_ studentlastname** in the location where your teacher instructs you to store the files for this lesson.

3 Switch to Normal view, if necessary.

4 Click between slides 3 and 4.

5 Click Home > Section ⬚.

6 Click Add Section.

7 Right-click between slides 7 and 8. Select Add Section.

8 Save changes, and leave the file open to use in the next Try It.

Creating a presentation section

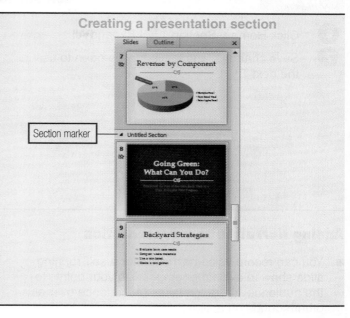

Section marker

Try It!   Renaming Presentation Sections

1 In **PTry11_studentfirstname_studentlast name**, right-click the presentation section bar between slides 7 and 8.

2 Select Rename Section from the content menu.

OR

Click Home > Section ⬚ > Rename Section.

3 In the Rename Section dialog box, type **Going Green** in the Section Name box.

4 Click Rename

5 Save changes, and leave the file open to use in the next Try It.

Rename Section dialog box

Try It!   Working with Presentation Sections

1 In **PTry11_studentfirstname_studentlast name**, right-click the presentation section bar between slides 7 and 8.

2 Select Collapse All.

OR

Click Home > Section ⬚ > Collapse All.

3 Right-click the Going Green section bar and select Move Section Up.

OR

Click the Going Green section bar and drag it up above the Default section bar.

4 Right-click the Untitled section bar and select Remove Section & Slides.

5 At the confirmation box, click yes.

(continued)

Try It!   Working with Presentation Sections *(continued)*

6 Click Home > Section 🔲 > Expand All.

7 Save changes, and leave the file open to use in the next Try It.

Collapsed Presentation Section

Slides	Outline	✕
▷ Default Section (8)		
▷ Going Green (6)		

- ◻ Rename Section
- ◻ Remove Section
- ◻ Remove Section & Slides
- ◻ Remove All Sections
- ▲ Move Section Up
- ▼ Move Section Down
- ◻ Collapse All
- ◻ Expand All

Adding Narration to a Presentation

- You can record voice **narration** for a self-running slide show to explain or emphasize your points to the audience. Narration takes precedence over all other sounds on a slide.

  ✓ *To do so, your computer must have a microphone, speakers, and sound card.*

- Before you begin adding narration to slides, make sure your microphone is working correctly.

- To record narration, use the Record Narration button on the Slide Show tab.

  - When you select whether to start at the beginning of the presentation or at the current slide, the presentation begins in Slide Show view so you can match your narration to each slide.

- You also have the option to record timings and narration or just narration.

- You will see that each slide to which you added narration has a sound icon displayed in the lower right corner. Viewers can click the icons to hear your narration, or you can use the Sound Tools Options tab to specify that the narration will play automatically.

- Before you begin, remember these tips.

  - Click through the entire presentation at least once, reading each slide's content.

  - Don't begin reading until the timing indicates 00:01.

  - If you make a mistake, keep reading (especially if you're also recording timings). Remember you can always go back and redo a single slide.

Try It!   Adding Narration to a Presentation

1 In **PTry11_studentfirstname_student lastname**, select slide 1, if necessary.

2 On the Slide Show tab, click the Record Slide Show 🕐 down arrow.

3 Click Start Recording from Beginning.

4 If you have a microphone attached to your computer, select both options in the Record Slide Show box. If you don't have a microphone set up, deselect the option for Narrations and laser pointer. Click Start Recording.

5 When the slide show opens, read the text on the slide as clearly as possible. Be sure to time your reading with the way the text appears on screen.

6 When you've finished with slide 1, click the screen to move to the next slide.

7 Continue recording the slide text until the end of the presentation.

8 Save changes, and leave the file open to use in the next Try It.

Record Slide Show dialog box

Try It!   **Correcting the Narration on a Slide within a Presentation**

1   In **PTry11_studentfirstname_studentlast name**, select slide 8.

2   Click Slide Show > Record Slide Show 🕐.

3   Click Start Recording from Current Slide.

4   Select only the Narration and laser pointer options and click Start Recording.

5   When the slide show opens, read the text on the slide as clearly as possible. Be sure to time your reading with the way the text appears on screen.

✓ *If you need to start over, click the Undo button � to restart the slide narration recording.*

6   When you've finished correcting the narration, click the Close button ✕.

7   Close the file, saving all changes, and exit PowerPoint.

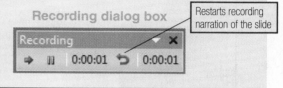

Recording dialog box   Restarts recording narration of the slide

Project 23—Create It

Adding Narration

DIRECTIONS

1. Start PowerPoint, if necessary, and open **PProj23** from the data files for this lesson.

2. Save the file as **PProj23_studentfirstname_studentlastname** in the location where your teacher instructs you to store the files for this lesson.

3. Create a footer with your name in it.

4. Click **Design** > **Fonts** Ⓐ > **Apothecary**.

5. Click **Design** > **Background Styles** > **Style 6**.

6. Click **Slide Show** > **Record Slide Show** 🕐 > **Start Recording from Beginning**.

7. If you have a microphone attached to your computer, select both options in the Record Slide Show box. If you don't have a microphone set up, deselect the option for Narrations and laser pointer.

8. Click **OK** to begin.

9. Read through the contents of each slide. When you are finished, click the ✕ to close the Recording dialog box.

10. Click **Slide Show** > **From Beginning** 📺 to view your changes.

11. Select slide 4 and in the Stage 2 box, place the insertion point at the beginning of the bullet point. Type **Hire a contractor** and press ENTER.

12. Click **Slide Show** > **Record Slide Show** 🕐 > **Start Recording from Current Slide**.

13. Select the same options in the Record Slide Show box that you chose for the initial recording and click **OK**.

14. Read the entire slide and then close the recording box.

15. **With your teacher's permission**, print slide 4. It should look similar to Figure 11-1.

16. Close the file, saving all changes, and exit PowerPoint.

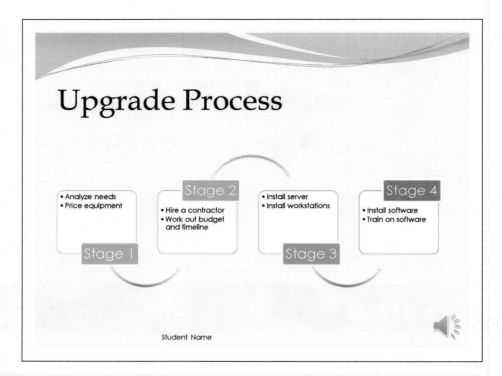

Figure 11-1

Project 24—Apply It

Organizing with Sections

DIRECTIONS

1. Start PowerPoint, if necessary, and open **PProj24** from the data files for this lesson.

2. Save the file as **PProj24_studentfirstname_studentlastname** in the location where your teacher instructs you to store the files for this lesson.

3. Right-click slide 2 and choose **Duplicate Slide**.

4. Click between slides 2 and 3 and click **Home** > **New Slide** > **Reuse Slides** to open the reuse slides pane.

5. Click **Browse** > **Browse File** and select the file **PProj23_studentfirstname_studentlastname** that you created in the previous project.

6. Click **Keep source formatting** and click each of the four slides to add them to the large presentation. Close the task pane.

7. Click between slides 1 and 2 and add a section.

8. Add a section marker between slides 6 and 7, 16 and 17, and 25 and 26.

9. Right-click the first untitled section marker and select **Rename Section**. Type **Upgrading Peterson's IT Equipment** and click **Rename**. When you are finished, click the arrow on the section marker to collapse the section.

10. Repeat the process to name each section according to headings on the Agenda.

11. You've just been informed that the new patient education portion of the presentation is going to be moved to another meeting. Remove that section and all of its slides.

12. Expand all the sections to see if this will cause any conflicts. You'll need to go through and remove the first line item from each of the three remaining agenda slides (2, 7, and 16).

13. Collapse all the sections.

14. **With your teacher's permission**, print slide 2. It should look similar to Figure 11-2.

15. Close the file, saving all changes, and exit PowerPoint.

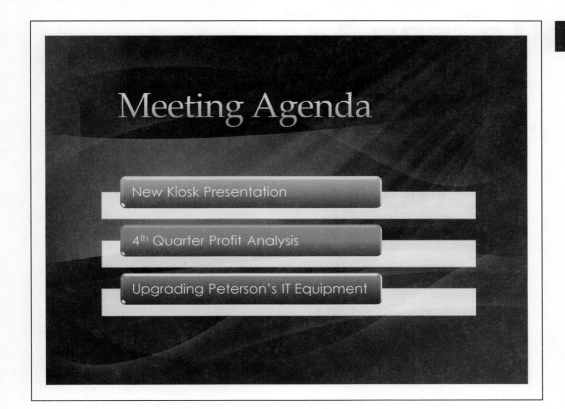

Figure 11-2

Lesson 12

Working with Actions

WORDS TO KNOW

Action
A setting that performs a specific action, such as running an application or jumping to a specific slide.

Target
The slide, show, file, or page that will display when you click a link on a slide.

➤ What You Will Learn

Using Advanced Hyperlink Settings
Working with Action Settings

Software Skills   Hyperlinks and action settings can be used to create interactive presentations that allow viewers to jump to different locations in the presentation, open other presentations or Web sites, send an e-mail message, run programs, or interact with objects on the slide.

Application Skills   Peterson Home Healthcare is starting the process of training employees on Microsoft Office 2010 after the installation of the new network and workstations. In this lesson, you will begin work on a presentation that employees can access from their own computers to learn more about Microsoft Office 2010. You will create links and action items to make it easy for employees to interact with the training materials.

What You Can Do

Using Advanced Hyperlink Settings

- You can use links to move from a presentation to another application to view data in that application. For example, you could link to Microsoft Excel data during a presentation.
- If the computer on which you are presenting the slides has an active Internet connection, you can also use a link to jump from a slide to any site on the Web.
- You can set up a link using text from a text placeholder or any object on the slide, such as a shape or picture.
- You have four target options to choose from.
  - Existing File or Web Page lets you locate a file on your system or network.

- Browse the Web button opens your browser to allow you to locate the page you want to use as a target.
- Place in This Document lets you select a slide or custom show from the current presentation. As you click a slide for the target, it displays in the Slide preview area.
- Create New Document allows you to specify the name of a new document and link to it at the same time. If you create a file with the name

Results.xlsx, for example, Excel opens so you can enter data in the Results workbook.

- The E-mail Address option lets you link to an e-mail address. You might use this option when setting up a presentation to be viewed by an individual on his or her own computer so that they can follow the link to send a message to the specified e-mail address.

■ If you want to provide a little extra help to a viewer about what will happen when a link is clicked, you can provide a ScreenTip.

Try It! **Inserting a Link to an External Document**

1 Start PowerPoint and open **PTry12** file from the data files for this lesson.

2 Save the file as **PTry12_studentfirstname_ studentlastname** in the location where your teacher instructs you to store the files for this lesson.

3 Select the Discussion object on slide 10.

4 Click Insert > Hyperlink 🌐 .

5 Click Existing File or Web Document.

6 Locate file **PTry12a** from the data files for this lesson.

7 Click OK.

8 Save changes, to **PTry12_studentfirstname_ studentlastname** and keep the file open to use in the next Try It.

The Insert Hyperlink dialog box

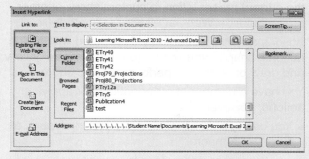

Try It! **Inserting a Link to an E-mail Address**

1 In **PTry12_studentfirstname_studentlast name**, select the information object on slide 17.

2 Click Insert > Hyperlink 🌐 .

3 In the E-mail address box, type **info@planet_ earth.com**.

4 In the Subject box, type **Request for more information**.

5 Click OK.

6 Save changes, and leave the file open to use in the next Try It.

Try It! **Creating a ScreenTip for a Hyperlink**

1 In **PTry12_studentfirstname_student lastname**, right-click the information object on slide 17.

2 Click Edit Hyperlink.

3 Click ScreenTip

4 Type **E-mail us for more information**.

5 Click OK two times.

6 Save changes, and leave the file open to use in the next Try It.

(continued)

Try It!   **Creating a ScreenTip for a Hyperlink** *(continued)*

Editing a hyperlink to add a ScreenTip

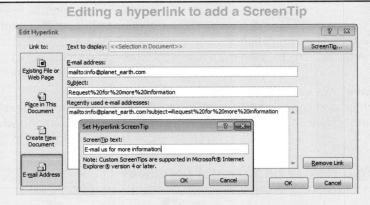

Working with Action Settings

- Like links, actions allow you to link to a slide in the current presentation, a custom show, another presentation, a Web page URL, or another file.

- Actions are most commonly associated with action buttons, shapes you select from the Shapes gallery and draw on a slide to perform specific chores.

- You have a number of other options for applying actions, however.
  - You can use an action to run a program, such as Excel, or a macro.
    - ✓ *You may have to respond to a security warning the first time you run a program.*
  - You can also use an action to control an object you have inserted on the slide; however, the object must be inserted using the Insert Object dialog box.

- ✓ *If you use an existing file, you can choose in the Insert Object dialog box to display the object as an icon on the slide.*

- You can use an action setting to play a sound effect or sound file.

- Use the action options, such as Hyperlink to, Run program, or Play sound, on the Action Settings dialog box to set the target for the action.

- Note the Highlight click check box in the Action Settings dialog box. When this option is selected, the shape or text to which you are applying the action setting will change size as you click it.

- By default, you set actions on the Mouse Click tab, which means that the action takes place when you click on the action object during the presentation.

- The Mouse Over tab contains the same options as the Mouse Click tab. Actions you set on this tab will take place when you hover the mouse pointer over the action object.

Try It!   **Working with Advanced Action Settings**

1 In **PTry12_studentfirstname_studentlast name**, click the action button on slide 9.

2 Click Insert > Action.

3 Click Run program.

4 Click Browse.

5 Click Desktop in the left pane and select one of the shortcuts on the Desktop.

6 Click OK twice.

7 Click the first action button on slide 2.

8 Click Insert > Action.

9 Click Play Sound.

10 Select Chime.

11 Click OK.

12 Repeat for the remaining two action buttons.

(continued)

13 Click Slide Show > From Beginning 📼 and watch the slide show, clicking all the action buttons as they appear.

14 Close the file, saving all changes, and exit PowerPoint

Edit Action Button dialog box

Project 25—Create It

Making an Interactive Presentation

DIRECTIONS

1. Start PowerPoint, if necessary, and open **PProj25** from the data files for this lesson.

2. Save the file as **PProj25_studentfirstname_studentlastname** in the location where your teacher instructs you to store the files for this lesson.

3. Start Word, if necessary, and open **PProj25a** from the data files for this lesson.

4. Save the file as **PProj25a_studentfirstname_studentlastname** in the location where your teacher instructs you to store the files for this lesson.

5. Display slide 2 and select the first bullet item.

6. Click **Insert** > **Hyperlink** 🌐 > **Place in this document** and select the Introduction slide. Click **OK**.

7. Repeat this process for each of the other bullet items on slide 2, linking them to the corresponding slide.

8. Select the object on slide 6. Click **Insert** > **Hyperlink** 🌐 > **Existing File or Web Page**.

9. Select the file **PProj25a_studentfirstname_studentlastname** from the data files for this lesson. Click **OK**.

10. **With your teacher's permission**, print slide 2. It should look similar to Figure 12-1

11. Close the file, saving all changes, and exit PowerPoint.

Figure 12-1

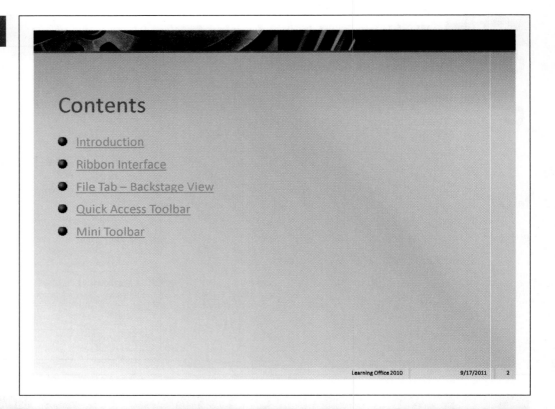

Project 26—Apply It

Flyer with Table

DIRECTIONS

1. Start PowerPoint, if necessary, and open **PProj26** from the data files for this lesson. Save the file as **PProj26_studentfirstname_studentlastname** in the location where your teacher instructs you to store the files for this lesson.

2. Open **PProj26a** from the data files for this lesson and save it as **PProj26a_studentfirstname_ studentlastname** in the location where your teacher instructs you to store the files for this lesson.

3. Select the shape at the top of the first slide in **PProj26a_studentfirstname_studentlastname** and create a hyperlink to **PProj26_studentfirst name_studentlastname**.

4. Close **PProj26a_studentfirstname_studentlast name.**

5. Select the word *here* in the last bullet item on slide 8 and link it to **PProj26a_studentfirstname_ studentlastname**.

6. Open Slide Master view. On the Title and Content layout (not the slide master), select the Questions text box and create a link to an e-mail address. Use the address **jpeterson@petersonhomehealth.com**.

   ✓ *This e-mail address is a dummy for setup purposes only.*

7. Select the More info box and create a link to the Office Online home page at **http://office. microsoft.com/en-us**.

8. Add the following ScreenTip to the More info link: **Visit Microsoft Office Online.**

9. Insert a Custom action button from the Shapes gallery to the right of the More info box and link the button to slide 2. Type **Contents** on the action button, and format the button with the same Quick Style as the text boxes but a different color, as shown in Figure 12-2.

10. Make sure all three boxes are the same height. Align top and distribute the three boxes horizontally. Then select the boxes, copy them, and paste them on all slide layouts except the title and section header layout and the picture layouts. Exit Slide Master view.

11. Display slide 4 and select the *Open Word* shape. Apply an action setting that will run Microsoft Word: Browse to **C:\Program Files\Microsoft Office\Office14\WINWORD**.

    ✓ *You may need to display hidden files to have access to the program files directory; consult your instructor if necessary.*

12. Select the *Open Excel* shape and browse to the same location, but select **EXCEL** in the Office14 folder.

13. You are ready to test your interactive presentation. Follow these steps in Slide Show view:

    a. On slide 2, test each of the links to slides, using the **Contents** action button to return each time to slide 2.

    b. Test the **Questions** and **More info** buttons. Close the e-mail message window without creating a message, and close the Web page after you are done viewing it.

    c. On slide 4, click the **Open Word** shape, and then click **Enable** when alerted to the potential security risk. Close Word, then click the **Open Excel** shape, Enable if necessary, and close Excel.

    d. On slide 6, click the **Test Your Knowledge** object to open a Word document with three questions. For extra credit, answer the questions and then save the document with a new name such as **PProj26b_studentfirstname_studentlastname**. Close the document to return to the presentation.

    e. On slide 8, click the link that takes you to **PProj26a_studentfirstname_studentlastname**. Use the link to navigate to the information on customizing the Quick Access Toolbar, then use the action button to return to the first slide and the button to return to **PProj26_studentfirstname_studentlastname**.

14. **With your teacher's permission**, print the document. It should look similar to Figure 12-2.

15. Close the file, saving all changes, and exit PowerPoint.

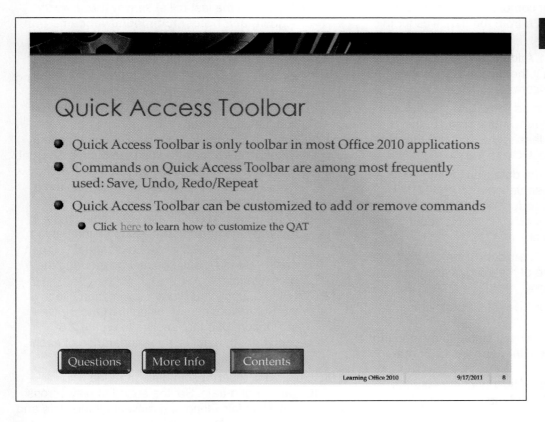

Figure 12-2

Chapter Assessment and Application

Project 27—Make It Your Own

Glacier National Park

Voyager Travel Adventures is preparing a presentation on their newest adventure location, Glacier National Park. In this project, you complete some final tasks on the presentation, including creating animations, inserting links, and adding action buttons.

DIRECTIONS

1. Start Word and open **PProj27a** from the data files for this project. Save the document as **PProj27a_ studentfirstname_studentlastname** in the location where your teacher instructs you to store the files for this project. Close Word.

2. Start PowerPoint, if necessary, and open your solution file **PProj20_studentfirstname_ studentlastname** from the location where your teacher instructs you to store the files for this project. If you did not complete project 20, you can open file **PProj27b** from the data files for this project.

3. Edit the photo album. Add the JPEG figure **PProj27c** and make it the third picture in the album. Update the album.

4. Save the presentation as **PProj27b_ studentfirstname_studentlastname** in the location where your teacher instructs you to store the files for this project. Close the file.

5. Open **PProj27** from the data files for this lesson. Save the presentation as **PProj27_ studentfirstname_studentlastname** in the location where your teacher instructs you to store the files for this project.

6. On slide 6 of **PProj27_studentfirstname_student lastname**, select one of the images and apply the following formatting.

   a. Apply the **Reflected Bevel, White** picture format.

   b. Use the **Picture Borders** button to change the border color to **Ice Blue, Accent 1, Lighter 40%**.

   c. Use the **Corrections** button to increase the sharpness by **25%** and the contrast by **20%**.

7. With the picture still selected, click **Home > Format Painter** twice.

8. Then click on each of the other pictures on the slide to transfer the formatting to each.

9. Animate the images using the **Zoom** effect, **From Center, After Previous** and with a **1.50** duration and a **00.25** delay. Use the Animation Painter to apply the same effect settings to each image in whatever order you wish.

10. Display slide 2 and create a link from the phrase Web cams in the last bullet item to **http://www. nps.gov/glac/photosmultimedia/webcams.htm**

11. Still on slide 2, insert actions as follows:

    a. Create a text box in the lower-right corner with the text **A brief look at . . .** Add an action setting to the text box that links to the **PProj27a_ studentfirstname_studentlastname** file in your solution folder.

    b. Draw a Custom action button about the same size as the text box and use the Mouse Over tab in the Action Settings dialog box to link to the first slide in the **PProj27b_studentfirstname_ studentlastname** presentation.

    c. Format the text button and action button as desired, and position the action button behind and slightly below the text box, so that you can easily rest the mouse pointer on it during the presentation.

12. On slide 3, apply the **Float In** animation effect to the SmartArt diagram, using the **One by One** Effect Option. Use the timeline to create **2.5** second delays to adjust the appearance of each element.

13. On slide 4, insert a sound file from the Clip Organizer of a train. Set the sound to play across slides if it is fairly long and move it off the slide and set the volume to medium.

14. On slide 7, make the following changes.

   a. Apply one of the soft edge picture formats to each image and change their shape to approximately 3.0 wide.

   b. Stack the images so they are centered on each other in the middle of the slide.

   c. Use motion path settings to move each picture to a new location on the slide. Make sure each uses the After Previous trigger.

15. On slide 8, apply emphasis or exit animation to the text.

16. Change *Student Name* in the Footer to your name.

17. Run the presentation to test your animations and links. Close the browser after testing the Web cams link; close Word after viewing the packages document; play the album slide show all the way through and then end it to return to your main presentation. Save your changes.

18. **With your teacher's permission**, print the presentation handouts, 4 slides horizontal in landscape orientation.

19. Compress the images in the presentation and save the presentation as a PowerPoint Show. Exit PowerPoint.

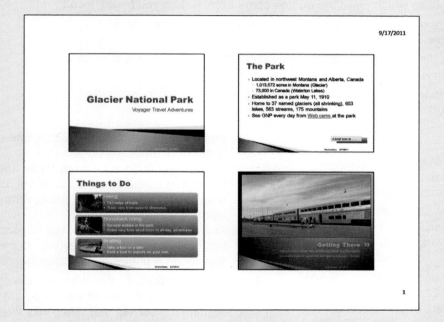

Illustration A

Illustration B

Project 28—Master It

Getting to Know Shakespeare

Your English Literature class is about to begin a unit on Shakespeare's plays. To get the class in the mood, your instructor has asked you to prepare a presentation that lists some famous quotes and common sayings that can be found in Shakespeare's plays.

To add interest, you will create the presentation in the form of a quiz to challenge students to guess which plays the quotes come from. Before you begin, locate:

- A picture of Shakespeare that you can download and save to your computer.
- A good dictionary of quotations (you can also use an online quotation dictionary).
- Information on Shakespeare's contributions to the English language, if desired.

DIRECTIONS

1. Start PowerPoint and begin a new presentation. You may use a blank presentation or use one of PowerPoint's online presentation templates.

2. Save the file as **PProj28a_studentfirstname_ studentlastname** in the location where your teacher instructs you to store the files for this project.

3. Insert an appropriate title and subtitle on the first slide. Place the picture of Shakespeare on this page and format as desired. (If you don't have access to the Internet, you can use the JPEG **PProj28** as the picture.)

4. Create an introductory slide that gives some information on Shakespeare's contributions to English language and literature.

5. Modify the slide masters to set up a main frame that will contain the quote, allowing room on the right for the names of plays and on the left for buttons you will use as triggers to identify the correct play.

6. Use the dictionary of quotations to identify a number of quotes that are familiar to you, or familiar sayings.

   a. Divide the quotations by the type of play: histories, comedies, and tragedies. If necessary, look up how Shakespeare's plays are assigned to these categories online or in a volume of Shakespeare's plays.

   b. Place the quotes on three slides, one each for history, comedy, and tragedy.

   c. Add answer buttons for each quote and text boxes that contain the names of the plays from which the quotes are taken, arranged in alphabetical order.

   d. Align and distribute the quotes, buttons, and text boxes to space them evenly on the slides. Illustration A shows one arrangement.

7. Set up animations so that when a viewer clicks the answer button to the left of the quote, the text box containing the correct play title blinks three times.

8. If you have the capability to add narration, use narration to explain on slide 3 how to use the answer buttons to trigger the correct answer. Test the presentation to check your triggers.

9. **With your teacher's permission**, print the presentation.

10. Set up the presentation to be browsed by an individual. Then save the changes to your presentation as **PProj28_ studentfirstname_ studentlastname**.

11. Save it as a PowerPoint Show, **PProj28b_ studentfirstname_studentlastname**.

12. Close the file, saving all changes, and exit PowerPoint.

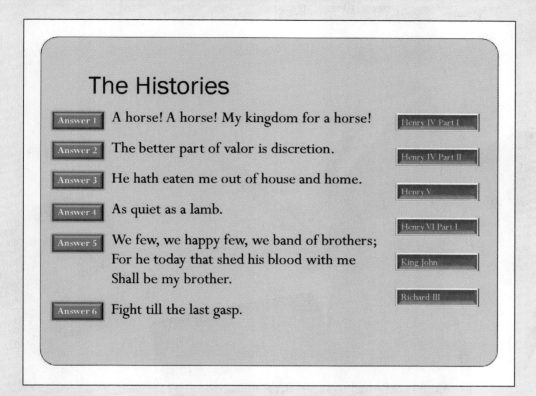

Chapter 3

Creating Presentations Using Tables and Charts

Lesson 13
Drawing and Adjusting Tables
Projects 29–30

- Drawing a Table
- Using the Eraser to Merge Cells
- Adjusting Column Width and Row Height
- Adjusting Cell and Table Size
- Changing Text Alignment and Direction

Lesson 14
Formatting Tables
Projects 31–32

- Applying a Table Style
- Modifying Cell Fill, Borders, and Effects
- Adding an Image to a Table

Lesson 15
Formatting Charts
Projects 33–34

- Applying Advanced Chart Formatting

Lesson 16
Adding Objects to Your Presentation
Projects 35–36

- Adding Existing Objects to Slides
- Using Paste Special to Embed or Link Object Data
- Copying Objects from Slide to Slide

End-of-Chapter Assessments
Projects 37–38

WORDS TO KNOW

Cell
A cell is the intersection of a table row and column.

Column
A column is a vertical segment of a table, and may include one or many rows.

Distribute rows and columns
Distributing table content means to evenly space the data or cells across the selected area.

Merge
To merge cells means to combine their space into one larger cell or section.

Row
A row is one horizontal segment of a table, consisting of a single or multiple columns.

Table
A table is a container that displays data divided into rows and columns. You can use tables to organize information so the readers can understand it easily.

Table handles
When you select a table, table handles appear in the corners and in the middle of each side so that you can drag the table border to either move it or change its size.

Text alignment
Text alignment refers to the way in which the text in the cell is arranged. Text can be aligned with the left margin, the right margin, or centered, and you can also choose to align the text vertically at the top, center, or bottom of the table cell.

Lesson 13

Drawing and Adjusting Tables

➤ What You Will Learn

Drawing a Table
Using the Eraser to Merge Cells
Adjusting Column Width and Row Height
Adjusting Cell and Table Size
Changing Text Alignment and Direction

Software Skills   One of the secrets to presenting information effectively on your PowerPoint slides is to keep the text brief and easy to understand. When you are presenting new concepts, comparing products, or designing a slide that needs to show contrasting items, it is tempting to try to cram a lot of information on the slide. Tables can help you present information clearly and succinctly by displaying information in a column-and-row format. Viewers will be able to understand your key points without reading through paragraphs of text.

Application Skills   Your local community college is offering a series of summer classes that give students a range of experiences in different fields. One of the professors asks you to create a PowerPoint presentation that tells a little bit about each class. At the end of the presentation, you want to include a table that shows the different features in each class so that students can easily decide among the course offerings. The table will include different column sizes, merged cells (for the title), and vertical text direction for the column labels.

What You Can Do

Drawing a Table

■ Add a **table** to your PowerPoint 2010 slides when you want to present information in a clear, easy-to-understand format.

- PowerPoint 2010 includes an Insert Table tool in the content placeholder of any slide, but when you want to draw your own custom table, use Draw Table.

- You find Draw Table by clicking the Insert tab and clicking Table in the Tables group. The Draw Table option is on the list that appears.

- After you click Draw Table, the pointer changes to a pencil, indicating that you can draw the table you want on the screen. Click and drag to draw the table.

- Add **rows** to the table by clicking the Draw Table tool in the Draw Borders group of the Table Tools Design tab. At the point in the left edge of the table where you want to begin a row, click and drag the pencil to the right edge of the table.

- Click Draw Table again and create **columns** by clicking along the top or bottom of the table and drawing a vertical line to create a column divider.

- Draw as many rows and columns as you like by drawing horizontal and vertical lines.

- You can change the color, style, and thickness of the lines you use to draw the table by using the Pen Style, Pen Weight, and Pen Color tools, also in the Draw Borders group.

  ✓ *If you click outside the table accidentally, the Table Tools contextual tab disappears. Click the table and then click the Table Tools Design tab to display the Draw Borders group again so that you can click Draw Table.*

Try It!   **Drawing a Table**

1 Start PowerPoint, and open **PTry13** from the data files for this lesson.

2 Save the file as **PTry13_studentfirstname_studentlastname** in the location where your teacher instructs you to store the files for this lesson.

3 Click Insert > Table 🔲.

4 Click Draw Table.

5 Draw a new table in the center of the slide area. Save changes and leave the presentation open to use in the next Try It.

Try It!   **Adding Rows and Columns**

1 In **PTry13_studentfirstname_studentlast name**, click Table Tools Design > Draw Table 🖉.

2 Click on the left side of the new table and drag the pencil to the right border.

  ✓ *Be sure that you click directly on the border of the table; otherwise, PowerPoint may create a table within a table. If you accidentally insert a new table by clicking in the wrong place, simply press* CTRL *+* Z *to undo the error and try again.*

3 Repeat until you have created four rows.

4 Click the top border of the table and drag the pencil down to the bottom border.

5 Repeat to create a third column.

6 Save changes and leave the file open on to use in the next Try It.

Drawing a table

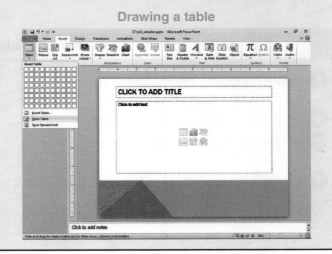

Try It!   **Changing the Look of Table Lines**

1 In **PTry13_studentfirstname_studentlast name**, click Table Tools Design > Pen Style drop-down list. Select one of the dotted line styles.

2 Click Table Tools Design > Pen Weight drop-down list and choose 3 pt.

3 Click Table Tools Design > Pen Color ✎ and select a red pen color.

4 Click at the top of the table to the right of the existing column lines, and draw a new line in the new style, weight, and color that extends to the bottom table border.

5 Choose a new Pen Style, Weight, and Color and draw a fourth line, similar to the third.

6 Save changes and leave the file open on to use in the next Try It.

Drawing new table lines with various styles

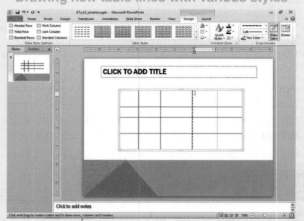

Using the Eraser to Merge Cells

- If you want to erase the last line you added to your table, you can simply press [CTRL] + [Z] or click Undo to reverse your last action.

- In some cases, however, you may want to **merge** cells to create a larger area. You might do this, for example, when you want to create a table heading that spans the width of the table, or when you want to combine a cell that will serve as a column label over two subheads.

- The Eraser tool is available in the Draw Borders group of the Table Tools Design tab.

- To erase a line using the Eraser, click the tool and then click the line segment you want to erase. You can also drag the eraser over the line to erase several segments.

- When you erase a row or column line, the cells in the affected row or column merge to make a larger cell.

- The Eraser tool remains selected until you click Eraser again or click a different tool.

Try It!   **Using the Eraser to Merge Table Cells**

1 In **PTry13_studentfirstname_studentlast name**, click the table.

2 Click Table Tools Design > Eraser ▦.

3 Click the first vertical segment in column 1 of your table.

4 Click the remaining vertical segments in row 1.

5 Click Table Tools Design > Eraser again to turn off the tool.

✓ *You can also merge cells in the table by selecting the cells you want to merge, clicking the Table Tools Layout tab, and clicking Merge Cells in the Merge group.*

6 Click in the new large cell and type **New Courses**.

7 Click outside the table and save your work. Leave the file open to use in the next Try It.

Adjusting Column Width and Row Height

■ PowerPoint 2010 makes it simple for you to adjust the column widths in your table. Simply position the mouse pointer over the column you want to change. When the pointer changes to a double-arrow, click and drag the column to increase or decrease the width.

■ Similarly, to adjust the row height, hover the mouse over the row you want to change. The mouse pointer changes to a double arrow; then click and drag the row to increase or reduce the height.

Try It! Adjusting Column Width and Row Height

1. In **PTry13_studentfirstname_studentlast name**, position the mouse over the rightmost column divider.

2. When the pointer changes, click and drag the column divider to the left, enlarging the column.

3. Release the mouse button and save your file.

4. Adjust the three columns on the right by dragging the column dividers until they look as though they are of equal width.

5. Position the mouse over the row divider in the bottom row of the table.

6. When the pointer changes, drag the row divider downward, enlarging the height of the middle row and making the table a little bigger.

7. Release the mouse button and save changes. Leave the file open to use in the next Try It.

Drag column dividers to make columns of equal width

CLICK TO ADD TITLE

New Courses

Adjusting Cell and Table Size

■ The tools in the Table Tools Layout tab give you what you need to adjust cell and table size.

■ If you want to control the size of the table or cell so that it fits a precise measurement, you can enter the precise width and heights in the Table Column Width and Table Row Height fields in the Cell Size group.

■ If you want to space the columns or rows evenly throughout the table, click the **Distribute Rows** or **Distribute Columns** tools.

■ In the Table Size group, you can enter size values for the Height and Width of the table.

■ Click the Lock Aspect Ratio check box if you want to preserve the shape of the current table no matter how you may resize it.

■ You can also drag a **table handle** or **border** to change the size of the table on the slide. If the Lock Aspect Ratio check box is selected, the table will be resized while still preserving its original shape if you enter new values in the measurement boxes.

Try It! Changing Cell Size

1. In **PTry13_studentfirstname_studentlastname**, click in the second row in the table.

2. Click Table Tools Layout, click in the Row Height box, and type **.75**.

3. Click Table Tools Layout, click in the Column Width box, and type **1.5**. Press Enter.

4. Save changes and leave the file open to use in the next Try It.

✓ Notice that the new column or row value is applied only to the current selection. To apply the new value to more than one column or row, select the additional columns or rows you want to change before entering the new value.

Try It!   Distributing Columns and Rows

1 In **PTry13_studentfirstname_ studentlastname**, click in column 2 in the table.

2 Click Table Tools Layout > Distribute Rows ⊞.

3 Click Table Tools Layout > Distribute Columns ⊞.

4 Save changes and leave the file open to use in the next Try It.

Try It!   Resizing the Table

1 In **PTry13_studentfirstname_ studentlastname**, select the table.

2 Click the Lock Aspect Ratio check box on the Table Tools Layout tab.

3 Click in the Height text box and type **4**.

4 To create more room for the table, drag the table to the left side of the slide.

5 Click the lower left corner of the table and enlarge the size of the table by dragging down and to the right until the Width shows 8.5.

6 Release the mouse button.

7 Save changes and leave the file open to use in the next Try It.

Resize the table with Lock Aspect Ratio

Changing Text Alignment and Direction

- The way you align your text can help readers make sense of the information you're presenting.

- PowerPoint 2010 enables you to align text along the left margin, center it between cell margins, or align it along the right cell margin.

- You can also change text direction so that text extends vertically in a cell. This is sometimes helpful when you have long column titles but don't want to use wide columns.

- PowerPoint gives you a number of options for changing text direction. You can choose Horizontal, Rotate All Text 90°, Rotate All Text 270°, or Stacked.

- You can also choose More Options in the Text Direction list to further control cell margins, alignment, and spacing options.

Try It!   Aligning Text

1 In **PTry13_studentfirstname_ studentlastname**, click in the second row of the table, and type the following in each of the cells:

    No.

    Course Title

    Instructor

    Days Offered

    Features

✓ *You may need to reduce the size of the font for the new column headings you have just added. To do this, simply highlight the cell text you want to change and click 16 in the Font Size list when the Mini Toolbar appears.*

2 Select the row of text you just entered and click Table Tools Layout > Center ▤.

3 Click Table Tools Layout > Center Vertically ▤.

4 Save changes and leave the file open to use in the next Try It.

Try It!   Changing Text Direction

1 In **PTry13_studentfirstname_studentlast name**, select the column labels if necessary.

2 Click Table Tools Layout > Text Direction ⬛.

3 Click Rotate All Text 270˚.

4 Click Table Tools Layout > Text Direction ⬛, then click More Options.

5 Click Table Tools Layout > Horizontal Alignment and choose Center ≣, if necessary.

6 Click Close.

7 Adjust the row height as needed to accommodate the text.

8 Close the file, saving all changes, and exit PowerPoint.

✓ You can format the text labels as you would format any text in your presentation, by changing the font, style, size, or effect of the text. You may also want to click to position the insertion point between the word "Days" and "Offered" and press Enter to format the label on two lines.

New text alignment

Project 29—Create It

Course Listing

DIRECTIONS

1. Start PowerPoint 2010 if necessary, and open the file **PProj29** from the data files for this lesson.

2. Save the file as **PProj29_studentfirstname_ studentlastname** in the location where your teacher instructs you to store the files for this lesson.

3. Select **slide 2** and click in the title placeholder. Type **Course Offerings** and click outside the box.

4. Click the **Insert** tab and click **Table** ⬛.

5. Choose **Draw Table** and move the pointer to the slide area.

6. Click and drag to draw a table that covers all but a small margin along the edges of the slide.

   ✓ Notice that the table is given a border using the same pen style, color, and weight you selected in the previous Try It! Exercise. You will learn how to change border settings later in this chapter.

7. Click the **Table Tools Design** tab, click the **Pen Style** drop-down list, and choose the solid line.

8. Click **Table Tools Design** > **Pen Weight** drop-down list and click **2¼ pt**.

9. Click **Table Tools Design** > **Pen Color** ✎ and choose a dark orange color.

10. Move the pointer to the table.

11. Click at the top of the table and drag the mouse down to the bottom to create a column divider.

12. Repeat this step three times so that you create five columns.

13. Click at the left side of the table and draw a line to the right side of the table.

14. Repeat this step four times so that you have a total of six rows in your table.

15. Click **Table Tools Design** > **Eraser** ⬛ and erase all the column segments in **row 1**. Click the **Eraser** ⬛ button a second time to turn off the tool.

16. To merge the last two columns, highlight all cells in the last two columns of the table and click **Table Tools Layout** > **Merge Cells** ⬛.

17. Resize the column on the right by dragging the column divider to the right.
18. Add the table title and column labels as shown in the following figure.
19. Select the column labels and click **Table Tools Layout > Center** ☰.

20. With the labels still selected, click **Table Tools Layout > Center Vertically** ☱.
21. **With your teacher's permission**, print the changed slide in the presentation. It should look similar to Figure 13-1.
22. Close the file, saving all changes, and exit PowerPoint.

Figure 13-1

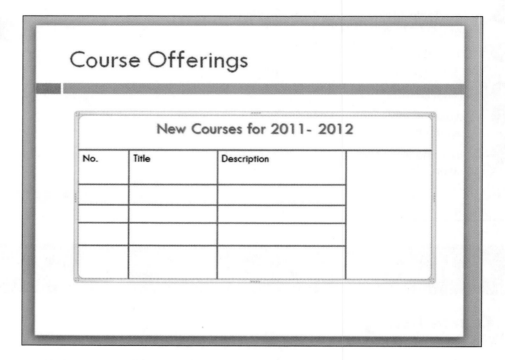

Project 30—Apply It

Course Listing

DIRECTIONS

1. Start PowerPoint 2010 if necessary, and open the file **PProj30** from the data files for this lesson.
2. Save the file as **PProj30_studentfirstname_ studentlastname** in the location where your teacher instructs you to store the files for this lesson.
3. Select a slide where you want to create a table and click in the title placeholder. Type a title for the slide and click in the main area of the slide.
4. Draw a new large table on the slide.
5. Select a pen style, weight, and color.
6. Draw four columns and seven rows.

7. Use the **Eraser** to merge the bottom two cells in each row so that you have a total of four columns and six rows.
8. Merge the cells in the top row to create one large cell, and add a table title.
9. Add the following column labels:

   Course name
   Instructor
   Days Offered
   Prerequisites

10. Change the text direction of the labels so that they rotate 270°.

11. Adjust the row height to accommodate the labels.

12. Change the column width so **Course Name** has the majority of the room and the other three columns are narrower.

13. Align the column labels so that the text appears centered in the cells.

14. Select the **Course Name**, center it horizontally in the cell, and align it at the bottom.

15. **With your teacher's permission**, print the changed slide. It should look similar to Figure 13-2.

16. Close the file, saving all changes, and exit PowerPoint.

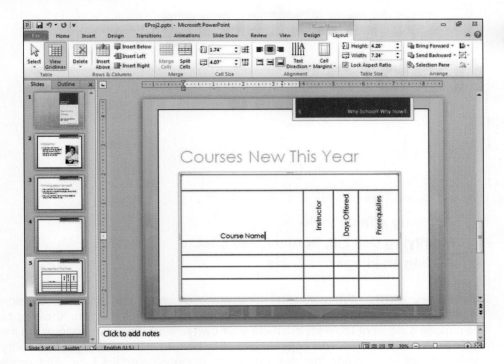

Figure 13-2

WORDS TO KNOW

Cell fill
To fill an individual cell or selected cells with color.

Gradient fill
To add color with a particular gradient to selected cells.

Table effects
You can add table effects to selected cells, sections, or the entire table by using the Effects tool in the Table Styles group of the Table Tools Design tab. Effects include shadows, reflections, or a beveled appearance.

Table shading
You can add shading to individual cells, table sections, or your entire table by choosing the Shading tool in the Table Styles group of the Table Tools Design tab. You can add a color, pattern, texture, or picture as shading in your table.

Table style
A table style is a set of formatting choices you can apply automatically to your table. You can choose a table style by clicking the example you want in the Table Styles gallery of the Table Tools Design tab.

Texture fill
Adding a textured visual effect (for example, Sand or Granite), to selected cells.

Lesson 14

Formatting Tables

➤ What You Will Learn

Applying a Table Style
Modifying Cell Fill, Borders, and Effects
Adding an Image to a Table

Software Skills   When you first draw a table on your slide, PowerPoint assigns a basic table style that reflects the overall theme of your presentation. Knowing how to choose a different table style, create your own custom styles, or change the look of individual cells, rows, and columns are all important skills, giving you the ability to tailor your tables and add that designer touch. Depending on the type of information you're displaying, you may want to add an image to the table as a background. This special effect can add "wow" to your presentation but you need to make sure you format the text carefully so the information in the table is still readable.

Application Skills   Your local wildlife organization is hosting a Habitat Stewards training, and you have been asked to create a presentation to help them spread the word. You want to create a table that showcases the training and lists the age groups, leaders, and locations. You want to create a table style that matches the organization's logo, and add a photo to the background of the table.

What You Can Do

Applying a Table Style

- A **table style** applies a particular color scheme, font selection, and background style to your table.
- You can use PowerPoint's built-in table styles and customize the look by adding Table Style Options.
- **Table shading** enables you to apply a **cell fill**, **gradient fill**, picture, or **texture fill** to selected cells or the entire table.

■ Click on the check boxes in the Table Style Options group to add specific elements to your table—Header Row, Table Row, Banded Rows, First Column, Last Column, Banded Column. These options control how shading is used in your table style.

■ Click the More button in the lower right corner of the Table Style gallery to display a large palette of table style choices. The table styles match the theme you have selected for your presentation; choose the one that best fits your content and audience.

Try It!   **Adding a Table Style**

1 Start PowerPoint, and open **PTry14** from the data files for this lesson.

2 Save the file as **PTry14_studentfirstname_studentlastname** in the location where your teacher instructs you to store the files for this lesson.

3 Click in the table to select it.

4 Click the Table Tools Design tab.

5 In the Table Styles group, click the More button to display the gallery of choices.

6 Click Themed Style 1, Accent 2.

7 Click the Banded Rows check box in the Table Style Options group.

8 Save changes and leave the file open to use in the next Try It.

Adding a table style

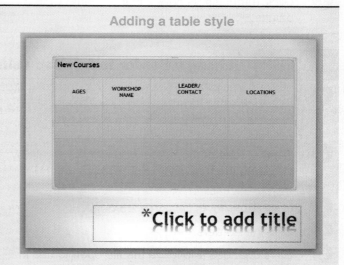

Modifying Cell Fill, Borders, and Effects

■ You can easily change the look and style of cells within the table by changing the **table effects**, or modifying the colors, borders, and effects of cells.

■ After you apply the table style to your table, you can fine-tune the look by changing the appearance of selected cells, rows, or columns.

■ One way to make a segment of a table stand out is to change the background color of the section.

■ You can also use borders to give a section of cells a special look.

■ PowerPoint 2010 also enables you to apply special effects to the table as a whole, adding a bevel effect, creating a reflection, or adding shadows.

■ The tools you need for fine-tuning the format of the table are on the Table Tools Design tab, which appears when you select the table.

■ The Shading, Border, and Effects tools are found in the right side of the Table Styles group.

  ✓ You can change the background of the table as a whole by choosing the Effects tool and clicking the Table Background option at the bottom of the list.

■ Each tool gives you a range of additional options from which to choose. Shading, for example, lets you select whether you want to add a cell fill color, a gradient, texture, or picture to the cell.

■ When you choose the Border tool, you can select from a list of 12 different border options. You can customize the look of the border by changing the pen color, style, and weight in the Pen Color group.

■ Choosing Effects displays a list of three effects choices: Cell Bevel, Shadow, or Reflection. Cell Bevel changes the look of the individual cell, while Shadow and Reflection apply to the entire table.

Try It!   **Changing Cell Shading**

1 In **PTry14_studentfirstname_studentlastname**, click the table and select the cells under Workshop Name.

2 Click Table Tools Design > Shading ⬦ .

3 Click Turquoise, Accent 2 in the Theme Colors palette.

4 Click Table Tools Design > Shading ⬦ > Gradient.

5 In the Light Variations palette, click the first gradient in the upper left.

6 Save your file and leave it open to use in the next Try It.

Try It!   **Adding a Border to Selected Cells**

1 In **PTry14_studentfirstname_studentlastname**, select the cells in the left column (below the column labels).

2 Set the color of the border you want to create by choosing the Pen Style, Pen Weight, and Pen Color settings before you add the border.

3 Click Table Tools Design > Borders ⬚ .

4 Click All Borders.

5 Save changes and leave the file open to use in the next Try It.

Adding a border to cells

New Courses				
AGES	WORKSHOP NAME	LEADER/ CONTACT	LOCATIONS	

*Click to add title

Try It!   **Adding Table Effects**

1 In **PTry14_studentfirstname_studentlastname**, select all the cells in the row containing the column labels.

2 Press CTRL + B to bold the labels.

3 Click Table Tools Design > Effects ⬤ .

4 Click Cell Bevel and click the Cool Slant bevel style.

5 Click outside the table to see the effect of the beveling.

6 Save changes and leave the file open to use in the next Try It.

✓ *If you want the text of the column labels to stand out a bit more, you may want to change the color of the column labels, or click the Home tab and in the Font group, click Text Shadow. This gives the text a 3-D effect on top of the beveling.*

Adding an Image to a Table

- You can add a special touch to your tables by including pictures.
- You might add pictures of products you're introducing, company logos, or images that represent particular programs or people.
- Add images by using the Shading tool in the table Styles group of the Table Tools Design tab.

- If you choose an image that is not large enough to fill the selected area, PowerPoint will tile the image so the amount of space you selected is covered.
- You can add an image to an individual cell or apply the image to the entire table background.
- If you add an image to the table background, be sure to preview your slides to ensure that the text shows up against the image you have added.

Try It!   Adding a Picture to a Cell

1 In **PTry14_studentfirstname_studentlast name**, click the top cell in column 4, just beneath the column label.

2 Click Table Tools Design > Shading 🖌 > Picture.

3 Navigate to the data files for this lesson, click **rick.jpg**, and click Open.

4 Resize the row height and column width if necessary to allow for the clear display of the photo.

5 Repeat with the three additional photos in the data files folder.

6 Remove the unused table row by right-clicking in the last row of the table and choosing Delete Rows.

7 Save changes and leave the file open to use in the next Try It.

Adding pictures to cells

Try It!   Adding a Picture to the Table Background

1 In **PTry14_studentfirstname_studentlast name**, click Table Tools Design > Shading 🖌 > Table Background.

2 Click Picture.

3 Navigate to the data files for this lesson and choose **background.jpg**.

4 Click Open.

5 Make text changes as necessary to ensure the text is readable against the picture background.

6 Close the files, saving all changes, and exit PowerPoint

Project 31—Create It

Program Spotlight

DIRECTIONS

1. Start PowerPoint 2010 if necessary, and open the file **PProj31** from the data files for this lesson.

2. Save the file as **PProj31_studentfirstname_studentlastname** in the location where your teacher instructs you to store the files for this lesson.

3. Click **slide 2** and enter the slide title **Our Most Popular Programs**.

4. Draw a table in the center of the slide area. Add four columns and five rows.

5. Merge the cells in row 1. Enter the title **Join Us!**.

6. Click the **Table Tools Design** tab and click the **More** button in the **Table Styles** gallery.

7. Click the **Themed Style 2, Accent 6** style to apply it to the table.

8. Click **Table Tools Design > Banded Rows**.

9. Click in the column labels row and type **Program, For Ages, Leaders,** and **Locations**.

10. Center the labels and click **Home > Text Shadow** 🅂 to make the characters stand out.

11. Highlight the last column on the right (from the column labels down) and click **Table Tools Design** > **Shading** ⬙.

12. Add a light red shade to these cells.

13. Click the table border.

14. Click Table **Tools Design** > **Pen Color** ✎ , and then choose a dark tan.

15. Click Table **Tools Design** > **Borders** ⊞, then click **All Borders**.

16. Highlight the row of column labels and click **Table Tools Design** > **Effects** ◌.

17. Point to **Cell Bevel** and click the first item in the gallery.

18. Highlight all cells below the column labels in **columns 1** through **3**.

19. Click **Table Tools Design** > **Shading** ⬙, and then click **Texture**.

20. Click the **Woven Mat** texture.

21. **With your teacher's permission**, print slide 2. It should look similar to Figure 14-1.

22. Close the file, saving all changes, and exit PowerPoint.

Figure 14-1

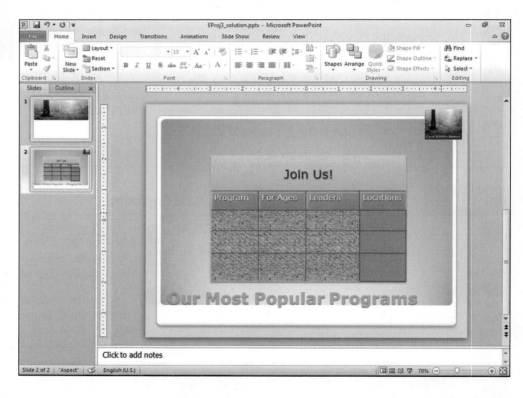

Project 32—Apply It

Program Spotlight

DIRECTIONS

1. Start PowerPoint 2010 if necessary, and open the file **PProj32** from the data files for this lesson.

2. Save the file as **PProj32_studentfirstname_ studentlastname** in the location where your teacher instructs you to store the files for this lesson.

3. Choose a slide where you want to add the table.

4. Type a title of your choosing for the slide.

5. Create a new table by clicking the Insert Table icon in the center of the slide and add columns for each of the following items:

    Program name
    Year started
    # of campers then
    # of campers now

6. Enter the data shown in Figure 14-2.

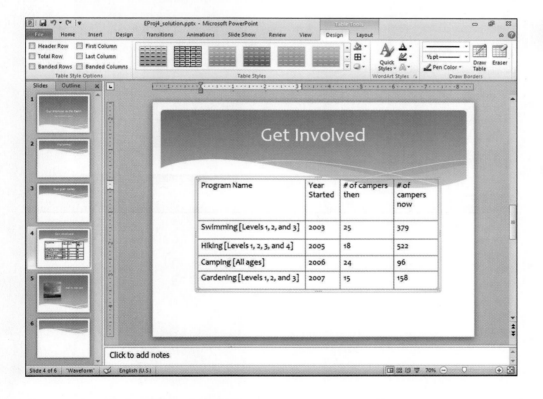

Figure 14-2

7. Apply a table style that complements the design.

8. Add any Table Options you feel fit what you want to show in this table.

9. Change the background color of the column that shows the number of campers in the various programs today.

10. Bevel the column label cells.

11. Right-click the column on the left and choose **Insert Column to the Right**.

12. Adjust the new column so that its width is **1 inch**.

13. Add a column label for the new column, select the text, and change the Text Direction.

14. Add the following photos from the data files to the background of the cells in column 2, then adjust the column width or row height as needed:

    Swimming – swimming.jpg
    Hiking – hiking.jpg
    Camping – camping.jpg
    Gardening – garden.jpg

15. Format the slide text as needed to ensure that the program names stand out against the table background.

   ✓ *You may need to change the text font, size, or color to increase the contrast so the text is readable.*

16. Click the table border and add a shadow effect to the entire table.

17. **With your teacher's permission**, print the slide. It should look similar to Figure 14-3.

18. Close the file, saving all changes, and exit PowerPoint.

Figure 14-3

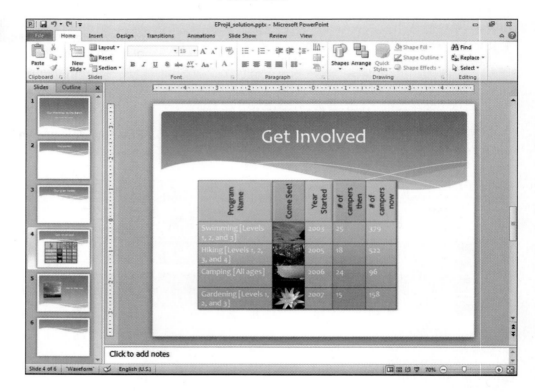

Lesson 15

Formatting Charts

➤ What You Will Learn

Applying Advanced Chart Formatting

Software Skills   Being able to present information in different ways is an important part of really connecting with your audience. Some people understand concepts best when they see them diagrammed; others like text; others like numbers and charts. PowerPoint includes an easy-to-use but fairly sophisticated charting tool that uses Excel 2010 as the basis for charts you create in PowerPoint.

Application Skills   A local YMCA has asked you to create a presentation that showcases their four fastest-growing children's programs. You have gathered video clips, photos, and quotes from kids in the different programs, and now you want to create a chart that will show viewers how much the different programs have grown over the last three years.

WORDS TO KNOW

Error bars
A chart feature available for some chart types that enables you to show a range of possible values.

Trendlines
A chart feature that displays a line showing the progression of value change over time.

What You Can Do

Applying Advanced Chart Formatting

- PowerPoint 2010 includes a number of features you can use to add advanced formatting to your **chart elements**.
- Two advanced tools that help you in analyzing and presenting your data are **trendlines** and **error bars. Trendlines** show the progression of your data over time, and **error bars** show the high and low range of values that are possible for the given data item.
- You'll find the tools you need in the Chart Tools Layout tab.
- The advanced options that are available will depend on the type of chart you have created and selected. For example, you cannot add trendlines to 3-D, radar, pie, doughnut, or surface charts.
- You can customize advanced formatting—such as trendlines and error bars—by changing the line color, style, regression type, and format.

Try It!   Adding Trendlines

1. Start PowerPoint, and open **PTry15** from the data files for this lesson.

2. Save the file as **PTry15_studentfirstname_studentlastname** in the location where your teacher instructs you to store the files for this lesson.

3. Click slide 3 and click in the chart on that slide.

4. Click Chart Tools Layout > Trendline 📈.

5. Choose Linear Trendline.

6. Save your changes and leave the file open to use in the next Try It.

Trendlines in a chart

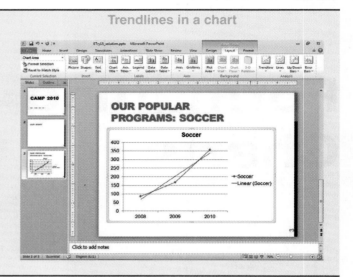

Try It!   Modifying Trendlines

1. In **PTry15_studentfirstname_studentlast name**, click the chart, then click Chart Tools Layout > Trendline 📈 > More Trendline Options.

2. In the Format Trendline dialog box, click Moving Average.

3. Click Line Color and select Solid Line.

4. Click the Color arrow and choose Red.

5. Click Line Style, and set Begin Type and End Type to Diamond Arrow.

6. Click Close.

7. Save changes and leave the file open to use in the next Try It.

Try It!   Adding Error Bars

1. In **PTry15_studentfirstname_studentlast name**, click slide 4 and select the chart.

2. Click Chart Tools Layout > Error Bars 📊 > Error Bars with Standard Error.

3. Click Chart Tools Layout > Error Bars 📊 > More Error Bar Options.

4. In the Add Error Bars dialog box, click the 2010 data series.

5. Click Line Color and choose Gradient Line.

(continued)

Try It!   **Adding Error Bars** (continued)

6 Click the Preset Colors arrow and choose Ocean.

7 Drag the Gradient Stops to set the color gradient as you'd like it to appear.

8 Click Close.

9 Close the file, saving all changes, and exit PowerPoint

✓ *Note that the changes are applied only to the data series currently selected. To modify another set of error bars, choose the data series in the Chart Elements setting in the Current Selection group of the Chart Tools Layout tab.*

The chart with error bars

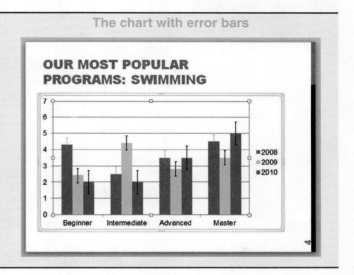

Project 33—Create It

Growth Chart

DIRECTIONS

1. Start PowerPoint 2010 if necessary, and open the file **PProj33** from the data files for this lesson.

2. Save the file as **PProj33_studentfirstname_ studentlastname** in the location where your teacher instructs you to store the files for this lesson.

3. Click **slide 3** and select the chart.

4. Click the **Chart Tools Layout** tab, then click the **Chart Elements** drop-down list in the Current Selection group.

5. Click Series **"Program 1"**.

6. Click **Chart Tools Layout** > **Error Bars** 📊 > **Error Bars with Standard Error**.

7. Change the look of the bars by clicking **Chart Tools Layout** > **Error Bars** 📊 > **More Error Bars Options**.

8. Click the **Line Color** setting and click **Solid Line**.

9. Click the **Color** arrow and choose a dark aqua color.

10. Drag the **Transparency** slider to **30%**.

11. Click **Close**.

12. **With your teacher's permission**, print slide 3. It should look similar to Figure 15-1.

13. Close the file, saving all changes, and exit PowerPoint.

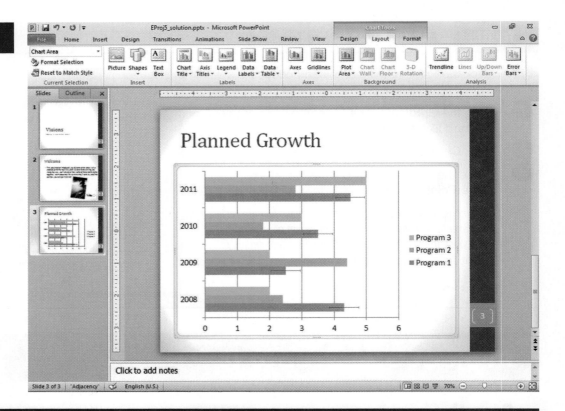

Figure 15-1

Project 34—Apply It

Growth Chart

DIRECTIONS

1. Start PowerPoint 2010 if necessary, and open the file **PProj34** from the data files for this lesson.

2. Save the file as **PProj34_studentfirstname_ studentlastname** in the location where your teacher instructs you to store the files for this lesson.

3. Click **slide 4** and select the **Program Changes** chart.

4. On the **Chart Tools Layout** tab, click **Series 3** in the **Chart Elements** drop-down list, found in the Current Selection group.

5. Add trendlines to the **"Waste Management"** series.

6. Change the look of the trendline by choosing a different color, line style, and weight.

7. Add a different set of trendlines to the data series **"Purchasing"**.

8. Customize the color, style, and weight of those trendlines to contrast against **"Waste Management"**.

9. Click the **Glow and Soft Edges** option in the **Format Trendline** dialog box, and add a **Glow** setting to one of the trendlines.

10. **With your teacher's permission,** print the presentation. It should look similar to Figure 15-2.

11. Close the file, saving all changes, and exit PowerPoint.

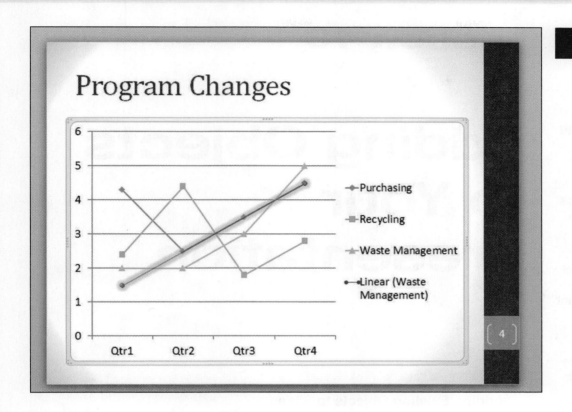

Figure 15-2

Lesson 16

WORDS TO KNOW

Embedding objects
When you embed an object in your PowerPoint presentation, the source file is copied and stored within the file.

Linking objects
When you link an object to your PowerPoint presentation, the content remains linked to the original file so that if you make changes to the original file later, the changes are reflected in your presentation.

Objects
An item like another presentation, a document, a worksheet, a picture, or a video clip you want to add to your slide.

Paste Special
Paste Special enables you to add objects to your presentation by copying them in another application and pasting them directly on to your slide.

Adding Objects to Your Presentation

➤ What You Will Learn

Adding Existing Objects to Slides
Using Paste Special to Embed or Link Object Data
Copying Objects from Slide to Slide

Software Skills   One of the great things about PowerPoint is that if you've created items in other programs that you'd like to show in your presentation, you can easily add the item as an object on your PowerPoint slide. PowerPoint enables you to create new objects or add existing objects to your presentation, and you can link the object or embed it, depending on how you plan to work with the object in the future.

Application Skills   You are a part owner in a new coffeeshop and one of your tasks has been to help the team come up with a presentation to show to potential investors. You have previously created a worksheet in Excel that you'd like to include in the presentation, but you want to link the file so that if you make changes in the original worksheet later, the presentation will update automatically.

What You Can Do

Adding Existing Objects to Slides

- If you've created other presentations, video clips, tutorials, interviews, graphic designs, or other items you'd like to add to your slides, you can add the elements as objects in your PowerPoint presentation.
- When you add an object to a slide, you have the option of linking the object or embedding it.

■ Linking an object enables you to maintain a link to the original file so that if you update the file later, the changes are reflected in the PowerPoint presentation.

■ If you choose to embed an object in the file, the information is included as part of the PowerPoint file. In some cases this can make the size of the PowerPoint file very large.

Try It!   Adding an Object to a Slide

1 Start PowerPoint, and open **PTry16** from the data files for this lesson.

2 Save the file as **PTry16_studentfirstname_ studentlastname** in the location where your teacher instructs you to store the files for this lesson.

3 Display slide 5 of the presentation.

4 Click Insert > Object 📄.

5 In the Insert Object dialog box, click the Create From File button.

6 Click Browse and navigate to the data files for this lesson. Click **energy_current.xlsx** and click OK.

7 Click the Link check box and click OK again to add the object to the slide.

8 Add a second object, **energy_green.xlsx**, on the right side of the slide, also linking to the source file.

9 Save your changes and leave the file open to use in the next Try It.

✓ *If you want to create a link to the object you have added so that any changes that are made to the original file appear in your PowerPoint presentation, click the Link check box before clicking OK.*

Inserting an object

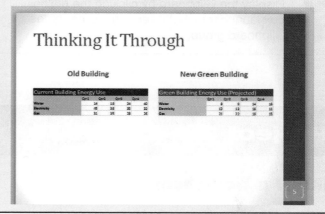

Using Paste Special to Embed or Link Object Data

■ You can also copy and paste an object from one application to another by copying the item in the original application and using Paste Special in PowerPoint.

■ You have the option of either linking or embedding the pasted file, just as you do when you insert the object on the slide.

■ The Paste Special tool is available when you click the Paste tool in the Clipboard group of the Home tab.

Try It!   Adding an Object Using Paste Special

1 With **PTry16_studentfirstname_studentlast name** open, navigate to open the Excel worksheet **PTry16_worksheet** from your data folder.

2 Select the chart in **PTry16_worksheet** and copy it by pressing CTRL + C.

3 Click on **PTry16_studentfirstname_ studentlastname**, then click slide 6.

4 Click Home > Paste 📋 > Paste Special.

5 In the Paste Special dialog box, click Paste Link.

6 Click OK.

7 Close **PTry16_worksheet**. Save changes in **PTry16_studentfirstname_studentlastname** and leave it open to use in the next Try It.

✓ *This process maintains a link to the original file so that when that file is changed the object on the slide will reflect the changes.*

✓ *If you want to include the data in the file instead of creating a link, select Paste and click OK.*

Copying Objects from Slide to Slide

- Copying an object from slide to slide in PowerPoint is a simple copy and paste operation.
- Click the object you want to copy and press CTRL + C or choose Copy from the Clipboard group of the Home tab.

- Click the slide where you want to paste the object and press CTRL + V or choose Paste from the Clipboard group of the Home tab.

Try It! **Copying and Pasting Objects from Slide to Slide**

1 In **PTry16_studentfirstname_studentlastname**, click slide 2, then click the photo.

2 Press CTRL + C to copy it.

3 Display the Clipboard by clicking the dialog box launcher in the lower right corner of the Clipboard group.

4 Click slide 5 so that you can paste the object.

5 Click the photo in the Clipboard.

6 Click Paste.

7 Close the file, saving all changes, and exit PowerPoint

Project 35—Create It

Insert a Worksheet

1. Start PowerPoint 2010 if necessary, and open the file **PProj35** from the data files for this lesson.

2. Save the file as **PProj35_studentfirstname_studentlastname** in the location where your teacher instructs you to store the files for this lesson.

3. Click **Home** > **New Slide** to add a slide to the presentation. Choose the **Title and Content** layout.

4. Click in the title area and type **Operating Expenses**.

5. Click **Insert** > **Object**.

6. In the Insert Object dialog box, click **Create From File**.

7. Click **Browse** and navigate to the data folder for this lesson.

8. Click the **PProj35_worksheet** file, click **Open**, and then click **OK**.

9. Click the added object and press CTRL + C.

10. Add a new slide.

11. Click **Home** > **Paste**.

    ✓ *If you want to see which objects are currently stored on the Clipboard, click the Clipboard dialog box launcher in the lower right corner of the Clipboard group.*

12. Resize the object by clicking the border and dragging in the direction you want to resize.

13. Add a gradient behind the worksheet to see which version you want to keep.

14. Delete the slide you don't want to use by right-clicking it and clicking **Delete Slide**.

15. **With your teacher's permission**, print the changed slide, which should look similar to Figure 16-1.

16. Close the file, saving all changes, and exit PowerPoint.

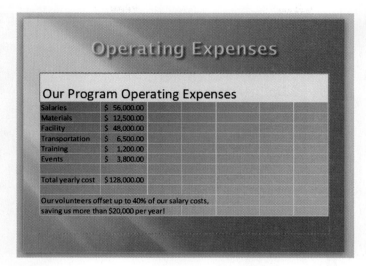

Figure 16-1

Project 36—Apply It

Link a Worksheet

DIRECTIONS

1. Start PowerPoint 2010 if necessary, and open the file **PProj36** from the data files for this lesson.

2. Save the file as **PProj36_studentfirstname_ studentlastname** in the location where your teacher instructs you to store the files for this lesson.

3. Create a new slide that will store the worksheet object.

4. Add a title for the slide.

5. Insert the object **wildlife_worksheet.xlsx** from the data files for this lesson.

6. Create a link from the file to the object on the slide.

7. Open **PProj36b** from your lesson data files.

8. Click the logo on slide 1.

9. Copy the logo (be sure to click both parts) and close the file.

10. In the original file, use Paste Special to add the logo to the slide.

11. Copy the new logo, and paste it in the lower right corner of the slide.

    ✓ *Alternately, you can add the logo to the slide master so that it will appear on every slide. Click the View tab and click Slide Master in the Master Views group. Paste the object at the place on the slide where you want it to appear and click Close Master View.*

12. **With your teacher's permission**, print the changed slide in the presentation. It should look similar to Figure 16-2.

13. Close the file, saving all changes, and exit PowerPoint.

Figure 16-2

Chapter Assessment and Application

Project 37—Make It Your Own

Children's Book Table

A local literacy organization is hosting a panel discussion for teachers on great children's literature. You have been asked to help them prepare a presentation they will introduce at the beginning of the session.

You will create a table to spotlight four favorite children's books for different ages, listing the title, author, showing a cover image (and attributing the copyright holder), and suggesting the appropriate age level. You will also create a chart to showcase the contribution children's literature makes to reading scores in the primary grades and incorporate a worksheet showing national reading averages.

DIRECTIONS

1. Start PowerPoint 2010 if necessary, and open the file **PProj37** from the data files for this project.

2. Save the file as **PProj37_studentfirstname_ studentlastname** in the location where your teacher instructs you to store the files for this project.

3. Create a new title and content slide and add a slide title.

4. Create a table on the new slide.

5. Choose the pen color, weight, and style you want to use and add four columns and six rows.

6. Add column labels (**Title**, **Author**, **Cover**, and **Age**) and format the labels as you'd like.

7. Increase the width of the **Title** column.

8. Increase the row height to make room for the cover images you will place later in this project.

9. Resize the table to maximize the amount of room it uses on the slide.

10. Enter the text shown in Illustration A.

Illustration A

BOOKS YOU HAVE TO READ

Title	Author	Cover	Age
Pat the Bunny	Dorothy Kunhardt		Toddler
The Very Hungry Caterpillar	Eric Carle		Preschool
Where the Wild Things Are	Maurice Sendak		Kindergarten-Grade 2
Eloise	Kay Thompson		Grade 2-Grade 4

9/7/2010   2

11. Center the column labels.

12. Left-align the table text.

13. Apply a table style, and add Table Options if you want to.

14. Select the cells beneath the **Age** column label, and change their shade to a color that complements the table style you selected.

15. Click **Table Tools Design > Border** and choose **All Borders** for those cells.

16. Right-click in the top cell of the table and choose **Delete Row**.

17. Highlight the column labels, click **Table Tools Design > Effects** , and click **Cell Bevel**. Click the second item in the gallery.

18. Click in the cell just beneath the **Cover** column label, and click **Picture Tools Design > Shading** .

19. From the data files for this project, add the cover for **Pat the Bunny** to this cell.

20. Continue adding the other cover images to the table.

21. Save the file and create **slide 3** using the title and content format.

22. Add the title **Our Research Shows**.

23. Insert a column style chart.

24. In the datasheet that appears, enter the information shown in Illustration B.

25. Add trendlines to show the progression of the **Read To** data series.

Illustration B

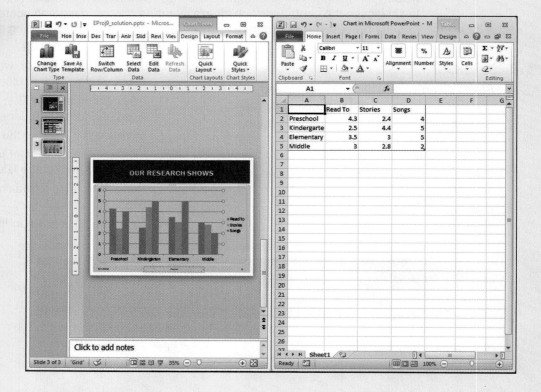

26. Customize the trendlines so they stand out in contrast to the chart.

27. Add a new slide with the title **National Statistics**.

28. Open the **PProj37b** file, click the table image, and press CTRL + C.

29. Return to **PProj37_studentfirstname_studentlastname**, click **Home > Paste > Paste Special**.

30. Click **Bitmap** and click **OK**. The image is added to your slide.

31. Resize the image as needed and add a picture effect, shadow, or other style if you'd like.

32. **With your teacher's permission**, print the changed slide in the presentation. It should look similar to Illustration C.

33. Close the file, saving all changes, and exit PowerPoint.

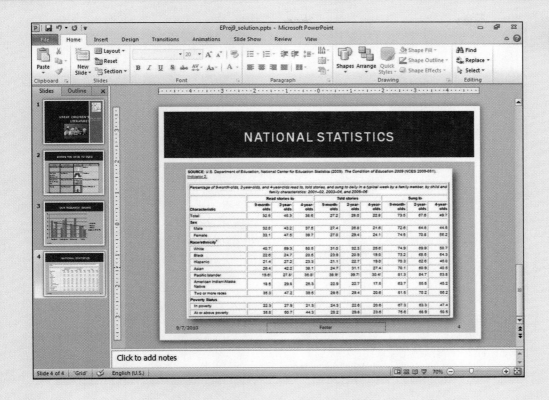

Illustration C

Project 38—Master It

Jazz Showcase

A local jazz ensemble is putting out a presentation that will share what they've done over the past year and invite jazz lovers to contribute to their upcoming event. They've asked you to help prepare the presentation they will use in their fundraising. One part of the presentation involves creating a table of jazz samples from their various performances.

In this project, you create and format the table, adding links to the sound clips and activating the object so that listeners will be able to hear the clips during the presentation.

DIRECTIONS

1. Start PowerPoint 2010 if necessary, and open the file **PProj38** from the data files for this lesson.

2. Save the file as **PProj38_studentfirstname_ studentlastname** in the location where your teacher instructs you to store the files for this lesson.

3. Click **slide 2** and title it **Jazz Samples**.

4. Create a table with three columns and six rows.

5. Choose the pen color, weight, and style you want to use.

6. Merge the top row into one cell and add a table title.

7. Add column labels (**Date**, **Event**, and **Sound Clip**) and center them.

8. Increase the size of the **Event** column.

9. Enter the text shown in Illustration A, left-aligning the table text and centering it vertically.

Illustration A

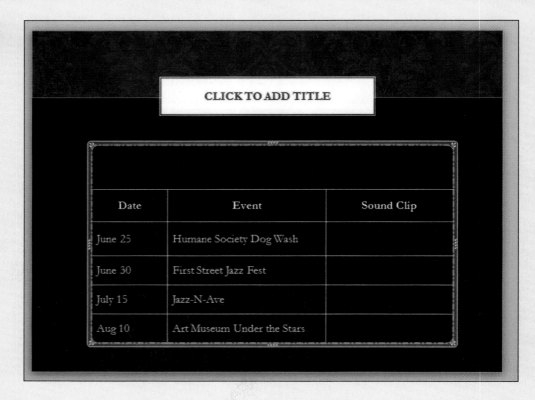

10. Lock the aspect ratio of the table and enter new values in the measurement boxes to enlarge it as much as possible.

11. Apply a table style that fits the overall theme of the presentation. Adjust the text and border colors as needed to complement the table style.

12. Select the table cells in the **Sound Clip** column and apply a lighter shade of background color.

13. Add the sound objects, one in each cell in that column.

14. Activate the sound objects by clicking each one and clicking the **Animations** tab, choosing **Add Animation**, **OLE Action Verbs**, and **Activate Contents**. Click **OK**.

15. Create slides 3 through 6 using the **Title and Content** layout for each.

16. Copy the first sound clip on **slide 2** and paste it in the brown box on **slide 3**.

17. Copy the second sound clip on **slide 2** and paste it on **slide 4**.

18. Repeat this copy and paste operation for the remaining two slides.

19. Save your work and press F5 to view the presentation.

20. On **slide 2**, click the first sound clip in the table to ensure that it plays correctly.

21. **With your teacher's permission**, print the changed slides in the presentation.

22. Close the file, saving all changes, and exit PowerPoint.

Index